VATICAN II

A PASTORAL COUNCIL

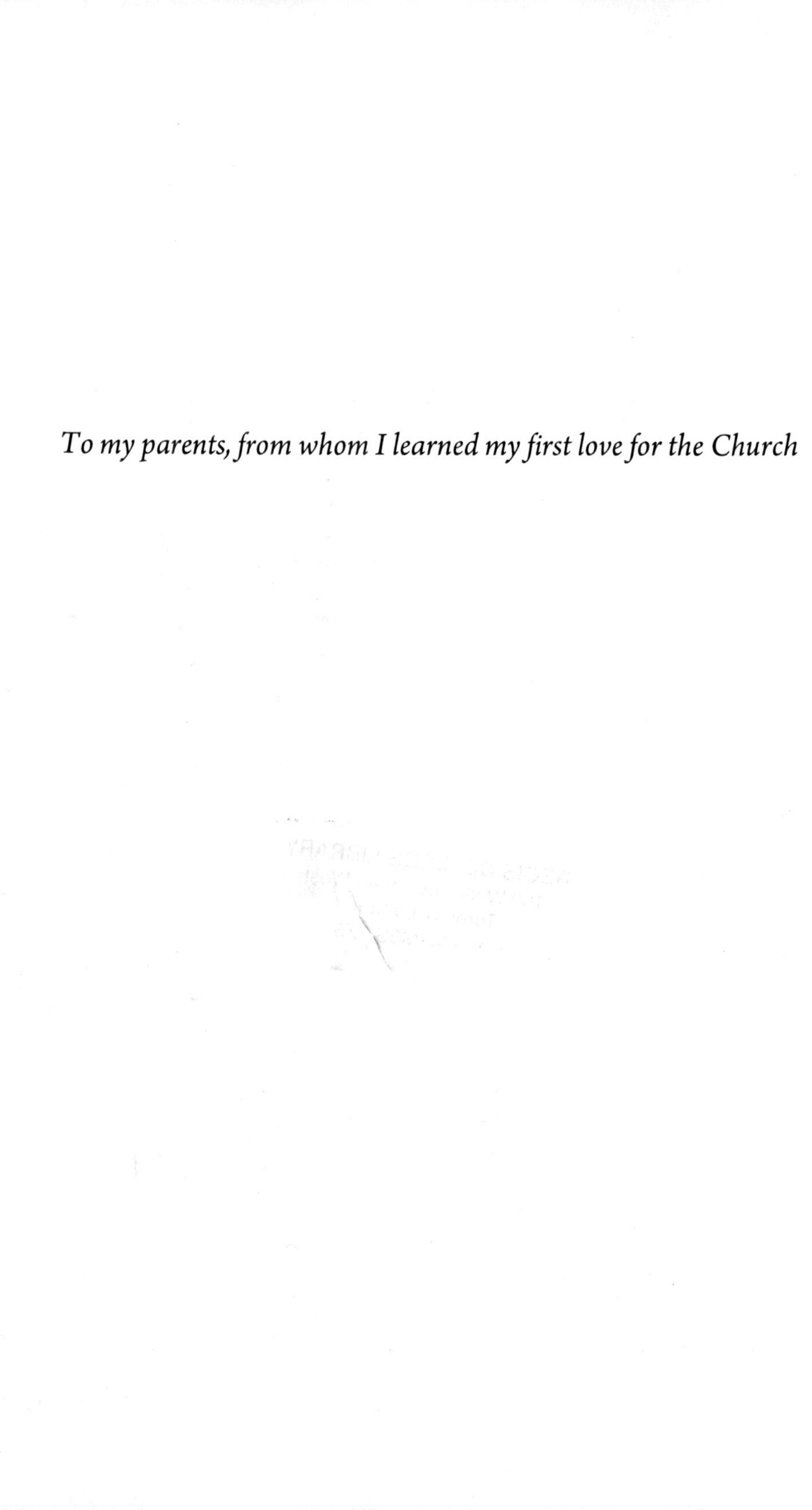

To my parents, from whom I learned my first love for the Church

VATICAN II

A PASTORAL COUNCIL

HERMENEUTICS OF COUNCIL TEACHING

SERAFINO M. LANZETTA

English translation by Liam Kelly

Published with the Assistance of

The Latin Mass Society

GRACEWING

First published in Italian as
Il Vaticano II, un Concilio pastorale. Ermeneutica delle dottrine conciliari
by
Edizioni Cantagalli S.r.l.,
Strada Massetana Romana, 12
Casella Postale 155
53100 Siena
Italy

English edition first published in 2016
by
Gracewing
2, Southern Avenue
Leominster
Herefordshire
HR6 0QF
www.gracewing.co.uk

ISBN 978 085244 888 5

Nihil obstat: Rev. William Wilson, Censor deputatis

Imprimatur: ✠ Rt. Rev. Philip A. Egan BA, STL, PhD, Bishop of Portsmouth 4 March 2016

The *Imprimi potest* and *Imprimatur* are declarations that a book or pamphlet is free from doctrinal or moral error. No implication is contained therein that those who have granted the *Imprimi potest* or *Imprimatur* agree with the contents, opinions or statements expressed.

Cover design by Bernardita Peña Hurtado

CONTENTS

ACKNOWLEDGEMENTS

I AM DELIGHTED TO present my book to an English-language audience. The book is the fruit of many years of research, conceived initially thanks to a Study Conference on the Second Vatican Council, organised by the religious Institute of the Franciscans of the Immaculate in Rome in December 2010, in which a variety of prelates and important theologians participated. The final result of my historical and theological work was successfully presented as a doctoral thesis for a lecturing post at the Theology Faculty of Lugano (Switzerland) in 2014.

For this English edition it is appropriate to thank His Lordship Mgr Philip Egan, Bishop of Portsmouth, for having welcomed me into his diocese as a religious among his clergy, and for the encouragement and support given in presenting this work to an English public. I would also like to thank the Latin Mass Society, in the person of Dr Joseph Shaw, for the closeness and assistance offered to me in this undertaking.

Appropriate and filial thanks must also go to the Founder of the religious family of the Franciscans of the Immaculate, Fr Stefano M. Manelli. Precisely due to that *sentire cum Ecclesia* which is appropriate to him, and thanks to which this new religious Institute was born in today's Church, in communion with the Church of all time, he encouraged me to undertake this research and to pursue it with commitment and diligence. With his blessing I began, and, from frequent discussion with him, I was able to draw so much richness: a forward-looking vision and a desire, imbued with love, to be able to offer a theological contribution for the unity and good of the whole Church.

Next I would like to thank those who made work and research possible in the various invaluable libraries and archives I visited.

My thoughts then go to the Friars Minor of the Austrian Province of Salzburg. I stayed with them for two consecutive summers, so as to be able to access the adjacent theological library at the State University, and so use the various sources and bibliography in German. To them and the personnel of this library, always helpful, despite my requests which were not always within the scheduled library times, is extended my gratitude.

I would then like to thank His Lordship Monsignor Giuseppe Sciacca, former Secretary of the Governorate of the Vatican City State, for his kind introduction of me and my research at the Vatican Secret Archives, where I worked for some time, finding invaluable material for the topic I was studying. I express my thanks to all the Archive personnel for their professionalism. Sincere thanks also go to the Archepiscopal Archive of the Diocese of Florence, and especially to the Archivist, Monsignor Gilberto Aranci, for the fraternal helpfulness shown to me in the consultation of the still-unexplored section concerning Cardinal Ermenegildo Florit and the Second Vatican Council.

Sincere thanks, once again, to the Poor Clares of the Immaculate in the monastery in Aulla (Tuscany) for the specialised work of reviewing the whole of the text, especially for the revision of the Latin, so that the written form might best mirror the thought and content of the work.

Last but not least, I would like to express my sincere thanks to Liam Kelly for the careful translation of the text and to the publisher *Gracewing,* thanks to whom this work will now see light in the land which, in the words of Shakespeare, is '*This precious stone set in the silver sea*' (Richard II).

May the Immaculate reward everyone, especially those whom I have not mentioned, but who in the silence of their prayers, and with their wise counsel, have been close to me in these years of work and endeavour.

ABBREVIATIONS

AAS	Acta Apostolicae Sedis, Vatican City.
AD I	Acta et documenta Concilio Oecumenico Vaticano II apparando. Series antepraeparatoria.
AD II	Acta et documenta Concilio Oecumenico Vaticano II apparando. Series praeparatoria.
AS	Acta Synodalia Sacrosancti Concili Oecumenici Vaticani Secundi.
ASV	Archivio Segreto Vaticano, Concilio Vaticano II.
AEF	Archive of Cardinal E. Florit, Archbishop of Florence, Second Vatican Council.
CCC	Catechism of the Catholic Church
CIC	Codex Iuris Canonici, Typis polyglottis Vaticanis, 1990.
CSEL	Corpus Scriptorum Ecclesiasticorum Latinorum, Vienna 1866-.
DH	H. Denzinger, *Enchiridion Symbolorum, definitionum et declarationum de rebus fidei et morum*, ed. P. Hünermann, Bologna: Dehoniane, 1995.
EE	Enchiridion delle encicliche, vols. 8 (1740–1995), Bologna: Dehoniane, 1994–1999.
ESV	Enchiridion del Sinodo dei Vescovi, vol. 1: 1965–1968, Bologna: Dehoniane, 2005.
EV	Enchiridion Vaticanum, Bologna: Edizioni Dehoniane, 1976ff.
f./ff.	Foglio/fogli.

$LThK^2$	Lexikon für Theologie und Kirche. Second edition, III vols., *Das Zweite Vatikanische Konzil*, Freiburg im B.: Herder, 1966–1968.
MANSI	G. D. Mansi, *Sacrorum conciliorum nova et amplissima Collectio*, eds. Louis Petit and J.-B. Martin, Paris-Arnhem-Leipzig 1901–1927.
PG	J. P. Migne, *Patrologiae cursus completus*, Ecclesia Graeca, Paris 1857–1866.
PL	J. P. Migne, *Patrologiae cursus completus*, Ecclesia Latina, Paris 1844–1864.
KT 1/1	S. Tromp, *Konzilstagebuch mit Erläuterungen und Akten aus der Arbeit der Theologischen Kommission*, Band I/1 (1960–1962), Herausgegeben von A. von Teuffenbach, Pontificia Università Gregoriana, Rome 2006.
KT 1/2	S. Tromp, *Konzilstagebuch mit Erläuterungen und Akten aus der Arbeit der Theologischen Kommission*, Band I/2 (1960–1962), Idem.
KT 2/1	S. Tromp, *Konzilstagebuch mit Erläuterungen und Akten aus der Arbeit der Theologischen Kommission*, Band 2/1 (1962–1963), Herausgegeben von A. von Teuffenbach, Bautz, Nordhausen 2011.
KT 2/2	S. Tromp, *Konzilstagebuch mit Erläuterungen und Akten aus der Arbeit der Theologischen Kommission*, Band 2/2 (1962–1963), Idem.
Hellín, *Dei verbum*	F. G. Hellín, *Concilii Vaticani II Synopsis in ordinem redigens schemata cum relationibus necnon Patrum orationes atque animadversiones. Constitutio dogmatica De divina revelatione Dei verbum*, Rome: LEV, 1993.
Hellín, *Lumen Gentium*	F. G. Hellín, *Concilii Vaticani II Synopsis. Constitutio Dogmatica De Ecclesia Lumen Gentium*, Rome: LEV, 1995.

FOREWORD

THE SECOND VATICAN Ecumenical Council (1962–1965) has oft been hailed as one of the most significant religious events of the twentieth century. This is certainly so for Roman Catholics. Its four plenary sessions were attended by most of the world's then two and a half thousand bishops, and by many ecumenical observers as well as theological experts and the secular media. All the great Catholic theologians of the last century were in some way involved: Yves Congar, Karl Rahner, Henri de Lubac, Edward Schillebeeckx, Bernard Lonergan, Hans Urs von Balthasar, Hans Küng, Karol Wojtyla (the later Pope St John Paul II) and Joseph Ratzinger (Benedict XVI). A number of preparatory commissions began working behind the scenes immediately the Council was announced in 1959. They drafted the sixteen documents the Council would issue, then redrafted or amended them as the debates and discussions went along. Afterwards, they enacted the follow-up. The Council was thus a dynamic, complex process lasting several years, marked by all the realities of human interaction, with tensions between modernisers and the 'old guard', different continental groupings, and local versus universal concerns. Once underway, it took on a life of its own. Indeed, the bishops soon realised that what was happening was an event of historical significance.

Vatican II was announced by Pope St John XXIII. Its central concern was: What does it mean to be the Church of Christ in the modern world? Pope John spoke of the need for an *aggiornamento*, an updating of the Church's life and teaching for the sake of Christian unity in order to evangelise the modern world. As the author of this study shows, many individuals and groups welcomed this with enthusiasm, whilst others, including some members of the Roman Curia, were more cautious or lukewarm. Ecumenical councils are usually called to deal with a crisis in doctrine or discipline, but this was to be a 'pastoral' council. As Fr Lanzetta convincingly argues, this made Vatican II unique. Unlike the previous twenty ecumenical councils, the twenty-first would not make any new definitions of doctrine. John XXIII wanted it to respond positively to modernity and to update those aspects of the Church that could be updated. It would occasion a spiritual renewal, a 'new Pentecost' to reinvigorate the Church's mission and the unity of Christians. It would open the windows to let in some fresh air.

The style, then, of the Council's documents would be 'pastoral'. As Fr Lanzetta argues, here were not canons and definitions but declarations of the Church's belief in such a way as to invite others to respond positively. Instead of dogmatic definition, we are given authentic ordinary Magisterium, albeit taught solemnly or extraordinarily by bishops gathered with the pope in a general council, but Magisterium 'with a purpose.' Moreover, unlike the councils of Trent or Vatican I, which evince a tightly defined conceptual framework, the texts of Vatican II are discursive; like a river with incoming streams, they synthesise numerous theological traditions and viewpoints. Biblical references alternate with historical analyses, citations of previous councils and papal Magisterium with legislative provisions. Their interpretation requires a process of investigating what was written, how it was written, and why it was written. Moreover, Blessed Paul VI wanted the final documents to be approved not only by the statutory two-thirds majority but overwhelming majorities. As a result, alternative formulations and positions, rather than being resolved in favour of one side or the other, are juxtaposed even in the same paragraph. The final products are consensus documents with many strands. They cannot be proof-texted in the manner of biblical fundamentalism, individual sentences or paragraphs taken in isolation. As with the Bible, so individual sentences and paragraphs and even whole documents must be read within the context of the whole, and, as Fr Lanzetta shows, within the context of the Tradition prior to the Council. One might add too, that the documents must also be read in the light of subsequent magisterial interpretation and pronouncements.

The Council issued sixteen documents: nine decrees and three declarations on specific areas of pastoral concern, and four great doctrinal constitutions (on the liturgy, the Church, Divine revelation, and the Church in the modern world). These assimilate all the new insights of twentieth century theology, especially those of the liturgical movement, modern Scripture scholarship and recent historical studies. They are marked by a two-fold *leitmotif* of *ressourcement* and *aggiornamento*, that is, going back to the source in the Bible and the Tradition and then applying what has been retrieved to the needs of the present. It is a process, as it were, of: 'What does Jesus say? What does the Bible say? What does the Church's Tradition say?' then 'In the light of this, what should the Church do now?' This is a remarkably different approach from the pre-conciliar Scholastic theology that was propositional and deductive. It is an approach that takes seriously history, culture, the modern world and human experience. In this way, Vatican II adopted an attitude of openness to the modern world, intentionally avoiding adversarial stances, open towards dialogue with anyone of good will. On the other hand, as Fr Lanzetta ably demonstrates, these at times uneven texts reflect unstable compromises between different theological approaches and positions. This is particularly evident in the three chief examples he studies: the relationship between Scripture and Tradition in *Dei Verbum*, the membership of the Church in *Lumen Gentium* and the conciliar teaching on the Virgin Mary that was eventually incorporated into *Lumen Gentium*'s last chapter.

Vatican II was closely related to the impressive scientific and technological advances of the period, the striking social and historical upheavals of the mid-twentieth century, the struggle between competing world politico-economic ideologies and the aftermath of two devastating global wars. It was preceded by, and itself initiated, a process of radical philosophical and theological renewal that has spawned today's theological pluralism—a variety of different positions coexisting without one being dominant—as well as intense specialisation, change and development. All the pre-Vatican II theological renewal movements (biblical, patristic, liturgical) continued after Vatican II. Freed from the pursuit of anti-modernism and the use of arguably out-dated methodologies, Catholic theology since the Council has entered a period of enormous vitality and creativity, with a welter of innovative theologies such as liberation theology, feminism, ecological theology and theology of religions. Yet the most significant outcome of the Council was the overthrow of Neo-Scholasticism and its a-historical and universalist world-view in favour of approaches to theology that take seriously historicity and culture. If the chief theme of nineteenth century theology was the relationship of faith and reason, culminating in the statement of Vatican I in *Dei Filius*, the chief theme of twentieth and twenty-first century theology is the relationship of history and theology.

In a 1968 essay, "Theology and Man's Future," Bernard Lonergan, the Canadian Jesuit philosopher-theologian (d. 1984), lists developments in five fields profoundly affecting Catholic thought. These are historical scholarship (the impact on theology of the historical-critical methods of scriptural exegesis together with an awareness of the historical evolution of doctrine), recent developments in philosophy (especially the pluralism of philosophies now in use by theologians), the impact of comparative religion, religious studies and the human sciences (such as psychology, economics, sociology and cultural anthropology), new methodologies (the exchange of Aristotelian-Thomist categories for critical and hermeneutical approaches) and new communications (the need to adapt to different cultural realities).

In the 1970s, the 'event' of the Council continued to dominate the Church's consciousness, causing the suspension of many pastoral and planning decisions. Thus there developed a sharp sense of a 'before' and an 'after', with the period after the Council being referred to as 'postconciliar'. In the fever of the times, it was not uncommon for popular speakers to suggest the Church had been reinvented at

Vatican II; a new era had opened up, with a 'return to the sources' that made the postconciliar Church much more similar to the early Church than the supposedly degenerate clericalism and pedantry of the intervening centuries. As a result, the situation within the Church today is marked by strong elements of pluralism and polarisation. Contention usually revolves around three key issues: church governance (authority), liturgy and anthropology (sexual morality). A canon of dissent is frequently heard, calling on the Church to abandon her traditional teaching against abortion and contraception, to allow divorcees to remarry, to change its doctrine on homosexual acts, to ordain women to the priesthood, to make priestly celibacy optional, to allow Catholics to receive communion at non-Catholic eucharists, to decentralise the Roman curia, and to change the style and exercise of ecclesial authority. Commentators frequently refer to ruptures, dislocations and fragmentation between 'conservatives' and 'progressives,' lay and clerical theologies, theologians and the Vatican dicasteries, theorists and pastors, the academic and the spiritual.

On the other hand, over half a century on, we can adopt a more historical perspective and recently, a number of new studies and theological analyses have appeared, such as this one. Even so, the Council continues to be so important for the Church that it will surely be many more decades, perhaps centuries, before a balanced and definitive evaluation can be reached. This is exactly what Newman argued in his *Essay on the Development of Christian Doctrine*, that while a stream might be clearest near its spring, the history of religious ideas is purer and stronger when their "bed has become deep and broad and full," and their vital elements have been disengaged from what is temporary and passing.

Fr Lanzetta notes how Benedict XVI warned against applying a 'hermeneutic of discontinuity and rupture' to Vatican II. Benedict's point was that the Council must be read within the flow of Catholic Tradition and teaching, even when there are specific discontinuities and developments. Vatican II was such a massive event for the Church that it inevitably engendered a strong sense of a 'before' and an 'after' and the post-conciliar period coincided with an era of explosive historical, social and technological upheaval. Whilst significant theological shifts occurred, the Council cannot be interpreted, Benedict argues, as *de facto* rupturing the Church into a pre- and post-conciliar reality. Nor should there be a juxtaposition between the 'spirit' of Vatican II and its 'letter,' as if the real message of the Council was its impulse towards the new, and not the fact that the texts themselves confirm many old things that some might deem no longer relevant. The only way to grasp the spirit of the Council is to steep oneself first-hand in its texts, in their background, genesis and subsequent development.

In fact, the sum of Vatican II is always greater than its parts. This Council was unique. Whilst Fr Lanzetta argues this largely in relation to the past, its uniqueness can also be seen in the on-going process that it opened up. Its documents continue to be alive, to prompt dialogue within the Church between competing positions, to encourage deeper understanding and ever-new applications. This is why the reception of the Council over the last fifty years is also part of the Council. The Council initiated a process and that process is still continuing. Within it, papal and episcopal Magisterium, the prudential judgments of the Roman curia, continuing discussion among theologians, as well as the on-going study of the documents by the Church as a whole, continue to be decisive for an authentic reception of its message. Fruits typical of this include the 1983 *Code of Canon Law* and the 1992 *Catechism of the Catholic Church*. Other fruits include important clarifications from the Holy See such as *Ad Tuendam Fidem* (1998), *Dominus Iesus* (2000) on aspects of Christology and ecclesiology, *The Collaboration of Men and Women in the Church and in the World* (2004) on the theology of being male and being female, and the *Response to Some Questions Regarding Certain Aspects of the Doctrine of the Church* (2007). As time goes on and new questions arise, there will no doubt be many more clarifications and developments. Unlike any other council before it, Vatican II is a work in progress.

I warmly recommend this study. It is another major contribution to our understanding of the intention, trajectory and formulation of key aspects of the teaching of Vatican II. Fr Lanzetta's meticulous research illuminates the background and some of the personalities involved. He cites his examples as 'epiphanies' typical of the Council's 'pastoral' intention, John XXIII's desire for *aggiornamento* and the promotion of mission and Christian unity. His thesis is that this pastoral intention makes Vatican II and the documents it promulgated unique among the ecumenical councils. Have we here a new 'form' of Magisterium? He argues provocatively that the theological status or qualification of the Council's teaching is at times contentious, whilst the documents themselves frequently espouse compromise formulations, sometimes at odds with common pre-conciliar positions and often the cause of on-going debate today. In this, Fr Lanzetta's penetrating, critical insights are a great help to the emergence of that higher viewpoint which the Church needs, if she is effectively, by God's grace, to proclaim the Gospel of Christ with the Spirit-filled dynamism the Council unleashed.

✠ Philip Egan BA, STL, PhD
Bishop of Portsmouth
4 March 2016

PREFACE

DURING THE CURRENT "Year of Faith" (11 October 2012–11 October 2013), devoted in particular to the 50th anniversary of the start of the Second Vatican Council, we are seeing a great proliferation of publications about the various conciliar documents and their interpretation. We find very different opinions, sometimes detached from the historical sources of the Council itself. Hence the need for systematic clarification, while taking into account the ample historical documentation. For the key points of a correct interpretation, we note *inter alia* the reception of Vatican II at the Extraordinary Synod of Bishops in 1985 and the magisterial discourse of Pope Benedict XVI given to the Roman Curia on 22 December 2005, to underline, against 'hermeneutics of rupture' from the 'right' and from the 'left', the need to present a 'hermeneutic of reform' to appraise the development that took place, while maintaining a continuity of substance with the preceding Magisterium. Fr Lanzetta's study furnishes a far-reaching approach, attentive to the historical sources and to the various proposals of interpretation in recent years.

The scope and methodology of the research

The 'Introduction' describes the scope and methodology of the research. Lanzetta sets out to provide 'a theological contribution for a more appropriate hermeneutic to be applied to Vatican II' (p. xxxvi), with particular attention to its 'pastoral' character. The 1985 episcopal Synod shows the need to differentiate the different rank of conciliar documents (Constitutions, Decrees, Declarations) and to take into account the cultural sensitivity which changed in the meantime. A particular challenge is the clarification of the relationship between dogma and pastoral teaching in the conciliar documents and therefore in the *mens* of Vatican II. To arrive at a hermeneutic consistent with the conciliar assembly, the author examines 'some conciliar teachings ... according to a criterion of the theological bearing of those teachings in development subsequent to the Council' (p. xlii): the relationship between Scripture and Tradition in *Dei verbum*, the concept of Church and belonging to it, as well as the figure of Mary in *Lumen Gentium*. Lanzetta underlines that the 'pastoral nature' of the Council should not be interpreted as the reversal of the classical relationship between doctrine and pastoral teaching, as suggested by some who want to 'overcome' the distinction between dogma and praxis with recourse to 'experience'. The proposed structure is presented with clarity. The author expresses the desire that Vatican II might be a 'council of unity for the Church'.

Historico-theological notes

The first of the five chapters examines 'The conciliar teaching as an act of the Magisterium. Historico-theological notes for an appropriate hermeneutic of Vatican II'. Starting from the masterful work of H. J. Sieben SJ (*Die Konzilsidee der alten Kirche*), Lanzetta reaffirms the intrinsic connection of the conciliar idea, in its origins, with divine tradition. Treasuring the contemporary research on the history of the Councils, the question is posed as to how to define an (ecumenical) 'Council'. Obviously unsuitable claims, such as a type of lay parliament, are rejected, but the relationship between the Pope and Bishops in the definition of the Council is greatly clarified.

When the author tackles the positioning of Vatican II 'between renewal and aggiornamento', he notes that the 'main tensions in the very planning of the Council' go back to the institutional polarity, already present in the preparatory phase, between the Doctrinal Commission and the promotion of ecumenism on the part of the Secretariat for Promoting Christian Unity. The theological consequences of the opening address of John XXIII, *Gaudet Mater Ecclesia*, which differentiated the deposit of faith from the way of presenting it, having recourse to a 'predominantly pastoral' Magisterium, can be seen. To grasp this message, there is a need to avoid a principled pluralism and an aggiornamento wishing to remove any uncomfortable messages of faith. To transmit the Word of God in the contemporary situation, the relationship between Sacred Scripture and Tradition must be explained well. Lanzetta presents some of the stances taken about the 'pastoral nature' of the Council in contrast with the authentic significance of dogma, presupposed by the documents of Vatican II itself, too, as in *Lumen Gentium*.

Then the author presents a summary of the discussion on the 'theological qualification of the documents of Vatican II'. He notes that already following on from Vatican I, in particular with Leo XIII, papal Magisterium assumed a broader significance, without leading to dogmatic definitions. There is unanimous agreement there were no dogmatic definitions at Vatican II. The observation that 'nothing was defined in strictly binding terms' (thus Cardinal Walter Brandmüller), is, however, contested by a position which posits the binding nature of all the conciliar texts (for example, J. H. Tück).

With O. Semmelroth and F. Sullivan 'three theological threads' can be distinguished to ascertain the magisterial rank of the conciliar documents: maximalist, minimalist and moderates. The 'minimalists' deny that the texts have any binding value, even, for example, on the sacramentality of the episcopate. The most qualified representative of the 'maximalists' is U. Betti, according to whom the text of the dogmatic constitution *Lumen Gentium* is irrevocable. The moderate position is represented, for example, by J. Ratzinger, Y. Congar and F. Sullivan. Even among these authors, however, there are different nuances: is this 'ordinary Magisterium' (Sullivan) or 'extraordinary' (Congar)? What is the distinction in the authority of the encyclicals?

The need for an appropriate hermeneutic is revealed in the opinions about how to evaluate, for example, the role of tradition, the relationship between spirit and letter, the intention of the Council Fathers and the importance of the 'signs of the times'. To find a common principle, there is research on the 'mens' of the Council. Vatican II as ecumenical Council in a global sense should be distinguished from its varied Magisterium at most levels. The 'mens sanctae Synodus' emerges from the texts and in the intentions of the Council Fathers. On the assent due to the council affirmations the three-fold distinction of the Motu proprio *Ad tuendam fidem* (1998) must be borne in mind. Anyone rejecting a teaching needs to rediscover the necessary distinctions of the theological notes and censures.

Status quaestionis *on the theological contribution to Vatican II*

The second chapter focusses on the *status quaestionis* of the theological interpretation of Vatican II. There is an overview of the theological contribution of the theologians and experts (periti) since the preparatory phase of the Council. Seven exemplary positions are examined: Cardinal Pietro Parente (a Council Father), Karl Rahner, René Laurentin, Hans Küng, Cardinal Umberto Betti (periti), Cardinal Leo Scheffczyk, and the 'School of Bologna' (among the theologians and historians in the reception of the Council).

The presentation begins with Pietro Parente, particularly interesting since he was a member of the Holy Office and the Theological Commission of Vatican II; he supported the openings of the Council, as well as making critical observations about its reception. The position is illustrated by the themes of religious freedom, collegiality (on which Parente was an expert) and ecumenism. For Karl Rahner, the Council seemed to be 'the beginning of the beginning' of a truly worldwide Church. Among the themes underlined by the influential theologian one finds first and foremost episcopal collegiality in his reflection in the 'episcopal council'. René Laurentin, too, reiterated the decisive importance of the reception of Vatican II, but also noted the limitations, the 'silences' and the 'ambiguities', including the term 'pastoral'. Hans Küng proposed a hermeneutic which led to a rift, when in his ecumenical approach he presented a model orientated to the Protestant Reformation. A figure of particular interest is the Franciscan Fr Umberto Betti. Having rejected, in 1963, Geiselmann's position on the material sufficiency of Sacred Scripture, in 1965 he wrote there was no quantitative supplement in Tradition. Despite that, Betti underlined that Vatican II did not clarify the debate that had arisen, but highlighted the link between Scripture and Tradition; the Council of Trent and Vatican II, however, highlighted the peculiarity of Tradition in the transmission of Revelation. Leo Scheffczyk is presented above all through his study on the 'Aspects of the Church in crisis', devoted to the interpretation of the ecclesiology of Vatican II. The conciliar teaching of *Lumen Gentium* offered at the same time both progress and continuity. A different hermeneutic, on the other hand, was to be found in the 'School of Bologna', which exalted the Council as an 'historic event'. According to Giuseppe Alberigo there is a 'priority of the council as event also with respect to its decisions'.

In the concluding observations on the theological contribution to Vatican II, Lanzetta raises the questions if the Council had been 'intrinsically compromised' and if it is hiding a fundamental metaphysical deficiency. A response is outlined which will be subsequently developed in more detail.

The example of the relationship between Scripture and Tradition

The third chapter reports on the first example carefully studied in the work of the Council: 'Pastoral epiphanies of the Second Vatican Council in the intentions and formation of the conciliar teaching on the "Scripture and Tradition" relationship'. The schema prepared on the theme *De fontibus revelationis* was not welcomed in the council chamber for pastoral and ecumenical reasons, in contrast with a more dogmatic and apologetic presentation. Lanzetta refers, inter alia, to a very careful German study (by H. Sauer) about the foundation of the 'pastoral principle' in the constitution *Dei verbum*; here one sees clearly the reason for the presentation of this example, believed to be 'the thorniest issue'. 'From this one could deduce a hermeneutic principle' for the Council 'in its entirety' and clarify the magisterial value of Vatican II.

For the study of the *iter* of the conciliar discussion, Lanzetta also uses sources hitherto unknown in theological considerations, especially from the Vatican Secret Archives. The most astonishing discovery was Paul VI's explicit desire to speak with clarity about the constitutive Tradition. Instead, for ecumenical reasons, the conciliar text does not have this teaching which had already emerged in the magisterial texts (for example, in Catechisms) of previous centuries, as the specific studies by H. Schauf underline.

There is also a presentation, *inter alia,* about the nuances of the positions of Rahner and Ratzinger on the theme of Revelation with their systematic impact. Cardinal Bea's influence encouraged the ecumenical outlook to the Protestant world and disadvantaged the consideration of the Orthodox Churches. The study of the relationship between Scripture and Tradition in the other documents of Vatican II, especially in *Dei verbum,* shows that the silence of the constitution on Divine Revelation on constitutive Tradition is in contrast to other texts, which, de facto, seem to support this conviction. According to Lanzetta, this stems from a careful reading above all of the constitution on the Church (*Lumen Gentium*) and on the liturgy.

The example of the conciliar teaching on the Church

The fourth chapter is devoted to 'Pastoral epiphanies of the Second Vatican Council in the intentions and formation of the conciliar teaching on the Church'. The author rightly notes that this is 'the central theme of the whole Council gathering' and outlines the originality of the setting for ecclesiology. The schema *De Ecclesia* is presented, already containing various teachings typical of the final text, such as the reference to the ecclesial 'elements' outside the visible whole of the Church.

There emerges, as one of the 'knots' to be examined, the thorny issue of belonging to (being a member of) the Church. The objections to the schema led to a new and complex redaction and the proposal of different new schema. In a 'first analysis', Lanzetta indicates the importance of the discussion about being a member of the Church and the collegiality of bishops. The preceding discussion during the preparatory phase of the Council is recalled. Among the 'Doctrinal elements in the *in fieri* text of *Lumen Gentium*' there is examination of belonging to the Church and collegiality. On being a member of the Church one sees the importance of ecumenism with the need to distinguish Christians and non-Christians in their relationship with the Church, on the one hand, and, on the other, the necessity of the Church for salvation. On the one hand, there is the fundamental importance of Baptism, and on the other the 'three bonds' are necessary (faith, sacraments and hierarchical communion). The conciliar text, due to the various difficulties which emerged in the discussion, does not use the term 'member' to speak about non-Catholic Christians. As regards collegiality, the question emerges whether 'it is a dual subject [of universal jurisdiction] which acts or one insufficiently distinct subject'. Lanzetta notes the need to distinguish 'collegiality as exercise of the *munus regendi*' from 'magisterial collegiality': 'One cannot speak of collegiality in the Magisterium, rather than universal Magisterium, in which the guarantee of the universality is the gathering of the bishops *cum Petro*' [p. 340].

In the final notes on the ecclesiology of *Lumen Gentium*, the author observes that 'the teaching on collegiality ... opened itself to many still unresolved questions' [p. 343]. The comment of J. Ratzinger is recalled, that the 'doctrinal text of the Council on the Church is not a theological treatise, nor a complete presentation on the Church, but a signpost ...' [p. 345]. As regards belonging to the Church, 'a sort of friction between the invisible Church and the visible Church seems to endure'. Leaving 'a lot of room for non-Catholics belonging to the Church ... has necessitated another document on ecumenism and then other clarifying magisterial documents which have appeared over time' [p. 354]. Even post-conciliar teaching, such as *Dominus Iesus* (2000), does not provide a totally satisfying clarification.

While the ecclesiological chapter treats widely the themes about belonging to the Church (the most enlightening point for the conciliar hermeneutic) and collegiality, the author presents more briefly a third theme emphasised in the conclusion and the bibliography: the sacramentality of the Church.

The pastoral and ecumenical formulation of Mariology

The third example chosen for the pastoral character of conciliar teaching is the fifth chapter: 'Pastoral epiphanies of the Second Vatican Council in the intentions and formation of the conciliar teaching on the Blessed Virgin Mary'. Especially in the wake of the initiatives of the Belgian Cardinal Mercier in coming to a dogmatic definition of Mary's universal mediation, there was a widespread desire, present in hundreds of votes for the preparation of Vatican II, to suggest magisterial clarification on the Blessed Virgin. This Marian trend clashed with the will, especially of Cardinal Bea and the German bishops, to avoid any strong outline of Mary's mediation so as not to stir up the Protestants. The integration of the Marian schema in the constitution on the Church might have appeared to many as a reappraisal of Marian teaching due to ecumenism with the evangelical world. The ecumenical desire had already manifested itself in the Marian schema *De Beata*, prepared by Fr Balić OFM (President of the International Pontifical Marian Academy), which, for example, avoided the term 'Co-redemptrix', while noting that this expression (which indicates co-operation in Redemption) was in itself 'very true'. Ecumenism was also a common thread in the written observations about the Marian schema. Ecumenical concern became problematic when the 'ancient traditions' clashed with the most recent magisterial teaching and when dialogue with Eastern Christians became marginalised in preference for meeting Protestants. The central theological problem here is the mediation of Mary, of which co-redemption is also a part. The two opposed positions clashed in the emblematic discourses of Cardinals König and Santos, and resulted in the paradigmatic voting on the integration or otherwise of the Marian schema in the constitution on the Church. This divided the Council Fathers into two almost numerically equal factions, although, by a small margin, the 'ecumenical' outline, which, according to Cardinal König, did not wish in the least to minimalise traditional Marian teaching, but support the encounter with the separated brethren, especially those from the Protestant world, triumphed.

A 'first analysis of an *in fieri* Mariology' raises some critical questions about the future prospects of a dialogue which encourages 'deep down a more pessimistic vision of human co-operation in salvation' [p. 399], as we see it in Protestantism. The Marian section concludes with the presentation of the discussion between Balić and Philips, the two authors of the Marian chapter in *Lumen Gentium*. Lanzetta also highlights the corrections which came from the appropriate subcommission working with Philips, who had the main responsibility for the drafting of the text. The author is of the opinion that the Marian chapter indicates 'significant Marian progression' and preserves the substance of traditional Mariology, but he also notes certain limitations which could encourage a doctrinal regression.

In his chapter devoted to Mary, without contradicting what has been rightly stated, the author has been able to note that the council teaching clearly describes Mary's active co-operation in salvation, leading, at least in fact, to an invaluable clarification of the disputed question about co-redemption, excluding a minimalist vision (of only indirect co-operation in Redemption). The council document preserves the doctrinal treasure, with important nuances on the relationship between Mary and the Church, although it is also true that from various points of view there are also limitations to the text which is placed in the stream of the tradition before and after the Council gathering.

Final proposals

At the end of his major work, Fr Lanzetta formulates the question if the Council wanted to inaugurate a 'new theological season' 'with a more pastoral outlook' so that 'metaphysical theology' might now in fact be 'unworkable'. In order to be able to respond, the author presents some 'concluding remarks', formulated in five points.

The first point, on hermeneutics (in general), reiterates the need to place the Council within the reality of the Church and not extrapolate it from its context in the name of the 'event' category. The pastoral choice of limiting itself to the level of authentic ordinary Magisterium, with the exception (according to various interpretations) of the sacramentality of the episcopate, is indicated as a *Leitmotiv* of Vatican II.

The second point of the summary concerns 'the position of the Council about the theological qualification of teachings'. Taking into account in particular the affirmations of the Doctrinal Commission of Vatican II and of Paul VI, Lanzetta speaks about 'the effective exercise of the authentic ordinary Magisterium, even though the form is that of the extraordinary or solemn Magisterium, because it is the teaching of an ecumenical council' [p. 431]. Such teaching is received 'with the religious deference of the intellect and the will in the field of an adherence which is not of faith, neither *credenda* nor *tenenda*, but is a "probable" adherence ...' [p. 431]. So 'the most suitable theological qualification for the teachings examined by us ... seems to be that of *sententiae teologicae ad fidem pertinentes*: questions on which the Magisterium has still not definitively pronounced, whose denial could lead to endangering others truths of faith and whose truth is guaranteed by their intimate link with Revelation' [p. 432].

As regards the relationship between Scripture and Tradition, for ecumenical reasons the Council did not pronounce on the material sufficiency or insufficiency of Sacred Scripture. Without doubting the progress of the constitution *Dei verbum*, especially on the description of Revelation, Lanzetta underlines the need, already affirmed during the Council itself by Paul VI, for a not just interpretative Tradition, but also constitutive. 'Only ... if full status is given back to the life-giving content of *Traditio fidei* in the theological universe is it possible to raise up the Church again ...' [p. 437]. For an in-depth examination, the author proposes the Eucharistic path, referring to 1 Co 11:23 (Paul transmits what he has received).

As regards ecclesiological teaching, the author makes his point above all about 'being a member' of the Church. In order not to hurt the sensitivities of the separated brethren, the Council did not clarify whether baptised non-Catholics are incorporated as members of the Catholic Church. According to Lanzetta, it seems better to underline the non-Catholic Christians being related to the Church so as not to separate 'drastically the visible and hierarchical aspect of the Church from the mystical and communion aspects' [p. 444].

The last passage of the conclusions concerns the form of the conciliar Magisterium. Lanzetta refers to the suggestion of a recent doctoral thesis according to which Vatican II (at least for the documents it examined) used 'a *munus praedicandi* more than *docendi*, as teaching which orientates praxis and is not exercised as *munus determinandi*' (a summary of the work of F. Kolfhaus). So the question is raised if a new era with 'a predicative or declarative Magisterium as a new form of the *munus docendi*' has begun [p. 448]. It is true that the Council texts lend themselves to the interpretation reported, above all on the basis of the statements of John XXIII and of Paul VI, but it must be underlined that the condemnation of errors, too, can be a pastoral necessity. Lanzetta believes that 'a more declarative form of Magisterium, that is to say, more pastoral, is both useful and necessary to reach the heart of the human person', but there is no need to 'neglect the proper dogmatic form which is definitive and infallible' [p. 451].

In Vatican II there are therefore 'different questions which still remain open'. To clarify these issues, the appropriate theological reflection is called upon 'to see the Second Vatican Council as part of a whole, a whole which is much greater: the Church' [p. 452]. To show this insertion of the last Council in the overall reality of the Church, Lanzetta proposes a dogmatic definition of the mediation of Mary. This proposal is also shared by other authors and church initiatives, especially since 1993, but certainly calls (so we might add) for a less optimistic evaluation of affinity with the Protestant world than found at the start of the 60s among influential protagonists, especially German-speaking, at the Council. It would be a theme to examine in depth, but that would be beyond the scope of our author's current work.

Lanzetta's work is a brilliant treatment of the chosen theme. The author is well aware of contemporary discussion and the sources of Vatican II. The thesis provides an original contribution both from an historical point of view (the material which emerged from archival research, in particular Paul VI's intervention on *Dei verbum*) and that of systematic reflection. The author does not content himself with just presenting the various positions (which he does in a precise manner), but also makes clarifying suggestions which can illuminate current debates. The central themes are examined (discussion about the sources of Revelation, ecclesiology, Mariology, the hermeneutic of the magisterial statements, etc.). All the various aspects are directed to gain a better understanding of the significance and import of council teaching. Enjoy reading it!

Professor Dr Manfred Hauke
Lugano, 31 May 2013
Feast of the Visitation of the Blessed Virgin Mary

INTRODUCTION

JUST OVER FIFTY years have passed since the solemn conclusion of the 21st ecumenical assembly of the Catholic Church, the Second Vatican Council (1962–1965), desired by Pope Saint John XXIII as a 'new Pentecost' for the whole Church. The Holy Father wanted to offer to the whole Church her own new awareness, and to the world a new message of hope. Almost on the threshold of a new millennium and after a fratricidal war, which deeply wounded the human condition, the occasion was opportune to revive the Gospel in the world, restoring trust and hope to humanity. The First Vatican Council had not been officially concluded and some of its teachings needed to be completed, such as that on the Church. We could say Vatican II was the most 'ecumenical' Council in the history of the Church, due to those present and the interest shown in its preparation and work. Numerous theologians took part as consultors to and experts for the bishops (*periti*), and they really had a decisive role: without doubt this was a great novelty.

Since the end of the Council there has been an abundance of most precious hermeneutic work and the birth of different study centres with a specific focus on Vatican II.[1] Alongside this, however, there has been no lack of disagreements and disputes about the very interpretation of the Council and, in church circles, about a correct hermeneutic to apply to the Council. What did Vatican II really mean?

1 Three French-speaking university institutions were established and began a research project on the hermeneutic of Vatican II: the Laval University (Québec), the Institut Catholique de Paris and the Catholic University of Louvain (Louvain-la-Neuve). A first congress was held in Paris from 5–6 October 2005. There are also two Italian institutions of note. One opened in 1998 and is affiliated to the Lateran University: Centro Studi e Ricerche 'Concilio Vaticano II', and the other, which had opened earlier in Bologna, with a specialist archive on Vatican II: Fondazione per le Scienze Religiose Giovanni XXIII.

What did it represent? A 'spirit of the Council', very often confused with the spirit of the world, prevailed, and the magisterial texts were simply ignored to make room for a 'spring' artificially created by some pastoral experts. The question arose about whether the Council was 'everything' for the faith, just like a new era of the Church, a path of no-return; on the other hand, it was presented as a hiccup, an error in judgement. For many, a starting point. For others, a halt. What was the last Council for the Church?[2] The question divides the Church like never before.

Into this panorama, of not easy and unambiguous reading, comes this work, too, which aims at being a theological contribution for a more appropriate hermeneutic to be applied to Vatican II, entering, so to speak, into the Council, reading its texts in their gradual magisterial formation, noting the significant theological contribution alongside a choice which frequently crops up: the pastoral nature of Vatican II. So, a hermeneutical work stemming from the current position of the Church and the Magisterium of Pope Ratzinger. In fact, it was above all with Benedict XVI, through his well-known address to the Roman Curia on 22 December 2005,[3] that the theme of the Second Vatican Council, especially with regard to its correct or incorrect interpretation, came to the fore again and asserted itself anew as an emerging question in historiographic and theological debate. In that address, the Pope called not just for the adoption of a correct hermeneutic of the 'reform' in the continuity of Vatican II with the whole Tradition of the Church, poles apart from that misleading hermeneutic of 'discontinuity and rupture', but also underlined—and this is important to note from the theological point of view—the different levels of the reform. In the Council, in the

---

2 The question of H.-J. Frings, *Aufbruch oder Betriebsunfall? Das II. Vatikanische Konzil und seine Folgen* (Ostfildern: Patmos, 2010), is interesting: during the pontificates of John Paul II and Benedict XVI the start was held back. So the author suggests the hypotheses for a Vatican III.

3 In AAS 98 (2006), pp. 40–53.

words of Benedict XVI, there is at the same time continuity in doctrine and in the unchanging principles and discontinuity in the historic or incidental forms which led to those principles: 'Basic decisions, therefore, continue to be well-grounded, whereas the way they are applied to new contexts can change'.[4] This was said with special reference to the issue of freedom of religion, offering also a summary of one of the predominant goals of the Council: 'to determine in a new way the relationship between the Church and the modern era'.[5] The theological-hermeneutic endeavour must channel itself in this direction: to co-ordinate theological continuity and discontinuity, bearing in mind the changed historical, philosophical, systematic panorama of the modern era, about which the Council principally called for discussion.[6]

Echoing this important indication is another teaching of the Holy Father Paul VI. In the course of a catechesis given at the General Audience on 12 January 1966, explaining the significance of the Second Vatican Council for the Church, as well as making it clear that

> The teachings of the Council do not constitute a complete, organic system of Catholic doctrine. Doctrine is much more extensive, as everyone knows, and it was not called into question by the Council nor substantially modified. Instead, the Council confirms, illustrates, defends, and develops it with a most authoritative apologia full of wisdom, vigour and confidence ...[7]

Pope Montini also provided an indispensable hermeneutical indication:

> We must not separate the teachings of the Council from the doctrinal heritage of the Church. Instead we must take a good look at where they fit into it and at how they are consistent

---

4 *Ibid.*, p. 50.

5 *Ibid.*, p. 48.

6 According to Ruggieri, the Council went beyond this alternative. Cf. G. Ruggieri, *Ritrovare il concilio* (Turin: Einaudi, 2012), p. 27.

7 Original Italian text in *Encicliche e Discorsi di Paolo VI*, vol. IX, 1966, (Rome: Paoline, 1966), p. 50.

> with it and supply it with added testimony, growth, explanation, and application. Then even the 'novelties' in doctrine or regulation coming from the Council will be seen in their proper proportions and will not give rise to objections about the Church's fidelity to its teaching function, but will acquire that true meaning which makes it shine with a higher light.[8]

Another significant epistemological and hermeneutical suggestion comes to us from the 1985 Extraordinary Synod of Bishops, called by St John Paul II to mark the 20th anniversary of the conclusion of the Second Vatican Council. The level of renewal of the Church according to the last Council, its reception, the difficulties encountered, errors or abuses in interpretation, as well as the application of the Council documents in the Church, were examined. In the summary of the responses submitted to the General Secretary of the Synod emphasis was placed on the repeated reference to the fact that the Council documents were 'scarcely known and often badly interpreted'.[9] To that was added another note of the Fathers: there was 'a crisis of identity about being Catholic just as there is a crisis of anthropological and ethical values in society'.[10]

In the proposals for the incipient Synod there was a desire to adopt a precise *method*: to limit the debate to the four conciliar constitutions, that on the liturgy, *Sacrosanctum concilium*, that on the Church, *Lumen Gentium*, that on divine revelation, *Dei verbum*, and finally that on the Church in the contemporary world, *Gaudium et spes*. This was because they 'encompass the whole doctrinal nucleus of the Council'; what's more 'the two constitutions *Lumen Gentium* and *Dei verbum* are like the framework for the whole of the conciliar Magisterium'.[11]

---

8 *Ibid.*

9 ESV n. 2687.

10 *Ibid.*

11 *Ibid.*, n. 2690. See also Congregation for the Doctrine of the Faith, *Note with pastoral recommendations for the Year of Faith*, 6 January 2012, which confirms this vision: the Constitutions are the pillars of the Council around which are arranged the Declarations and Decrees which in turn address some of the

It was then pointed out that the 'original and decisive insight of the Council was to be identified either in the renewal (aggiornamento) or new Pentecost of the Spirit or in the spiritual impulse'.[12]

The Synod had to divide its study commitment distinguishing the Church *ad intra* and *ad extra*. As regards the Church looking out, it was clearly stated that the 'Constitution *Gaudium et spes* constitutes a new literary genre in the theology of the councils'.[13] It recalled the 'optimism with which the Council characterised the Church's relationships with the world. However, today one sees there is a widespread cultural pessimism in the face of the daily situations, where there is the race to armaments, the scourge of hunger, the pollution of the living environment, the threats to human life'.[14] Which is to say that *Gaudium et spes*, inaugurating a new magisterial genre, was in truth not very prophetic. This is important in correctly developing an appropriate conciliar hermeneutic, starting from distinguishing the four constitutions from the nine decrees and the three declarations. Then, distinguishing within the two dogmatic constitutions themselves, the liturgical and pastoral; the latter is at an inferior level, as regards the first two, while the liturgical is as at a middle level. The Council is not a complete whole, an undifferentiated homogenous teaching: those who see it as *unicum*, quickly either take it in a block as infallible or are forced to reject it as dangerous to the faith. It is my opinion that to understand the Council correctly very often it is necessary to distinguish.

The final report of the said Synod bears the title *Exeunte coetu secundo*, a report given by Cardinal Danneels, Archbishop of Brussels-Malines (7 December 1985). Here, repeating the need to devote special attention to the four major constitutions, as 'interpretative keys of the other decrees and declarations',[15] the following is added:

---

major challenges of the day.

12 *Ibid.*

13 *Ibid.*, n. 2695.

14 *Ibid.*

> It is not licit to separate the pastoral character from the doctrinal vigour of the documents. In the same way, it is not legitimate to separate the spirit and the letter of the Council. Moreover, the Council must be understood in continuity with the great tradition of the Church, and at the same time we must receive light from the Council's own doctrine for today's Church and the men of our time. The Church is one and the same throughout all the councils.[16]

Again, reflecting on the sources by which the Church lives, Scripture, Tradition and Magisterium, once again the concept of what is doctrinal and what is pastoral is clarified, without placing opposition between the two different angles, which, on the other hand, as we will see, often permeated the debate in the General Congregations of the Council and the Doctrinal Commission itself:

> The false opposition between doctrinal and pastoral responsibilities must be avoided and overcome. In fact, the true intent of pastoral work consists in actualising and making concrete the truth of salvation, which is in itself valid for all times. As true pastors, the bishops must point out the right way to the flock, strengthen the faith of the flock, keep dangers away from it.[17]

The antithesis, which was pressing, must be avoided. In fact, rightly so, here the Synod re-stated the classical concept of doctrine and the pastoral: the pastoral which, emanating from dogma, makes concrete the fulfilment of salvation *hic et nunc* of the brethren. Dogmatics, on the other hand, sheds an unequivocal light on the elements of the faith. The question which I will raise in this work could now be anticipated thus: does Vatican II abide by this traditional distinction between doctrine and the pastoral, or—as I believe—leaving the two concepts in a sort of general fluctuation, without a prior *explicatio terminorum*, sometimes unites them, sometimes replaces one with the

---

15 *Ibid.*, n. 2724.

16 *Ibid.*

17 *Ibid.*, n. 2733.

other (mostly pastoral for the doctrinal), sometimes prefers not to enter into 'issues of schools of thought' in order to respect its aim, that of giving a decisively new *form* to the whole of its doctrinal teaching? It is not always easy to distinguish the *mens* of the Council precisely on this harmonious relationship between doctrine and the pastoral. Ecumenism had to express a teaching to restore the unity of Christians, echoing the ecclesiological vision of *Lumen Gentium* (did this always happen or just sometimes?), but also had to—or was able to—characterise in a prevalent manner the pastoral aim of the Council. I believe this was one of the central difficulties for a hermeneutic which, while respecting the doctrinal of Vatican II, does not exacerbate it to the point of placing it in an absolute self to the detriment of the whole of the Tradition of the Church and all its preceding Magisterium.

The so-called 'aggiornamento', too, the concept which became like a mirror of the Council, was clarified by the 1985 Synod in its correct meaning:

> From this paschal perspective, which affirms the unity of the cross and the resurrection, the true and false meaning of so-called 'aggiornamento' is discovered. An easy accommodation that could lead to the secularisation of the Church is to be excluded. Also excluded is an immobile closing in upon itself of the community of the faithful. Affirmed instead is a missionary openness for the integral salvation of the world.[18]

So 'dialogue must not be opposed to mission'.[19] The opposite of conservative is not progressive, as Ratzinger said in the same year to the journalist V. Messori, but missionary.[20] Behind it all there is a correct hermeneutic which uses the word *aggiornamento*: to return effectively to the sources, allowing them to live in their uninterrupted

---

18 *Ibid.*, n. 2751.

19 *Ibid.*, n. 2753.

20 Cf. J. Ratzinger, *The Ratzinger Report. An Exclusive Interview on the state of the Church* (Leominster: Fowler Wright Books, 1985), p. 11.

being handed on, or to make history more comfortable.[21] What did the Council want on this point? Did perhaps the logic of an opposite reform impose itself—as Ratzinger again recalled in his address at the *Katholikentag* of Bamberg in 1966[22]—compared to that desired for example by St Teresa of Avila for her Carmel, by St Catherine of Siena for the Roman Curia, by St Maximilian Kolbe for the Franciscan Order? Was there really a return to the sources, or, often, did that *ressourcement* impose the rule of adapting to the times, to modernity, to history? However, the sources are alive in their uninterrupted being handed on.

So what is the goal I suggest in this book? As indicated, to offer a hermeneutic principle of the Second Vatican Council, which is consistent with the assembly, examining some conciliar teachings chosen by us according to a criterion of the theological bearing of those teachings in development subsequent to the Council: in *Dei verbum* I will focus on the relationship between Sacred Scripture and Tradition, in *Lumen Gentium* I will analyse the concept of Church in its entirety and in particular I will focus on the question of belonging to the Church, on the consideration given to 'members' of the Church and to collegiality. Again in the Constitution on the Church, I will finally examine the chapter devoted to the Blessed Virgin Mary in the mystery of Christ and the Church, reconstructing the genesis of the Marian teaching, the *iter* and choices which ended, after a paradigmatic vote, mirror of the problem which I propose to examine, in the promulgation of Chapter VIII as the concluding chapter. The study of these teachings will help us to understand the nature and goal of

---

21 Cf. J. Ratzinger, *Salt of the Earth. Christianity and the Catholic Church at the End of the Millennium. An Interview with Peter Seewald* (San Francisco: Ignatius Press, 1997), p. 75 (original German *Salz der Erde. Christentum und katholische Kirche an der Jahrtausendwende. Ein Gespräch mit Peter Seewald,* Stuttgart 1996).

22 Cf. J. Ratzinger, *Mon Concile Vatican II. Enjeux et perspectives* (Perpignan: Artège Spiritualité, 2011), p. 264. See the original text 'Der Katholizismus nach dem Konzil', in Id., *Zur Lehre des Zweiten Vatikanischen Konzils,* II (Gesammelte Schriften 7/2), (Freiburg im B.: Herder, 2012), pp. 1003–1025.

the Council—'*Ratione habita,... tum finis peculiaris huius Concilii, qui est principaliter pastoralis*'[23]—just as presented by the Popes who guided the assembly and as interpreted by the Council Fathers, showing how easily pastoral and doctrinal intersected in the Council. For the Fathers, did the pastoral always depend on the doctrinal? As regards the goal of the Council, did its ecumenical pastoral nature especially influence the presentation of Catholic teaching? This is a hermeneutical criterion that should not be underestimated.

So I will examine the Council, wanting to discover above all its *mens*, what animated the Fathers and what they asserted, which then determined choices and decisions. The pastoral field is not always clearly distinct from the doctrinal field for the simple fact that no definition was given of one or the other, but often, the two terms used in their traditional meaning, serve sometimes to confirm sound theology, sometimes to still leave the doctrinal to theology, sometimes to give rise to a development which necessarily involves the faith and its teaching.

Our theological horizon and criterion of assessment, as the 1985 Synod already proposed, are therefore placed within the classical distinction between dogmatic and pastoral.[24] Dogmatics, which is to do with doctrine, the dogma of faith, must illuminate the discipline, the customs, and offer truthful theoretical premises for the catechetical and missionary proclamation, with the aim of spreading the truth of Christ and preserving it pure and sincere in those who accept it.[25]

---

23 AS II/6, p. 305: it is the official response of the General Secretariat of the Council about the theological qualification of the conciliar teaching, dating back to 29 November 1963, in the 78th General Congregation. See also AS III/8, p. 10: declaration of the Doctrinal Commission, 6 March 1964, about the theological qualification of the teaching on the Church. Here is taken up again the idiom about the pastoral goal of the Council.

24 On the other hand, what Schillebeeckx writes in his Notes is symptomatic: 'The *pastoral council* becomes *doctrinal*, precisely on account of its pastoral character. Pastoral demands call for *doctrinal deepening*', E. Schillebeeckx, *The Council notes of Edward Schillebeeckx 1962–1963* (Leuven: Peters, 2011), p. 37.

The pastoral depends on the dogmatic. Vice-versa, the pastoral can constitute a challenge which leads to a deepening of doctrine. Dogma, however, must guide praxis, just like the Good Shepherd who feeds his sheep with the food of the Word, which is spirit and life (cf. Jn 6:63), to the point of giving his life for them (cf. Jn 10:11).

Vatican II certainly inaugurated a new way of being Council, which however must be protected from an excessive enthusiasm, which easily absorbs the text in the event and above all in the latter the constant teaching of the Church. Its documents prefer not the assertive or censorious form, but rather the declamatory, descriptive or narrative. A new conciliar style like a passage from *what* to *how is the Church*?[26] A new conciliar paradigm?[27] If the response is yes, but without the appropriate distinction of the conciliar *mens* from the differentiated nature of the documents, up to the different rank of the Council's magisterial authority even within the same document, then the path is thrown wide open to make Vatican II almost the only council of the Church.

This decisive change of compass places before us the 'principle of the pastoral nature' of the Church in its beginnings. In our opinion it is precisely here that one of the problems lies hidden: if Vatican II is the start of the pastoral nature of the Church, were all the previous councils which condemned errors about faith and morals not pastoral? Again, what then does the pastoral nature in Vatican II mean?

---

25 In this regard it is good to refer to a sort of definition of the *munus pastoralis* of the Church, expressed by Blessed Pius X in the Dogmatic Constitution *Pastor aeternus*: 'Huic pastorali muneri ut satisfacerent, praedecessores Nostri indefessam semper operam dederunt, ut salutaris Christi doctrina apud omnes terrae populos propagaretur, parique cura vigilarunt, ut, ubi recepta esset, sincera et pura conservaretur', DH 3069.

26 Cf. J. W. O'Malley, 'The Style of Vatican II. The "How" of the Church changed during the Council', in *America* 188/6 (2003), pp. 12–15, echoed by G. Routhier, 'Il Vaticano II come stile', in *La Scuola Cattolica* 136 (2008), pp. 5–32.

27 Cf. Ruggieri, *Ritrovare il concilio*, p. 115.

Would the pastoral lead to the doctrinal and no longer vice-versa? According to the very careful study of H. Sauer, Vatican II inaugurated the theological principle of pastoral nature through the Constitution on Divine Revelation, before then finding its explanation in the Constitution on the Church in the contemporary world. What's more, with its highest magisterial authority, it bound the Church to its pastoral principle.[28] The term 'pastoral' here is not seen as a consequence of 'dogmatic', or as an instrumental mediation in the application of the truth of faith inferred in a positive way from Revelation. In such case the pastoral plan would be only secondary: while dogma would remain invariable and closed in on itself, the vital, historical and social process would not influence the dogmatic and metaphysical vision. Dogma would relativise praxis, vice-versa there is no knowledge of a principle which questions dogma, which instead would be seen as *contradictio in adiecto*. Vatican II, placing the emphasis on the Church as a sign of herself and Revelation as self-communication of God Himself through words and signs, changes tack, according to Sauer: it conforms with a sort of perichoresis between dogma and pastoral, which constitute like two poles of a whole. Two poles which are not one above the other but which are related one to the other. That will enable uniting experience and faith, no longer in a deductive manner, so as to finally overcome a sort of dogmatism, of externalism and of anti-modernism, which negates the quality of the human experience. First, in the name of the transcendence of God the immanence and concreteness of faith was revealed, but now instead, as in faith, immanence and transcendence in a mutual inter-penetration can be tightly bound one to the other.[29] Having carefully recon-

[28] Cf. H. Sauer, *Erfahrung und Glaube. Die Begründung des pastoralen Prinzips durch die Offenbarungskonstitution des II. Vatikanischen Konzils* (Frankfurt am Main: Peter Lang, 1993), p. 8: 'das Konzil hat die Kirche mit höchster lehramtlicher Autorität auf ihr pastorales Prinzip festgelegt'.

[29] Cf. *Ibid.*, pp. 6–8: 'Mit diesem theologischen Ansatz überwindet das Konzil grundsätzlich den Extrinsezismus, der im Namen des transzendenten Gottes die Immanenz (und somit die prinzipielle Bedeutung der Inkarnation Gottes)

structed the genesis of *Dei verbum*, and having pointed out the overcoming of 'Ottaviani's dogmatism' as a rejection of a theological position,[30] Sauer, along with Rahner as well as Kant, is thus able to articulate his leading idea: 'experience as principle of theology' and that by reason of the fact that there is a fundamental experience (*Grunderfahrung*) of faith, and starting from Revelation as a living principle of the transmission of faith.[31]

On the line of the Council as initiator of the 'principle of pastoral nature'—which unites various exponents from the School of Bologna—we also find C. Theobald, who places his hermeneutical work more from the point of view of the reception of the Council. Theobald establishes the said principle of pastoral nature by asking: what is the relationship between the so bold and surprisingly new project of Vatican II in particular in relation to the Council of Trent and Vatican I?

The answer to the question is not easy, and remained implicitly in suspense throughout the whole of the Council and also afterwards. *Gaudet mater Ecclesia* provided a first response in its manner of assessing the historical context and immediately situating the 'dogmatic', beyond an alternative phase between a doctrine without the pastoral and a pastoral without the doctrine, at the point in which the two find themselves dividing: overcoming the Tridentine distinction between *fides* and *mores* (doctrine and discipline), the Pope insisted, with theological modernity, on the form of the Christian faith, displacing it however from its rational credibility (Vatican I) to its historical-practical rootedness (Vatican II). ... the *paradosis* is here conceived as a *way of doing*, or as a believing and acting pastorally (or apostolically)

verrät und damit den Tatsachenbezug des Glaubens aufgibt, statt Transzendenz und Immanenz in ihrer gegenseitigen Durchdringung als im Glauben voneinander untrennbar erfassen zu können', *Ibid.*, pp. 7–8.

30 'Das Konzil hat mit der Ablehnung des Schemas "De Fontibus" nicht nur ein Schema abgelehnt (aufgrund einer zu abstrakten Sprache, einer unangemessenen Gliederung oder sonstiger formaler Elemente), sondern eine theologische Position, die sich in diesem Schema artikuliert', *Ibid.*, p. 508.

31 Cf. *Ibid.*, especially pp. 584–607.

intimately linked between them and situated in a continual process of historical re-interpretation of the mystery *in its fullness*.[32]

The title of our work could give rise to the understanding that in some way I am on the same lines. Instead, I do not intend to establish a 'principle of pastoral nature' in some new fashion, to the point, nevertheless, of having to characterise the Church and the whole of the conciliar and post-conciliar Magisterium with the qualification 'pastoral', which in some way subsumes and determines doctrine. I will embrace the idea that the *proprium* of Vatican II consisted in this: a new way of being council and then Church of the Council, in which the doctrinal necessities cannot be dictated by pastoral motives and by the changed and changing needs of the time. All that depended on the programmatic discourse of John XXIII, *Gaudet mater ecclesia*, so dear to the School of Bologna so as to bind there in some way all the hermeneutical consequences of Vatican II, reproaching any distancing from it almost as a betrayal of the Council. Is it an a priori hermeneutic to lead back the whole of the history of the Church to a recommencement after a thousand-year gap? One cannot make one Pope or one speech almost the rising star of a new era. That necessarily implies historical and theological bias.

Precisely on this point I wish to provide a degree of clarity with our contribution: with Vatican II, especially in the receptive phase of the Council, did the doctrinal and the pastoral come together without further distinguishing between the two? I believe not, and that this 'no' must remain in Christian tradition in order to distinguish the revealed from the historical plan, the mystery from the varied anthropological conceptions and from the different theological systems. But to say no it is necessary to ascertain that there is a certain unification there. It is a positioning of the Council and to study it one has to enter into the Council.

---

32 C. Theobald, *La ricezione del Vaticano II*, 1, *Tornare alla sorgente* (Bologna: EDB, 2011), p. 202 (French original, *La réception du concile Vatican II*, I, *Accéder à la source*, Paris: CEF, 2009).

My intention, once again, is that of seeing how the pastoral was predominant at Vatican II, to the extent that it dictated the agenda and the direction of the debates, to the extent of preferring some doctrinal elements and neglecting others, but not to the point of having to make of it an archetypal theological principle for the conciliar hermeneutic and for theology itself. Otherwise one runs the risk of absorbing the theology and doctrine of Vatican II in the history, in the present moment, and having to make of every possible historical moment of the Church in the world that favourable one for a true hermeneutic of the Second Vatican Council. This seems to us to be the real problem. In my opinion the Church can get out of the doctrinal *impasse* and the crisis of faith in which she is living, only to the extent that the dogmatic field will once again be very clear and distinct from the practical-pastoral one, where praxis, such as ecumenism, depends on truth, on doctrine. Praxis must be guided by dogma, but this will not be possible without a defining Magisterium (not necessarily or only *ex cathedra*), in which the preconception of the experts is not admitted, but simply says to the faithful what is to be believed and what is to be lived.

So I would like to clarify and indicate a possible hermeneutical principle, to orientate a more faithful reception of the Second Vatican Council, which respects the Council in its precise identity and so gives the doctrines their right place in the revealed and defined structure. This hermeneutical research allows us to thus get into the conciliar teachings: from analysis of them I will infer a criterion for their correct interpretation, which can then serve in some way as a 'model' for a wider conciliar interpretation, applicable to other documents and to other teachings. I will limit myself to some conciliar teachings, in my opinion believed to be typical, from which can be inferred the endeavour of doctrinal renewal proposed by the Fathers and finalised in the two Constitutions *Lumen Gentium* and *Dei verbum*, and also the will, often pastoral and ecumenical, which determined their formulation, leaving them however sometimes with a lack of precision which lends itself or lent itself in the subsequent theological hermeneutic and reception to misunderstanding, as well. It is the doctrinal in itself, deliberately taught in a broader and colloquial manner, which must be carefully assessed and analysed, to discover sometimes the limit of it being set out and also to suggest some possible developments of the same along the line of the uninterrupted Tradition of Church. This allows us also to arrive at a theological qualification of our teachings, as appropriate as possible to the character of the documents, at the insistence in proposing that teaching, and at the same time the way of expressing it, that it is to say, in conformity with the common rules of theology, confirming their level of magisterial authority.

Certainly the doctrinal element of Vatican II is to be read in the light of the perennial Tradition of the Church and the Council cannot but be inscribed in this uninterrupted Tradition. On the other hand, reading the whole and uninterrupted Tradition in the light of Vatican II is more complex. This latter movement cannot be taken for granted. Primarily, because the *whole* Tradition of faith is not in Vatican II. Then, because we are dealing with a Council, every time Vatican II teaches the new teaching does not necessarily develop the previous one. On this point there can be no generalities. There is a need to indicate precisely the teachings which are a progression and those which still leave room for a perfective development. It is a sign of the level of magisterial assertion in which Vatican II places itself. Can it be claimed, for example, that the ecclesiology of *Lumen Gentium* in general is a development compared to the ecclesiology of Vatican I? Yes, if we speak of a new, broader theological reflection on the Church in her different properties and in the different attributes which make up the Church; no, on the other hand, if we wish to place with that on the same magisterial level the Primacy of the Roman Pontiff and his infallible Magisterium[33] and the episcopal collegiality of *Lumen Gentium* 22. In *Pastor aeternus* we have a dogmatic definition[34] and

33 Cf. DH 3050–3075.

34 Cf. *Ibid.*, 3074.

some canons[35] which establish infallibly faith in this truth, in *Lumen Gentium* we have infallibility only where there is a reiteration of it, but generally the Constitution on the Church is placed doctrinally on the level of authentic ordinary Magisterium. There is normally an expansion of the theological vision, a development and a deepening, but this is not always and necessarily followed by an enforceability of faith as certain assent. The development of a teaching, declared as such by the Magisterium, requires that corresponding to it there is also the obligation to adhere to it with theological faith. Where does Vatican II obligate with an act of theological faith? So it is about evaluating its teachings carefully, taking into account what seems to us to be decisive: the teaching for that historical moment, for that situation. This does not prevent having to not only express the teaching today in an *already* different manner, but also to have to express it in a more effective, more precise, less colloquial manner, in order to prevent streams of other possible interpretations of the Council.

To that end, my work will be divided into five chapters. The first chapter will help the reader to enter into the hermeneutical theme. I will develop some historical-theological notes to tackle the theme of Vatican II and to thus also situate my interpretative effort. I will also offer, with the Magisterium, the doctrinal elements to set out the discourse about the qualification of the Council teachings and I will recall the need of the theological notes and respective censures, which sadly fell into disuse but remain invaluable to guide the work of the theologian in a systematic manner. In the concluding reflections, on the other hand, I will propose the *status quaestionis* of the theological qualification of the Council teachings as emerged from the study of the Council and I will give my interpretation.

In the second chapter I will make the point about the theological interpretation of the Council and some of its teachings in theologians, among whom I have chosen seven positions: a Father, some periti and others, instead, theologians/historians in the reception of the

35 Cf. *Ibid.*, 3058, 3064, 3075.

Council. In my opinion the seven stances chosen by me are well representative of the different theological threads which developed in the Council and immediately after. This theological status of the 'Vatican II' question and its teachings will help us to gain a greater awareness of the need for a hermeneutic as much as possible in conformity with the Council. The theological contribution is an indication of the major role played by theology at Vatican II, of the problem of the hermeneutic which in some way arose from the Council itself and among the interpreters themselves, unravelling more possible paths. So it is absolutely essential for a theological memory looking to the future with certainty.

With the third chapter I come to the heart of my task. I will study the Scripture-Tradition relationship in *Dei verbum,* starting from the first schema *De fontibus* and arriving at the promulgation of the Constitution on Divine Revelation. For every teaching studied I will begin my examination locating the research in the preparation for the Council, in its development and its definitive decisions, passing through the great theological work of the Commissions and Sub-commissions devoted to it.

In the fourth chapter I look at the mystery of the Church as presented first in *De Ecclesia* and then in *Lumen Gentium*. I will focus on the debate about the schema and then I will enter *in media res* of some particular teachings: the 'members' of the Church and therefore the *visible* and *invisible* aspect of the mystical Body and their intimate unity and inter-dependence, showing the Church as the only necessary means for salvation even though this is realised also outside her visible confines; I will then speak about collegiality in the conciliar debate and the Church as *sacramentum*.

The fifth chapter will be devoted to the Marian schema *De Beata Virgine Maria,* to the debate about its inclusion in that on the Church or its independence as another conciliar document. With such a sensitive decision and the narrow voting margin there was a great change in the Council. It was this which was rather the 'pastoral change' of Vatican II and not just the programmatic discourse of John XXIII. The subsequent work of two great theologians, Balić and Philips, called to collaborate on the redaction of a Marian schema in conformity with the pastoral needs of the Council, highlights both the desire to provide teaching on the Mother of God from the relationships never before known, and the shrewdness of avoiding some teachings, such as maternal mediation and co-redemption, since they were very sensitive issues at the ecumenical level.

In the concluding remarks, by way of summary I will present what has emerged from the work. As well as the *normal* testifying of the Council on ordinary authentic Magisterium, there are also three important points for an overall evaluation: the magisterial position which I have defined 'neutral' about the relationship 'Scripture and Tradition'; the absence of the theme of the 'members' of the Church and the movement of the question of the *plene/non plene* belonging of non-Catholic Christians to the Church; finally, the new magisterial form which seems to emerge from Vatican II, which I believe it is possible to call *declaratory*.

In this work I will make use of numerous archive documents, which have been invaluable sources in reconstructing some key passages, both historical and theological, and at the same time in offering an interpretation much more in conformity with the facts and the faith of the Church. For example, I found myself before the Holy Father Paul VI, who followed the work of the Council with care and eager watchfulness, strongly asking that the constitutive value of Tradition be expressed or that, in chapter III of *Lumen Gentium*, the fundamental dependence of the authority of the episcopal College on the consent of the Roman Pontiff be clarified. However, the assembly was not always and in everything attentive to this voice, to the point that Ottaviani was able to risk directly with the Pope the idea of inserting a special note in *Dei verbum*, too. Such documents are invaluable and, along with another great quantity still to be archived, indicate that a great part of the story of Vatican II is still to be written. Hence the limitations and verifiability of so many personal diaries.

Can Vatican II be a council for the unity of the Church? This is my wish, desired through the mediation of the Blessed Virgin Mary, Mother of the Church. In this I will raise many questions, much more than answers. I hope at least to have got the right ones.

I

COUNCIL TEACHING AS AN ACT OF THE MAGISTERIUM

HISTORICAL-THEOLOGICAL NOTES FOR AN APPROPRIATE HERMENEUTIC OF VATICAN II

THE FIRST QUESTION in my study is to outline what a council is for the Church and with respect to the Church. The question is not so simple to illustrate. Suffice to recall—as I will do subsequently—the fact that the CIC of 1917 and then that of 1983 provide a definition which betrays the theological formulation of the time: the former, taking note of the conciliar teaching of the second millennium, places the emphasis on the coming together of all those who in the Church participate in the 'supreme power of jurisdiction' to exercise it together with the Pope and under his authority in doctrinal and disciplinary matters. The new Code, taking note of the teaching of the Church-communion, places the emphasis on the council as a collegial act. The council turns out to be one of the ways of such a collegial exercise of the bishops in communion with the Pope.[1]

---

1 Here according to Theobald it would be a relativisation of ecumenical conciliarity and at the end of the day an *exploitation* at the service of the central governance of the Church, 'while Vatican II understood it above all as *expression* and *universal representation* of the particular Churches and their bishops' (Theobald, *La recezione del Vaticano II*, p. 43), according to *Lumen Gentium* 22 on the college of bishops and *Lumen Gentium* 23 about the fact that the one and only universal Church exists in the particular Churches and starting from them.

Right from the first council of Jerusalem, recorded in Acts 15, the Church perceived the need to come together to decide on doctrinal or also disciplinary matters, having, however, relevance to the believed truths. So various types of assemblies or provincial councils took shape, necessitated by the fact that, from time to time, new problems arose due to the heresies which threatened the doctrinal stability and the very social tranquillity of the Church and consequently the State. This until, in 325, with the first ecumenical Council of Nicaea, a major step forward was taken: not only is it important to note the doctrine defined against the Arian heresy, but also the ecumenical convocation by the Emperor and the consequent ratification by the Pope. A very important factor which groups all the councils of antiquity and which in some way also goes beyond the proper definition of 'ecumenical council', which distinguishes Nicaea from the local councils—in St Athanasius († 373) the distinction between Nicaea and the other previous councils was still not clear, but the *faith* taught against errors remained normative—is the *parádosis* as the norm which guides the conciliar assembly, according to the saying of the Apostle Paul: *to hand on what has been received* (cf. 1 Co 11:23 and 15:3). That emerges in a unique way in the Nicaean Symbol of faith: the most that can be said is affirmed and this was the apostolic faith, the faith of the Catholic Church. So on the faith of the Council is conferred the dignity and authority of the *parádosis*, of divine tradition.[2] Therefore the constant conformity of conciliar teaching with Sacred Scripture

---

2 Cf. H. J. Sieben, *Die Konzilsidee der alten Kirche* (Paderborn: Schöningh, 1979), p. 39. The Synod fathers of Nicaea for the first time were called 'Fathers' or 'blessed Fathers' by St Athanasius due to the fact that they were the organs and transmitters of the *parádosis*. The title of 'Fathers': transmitters of the *didaskalìa* of 'Fathers in Fathers', was attributed to them because for St Athanasius it was clear that the Nicaean Symbol, in its positive formulation, was the divine *parádosis*, cf. *Ibid.*

and with tradition is necessary[3]: hence the guarantee of the *antiquitas* of the teaching and therefore the horizontal *consensus*.

Pope Gelasius I in Letter 26 in 495 would clarify, in the wake of St Leo the Great, the principle of the impossible revision of a conciliar definition, on the basis of the explanation of five criteria: 1) conformity of the doctrine with Sacred Scripture; 2) conformity with the tradition; 3) observance of the canons; 4) reception on the part of the universal Church; 5) confirmation on the part of the Apostolic See.[4] A council had to assert itself not first of all for its ecumenism but for the positive norm of the faith defended and taught in an authoritative manner and received universally. It is the revealed *content* which gradually raises consciousness of the *form* of the teaching of such truth, which in turn experiences a gradual development. What is unquestionable is that the first Fathers of the Church 'see in the tradition the very essence of the Council'.[5] So we move towards the problem of the *form* of a council, which remains nevertheless and always attached to the principle of the faithful transmission of the teaching of Christ and of the Apostles.

---

3 The decisive argument at the Second Council of Nicaea (787) for rejecting iconoclasm was the 'teaching of our Holy Fathers' (especially St. Basil, *De Spiritu Sancto* 18, n. 45, PG 32, 149C) and the 'tradition of the Catholic Church': anyone who venerates images, venerates the image par excellence, the Cross of Christ, and in it the Person who is portrayed. Hence the necessary recognition of the whole tradition of the Church ('*pasan parádosin*'), written and unwritten (cf. DH 600, 609). Thus, too, at the Fourth Council of Constantinople (869–870), against the schism of Photius (859), aimed at establishing the veneration of images, the tradition as a rule of faith was invoked. With that are preserved the rules which have been handed on 'to the holy, Catholic and apostolic Church both by the saints and glorious apostles, by the universal and local councils of orthodox bishops, and by every father, bearer of the word of God and doctor of the church', cf. DH 650–652.

4 Cf. Sieben, *Die Konzilsidee der alten Kirche*, pp. 275–277.

5 W. Brandmüller, 'Il Concilio e i Concili. Il Vaticano II nel contesto della storia conciliare', in W. Brandmüller et al, *Le "chiavi" di Benedetto XVI per interpretare il Vaticano II* (Siena: Cantagalli, 2012), p. 59.

1. The form of a council

The novelty of the Council of Nicaea lay in the fact that the need to teach the truth as a spiritual gift was now formulated as a principle. The fundamental problem of a council, right from the outset, was not infallibility but the need to teach the truth. However, this necessity was not immediately recognised before the Council of Nicaea, but, after a long process, the conviction that the Church must be in the position to preserve the Faith from errors, not just once but every time it was necessary, was affirmed. In this way, the ecumenical councils began to distinguish the faith from the heresies, but the concept of infallibility (*Unfehlbarkeit*) was unknown to the ancient Church. This still ambiguous term was used in relation to the councils of the fourteenth century, when in an adversarial manner there was an attempt to subordinate the authority of the Pope to that of the council. Formally the infallibility of the general councils was defended above all by the councils of Basle (1431–1449). In fact, it was precisely the Council of Basle, comments K. Schatz,

> to first claim and very clearly 'infallibility', also independently from the consensus of the church. This can already be easily understood from the fact that from the Council of Pisa onwards the councils found themselves in a situation of conflict. They fought for their reception on the part of the church and so were unable to base themselves on it. Precisely for this starting from the Council of Pisa conciliar authority was underlined with particular emphasis.[6]

The critics of the papacy did the same in the fourteenth century, making infallibility of the general councils derive from that of the Church with the help of the concept of 'representation'. The concept of the infallibility of the councils became a fundamental axiom

---

6 K. Schatz, *Storia dei Concili. La Chiesa nei suoi punti focali* (Bologna: EDB, 1999), p. 141 (German original, *Allgemeine Konzilien. Brennpunkte der Kirchengeschichte*, Paderborn: Schöningh, 1997).

(*Grundaxiom*) only in relation to the manifest rejection of the infallible councils by Luther. In the Greek Church, too, we find the declarations on the infallibility of the councils in a context orientated against the authority of the Pope.[7]

A very important term for understanding how to formulate the 'ecumenical council' question is *repraesentatio*, which came with the institution of the council itself. In Tertullian[8] 'representation' or 'representative' is not meant in a legal but a spiritual sense. It was at the IV session of the Council of Chalcedon that the Egyptian bishops opted for a representation of a legal nature, not being able to represent all the bishops because of the small number of them summoned there. The concept of council as legal representation is based on a conception of Church as *congregatio fidelium*, which as such originally possesses every right. With the Dominican Johannes Quidort can be seen for the first time the exchange between two concepts: that of popular sovereignty with that of the representation with a view to a council, and this in connection with the justification of the removal

7 Cf. H. J. Sieben, *Studien zur Gestalt und Überlieferung der Konzilien* (Paderborn: F. Schöningh, 2005), pp. 19–20. On the infallibility of the Church gathered in Council and in the limitations of the Council see what the Greek Emperor believed about the Council of Florence (cit. in *Ibid.*, footnote 24): 'Ich bin der Meinung, daß die heilige Kirche sich auf keine Weise in ihren heiligen Lehrsätzen irren kann, vorausgesetzt sie erörtet sie gemeinsam und im Rahmen eines Konzils' (Syropoulos, IX, 22; CFl 9, 456, 32). About the infallibility of the general councils see H. J. Sieben in his work *"Die Quaestio de infallibilitate concilii generalis" (Ochhamexzerpte) des Pariser Theologen Jean Courtecuisse († 1423)*, (in *Ibid.*, pp. 153–176). Sieben shows that the Parisian theologian normally refers the opinion of other theologians, not being in agreement with the rigorists nor the minimalists. If one asked what was his vision of a general council, it could be said that for Jean Courtecuisse the fallibility of a council appeared cumbersome and difficult but at the same time he did not see its clear foundation with natural reason and in Tradition. Anyone can choose the path they believe to be more trusted and more probable.

8 Cf. *De jejunio* 13, CSEL 20, 1; 292, 13, cit. in *Ibid.*, p. 24.

of a Pope through the council. Hidden at the root of this idea is the presentation of a council which acts *loco ecclesiae, loco totius populi.*[9]

The conciliarists of the fifteenth century, then, used the concept of 'representation' of the council to subordinate the Pope to the conciliar assembly, and this as a maximum punishment in case of argument. Making a comparison between the Pope and the council as representatives of Christ, the former, in the conciliarist logic, is less representative than the latter.[10] Hans Küng would take up again this concept of 'representation' on the occasion of Vatican II, rooting here his proposals about the new form to be assigned to that tradition of councils: a council which *expresses* the Church (a Church, consequently, which transforms itself into a permanent council), and the request for the participation of the laity, as well.[11]

9 Cf. Sieben, *Studien zur Gestalt,* p. 24.

10 The structural peculiarity of the conciliarist logic applied to the council (Pisa: 1409 and Basle: 1431–1449, passing through Constance: 1414–1418) lies in the fact that it takes up again the model of the 'general assemblies of Christianity' more than the 'papal councils'; these, then, 'reclaim and strengthen, in the composition and conception they have of themselves, the character of "representation" of the universal church proper to the "papal" councils of the Dark Ages, with the sole difference that now no longer are they understood as consultative organs of the Pope, and not even as an assembly of the local churches (like the ancient councils), but as supreme court of the universal church understood in the corporative sense... The Fifth Lateran council, summoned as "counter-council" in response to the "conciliarist" Pisa Council of 1511–1512, represents a return to the type of "papal" councils of the Dark Ages', Schatz, *Storia dei Concili,* p. 14.

11 Cf. Sieben, *Studien zur Gestalt,* p. 25. In opposition to Küng about the new conciliar form to be applied to the councils and the request about the participation of the laity, to express as well as possible the representation of the Church, we find Joseph Ratzinger, according to whom the Council does not represent the Church but is 'wesentlich eine Versammlung derer, die den Auftrag ihrer Leitung innehaben. Das sind nun einmal in der konkreten Ordnung der Kirche die Bischöfe' (*Das neue Volk Gottes. Entwürfe zur Ekklesiologie,* Düsseldorf 1969, p. 161, cit. in *Ibid.*, p. 26). What's more, Küng had suggested interchanging the features of the Church, *one, holy, Catholic*

A considerable difference is noted, then, as I said at the start, by comparing the 1917 CIC[12] with that of 1983 as regards the role of the council and the very way of understanding it in relation to the Pope who convenes it and approves it and to the college of bishops summoned to it. In fact, the last Code takes into account the re-evaluation of the episcopal college. However, while it does not add any new article about it, it simply integrates there the concept of 'episcopal college', putting it on the level of other collegial forms, from which the Pope can choose according to the needs of the Church.[13]

---

and *apostolic* with the council itself, so as to reflect the structure of the Church and encourage the *encounter* between the divine call, the Church, and the human one, the council. Ratzinger would point out to Küng that the council is not to be confused with the New Testament *ekklesía*, but it is *synedrion* and therefore does not represent the Church, just like each eucharistic celebration, but is just a particular *service* which takes place in it. On this element see the more in-depth study of H. J. Sieben, *Katholische Konzilsidee im 19. und 20. Jahrhundert* (Paderborn: F. Schöningh, 2005), pp. 258–265 [the idea of Küng], pp. 273–274 [Ratzinger's criticism]. The whole study (*"Zur Theologie des Konzils". Wesensbestimmung zu Beginn des Zweiten Vatikanums*, pp. 244–277), starts from the fact that from the announcement of the Council, made by John XXII on 25 January 1959, many people, journalists, bishops, theologians, politicians, expressed their opinion on the imminent gathering, and the theologians, in particular, formulated a 'theology of the council'. Two positions faced each other: the 'traditional', which saw the council as a congregation of bishops, whose authority (secondary, compared to the primary authority of the Pope) derived from the Roman Pontiff, and the 'new' (Congar, Küng and Rahner), which urged the balancing of the Pope-Council bipolarity, which had become polarity at Vatican I, with the unity and importance of the episcopal body of the imminent Vatican II.

12 Cf. Can. 222. § 1: Dari nequit Oecumenicum Concilium quod a Romano Pontifice non fuerit convocatum.§ 2: Eiusdem Romani Pontificis est Oecumenico Concilio per se vel per alios praeesse, res in eo tractandas ordinemque servandum constituere ac designare, Concilium ipsum transferre, suspendere, dissolvere, eiusque decreta confirmare.

13 Taking into account *Lumen Gentium* 20–24, canon 338, § 1 of the CIC states: 'It is for the Roman Pontiff alone to convoke an ecumenical council, preside over it personally or through others, transfer, suspend, or dissolve a council,

Here there is certainly a positive reading. Rather than a manipulation of the council in favour of the jurisdictional power of the Pope over the whole Church, there emerges an appraisal of collegiality on behalf of the Church and seeing it at the service of the Church in accordance with the hierarchical order and the communion of the particular Churches in the universal Church. In my opinion, it seems the question: what is a council? remains without a definitive response, at least as far as the previous question: who is the subject of the supreme legal authority? The Pope and the college of bishops or the college of bishops with the Pope at its head? For Semmelroth, Rahner and Congar the second possibility is valid. The response bears witness, however, to the value given to the Nota praevia of *Lumen Gentium*, which for some theologians, as we will see, brought no progress to the understanding of episcopal collegiality. However, what is certain is that, with Vatican II, the college of bishops exercises an ordinary power and not delegated by the Pontiff.[14]

2. *The Second Vatican Council (1962–1965) between renewal and aggiornamento*

The definition of the infallibility of the Pope at the First Vatican Council had put an end in a definitive manner to the thought that a

and to approve its decrees'. And § 2 states: 'It is for the Roman Pontiff to determine the matters to be treated in a council and establish the order to be observed in a council. To the questions proposed by the Roman Pontiff, the council fathers can add others which are to be approved by the Roman Pontiff'. Cf. Sieben, *Studien zur Gestalt*, p. 34. To examine the matter in depth, see the reading indicated by Sieben in *Ibid.*, footnote 84.

14 For a systematic vision for now I refer again to Sieben, *Katholische Konzilsidee im 19. und 20. Jahrhundert*, pp. 330–350. It is exemplary what Theobald asserts in relation to the historical research on the form of a council: 'our interest in the conciliar form and the relation between those who transmit the faith (tradentes) must not allow us to forget that the council meets to find an understanding of what is to be transmitted (traditum) or what is true…', Theobald, *La recezione del Vaticano II*, p. 127.

council might be necessary for the Pope to resolve a doctrinal or disciplinary controversy. It was thought that now the time of councils was over, according to the statement of Cardinal Billot, because besides they were 'so costly, uncomfortable, and full of problems and dangers of every kind'.[15] So leading to Vatican II was not the request for a council—by now the conciliar decree *Frequens* had already been abundantly superseded—but rather some ideas of reform and the very social and cultural transformations which they affected.

The main tensions in the very planning of the Council came about by reason of the fact that the 'Secretariat for Promoting Christian Unity', a new body desired by John XXIII and entrusted to Cardinal Bea, in co-ordinating all the ecumenical relations had equal importance as the other ten preparatory commissions, in the task of preparing schema for decrees, 'which was naturally tantamount to programming a priori tensions with the other commissions, in particular the Theological Commission'.[16]

Already in the preparatory phase two opposed poles were created, one intent on safeguarding doctrine and promoting its defence, represented by the Doctrinal Commission led by Cardinal Ottaviani, and the other intent on promoting ecumenism and strategic paths for the participation of observers at the Council itself, represented by the Secretariat for Promoting Christian Unity, led by Cardinal Bea.

> According to the Theological Commission, other commissions were responsible for the 'pastoral' aspect, and for their part those commissions were concerned with secondary questions of a pragmatic and legal nature. Only in the Secretariat for Promoting Christian Unity and in the Liturgical Commission did they really take into account the 'Johannine' conception of 'aggiornamento'...[17]

---

[15] Reported by Schatz, *Storia dei Concili*, p. 249.

[16] *Ibid.*, p. 263.

[17] *Ibid.*, p. 264.

According to Theobald, who, along with others, saw in the inaugural discourse of John XXIII the foundation of the 'pastoral principle', the said principle was only accepted with difficulty and gradually during the whole conciliar journey, when a certain number of Fathers, making reference to the Council of Trent, proposed separating the dogmatic need from the pastoral: 'deep down they did nothing other than show up to what point the history of the conciliar programmes was in tension with the principle set by John XXIII and often taken up again in terms of "pastoral nature of doctrine"'.[18] So is it right to ask from now on: did the Council with John XXIII really want to inaugurate the 'pastoral principle'? From where did Pope Roncalli obtain his pastoral perception of the conciliar Church?

2.1 The theological consequences of a pastoral aggiornamento

In John XXIII's opening address, *Gaudet mater ecclesia*,[19] a real key for understanding the Council,[20] the major theological perspectives of the imminent Assembly were outlined: to 'proclaim' in a new way the doctrine of the Church, which in itself remained always identical.

---

18 Theobald, *La recezione del Vaticano II*, p. 225 (also pp. 230–286 in which the reception of the pastoral principle and the gradual aggiornamento of its implications is traced). See also G. Ruggieri, *The First Doctrinal Clash*, in G. Alberigo (ed.), *History of Vatican II, Vol. 2. The Formation of the Council's Identity* (Maryknoll / Leuven: Orbis / Peeters 1997), pp. 233–266.

19 AS I/1, pp. 166–174.

20 Cf. R. De Mattei, *Il Concilio Vaticano II. Una storia mai scritta* (Turin: Lindau, 2010), p. 199. De Mattei writes: 'The Council had been convoked, not to condemn errors or formulate new dogma, but to propose, in a language adapted to the new times, the perennial teaching of the Church. The pastoral form, with John XXIII, became the form of the Magisterium par excellence. This prospective was destined, according to Alberigo, to make the Council an event, rather than a place of the elaboration and production of norms. The main identity of Vatican II appeared to be that of "*aggiornamento*", understood as the "*rejuvenation of the Christian life and of the Church*" and the "*willingness and attitude of the search for a renewed inculturation of the Christian message in the new cultures*"', *Ibid.*, pp. 201–202.

One thing was the faith, another the way of expressing it, which needed rejuvenation. And precisely on this way of proclamation, largely pastoral, the Pope gambled the convocation of a council. In one of the important passages of the discourse he said:

> The substance of the ancient doctrine of the Deposit of Faith is one thing, and the way in which it is presented is another. And it is the latter that must be taken into great consideration with patience if necessary, everything being measured in the forms and proportions of a Magisterium which is predominantly pastoral in character.[21]

For its declarations, the Council chose a new measure and a new approach to the sources; to express it better, it wanted to 'return' to the sources: Sacred Scripture and the great theology of the Fathers. It did not want to give a simple dogmatic response to problems, but to seek people; it did not apologetically defend the faith, but suggested it drawing close to the people. However, for theology in general and dogmatics in particular this caused a new situation, explained as follows in the essential lines of W. Beinert:

> Its original sources became the Sacred Scriptures once again; therefore it had to be aware of the results of the historical-critical method of exegesis and apply this method to the

---

21 AS I/1, pg. 172. In the Latin, the request for a method of exposition suitable for the Magisterium, whose nature would be largely pastoral, the text reads: 'Huic quippe modo plurimum tribuendum erit et patienter, si opus fuerit, in eo elaborandum; scilicet eae inducendae erunt *rationes res exponendi*, quae cum magisterio, cuius indoles praesertim pastoralis est, magis congruent' (my italics). On this passage Sullivan notes: 'It was this last few words that set the tone and the agenda of the council. Its exercise of teaching authority was to be predominantly pastoral in character. But what did this mean? While most agreed that it meant there would be no *anathemas*, it soon appeared that there were very different notions of what was meant by a "pastoral Magisterium"', F. Sullivan, 'Evaluation and Interpretation of the Documents of Vatican II', in *Creative Fidelity: Weighing and Interpreting Documents of the Magisterium* (New York: Paulist Press, 1996), p. 163.

> propositions of faith. The importance of church teaching was not excluded, but was certainly placed after the Scriptures. A consequence for dogmatic methodology was that the Church was no longer the main argument of theology, but rather the Lord of the Church, that Jesus Christ, whom the New Testament had proclaimed. For the other things [theology] was challenged to think and work more on what had been solely pastoral up to now. Now, no longer exclusively important were the things of faith to be contemplated in themselves, that is, to identify within the given system and not to be brought into discussion, but rather to show above all their plausibility and their actuality for contemporaries. But since this contemporary is no longer the product of an ideologically closed *milieu*, it is rather the contemporary human person subject to a more diversified ideological influence, one can no longer conceive of just one form of response. In fact, according to the ideological basis of people, different ways had to be developed. Just one system was no longer possible. The plurality of theologies, which in one way or another, as had always already happened, became hypothesised and soon also event... This is the problem of present theology and dogmatics: how do each relate to the Tradition, which is indispensable, and the missionary concern for people today, which by the Church equally is led in a vital manner?[22]

In a particular way, in Rahner's words, this transformation came about by virtue of the Council: from a *Weltkirche* to a *Welttheologie*, from a world church inaugurated by Vatican II to a world theology, whose heart would be pluralism as the overcoming of the European or non-Scholastic boundaries to open itself to world cultures.[23] The

---

22 W. Beinert, *Dogmatik studieren. Einführung in dogmatisches Denken und Arbeiten* (Regensburg: F. Pustet, 1985), pp. 99–100.

23 Cf. K. Rahner, 'The Abiding Significance of the Second Vatican Council', in Id., *Theological Investigations*, vol. 20, (London: Darton, Longman & Todd, 1981), pp. 90–102 (German original, 'Die bleibende Bedeutung des II. Vatikanischen Konzils', in Id. *Schriften zur Theologie*, vol. XIV (Einsiedeln:

German Jesuit, along with other authors, greeted this epochal moment as *Abschied von Trient,* a leave-taking of Trent, where this means 'not a leave-taking from dogma as a living reality, which at Trent as in other two subsequent councils, it expressed itself, rather a leave-taking from a specific form *of* theology, in which and with which this dogma which remains is asserted'.[24]

So dialogue between the theologies becomes necessary. One no longer produces a theology of the Church but ecclesial theologies, whose difference compared to the one profession of faith contributes to strengthening the knowledge itself of the creed. What's more, in Rahner's words, the theologies become their philosophies with which they interact. The pluralism of philosophies, practiced in theology, is the foundation and a moment of the pluralism of the ecclesial theologies. The aim of theology therefore will not be that of formulating new dogmas, but a radical understanding of the Revelation of God, of his grace, of his mediation, of responsibility for the world and eschatological hope.

Here Rahner suggests an 'anthropological concentration', which 'could mean, that in all theological affirmations, the relationality of its content with the human person as subject, as freedom and author of his / her world becomes ever clearer'.[25]

Benzinger, 1980), pp. 303–318 (*Stimmen der Zeit* 12 [1979], pp. 795–806).

24 Cf. K. Rahner, 'Die Zukunft der Theologie', in J. Bielmeir (ed.), *Abschied von Trient. Theologie am Ende des kirchlichen Mittelalters* (Regensburg: F. Pustet, 1969), p. 122: 'Insofern bedeutet der Abschied von Trient nicht Abschied von Dogma als lebendiger Wirchlichkeit, das sich in Trient oder in den zwei weiteren Konzilien der Kirche ausgesprochen hat, sondern einen Abschied von der bestimmten Gestalt *der* Theologie, in der und mit der sich dieses bleibende Dogma ausgesagt hat'.

25 *Ibid.*, p. 127: 'Aber eine solche anthropozentrische Konzentration könnte bedeuten, daß in allen theologischen Aussagen die Bezogenheit ihrer Inhalte auf den Menschen als Subjekt, als Freiheit, als Täter seiner Welt immer deutlich wird'. See also the other contributions of this volume along the same lines. For example, J. Gründel, *Vom Gesetz zur Freiheit,* pp. 27–38; L. M. Weber, *Seelsorge oder Sorge um den Menschen,* pp. 75–91.

Now, fifty years after the closing of the Council, and looking retrospectively at all the varied theologies which were produced often in the name of the 'anthropological concentration' and a philosophical pluralism adopted as the measure of theological pluralism, we can ask: is a theology which loses its identity to pour itself out in the plurality of the fact of the philosophical and human sciences in general far-sighted? Has not this great pastoral opening produced, largely, a varied and often contradictory theological output? Is varied theological output always a sign of a legitimate pluralism or rather of a confusion about the starting-point?

The starting-point, for Rahner, was, in a certain way, still the Second Vatican Council, where two theologies stood beside each other: one rigidly Neo-scholastic, fixed on monogenism and the doctrine of limbo, and the other, instead, more biblical, which did not derive its repertoire from that of the Neo-scholastics and which used the restrain of caution, especially in the Marian sphere. The theology which won out was the one capable of becoming 'worldwide', like the Church, overcoming the cultural boundaries of Christianity. *Welttheologie* also means a theology capable of broadening the horizons about the problem of salvation: before, one asked how many people might be saved from among the 'damned mass', according to a classical Augustinian expression, but today, instead, one asks if all might be saved. The present position, matured therefore in the epochal process of post-conciliar theology, would have a more Christological awareness.[26] In truth, for the German Jesuit, the real theological awareness is to say to the world, by virtue of the Council, that despite all the abysses of its history and all the shadows of its future it is embraced by God and by his will and God with his self-communication offers himself as foundation, strength and end.[27]

---

[26] Cf. on this K. Rahner, 'The Abiding Significance of the Second Vatican Council', pp. 90–102.

[27] Cf. *Ibid.*, pp. 100–102.

Here, unfortunately, there is no longer a clear identity of the Church. The basic idea is that the identity—which cannot but come from the homogenous development of the Tradition of the faith—is to be acknowledged solely in multiplicity.[28] The identity loses its way when the essence of the Church, its mystery, is clouded. In my opinion, the clouding arises from having misled—and thus multiplied—the concept of *Traditio Ecclesiae,* often diluting it in the content of the Scriptures, even to the point of the two being almost identical.

So a new balancing between Sacred Scripture and Sacred Tradition, which together constitute the unique divine Revelation, the Word of the living God, is necessary. This supreme Word is not identified with Scripture,[29] but knows, in human language and salvation history, an analogous use, which gives rise to a 'symphony of more voices', as recognised by the Synod of Bishops on the Word of God and as taught by Benedict XVI's *Verbum Domini.* The heart of the Word of God is the Word of God 'through whom all things were made' (Jn 1:3) and who 'became flesh' (Jn 1:14). Christ is the Word of God, a Word made flesh:

---

28 See Beinart's criticism of Rahner on this issue: a loss of the Catholic identity and its Rahanerian rediscovery only in multiplicity: 'Rahner hat keine Angst vor Identitätverslust. Er setzt freilich voraus, daß die Identität nur in der Vielfalt ist', W. Beinert, *op. cit.*, p.100.

29 In an emblematic way, Congar, in disentangling his idea of the council as congregation and as fundamental conciliarity of the Church, wanted the council itself not to separate itself from the measure of the Scriptures and at the same time from historicity, as relationship between salvation history and human history. The council, in its historicity, would be a sort of revelation of the (biblical) structure of the Church, 'eine gewisse Struktur', which remains tied to the words of Scripture (above all Mt. 28:18–20, in relation to Mt 18–20), cf. Y. Congar, 'Konzils als Versammlung und grundsätzliche Konziliarität der Kirche', in J. B. Metz et al (eds.), *Gott in Welt. Festgabe für Karl Rahner* (Freiburg im B.: H. Herder, 1964), pp. 135–165 (154–155). Cf. also the critical exposition of Congar's 'theology of the council' by Sieben, *Studien zur Gestalt*, pp. 253–258.

> All this helps us to see that, while in the Church we greatly venerate the sacred Scriptures, the Christian faith is not a 'religion of the book': Christianity is the 'religion of the word of God', not of 'a written and mute word, but of the incarnate and living Word'.[30]

From the theological point of view, the Apostolic Exhortation quoted above stated[31] that it is necessary to deepen the articulation of the various meanings which can be attributed to the expression 'Word of God': more levels, of which the *analogatum princeps* is Christ the centre and culmination of Revelation. In summary, this 'symphony of the Word' knows four levels: its natural expression in the *liber naturae,* first and fundamental reflection of the creation made by means of Christ and in view of Him (cf. Col 1:16); its expression throughout the whole history of salvation, culminating in the mystery of the incarnation, death and resurrection of Christ; its preaching made by the Apostles, constituting the living Tradition of the Church, which unwaveringly transmits this divine Word; finally its attestation and canonical fixation by virtue of divine inspiration in the Sacred Scriptures.[32] Overall it constitutes a harmonious articulation, which highlights the presence in the world and in the Church of the one Christ, the way, the truth and the life (cf. Jn 14:6).

The Church thus becomes the 'place' where this divine Revelation lives and the possibility itself so that this might be transmitted to humanity. There is no Magisterium outside this Word of God and there is no Word of God which excludes the Magisterium and thus encourages a parallel Magisterium of the theologians.

Thus the endeavour of 'pastoral aggiornamento' could not signify a theological reorganisation omitting some truths of faith—perhaps

---

30 Benedict XVI, Apostolic Exhortation *Verbum Domini,* 30 September 2010, n. 7: AAS 52 (2010) 688. The quotation within the extract is from St Bernard of Clairvaux, *Homilia super Missus est,* IV, 11: PL 183, 86 B.

31 Propositio n. 3, *Verbum Domini,* 7.

32 Cf. *Verbum Domini,* 7.

those most insidious for ecumenical dialogue—and above all the theological places of the Tradition of the Church, concentrating on the moment of pluralism and the cogency of anthropological issues. Rather it should signify a proclamation not cut off from dogma; a proclamation up-dated to today which, moving from dogma, explains to men and women the essential nature of the faith as received and faithfully handed on down the centuries: that cosmic symphony of the one Word of God.

2.2 Vatican II as "dogmatic pastoral"?

Still on the lines of 'anthropological concentration', which had a strong resonance in the reception of the Council, there was a further development, again starting from the conciliar reorganisation: from dogma as definition of the faith and in some way coercibility of the same in narrow parameters, there was a move from a phase in which more willingly faith is seen as confession rather than as formulation of a doctrine, in which the focal points are the anchoring to the Scriptures and the genuine witness of the liturgy of the Church.[33] Briefly: Vatican II would end the post-Tridentine phase persistent up to Vatican I. Therefore, the post-conciliar phase of theology should no longer be dogmatic *scrictu sensu,* but rather of proclamation or kerygma. The post-conciliar period would see at the most new definitions but no longer new dogma.

Passing over the major dispute created by H. Küng's book, *Unfehlbar? Eine Frage,*[34] dividing theological feeling in a for and against

---

[33] Cf. H.-J. Schulz, *Bekenntnis statt Dogma. Kriterien der Verbindlichkeit kirchlicher Lehre* (Freiburg-Basel-Vienna: Herder, 1996). Schulz does not want to exclude dogma, but offers a new transparency of it, aiming above all at the tradition behind it and which in the late eighteenth century led to its conceptualisation. That is, he proposes going to the sources of dogma, offering a biblical-liturgical hermeneutic of it, so as to demonstrate its freshness. And free it from superstructures? In his way of seeing it, Vatican II offered principles for such retrovision work, cf. for now *Ibid.,* pp. 13–18.

[34] Zürich: Benziger, 1970 (English translation, *Infallible? An Enquiry,* London:

(however there were those who attempted mediation between Küng and the traditional position, such as, for example, W. Kasper, E. Schillebeeckx),[35] the position of K. Rahner remains however exemplary, for, in replying precisely to Küng on infallibility, he revealed his perplexities about the possibility that the post-conciliar Church might proclaim new dogmas. His *Grundbegriff* returned: since with the Council the Church became aware of cultural, philosophical and theological pluralism, it would almost be anachronistic to present a new dogmatic provision along the lines of the dogma defined in 1854 by Blessed Pius IX or in 1950 by Venerable Pius XII. Here are his thoughts:

> It is envisaged that no new definition will be given in time; the future situation which lies before us makes impossible an exercise of the full magisterial power which defines infallibly in the *way* in which was thought before ... Nothing was defined at Vatican II. Today the no longer adequate synthesisable pluralism of the cultural regions, of the philosophies, of the terminologies, of the horizon of understanding, of the theologies, and so on, has so clearly entered into the consciousness of the Church, to the point that I cannot myself imagine that a new precise and certainly real proposition can be thus expressed, that it as an expression of the consciousness of faith of the whole Church everywhere felt, can be thus defined.[36]

Collins, 1971).

35 For an overview of the problem of the infallibility of the Church posited by Küng (who de facto negates it because only God is infallible) and acknowledged by theologians, see the study by Sieben, *Katholische Konzilsidee im 19. und 20. Jahrundert*, pp. 386–407 ('Unfehlbarkeit, Rezeption und Hermeneutik der Konzilien').

36 K. Rahner, 'Zum Begriff der Unfehlbarkeit in der katholischen Theologie', in K. Rahner (ed.), *Zum Problem Unfehlbarkeit. Antworten auf die Anfrage von Hans Küng* (Quaestiones disputate, 54) (Freiburg im B.: Herder, 1971), p. 10 (Italian translation: K. Rahner [ed.] *Infallibile? Rahner, Congar, Sartori, Ratzinger, Schnackenburg e altri specialisti contro Hans Küng*, [Punti scottanti di teologia, 69] Rome: Paoline, 1971).

According to A. Ganoczy, Rahner is right to say—with respect to the past—that there will be no new dogmas, considering the method of teaching of the Magisterium in the last 150 years and comparing it with today's pluralism of the world community. But the question remains about the future: if the new development must not be a revision of the old concept of dogma, rejecting narrow, technical and defining formula. In fact, a methodology of the interpretation of dogma is necessary, which will emanate from a new theological vision from the same.[37] Vatican II would inaugurate this new criterion already from the fact that its two dogmatic constitutions, *Lumen Gentium* and *Dei verbum*, set out the doctrine of the faith, but without new dogmatic definitions. Never had a council so widely acknowledged the results of a modern theological work with the historical-critical method:

> An unknown but well-informed academic, wrote Ganoczy, could find it sometimes even moving how much intellectual talent and diplomacy was deployed, to recognise a declaration of Trent or Vatican I now surpassed at the levels of linguistics and content, to the point that a correction of meaning did not come out.[38]

And there were corrections, explained Ganoczy, and they concerned, for example, salvation outside the Church, the theory of the two sources of Revelation, the danger of religious freedom, etc., without, however, losing a centuries-old Tradition. The reason for that is to be seen in the fact that Vatican II wanted to look at each doctrine with a new understanding of the 'dogma', wider and freer than that of the

---

37 A. Ganoczy, *Einführung in die Dogmatik* (Darmstadt: Wissenschaftliche Buchgesellschaft, 1983), p. 123.

38 'Ein außenstehender, aber gut informierter Gelehrter mag es manchmal geradezu rührend finden, wieviel Geschick und intellektuelle Diplomatie entfaltet wird, um eine heute sprachlich und inhaltlich überholte Äußerung des Tridentium oder des I. Vaticanum so zu rezipieren, daß sie dabei einer Sinnkorrektur nicht entgeht', *Ibid.*, p. 53.

Dark Ages Church, which had translated Revelation into a form of language and the Gospel into a form of teaching. Not to be forgotten, then, Ganoczy says again, is that the reformers, Luther and Calvin, in this sense were not enemies of dogma.[39] Here one sees the real change, according to some, which Vatican II inaugurated: a 'doctrinally pastoral' ecumenism; and neither pastoral, but not even solely doctrinal, because in both cases there would have been no progress, especially in dialogue with the Reformation.[40] On the other hand, I believe it useful to recall that the Reformation moved the importance of the explanation of Revelation to the concept of the proclamation (*Verkündigung*), and of faith (*Glaube*), protecting the authoritative and theocentric character of the Word of God, identified ever more strongly with Sacred Scripture.[41]

From what has been said up to now, it can be argued that the problem of the dogmatic and / or pastoral of the Council is twofold: on the one hand the perception of the doctrinal corrections brought to Catholic doctrine by Vatican II is clear,[42] or, for others, of contribu-

39 Cf. *Ibid.*, p. 54.

40 I refer the reader to my Editorial in *Fides Catholica* 1 (2011), pp. 5–14: 'Il Vaticano II: un Concilio Ecumenico della Chiesa cattolica. Perché tanti abusi post-conciliari?' In my opinion, the abuses testify largely to an unclear definition of what is 'pastoral' in the Council and in its reception. The term is easily interchanged with 'doctrinal', and this, sometimes, to justify doctrinal changes without disturbing dogma.

41 Cf. H. Waldenfels, 'Die Lehre von Offenbarung in der tridentinischen Ära', in Id.—L. Scheffczyk, *Die Offenbarung von der Reformation bis zur Gegenwart*, (Handbuch der Dogmengeschichte, I/1 b), (Freiburg im B.: Herder, 1977), pp. 5–20. Significant in this regard are the words of G. Ebeling, Luther [(T 1964), cited in *Ibid.*, p. 8, footnote 14]: 'Weil die Offenbarung Gottes im Kreuz geschieht, darum ist hier alles auf Worte und Glaube gestellt. Wort und Glaube—das ist die Signatur der unter dem Gegensatz verborgenen Offenbarung'.

42 Inter alia cf. K. Richter, *Das Konzil war erst der Anfang. Die Bedeutung des II. Vatikanums für Theologie und Kirche* (Mainz, M. Grünewald, 1991) (opening with the text of J. B. Metz, which echoes an expression of Rahner: *Das Konzil—"der Anfang eines Anfangs"?*); H. J. Frisch, *Aufrbrurch oder Betriebsun-*

tions to the renewal of Catholic life and thought,[43] of developments,[44] of '*micro-ruptures*',[45] or even changes in conflict with the Tradition[46] (the perception of the renewal is not unambiguous); on the other hand, the general awareness prevailed that such corrections or developments had not forced dogma: rather, they explained it in a new manner. But we must ask: with a new dogmatic language or with a new perception of the dogma? At first it seems they are both sides of the conciliar coin. The conflict of interpretations expands also into a question of a break or not with the preceding Tradition of the Church.[47]

---

fall? Das II. Vatikanische Konzil und seine Folgen.

43 Cf. F. Sullivan, *Magisterium. Teaching Authority in the Catholic Church* (New York: Paulist Press, 1983), p. 75.

44 Cf. M. L. Lamb—M. Levering, *Vatican II: renewal within tradition* (Oxford: Oxford University Press), 2008.

45 O. Rusch, *Still interpreting Vatican II. Some Hermeneutical Principles* (New York, Paulist Press, 2004), pp. 25–26. Rusch, along with J. W. O'Malley ('Reform, Historical Consciousness, and Vatican II's Aggiornamento', in Id., *Tradition and Transition: Historical Perspectives on Vatican II* (Wilmington: M. Glazier, 1989), p. 45), and H. Pottmeyer (*A New Phase in the reception of Vatican II*, pp. 37–39) and O. H. Pesch (*Das Zweite Vaticankische Konzil: Vorgeschichte-Verlauf-Ergebnisse-Nachgeschichte* (Würzburg: Echter, 2001), pp. 150–154) is convinced by the presence of compromises, ambiguities and juxtapositions from conflictual points of view in the final documents of Vatican II. Therefore, he asks, can one speak of a common 'mind of the Council'?, cf. *Ibid.*, pp. 27–28.

46 B. Gherardini, *Concilio Ecumenico Vaticano II. Un discorso da fare* (Frigento: Casa Mariana Editrice, 2009); Id., *Concilio Vaticano II. Il discorso mancato* (Turin: Lindau, 2011).

47 O. Rusch, supporting the vision of J. W. O'Malley (*Vatican II: A Matter of Style*, in *Weston Jesuit School of Theology 2003 President's Letter*, Cambridge: Weston Jesuit School of Theology, 2003, p. 3), asks: 'The Council may well speak of continuity in the "what" of being church; but does Vatican constitute a definite break in the "how" of being Church? Here I believe it is possible to speak of a deliberately intended micro-rupture with other eras, particularly the ecclesial style of the Pian era (Pius IX-Pius XII). Not only in the rhetorical style, but also in the vocabulary of the Council, the letter reveals the spirit through its new "how" for Church teaching-persuasion', cf. O. Rusch, *Still*

So the question remains: have the corrections (which if we wish we can indicate as 'corrections of meaning') which have been made to the teaching modified the dogma simply by dint of the fact that there was a new concept of dogma? Is it then simply a problem of a new dogmatic language?

In reality, dogma, according to the words of Scheffcyzk, is a 'crucial point of Tradition'[48] (*Brennpunkt*). Per se it makes reference to the *pertinere ad fidem*: the equivalent assigned by the Council of Trent to the word 'dogma'.[49] Vatican I, then, without using the word, made reference to it when it said 'all those things are to be believed with divine and Catholic faith which are contained in the Word of God, written or handed down, and which the Church, either by a solemn judgment, or by her ordinary and universal Magisterium, proposes for belief as having been divinely revealed'.[50]

Vatican II also uses the same meaning when, in the decree on ecumenism (*Unitatis redintegratio* 14), it speaks of the 'basic dogmas of the Christian faith concerning the Trinity and the Word of God made flesh from the Virgin Mary... defined in Ecumenical Councils... '. Especially, then, in the constitution on the Church (*Lumen Gentium* 25) reference is made when it alludes to the charism of the infallibility of the Bishops in union with the Roman Pontiff. This infallibility 'in defining doctrine pertaining to faith and morals, is co-extensive with the deposit of revelation', and by virtue of it 'teaching concerning matters of faith and moral... is to be held definitively and absolutely'.

---

interpreting Vatican II, pp. 38–39.

48 L. Scheffczyk, *Grundlagen des Dogmas. Einleitung in die Dogmatik, Katholische Dogmatik*, vol. I (Aachen: MM Verlag, 1997), p. 131. See the whole exposition on the need for dogma from pp. 132–175.

49 Cf. DH 1501.

50 Cf. DH 3011: 'Porro fide divina et catholica ea omnia credenda sunt, quae in verbo Dei scripto vel tradito continentur et ab Ecclesia sive solemni iudicio sive ordinario et universali magisterio tamquam divinitus revelata credenda proponuntur'.

Therefore the corrections cannot be dogmatic, in the canonical sense of the word as developed by the Magisterium. Instead they could be additions, improvements, revisions, concerning instead the '*fundamentalia dogmata*', such as, for example, the principle stated in *Unitatis redintegratio* 11 about the '*hierarchia veritatum*', according to which, above all in consideration for ecumenical dialogue, dogmatic knowledge recognises an order and gradation of dogma, but without this encouraging arbitrary judgements or leaving room for choice[51]. Often, however, a new (pastoral) language encouraged a new perception of dogma, pushing on some fundamental theological principles of Vatican II, the specific use of which means the interpretation of teaching is either easily falsified or in conformity with Tradition.[52]

One of the principles which lends itself most to this ambiguous interpretation is that of the 'hierarchy of truths', of which the current renewed understanding of dogma takes advantage. That is due to the fact that such a principle would lend itself to distinguishing, as suggested in the Council by the Archbishop of Gorizia, A. Pangrazio,[53] some truths belonging to the *order of the ends* (the Trinity, the Incarnation and the mystery of Redemption, charity and Grace, eternal life, etc.) and others to the *order of means* (the septenary number of the sacraments, the hierarchical structure of the Church, apostolic succession, the primacy of the Roman Pontiff, etc.). The

[51] Cf. Scheffczyk, *Grundlagen des Dogmas*, pp. 139–140.

[52] In an address given at a conference on Vatican II, organised in Rome by the Franciscans of the Immaculate (16–18 December 2010), I believed it appropriate to identify in Vatican II three fundamental theological principles, on which, in my humble opinion, depends the historical-theological vision of the Council overall (as 'event' or simply celebration of solemn Magisterium) and the correct / erroneous interpretation of council teaching, cf. S. M. Lanzetta, 'La ricezione teologica del Vaticano II, Status quaestionis', in *Fides Catholica* 1 (2011), pp. 121–158 and in S. M. Lanzetta—S. M. Manelli (eds.), *Concilio Ecumenico Vaticano II: un concilio pastorale. Analisi storico-filosofico-teologica* (Frigento (AV): Casa Mariana Editrice, 2011), pp. 189–230.

[53] Cf. AS II/6, pp. 32–35. See also LThK^2, *Das Zweite Vatikanische Konzil*, II, pp. 88–90.

latter concern the means which Christ has given to his Church in the earthly pilgrimage, and after they will come to an end.[54] Archbishop Pangrazio was very optimistic: if one looked at the actual ecumenical situation, he thought, one would notice that many doctrinal differences between Christians concern the truths belonging to the order of means, even less those concerning the order of ends, to which they are subordinate. He hoped that in the schema *De oecumenismo* the distinction *secundum hierarchiam veritatum et elementorum* would be used explicitly, so that, he said, 'it may appear better, as I esteem, the unity existing between Christians, and to all Christians, as a family at least already united in the primary truths of the Christian religion'[55].

According to H. J. Schulz the principle of the 'hierarchy of truths', welcomed by O. Cullmann 'as the most significant point of the whole schema for future dialogue'[56] and the entire paragraph 11 (of *Unitatis*

54 From that A. Ganoczy, applying this understanding of the 'hierarchy of truths' to the Marian dogmas, infers that the divine motherhood of Mary behaves like a main phrase in German (*Hauptsatz*), while the other dogmas are like secondary phrases (*Nebensatz,* which does not mean something secondary, *Nebensache,* in the current meaning) (cf. Ganoczy, *Einführung in die Dogmatick,* p. 86). For this same reason it will be contrary to the theological use of the qualifications and censures, as we will see subsequently, to remain in the freedom of the dogmatic discussion of Vatican II, which 'hat nichts definiert, weder Qualifikationen noch Zensuren verteilt, sondern nur den faszinierenden Glaubensgegenstand, so gut es konnte, zu beschreiben und anzubieten gesucht', *Ibid.,* p. 118.

55 AS II/6 p. 34. In footnote 10, p. 35, Archbishop Pancrazio explains: 'Unitatis vero christianorum praecise consistit in communi fide et professione veritatum pertinentium ad ordinem finis'. I believe, instead, that such a distinction between truth belonging to the order of ends and truth belonging to the order of means is somewhat surreptitious and ambiguous. The Christian truths, while they have a different analogical relationship with the foundation which is the revealing God—only by reason of which there is a hierarchy—are between them at the same dogmatic level, as revealed. As regards then the assent of faith there is also a hierarchy, in consideration of the level of theological certainty which they have.

56 Quoted in Schulz, *Bekenntnis statt Dogma,* p. 34.

redintegratio) as 'the most revolutionary phrase not just in the decree in ecumenism, but among all the texts of the present council',[57] is a hermeneutical principle of the Tradition in Vatican II, showing the historic-revelatory transparency of the scriptural exposition. What's more, such a principle represents the quintessence of the communication of the Christ-event, where the 'visual hierarchy of the truth is not concerned primarily with a conceptual arrangement, but rather, above all with a stronger consideration of the fundamental truths through the intensifying anamnesis and confession (of the faith)'.[58] Rightly, therefore, according to Schulz, *Dei verbum* corrects the primordial schema *De fontibus,* which presented two sources of Revelation, almost one beside the other, Scripture and Tradition. Only with their unification and complementarity can one understand the constitutive function of the Scriptures by the exposition of the apostolic Tradition and thus its character as a benchmark and rule for that post-apostolic function as well. In short, there is always a priority of the Scriptures (of the New Testament over the Old)[59] and of their proclamation. Therefore, from *dogma* one can go to the *kerygma* which prepared it.

Of course, it is a feasible and laudable operation. However, in doing so does a large part of the post-conciliar theology not risk forgetting dogma or declaring it to be surpassed, in order to return to the *kerygma* of the faith? Does appealing to the work of the revision of Vatican II, due to its discursive and predicative positioning compared to the defined dogma, not risk separating the Church of today from that of

---

57 Quoted in *Ibid.*

58 *Ibid.*, p. 37.

59 Cf. *Ibid.*, pp. 17, 49–55. Schulz's intention can be well summed up in a question posted in IV on the cover: 'Does the Pope lose his authentic magisterial authority, when his Magisterium, like that of Saints Pope Leo I and Pope Gregory I, instead of being infallible and defining, returns to being circumscribed as episcopal proclamation of the Gospel at the centre of the ecclesial community?'

before? And to easily renounce the dogmatic truths in the proper sense, or encourage a choice of them according to historic necessity?

In the absence of a metaphysical vision of the Council, the term 'hierarchy' is no longer seen in terms of analogy but subordination. According to my way of seeing things, one cannot support the new concept of dogma or the principle of the 'hierarchy of truths' to bring about a real reorganisation of the faith and consequently of the Church. The operation would be partial and what's more not take account of the Council in its entirety: its nature, its aim, the different tenor of its documents, with the greater risk of suggesting that the relative truths would have become with the Council 'subjective'. The problem must shift to the correct hermeneutic of Vatican II, which cannot set aside any metaphysical and therefore indisputable principles which I will set out subsequently. It is necessary to testify to the whole magisterial import of Vatican II and to place the latter, by reason of its genesis and its method, in the right place which it chose: an effort principally for the unity of Christians and dialogue with the modern world. For example, contrary to Cullmann, I do not believe that *Unitatis redintegratio* 11 is a text for the Council as such, but which must be contextualised in the ecumenical field.

3. The theological qualification of the Vatican II documents

It is a difficult task to assign a definitive theological qualification to the constitutions, decrees and declarations of Vatican II.[60] There is

[60] On the theological qualification of the Vatican II documents see: Sullivan, 'Evaluation and Interpretation of the Documents of Vatican II', pp. 162–174; D. Iturrioz, 'La autoridad doctrinal de las constituciones y decretos del concilio Vaticano II', in *Estudios Ecclesiásticos* 40 (1965), pp. 282–300; H. Lavalette, 'Réflexion sur la portée doctrinale et pastorale des documents de Vatican II', in *Etudes* 323 (1966), pp. 258–269; O. Semmelroth, 'Zur Frage nach der Verbindlichkeit der dogmatischen Aussagen del II. Vatikanischen Konzils', in *Theologie und Philosophie* 42 (1967), pp. 236–246; P. Delhaye, 'L'autorité théologique des textes de Vatican II', in *Communio* 4 (1971), pp. 193–227.

still no unanimity among theologians about the magisterial rank to be assigned to the conciliar pronouncements.

However, I believe it is necessary to make brief reference to the historical development of the ordinary Magisterium (of the Pope). In fact, something rather new happened after Vatican I: with Leo XIII (1878–1903), through the encyclicals there was an almost constant use of the 'ordinary' Magisterium of the Pope and from this Pope onwards the ordinary exercise of the Magisterium, especially through the encyclicals, would be the normal way of responding to the most important problems about dogma, morals and the social doctrine of the Church. This would then become the ordinary way for magisterial practice, with infallible definitions remaining a rare and limited case. From now onwards, the Magisterium would also have a somewhat new form: it would not be above all a Magisterium of prohibitions and the condemnation of errors, but also a purposeful writing rich in theology, capable of addressing the faithful in the present time. From now there was an increasing development of the awareness of an 'ordinary infallibility' of the Magisterium of the Pope almost as a sort of halo which crowned the common magisterial practice of the Church. Thus the authentic papal Magisterium began to carry out that function of infallibility which at Vatican I had been defined as a special quality of the Magisterium of the Pope *ex cathedra*.[61]

[61] On the historical development of the papal Magisterium as far as *ex cathedra* definitions are concerned, see K. Schatz, 'Welche bisherigen päpstlichen Lehrentscheidungen sind 'ex cathedra'? Historische und Theologische Überlegungen', in W. Löser et al (eds.) (Würzburg: Echter, 1985), pp. 404–422. Here the author reaches this conclusion: theology after Vatican I was not capable of saying precisely which papal teachings were *ex cathedra*. However, what is fundamental is that the principle of the resolution remains always 'Scripture and Tradition', not just the Pope, nor just Scripture. On the infallibility of the Pope at Vatican I, still as balance between Scripture and Tradition (historical development), see by the same author 'Päpstliche Unfehlbarkeit und Geschichte in den Diskussionen des Ersten Vatikanums', in *Ibid.*, pp. 186–250. Cf. also F. Ardusso, *Magistero ecclesiale. Il servizio della Parola* (Cinisello Balsamo: San Paolo, 1997), pp. 245–247.

On the other hand, what is unanimous is that at Vatican II there were no dogmatic definitions as in previous councils, not even in the dogmatic constitutions, and that is surely to be ascribed to the choice of a more pastoral Magisterium made by John XXIII.[62] But does this also mean—O. Semmelroth asks—that in the Council there were no declarations whose magisterial import can be founded on the level of infallibility? It is difficult to respond. In fact, Semmelroth only raises other questions.[63] Here one sees the singularity of Vatican II, which 'sensed in a charismatic manner the historical consciousness of our time, making it bear fruit for the consciousness of the very essence of the Church'.[64] Hence many theologians, without great difficulty, do not attribute to the conciliar declarations a higher level than the qualification 'theologically certain'. However, this does not mean that such declarations cannot be developed to the point of rising to a higher level; vice-versa, the affirmations 'de fide' are not rejected by the Council.[65] Recently, Cardinal W. Brandmüller, President Emeritus of the Pontifical Committee for Historical Sciences, has intervened on the matter, writing:

> Vatican I... did not exercise jurisdiction nor legislate, nor deliberated over questions of faith in a definitive manner. Rather it was a new type of Council, in that it was conceived as a pastoral Council, which wanted to explain to the world of today the doctrine and teachings of the Gospel in a more attractive and instructive way... So, as we know twenty-five

62 Cf. Semmelroth, 'Zur Frage nach der Verbindlichkeit', pp. 241–242. The Council, while treating 'dogmatic issues', did not take into consideration canon 1323 § 3 of CIC (1917), which states: 'Declarata seu definita dogmatice res nulla intelligitur, nisi id manifeste constiterit', as Semmelroth notes, cf. *Ibid.*, p. 241.

63 Cf. *Ibid.*, pp. 243–245.

64 'das Konzil in charismatischem Gespür das Geschichtsbewußtsein unserer Zeit aufgenommen und für die Erkenntniss des der Kirche eigenen Wesens fruchtbar gemacht hat', *Ibid.*, p. 245.

65 Cf. *Ibid.*

> years after the end of the Council,[66] it would have written a glorious page, if, following in the footsteps of Pius XII, it found the courage to pronounce a repeated and express condemnation of Communism. Instead, the fear of pronouncing both doctrinal censures and dogmatic definitions ensured that at the end there emerged conciliar pronouncements whose level of authenticity and therefore being obligatory were totally varied. So, for example, the constitutions *Lumen Gentium* on the Church and *Dei verbum* on Divine Revelation certainly have the character and cogency of an authentic doctrinal pronouncement, although here, too, nothing was defined in strictly binding terms, while, on the other hand, the declaration on religious liberty, *Dignitatis humanae,* according to Klaus Mörsdorf, takes a stance on issues of the time without an obvious normative content. Therefore each conciliar text has a different grade of cogency. This, too, is a totally new element in the history of the Councils.[67]

Generally there exist three theological threads, which attempt to confirm the magisterial rank of the conciliar documents. The theologians who belong to these are distinguished by Sullivan as maximalists, minimalists and moderates.[68] Among the minimalists are placed

---

66 This was the time the Cardinal composed the article, taken up again in the recent publication.

67 Brandmüller, *Il Concilio e i Concili*, p. 53–55. Mainly in response to Brandmüller's stance, which also supports the discourse of the then Cardinal Ratzinger to the Bishops of Chile on 13 July 1988, in which Ratzinger underlined the modest rank of pastoral council chosen by Vatican II and the temptation to make it instead rise to superdogma (cf. "Cuaderno Humanitas", Centro de Extensión de la Pontificia Universidad Católica de Chile, Santiago, December 2008, n. 20, p. 38, cit. in *Ibid.*, pp. 61–62) writes J.-H. Tück ('Ein "reines Pastoralkonzil"? Zur Verbindlichkeit des Vatikanum II', in *Communio* 41 [2012] 441–457), who instead aligns with the thesis of Cardinal Kasper on the enforceability of the conciliar decrees and declarations.

68 Cf. Sullivan, 'Evaluation and Interpretation of the Documents of Vatican II', pp. 164–169. The same three-fold division was made by Semmelroth, 'Zur Frage nach der Verbindlichkeit', pp. 238–241, with particular reference to the

those who see in the fontal pastoral nature the negation of any binding value of the doctrinal declarations of Vatican II, especially that of the sacramentality of the episcopate and the collegial nature of the Church. Among these, of note are the articles of G. Hering, U. Lattanzi and A. Gutierrez, published in two important Italian theological journals.[69] The maximalists, on the other hand, include the Franciscan Fr U. Betti, who in his article[70] on the theological qualification of the constitution *Lumen Gentium,* reached the conclusion that the chapters of the said constitution have equal doctrinal value compared to those of the constitutions of the previous councils (particularly Trent and Vatican I). The difference between Vatican I and Vatican II lies in the fact that, at the latter, there were no dogmatic definitions in the proper sense, and their negation does not lead into heresy. But, even if infallibility and irreformability are not explicitly declared, that does not mean they do not exist. According to Fr Betti the teaching of *Lumen Gentium* would be irrevocabale. Ratzinger criticised this vision, saying that in such a way many conciliar affirmations could be de facto credited with the level of dogma.[71] Among the

papal interventions about the magisterial value of the conciliar declarations: cf. Paul VI, 14 September 1964, in AAS 56 (1964) 809; Id., 21 November 1964, in AAS 56 (1964) 1010; Id., 6 December 1965, in AAS 58 (1966) 68ff.; Id., 21 September 1966, Letter to Cardinal Pizzardo, in AAS 58 (1966) 879.

69 *Palestra del Clero* 44 (1965), pp. 577–592 and *Divinitas* 9 (1965), pp. 393–414; 421–446.

70 U. Betti, 'Qualificazione teologica della Costituzione', in G. Baraúna (ed.), *La Chiesa del Vaticano II, Studi e commenti intorno alla Costituzione dogmatica 'Lumen Gentium'* (Florence 1967[3]), pp. 267–274.

71 J. Ratzinger, *Kommentar zu den Bekanntmachungen,* in LThK[2], *Das Zweite Vatikanische Konzil,* I, pp. 349–350. For Ratzinger, clearly, there was no new dogma in the Council, at any stage. But this does not mean that its teaching is not binding. The pastoral is founded on what is doctrinal and doctrine is with a view to the realisation of Christianity in today's world. Joining truth and love, doctrine and pastoral concern, one can overcome the division between pragmatism and doctrinairism, precisely just as in Christ the properties of Logos and Shepherd are inter-changeable: Christ as Logos is Shepherd

moderates are Ratzinger himself,[72] and Y. Congar.[73] The former states that the documents of Vatican II surpass by a long way the level of the Pope's ordinary Magisterium, especially that expressed in the encyclicals; by reason of that, they acquire a first-rate importance among modern doctrinal texts. According to Congar, on the other hand, the only passage in which there is a dogmatic declaration of the conciliar Magisterium is that concerning the sacramentality of the episcopate (cf. *Lumen Gentium* 21). Even though the tenor of the expression is no different from the one usually used, the subject matter is so important that it is difficult to say that it is not a definitive judgment of the Magisterium. In the same vein is Schmaus, basing himself on the address of Paul VI at the last public session of the Council on 7 December 1965.[74] So, according to Congar, with a unanimous act of extraordinary Magisterium, the Council proposed a common doctrine of the ordinary universal Magisterium.

Sullivan, while accepting along with other theologians the enforceability of the doctrine about the sacramentality of the episcopate, dissents from Congar about the use of the expression 'extraordinary Magisterium' applied to Vatican II, and this due to what is stated by Vatican I. For Vatican I, 'extraordinary Magisterium' was to be reserved to solemn judgements, in other words dogmatic definitions, in contrast to the ordinary Magisterium which included everything except definitions.[75] So, according to Sullivan, Vatican II exercised 'ordinary Magisterium', therefore non-defining, this remaining a singular characteristic of the last Assembly.[76] According to that, is the

---

and as Shepherd, Logos, cf. *Ibid.*, p. 350.

72 J. Ratzinger, 'La collegialità episcopale: spiegazione teologica', in Baraúna (ed.), *La Chiesa del Vaticano II*, pp. 757–760.

73 Y. Congar, 'En guise de conclusion', in *Ibid.*, pp. 1366–1367 (cit. in *Ibid.*, pp. 166–167, footnote 14).

74 Cf. M. Schmaus, 'Mariology', in K Rahner et al. (eds.), *Sacramentum Mundi*, 3 (London: Burns & Oates, 1969), p. 376ff.

75 Cf. DH 3011.

76 'since Vatican II nowhere expressed its intention to define a dogma, its exercise

overall magisterial importance of Vatican II comparable to that of papal encyclicals? According to Ratzinger, no,[77] because the Council, as extraordinary assembly and collegial work of the bishops, has a greater importance concerning the nature of theological obligation. For Sullivan, on the other hand, it is about distinguishing two ways of exercising Magisterium, in which the one who holds supreme magisterial authority (the Pope alone and a Council with the Pope), chooses instead to exercise it at a lower level and in a non-definitive manner. Therefore the equivalence between the encyclicals and Vatican II does not lie in the document *per se* (without doubt a Council is more than an encyclical) but in the *form* of teaching chosen.[78] Vatican II, for reasons suitable to the vision of John XXIII, chose the ordinary (only in this way can the 'pastoral' meaning attributed to the conciliar Magisterium be explained, too, otherwise it would be doubly ambiguous: it would mean that the infallible declarations do not have a pastoral aim, sic!); in turn, the ordinary magisterial form admits in itself various levels of authority and enforceability, but excludes *per se*—obviously, not *per accidens*—infallibility. So it is a matter of distinguishing, with good theological rules, the various levels of the magisterial authority of the Council.[79] With Vatican II, and this is a novelty which theology must necessarily note, the teaching of the Pope and that of the college of bishops gathered in council, sometimes presents the same characteristics. Recently Kolfhaus wrote:

> It is not to be excluded a priori that the college of bishops convoked by the Pope might not speak in an infallible manner, but rather seeks other levels of enforceability, as the Pope can and effectively does alone in the exercise of his Magisterium.[80]

---

of Magisterium belongs in the category of "ordinary", that is to say, non-defining Magisterium', Sullivan, *Creative Fidelity*, p. 167.

77 Ratzinger, *La collegialità episcopale*, p. 759.

78 Cf. Sullivan, *Creative Fidelity*, pp. 168–169.

79 Cf. *Ibid.*, p. 169.

3.1 Vatican II and the need for an appropriate hermeneutic

Since the closure of the conciliar Assembly questions have arisen about the correct hermeneutic of the Council. The at-times agitated spirits who led the conciliar discussions, the modifications and finally the votes, were not always in unison. Soon Vatican II became like the meeting or the clash of a minority and a majority,[81] or, as in the view of de Mattei,[82] of two minorities, where the progressives succeeded catalysing favour and consensus even from the rather indecisive majority. This dialectic is highly recognisable in the very drafting of the texts, which, to reach the consensus of two-thirds of the Fathers, often had to find compromises,[83] so that the result was somewhat disjointed and hesitant as a summary of different views. Hence the problem: the rules of classical hermeneutic interpretation are not sufficient, it is essential to go back to the *mens* which preceded the texts. Compared to the previous councils, the texts of Vatican II are of a different nature. For the first time a pastoral Constitution appears (at first it sounds like a theological oxymoron). Normally, the previ-

---

80 F. Kolfhaus, *Pastorale Lehrverkündigung—Grundmotiv des Zweiten Vatikanischen Konzils. Untersuchungen zu "Unitatis Redintegratio", "Dignitatis Humanae" und "Nostra Aetate"* (Berlin: LIT, 2010), p. 24. Interesting, too, is the theological *status quaestionis* presented by the author about the five interpretative models of the magisterial exercise of Vatican II. 1st model: exercise of the solemn extraordinary Magisterium; 2nd model: exercise of the ordinary universal Magisterium; 3rd model: exercise of the authentic Magisterium; 4th model: exercise of a homiletic Magisterium; 5th model: exercise of a differentiated Magisterium, cf. *Ibid.*, pp. 25–34.

81 Cf. Schatz, *Storia dei Concili*, pp. 273–275.

82 Cf. De Mattei, *Il Concilio Vaticano II*, pp. 28–283.

83 Cf. Sieben, *Katholische Konzilsidee im 19. und 20. Jahrhundert*, cit., pp. 415–416 ('Unfehlbarkeit, Rezeption und Hermeneutik der Konzilien'): 'Ein besonderes Problem der Texte des Zweiten Vatikanischen Konzils besteht ferner darin, daß sie oft Kompromisse zwischen den Positionen der Mehrheit und der Minderheit enthalten. Die Position der progressive Mehrheit steht in nicht wenigen Fragen unvermittelt, ohne in eine höhere Synthese geführt zu sein, neben der Meinung der konservativen Minderheit'.

ous councils, alongside the exposition of doctrine, condemned the ideas which were false and pernicious to that teaching: that meant, above all, offering unquestionably the correct rules for interpreting teaching, contrary to what was condemned. Vatican II preferred not to condemn, and so was always very positive and optimistic. Moreover, its 'pastoral' character, lending itself to a verbose and narrative exposition, did not encourage dogmatic precision and clarity. So, very soon the problem arose of the opposition between the letter and the spirit of the Council. For many people, the conciliar 'new Pentecost' had inaugurated a rather practical and current interpretation of Vatican II, where the spirit, the hidden intention and the interpretation most suitable for the time, easily led to isolating some declarations, letting everything fall into an exasperating radicalisation and a fracture between the pre-conciliar and the post-conciliar Church. A real conflict of contrasting interpretations was created.[84] Different models of the Church clashed. Already there was a feeling that something in the Council had not worked well. It is not denigrating Vatican II and the solemn and supreme Magisterium if it is stated that the problem of Vatican II and in the majority of the post-conciliar period is identified in the Council itself. It is not a question of *post hoc propter hoc*, but of taking into consideration the Council itself, what it was for the whole Church, the multiplication of hermeneutics driving the reception in this or that direction. Here too: reception of the Council, of its texts, or of the doctrine of the faith and morals which it taught along with a new pastoral vigour?

C. Theobald notes there are different responses to the question *how to interpret Vatican II today*. Some respond by taking into consideration its documents and placing them in the great Tradition of the Church; others insist on the state of compromise of such documents, trying to

---

[84] See G. Angelini, 'Dibattito—Vaticano II: la recezione del Concilio. Sul conflitto delle interpretazioni', in *Il Regno*, 53/10 (2008), pp. 297–303; G. Ruggieri, 'Recezione e interpretazioni del Vaticano II. Le ragioni di un dibattito', in *Cristianesimo nella storia* 28/2 (2007), pp. 381–406.

shift the principle of interpretation towards the category of 'event'. In truth, behind all this looms the unique question about the *identity* of Vatican II, which in the various, and at times conflicting attempts at reception, seemed assured or simply assumed. But in his judgment there remains another question: 'Is the cause of the post-conciliar problems to be sought for the most part in that synod itself?'[85] Theobald identified three symptoms which make one think that the problem lies in the great synod: 1) never before Vatican II had the awareness been expressed in such a clear manner that 'a new age of human history' (*Gaudium et spes* 54) demanded a global reinterpretation of the tradition. One can also differ from the French Jesuit as far as this awareness turned towards the reinterpretation, but the fact remains that Vatican II lies historically at one of the rarest and greatest crossroads of Christianity in its two-thousand year old history; 2) the exceptional dimension of the magisterial *corpus* of Vatican II, occupying almost a third of the whole documentary space of the 21 councils in their entirety, considering also the absence of anathemas which usually accompanied the other councils. A teaching of such proportions and such a wide and varied range of interests which raises per se a problem about the consequent interpretation; 3) the hesitation of John XXIII about the choice of a conciliar model. First of all the assembly seemed to him like a new Pentecost recalling the first (in Ac 2) and the discussion in Jerusalem (in Ac 15), then the model became clearer especially with Paul VI.[86] However, in Theobald's opinion, which I am inclined to share, both the Popes 'demanded from reception [of the Council] the difficult task of preserving both its Pentecostal or theological opening and the clarity of its specific profile'.[87]

85 Theobald, *La recezione del Vaticano II*, p. 14.

86 Cf. *Ibid.*, p. 15.

87 *Ibid.*, pp. 15–16. Fr Theobald himself aligns his work rather in the line of reception rather than conciliar hermeneutics. He establishes an intrinsic unity between *tradentes* and *traditum*, that is between the form of truth and truth: 'the only absolute in history', which 'commits to overcoming *both* the kerygmatic adaptation *and* the doctrinal flattening of the *paradosis*', (*Ibid.*, p. 211).

So, good or bad use can be made of Vatican II, not because the Council was at the same time both good and bad: that would be a contradiction, but because, given its pastoral nature, the diversity of the theological statute of its documents and therefore their diverse magisterial importance, an incorrect hermeneutical criterion could easily unbalance the whole interpretation, making the Council either an error or the only truth of the faith. The only thing that can act as guide in the understanding of Vatican II is the *entire Tradition of the Church*: Vatican II is not the only nor the last council of the Church, but a moment in its history; to speak of Tradition means putting before the Council the mystery-Church, without indulging in a sort of identification between the two, with the risk of transforming the Church into an everlasting Council, or, as Congar would have it, of perceiving that 'profound conciliarity of the Church':[88] here the risk is to confuse the concept of 'communion/collegiality' with 'conciliarity' and therefore substitute mystery-Church with the latter. It is a confusion of the historic with the theological level. The Church would become 'com-

---

This allows him to see Vatican II, in its whole as *corpus* and event, starting from the 'pastoral principle', as a *re-framing* of the entire tradition of the Church, understood as re-interpretation (without thereby denying the beginnings) especially in the light of *Dei verbum* and therefore of the new way of establishing the relationship between Council and Sacred Scripture. Vatican II seen in its *theological character* leads to taking into account not only what is transmitted and who is transmitting but also the experience of the recipients, who necessarily add something new. Thus one reaches a reception as *unpredictable* and not programmed process, which would be part of Vatican II. It all moves towards a new paradigm inaugurated by the last Council, in which, without necessarily being distinguishable, the doctrinal task and practical praxis, proclamation of the Gospel and the ecumenical pastoral, are joined (Cf. *Ibid.*, especially pp. 547–599). I would ask: it is objective to see Vatican II as a *re-framing* or is this already an assumption?

88 Y. Congar said this in relation to the reception of the Council as extension of the conciliar process and visibility of the conciliarity itself of the Church, 'La "Reception" comme réalité ecclésiologique', in *Revue des sciences philosophiques et théologiques* 56 (1972), p. 396.

munion-conciliarity', against its hierarchical constitution, which is nothing but the divine origin and therefore non-horizontal nature of the Church. The Church is not a council, nor is a council the Church.

The perennial *Traditio Ecclesiae* is, therefore, the first hermeneutic criterion of Vatican II from which arise other more detailed ones, too. Various authors,[89] according to this hermeneutic need, have formulated some theological principles to be respected and followed to understand Vatican II as an integral part of the whole doctrinal patrimony of the faith. For example, G. Dejaifve has four: 1) consideration of the historical context; 2) consideration of the intention of the defining Council Fathers; 3) the theological conditioning of their choice; 4) the significance of the teaching.[90] On this line Cardinal W. Kasper, too, had outlined four 'special principles' for the interpretation of the conciliar declarations: 1) the texts of Vatican II must be understood and realised integrally; 2) the letter and spirit of the Council must be understood as a unity; 3) in a way corresponding to its intention, Vatican II, like every other council, must be understood in the light of the uninterrupted Tradition of the Church; 4) the intention of Vatican II allows it to be contextualised and relativized with respect to the concrete situation with which it is in dialogue.[91] The Council, in fact, is a response to the 'signs of the times' and must make reference to these times.

For others, instead, these 'signs of the times' represent the real hermeneutic imperative: to historicise the Council, so that as 'event' it might now enter into the history of the Church and represent an

---

[89] See, inter alia, G. May, 'Deutung und Mißdeutung des Konzils', in *Archiv fur katholisches Kirchenrecht* 135 (1966), pp. 444–472; H. J. Pottmeyer, *Ist die Nachkonzilszeit zu Ende?*, in H. J. Pottmeyer et al. (eds.), *Die Rezeption des Zweiten Vatikanischen Konzils* (Düsseldorf: Patmos, 1986), pp. 47–65.

[90] Cf. G. Dejaifve, 'Pour un bon usage des conciles', in *Nouvelle Revue de Théologie* 101 (1979), pp. 801–814.

[91] Cf. W. Kasper, 'Die bleibende Herausforderung durch das II. Vatikanische Konzil. Zur Hermeneutik der Konzilsaussagen', in Id., *Theologie und Kirche* (Mainz 1987, pp. 290–299).

epoch-making change, the turning-point of pastoral teaching, in other words historical, in the doctrinal field, renouncing the denunciations and condemnations and aiming above all at ecumenism.[92] Here, however, the criterion is somewhat historic and the historic is subordinate to the theological, with the danger of transforming the Church in its transient moments and within these to choose and absolutise the one most in tune with one's own point of view. Once again, the Church is not to be identified with history, nor with a council. It is more. It is the transcendent mystery which lives in time, watched over in its visible ecclesial Body.

More recently, along these lines of 'Council-event', O. Rusch has formulated four hermeneutical principles to faithfully interpret Vatican II.[93] Rusch's effort is to overcome a conflicting hermeneutical vision, resulting from the juxtaposition of two theological visions: the Augustinian (God against the world, represented by Ratzinger, de Lubac, more conservative) and the Thomist (God for the world, represented by Rahner, Congar, Chenu, progressive). Rusch aims to accomplish a hermeneutical effort by a circular movement from the 'whole' to the 'parts' and again to the 'whole', imaging the 'part' as an end to the 'whole' and vice-versa. There are three hermeneutical moments and they must be used together:

1. the hermeneutic of the author, that is to say the intention the bishops wished to communicate in the texts. That means, to use the words of P. Ricoeur, to examine the 'world behind the text' and the historical factors which have determined it; in other words, it is reading the 'mind' or the 'spirit' of the Council.

---

92 Along these lines is above all the School of Bologna, which I will examine in more depth in Chapter III. For now, see G. Alberigo, 'Fedeltà e creatività nella ricezione del concilio Vaticano II', in *Cristianesimo nella storia* 2 (2000), pp. 384–387; G. Ruggieri, 'Per una ermeneutica del Vaticano II', in *Concilium* 35/1 (1999), pp. 18–34.

93 Cf. O. Rusch, *Still interpreting Vatican II.*

2. the hermeneutic of the texts, that is to say of the letter. While the first movement encourages a diachronic approach to the Council (the historical origin of the texts), this privileges the synchronic approach (the text in itself), recognising in the texts their own genre, style and rhetoric. In short, Rusch would say, with O'Malley, that 'the style is the Council'.[94] Spirit and letter must be read together, but this, I think, is insufficient for the Council to be correctly interpreted. It is necessary to hark back to another principle.
3. the hermeneutic of the reception, that is to say, of those who receive the Council, reading it and putting it into practice. Who are the recipients? For *Lumen Gentium* 12 it is the whole People of God who receive the Council. This highlights the *sensus fidei* as fundamental hermeneutic principle for a correct conciliar reception.

Then again, Rusch is aware of a plurality of receptions of the Council, at times also conflicting. Here, Rahner seems right,[95] for, as we have seen, he grasped the permanent significance of Vatican II in the transformation of the Church into a worldwide-Church. Consequently, this justifies the multiplicity of the *loci receptionis* of Vatican II in having, for example, a reception for Latin America, one for Australia, one for Canada, etc., by reason of the effort in understanding and the realisation of the conciliar provision. Would multiplicity be a factor of unity?

To resolve this problem Rusch suggests his 'fourth', more theological hermeneutical criterion: Vatican II as 'new Pentecost', which generates a new pneumatology and this becomes the real criterion to overcome the dialectic moment of the different models of conciliar

---

94 J. W. O'Malley, 'Vatican II: Historical Perspectives on its Uniqueness and Interpretation' in L. Richard—D. J. Harrington—J. W. O'Mallley (eds.), *Vatican II, The Unfinished Agenda: A Look to the Future* (New York: Paulist Press, 1987), p. 25, cit. in *Ibid.*, p. 37.

95 Cf. *Ibid.*, p. 56.

reception. For Rusch 'a pneumatology of *aggiornamento* is necessary which incorporates the discontinuity with the continuity'.[96] In his way of seeing things,

> Vatican II was a call to a new model of transmission and reception of the past, which it itself has incorporated. This model calls for a receptive pneumatology which not only gives suitable emphasis to *both* continuity and discontinuity, but conceives the Holy Spirit as the *true source of this divine discontinuity,* for the cause of the continuity with the great *tradition.*[97]

It would seem to be a hermeneutical contradiction, and yet, according to Rusch, who takes up above all the hermeneutic idea of O'Malley, Vatican II lends itself to this necessary overall picture of continuity as regards the essence of dogma and of discontinuity as regards the 'how' to be Church today, where, however, in my opinion, the concept of 'great tradition' appears rather weak,[98] since it is *already* based on the historical conciliar discontinuity and not, in truth, on the theological dogmatics beginning from the Apostles up to Vatican II.[99] Continuity and discontinuity according to the different levels are inevitable. But to justify the overall vision according to the superactive-synthetic moment provided by the 'epoch-making turning point' of Vatican II,[100]

---

96 *Ibid.*, p. 75.

97 *Ibid.*, pp. 79–80, author's italics.

98 'Tradition is accordingly portrayed not simply as a collection of traditions, but as a living process in which the Church offers to the whole world the opportunity of responding in loving faith to God's outreach to humanity through Christ in the power of the Spirit. This is the "great traditio", the deposit of faith, the great treasure given to the Church in trust. All else is in service of that mission' (*Ibid.*, p. 66). A definition which seems verbose but without the elements which explain what *living process* consists in. According to the mind of the Council it should be aggiornamento. And does aggiornamento explain the 'great tradition'? It is impossible to get out of this circle without a dogmatic element which precedes Vatican II and which I have indicated in the (dogmatic) Tradition of the Church.

99 Cf. *Ibid.*, pp. 4–7.

100 Cf. *Ibid.*, pp. 74–75.

seems impossible and after all inconclusive: one remains in the *today* which however will already be different from *tomorrow* and the Council could be *what you want* for today and for tomorrow.

The most difficult hermeneutic moment to tackle remains, however, the key pair, also defined as 'paralysing', of spirit and letter. Not the alternative event or texts but the experience of the Council which influences the texts to the point of determining the craftsmanship itself.[101] The only way to overcome the stalemate would therefore be the experience, that is, the transformation produced by the event on the participants in the Council, in order to encourage them to then devise an appropriate teaching. For example, the teaching about collegiality would stem from the life experience and collegial analysis which the Fathers had at the Council. This experience thus led to an appropriate self-awareness of the Church in herself—which could be extended to the entire history of the Church—which unravelled in history according to the experience of Catholicity, widespread at the Council in a unique manner.[102] This principle would allow uniting practical experience to doctrine and to faith itself. The faith would be ever more conscious of itself in time. The problem here, however, is that experience generates self-awareness of faith determining its understanding in a specific time, provoking, in such a way, an everlasting arriving at the letter, of the dogmatic and magisterial texts in general. Who becomes the key interpreter of the Council? The Council texts would thus become simply the initial moment of self-understanding of the Church and not the level of compulsoriness of faith to discern objectively the mystery of the conciliar event. To

[101] Cf. J. A. Komonchak, 'Vatican II as an "Event"', in *Theology Digest* 46 (1999), pp. 337–352.

[102] G. Routhier, 'La recezione dell'ecclesiologia conciliare: problemi aperti', in *Associazione Teologica Italiana, La Chiesa e il Vaticano II. Problemi di ermeneutica e recezione conciliare,* ed. M. Vergottini (Milan: Glossa, 2006), pp. 20–21. See also Id., *Il Concilio Vaticano II. Recezione ed ermeneutica* (Milan: Vita e Pensiero, 2007) (French original, *Vatican II. Herméneutique et réception,* Montreal: Fides, 2006).

see Vatican II in the light of the Church and all its councils, to the point of not isolating the last council to the detriment of the entire history of the Church, implies the authentic recognition of its texts, to which we must bring the spirit. If then the texts are advocate of a new spirit that is another thing. It is necessary to offer a hermeneutic of the texts responding to the will of the Council itself. Not a generic will, but the one which results from the motives which determined the Fathers' choices. The *corpus magisterialis* of Vatican II is in its documents. The event, which can be of greater interest to the historian or sociologist, if not brought back to the texts easily transcends its circumstances. The texts then as a *corpus* cannot be read as if they were great islands, but necessarily demand recourse to the theological rules of interpretation and the preceding Magisterium, indicating a development where it is expressly stated and not necessarily whenever Vatican II speaks. The difficult point of interpretation is precisely this: where and how is magisterial development seen in Vatican II?

The hermeneutical moment of the Council in itself requires, as can be perceived, a further passage: what is the magisterial value of Vatican II in the light of the preceding Councils, and therefore how can one see its effective dogmatic importance, united with but distinct from the pastoral, for the faith of the Church?

3.2 In search of the *mens sanctae Synodus*

To the question about the hermeneutic interpretation of Vatican II is intrinsically linked another, about the normative-magisterial value of the Council. Here, too, we do not yet have an unambiguous hermeneutic which highlights in an indisputable way the magisterial value of the conciliar texts.[103] To my way of thinking, there is still a degree of confusion about this, generated by the fact that a convenient distinction is not made between Vatican II as magisterial *unicum*,

[103] On this point see H. J. Pottmeyer, 'Una nuova fase della ricezione del Vaticano II. Vent'anni di ermeneutica del concilio', in G. Alberigo—J. P. Jossua (eds.), *Il Vaticano II e la Chiesa* (Brescia: Paidea, 1985), pp. 41–64.

because an ecumenical council, and Vatican II as Magisterium at various levels, according to a variation in its teaching in the different typology of its documents and in the different tenor of its teaching. It is about distinguishing unity from the multiplicity. Then to avoid losing the magisterial unity of Vatican II in a vague and fluctuating multiplicity, it is essential that this unity be sought at a more original and hidden level, that which de facto generated and guided the very magisterial desire of the Fathers. So it is about confirming and verifying the *mens* of the Council, the true hermeneutical soul of the texts and the measure of the correct interpretation of their being obligatory. In doing this is there a risk of opposing here, too, the spirit to the letter? No, but only to make explicit a hidden will for obvious pastoral and ecumenical reasons and to be able to keep firm the appropriate distinction between the whole (the Council) and its parts (the different documents).

Various theological attempts in this area very often ended up in two opposing and extreme directions. F. Ardusso, endorsing the interpretative line of F. Sullivan, recognises that, given the absence of a desire to define in a technical sense, in Vatican II we are in the presence of a 'non-defining' teaching but at the same time binding as far as it is the supreme Magisterium of the Church. It is a 'being obligatory' of the conciliar Magisterium of a different grade and this grade is recognisable by reason of the mind itself of the sacred synod. Therefore, a certain hermeneutic path is to qualify the different magisterial tenor of the documents of Vatican II according to the *mens sanctae Synodus*, as expressly formulated by the note of the Doctrinal Commission of the Council (6 March 1964), reported in the notifications made by the Secretary of the Council (123rd Congregation, 16 November 1964), which, in the important parts, stated:

> Taking into account conciliar practice and the pastoral purpose of the present council, the sacred synod defined as binding on the church only those matters of faith and morals which it has expressly put forward as such. Whatever else it

> proposes as the teaching of the supreme Magisterium of the church is to be acknowledged and accepted by each and every member of the faithful according to the mind of the council which is clear from the subject matter and its formulation, following the norms of theological interpretation.[104]

What must be borne in mind, in the interpretation of *Lumen Gentium* and the conciliar texts in general, is the *material treated* and the *mode of expression,* following the traditional theological norms. There is nothing more to be said. The hermeneutical work is thus transferred wholly to theology.

Sullivan, who Ardusso echoes, sees the different levels of magisterial compulsory character reflected in three specific moments:

1. a first indication of the mind of the Synod comes to us from the different theological distinction of the documents, divided into three, the constitutions, decrees and declarations, about which, however, the Council provides no explanation, even if it recognises their magisterial diversity, when, after a hiccup, there was a desire to re-introduce the attribute 'dogmatic' for the constitutions on the Church and on Divine Revelation, after they both disappeared in the revision of the schema.[105] This is still insufficient. Therefore, Sullivan suggests, it is important to go to the *acta* of the Council,

---

104 AS III/8, p. 10 and AAS 77/1 (1965) 72.

105 Fr Betti reports the matter in his *Diario*: 'The new Schema of the Constitutions *De divina Revelatione* and *De Ecclesia* were sent to the Fathers. From both, the word "dogmatic", which had up till then qualified them, had disappeared. A naïve deception, but not much, devised as ever by Fr Tromp, with the aim of lessening the value of the two Documents. Furthermore, in n. 8 of *De divina Revelatione,* in the text inspired by Jude (1:3), "*eosdem semel traditae sanctis fidei supercertari deprecantur*", the same hand had altered *semel* to *simul,* perhaps to give greater independence to Tradition compared to Scripture. It was clutching at straws' (U. Betti, *Diario del Concilio. 11 ottobre 1962—Natale 1978* [Bologna: Dehoniane, 2003], pp. 50–51). According to a careful listening of the tape recordings it was not Fr Tromp who devised that solution. However, the attempt to eliminate the adjective 'dogmatic' to define the constitution is attested to also by J. Ratzinger, *La collegialità episcopale,* p. 757.

where the doctrinal vale of a declaration can be effectively ascertained, taking into the account the gravity of the discussion, the historical *iter* of the documents, at times so tormented as to require an intervention from the Pope aimed at resolving the issue;[106]

2. another indication lies in the use of the phrase '*docet sancta Synodus*', used somewhat rarely and to introduce an important doctrinal affirmation (cf. for example *Lumen Gentium* 14,[107] 18,[108] 20 and 21[109]). At times, on the other hand, the verb *declarare* is used to introduce an important teaching;[110]
3. the use of the word '*credimus, creditor*' when introducing an expression of the kind: 'It is the faith of the Catholic Church that...' (in

---

106 On the theological importance of the *Acta Synodalia* of Vatican II to verify the conciliar *mens*, see Sullivan, *Creative Fidelity*, pp. 170–171.

107 On the need for the Church as means of salvation: 'Docet autem, Sacra Scriptura et Traditione innixa, Ecclesiam hanc peregrinantem necessariam esse ad salutem'.

108 On the hierarchical constitution of the Church divinely revealed and appealing to Vatican I ('vestigial premens'): 'Haec Sacrosancta Synodus, Concilii Vaticani primi vestigia premens, cum eo docet et declarat Iesum Christum Pastorem aeternum sanctam aedificasse Ecclesiam, missis Apostolis sicut Ipse missus erat a Patre (cf. Io 20,21); quorum successores, videlicet Episcopos, in Ecclesia sua usque ad consummationem saeculi pastores esse voluit'.

109 On the sacramentality of the episcopate: 'Docet autem Sancta Synodus episcopali consecratione plenitudinem conferri sacramenti Ordinis, quae nimirum et liturgica Ecclesiae consuetudine et voce Sanctorum Patrum summum sacerdotium, sacri ministerii summa nuncupatur'.

110 In DH the phrase '*haec Synodus declarat*' occurs: 'Haec Vaticana Synodus declarat personam humanam ius habere ad libertatem religiosam' (2); 'Quae de iure hominis ad libertatem religiosam declarat haec Vaticana Synodus, fundamentum habent in dignitate personae, cuius exigentiae rationi humanae plenius innotuerunt per saeculorum experientiam' (9). We find *declarat* in reference to the Sacred Synod in *Sacrosanctum concilium* 4 (et alia), in a generic fashion in the introduction in *Presbyterorum ordinis* 1 along with *decernit*. In *Lumen Gentium* only in 18 do we find *docet* linked with *declarat* and both linked to the teaching of Vatican I. Then in *Unitatis redintegratio* 16, 17, 18 and in *Christus Dominus* 20, etc., does *declarat* in place of *docet* express a different level of teaching?

Lumen Gentium 39[111] and *Unitatis redintegratio* 3d[112] and 4b[113], *Dignitatis humanae* 1b[114]).

Considering that assent to the conciliar Magisterium is varied and not unambiguous: fundamentally and generally it is not about assent of *divina* and *catholica* faith but *ecclesiastica* faith, as given to *res tenendae* (not revealed but word of the Magisterium, different from *res credendae*, revealed and therefore Word of God) and so there also remains a question about rejection of the conciliar Magisterium. *Strictu senso* it would not be formal heresy, except when the matter denied has not already been raised to the level of dogma or *definitive tenenda* teaching. So rejection of the Council in its totality or at least in its main content would however, according to Sullivan, be an estranging from the main tendency of the Catholic Church.[115]

More recently B. Gherardini has intervened on the issue of the conciliar Magisterium, distinguishing four magisterial levels in Vatican II, which would consequently entail a level of differentiated adherence, even if that is not explicitly stated:[116]

---

111 On the holiness of the Church as ontological feature: 'Ecclesia, cuius mysterium a Sacra Synodo proponitur, indefectibiliter sancta creditur'.

112 On the unicity of the visible Body of Christ on earth: 'Uni nempe Collegio apostolico cui Petrus praeest credimus Dominum commisisse omnia bona Foederis Novi, ad constituendum unum Christi corpus in terris, cui plene incorporentur oportet omnes, qui ad populum Dei iam aliquo modo pertinent'.

113 On the hope for unity of all Christians in the unique Eucharistic celebration and in the one and only Catholic Church: 'in unius unicaeque Ecclesiae unitatem congregentur quam Christus ab initio Ecclesiae suae largitus est, quamque inamissibilem in Ecclesia catholica subsistere credimus et usque ad consummationem saeculi in dies crescere speramus'.

114 On the one true religion: 'Hanc unicam veram Religionem subsistere credimus in catholica et apostolica Ecclesia, cui Dominus Iesus munus concredidit eam ad universos homines diffundendi...'.

115 See Ardusso, *Magistero ecclesiale*, pp. 212–214; Sullivan, *Magisterium. Teaching Authority in the Catholic Church*, p. 60ff.

116 Cf. B. Gherardini, *Indole pastorale del Vaticano II: una valutazione*, in S. Manelli—S. Lanzetta (eds.), *Concilio ecumenico Vaticano II, un concilio*

1. generic level, of the ecumenical Council as ecumenical Council;
2. the specific level of the pastoral style;
3. that of the appeal to other Councils;
4. that of the innovations, in which the author places the majority of the conciliar teachings, which in his opinion jar with the Tradition of the Church.

To this four-fold distinction B. Lucien feels the need to bring some corrective remedies, mainly on the second and fourth points. The fact that the Second Vatican Council had a specifically pastoral spin does not mean that it never exercised dogmatic and infallible Magisterium, even though in an ordinary and universal and not defining form. In his work, Lucien tries to show principally that Vatican II truly exercised magisterial authority which, when it is explicit, ascends also to the level of infallibility. For this reason Lucien criticises the sub-distinction of the conciliar 'innovations', without inserting them into a specific level of magisterial authority. The fact that the faithful do not see the link of the new teaching with the deposit of faith does not cancel the value of the magisterial intervention, with the obligation to adherence which it implies. Something new, Lucien says, could be inserted into a passage of the authentic authoritative Magisterium or that which he defines as pedagogical Magisterium.[117] However, what can be inferred from these authors is that the level of magisterial authority of Vatican II is seen in its acts: in the texts, and if it were still not sufficiently clear, in the very intentions of the Council Fathers. The Council presents one of the greatest hermeneutical difficulties precisely with regard to the magisterial evaluation of its teaching and the respective level of assent which its teachings demand. There is no fixed remedy for that but it must be seen with patient theological scrupulousness.

---

pastorale. Analisi storico-filosofico-teologica (Frigento: Casa Mariana Editrice, 2011), pp. 164–166.

117 Cf. B. Lucien, 'L'autorité magistérielle de Vatican II. Contribution à un debat actuel', in *Sedes Sapientiae* 119 (2012), pp. 71–78.

3.3 The assent due to Church Magisterium

To that end it is very important to recall the levels of assent due to the Magisterium of the Church. It was John Paul II who, with the Motu proprio *Ad tuendam fidem* of 18 May 1998,[118] wanted to fill a gap in the CIC, about the triple distinction in the assent to be given to Church Magisterium, made by the *Professio fidei et iusiurandum fidelitatis in suscipiendo officio nomine Ecclesiae exercendo* from the Congregation for the Doctrine of the Faith, dated 9 January 1989.[119] With the absence in the CIC (and that of the Eastern Churches, too) of a canon about the firm and irrevocable assent to be given to the doctrines of the faith or morals proposed in a definitive manner both through a solemn judgment and the ordinary and universal Magisterium, Canon 750 turned out to be composed of two paragraphs, which along with Canon 752, constitute the three distinct levels of assent to be given to ecclesiastical Magisterium. So, Canon 750 §1 states:

> A person must believe with divine and Catholic faith all those things contained in the word of God, written or handed on, that is, in the one deposit of faith entrusted to the Church, and at the same time proposed as divinely revealed either by the solemn Magisterium of the Church or by its ordinary and universal Magisterium which is manifested by the common adherence of the Christian faithful under the leadership of the

[118] In AAS 90 (1998) 457–461.

[119] In AAS 81 (1989) 104–106. The three magisterial levels are thus distinguished in the *Professio fidei*: '1) Firma fide quoque credo ea omnia quae in verbo Dei scripto vel tradito continentur et ab Ecclesia sive sollemni iudicio sive ordinario et universali magisterio tamquam divinitus revelata credenda proponuntur. 2) Firmiter etiam amplector ac retineo omnia et singula quae circa doctrinam de fide vel moribus ab eadem definitive proponuntur. 3) Insuper religioso voluntatis et intellectus obsequio doctrinis adhaereo quas sive Romanus Pontifex sive Collegium Episcoporum enuntiant cum Magisterium authenticum exercent etsi non definitivo actu easdem proclamare intendant' (*Ibid.*, p. 105). See also Congregation for the Doctrine of the Faith, *Doctrinal Commentary on the Concluding Formula of the Professio fidei*, 29 June 1998, in AAS (1998) 542–551, which takes note of *Ad tuendam fidem*.

> sacred Magisterium; therefore all are bound to avoid any doctrines whatsoever contrary to them.

Here is required an assent of theological faith (divine and Catholic) to the magisterial pronouncement. Therefore the truth taught is proposed as divinely revealed. It is teaching *de fide credenda,* that is to say teaching whose assent is based directly on faith in the authority of the Word of God. Rejection of such teaching can be described as heresy (cf. also Canon 751).

Canon 750, §2 states:

> Each and every thing which is proposed definitively by the Magisterium of the Church concerning the doctrine of faith and morals, that is, each and every thing which is required to safeguard reverently and to expound faithfully the same deposit of faith, is also to be firmly embraced and retained; therefore, one who rejects those propositions which are to be held definitively is opposed to the doctrine of the Catholic Church.

Here the truth, taught in a solemn manner or with ordinary universal judgment, is presented as *connected* to divine Revelation and therefore must be believed as a definitive verdict. Some authors speak of assent of ecclesiastical faith or firm and definitive assent. They are teachings *de fide tenenda,* that is to say, teachings whose assent is based on faith in the assistance of the Holy Spirit to the Magisterium and in the Catholic doctrine of the infallibility of the Magisterium. Rejection of such a definitive judgement is a rejection of Catholic teaching and rejection of communion with the Catholic Church.

Then we have Canon 752, which, recalling *Lumen Gentium* 25, states:

> Although not an assent of faith, a religious submission of the intellect and will must be given to a doctrine which the Supreme Pontiff or the college of bishops declares concerning faith or morals when they exercise the authentic Magisterium, even if they do not intend to proclaim it by definitive act;

therefore, the Christian faithful are to take care to avoid those things which do not agree with it.

Here the doctrine is taught in an authentic but not definitive manner. The teaching is per se *in fieri* and respectful adherence as '*religiosum voluntatis et intellectus obsequium*' (*Lumen Gentium* 25) must be given in keeping with the will of the Magisterium itself (of the Pope principally and of the College of bishops in communion with him). Such will is inferred from the character of the documents, or from the insistence in proposing a certain teaching, or from the mode of expression (cf. *Ibid.*). Adherence to this authentic Magisterium which we can call 'probable', as explained by the Instruction from the Congregation for the Doctrine of the Faith, *Donum veritatis*, dated 24 May 1990,[120] must however move in the logic of obedience of the faith, while not blocking the theologian from raising respectful questions about the convenience, form or content of a magisterial intervention. Rejection can be described as erroneous teaching or reckless or dangerous in the case of prudential teachings. Therefore *Donum veritatis* clarifies that here the Magisterium, without the intention of establishing a 'definitive' act, teaches a doctrine to help to have deeper knowledge about Revelation, or to recall the conformity of a teaching with the truth of faith or finally to guard against ideas incompatible with these truths themselves. This is an area for prudential magisterial judgments, which does not exclude per se *deficiencies* (they are not '*a defectibus immunia*') and therefore a subsequent perfectibility, while however as a rule the will for real deference remains.[121]

In this third level of Magisterium, ordinary authentic, which always demands religious deference, one can confirm, consequently, the request for a differentiated adherence, by reason of what I recalled before in reference to the manifestation of the magisterial mind and will. Here again greater caution and scrupulousness is called for, considering, to say it again, the nature of the documents, the frequent

[120] In AAS 82 (1990) 1550–1570.

[121] Cf. 23–24 of *Donum veritatis*, in *Ibid.*, pp. 1559–1561.

re-proposal of the same teaching and finally the tenor of the verbal expression. A labour demanded of theologians.

4. The theological notes and censures: a considerable loss

Like F. Ardusso I am of the opinion that 'the maximalism and minimalism which one sees today in the Catholic Church about the ordinary non *ex cathedra* Magisterium cry out for the theological notes and censures which both the Magisterium and the *probati auctores* once used. Sadly, they have almost completely disappeared. And if that involves as a positive consequence a less legalistic exercise of the Magisterium, it also brings with it, as a negative effect, uncertainties about the type of assent to give to a proposed teaching, or to a re-experienced teaching'.[122]

Unfortunately the new manuals of theology have forgotten almost completely the theological importance of the levels of assent to give to the revealed and defined truths of the Magisterium or simply taught by the Magisterium with a non-infallible act. Therefore I believe it appropriate to offer a framework of the main theological notes with the relative grades of assent, to which correspond, then, when the teaching is rejected, a theological censure.

Usually, the notes are sub-divided thus by the authors:[123]

1. *de fide divina*: a truth contained formally and immediately in Revelation (material dogma);
2. *de fide divina et catholica*: a truth revealed by God and defined as such by the Magisterium (formal dogma);

---

[122] Ardusso, *Magistero ecclesiale*, p. 268.

[123] Cf. L. Ott, *Grundriss der Katholischen Dogmatik* (Freiburg im B.: Herder, 1978^9), pp. 11–12; H. Waldenfels, *Teologia fondamentale nel contesto del mondo contemporaneo* (Cinisello Balsamo: Paoline, 1988), p. 625; S. Cartechini, *De valore notarum theologicarum* (Rome: Pontificia Università Gregoriana, 1951); W. Beinert, *Theologische Erkenntnislehre*, in Id. (ed.), *Glaubenszugänge. Lehrbuch der Katolischen Dogmatik*, vol. I (Paderborn: Schöningh, 1995), p. 149.

3. *de fide ecclesiastica*: Catholic truths or ecclesiastical teachings (not contained in Revelation formally and directly) on which the Magisterium of the Church has pronounced in a definitive manner. The certainty of these truths is infallible and, like dogma, they call for an assent of faith;
4. *sententia fidei proxima*: a truth which is believed to be revealed according to the consensus of theologians, but not yet proposed as such by the Magisterium;
5. *sententia ad fidem pertinens* or *theologice certa*: a proposition on which the Magisterium has not yet pronounced in a definitive manner, the rejection of which could endanger another truth of faith and whose truth is guaranteed by its intimate connection with Revelation (one speaks of *conclusiones theologicae*);[124]
6. *sententia communis*: a teaching formulated by theologians and for a long time never contradicted;
7. *opiniones theologicae*: theological teachings about the faith and morals which are not clearly contained in Revelation, nor has the Magisterium pronounced on them. These opinions in turn can be qualified in different ways: as *sententia probabilis, sententia probabilior, sententia bene fundata, sententia pia* and finally as *opinio tolerata*: weakly founded but tolerated by the Church.

Up to a few years ago, as well as these notes theology knew different levels of censure, when the widespread teaching was not in conformity with the faith of the Church or seemed rash with respect to the judgment of theologians. The classic schema envisaged the following censures:[125]

124 More broadly speaking, the *conclusiones theologicae* are divided into two categories: conclusions where both the premises are directly and formally revealed by God, and thus one reaches a truth which demands an assent of divine and Catholic faith (or *immediate divina*), and conclusions of which only one of the premises is directly and formally revealed by God, while the other is revealed virtually or indirectly. Here one reaches a truth which demands an assent of ecclesiastical faith (or *mediate divina*), cf. F. Diekamp, *Katholische Dogmatik*, vol. I (Münster: Aschendorff, 1949), pp. 22–23.

125 Ott, *Grundriss der Katholischen*, p. 12; Scheffczyk, *Grundlagen des Dogmas*, pp. 128–129: here Scheffczyk, to the different level of certainty of a teaching,

1. *propositio haeretica*: denial of a formal dogma;
2. *propositio haeresi proxima*: denial of a *sententia fidei proxima*;
3. *propositio de haeresi suspecta* or *propositio erronea*, which in turn can be:
   - 3.a *error in fide ecclesiastica*: denial of a truth not formally revealed by God but definitively taught by the Magisterium;
   - 3.b *error theologicus*: denial of a *sententia communis* of theologians;
4. *propositio falsa*: contradictory dogmatic fact;
5. *propositio temeraria*: without foundation and divergent from common teaching;
6. *propositio piarum aurium offensiva*: which harms popular piety;
7. *propositio male sonans*: contradictory in the way of expression;
8. *propositio captiosa*: insidious because of its ambiguity;
9. *propositio scandalosa*.

These theological qualifications and the corresponding censures remain of great value; they are a sign of the fact that dogmatics are aware of a different gradation both about the certainty and the obligatory nature of its teachings, and the same objective certainty and the same subjective obligation is not to be given to all its theological propositions.[126] To return to their use seems pedagogically essential, to take note, above all after the post-conciliar theological change, of a Magisterium differentiated according to different levels, and to avoid making infallible, or, on the contrary, to reject easily, both the Magisterium and the theological statements themselves which support it, in relation above all to Church teachings.

---

corresponds with a censure in case of rejection.

126 Cf. Scheffczyk, *Grundlagen des Dogmas*, p. 129.

II

THE THEOLOGICAL CONTRIBUTION TO VATICAN II

STATUS QUÆSTIONIS

1. Vatican II: a council and the theologians

WITHOUT DOUBT THE theologians had a most significant role at the Council. There was something new and also surprising about the enormous amount of theological work prepared by many who, first of all, arrived as personal theologians of the Bishops, and were then nominated as periti to the Council. K. Schatz states that 'in this, the Second Vatican Council was obviously, in a way in which only prior to this the councils of Constance and Basle had been, a council of "experts" or of "theologians"'.[1]

---

1 Schatz, *Storia del Concili*, p. 277: 'The role undertaken at Trent by the congregations of theologians could be equated—as regards the council—to those very-well attended meetings—while not being official structures—in which periti such as Rahner, Ratzinger, Schillebeeckx, de Lubac, Congar and many others communicated their theological perspectives to the bishops, proposed their own texts and were consulted on how to proceed. That was necessarily determined by the situation. Even the majority of the "progressive" Fathers had still not effectively perceived, and even less contributed to realising, that epoch-making transformation which had intervened in theological reflection in recent decades. In general, they came to the council simply with a generic open-mindedness and, without their theologians, would rather have been somewhat impotent and uncertain. Without this intense learning process—still completely unknown in all its detail—which happened in the

B. Mondin, too, concurs with this point about the strong theological significance at Vatican II:

> It was the Council which brought out the theologians in all their prominence, for they were its main authors and protagonists. Their presence at Vatican II was massive. There were more than two hundred official and private periti. Like the Bishops, the theologians came from all over the world, and this contributed to giving to the 'theological' thought of the Council that Catholicity which allowed it to overcome the narrow horizons of curial theology. The contribution of the theologians to the work of the Council was substantial, constant and decisive: their opinions were continually listened to and their proposals welcomed. To them was entrusted the drafting of all the conciliar texts which were then approved by the Fathers. It can definitely be said that the theology of Vatican II is that of the theologians who took part in it (Parente, Colombo, Congar, Daniélou, Rahner, Ratzinger, Chenu, etc.) ... The Council represents the happy conclusion of the great renewal which had taken place in Catholic theology since the Second World War.[2]

For R. Laurentin, the fundamental problem to resolve in post-conciliar theology, owing to the demands of the Council, is the preceding theology, wasting away, in as far as it had lost contact with the sources of Revelation and with life, and had become a collection of a system of theses.

> The remedy, he said, came from the theologians themselves who worked assiduously in the shadows. Vatican II gave recognition by right to the acquisitions of this trend which

council itself and then quickly had international repercussions, it would be impossible to understand what effectively happened at the Second Vatican Council'.

2 B. Mondin, *Storia della teologia*, vol. 4 (Bologna: Studio Domenicano, 1997), pp. 619–620.

assumes in just one movement the revealed sources and the living realities of salvation.[3]

To evaluate more broadly this presence of theologians, their great influence over the bishops[4] and their capacity to direct the work of the preparatory Commissions along other paths, it is essential to recall their work in the two moments which characterised the conciliar process *in fieri*, awaiting the solemn opening of the work: 1) the ante-preparatory phase (1959–1960), 2) the preparatory phase (1960–1962), from which follows 3) the phase of the work of the Council, up until its closure on 8 December 1965. In the ante-preparatory phase (1959), of note were two purely theological interventions from Y. Congar, the first of which was published anonymously three weeks after the announcement of the Council. Congar expressed the hope that the Council might abstain from any new definition of faith on the Virgin Mary, that it might balance the function of the Pope and the bishops, that there might be development of horizontal communion between the local Churches, greater impulse given to ecumenism, for which there was no qualified contact in the Vatican. The same year, at a conference held in Belgium, the French Dominican called on the Council to draw up teaching on episcopal collegiality and clarify the relations between Sacred Scripture and Tradition.[5] In the years of the Council, too, the book by H.

---

3 R. Laurentin, *Bilan du Concile Vatican II* (Paris: Edition du Seuil, 1967), p. 369 (Italian edition, *Bilancio del Concilio* [Milan: IPL, 1967]).

4 It is interesting what Rusch says in this regard, interpreting what L. Örsy wrote (*The Church Learning and Teaching* [Dublin: Dominican Publication, 1987]): 'As an attempt at *aggiornamento* through *ressourcement* of the tradition, the Council's final documents were the result, in part, of a dialogue whereby at night bishops became learners and theologians the teachers, and by day the theologians listened as learners and the bishops once again assumed their teaching role. In effect, this reception of contemporary scholarship was a reception of "history" in its broad sense', Rusch, *Still interpreting Vatican II*, p. 12.

5 See É. Fouolloux, *Comment deviant-on expert à Vatican II? Le cas du Père Y.*

Küng on unity understood as renewal of the Church[6] received widespread circulation. The origins of this book lay in a conference held in Basle at the invitation of K. Barth on the Church *semper reformanda*, a week before the announcement of the Council. Here it was announced that the Council would lead to a change in the general climate for a reform of the Catholic Church, consistent with welcoming the just proposals of Luther's reform, so as to overcome divisions.

Among the *vota* of the future Fathers (1959–1960) the contribution of theologians, even if this time fairly meagre, can still be seen. One significant example is the *votum* presented by Mgr Michael Keller of Münster, into which were inserted different proposals drawn up by the local Faculty of Theology, whose Dean was Professor Hermann Volk, whose very significant text was widely reported by Keller:

> It must be solemnly affirmed that Sacred Scripture is the main source of Catholic truth, while Tradition, while not being creative of revelation, is a source by which revealed things are manifested to us. The popular idea according to which the Catholic Church lives by the sacraments, while the Protestants are nourished by the spoken and preached word, must be overcome. Starting from the *Letter to the Hebrews*: 'Indeed, the word of God is living and active, sharper than any two-edged sword' (4:12), the Council must highlight the salvific virtue

---

Congar, in *Le deuxième Concile du Vatican 1959–1965* ("Collection de l'école française de Rome" 113), Rome 1989, pp. 312–313; J. Wicks, 'I teologi al Vaticano II. Momenti e modalità del loro contributo al Concilio', in *Humanitas* 5 (2004), p. 1013.

6 *The Council and Reunion* (London and New York: Sheed and Ward, 1961) (German original, *Konzil und Wiedervereinigung: Erneuerung als Ruf in der Einheit*, Freiburg im. Br.: Herder, 1960). It is interesting what Wicks says ('I teologi', footnote 6, p. 1014): 'On the origin of the work, see the memories of H. Küng, *Erkämpfte Freiheit. Erinnerungen* (München-Zürig: Piper, 2002), pp. 227–230 and 249–253. On the eve of the opening of the Council, the same author opened up forgotten horizons to ecclesiology with his work *Strukturen der Kirche*, welcomed by Rahner in the series "Quaestiones Disputate" (Freiburg im. Br.: Herder, 1962)'.

> of the word read in the liturgy, applied in the homily and explained in catechesis according to the sense believed to be true by the Church.[7]

In the ante-preparatory phase there were also many important *studia* prepared by the pontifical Faculties for the orientations of the Council. On 18 July 1959 Cardinal Tardini sent a letter to 62 Catholic faculties, asking them to provide an illustrative contribution by April 1960; of these, 53 faculties succeeded in delivering texts.[8] Among these, highlighted for its importance, is a sort of syllabus drawn up by the Rector of the Lateran University, Mgr Antonio Piolanti, subsequently elected a member of the preparatory Theological Commission and therefore peritus at the Council. In his preparatory study, Piolanti denounced the errors which were spreading in the *nouvelle théologie,* compared with the principles enunciated by Pius XII in *Humani Generis* (1950). Piolanti also indicated the names of the theologians who were propagators of these tendencies: H. Bouillard and M. D. Chenu, accused of relativism in doctrinal terminology, alongside H. De Lubac, J. Daniélou and H. U. von Balthasar belonging to the School of Lyons, which promoted Patristic theology as an alternative to Scholastic theology. According to Piolanti, these theologians illustrated their theses deriving their validity not from objectivity but their religious experience. Therefore he called on the Council to take a stance to reaffirm the immutability of the truths of the faith and the need to refer to the Magisterium. His proposal, made its own by the Congregation for Seminaries and Studies, was handed over as a written text (without the implicated names) of the Congregation for the ante-preparatory consultation, unaware, however, of

---

7 The *votum* of Mgr Keller is reported in *Acta et Documenta,* Ser. I, vol. II/2 pp. 629–633, that of the Faculty in *Ibid.,* Ser. I, vol. IV/2, pp. 799–803; Wicks, 'I teologi', p. 1017.

8 Published in three volumes in *Acta et Documenta,* Ser. I, vol. IV, comprising three parts.

the subsequent stances against a very marked interference by the Roman curial theology.[9]

So one comes to the work of the particular preparatory Commissions (1960–1962), among which the Theological Commission, led by Cardinal Ottaviani and by Mgr Parente, with Fr S. Tromp as secretary, assumed a significant role. There were 27 members, of whom 16 were theologians. These included A. Piolanti, S. Garofalo, L. Cerfaux, J. Fenton, L. Ciappi and C. Balić. There were 20 consultors, including Y. Congar, H. de Lubac, B. Häring and J. Lécuyer. The preparatory Theological Commission drafted 8 constitutional schema in 25 files of 480 pages. Of these schema only six were examined in the sessions from November 1961 to June 1962. In November 1961 a new model of the profession of faith was also discussed, thus arriving at a total of nine prepared schema.[10] However, only the following were examined and discussed:

1. The sources of revelation (co-ordinated by S. Garofalo)
2. The custody of the purity of the deposit of faith (L. Ciappi)
3. The Christian moral order (F. Hürth)
4. Chastity, marriage, the family and virginity (E. Lio)
5. The Church (R. Gagnebet)
6. The Blessed Virgin Mary (C. Balić)

However, none of the schema reached promulgation through voting in the Council chamber. Immediately they were the object of considerable discussion and objections, resulting in replacement with new texts or partial integration in other schema. By now the premises for

9 Cf. Wicks, 'I teologi', pp. 1018–1019.

10 For an historical overview of all the preparatory Commissions and Secretariats of the Council and the relative proposals for the schema of constitutions and decrees, see G. Caprile, 'Entestehungsgeschichte und Inhalt der Vorbereiteten Schemata', in *Lexikon für Theologie und Kirche, Das Zweite Vatikanische Konzil*, III (Freiburg-Basle-Vienna: Herder, 1968), pp. 665–726 (p. 725 for an overall picture).

the change wanted by the Fathers—especially those from beyond the Alps, at the advice of the German periti—had been realised, that the Council might not be something already pre-ordained or monopolised by a certain Roman and curial theology, but, in the Council chamber, there be a real opportunity to discuss and broaden the very horizons of theology, as prophesied by some theologians. In a certain sense Y. Congar became the champion of this position, pointing out its reasons. The fundamental one was the strong influence exercised over the work of the Theological Commission by the mindset of the Holy Office, alienated from the indications of openness given by John XXIII. For example, the schema *De deposito fidei* in ten chapters, had as a goal that of correcting the errors of the twentieth century about the possibility of knowing truth, the creation and evolution of the world, objective revelation through God's expressions, the correct distinction between nature and grace, the existence of original sin, etc. The Council, instead, did not have to stop to condemn the errors, but had to encourage dialogue with the world, and above all provide an impulse to free theological research and welcome the significant progress, which up to then had taken place especially in the area of biblical studies. Among the failures of this schema, Congar included the lack of dialogue between the Theological Commission and the other commissions, especially with the Secretariat for Promoting Christian Unity, therefore the ecumenical efforts appeared to be in vain and without any bearing on the doctrinal work.[11] Likewise, in his

---

11 Cf. Y. Congar, *My Journal of the Council* (Collegeville MN: Liturgical Press 2012), p 28ff. Congar criticises the handbook-like and scholastic procedure, hardly ecumenical and biblical, used in the drawing up of the definitive texts of the ante-preparatory Theological Commission and denounces an 'obscurantist clique (Fenton-Ottaviani-the Lateran)' which wanted to secure the work of drafting the *De Ecclesia* schema (cf. *Ibid.*, pg. 40). See also, Wicks, 'I teologi', pp. 1023–1025. As regards the ecumenical effort, it is interesting to note a 1960 work by Fr Giuseppe D'Ercole (Professor in the History of Canon Law at the Pontifical Lateran University), presented, as a suggestion, to the ante-preparatory Commission of the Council about the problem of ecumen-

opinion, the curial hierarchy was reflected in the division of the conciliar commissions and this was an 'original sin' of John XXIII, the consequences of which would be paid for in the Council.[12]

On 10 November 1961, the Theological Commission presented through Cardinal Ottaviani a new formula for the Profession of Faith (comprising 12 pages), which, however, was set aside; in its place was chosen that prescribed by the Supreme Pontiffs Pius IV and Pius IX.[13]

---

ical union with the separated brethren. In the foreword he says: 'In announcing his intention to convene the celebration of an Ecumenical Council, the Holy Father has indicated the return of dissidents to the Church as one of the main objectives of the same Council. Subsequently, this goal has been less repeated in public, so at the moment one has the sensation that an almost discreet veil has descended on this objective' (*Voto per la Pontificia Commissione Antepreparatoria per il Concilio Ecumenico*, Rome: SIGAP, 1960, p. 5). And he adds an interesting fact about the desired pastoral goal of the same document, which the Council then had to formulate: 'Even if union were not an openly specific theme of the Council, the Fathers are aspiring to it and preparing it with a solemn document, which almost constitutes its *magna charta*. The author believes that it would be equally appropriate for the purpose, if the proposed document were not drawn up in the form of a dogmatic constitution, followed by canons, with sanctions, but had the form of a letter of the Fathers to the dissidents, in which they might be encouraged to return to the unity of the Church, suggesting to them the elements of the Catholic faith on the controversial issues which have caused disagreements' (*Ibid.*, p. 6). It is also true, however, that D'Ercole, in formulating his proposal for union, justly taking advantage of the biblical element to approach the Protestants, also says that the goal of the Church is not really the salvation of souls (in a restrictive sense) but would be 'to confer vitality, and health and really to procure salvation, because the Church realises its goal in time and the phase of the beyond is outside its direct mandate' (*Ibid.*, p. 32). The Church, on the other hand, also in the 1983 CIC (canon 1748), reiterates that the aim of the Church is the salvation of souls.

12 Cf. Congar, *My Journal of the Council*, p. 464.

13 This formula comprised 18 chapters: it began with the Nicaean-Constantinopolitan Symbol, united with the Tridentine Profession of faith with the anti-modernist oath, it reported some new errors, already denounced by the Encyclical *Humani generis*, as well as some erroneous opinions on the virginity

The most discussed and difficult schema were the first two: *De fontibus* (20 pages)[14] and *De deposito fidei puro custodiendo* (7 booklets, 84 pages).[15] In the Central Preparatory Commission which examined the schema of the particular preparatory Commissions a rift appeared: some of the Roman Curia, and not just the Cardinals, said they were in favour of the two schema mentioned but others

of and the veneration of Our Lady, on the ontological distinction between the common and the ministerial priesthood, some errors concerning the last things, particularly in reference to judgment and hell, etc.. Cf. Caprile, 'Entestehungsgeschichte und Inhalt', p. 666.

14 This schema began with the following words: 'De fontibus revelationis: Iuxta ea quae a Summis Pontificibus recentius edita sunt, exponatur doctrina catholica de Sacra Scriptura (de sacrorum librorum historicitate; de obsequio quo exegetae erga Traditionem sacram et Magisterium ecclesiasticum tenentur) ...'. It was divided into five parts: 1. *De duplici fonte revelationis* (Scripture and Tradition: their mutual relationship and their relationship with the Magisterium); 2. *De S. Scriptura inspiratione, inerrantia et compositione litteraria*; 3. *De Vetere Testamento*; 4. *De Novo Testamento*; 5. *De Sacra Scriptura in Ecclesia*, cf. *Ibid.*

15 This schema was presented to the Central Commission on 20, 22 and 23 January 1962. It comprised 11 chapters: 1) *De cognitione veritatis*; 2. *De Deo*; 3. *De Deo creatore et evolutione mundi* (including the teaching of the faith and scientific research on evolution); 4. *De revelatione et fide*; 5. *De progressu doctrinae*; 6. *De distinctione et convenientia ordinis naturalis et supernaturalis* (condemning some positions which did not adequately distinguish between the natural and supernatural orders or which on the contrary paid tribute to naturalism and false humanism); 7. *De spiritismo et novissimis*; 8. *De peccato originali*; 9. *De unitate seu de communi origine generis humani* (affirmation of monogenism); 10. *De sorte infantium absque baptismo decedentium* (on the need for infant baptism, and the fate of those who die before baptism); 11. *De satisfactione Christi*. However, the schema was already improved by the Sub-commissions, and instead of 11 chapters with 52 paragraphs, a text with 10 chapters and 59 paragraphs was presented. Chapter 10 was eliminated. Already in chapter 9 *De novissimis* the problem of the eternity of hell and paradise was tackled. Since the Commission trusted in the mercy of God, it no longer wanted to talk about the fate of children who died without being baptised (cf. *Ibid.*, pp. 667–668). For a complete presentation of the schema see *Ibid.*, pp. 665–726.

moved over to the opposition, behind the increasing influence exercised by Cardinal Bea who examined the schema in advance.[16] Among the opponents of the schema *De fontibus* were, inter alia, Cardinals J. Döpfner (Munich), J. Frings (Cologne), B. Alfrink (Utrecht), F. König (Vienna), Mgr D. Hurley (Durban, South Africa), and the Patriarch of the Chaldean Church, Fr Cheikho.

F. König had K. Rahner as theologian for his interventions in the Central Commission.[17] König complained about the fact that it was necessary to begin with the updating of the teaching of Vatican I on Revelation and then move on to the problem of the sources, to which the Viennese Cardinal rebuked a defence at all costs of the statute of the Tradition at the expense of Scripture. For König, Scripture was the primary source of the Church, as sacred and inspired Word. Always under Rahner's guidance, König had complaints about the schema *De deposito*, judged by him to be muddled, because instead of proposing revealed truth in a positive manner, with particular attention to people of goodwill who did still not adhere to it, it was concerned in an apologetic way with defending the Deposit of faith.[18] Rahner, while he continued to assist Cardinal König, also sent his comments to Cardinal Döpfner when the first schema arrived.[19] Congar, instead, advised Mgr J. J. Weber of Strasbourg;[20] J. Daniélou wrote his assessments of the two schema above and sent them to the

16 Cf. Wicks, 'I teologi', p. 1025. Wicks' footnote (p. 1028, no. 38) is interesting: 'Especially with regard to the schema De Deposito, the theological Preparatory Commission presented many themes which are beneath the level of the dignity of a Council'.

17 See Rahner's comments on the preparatory schema of the period January-June 1962: 'Konzilsgutachten für Kardinal König', in H. Vorgrimler (ed.), *Sehnsucht nach dem geheimnisvollen Gott. Profil-Bilder-Texte* (Freiburg i. Br.: Herder), 1990, pp. 95–149.

18 Cf. Wicks, 'I teologi', pp. 1025–1026.

19 Cf. K. Rahner, 'Konzilsgutachten', pp. 149–163.

20 Cf. J. Wicks, 'Congar's Doctrinal Service of the People of God', in *Gregorianum* 84 (2003), pp. 519–520.

Coadjutor Archbishop of Paris, P. Veuillot, who for the most part made them his own as *animadversiones*[21]. Schillebeeckx collaborated with Brouwers and 50 pages in Dutch were prepared, with Latin and English translations, and 2,700 copies distributed to the episcopates.[22]

Some theologians prepared and circulated alternative texts to the schema. Among these was that of J. Ratzinger and K. Rahner on revelation in Christ,[23] the conciliar Credo of Y. Congar,[24] along with his text *De traditione et Scriptura* prepared for a group of French bishops.[25]

There was also a lot of fruitful activity undertaken by the theologians in Rome as speakers for groups of bishops. Here of note is the peritus of Cardinal Frings, J. Ratzinger, who on 10 October 1962, in an address to the German bishops, explained the problems with the schema *De fontibus*. According to Ratzinger, instead of examining *in primis* God's action which is revealed to his people, it highlighted our knowledge of Revelation through testimonies. Ratzinger underlined, with St Thomas and St Bonaventure, the presence of all the truths of faith in Scripture, while *De fontibus* was determined to condemn them. As regards biblical inspiration, Ratzinger criticised the schema for the emphasis it placed on the canonisation of the dogmatic manuals about the manner of the inspiring influence, ignoring instead the exegetical data acquired on the redaction itself of the biblical texts. Finally,

21 Cf. P. Pizzuto, *La teologia della rivelazione di Jean Daniélou. Influsso su Dei verbum e valore attuale* (Rome: Pontificia Università Gregoriana, 2003), pp. 32–39.

22 Cf. J. Brouwers, 'Vatican II, derniers préparatifs et première session. Activitès conciliaires en coulisses', in É. Fouilloux (ed.), *Vatican II commenc... Approches francophones* (Leuven: Bibliotheek van de Faculteit der Godgeleerdheid, 1993), pp. 353–357.

23 *De revelatione Dei et hominis in Jesu Christo facta*, of which *c.* 2,000 copies were duplicated and distributed.

24 Published in Latin and German in E. Klinger—K. Wittstadt (eds.), *Glaube im Prozess. Christsein nach dem II. Vatikanum* (Freiburg im.Br.: Herder, 1984), pp. 51–64.

25 Text published in U. Betti, *La dottrina del Concilio Vaticano II sulla trasmissione della rivelazione* (Rome: Antonianum, 1985), pp. 303–306.

chapter III of the schema omitted, according to Ratzinger, the immense historic period of the Old Testament, including the origins and the call of Abraham.[26] Along the same lines, and in a more pronounced manner in opposition to the duplicity of the sources of Revelation, we also find the peritus of Cardinal Florit (Archbishop of Florence), U. Betti, as his *Diario del Concilio* records. For Fr Betti, the Council was also a school and therefore needed to update the teaching on the duplicity of the sources to make room for the new position: Tradition as transmission of Scripture, putting to one side the question of the material sufficiency / insufficiency of Scripture. According to Betti, Tradition did not transmit those truths which were not in any way contained in Scripture.[27]

Due to this feverish theological activity by the periti, we can say that the Council experienced a considerable change in compass, which went well beyond the forecasts in order to achieve un-hoped for objectives at the Council assembly. This success was also noticed by G. Alberigo, who wrote:

> Despite considerable correspondence between many of those expectations and the conclusions, nevertheless it seems that Vatican I… had on the whole surpassed expectations, bringing about a more profound and systematic 'change' than the entreaties on the eve [of the Council] had the foresight and courage to hope for.[28]

---

[26] Cf. J. Ratzinger, *Bemerkungen zum Schema De fontibus revelationis* (10 October 1962), kept in the Vatican II Archive P. F. Smulders, Kathliek Documentatie Centrum, Nijmegen, Netherlands: see J. Wicks (who consulted this archive), cit., footnote 48, p. 1030, and footnote 37, p. 1027. The text has now been published in J. Ratzinger, *Zur Lehre des Zweiten Vatikanischen Konzils*, I, (Gesammelte Schriften 7/1, Freiburg im B.: Herder, 2012), pp. 157–174.

[27] Betti, *Diario*, p. 28: 'il Concilio è anche una scuola, che vale più d'ogni altra finora frequentata o tenuta'.

[28] G. Alberigo, 'Il Vaticano II dalle attese ai risultati: una 'svolta'?' in J. Doré—A. Melloni (eds.), *Volti di fine concilio* (Bologna: Il Mulino, 2000), p. 415. Laurentin's judgment on the 'change' made at the Council is as follows: 'the work of the Council, today ended, shows us all its coherence. The contrast

Congar had read this change in compass right from 13 October 1962, the day on which Cardinal Liénart had intervened in the Council to postpone for a few days the voting on the members of the ten commissions which would discuss and approve the preparatory schema, and he said:

> Between the supreme head (and his Curia) and the individual bishops, there are intermediate groupings. One of the results of the Council ought to be that of giving them more power and independence. The importance of this was demonstrated on the very first day. What I foresaw is happening: the Council itself could well be very different from its preparation. So, for Congar, this novelty and the unique importance of this moment lay in the fact that 'this is the first conciliar act, a refusal to accept even the possibility of a prefabrication.[29]

1.1 Cardinal Pietro Parente (1891–1986): the Council for a Christian *Weltanschauung*

In a conference held in 1961 about the forthcoming Ecumenical Council, Mgr Parente, then assessor at the Sacred Congregation of the Holy Office, outlined the desires of the Holy Father John XXIII: desires aimed at making the face of the Church shine out with new beauty. More than being about one or other point of teaching and discipline, it was about giving back value and substance to human and Christian life (address of 14 November 1960). Having traced a quick overview of the twenty previous Ecumenical Councils, Mgr Parente focussed also on the aims and prospects of the next Council,

> Conditioned by the profound analysis of the reality of the modern world. A brutal war and draining post-war period have

with the work of the preparatory commissions is enormous: there was a great cluster of things where incompatible and divided things were to be found randomly. Such coherence is not by chance. Already in 1962 it was noticed that the preparation was flawed', Laurentin, *Bilancio del Concilio*, p. 35.

29 Cf. Congar, *My Journal of the Council*, p. 92 (for stylistic reasons I have not reproduced the capital letters Congar uses to underline points in the text).

> sown in people's hearts scepticism and contempt for any ideology or institution of the past and an adventurous sense of newness in all areas of learning and life. In such a way, trust in the Church, in truth, even revealed truth, in the moral law, in the old social structure, has been shaken. A materialistic ideology realised in a political-social structure, in which spiritual values are replaced by technology, has taken advantage of this state of mind in turmoil.[30]

In Parente's judgment, to a materialist and atheist *Weltanschauung* the Council would have to offer a 'Christian *Weltanschauung* opposed to the materialist one, so that divided and lost humanity might resume the path of its real progress and supreme end, to which it has been destined by the Supreme Wisdom and First Love'.[31] In fact, the tension between the Soviet bloc and the Western one was very high, with the birth of a Cold War, the possibility of degenerating into a nuclear war, which would result in the destruction of humanity[32]. Precisely in this tormented situation 'the Second Vatican Ecumenical Council', Parente said, 'can be the ferment of this healing and regenerative action of the modern world'.[33]

---

30 P. Parente, *Il prossimo Concilio Ecumenico tra passato e l'avvenire.* Address given in Rome, 18 May 1961, edited by Banco di Roma, Stab. A. Standerini, Rome 1961 (?), p. 39.

31 *Ibid.*, p. 41.

32 Cf. *Ibid.*, p. 40.

33 *Ibid.* The speaker on that occasion was introduced by two important figures. By Cardinal Ottaviani, who said: 'in the Ecumenical Council we must see a great means, a significant tool, not just for the religious, spiritual re-edification of peoples, but also for the pacification of peoples' (cf. *Ibid.*, p. 21). The other figure was Tommaso Sillani, General Secretary of the Italian Centre of Studies for International Reconciliation, who, in speaking at the start of the event, said: 'Today, there are no longer heresies fighting against revealed truth; the Emperors no longer interfere in religious affairs. There are only great hopes, whose realisation would increase the authority of the Church and make it more resolute and powerful in the face of the current subversions of those without faith, much more ruthless and dangerous [in the face of] the doctrinal

The work of Cardinal Parente at Vatican II was very fruitful and laborious: his numerous interventions at the Doctrinal Commission, his meritorious theological work as a peritus and relator on the notion of 'collegiality' (as we shall see), his active interest in the Council, manifested starting from his letter-voto of 25 August 1959 to the Commission established by John XXIII to prepare the Council, when he was Archbishop of Perugia.[34]

Some years after the end of the Council assembly, in 1983, Parente published a paper on the question of Vatican II, on its degenerate interpretability due to a previous opposition of two opposed currents, which both, each in their own way, manipulated the Council. The title of this paper is significant: *La crisi della verità e il Concilio Vaticano II,*[35] which already casts a shadow over the fundamental problem the Council faced: to confirm the traditional patrimony of the Church, but re-thinking it and integrating it 'according to the needs of the changed modern mentality. Certainly a risky undertaking, but brought to a conclusion without disasters'.[36]

The culture of the Council years had to deal with the problem of the truth. In another paper, twenty years after the end of the Council assembly, Parente would write:

> Generally, the decisive cause of a Council is a crisis of the Church or the world or both. Vatican II responded to the needs of a crisis internal to the Church and to a crisis of the modern world.[37]

---

errors and disagreements of the first centuries' (*Ibid.*, pp. 16–17).

34 A book was recently published bringing together all the theological work of Cardinal Parente at Vatican II: P. Parente, *Proposte, interventi e osservazioni nel Concilio Vaticano II*, ed. His Grace Mgr Michele di Ruberto (Vatican City: LEV, 2010). See the interesting theological introduction to Parente's work at the Council, traced by one of his disciples, B. Gherardini, in *Ibid.*, pp. 9–27.

35 P. Parente, *La crisi della verità e il Concilio Vaticano II* (Rovigo: Istituto Padano di Arti Grafiche, 1983).

36 *Ibid.*, p. 167.

37 P. Parente, *A vent'anni dal Concilio Vaticano II. Esperienze e prospettive* (Rome:

For P. Parente, then a nonagenarian Cardinal, the problem was not recognisable in the Council and therefore not to be resolved by referring merely to its pastoral nature. Parente clearly states that the Council, 'despite all the abuses of interpretation, presented itself, besides being pastoral, as doctrinal, too'.[38] The problem, therefore, is not the Council, but a crisis which assailed theology many years previously, precisely in the 1940s, when, as long as the dubious and erroneous claims of Modernism remained alive, theology felt a need for aggiornamento and a return to the sources of the thought of faith, to the Fathers and to Scripture above all, because, according to some, Scholasticism and its theological method had led to an estrangement from the freshness of the original. In with this desire for renewal, already supported in its just claims by the great Pope Pius XII—suffice to recall his Encyclical *Mystici Corporis* on the Church and *Humani generis* in which he denounced the abuses of the new theology and encouraged careful study of the progress of modern culture—were mingled motives of honest theological development, thanks to theologians both competent and at the same time faithful to the Magisterium, and motives of expediency, to support instead a desire for supine acquiescence to the secular culture of Modernity, even at the price of the manipulation of faith, become, due to barely orthodox theologians, ambiguous and sometimes clearly heretical. Parente offers us a reasoned and wise summary of this critical unravelling. Even in 1952, he published a paper entitled *Teologia*,[39] in which, speaking about the Encyclical *Humani generis*, he expanded the outlook to theological

---

Città Nuova, 1985), p. 8.

38 Parente, *La crisi della verità*, p. 15. And he adds: 'At the express order of Pope John XXIII, the Council had to proceed with pastoral criteria. However, this word lends itself to misunderstanding, because one can think that pastoral is of a practical, not doctrinal nature; but pastoral which is not also doctrinal is not possible... And so Vatican II, despite any suggestion to the contrary, is necessarily doctrinal, even if it did not want to adopt the technical style of the other councils (with definitions, formula, anathema)', *Ibid.*, p. 38.

39 In the *Universale Studium* series, n. 14, Studium, Rome 1952.

affairs, tracing a path from the modern era up to the crisis at the time of the angelic Pope. The theological revival, so to speak, started with an article by Jean Daniélou in 1946, which appeared in a journal *Études* under the title 'Les orientations présentes de la pensée religieuse', in which the French Jesuit gathered the claims of modern thought in the face of Scholastic philosophy and theology. He called for a return to the sources (Scripture and the Fathers). Thus Daniélou, along with de Lubac, in order to bring about this desired new theology, gave life to two great publishing undertakings: *Sources chrétiennes* for the study of the works of the Fathers, and the series *Théologie* to re-present theological issues with new methodological criteria. The Dominicans of the *Revue thomiste* reacted harshly to this initiative, publishing in 1947 a booklet entitled *Dialogue théologique,* in which they refuted the new claims of the Jesuits and defended Scholasticism and especially St Thomas. Parente noted that the Dominicans' critical observations in any case had the value of halting the bold claims of the Jesuits which offended the Thomist tradition, made its own also by the Church's Magisterium. Among these of note is included Bouillard.[40] In this period the figure of Pius XII was vigilant,

> Who while [he] defended the essence of the traditional teaching, carefully followed the contemporary development predicting the future with its crisis, which resulted in Vatican II.[41]

Cardinal Parente went on:

> All the currents of thought developed from 1940 onwards merged in to the great Ecumenical assembly of Vatican II through the Bishops and later still through the Periti, who exercised a strong influence over the Fathers. So the Council can be considered to be a starting point, not however such as

---

40 H. Bouillard, *Conversion et grâce chez S. Thomas d'Aquin* (Paris: Aubier, 1944), in which it is stated that if theology is not current it is false and therefore must adapt to the times in its way of expression, which, ultimately, is never absolute but always inferior to the truth of God. Cf. Parente, *La crisi della verità,* p. 30.

41 *Ibid.*

> to satisfy at the moment of its closure all the claims of the new Theology… Therefore the work of the Council disappointed the conservatives, but did not satisfy the progressives, who would have desired something broader and more audacious.[42]

According to Parente, the post-conciliar period was a hotbed of the most diverse interpretations of the Council. Theology was largely renewed and adapted to the new style of Vatican II. Here one must underline some respected works but with different emphases and very often contradictory. First of all, a conference of theologians at the Faculty of Posillipo (Naples), under the direction of Mgr Carlo Colombo, to give a strong impulse to theological renewal. The fruit of the conference was the book *L'insegnamento della teologia dopo il Vaticano II* (Milan: Ancora, 1967). That occasion also saw the birth of the Italian Theological Association. A larger and more profound contribution came from the volume edited by J. M. Miller, *La teologia dopo il Vaticano II* (Brescia: Morcelliana, 1967, where the names of Rahner, De Lubac, Congar, Häring, etc. appear). Immediately after the Council in the period 1965–1970 of note was the work of Y. Congar, *Situation et tâches présentes de la Théologie* (Paris: Cerf, 1967), in which there was an overview of the crisis before, during and after the Council. Parente respectfully and in some cases admirably underlines the work of Congar, who, along with De Lubac and Daniélou, was one of the main instigators of the *Théologie nouvelle*. Congar tended to justify the crisis seeing it as spontaneous movement of the old theology, considered abstract and cut off from the modern culture. Instead the Council enabled discussion about Scholasticism and the progressives, inspired by the thought of John XXIII, who had distin-

42 *Ibid.*, p. 59. Previously, Parente had said: 'an unpleasant phenomenon must be underlined: the appraisal of the Council between two opposite sides, that of the rigid conservatives, who saw in the Council the denial of the whole of Tradition; and that of the progressives, who, not satisfied by the promulgated documents, strove persistently to interpret the documents themselves in this or that phrase, separated from the context or exaggerating the openness of the Council to justify their audacious and often heterodox positions', *Ibid.*, p. 38.

guished between the substance of the faith founded on Revelation and its expressive form. So the Council had opened the path to theological renewal according to the claims of the new theology, but without renouncing traditional theology.[43]

But a matter of some concern in this theological progress and aggiornamento was represented by the Theological Congress which took place in Brussels in 1970, promoted by the journal *Concilium*, on the theme *The future of the Church*. President of the Conference was E. Schillebeeckx from the University of Nijmegen (Holland). Speakers included Cardinal Suenens, Schillebeeckx himself, Chenu, but, without being concerned in any way about magisterial authority, they began to set themselves up as champions of popular pamphlets and renewal often to the very limit of what was tolerable. The Congress approved 12 theses and four supplements (including total freedom of theology and the legitimacy of theological pluralism, the autonomy of the Magisterium, the abolition of celibacy, a re-thinking of the theological formulae of the past, the admission of women to sacred ministries, the need for adaptation to the modern world, Christological errors, etc.). Parente drew this conclusion from the Congress:

> Overall and in its details, the Congress echoed almost all the problems of the post-conciliar period, without any significant contribution of acceptable solutions.[44]

In a calm and wise reflection, from someone who had experienced at first-hand deviations and abuses, alongside the birth of a renewed hope for the Church, Parente said this about the post-conciliar crisis:

> After Vatican II the dynamism of Christian thought became more pronounced and developed in different ways: there were the serious theologians, such as De Lubac and Daniélou, who followed the impulse but controlled themselves and sought to enrich Theology by purifying it, with ever better organisa-

---

43 Cf. *Ibid.*, pp. 65–66. Congar's thoughts on this are to be found in the work quoted above, pp. 21–23.

44 *Ibid.*, p. 71.

> tion ... Then there were the enthusiastic, adventurous theologians, who preferred the novelties, the paradox, the originality at all costs and published misleading works. These two threads continue even up to today and perhaps will do so forever.[45]

However, the danger of adventurous theology is that of depreciating Revelation in a jumble of themes, therefore a disorientating fragmentation, which hides a vein of scepticism with regard to the truth.[46] The problems that would then give rise to a 'theological adventure', in the sense of a gap between progressives and conservatives, with a notable emphasis on the former, a gap which in Parente's words was exaggerated and harmful,[47] were acknowledged by Parente in the following terms: culture, freedom, pluralism, nature and the human person. In the area of culture the problem was raised about the evolution of the revealed Truth of God as present in the conscience of believers, which evolves and develops in time.

> The Modernists and Progressives of the 'Théologie nouvelle' believe that dogma is the fruit of the religious experience of the human conscience, which reflects on the Word of God; therefore they acknowledge the intrinsic evolution of dogma.[48]

---

45 *Ibid.*, p. 82.

46 Among the 'outlandish' works which came to light as post-conciliar criticism and turmoil, Parente included the following: 'In the last decade have come to light the works of Hans Küng, of Schoonenberg, of Schillebeeckx, of Rahner, and their followers, who have changed the whole of theology in the various areas, almost emptying the defined Dogma of faith and disregarding the infallible Magisterium of the Church' (*Ibid.*, p. 84). Again Parente criticised this way of doing theology in his *L'Io di Cristo* (Rovigo: Istituto Padano di Arte Grafiche, 1981); and *Terapia tomistica. Per la problematica moderna da Leone XIII a Paolo VI* (Rome: Logos, 1979). Parente also aimed a critique at B. Mondin, who delighted in speaking of 'Theologies and Christologies of today', as if they were good simply because they were of today and are in the plural. Cf. especially Parente, *La crisi della verità.*, pp. 84–85. For Parente, the 'pleasure of the progressives' is precisely the 'anti-systematic fragmentation', cf. *Ibid.*, p. 85.

47 Cf. *Ibid.*, p.86.

Actually, the classic text of St Vincent of Lerins (quoted by Vatican I, Dogmatic Constitution *Dei Filius*, chapter IV), suggests in primis a subjective development from knowledge of dogma to which can be added—but not as Bouillard[49] does or Schillebeeckx[50] in an even more audacious manner—an also objective perfectibility but only under the control of the Magisterium of the Church, the sole authentic interpreter of Revelation.

The other theme which produced real bedlam was that of freedom: to justify it in a surreptitious manner there was recourse to the concept of pluralism, as Rahner does, for example.[51] Such a theme, in fact,

> From Modernism onwards was driven to the point of compromising the unity and homogeneity of the doctrine of the faith. Saint Pius X in the Encyclical *Pascendi* and Pius XII in the Encyclical *Humani generis* had condemned similar excesses. But today, after Vatican II, the progressive theologians returned to the position of the Modernists and surpassed it, stating that one can and must adopt an integral pluralism, not just in form, but also in content, so as to be able to construct so many different theologies as there are varied modern theologies, under the impulse of the evolution of the individual and collective religious experience, through which revelation must pass to express itself and formulate itself in ever more diverse ways according to the different historical moments.[52]

The supine and submissive adaptation of modern philosophies, run through with phenomenalism, immanentism and existentialism, combined together by the identification of being and thought, constricted the stability of dogma and the unity of faith. Being and thought, identified, evolve continuously. Or better still, thought, in

---

48 *Ibid.*, p. 100.

49 H. Bouillard, *Conversion et grace chez Saint Thomas d'Aquin* (Paris: Aubier, 1944).

50 AA.VV., *Théologie d'aujourd'hui et de demain* (Paris: Cerf, 1967).

51 Cf. Parente, *La crisi della verità*, p. 103.

52 *Ibid.*, pp 113–114.

developing, has led to a substantial development of being, too, and therefore, in the final analysis, a development in revealed truth, too. The real problem is that philosophical pluralism has become theological pluralism, in which there is an attempt to defend systems which are in contradiction with each other. Thus there is talk of Christologies and theologies which have ended up changing the face of the Church and presenting a different Church. With pluralism an inconsistent ecumenism was also justified. Instead there is one faith in Christ and one Church founded by him, and so whoever is cut off from the one tree must return to it. Truth must be witnessed to even to the shedding of blood, just as Christ and the martyrs did.[53]

Finally, the last point tackled by Cardinal Parente is the concept of nature and person, to which many have clung, but falsely, to acccuse classical theology of being Hellenised. Parente underlines the ambiguous Christological and Trinitarian novelties, based on these concepts, of theologians such as Küng,[54] Schillebeeckx,[55] Schoonenberg[56] and finally Rahner,[57] who do not really demonstrate progress, but a deformation of

---

53 Cf. *Ibid.*, p. 117, 121.

54 H. Küng, *On Being a Christian* (London: Collins, 1977) (Original German, *Christ sein*, Munich: Piper, 1974). Parente points out to Küng that to appeal to the Hellenisation of Christianity according to the categories of nature and person and therefore to justify one's own rejection of the Christological and Trinitarian dogma for that reason, is simply surreptitious. In fact, the Arianism condemned at Nicaea was a Hellenistic conception which seduced Arius, by which the Logos could not be Son of God due to the fact that for the Platonists God was not generated (*agennetos*). For Arius, the Word is a creature and not the Son of God of the same nature as the Father (cf. Parente, *La crisi della verità*, p. 124). Küng defended himself, worsening his position, in *Does God Exist?* (London: Collins, 1980). For a critique of this text of Küng, see L. Immarrone, *Teologia e cristologia: 'Dio esiste?' di H. Küng* (Genoa: Quadrivium, 1982).

55 E. Schillebeeckx, *Jesus: an experiment in Christology* (London: Collins, 1979).

56 P. Schoonenberg, *The Christ* (London: Sheed & Ward, 1972). Schoonenberg, a Dutch Jesuit, was one of the main authors of the Dutch Catechism.

57 In particular his *Foundations of Christian Faith: an introduction to the idea of Christianity* (New York: Crossroad, 1997) (Original German, *Grundkurs des*

Christian truth. Parente focusses largely on Rahner who, 'while not denying nor abandoning the whole of classical Theology, welcomes many claims of modern theories, creating new problems and reaching conclusions which, if not being heresy, already open the path to errors, into which in fact fall some of his students, less prepared and cautious than him. This also happens due to his generally obscure, even inscrutable style'.[58] Rahner reveals himself to be very amenable and open to modern theories such as Existensialism, Immanentism, and Phenomenalism. In short, Parente says, 'he has no fear of manipulating the teaching of the Christian faith to accommodate it in some way to so-called modern culture'.[59] Rahner insists too much on two concepts: God's *self-communication* and humanity's *self-transcendence*. God communicates himself necessarily and this self-communication is understood by Rahner as essential, so as to endanger God's freedom, while the human person is simply a free *Geist*. The self-transcendence of the human person, on the other hand is also a tendency, above all ontological, compromising the transcendence of the supernatural world. With these two theological signposts, Rahner presents the Christian faith as close to the modern environment which loves evolutionism. So, Rahner formulates an ambiguous and obscure Christology ultimately incomprehensible even to the modern theologians: for Rahner, the grace of the hypostatic union and grace as participation in the divine life can be conceived together and only in their unity signify the unique free plan of God to establish a supernatural salvific order.[60]

Finally, Cardinal Parente draws up the conclusions of his analysis and feels he almost has to make an apology for the Council 'accused in a paradoxical manner by the monolithic and rock-like conservatives, and by the agitated progressives'.[61]

Galubens. Einführung in den Begriff des Christentums, Freiburg im B.: Herder, 1977) and *Theological Investigations*, vol. IV (London: Darton, Longman & Todd, 1966) (Original German, *Schriften zur Theologie*, vol. IV, Einsiedeln: Benziger, 1964).

58 Cf. Parente, *La crisi della verità*, p. 129.

59 *Ibid.*, p. 131.

60 Cf. *Ibid.*, pp. 131–135.

61 *Ibid.*, p. 143. Twenty years on from the Council, Parente published another

At the end of his study of Vatican II, Cardinal Parente assesses his reflections (twenty years after the celebration of the Council), checks the effects, and thus summarises the results:

The Church must not become the world, but must remain identical to itself while being in dialogue with the world and with culture. Parente harshly contests the incorrectly understood principle of the aggiornamento: the Church should move towards the world not to win it over to Christ, but to adapt itself to its mentality. The Council encouraged the opening to the new needs of culture and taking into account the progress of secular culture itself, so as to open a dialogue in which the interlocutors can really interact. The Council's open attitude was interpreted as a rebellion with regard to the past and like a Copernican discovery, an integral newness of substance and form. This caused perplexity among the conservatives, while it became a Trojan horse for the innovators. Parente tackled the problems which would lend themselves to misunderstanding but which, in an authentic interpretation, fall back into their right order.

a) Vatican II did not endorse a change in the substance of dogma

The Council documents do not authorise nor lead in themselves to the affirmation of a dogmatic development understood as a substantial change of dogma and the faith. In fact, says Parente,

> This statement is arbitrary in reference to this problem, because the Council reaffirms the entire essential content of Christian doctrine, founded on divine Revelation matured

---

book as a retrospective look at the crisis and a positive statement, through the conciliar progress seen as dynamic spirals of Catholic teaching matured and deepened in Vatican II: *A vent'anni dal Concilio Vaticano II. Esperienze e prospettive* (Rome: Città Nuova, 1985). Here, with great pride, he adds that as well as having been a speaker at the Council and defender of episcopal Collegiality, he was also a tireless defender of the Mediation of Mary, 'for whom', he says, 'I fought strongly, in a favourable sense, at the Doctrinal Commission' (*Ibid.*, p. 44). Collegiality and the Mediation of Mary were, for Parente, 'two jewels of the Constitution which is the summit of the Vatican' *Ibid.*

> down the centuries, under the action of the Fathers and the Theologians, under the action of the Holy Spirit and the vigilant control of the Church's Magisterium.[62]

The identity and perpetuity of the sacred Deposit are clearly expressed in *Dei verbum* (7–8). Here is stated the divine origin of Revelation, the need to transmit it faithfully, as well as the inspiration of the sacred books. *Dei verbum* 8 speaks of a progress of Revelation, recalling St Vincent of Lerins, quoted by Vatican I. *Dei verbum* 8[63] states:

> This tradition which comes from the Apostles develops in the Church with the help of the Holy Spirit.[64] For there is a growth in the understanding of the realities and the words which have been handed down. This happens through the contemplation and study made by believers, who treasure these things in their hearts (see Luke 2:19, 51) through a penetrating understanding of the spiritual realities which they experience, and through the preaching of those who have received through Episcopal succession the sure gift of truth. For as the centuries succeed one another, the Church constantly moves forward toward the fullness of divine truth until the words of God reach their complete fulfilment in her.

From these words, Parente explains, no wise and careful reader could deduce an admission of an intrinsic evolution of the revealed truth and the dogmatic formula themselves. And yet, Parente writes,

> Certain progressive Theologians believe that Vatican II reaffirmed the evolution of dogma, already condemned at the time of Modernism under Pius X... In conclusion we can state that the post-conciliar deviations are abuses by inattentive and hardly loyal readers, who seek to justify their errors and their uncontrolled tendencies with the authority of the Council.

---

62 Parente, *La crisi della verità*, p. 151.

63 Quoted by Parente in *Ibid.*, p. 152.

64 Here the Council refers to Vatican I, the Dogmatic Constitution on the Catholic Faith, *Dei Filius*, chapter 4: Dz 1800 (3020) [Collantes 1.085].

> This abuse can be seen in other points of the Council, too, which at first seem to be an absolute novelty compared to Tradition; but a careful reflection puts things back in place.[65]

b) The singularity of the Catholic Religion

On this fact, too, the Council presents statements which lend themselves to discussion, especially about the singularity of the Catholic religion, which we, according to divine Revelation, believe to be the only salvific religion,

> With divine right to win over humanity to the Kingdom of God and the Gospel which is its code. This correct sentiment determined in the Middle Ages language, customs and attitudes, which today clash against consciences; one thinks of the phrase 'Catholicism as State religion', with the consequence that the Church benefited from every privilege, while the other religions were 'tolerated' without the faculty to publish their professions [of faith].[66]

Parente notes that the subject of religion is the human person, conscious and free, who has the right to think and choose his or her own credo autonomously, subject to respect for social order and public morality. Thus the Council highlighted an undeniable fact, that is to say, religious liberty and freedom of conscience. 'The abuses of the Inquisition cannot be justified simply by recourse to the divine right of the one true Religion, without considering human psychology, in which reason and freedom dominate'.[67]

c) Collegiality

Another factor, which, according to Parente, caused scandal among the conservatives, was collegiality, which 'would be a disastrous novelty which harms the Primacy of the Roman Pontiff!'[68] Instead,

---

65 Parente, *La crisi della verità*, p. 153.

66 *Ibid.*, p. 154.

67 *Ibid.*, pp. 154–155.

68 *Ibid.*, p. 155.

Parente, who knew about this issue very well, as speaker, too, in the Doctrinal Commission,[69] replied simply by saying that in its most genuine form, it was desired by Christ himself who founded the apostolic College with Peter and the other apostles as members, who participate, subordinately to Peter, in all the Sacred Power of Christ. The Primacy of Peter is not a tyranny, but a paternal primacy of love and the realisation of communion. The Holy Roman Empire, with the figure of an Emperor who personified all the power of the Western world, certainly influenced the Church, creating a sort of absolutism of the Roman Pontiff. This somewhat mortified ecclesiology lasted until Pius XII, who, in *Mystici corporis*, recalled the authentic nature of the Church and its supernatural whole. Vatican II, while confirming the teaching of Vatican I on the infallibility of the Pope, softened its absolutism—for a theological reason—shedding light on the doctrine of collegiality, recalling directly the concept of hierarchy, understood as the sacred principle of the ecclesial communion of the whole people of God.[70] In this way the Council also encouraged the theological

[69] Parente says: 'On this text (chapter III of *Lumen Gentium* 22) I spoke on 21 September 1964, [an address] received with great applause. The following 21 November there was a vote on the overall text, with the result: Fathers voting, 2156; Yes, 2151; No, 5. Perhaps no other Council document received such unanimity. So no Christian, even less a priest, can deny his assent to the text thus voted, treating it as an act of the solemn Magisterium of the Church. I quote from the end of my address: 'Our schema is not based on new opinions, but on the pure sources of the Ecclesiology of the Fathers of the Church, which more adheres to the teaching of St Paul on the mystical Body, and therefore better reflects the thought of Christ', *Ibid.*, pp. 160–161, footnote 16.

[70] However, Cardinal Suenens did not agree with this, and along with Agagianian, Döpfner and Lercaro, was promised the appointment as legate of the Council, but was then appointed by Paul VI only as moderator (to manage personal relations with the Pope), due to the fact that the Council's Presidency Council, according to Montini, was not very functional. In an interview, Suenens said: 'The text of Vatican I on papal primacy and that of Vatican II on collegiality were simply put one beside the other, without undertaking the necessary integration', 'Quando il Vaticano II trovò finalmente la sua strada. Intervista al Cardinale Leo Jozef Suenens', in G. Svidercoschi, *Inchiesta sul*

deepening of the role of the laity in the Church and their liturgical-sacramental participation in the life and mission of the Church, by reason of their common priesthood. Thus, Vatican II, recalling directly the example of Christ, highlighted the concept of *service* of Authority to edify the communion of all the members.[71]

d) Ecumenism and missionary work

On the ecumenical and missionary level, the Council held firmly to the teaching of the uniqueness of the Church of Christ, which is the Catholic Church. At the same time, however, it recalled the need to not condemn and reject those separated from it, but to establish a dialogue with them, with the aim of building up the unity of all Christians in the one Church. The separated belong to Christ, they are also his members (even if not fully).

> Therefore not just the Holy See, but every particular Church, every Christian must feel the duty, even the need, to participate in the ecumenical and missionary movement to win over everyone to the Faith and to the Heart of Christ.[72]

Concilio. Parlano i protagonist (Rome: Città Nuova, 1985), pp. 29–20.

71 Cf. Ibid., pp. 155–161. B. Gherardini relates that one day he was called by the then Mgr Parente, who asked his opinion about episcopal collegiality, since he knew they disagreed about some things. Gherardini noted that the reason for his disagreement was based on the fact that the Council, distancing itself from the Scholastic models, could not succeed, essentially, in correctly applying the *real inadequate distinction* postulated by Parente to define the relationship between the Roman Pontiff and the college of Bishops. To the Pope belonged 'potestas plena et suprema' and this 'abitu et actu', while to the Bishops only 'abitu', because translated into action by the Pope, by reason of his *potestas iurisdictionis*. Gherardini asked, in the application of the above-mentioned metaphysical distinction: where is the whole and where is the part? Cf. his *Introduzione* to the work of Parente, *Proposte, interventi e osservazioni*, pp. 18–19.

72 *Ibid.*, p. 159.

1.2 Karl Rahner (1904–1984): the Council, the 'beginning of the beginning'

K. Rahner was a very influential theologian throughout the theological world in the twentieth century and had a very important role in the Council. At the start, in 1961, he was appointed simply a consultor to the Commission for Discipline of the Sacraments, and then, during the Council, was theological peritus of Cardinal König.[73]

In Rahner's conference on the occasion of the solemn closing ceremony of the Second Vatican Council in Herkules-Saal in Munich (12 December 1965), Rahner praised above all the role of the 'episcopal council' and said:

> It would be very difficult ... to predict precisely how or whether the recent proclamation of the collegial-synodal principle of the Church will take concrete form and be put into actual operation. It is impossible to foretell whether the newly founded senate of bishops will be merely consultative or whether it will comprise in theological essence a Council itself by carrying out the mandates of the Second Vatican Council (even though frequent interference and restrictions may hamper it in this task).[74]

Thus Rahner also clarified his theological thought about the Council in relation to faith:

> It was a Council in freedom and love. The Council, within the freedom of that grace which joined all its members in steadfast devotion to our Lord Jesus Christ, explored the growing *understanding* in faith of the dogmas of the Church while remaining

[73] In January 1961, Cardinal Döpfner proposed Rahner as a member of the Council's Preparatory Theological Commission, but, due to the reluctance of the President, Cardinal Ottaviani, because there were still 'pending issues' about the German Jesuit in the Holy Office, he suggested Rahner for the Sacraments Commission, cf. K. Wittstadt, *Julius Kardinal Döpfner (1913–1976)* (Munich: Don Bosco, 2001), p. 183; Wicks, 'I teologi', p. 1023.

[74] K. Rahner, *The Church after the Council* (New York: Herder and Herder, 1966), pp. 11–12 (Original German, *Das Konzil—ein neuer Beginn,* Vienna-Freiburg-Basle: Herder, 1966).

> equally loyal to the already accepted faith of the Church. Truly, it was a Council in freedom, that I can assure you.[75]

For Rahner, freedom was the ability the Council gave to everyone to support their own ideas and thus arrive at unity (at consensus) but in respect for personal liberty. All this considering the Council 'through the miracle of the Spirit'.[76] In fact,

> One can easily get the impression nowadays that freedom has caused, at least in the field of theology, discord, and that only by the show of authority can one make any appreciable advances in thought or activity.[77]

---

75 *Ibid.* The italics are Rahner's who thus wishes to underline faith as a concept (*Begriff*). This is Rahner's fundamental assumption, clearly outlined in his *Foundations of Christian Faith: an introduction to the idea of Christianity* (New York: Crossroad, 1997) (Original German, *Grundkurs des Galubens. Einführung in den Begriff des Christentums*, Freiburg i. B.: Herder, 1976). Y. Congar is also along the same lines: 'Today this is the atmosphere of the Council: a pastoral climate, a climate of freedom and dialogue and openness. Back then, it was the climate of the 'Holy Office' and of the professorships of the Roman Colleges. One was neutralised by a tacit but powerful code, by very strong social pressure against which one did not push back to the point where it would have been necessary to put everything in question', Cf. Congar, *My Journal of the Council*, p. 145

76 Rahner, *The Church after the Council*, p 13.

77 *Ibid.*, p. 14. When on 14 July 1966, Cardinal Ottaviani, Pro-prefect of the Congregation for the Doctrine of the Faith, sent to the Presidents of the Bishops' Conferences a letter about some dangerous tendencies inherent in a certain theology, Rahner responded to the Cardinal in a booklet entitled *Magistero e teologia dopo il Concilio* (Giornale di Teologia, Brescia: Queriniana, 1967; German original, 'Lehramt und Theologie nach dem Konzil', in *Stimmen der Zeit* 91/7 [1966]). Here, starting from the fact of the current problem inherent in theological knowledge, it could no longer be said with precision what is true and distinguish it clearly from what is false, while he praises Ottaviani's concern, he overcomes it by reason of the 'possibility of error' inherent also in the decision of a bishop, perhaps with regard to a censured theologian (cf. *Ibid.*, p. 53). This 'overcoming' of truth with freedom and dialogue, in the final analysis goes back to Vatican II, which could be a

Rahner recognises that the primacy of theological freedom should triumph over the already fixed choices and over the schema themselves and the outcomes of the preparatory commissions. There was a desire for an ecumenical council which Rahner defined 'of the liturgy... and of the missions'.[78] The issues which were most dear to the Council's heart, after a careful selection, were listed by Rahner as follows:

> The collegial principle in the Church... the significance of the charismatics in the Church... the local congregation as Church... the salvation of the non-Christian... the hierarchy of significance among even the defined truths of the faith... the Scripture which serves the Church and her teaching office... the general priesthood... the plurality of equally valid theologies in the one Church... the personal freedom of belief... the significance and rightness of a historical-critical theology... the falsity of a two-storey theory of a higher and a lower morality and sanctity in the Church... the meaning of the Service of the Word, and so forth.[79]

For Rahner, what the Council did remains only 'the beginning of the beginning'.[80] This beginning of the beginning, which is read by Rahner also as a 'new beginning'[81] of the Church, is understood in this way:

---

middle course between a 'planned monolithism' (or 'stagnant conservatism', *Ibid.*, p. 23) and a 'theological iconoclasm' (cf. *Ibid.*, p. 24). In fact, Rahner says: 'Vatican II preferred another method, it was more prudent and reserved in its dogmatic pronouncements, it granted more space to "dialogue" within the Church, it allowed different trends within theology to express themselves more freely, etc. It seemed that in some issues the formulation of a clear and binding formula is less easy than was thought even twenty years ago. In recent decades opinions about issues, terminology and theological methods have so quickly differentiated, that it has become much more difficult to explain with accuracy what a theological opinion intends to say, when it is "translated" into another theological language, whose "translation" is nevertheless necessary in today's theological pluralism', *Ibid.*, pp. 25–26.

78 Rahner, *The Church after the Council*, p. 19.

79 *Ibid.*, p. 16.

80 *Ibid.*, p. 19.

> So that Jesus Christ and his Church may truly encounter the spirit of this age and the future age. Therefore, the Council was the beginning of beginnings for the Church of the limitless grace of God; for a Church of our Lord and Saviour; for a Church of the word of God, of brotherhood, of hope, of humble love and service.[82]

This way of arguing presupposes in Rahner his globalising vision attributed to Vatican II, which would have led the Church to pass once again—after the intermediate stages—from a Judaeo-Christian to a pagan-Christian phase. By now with the Council the Church had encountered the world, and in itself had opened out to the world dimension, thanks to the episcopate which participated in it. Unlike Vatican I, in which there predominated 'an episcopate of exported European missionary bishops',[83] at Vatican II the bishops came from all over the world. Therefore Rahner would express this conviction:

> The Council—without thereby denying any previous ones—was the first act in history in which the world Church (*Welt-kirche*) began to officially be realised as such.[84]

Everything remains to be done in a Church which through the Council wanted to make a new beginning, passing from a Western to a worldwide form.[85] Still remaining to be done was the transformation into concrete form of the directives on the liturgy, the institution of

81 'And there is much, almost too much that needs to be done in order to initiate this beginning', *Ibid.*, p. 21. Had the Church done nothing up to the Council? This beginning would then give rise to a hermeneutic 'of discontinuity and rupture', according to Benedict XVI's expression.

82 *Ibid.*, p. 20.

83 K. Rahner, 'Interpretazione teologica fondamentale del Concilio Vaticano II', in *Sollecitudine per la Chiesa* (Rome: Paoline, 1982 (Nuovi Saggi, 8) p. 364 (German original, 'Theologische Grundinterpretation des II. Vatikanischen Konzils', in *In Sorge um die Kirche,* Einsiedeln: Benziger, 1980, pp. 287–302 [*Schriften zur Theologie,* Band. XIV]).

84 *Ibid.*, p. 363.

85 *Ibid.*, p. 355.

the permanent diaconate, the reformation of the Code of Canon Law, beginning ecumenical dialogue with courage and hope, the dialogue with atheism and with the urgent need of faith in the world of today, etc. However, there was a need more than anything else for a 'theology which is worthy of Vatican II and of the task assigned to the Church',[86] more dynamic and more acute to penetrate the depths of God and of time. Rahner thus makes himself a promoter also of the new needs which await post-conciliar theology:

> [to] speak of God, and his existence in the midst of mankind, in such a way that the words can be understood by the men of today and tomorrow; how it can proclaim Christ in the midst of an evolving universe that the word of the God-man and the incarnation of the eternal Logos in Jesus of Nazareth do not sound like myths which men cannot any longer take seriously; how it can relate human ideologies and plans for the future with the Christian eschatology; how it can assure humanity that in the *eschaton* redemption has already been achieved, so that men do not relapse into the position of the men of the old covenant who dreaded death as though it meant separation from the God of life; how it can show that love of God and love of neighbour always form in a new and epochal way an absolute unity.[87]

Therefore, the tasks awaiting the Church, too, were different. The immediate future, in fact,

> [d]oes not ask the Church for the precise details of our ecclesiology, nor for a more exact and lovelier ordering of the liturgy, nor for more precise distinctions in controversy with the theologies of non-Catholic Christians, nor for a more or less ideal regulation of the Roman bureaucracy, but, rather, whether the Church can so faithfully testify to the redeeming and fulfilling presence of that ineffable mystery which we call God.[88]

---

86 Rahner, *The Church after the Council*, p. 24.

87 *Ibid.*, p. 25.

88 *Ibid.*, p. 26.

It is always necessary to read in the light of this liberty which is at the heart of Rahner's theology, his reformulation of pastoral theology, understood as theology of praxis, political theology, too, and therefore 'intrinsic and extrinsic organising principle of the whole of theology'.[89] Pastoral theology as science of practical reason, that is, of freedom, has a priority with respect to dogma. Rahner writes:

> If one gives priority to practical reason (reason, not emotion or free will, to which the name liberty is given!), due to the fact that it is the reflected existence of that action which signifies salvation which is conceived solely and totally in itself, not on the basis of anything else, then one can confer on Pastoral Theology, understood as the representative of the self-reflection of this practical reason in the church, a priority in global theology. In itself, this should not be surprising. To free love (and hope) must be recognised a certain propriety with regard to dogmatic faith.[90]

1.3 René Laurentin: a Council between limits, ambiguities and hopes

Another witness, chosen to confirm the impact of Vatican II in the immediate post-conciliar period, is the French Mariologist R. Laurentin, first a member of the Council's Preparatory Commission and then peritus at the work of the Council. A year after the end of the Council, Laurentin provided an analysis of the pastoral and doctrinal legacy left by the Council.[91] He noted a paradox:

> Vatican II, pastoral Council, paradoxically became the Council of doctrinal renewal. The theologians there found an unprecedented audience. 'Council of the experts' was said right from

89 K. Rahner, *Teologia pastorale*, in *Dizionario di pastorale*, ed. K. Rahner et al (Brescia: Queriniana, 1979), p. 798 (German original, *Lexikon der Pastoraltheologie*, Freiburg i Br.: Herder, 1972).

90 *Ibid.*

91 Laurentin, *Bilancio del Concilio.*

> the first session, with a justified critical note about what was excessive: but the mere fact had its justification.[92]

The justification, acknowledged by Laurentin in a necessary revision of the theology and its aggiornamento, was broadened in his analysis to the point of highlighting the limits of the Council, the silences and the indecision, the incompletenesses and the ambiguities, and, finally, the tasks which awaited the post-Conciliar Church. Among the limits, Laurentin acknowledged above all the absence of any decisions about burning issues:

1. *mixed marriages*: 'the most perceptible disappointment was expressed by the Protestants as regards the Council'.[93] Laurentin noted that the conciliar plan, as a vote to remove the obstacles of the restrictions, did not have any repercussions in the Council, but the problem was ratified only afterwards, on 18 March 1966, with the Instruction from the Congregation for the Doctrine of the Faith *Matrimonii sacramentum*, bearing the signature of Cardinal Ottaviani, representing for some a step backwards with regard to the conciliar vote, but for Laurentin progress with respect to the previous legislation.[94]
2. *Birth control*, causing, according to Laurentin, an en masse estrangement of many of the faithful, due to the rigidity of Christian teaching. However, the French Mariologist recognised that, after the favourable judgment of the theological Commission entrusted with the task of examining the issue, the last word belonged to the Pope: 'the Council did a lot to give the measure of these difficulties'.[95]
3. *The problem of priestly celibacy*, posed by some Latin American bishops, to resolve the problem of the lack of vocations and

---

92 *Ibid.*, p. 220.

93 *Ibid.*, p. 200.

94 Cf. *Ibid.*, pp. 200–201.

95 *Ibid.*, p. 202.

> the isolation of priests. Some wrote directly to the Pope about this, but, says Laurentin, the Council 'cleared up the basic problem with an unambiguous light and consciously confirmed the status proper to the East and to the West'.[96]

Among the 'silences' of the Council, Laurentin listed extra-sacramental ministry, including that undertaken by women. This problem 'was not tackled with clarity at the Council due to the insufficient participation of female representatives... If women do not find their true place in the Church, they will seek their advancement elsewhere'.[97]

Another unacceptable silence was the theology of the Angels, of whom no mention was made, as well as the worship of the saints and the problem of hell, 'tremendous mystery of the rejection of love and its consequences which should never be set aside'.[98]

From this with parrhesia Laurentin reached the most burning issue of the 'defects and the ambiguities' of some of the conciliar documents. These ambiguities, in particular 'that of life in its stages of development', 'do not affect the Council but constitute a risk for many Christians'.[99]

Among these it is important to list:

1. the ambiguity about ecumenism, indicated by O. Cullmann: 'When we go back to our ranks, we will have to fight, above all among the laity, the false ecumenical sentimentality'.[100] For Laurentin, this ambiguity was not of Vatican II, but such false sentimentality was one of the risks of the rapid post-conciliar expansion of ecumenism. So, 'it is essential to be on guard against an ecumenical triumphalism'.[101]

---

96 *Ibid.*

97 *Ibid.*, p. 206.

98 *Ibid.*, pp. 206–207.

99 *Ibid.*, p. 208.

100 Conference of 2 December 1965, cit. in *Ibid.*

101 *Ibid.*

2. Another ambiguity was aggiornamento, also denounced by Cullmann. Some, in fact, read it as adaptation to the modern world, while the Council wanted to enlighten human activity with the light of the Gospel. The risks, stated Laurentin, 'are linked to the ambiguity of the term "world", which formed the object of examination by the Council'.[102]
3. Besides these two, there is another 'which has affected the Council itself: the ambiguity linked to the term "pastoral"'.[103] Here is a longer quotation in which Laurentin describes this issue, which, in my opinion, is a very serious historical and theological crux:

> This adjective [pastoral] launched by John XXIII was fortunate. It undoubtedly responds to a profound intuition: the need to restore the link between life and truth, between doctrine and salvation. However, its use remained vague and pragmatic during the first session. But with the second session some fell into the error of considering the term 'pastoral' as contrary to 'doctrinal'; thus hierarchical 'collegiality' and matrimonial love belonged to the 'pastoral', not the 'doctrinal' sphere. There was a desire in some way to find a solution to the opposite tendencies: the pastoral sphere eluded the need for rigour proper to doctrine: approximate terms and words would suffice. Right at the start of the session Cardinal Silva expressed surprise that such a principle had found a place even in the official explanation of the amendments to Schema 13. The rift between theology and life was one of the most serious deficiencies of these last few centuries. It would be an illusion to want to remedy this fact, creating a type of life crammed with doctrine: an illusion more damaging than the first.[104]

---

102 *Ibid.*, p. 209.

103 *Ibid.*

104 *Ibid.*, pp. 209–210.

In Laurentin's opinion, Vatican II lay between Scylla and Charybdis: between the fear of tackling the problems and the abuses of freedom; the freedom of research proclaimed by the Council always bears its own risks. A lot has been said about the oppression experienced by the progressive theologians, less has been said on the other hand about the proliferation of crypto-heresies of the right and the left, like mushrooms which are discovered from time to time in the most obscure places. In fact, 'if the restrictions and the closures cause secret revolts, misunderstood freedom can also unleash negative forces: superficiality, heresy, scandal'.[105] Therefore, said Laurentin, 'Vatican II, which is a council about return to the sources, must preserve contact with the whole of Tradition'.[106] There were things to be up-dated, of course, but they were to be done and read in the light of openness to God and the desire to reach out to the world, taking into account the rapid changes which characterised it. The Church recognised the autonomy of earthly values and the authenticity of human progress. So, 'Vatican II, without abandoning the absolute need which inspired the *Syllabus*, overcame its spirit of mistrust and rigidity'.[107]

Of course, if the Church came out of the Council losing a certain type of security, it developed the sense of research. It rediscovered the sense of the essential, that is to say, the Father's plan. At last the 'great unknown', the Holy Spirit, also found a place again, the Spirit who, according to Laurentin, while the Spirit's pre-eminence had been recognised in the first centuries, had then lost its importance to the point of being forgotten. According to the judgment of the French Mariologist, Vatican II 'would go down in history as the first stage of the rediscovery of the Holy Spirit'.[108]

The future of the Church, therefore, must be marked by putting into practice these pastoral-dogmatic initiatives, so as to truly have a

---

105 *Ibid.*, p. 211.

106 *Ibid.*, p. 210.

107 *Ibid.*, p. 215.

108 *Ibid.*, p. 217.

post-Conciliar Church, the model of which Laurentin saw in the post-conciliar bishop, in the lay person, in the priest, and finally a post-conciliar theology, still taking its first but promising steps given the size of renewal proposed by the Council.[109] So the Council must be like a 'continuing creation', seeking to establish with *Unitatis redintegratio* 12 that order or hierarchy of truths according to their relationship with the foundation of faith and highlighting in a better way the suggestion initially made by John XXIII, to distinguish between the 'substance' and 'formulation' of the teaching of the faith, but not developed neither by the Pope nor the Council. In closing, for the French Mariologist, the whole of the Council lay, so to speak, in the post-Conciliar period.[110]

1.4 Hans Küng: the Council, *path* to re-unification

Küng represents, for the work at the Council and his symbolic position of fracture, a very interesting author, whose close examination highlights the significance of a hermeneutic which, when separated from the living context of the Church, that is to say isolated in a solitary work of a theologian, leads to a necessary rift with the Subject-Church: a rift which by now Küng has celebrated with the Church, above all due, to his way of seeing things, the betrayals of the Council by the Magisterium itself. Küng had a very important role at the Council as peritus and then as theologian for the application in the post-Conciliar period. One of the themes examined more in depth by him and seen as hope for the real unity of the Church with the Protestants was that of ecumenism. It is interesting to report the testimony of Cardinal W. Kasper, who was his assistant in the chair of fundamental theology:

---

[109] Cf. *Ibid.*, pp. 218–227. On theology, Laurentin said: 'Theology experimented on particular points such as collegiality, priesthood, the laity, Revelation, and ecumenism; they passed into the work of the Council with an unpredictable rapidity and ease. But the work is still in its early stages, the teaching has still not reached full maturity', *Ibid.*, p. 220.

[110] Cf. *Ibid.*, pp. 220–221.

> At the start there were many things which were fascinating about Hans Küng: his youthful and fresh pose, his spontaneous and unconventional vision of the church and many reforming ideas, too. His book *The Council and Reunion*, which rapidly became a *bestseller*, gave expression to the expectations which many placed in the Council; it became also a sort of catalyst, over which many spirits were divided. Even my teacher Geiselmann frowned.[111]

A fundamental and inescapable issue also for understanding Küng's very hopeful and hasty ecumenical stance is that of the Church's Tradition, in the context of the discussion which was tackled by the Doctrinal Commission, for the formation of the Schema which was to lead to the promulgation of *Dei verbum*, a schema which had avoided proposing again the problem of the duality of the sources of Revelation. An authoritative expert on the problem, which Küng's ideas presuppose, was J. R. Geiselmann.[112] Taking up again the Tridentine theme and Luther's charge against Tradition (more a charge against ministry in the Church), Geiselmann believed that Vatican II had abandoned the *partim* idea (part of the revelation contained in the Scriptures and part in Tradition) to be satisfied with the conjunction *et*. From this Geiselmann inferred that the idea of the duality of the sources of Revelation was abandoned by Vatican II or at least was not expressly defined. From such a conviction stemmed his idea, according to which, essentially, a Catholic, too, can reach the

---

[111] W. Kasper—D. Deckers, *Al cuore della fede. Le tappe di una vita* (Cinisello Balsamo (Milan): San Paolo, 2009), p. 42 (German original, *Wo das Herz des Glaubens schlägt. Die Erfahrung eines Lebens*, Freiburg-Balse-Vienna: Herder, 2008).

[112] Testimony to his significant influence in council discussions, too, leading them from disputes between different theologies to a unanimous Catholic reflection on its essential foundations, is also J. Ratzinger, 'Un tentativo circa il problema del concetto di tradizione', in K. Rahner—J. Ratzinger, *Rivelazione e Tradizione* (Brescia: Morcelliana, 2006[2]), p. 32 (German original, *Offenbarung und Überlieferung*, Freiburg im B.: Herder, 1965).

conception of the material sufficiency of Scripture (all the revealed truths are contained in Scripture) and that, again as a Catholic, can believe that Scripture delivers Tradition to us in a sufficient manner.[113] In this way, therefore, the Catholic concept of Tradition, as a channel of Revelation and knowledgeability of Tradition along with Scripture, disappeared. One can immediately imagine the jubilation and approval which such an idea found among those who worked hard for a calm dialogue with Protestantism, offering totally new possibilities for a new encounter between Catholics and Evangelical Christians in particular. Among the Council Fathers should be noted in particular Cardinal Döpfner, who in the Council said that Sacred Scripture and Sacred Tradition were not to be venerated with the same reverence.[114]

Küng placed himself in this ambit;[115] he would renounce the Catholic concept of Tradition in an ever more marked manner, considering the interventions of the Church simply as a consequence of a specific historic moment, and thus would deprive from within the

113 See his fundamental work: J. R. Geiselmann, *Die Heilige Schrift und die Tradition: zu den neuren Kontroversen über das Verhältnis der Heiligen Schrift zu den nichtgeschriebenen Traditionen* (Freiburg im B. 1962) (Italian translation, *La Sacra Scrittura e la tradizione* [Brescia: Morcelliana, 1974]). Distancing himself from Geiselmann in a critical way is J. Ratzinger, 'Un tentativo', pp. 34–51.

114 This is from a testimony reported by Fr Betti in his *Diario*, p. 76: Fr Betti reports that Mgr Franić was complaining that in the position read about a procedure of the schema *De divina Revelatione* 'the extremist position of those Fathers who believed that the whole of Revelation is contained in Scriptures, like Cardinal Döpfner, who said in the Council that *Scriptura et Traditio non sunt pari pietate venerandae* was being favoured; while *impugnari immo et aliquantulum irridere videntur* the Fathers who say the opposite'.

115 See the summary of all those who adhere to this trail of dialogue opened by Geiselmann with his new interpretation of the relationship between Scripture and Tradition, provided by H. Küng, *Karl Barths vom Wort Gottes als Frage an die katholische Theologie*, in J. Ratzinger—H. Fries (eds.), *Einsicht und Glaube* (Freiburg: Herder, 1963[3]), p. 105, footnote 25.

normative content of Tradition.[116] His theological influence would inaugurate a new way of advancing the ecumenical movement, as a call to unity: imperative of Vatican II.

This new way, for example, can already be seen in his book—which according to Cardinal Kasper was a real bestseller in this sense, which went far beyond Geiselmann's expectations—on the Council and unity (of the Church?): here the renewal of the Council was seen as a call to unity (a subtitle suggested to him by K. Barth). Küng asked: 'How can Catholics and Protestants come together again?'[117] And he replied indicating the path inaugurated by John XXIII, that is, the path of the 'renewal of the Church to reunion'.[118] For Küng this meant: '*Not passive appeals to return to the unity of the Church*';[119] '*Not simply individual conversions*';[120] '*Not simply "moral reform"*',[121] because the division of the Church does not belong to the order of capital vices and therefore to the eternal vices of humanity, but since it came about historically 'unlike the seven deadly sins, it can, by the grace of God, be brought to an end'.[122] So therefore for Küng renewal must come about in the Catholic Church, which starting from its founding essence (as Barth said), realises the true spirit of the Gospel. And thus he summarised in a symbolic way his thought about this necessary renewal:

---

116 See his main works on this issue: *Kirche im Konzil* (Freiburg im B.: Herder, 1964²); *Structures of the Church* (New York: Thomas Nelson and Sons, 1962) (German original, *Strukturen der Kirche* [Freiburg im Br.: Herder, 1963²]); *The Council, Reform and Reunion* (New York: Sheed and Ward, 1961 (German original, *Konzil und Wiedervereinigung: Erneuerung als Ruf in der Einheit* [Freiburg im Br.: Herder, 1961³]).

117 Küng, *The Council, Reform and Reunion*, p. 93.

118 *Ibid.*

119 *Ibid.*, and p. 94: 'It cannot be a matter simply of the others' "returning", as though we had no responsibility for the split, as though *we* therefore had nothing to make good, as though it were not in the least up to *us* to go to meet them, and as though they had nothing whatever to bring with them—they, our brothers, lovers of Christ our Lord!'.

120 *Ibid.*, p. 94.

121 *Ibid.*, p. 95.

122 *Ibid.*, p. 95–96.

> To whatever extent the Protestant protest is justified, it is the Catholic Church herself, against whom the protest is made, who must take it up and provide the remedy which will make the protest pointless. True, the Church, being of men and sinners, will remain an *ecclesia reformanda* until the end of time.[123]

Thus Küng ultimately saw his programme of renewal: the Protestant Reformation was that just and human aspiration for reform, which gives to the Catholic Church the model of a real return to the Gospel, and to us Catholics, returning to the Gospel, in this historical/historist logic of reform, we return to unity with the Protestants. But you might ask: unity where? In which Church? Ultimately, what unity was Küng talking about? With the passage of time, however, from the enthusiastic hosannas to John XXIII, which drove him to ride the wave of conciliar renewal and the new ecumenism—which shines through in the preface of this book[124]—he would pass to a qualified criticism of the Magisterium, and would accuse the Church of having betrayed the Council.[125]

---

123 *Ibid.*, p. 96.

124 The book is also the proud bearer of an Introductory Message from Cardinal König (cf. *Ibid.*, Introductory Message), thanks to which, as Küng says in the preface (cf. *Ibid.*, p. 8), it succeeded in overcoming reluctance and closure.

125 See, for example, H. Küng—N. Greinacher (eds.), *Contro il tradimento del Concilio: dove va la Chiesa cattolica?* (Turin: Claudiana, 1987) (German original, *Katholische Kirche—wohin? Wieder der Verrat am Konzil* [Munich: Piper, 1986]). See also Küng's analysis of the Council in 2005, celebrated particularly by the journal *Concilium*, which devoted a special edition to it with a series of essays: 'Is the Second Vatican Council Forgotten?', in *Concilium* 4 [2005] 108–117; (German original, 'Das vergessene Konzil', in *Concilium* 4 [2005] 425–433). Here Küng examines the conciliar legacy and lists a series of points, which highlight that, 'if the Council had not taken place', the Catholic Church would have remained centuries behind. The reasons for the renewal, as conceived by him, which had to 'provide' a new Church are thus listed and examined: 1) religious liberty and tolerance; 2) ecumenism; 3) other world faiths; 4) liturgy in the vernacular; 5) the centrality of the Bible; 6) the distancing from a supernatural 'Imperium Romanum'; 7) the positivity of the secular world. He then identifies the tasks: 1) reform of the Curia understood as decentralisa-

1.5 Cardinal U. Betti (1922–2009): the eloquent silence of Vatican II and the examination of Vatican I

A very interesting and representative figure, more than for a vision of the Council as such, as for a more in-depth understanding of some key teachings of Vatican II, is the Franciscan Fr Umberto Betti, personal theologian of Cardinal E. Florit, Archbishop of Florence. Fr Betti was peritus at the Council and secretary to two sub-commissions: for the drafting of *Dei verbum* and for the drafting of *Lumen Gentium*, intervening here in the drafting of Chapter III, about the hierarchy of the Church and the episcopate.[126] He was created

tion and internationalisation to establish a 'cabinet' of reformers; 2) a convincing encyclical about sexuality, and instead Paul VI's *Humanae Vitae* came along; 3) the abolition of the law of celibacy, the election of bishops through presbyteral and pastoral councils, now created after the Council; 4) the transfer of the election of the Pope from the College of Cardinals to the Synod of Bishops. 'In any case', he says, 'one thing is certain in spite of all resistance and regression: the Second Vatican Council marked even for the Roman Catholic Church the end of the Middle Ages including the Counter-reformation! To be more precise: the Roman-medieval, anti-modern paradigm of the Counter-reformation has had its day! Many of the concerns of the Reformation and the Enlightenment have been taken up by the Catholic Church, and *the paradigm shift towards a post-modern constellation*, whilst being slowed down from above, is far advanced from below. Despite all the disappointments: the Council was worthwhile, its resumé on the whole positive! The Church after the Council is a different one from the pre-conciliar one, no doubt about it. The big debate about the future shape of the Catholic Church and Christianity as a whole however continues' (*Ibid.*, p. 117). On the same wavelength is his 2010 'Open Letter' contesting the Magisterium of Benedict XVI who, from being colleague and friend, has become his bitter enemy. An English version can be found at the following website address: http://www.indcatholicnews.com/news.php?viewStory= 15996

126 His work on the teaching about the episcopate in *Lumen Gentium* is distinguished, contained in Chapter III of this Constitution on the Church. Cf. especially U. Betti, *La dottrina dell'episcopato nel capitolo III della 'Lumen Gentium'* (Rome: Città nuova, 1968) in which the historical-theological iter is reconstructed through published and unpublished documents. In the course of the presentation of the thoughts of the Franciscan, I will leave aside this teaching, given its quiet reception, and I will focus on his theological contri-

Cardinal by Benedict XVI in November 2007 for his theological prestige. I will focus on his thought about Vatican II, above all seeing it in its implications which gave significant impulse to the two major conciliar documents just mentioned.

His theological work in preparation for the constitution on Divine Revelation was very intense, work which lasted throughout the Council and which highlighted, in such a way, an arduous element according to the not always easy dyadic relationship between Scripture and Tradition. Fr Betti was an expert in Vatican I and especially *Pastor aeternus*; this enabled him to always explain the rooting of the teachings of Vatican II in the perennial Tradition of the faith. I will follow the path of his thought about the teaching on the Church's Tradition: this seems to override all his other theological interests and explains, at a time, the significant passage which he had at Vatican II, after the rejection of the schema *De fontibus*, with the aim of better balancing the Scripture-Tradition relationship.

In 1963, Fr Betti asked, in a study which certainly indicated the course of the work of the doctrinal sub-commission: 'La Tradizione è una fonte di rivelazione?'[127] The common teaching rooted in the

---

bution about Revelation handed down to us by Scripture and Tradition, a theme which presents not a few peculiarities and which will enable us to tackle an issue which, in my opinion, is typical for ascertaining one of the pastoral epiphanies of Vatican II.

[127] U. Betti, 'La Tradizione è fonte di rivelazione?', in *Antonianum* 38 (1963), pp. 31–49. This article was appreciated by a variety of people. From Cardinal Siri, who, in a letter sent to Fr Betti (8 March 1963), said: 'The argument is delicate today because it was treated at the Council by some in such a way that it can be justified only by, perhaps subconsciously, Protestant infiltration' (Betti, *Diario*, p. 16). The other was a Waldensian, Professor Vittorio Subilia, an observer at the Council, who said he discovered the Catholic conviction about the matter there (cf. *Ibid.*, p. 17). I found the letter of Professor Subilia, from the Waldensian Faculty of Theology in Rome, to be very significant. He wrote this to Betti on 5 April 1963: 'Allow me to express to you my appreciation for the clarity with which, in the documents, you supported a thesis which seems to me to belong unquestionably to the central and constant line of Catholic

Catechism of those years was unanimous: Tradition is a source of revelation truly distinct from Scripture, manifesting furthermore the material insufficiency of the latter: some revealed truths can be known only through Tradition. Scripture and Tradition are two sources of the faith, through which, the Church, with the assistance of the Holy Spirit, receives its teaching.[128] This teaching is rooted in the decree *Sacrosancta* of the Council of Trent, promulgated in the IV session on 8 April 1546, which states:

> This truth and discipline are contained in the written books, and the unwritten traditions which, received by the Apostles from the mouth of Christ himself, or from the Apostles themselves, the Holy Ghost dictating, have come down even unto us, transmitted as it were from hand to hand; (the Synod) following the examples of the orthodox Fathers, receives and venerates with an equal affection of piety, and reverence, all the books both of the Old and of the New Testament—seeing that one God is the author of both—as also the said traditions, as well those appertaining to faith as to morals, as having been

---

thought. I confess to not understanding how theologians along the line of Geiselmann can in a certain way contest this thesis. As an observer at the Council I received an impression of disorientating confusion in ascertaining the support given to this dispute. It seems to me that to contest this thesis means posing serious problems for Catholic theology and in any case orientate it towards a different direction from the traditional direction of Catholicism. Is this legitimate from a Catholic perspective? Or, under the guise of a terminology which seems to draw close to Protestant positions, are we faced with a process of greater Catholicisation of Catholicism? I believe that due to the Christian and ecclesiastical responsibility we mutually hold, we must, on this fundamental point as on others, be animated by that spirit of clarity which animates the pages of your work', in AEF, Cartella n. 3, Schema "De divina Revelatione".

128 U. Betti, *La Tradizione è fonte di rivelazione?*, p. 31. Here Fr Betti quotes (footnote 1), while verifying the affirmative answer according to the common teaching, the *Catechismo della dottrina cattolica* (Milan-Rome 1957), p. 93 (German original, *Katholischer Katechismus der Bistümer deutschlands*, Freiburg im Br. 1955).

> dictated, either by Christ's own word of mouth, or by the Holy Ghost, and preserved in the Catholic Church by a continuous succession.[129]

Fr Betti recognised that this text from Trent was in his days the object of discussion among Catholic theologians, a discussion which focussed, more than anything, on the hermeneutic of the text. A good number of the theologians were moving for a reappraisal of the effect of Tradition.

Some, he said, moved above all by the laudable intention of finding a common basis for dialogue with the separated brethren, rooted in the principle of 'Scriptura sola', believe that in fact this principle was not substantially rejected by the Council of Trent. Proof of this would lie in the fact that the formula of the primitive text 'hanc veritatem *partim* continere in libris scriptis, *partim* sine scripto traditionibus', from which could only be meant that revelation is contained partially in Tradition, too, was replaced with the text reported above.[130]

In the definitive text the preposition *partim* disappeared and was replaced by the somewhat innocuous conjunction *et*, on its own incapable of defining Tradition as a channel of Revelation, distinct and independent from Scripture. For these critics, the Council assumed an agnostic stance, limiting itself to stating that alongside Scripture there were also non-written apostolic traditions. So they concluded, as Betti summarised, that

---

[129] DH 1501: 'hanc veritatem et disciplinam contineri in libris scriptis et sine scripto traditionibus, quae ipsius Christi ore ab apostolis acceptae, aut ab ipsis apostolis Spiritu Sancto dictante, quasi per manus traditae, ad nos usque pervenerunt: orthodoxorum patrum exempla secuta, omnes libros tam veteris quam novi testamenti, cum utriusque unus Deus sit auctor, nec non traditiones ipsas, tum ad fidem, tum ad mores pertinentes, tamquam vel oretenus a Christo, vel a Spiritu sancto dictatas, et continua successione in Ecclesia catholica conservatas, pari pietatis affectu ac reverentia suscipit ac veneratur'.

[130] Betti, *La Tradizione*, pp. 32–33.

1. Scripture contains the whole of Revelation ('this the principle, common both to Catholics and Protestants, of the material sufficiency of "Scriptura sola"');[131]
2. Scripture to be correctly understood needs Tradition (the principle of the formal insufficiency of the Scriptures, not held in common with the Protestants);
3. consequently Tradition has only an interpretative and declaratory function of Scripture.[132]

For other theologians, on the other hand, to have replaced *partim* with *et* did not imply a substantial change of thought, but, however, a desire to say that Scripture and Tradition are two sources of Revelation, since the latter is contained in both and neither of the two contains it sufficiently or wholly. For this reason, both are venerated with feelings of equal piety and reverence: each in its own way transmits something which is not transmitted by the other.[133] With frank lucidity, Betti, comparing the two theological positions, said:

---

[131] *Ibid.*, p. 33. Here one can object to Fr Betti that the principle of the material sufficiency of the Scriptures was not common between Catholics and Protestants, for the same reasons that it said at the start and as will be seen subsequently through Vatican I up to the preparatory schema of Vatican II, *De fontibus*.

[132] Noteworthy among these authors are: J. R. Geiselmann, 'Das Missverständnis über das Verhältnis von Schrift und Tradition und seine Überwindung in der kathlischen Theologie', in *Una Sancta* 11 (1956), pp. 131–150; Id., *Die Heilige Schrift.*; Y. Congar, 'Traditions apostoliques non écrites et sufficience de l'Écriture', in *Istina* 6 (1959), pp. 279–306; Id., *La Tradition et les Traditions*, Fayard, Paris 1960; P. De Vooght, 'Écriture et Traditions d'après des études catholiques récentes', in *Istina* 5 (1958), pp. 183–196; see Betti, *La Tradizione*, p. 33, footnote 2.

[133] Of note among these theologians: H. Lennerz, 'Scriptura sola?', in *Gregorianum* 40 (1959), pp. 38–53; F. Bruno, 'Le Tradizioni apostoliche nel Concilio di Trento', in *Studi di scienze ecclesiastiche* (Aloisiana, 1) Naples 1960, pp. 317–334; see Betti, *La Tradizione*, p. 34, footnote 2.

> Leaving aside the greater or lesser validity of these two particular interpretations of the Tridentine decree, this much is sure: that the first is motivated by the concern to give a new orientation to the theology of the Tradition; the second aims to be simply a justification of what had been for four centuries the common teaching of Catholic theology.[134]

Fr Betti concluded his research and asked how Vatican I stood before the Tridentine teaching about the theological factor of the two sources of Revelation. The main text of Vatican I which deals with it is the Constitution *Dei Filius*, promulgated at the III session on 24 April 1870, which, while reproducing almost verbatim the Tridentine decree *Sacrosancta*, dwells more broadly on Scripture, to respond to the problems and the needs of that time. The Fathers at Vatican I fundamentally asked two things of the primitive text of Trent, and removed those small additions which had been introduced.[135] So the definitive text states:

> This supernatural revelation, according to the faith of the universal Church, as declared by the holy synod of Trent, is contained 'in the written books and in the unwritten traditions which have been received by the apostles from the mouth of Christ Himself; or, through the inspiration of the Holy Spirit have been handed down by the apostles themselves, and have thus come to us'.[136]

Fr Betti, a fine expert on Vatican I, commenting on this text of *Dei Filius*, recognised that even in the previous formulations of the text, this 'doubt about the equal importance of the written and unwritten word of God had never emerged'. Therefore, 'it is not arbitrary to think that if the

---

134 *Ibid.*, p. 34.

135 Cf. *Ibid.*, p. 40.

136 DH 3006: 'Hæc porro supernaturalis revelatio, secundum universalis Ecclesiæ fidem, a sancta Tridentina Synodo declaratam, continetur in libris scriptis et sine scripto traditionibus, quæ ipsius Christi ore ab Apostolis acceptæ, aut ab ipsis Apostolis Spiritu Sancto dictante quasi per manus traditæ, ad nos usque pervenerunt'.

Council Fathers had had the opportunity they would also have given Tradition some official teaching in conformity with the common conviction they held. And that was precisely that Tradition is a source of Revelation in the same way that Scripture is'.[137]

Betti concluded his very rigorous study as far as an analysis of Trent and Vatican I is concerned, with his own reflections, very interesting

[137] Betti, *La Tradizione*, p. 41. Betti reports and comments on the other passages from Vatican I which speak about the two sources of Revelation. For example the Introduction to the Constitution *Dei Filius* refers to it when it says: 'innixi Dei verbo scripto et tradito, prout ab Ecclesia Catholica sancte custoditum et genuine expositum accepimus...' (DH 3000). Here Betti says: 'if Tradition were considered not as a distinct source, but only as a means or norm for correct interpretation of Scripture, the text would be at least superfluous' (Betti, *La Tradizione*, p. 42). In chapter III of the same Constitution it says: 'Porro fide divina et Catholica ea omnia credenda sunt, quæ in verbo Dei scripto vel tradito continentur, et ab Ecclesia sive solemni judicio sive ordinario et universali magisterio tamquam divinitus revelata credenda proponuntur' (DH 3011). In chapter IV of Pastor aeternus, defining the infallibility of the Roman Pontiff, it says: 'ea tenenda definiverunt, quae sacris Scripturis et apostolicis traditionibus consentanea, Deo adjutore, cognoverant' (DH 3069). About this, Betti reports an interesting testimony: 'justifying the definition of the primacy itself, the official speaker of the deputation of the faith, Schrader, reminded that, as a doctrinal fact of peaceful possession, beyond so-called exegetic Tradition, which was verified in the case in point, there was also the so-called constitutive Tradition, that is, capable alone of transmitting revealed Truth' (Betti, *La Tradizione*, p. 45. See also on this matter Pius IX's letter *Inter gravissimas*, 28 February 1870, addressed to the German episcopate, against those who, by denying the dogma of infallibility, did not believe that Scripture and Tradition were sources of divine revelation). Chapter VII *De ecclesiastico magisterio*, of the schema of the II dogmatic constitution on the Church, too, while never actually getting to the stage of being promulgated, carried the same teaching, stating that the primary object of the Magisterium consisted 'in ipso verbo Dei scripto vel tradito' (Mansi 53, 313C, cf. Betti, *La Tradizione*, p. 45). From all of this it can be concluded, according to Betti, that 'the First Vatican Counci... aimed to present Scripture and Tradition as two distinct sources of revelation. Which however can contain and transmit the revealed deposit differently not just as to the how, but also as regards the objective entity', *Ibid.*, p. 46.

in order to understand then his 'passage' to the teaching of Vatican II. It does not matter if instead of 'sources' of Revelation one wants to speak of 'means' of transmission of the same, as long as the word is not meant in too materialistic a sense.[138] However it is important to indicate that Tradition is a different means from Scripture in the transmission of Revelation, above all due to the fact that by this we are enabled to know something objectively new from what is contained in Scripture.

And then, recognising what in my opinion would be the tendency and primary question of Vatican II, he writes:

> Certainly remaining rooted in the doctrinal position which believes that Tradition, with whatever name is given to it, is a vehicle of some revealed truth which is not contained in Scripture, does not facilitate reconciliation with the separated brethren. But, looking at it more closely, the probabilities of a hoped-for meeting from the withdrawal of that position seem more of a psychological than theological character. The real difficulty would remain the same: that of admitting a divinely-instituted hierarchical Magisterium, always authoritative interpreter of Tradition, in whatever way it might be considered. It seems to go back to what was said at the First Vatican Council, in similar circumstances, by the Archbishop of Utrecht, Schaepman, responding to those Fathers who saw in the definition of papal infallibility an obstacle to the return of the Protestants: 'Nihil eorum interest utrum infallibile Magisterium soli attribuas corpori pastorum in ecclesia, an idipsum etiam penes Romanum pontificem esse docet: auctoritas est, quam odio habent'. One is unsure whether to deplore more, in these words, the lack of any ecumenical and pastoral inspiration, or to be satisfied by the clarity of the basic ideas. It would be best to reconcile both.[139]

---

[138] With a similar language Pius XI also called the sacraments 'sources' of grace, cf. *Mortalium animos* of 6 January 1928, in AAS 20 (1928) 8.

[139] Betti, *La Tradizione*, p. 48.

Nevertheless, Betti recognised that Tradition, as a source of revelation distinct from Scripture, found itself in a more advantageous dogmatic position compared to other questions debated instead, such as, for example, the sacramentality of the episcopate. To resolve the latter in favour of the espicopate as sacrament truly distinct from the presbyterate and to abstain from declaring Tradition object source of revelation would have been to use double standards.[140]

On 15 November 1965, on the occasion of the inauguration of the academic year of the Pontifical Athenaeum the Antonianum, Fr Betti gave an address entitled *De sacra Traditione in Concilio Vaticano II*. In following his exposition one can ascertain the initial fact present in the preparatory Schema *De fontibus,* and the choice then of the new schema *De divina Revelatione.* In the old schema Tradition was presented as a source of Revelation distinct from Scripture, not so much according to the mode of transmission as for the object transmitted. The Theological Commission deputed with the revision and formation of the new schema, in March 1963, presented a new one, in which Tradition was spoken of in the first chapter 'De Verbo Dei revelato', but the problem of the relationship between Scripture and Tradition was not examined in depth, limiting itself to saying that both constituted the unique deposit of faith. In June that same year a new schema was sent to the Fathers, so that up to the first months of 1964 many observations were made about the text, aimed at enriching somewhat the content on Tradition. Chapter II was devoted to it, affirming that it has divine origin and transmits divine things, not just words but also the institutions, the rites and examples coming from the Apostles. Thus it was acknowledged that Tradition was broader than Scripture, but not also for those things which have no basis in Scripture itself. Thus more emphasis was given to the greater intensity of the expression than to the greater quantity of the object transmitted.[141] Such a schema, then, was amended, discussed in the Council

---

140 *Ibid.*, pp. 48–49.

141 Cf. U. Betti, 'De sacra Traditione in Concilio Vaticano II', in *Antonianum* 41

in the period 30 September—6 October 1964, and welcomed by the majority of the Fathers. The observations made in the aula were reconsidered and the definitive text approved by the Doctrinal Commission was distributed to the Fathers for the definitive vote in the fourth and last period of the Council (14 September—8 December 1965). Betti observed that in this definitive text, as regards Tradition, there were two things to note, highlighting the 'munus in divina Revelatione transmittenda';[142] 1) it is expressly stated that the Word of God is wholly transmitted by it, and 2) by means of it one can know the canon of the sacred books in an integral manner.[143] The vote on chapter III (about Tradition) took place on 21 September 1965, with this outcome: there were 2,246 voters; 1,874 placet; 9, non placet; 354 placet iuxta modum; 9 null votes. The high number of Fathers who had approved that chapter *iuxta modum* refers to some amendments to be made to the text, above all about the declaration that not every Catholic teaching can be found in Scripture alone but that for a full awareness of Revelation Tradition is indispensable. Thus the Doctrinal Commission, at the request of the Supreme Pontiff on 19 October, by a secret vote, chose from the 7 formula suggested for amending chapter II, the following: 'quo fit ut Ecclesia certitudinem suam de omnibus revelatis non per solam sacram Scripturam hauriat'. In this way, Betti said, the judgment which said that Tradition transmits wholly the Word of God was made more explicit.[144]

(1966), pp. 3–5. As regards what was proper to chapter II of Dei verbum, Betti says: 'Per has affirmationes conceditur quidem Traditionem Scriptura latius patere, non autem eo usque ut quaedam eidem adscribantur, quae nullum in Scriptura habeant fundamentum: agitur potius de maiore intensitate expressionis quam de maiore quantitate obiecti transmissi', *Ibid.*, p. 5.

142 *Ibid.*, p. 6.

143 Cf. *Ibid.*

144 'Hisce additis verbis textus immutatus manet quod substantiam, perficitur autem quoad expressionem: explicitor namque redditur sententia qua dicebatur Traditionem verbum Dei integre transmittere', *Ibid.*, p. 7.

Hence the Franciscan friar concluded that Vatican II considered Scripture and Tradition as two communicating realities. On the one hand, it must be recognised that the Church does not have the certainty of what is believed in Scripture alone, but on the other that Tradition should not be considered as a quantitative supplement to Scripture.[145] 'To the rejected principle of Scripture alone is not opposed, however, that of Tradition alone; it is judged Catholic only that teaching, sanctioned by a constant practice of the Church, according to which divine Revelation is transmitted and known by means of Scripture and Tradition'.[146] Thus the greater question about the objective breadth of Tradition compared to Scripture remained unresolved, said Betti. The silence kept by the Council, which did not forbid open research, did not want to lead to the separation of the two sources of Revelation, but in some additional things even silence, too, had its voice.[147]

Vatican II was, for Fr Betti, as I have said, a school, which taught him also to put aside theological positions perhaps learned previously, especially that of the material insufficiency of the Scriptures.[148] One

---

145 *Ibid.*, p. 12: the Council, 'numquam Traditionem veluti quantitativum Scripturae supplementum considerat'.

146 *Ibid.*: 'Principio igitur de Scriptura *sola* rursus reiecto, non eidem opponitur principium de Traditione *sola*; at tantum doctrina statuitur catholica, costanti Ecclesiae praxi sancta, iuxta quam divina Revelatio transmittitur et cognoscitur per Scripturam *et* Traditionem'.

147 'Quaestio de maiore amplitudine obiectiva Traditionis comparative ad Scripturam theoretice insoluta manet, ideoque liberae inquisitioni obnoxia. Silentium autem, quod Concilium consulto hac in re tenere intendit, serio suadet ne qualiscumque inter utramque separatio inducatur, quae in utriusque cederet damnum. In certis enim rerum adiunctis etiam silentium suam habet vocem' (*Ibid.*, p. 14). Fr Betti, leaving to the theological *munus* the task of indicating how a teaching is contained in the Deposit of faith, when it is taught by the Magisterium as divinely revealed (cf. *Ibid.*, p. 14), chose the way of St Bonaventure, alluding however to a certain material sufficiency of the Scriptures: 'Prudentius silentio tegitur quod Scripturam testimoniis non probatur', St. Bonaventure, *Apologia pauperum*, IX, 5, VIII, 269[a], cit., in *Ibid.*, p. 15.

could nevertheless ask the Franciscan friar why the Council wanted to limit the importance of Tradition solely to the two cases mentioned: to reveal the canon and interpret the Scriptures. Explaining in some of his publications[149] the strenuous iter of *Dei verbum*, while he verifies the only two cases in which Vatican II highlights the dogmatic value of Tradition (while not excluding a priori that there can be others, when, that is, the Church is anchored in itself to propose a truth as divinely revealed),[150] he provides the reasons. First of all because Tradition here is considered solely in relation to Scripture and not in relation to Revelation. Then also because the Council believed that there were not sufficient reasons to be able to say more, ascertaining, according to Betti, there were no cases in which there had been dogmatic definitions based solely on Tradition.

---

148 He reports in his *Diario*, on 13 January 1964 (p. 28): 'I received a letter, not dated, from Mgr Florit. The exemplars of the exposé of 9–12 have increased, destined for the Secretary of the Council and, through Mgr Castelli and Mgr Giuliani of the Secretariat of the Italian Bishops' Conference, to the Italian bishops. But in the meantime he is full of scruples about my expression in which Tradition is recognised as "*Complementum Scripturae* ... "Is this supposition perhaps not contestable?" It is extremely difficult for him to abandon the conviction that Tradition transmits some revealed truth which in no way is attested to in Scripture. It wasn't easy even for me. But the Council is also a school, which is worth more than any attended or given up to now. To think of having nothing to learn would be like freezing one's own intelligence, to retire it due to premature old age'.

149 U. Betti, *La Rivelazione divina nella Chiesa* (Rome: Città nuova, 1970); Id., *La dottrina del Concilio Vaticano II sulla trasmissione della rivelazione* (Rome: Spicilegium Pontifici Athenaei Antoniani, 1985). These are fundamentally two similar publications, in which Fr Betti traces the historical-theological iter which brought about the gradual maturation in the Fathers which led to the Constitution *Dei verbum*, especially in its second chapter, concerning Tradition. In the last work the treatment of the subject matter is simply expanded, with the final addition of a very interesting appendix of complementary documents (for example the interventions about the issue by Congar and Rahner).

150 Betti, *La Rivelazione*, p. 236.

Betti recalled there was a group of Fathers who instead wanted the Council to recognise the existence of a constitutive Tradition, as far as those truths which come to us solely from this source were concerned, petitioning the intervention of the Pope himself, too. Among the truths which were offered as proof of that figured: the virginity of the Madonna after giving birth, her assumption into heaven, the seven-fold number of the sacraments, the need for infant baptism, the sacramental character, the sacramentality of marriage and confirmation. The Commission did not examine in any detail these theological places of the manifestation of the unicity of the Tradition as far as believed and defined truths were concerned, but it was evident, according to Betti, that each of them, as was clear to the suppliants themselves, that one could not however deny a certain biblical foundation. The solution proposed by the official relator was that of saying that the proper function of Tradition which attested to the inspired books, was not repeatable for any other revealed truth.[151]

[151] Cf. *Ibid.*, pp. 240–241. Fr Betti, too, was convinced of the at least implicit biblical foundation for these truths attested by Tradition alone. In fact he said: 'It will be observed that to deduce these truths from Scripture is to carry out an insincere exegesis. I would reply simply that the Church does not do any exegesis; only refer to Scripture to give authenticity to the Tradition. Which means that this is believed convinced, in these cases, in that it links to Scripture. When on the other hand one refers to Tradition alone, it is done to establish the legitimacy of a practice, not to affirm the immutability. An example can be found, just to offer one, in the Council of Trent, Session XIII, Decree *De SS. Eucharistia*, chapter VIII: Denz. 881 (1648): "As regards the reception of the sacrament, it has always been the custom in the Church of God that laity receive communion from priests, but that priests when celebrating communicate themselves, which custom ought with justice and reason to be retained as coming down from Apostolic tradition"' (*Ibid.*, pp. 240–241, footnote 102). Here, however, one could ask: is this same reasoning true also for the definition of a dogma, such as the Assumption or the Immaculate Conception itself? That there is an at least implicit foundation in Scripture is beyond doubt and right and proper, but that according to Scripture the foundational contribution of Tradition must be silenced seems to be somewhat disrespectful.

What emerges from this analysis is the following: Vatican II opted for a very precise pastoral choice. It left unresolved the question about the material sufficiency of Scripture, even though the fact was attested to by magisterial reiteration, limiting itself to saying, in a very 'broad' fashion: 'it is not from Sacred Scripture alone that the Church draws her certainty about everything which has been revealed' (*Dei verbum* 9), so as to save the dogmatic need for Tradition and its 'non-overabundance' or 'competition' compared to Scripture. There was no desire to have a Council just about Tradition. In such a way—this seems the perspective—ecumenical dialogue was encouraged, linking the teaching and the pastoral, as Fr Betti said. However, the fact remains: one denotes a certain discontinuity of Vatican II compared to Trent and Vatican I in the teaching about the peculiarity of Tradition in objectively attesting to the existence of Revelation in the truths contained in the Deposit, a teaching which instead was definitively acquired. Has attributing the role of Tradition essentially to the interpretation of Scripture—as resulted then in a more abundant manner in post-conciliar theology—and for clear pastoral reasons, improved the position of the Church internally? I believe that a pastoral analysis of the approach to the revealed Deposit is necessary to better reintegrate what was on the other hand the common patrimony of the Church's Magisterium.

1.6 Cardinal Leo Scheffcyzk (1920–2005): aspects of the Church in crisis

Leo Scheffcyzk, a German dogmatic theologian, friend and colleague of J. Ratzinger, raised to cardinalate status for his theological merits, is a testimony of a theology of some import—as J. Ratzinger acknowledged in his introduction to the Italian translation of his work, which I will be examining—by reason of 'his extraordinary knowledge of the sources, his sharp view of the problems and tasks of the present, as well as his profound faithfulness, rooted in faith, to the Magisterium'.[152]

---

[152] J. Ratzinger, *Presentazione* to the book of Leo Scheffczyk, *La Chiesa. Aspetti*

For Scheffczyk the problem of the post-conciliar crisis can be traced back to an ecclesiological crisis, and that is to research on the 'Church' believed for a variety of reasons to be already exhausted, in an era of strong post-modern irrationalism, which contains in itself post-Christian elements. So,

> [i]gnoring this situation, he wrote, and considering the hasty and non-critical fraternisation of Christianity with the spirit of the time, it is easy to predict within the church, too, tendencies towards irrationalism will appear, such as a vague religiosity and a gnostic presumption, involving itself thus in the plot of the 'faint conspiracy'.[153]

These reflections are formulated by the author, as an invitation,

> In the beautiful revolutionary ferment, to the understanding of what is permanent in the church ... The possible risk is that in a near future the tragic words of the time of Arian chaos might return to be current: 'The world mourns and wonders if it has become Arian'. All Christians really concerned about the Church should find in the Second Vatican Council a meeting point.[154]

Scheffczyk, in his essay on the *Aspetti della Chiesa nella crisi. Per la scelta di un Concilio autentico,* as a more literal translation of his work on the aspects of the post-conciliar crisis would sound, focussed on the theme 'Church', tracing a renewed theology in the light of Vatican II, but without betraying or watering down the dogmatic element acquired by Tradition and preceding theological reflection. For Scheffczyk the crisis was a crisis of the Church as mystery. It can seem strange, given the ecclesiological emphasis of post-conciliar development, and yet the real crux can be traced back, according to Scheffc-

---

della crisi postconciliare e corretta interpretazione del Vaticano II (Milan: Jaka Book, 1998), p. 11. (German original, *Aspekte der Kirche in der Krise. Um die Entscheidung für das authentische Konzil* [Siegburg: Franz Schmitt, 1993]).

153 Scheffczyk, *La Chiesa. Aspetti della crisi*, p. 13.

154 *Ibid.*, p. 14.

zyk, to the loss of a metaphysical concept of participation of the mystery-Church. The anti-clerical passions at the end of the 1800s and the 1900s, provoked largely by liberal Protestantism, as demands of democratisation, the abandonment of authority, freedom from dogmas, liberality and equality—almost all welcomed by the evangelical Church—continued to challenge the Catholic concept of Church. For Protestantism, one fact was certain, Scheffczyk said: 'One can react to the crisis not with external changes, but solely through an inner change of the nucleus of faith'.[155] And thus the internal disputes within Protestantism and the external downturn were much more extensive and dangerous than those presented in the Catholic Church. In the Catholic sphere, instead, said Scheffczyk,

> The real pruning in the development of the Church's conscience took place after the Second Vatican Council, over whose legitimate aspirations of reform were superimposed tendencies to a restructuring thought in other terms. They are remembered today both in the evangelical and Catholic fields and are visible first of all in external aspects.[156]

However, one fact is certain: the ecclesiological teaching of Vatican II was to be read as progress and continuity. *Lumen Gentium* describes the Church as *mysterium*, thus clearly reconnecting it to Tradition. The Church is the mystery of the Triune God, becoming in Him sign of the divine life among humanity. From this one passes to another definition of the Church: 'The Church is sacrament, this a definition rooted in Tradition, but transported here in a new dimension'.[157] *Lumen Gentium* 1 says that the Church is 'in Christ like a sacrament or as a sign and instrument both of a very closely knit union with God and of the unity of the whole human race'. This formula, Scheffczyk noted, with which the Church is described as 'indissoluble sacrament

155 *Ibid.*, p. 16.

156 *Ibid.*, pp. 16–17.

157 *Ibid.*, p. 22.

of unity', was already present in Cyprian of Carthage († 258), according to whom the formula is to be referred

> To the internal unity of the church and signifies above all the unity with the legitimate bishop. For this those who are not included in this unity are 'outside the Church'. Addressing the heretics, Cyprian underlines in this context that unity with the church is necessary for the salvation of souls.[158]

So Scheffczyk noted that, despite the Council not citing Cyprian's classic formula that 'outside the Church there is no salvation', there nevertheless remained in Vatican II the same image of the Church, in which is highlighted the sacramental features of unicity, the need for salvation and the fullness of salvation in Christ and in the Holy Spirit. This is the 'one Church of Christ which in the Creed is professed as one, holy, catholic and apostolic' (*Lumen Gentium* 8).[159]

This concept of Church–sacrament allowed the Council to move carefully from Christ sacrament to Church sacrament, whose most profound Christological root is

> The image of the body of Christ... Pius XII recognised in it 'the most significant and most divine definition of the substance of the Church'. The Second Vatican Council also held this image in great respect, when it considered the church 'by no weak analogy... compared to the mystery of the incarnate Word' (*Lumen Gentium* 8).[160]

In this way the Council did not have any formal innovation in ecclesial thought. It simply gave further recognition to a biblical idea founded in Tradition. In fact, already Vatican I had defined the Church as 'the sign arisen among the people', referring to Is 11:12. Therefore 'recognising in the church this character as sign guarantees the diversity between Christ and the church and recognises the latter as

[158] *Ibid.*, where he quotes *Cyprian*, Epistle 69, 6.

[159] Cf. *Ibid.*, pp. 22–23.

[160] *Ibid.*, p. 35.

a reality which exists starting from its relationship with Christ'.[161] The Church 'faces' Christ and is not identified with Him. The correct Christ-Church relationship is fundamental also for understanding the salvific significance of Christ in the Church and always through the Church. Christ founded his Church and preserves it in being. He is present in his Church and his presence 'is not exhausted in the Church, but he remains above: Christ lives in the Church and at the same time is superior to it; the Church is included by Christ, while it cannot contain him in a complete way'.[162] In this sense the Church is always instrument and organ of Christ.

Alongside the concept of 'sacrament', the Council also used the concept of 'people' to describe the Church. This profoundly biblical image expresses the fact according to which the Church is a living communion of brothers and sisters, which incarnates its communional, dynamic and historic nature. Certainly the mission of this people of God is not of a political or social order, but *Gaudium et spes* 42 says 'the purpose which He set before her is a religious one'. However, there was no lack of political and social interpretations of this term Church-people. Starting from the current concept of people as emerged from Romanticism, it was linked to the spirit of the people, to popular sovereignty, to people as a primitive force which determines rights and customs. Thus someone cried: 'We are the people', '*wir sind Kirche*'. But, Scheffczyk noted,

> The Council does not offer any foundation for this interpretation, since it understands in the image of the people the sacramental community of the 'body of Christ', which is comprised of not just the 'people', but also a head and a sacramental body composed of members. In the meantime, in the post-conciliar period, in which there was a desire to continue the council solely according to its 'spirit', without conforming to the meaning and content expressed by it, the

161 *Ibid.*, p. 39.

162 *Ibid.*, p. 53.

> concept of 'People of God' was repeatedly misunderstood and interpreted according to a democratic model.[163]

Another central concept of the conciliar ecclesiology is the concept of *communio*, unfortunately it, too, becoming misunderstood and contradictory in the post-conciliar period. This does not, however, devalue its correct significance attributed to it by Vatican II, according to which, 'they are fully incorporated in the society of the Church [those who are linked to Christ through the bonds of the] profession of faith, the sacraments, and ecclesiastical government and communion' (*Lumen Gentium* 14). Here communion is in its Trinitarian and hierarchical whole (that is, it has sacred origin) and therefore is a hierarchical communion or a hierarchy for the communion of the Church.

Alongside the progress of the mystery of the Church, there developed, largely in the post-conciliar period, an erroneous interpretation of this communion, too. Scheffczyk described three models of errors which manifested themselves in contemporary theology:

1. according to Hasenhüttl 'communion is, in its pre-institutional truth, community of fulfilment; church is a determination of relationships from man to man';[164]
2. for E. Schillebeeckx the church reduced to community is a 'pastoral unity', to which belongs the task 'above all of building a living community of people' of a 'pluralist nature';[165]
3. according to the exegete P. Hoffman, the aim of the community of Jesus was and remains 'a free configuration of interpersonal relationships, through which one becomes brother and sister'. The Church of today appears to Hoffmann like 'a cold

---

163 *Ibid.*, p. 25.

164 G. HasenhÜttl, *Kritische Dogmatik* (Graz: Styria, 1979), p. 172, cit. in *Ibid.*, p. 75.

165 E. Schillebeeckx, *Das kirchliche Amt* (Düsseldorf: Patmos, 1981), p. 194f., cit. in *Ibid.*

> bureaucracy of power' which 'is differentiated from other authoritarian systems only by ideology'.[166]

This community conception of Church was belittled by an intervention from a Dutch priest in a book edited in fact by Hoffman, with the title *Una lettera dall'Olanda*, expressing a desire to bring egalitarianism into the community; so a claim was made for women priests and the desire that 'homosexual brothers and lesbian sisters might exercise their office precisely starting from their concrete life experiences'.[167] This would have brought the Church's mission to maturity. Evidently here the concept of 'political democracy' and 'social praxis' ended up completely superseding the real content of *communio*. The transcendental horizon had been lost.

In this way, in fact, Vatican II also read the careful and ontological distinction between the common and ministerial priesthood. The priesthood as 'sign' which continues the salvific work of Christ lies, just as Christ himself, before the community of believers. If it were not him alone representing Christ, but all the faithful, then the significance of the sign would be lost and salvation would no longer have its origin in Christ.[168] This certainly blocks a servile subordination of believers by the fact that the ministerial priesthood is possible only as service and sanctification of the brethren. The presbyterate is for the Christian people Christ, while the priestly office 'contains in itself also a spiritual subordination of the priest to believers'.[169]

Finally, Leo Scheffczyk confirmed the continuity of the Tradition in two other factors of conciliar ecclesiology: the fact that the Catholic Church is the sole Church of Christ and the fact that outside the

---

166 P. Hoffmann, 'Christliche Gemeinde/Kirche', in *Orientierung* 55 (1991), pp. 165, 166, cit. in *Ibid.*

167 K. Derkesen, 'Ein Brief aus den Niederlanden', in P. Hoffmann (ed.), *Priesterkirche* (Düsseldorf 1987), p. 276f., footnote 15, cit. in *Ibid.*, p. 76.

168 Scheffczyk, *La Chiesa*, p. 96.

169 *Ibid.*, p. 94.

Church there is no salvation. They are two different problems, one ecumenical and the other concerning inter-religious dialogue.

Vatican II never speaks of a restoration of the unity of the Church, but only of Christians. If one were to restore the unity of the Church in itself, it would signify that Christ has recalled, so to speak, from it his incarnation and it would deny his promise to remain in it until the end of time. The more sensitive problem raised is how the Council referred to the concept of subsistence to describe the one true Church: the Church of Christ subsists in the Catholic Church (cf. *Lumen Gentium* 8), and did not state that it *is* the Catholic Church. Here one sees the theological opening to the concept of ecumenism and the desire to root it in a theology of the *elementa Ecclesiae.* There are certainly ecclesial elements present in the other Christian communities or particular Churches separated from Rome, too, but, said Scheffczyk,

> 'Ecclesiality' is not yet 'church', just as (to provide an example) the particular characteristics and connotations of a people do not yet form a State, even if for a State they assume great significance.[170]

Unity and multiplicity, the mystery of the universal Church (preceding in an ontological and chronological manner) and that of the particular Churches must therefore be thought out in a correct manner. The unity of the Church precedes multiplicity: it is its measure and purpose. Multiplicity, in fact, 'does not involve the essence, but rather the external modalities; not the substance, but rather the form, nor the truth but rather its expression (as theology and devotion)'.[171]

The other important element, but it, too, strongly and deliberately misunderstood, is inter-religious dialogue and the salvation of non-Christians which can only be achieved in and through the Church. First of all Scheffczyk confirmed that the Council teaching did not deny the classic axiom of patristic origin according to which 'outside

[170] *Ibid.*, p. 143.
[171] *Ibid.*, p. 147.

the Church there is no salvation', which, furthermore, is only understandable starting from the historical conditions of the period to which it dates back. Right from Origen and Cyprian, Scheffczyk observed, it was aimed against the divisions and wounds of the Church and wanted to contest the right of the particular Churches to present themselves as salvific organisations alongside the one true Church. So, Scheffczyk said,

> Even in the Church Fathers, rigorous judges, who supported this principle, there are no lack of references to the 'hidden saints' of paganism and the possibilities of salvation for non-Christians, since grace is offered to everyone and all people of goodwill can recognise it.[172]

Another factor must be clearly borne in mind: the fact that the Church condemned the Jansenist phrase according to which 'outside the Church there is no grace'.[173] Therefore Scheffczyk said,

> [t]he church ... also repeating the traditional principle up until yesterday, in no way contests the possibility of salvation for those who are outside it, just as it, on the other hand (it is important to note this) does not guarantee to the individual Christian salvation on the basis of belonging to the church.[174]

Therefore it is not the Council endorsing new interpretations according to which all religions, being objective facts, would be paths to salvation and it would be sufficient that each person strives to be what they are: a good Muslim, a good Hindu, etc. For example, Küng wanted the religions to commit to the 'common search for truth'.[175] It is true that the Council,

> Did not clarify the difficult questions about the relationship between Christianity and the other religions. But there was a

[172] *Ibid.*, p. 161 where he quotes Augustine, *De catechizandis rudibus*, 22,40.

[173] DS 2429, cit. in *Ibid.*

[174] Scheffczyk, *La Chiesa*, p. 161.

[175] H. Küng, *Christsein*, p. 105, cit. in *Ibid.*, p. 154.

> fundamental decision whose consequences it is good to observe… with the coming of Christ something happened objectively (understandable only in the faith of the Christian), which is equivalent to a fundamental criticism, to an increase and (both in a negative and a positive sense) to an 'abolition' of religions in the fullness of Christ. And since the rays of truth present in some way in the religions 'are now gathered in the church given by Christ, the action of bestowing grace outside the church does not happen *without* the church and not even *outside* it. The church remains the universal sacrament of salvation from which comes grace and towards which grace is directed'.[176]

1.7 The School of Bologna: the Council as 'historic event'

A major role in the hermeneutic and reception of the Council was played by the School of Bologna, founded by G. Dossetti with the creation of an Institute for Religious Sciences, led by G. Alberigo, director of the imposing five-volume *History of Vatican II*. A work of international renown, in which the hermeneutic criteria of the Council are traced back first of all to the very historical importance of the Council, a category which enables Vatican II to be seen as an 'event' with great participation and mass-media amplification. The criterion of historical significance means the fontal pastoral-ecumenical imprint of the conciliar event can be well understood; which ultimately allows the examination in a cross-the-board manner, with notable meticulous work, of the more obscure aspects of the Council, too. These aspects are not exhausted in the celebration of the event as such; but according to a 'spirit of the Council', the latter could be read like an ever present law of 'conciliarity'—a dominant theme in the Bolognese reading of the conciliar hermeneutic—in a way that Vatican II is also a future ferment of continual renewal. This we see, for example, in the historical close examination done by Alberigo forty years after the celebration of Vatican II and at the end of the publication of the five-volume history of the Second Vatican Council.[177]

176 Scheffczyk, *La Chiesa*, p. 162.

Alberigo wrote: 'Investigating the history of Vatican II opens up the possibility of a "hermeneutical turning"'.[178] Alberigo also noted that 'it would not be unreasonable to regard the movements of the first half of the twentieth century (liturgical, ecumenical, biblical, for the promotion of the laity) as a genuine 'pre-council'. On the other hand, post-modernist crisis diffidence also had a 'holding back' effect on the outcomes of theological research'.[179]

The reading of Vatican II as 'event' would be necessary to overcome the problematic moment of the celebration of the event and its reception, that dispute between doctrine and pastoral. Again, Alberigo wrote in the introduction to the first volume of the History of the Second Vatican Council:

> Satisfaction with a vision of the Council as a collection of several hundred pages of often prolix and sometimes short-lived conclusions has until now hindered the perception of its more fruitful meaning as a stimulus to the community of believers to accept the disquieting confrontation with the word of God and with the mystery of human history... It is ever more pertinent to recognize the priority of the conciliar event itself, even in relation to its decisions, which are not to be read as abstract normative prescriptions but as an expression and prolongation of the event itself. The task of renewal, the anxious searching, openness to the gospel, fraternal attention to all human beings: these characteristics of Vatican II were not elements of folklore nor at all marginal and transient features. On the contrary, they sum up the spirit of the conciliar event, which any sound and correct interpretation of its decrees must take into account.[180]

177 See G. Alberigo, 'Vatican II and its History', in *Concilium* 4 (2005), pp. 9–20.

178 *Ibid.*, p. 16.

179 *Ibid.*, p. 15. The words in brackets are the author's addition. The 'holding back' factors Alberigo notes particularly with regard to episcopal collegiality and ecumenism, the lack of a theology of peace, a theology of marriage, or of any of the analogous 'social' questions, cf. *Ibid.*

180 G. Alberigo, *Preface: 1965–1995: Thirty Years After Vatican II*, in *History of*

The post-conciliar period must be the moment of 'a historical treatment of Vatican II, not in order to dismiss it by relegating it to the past, but to make it easier to move beyond the phase of controversy that marked its reception by the church'.[181] That will only be possible to the extent that 'the spirit and dialectic that inspired and characterized the assembly'[182] will be allowed to shine out. This close examination, according to Alberigo, is interesting because of the emergence of 'a gap between the event of the Council as a collective happening and the final decisions made by the assembly'.[183] This again underlines how

> The event of the Council could not be reduced to the body, wide though it was, of its decisions: the collegiality of the Council had much greater depth and coherence than the expression of it in *Lumen Gentium*. The Constitutions and Decrees do not reflect all the shades of opinion that had been expressed over the course of the Council.[184]

Thus it opens the possibility of transverse researches which

> Bring to light the recurring and often determining presence of crucial factors in the spirit of the Council: liturgical and ecclesiological renewal, reaching beyond the limitations of the two corresponding Constitutions; ecumenical concern, deeper and more consistent than that expressed in the decree *Unitatis redintegratio*; the rediscovery of the Word of God, expressed in more than *Dei verbum*; the fundamental need for religious freedom, which the Fathers gradually came to appreciate, above all as a dimension of their Christian charter.[185]

Vatican II, edited by G. Alberigo, vol. I, *Announcing and Preparing Vatican Council II—Toward a new Era in Catholicism* (Maryknoll / Leuven: Orbis / Peeters, 1995), pp. XI-XII.

181 *Ibid.*

182 *Ibid.*

183 Alberigo, 'Vatican II and its History', p. 16.

184 *Ibid.*

185 *Ibid.*, pp. 16–17.

In a lecture given in Münster on 18 June 1999, Alberigo revisited his hermeneutical criteria, drawn up for the undertaking of a history of the Council. Substantially the same, they were listed and developed in the following way:[186]

1. *the council-event as hemeneutical canon,* as essential context for a rigorous interpretation of the conciliar *corpus* and premise for a faithful reception.
2. *the intention of John XXIII,* seen as 'primatial desire' of the Pope, true protagonist of the Council and model of a faithful but creative reception of the Council. Creative understood as distancing of the Council from the curial normativism, preferring its 'new Pentecost' aspect, now free from suffocating normative impostures (both in reference to models of previous pontificates and to previous councils).
3. *the pastoral nature of the Council.* Vatican II made the pastoral character its own especially at two moments: in rejecting the preparatory schema and in leaving aside condemnations and the formulation of canons.
4. *aggiornamento as purpose of the Council.* This was to indicate more than a reform of the Church, an attitude: readiness and commitment for a renewed inculturation of the Revelation.
5. *hermeneutic significance of the 'compromise' and 'unanimity',* understood as significant hermeneutic element of the Council: the doctrinal, pastoral, cultural, geographical differences were not resolved but simply muted. So, to understand the texts, it is about taking into consideration the next consensus often close to unanimity, even if at times at the cost of potentially ambiguous compromises.

For the School of Bologna the criterion of the *pastoral nature* of the Council is indispensable for distinguishing a level of the temporary

[186] Cf. Alberigo, 'Fedeltà e creatività', pp. 384–387; pp. 395–397 for the guiding criteria for a faithful and creative conciliar reception.

and historical forms and a level of the principles of faith, without, however, the two levels appearing to be in discontinuity between themselves; the work of the theologian and of the Magisterium start out from the historic and the apparent contingent historicity of the pastoral forms would be supported on the one hand by the hierarchy of truths in *Unitatis redintegratio* 11[187] and on the other by a doctrinal nucleus, which as a whole remains the same while becoming fragmented.[188] Alberigo saw the turning point of John XXIII in summoning a pastoral council as

> [t]he overcoming of the centuries-old 'Constantinian' period, during which the Church frequently had recourse to the support of the social and political institution ... To this day it is still on-going to the extent in which 'pastorality' and 'aggiornamento' are asserted as guidelines on the basis of a globally united vision of Christianity itself, governed by the communion between the one Pastor, Christ and the faithful.[189]

---

187 For a correct reception of Vatican II, G. Alberigo indicated in the hierarchy of truths in *Unitatis redintegratio* 11, 'the basis for a renewal of the criterion of theological qualification. Compared with the note on the theological qualification of the conciliar decisions drawn up in September / October 1963 (*History of Vatican II*, III, 63, 77, 115 footnote 369; Editio typica, 214–215), on the basis of which the decisions were separated into constitutions (dogmatic, pastoral), decrees, declarations, appears to be of relatively secondary importance', in *Ibid.*, p. 386, footnote 11.

188 On this see G. Ruggieri, 'Ricezione e interpretazione del Vaticano II. La ragioni di un dibattito', in A. Melloni—G. Ruggeieri, *Chi ha paura del Vaticano II?* (Rome: Carrocci, 2009), pp. 17–44; C. Theobald, 'The Theological Options of Vatican II: Seeking an 'Internal' Principle of Interpretation', in *Concilium* 4 (2005), pp. 87–107.

189 G. Alberigo, 'Le ragioni dell'opzione pastorale del Vaticano II', in *Synaxis* 3 (2002), pp. 503–504. Alberigo sees precisely in the pastoral nature of the Council a participation and new context in which Vatican II took place. This new context 'enables to discover in it an experience of total sharing of the council-event. Total sharing which was possible perhaps precisely because purposes of theological consent were not suggested. To the extent that there is a basis to believe that among the non-Catholic observers and members at

Pastorality, therefore, while hiding the danger of discrediting the Council,[190] for Alberigo, read in the right way (as council-event), would open the Church to new and unexpected horizons. One of the principles is the 'in-depth modification of the Roman Pontiff. "Roman nature" is no longer the characteristic of papal service, but—on the contrary—the pastoral needs of the church govern the service of presidency'.[191] According to Alberigo, this pastorality succeeded in changing the course of the Council and moving from a restrictive vision of doctrinal ecumenism to a pastoral one instead, synonymous with consent, with openness. He wrote:

Vatican II there was an habitual communion which even implied a "communicatio in sacris" both at the level of contribution for the formation of the will of the Council and at the level of prayer, it becomes difficult to deny that they were not in some way real and proper members of the council itself' (*Ibid.*, p. 509). According to my way of seeing things, this text is symptomatic on the one hand of the goal to which the pastorality of the Council aimed—when absolutised in the way seen by the School of Bologna—and on the other, of the risks and errors which were hidden therein and which still continue to hide themselves there, when in a certain way it is dogmatised, without any longer knowing that its true goal is praxis and not teaching: it starts from the teaching for a practical goal and never vice-versa. For M. D. Chenu, as well, Vatican II indicated the end of the Constantinian era and the start of an epoch-making change, which enabled the Church to move out from the 'Christian season' to introduce it into the universal one, now as presence among the different nations. Cf. his essay 'La fine dell'era costantiniana', in J. P. Dubois-Dumée et al. (eds.), *Un Concilio per il nostro tempo* (Brescia: Morcelliana, 1962), pp. 47–70 (French original, 'La fin de l'ère constantinienne', in *Un concile pour notre temps* [Paris: Cerf, 1961]).

190 Alberigo wrote: 'The Jesuit Tromp was particularly peremptory stating that a modern person was being spoken about who doesn't exist. One wants to be "pastoral". But the first pastoral duty is the "teaching". Marcel Lefebvre did not deny that the characteristic of this council was precisely a pastoral one. This will be an idea which progressively will take hold of the minority, too, but to deny doctrinal dignity to Vatican II, therefore interpreting the pastorality in a different sense from that understood by John XXIII', Alberigo, 'Le ragioni dell'opzione pastorale', p. 503.

191 *Ibid.*, p. 508.

> The 'pastorality' also called into question the 'doctrinal' ecumenism, advocating a global setting of the search for unity. It is the very idea of unity which finds in the pastoral vision of Christianity an impulse to describe itself in articulated and flexible terms. The overcoming of the hegemony of the 'theology' appears today equivalent to the overcoming of the hegemony of the 'juridical', and like that full of complexes and rich consequences.[192]

The same applies to the declarations of the Magisterium, now no longer proposable as condemnations; even the same condemnations of before show themselves to be conquerable by reason of their historicity and new pastoral setting.[193] Pastorality, then, is, in a certain way, synonymous with ecumenicity. In fact, according to C. Theobald,

> The representatives of the Secretariat for Christian Unity, Cardinal Bea, Bishop de Smedt, and Bishop Volk, who at the time crystallized the views of all those who opposed the preparatory schemas, seized on this internal link between pastoral and ecumenical form in the council document to be composed.[194]

192 *Ibid.* No. 1 (2000) of *Cristianesimo nella Storia* devoted to John Paul II's 18 May 1998 Motu proprio, *Ad tuendam fidem*, is interesting, seen as imposition of a doctrinal Magisterium, so as to be no more, as Vatican II wished, on the other hand, a pastoral Magisterium of consent and the search in common, in dialogue, for the truth. Among the various studies of note in particular is that of A. Melloni, 'Definitivus/definitive', in *Ibid.* 1 [2000] 171–205, according to which the 'definitive judgment' introduced by the Pope's Motu proprio would have the sense of a legal verdict in public law, would be of legal origin and pass from *Lumen Gentium* 25 to the Code of Canon Law in an ambiguous fashion: it would transfer a question of theological debate to the Code, in an (historic) anachronistic manner, and this would be a return to arms of the severity of the Magisterium, against John XXIII's medicine of mercy.

193 Cf. Ruggeri, 'Ricezione e interpretazione', pp. 24–25.

194 Theobald, 'The Theological Options of Vatican II', p. 94. Here Theobald cites Volk, who noted that '*De Ecclesia* 'has not enough of the flavour of the gospel for the Catholic faithful, for those who are separated from us, and for the whole world: dogmatic teaching on the Church itself should be put forward by the

The pastoral vision of the School of Bologna, which succeeds in welding into unity the event with the teaching, that is to say, the fact of faith with its communicability, can be traced back, I believe, to this expression of Theobald:

> Is the relationship between scripture and tradition really a problem of truths or of points contained in the 'deposit'? Is doctrine not rather one way of establishing, in different contexts, conditions under which the kerygmatic or pastoral event can be truly produced, in all its dimensions, at the very heart of tradition? This must be what John XXIII had in mind when he spoke of the 'forms and proportions of a Magisterium which is predominantly pastoral in character'.[195]

On the historicity front of Vatican II lies also B. Forte. He defined the Second Vatican Council as 'the Council of history', in the sense that,

> Vatican II started a 'history of the Council', an itinerary of reception through which the promise which reverberated in the conciliar event could take flesh in people's lives.[196]

In this way Vatican II assumes the 'history of self-awareness of the faith',[197] putting it in relation to truth. For Forte, the most important document of Vatican II is *Dei verbum*:

> The most incisive contribution which magisterial reflection gave to the problem of the historical mediation of revelation.

Council as Gospel, which means Good News; and it is in this way that dogmatic teaching is in itself truly pastoral. If teaching has no saving power in itself, pastoral work can no longer add this. This is the reason why the two must not be separated. Such evangelical teaching also serves ecumenical requirements at the same time… ', AS I/4, p. 388, cit. in *Ibid.*, pp. 94–95.

195 *Ibid.*, p. 96.

196 B. Forte, 'Le prospettive della ricerca teologica', in R. Fisichella (ed.), *Il Concilio Vaticano II: recezione e attualità alla luce del Giubileo* (Cinisello Balsamo: San Paolo 2000), p. 423. See also Id., 'Ripensare il Vaticano II tra memoria e profezia', in *Communio* 142 (1995), pp. 69–84.

197 B. Forte, 'Le prospettive della ricerca teologica', cit.

> The moving on from the teaching of the two sources, Scripture and Tradition, in that one *traditio Verbi ex fide in fidem*, which has its normative movement in the word recorded in the sacred text, but which lives in permanent newness of telling and interpretation under the action of the Holy Spirit in time.[198]

Along the lines of pastorality understood as historical significance one also finds the episcopal witness of the Council, one of the youngest participants at Vatican II, L. Bettazzi. Precisely due to the pastorality of the Council, one can overcome, in a certain way, that discontinuity provoked instead by the preceding councils as dogmatic. Vatican II would always be current/historical because pastoral.[199]

2. *Concluding observations on the theological contribution to Vatican II*

At this point of our theological journey, which has led us to check certain stances on the Second Vatican Council, chosen because they seemed to be exemplars, we can deduce, from the study of the problem as a whole, some key elements. In my opinion, these elements underline on the one hand the complexity of the theological fact which presents itself in its totality as 'the Second Vatican Council', and on the other enables the emergence of the crux of the problems which gradually presented themselves, and which can be summarised

---

198 *Ibid.*, p. 420.

199 L. Bettazzi, *Non spegnere lo Spirito. Continuità e discontinuità del Concilio Vaticano II* (Brescia: Queriniana, 2006), pp. 9–10 in particular. The Neapolitan Jesuits also attested to this historical dimension of Vatican II. See the three-volume work AA.VV., *Il Concilio venti anni dopo* (Rome: Ave, 1984–1985–1986). In particular, P. J. Rosato SJ writes: 'The already-mentioned attempts to place the classical metaphysic in the new historical context concern not just the main concept (the being understood as *event*), but also its corollary: that the being, that is, species in its human manifestation, is expressed as *dialogue*', in M. Simone (ed.), *Il Concilio venti anni dopo. Le nuove categorie dell'autocomprensione della Chiesa*, vol. 1, (Rome: Ave, 1984), p. 81.

in two points: 1) Is Vatican II intrinsically compromised? 2) Is Vatican II hiding a fundamental metaphysical deficiency?

2.1 Is Vatican II a 'compromised text'?

The theme is somewhat sensitive and pressing, despite the fact that we have seen that Laurentin also had no fear in denouncing the imprecision of the Council documents. A case sufficiently singular and certainly without any doubts is that of O. H. Pesch who—to express it in a somewhat biting and sarcastic manner—accused the Council of being a compromised text: 'Often', he said, 'in extreme cases it is to do with 'the compromise of contradictory pluralism''.[200] By contradictory pluralism Pesch means for example the fact that very often the schema were formulated as a *do ut des*: if you accept my text I'll approve yours. A similar way of preceding was presented in the voting in the Commissions, as regards, for example, episcopal collegiality: first significant openings were made, then, for a conservative minority, steps back were taken, increasing the references to the *potestas* of the Roman Pontiff: a similar procedure is verified, according to Pesch, above all in the final outcome.[201]

On this matter, P. Hünermann responded to Pesch, criticising this extreme position, for the fact that the Council documents are not to be seen as documents of human and civil constitution. The possibility of speaking of 'contradictory pluralism' applied to *Lumen Gentium* would exist 'if one starts out from a conciliar text which in terms of genre has the form of a law or a judgment'.[202] For Hünermann, in line with the idea of the School of Bologna, there was a need to strictly evaluate the genre of the Council texts above all in their reception, taking into account the genesis and unfolding of the Council. In fact,

200 O. H. Pesch, *Il Concilio Vaticano II. Preistoria, svolgimento, risultati, storia post-conciliare* (Brescia: Queriniana, 2005), p. 148 (German original, *Das Zweite Vatikanische Konzil* [Würzburg: Echter, 1994]).

201 Cf. *Ibid.*, pp. 149–150.

202 P. Hünermann, 'The Ignored 'Test' On the Hermeneutics of the Second Vatican Council', in *Concilium* 4 (2005), p. 129.

Vatican II is integrated into the tradition of Trent and Vatican I, but, unlike these, does not make any demarcations in terms of definitions. The meaning of Vatican II, of a pastoral nature, is to be seen above all in the will of the Popes, and in particular in the work of the first session. This would facilitate the adoption of 'the corpus of the texts of Vatican II as *lasting guide lines*. Its true character will only come to the fore if it is not merely regarded as fulfilling a one-off function, but if it used *time and time again* for the resolution of the respective problems of different times'.[203] For Hünermann, however, one could 'describe the genre of the text of Vatican II as a 'constitution of faithful ecclesial life' or for short as 'constituent of faith''.[204]

So we ask ourselves does this resolve the problem of 'contradictory pluralism'? I believe not, due to the fact that the documents of a council in general do not *constitute the faith*, they express it, they define it in a solemn manner. They could constitute it only in a dogmatically pastoral sphere, seen from a historical slant as the School of Bologna wishes. But the Council was not this, nor did it want to be.

I also believe that a certain contradictory pluralism does appear, and was inevitable, for various reasons,[205] all innervated however by the lack of clarity of the boundaries between what is pastoral and what is dogmatic.[206] Are the two dimensions of the one theology equiva-

---

203 *Ibid.*, p. 131.

204 *Ibid.*, p. 128.

205 In 1961 Congar maintained: 'The whole of this week has taught me a lesson concerning the psychology of meetings which will probably apply also to the Council: 1) When one persists in one's objection or criticism, one always ends up by gaining something; 2) when there is discussion and opposition, the person who calmly suggests a formula has a good chance of being listened to. This often happens with Mgr Philips', Congar, *My Journal of the Council*, p. 55.

206 Thus Congar states in a way which to me seems emblematic of the hermeneutical problem tied to Vatican II: 'The pastoral is no less doctrinal, but it is doctrinal in a way that is not content with conceptualising, defining, deducing and anathematising: it seeks to express the saving truth in a way that reaches out to the men and women of today, takes up their difficulties, and replies to their questions', (Y. Congar, 'Le Concile du Vatican II. Son Église peuple de

lent? Can they be distinguished? Is one subordinate to the other? Hence, an exhaustive reply cannot be given to the question formulated and nor could one verify at a theological level the continuity/discontinuity of the teachings of the Council with the Tradition of the Church, without referring to another level, which I will indicate subsequently.

2.2 Vatican II as a metaphysical problem: a problem of substance and form?

The 'Vatican II' problem, more than one of 'contradictory pluralism', is that of an unclear elucidation of its nature and consequently of the tenor of its documents, in whose perspective are to be read the so-called innovations or rather theological-magisterial in-depth analyses. If the notion that the Council was pastoral remains strong (not

---

Dieu et corps du Christ', in *Théologie historique* 7 [1984], p. 64, cit., in Ibid., p. 46. É. Mahieu, on this passage just quoted, observed: 'On this Congar would clash very quickly with men such as Cardinal Ottaviani or Fr Tromp, for whom the pastoral is, like ecumenism, a purely practical question, reserved to other bodies (*Introduction,* in *Ibid*). For example, concerning the schema *De oecumenismo,* which like others did not make it to the council chamber, Congar said on Wednesday 22 November 1961, again along the same lines: 'Continuation of the Constitution on Ecumenism. A Dogmatic Constitution of this kind cannot but be a disappointment from the ecumenical point of view. On the one hand, all it can do is to proclaim general principles, which are always valid, whereas ecumensim is a fact, a movement, entirely dependent on the will of God recognised as such in our own day; on the other hand, at the level of dogmatic principles, one can hardly find anything other than very rigid statements about the oneness of the Church and warnings against indifferentism, against *communicatio in sacris* [sharing in the sacraments], against false irenicism. I asked for the Constitution to express its own proper limits and that it should refer specifically to more positive pastoral and practical indications to be supplied either by the Secretariat or by the Congregation for the Eastern Churches. I was told that: 1) this would happen of its own accord when this Constitution came to be published together with all the other documents; 2) when all the documents were about to be published would be the time for inserting something along the lines I was suggesting', *Ibid.*, p. 66.

in the historical significance sense understood by Rahner: to glean the theological presuppositions from praxis and the secular sciences, but in the theological sense understood by the Magisterium) and the fontal tenor of the Magisterium is authentic and ordinary, infallible only to the extent that the facts already *definiti* or *definitive tenenda* of Tradition are reiterated, then the improvements and in-depth analyses of the Council, which could also give rise to regressions due to theological innovation, are to be verified in the light of the sane method of theology. The theology which enlightens the Magisterium can verify the *status* of these in-depth analyses and provide the Magisterium with a criterion for a pronouncement (perhaps also only ordinary) aimed at dissipating all the misunderstandings gathered around it. In such a way the Magisterium could say, with authority, that continuity alone is the correct hermeneutic to apply to the Council and how the innovations are to be read in this continuity of the Tradition. The possible discontinuities which might be encountered are not dogmatic (in the sense that they harm dogma or change it; more than anything they explain it or try to explain it) but theological, and are susceptible to revision and renewal, given their non-definitive magisterial character. Modernism does not insinuate itself into Vatican II as dyadic relationship of 'council-mystery'. It would be blasphemous even to think it. Perhaps this was present in some periti and theologians, but the Council was Catholic, summoned and approved by the Roman Pontiff; its documents remain, *natura sui*, a teaching of the supreme Magisterium of the Church.

III

PASTORAL EPIPHANIES OF VATICAN II

IN THE INTENTIONS AND FORMATION OF THE CONCILIAR TEACHING ON THE 'SCRIPTURE AND TRADITION' RELATIONSHIP

1. The Scripture and Tradition relationship in **Dei verbum***: a laborious historical-theological path:*

IN THE AUDIENCE on 2 July 1960, John XXIII had given the conciliar preparatory Commissions the questions to be studied and on the basis of which to draft the schema of the constitutions then to be discussed in the Council. Five areas for study were entrusted to the Theological Commission, chaired by Cardinal Ottaviani, with the Jesuit Fr S. Tromp as secretary: 1) *De fontibus revelationis,* 2) *De Ecclesia Catholica,* 3) *De ordine supernaturali praesertim in re morali,* 4) *De matrimonio,* 5) *De doctrina sociali.*

The thorniest theme, as we will see, which led to a lively discussion and strong opposition and which finally generated a decisive change of direction in the Council, was precisely *De fontibus,* which was per se, at the Pope's request, to set out Catholic teaching on Sacred Scripture, that is to say the historicity of the sacred books and the reverence to which Catholic exegetes were bound by Sacred Tradition and the Church's Magisterium; it was to condemn the errors in this area and provide exegetical norms to be followed.[1]

The schema prepared by the Theological Commission was discussed at the Central Commission, approved on 9 November 1961 and presented in the council chamber for debate on 14 November 1961. The text did not have a happy outcome. Right from the first discussion in the Central Commission there was evidence of friction between Ottaviani and Bea, between a doctrinal sense and condemnation of exegetical errors and instead a sense of being more respectful to the new achievements of exegetical knowledge; friction which, in the council chamber, would be transformed into two opposite ways of perceiving the Council: a doctrinal council for pastoral ends and instead a pastoral and ecumenical council with a new methodology for the exposition of doctrine. The schema would be withdrawn from discussion and, at the behest of the Pope, subjected to a re-writing by a commission chosen ad hoc, which saw some synergy between the Doctrinal Commission and the Secretariat for Promoting Christian Unity. The new schema was to be a via media between Ottaviani's vision and that of Bea and above all Bishop De Smedt. The desire for the pastorality of the Council, without renouncing truth, but presenting it in an 'ecumenical way', gave a decisive orientation to the whole assembly, and this could be seen right from the first discussion on the schema *De fontibus*.

---

1 Cf. AD II/2.1, p. 408.

I will go over the historical progress of the schema,[2] focusing above all on the relationship between Scripture and Tradition, which is one of the most important cruxes for examining, in the perspective of the whole discussion about *De fontibus*, and then on the dogmatic constitution *Dei verbum*, the *mind* of the Council, or at least a significant effect of this conciliar desire. From this one can deduce a hermeneutical principle to then apply to the Council in its entirety. In fact, 'going over the discussion which led to the withdrawal of *De fontibus*, some valid guidelines begin to take shape for all the conciliar documents'.[3] Analysing what the Council desired, what was its position as regards doctrine, which always intersects with pastoral and ecumenical endeavour, we will also be able to give a response to the question: what is the magisterial value of Vatican II where it touches such an important point as Revelation and its transmission?

---

2 For an overall vision of the long generative process of *Dei verbum*, through analysis of its stages, see U. Betti, 'Storia della Costituzione dogmatica 'Dei verbum'', in AA.VV., *La Costituzione dogmatica sulla divina rivelazione* (Turin: Elle Di Ci, 1967), pp. 14–68; E. Stakemeier, *Die Konzilskonstitution über die göttliche Offenbarung* (Paderborn: Bonifatius, 1967²); J. Ratzinger, *Dogmatische Konstitution über die göttliche Offenbarung. Einleitung*, in LThK², *Das Zweite Vatikanische Konzil*, II, pp. 498–503 (abbreviation: Ratzinger, *Einleitung*); R. Burigana, *La Bibbia nel Concilio. La redazione della costituzione 'Dei verbum' del Vaticano II* (Bologna: Il Mulino, 1998). Here the author, on the basis of the methodology promoted by the School of Bologna, situates his research in the wake of the process of the historicisation of Vatican II, according to the historical-critical method (cf. *Introduzione*, p. 17); H. Sauer, *Erfahrurng und Glaube. Die Begründung des pastoralen Prinzips durch die Offenbarungskonstitution des II. Vatikanischen Konzils* (Frankfurt am Main: Peter Lang, 1993); G. Montaldi, *In fide ipsa essentia revelationis completur. Il tema della fede nell'evolversi del Concilio Vaticano II: la genesi di DV 5–6 e i suoi riflessi su ulteriori ambiti conciliari* (Rome: Pontificia Università Gregoriana, 2005, doctoral thesis). On the discussion in the third period of the Council, with a significant title with the same vision as this author, see Sauer, 'The doctrinal and the pastoral: the text on Divine Revelation', in *History of Vatican II*, vol. 4, pp. 196–233.

3 Montaldi, *In fide ipsa essentia revelationis.*, p. 219.

1.1 The definitive text and its references in footnotes

I will take things in reverse. I will begin with the promulgated text of *Dei verbum,* with its footnotes. Then diachronically I will start with the first schema, *De fontibus,* to gradually trace the significant passages and amendments, to reach the promulgated text.

Chapter II of *Dei verbum* is devoted to 'Handing on Divine Revelation'. God himself has established that what has been revealed be handed on to all generations. To this end Christ the Lord commissioned the Apostles to preach the Gospel handed over by him and promulgated in his very person, as source of all saving truth and moral teaching. The Apostles, then, who were faithful to this command, so that the Gospel might be preserved whole and alive, chose successors to whom was entrusted their same task as teachers. Thus, the sacred tradition and Sacred Scripture are referred to as a mirror in which the Church looks at God and from whom she has received everything (cf. *Dei verbum* 7). Paragraph 8, on the other hand, is devoted to the sacred tradition. It asserts, inter alia:

> Now what was handed on by the Apostles includes everything which contributes towards the holiness of life and increase in faith of the peoples of God; and so the Church, in her teaching, life and worship, perpetuates and hands on to all generations all that she herself is, all that she believes. This tradition which comes from the Apostles, develops in the Church with the help of the Holy Spirit.[4]

This tradition enables the Church to know the full canon of the Scriptures and understand its significance, made unceasingly active in her (cf. *Dei verbum* 8c). Paragraph 9 then moves on to study the inter-dependent relationship between Scripture and tradition, between which there is a 'close connection and communication'. Their intrinsic unity is thus explained by the Constitution:

---

4 As regards the advance of the Tradition and the increased understanding of the faith brought by it, the text refers to the First Vatican Council, Dogmatic Constitution on the Catholic faith, *Dei Filius,* chapter 4, DH 3020 [Collantes 1.085].

> For both of them, flowing from the same divine wellspring, in a certain way merge into a unity and tend toward the same end... Consequently it is not from Sacred Scripture alone that the Church draws her certainty about everything which has been revealed. Therefore both sacred tradition and Sacred Scripture are to be accepted and venerated with the same sense of loyalty and reverence (*Dei verbum* 9).[5]

Finally, paragraph 10 is devoted to the relationship between Scripture, tradition and the Magisterium. Sacred tradition and Sacred Scripture constitute 'one sacred deposit of the word of God, committed to the Church' (*Dei verbum* 10a). The task of interpreting the Word of God 'whether written or handed on' has been entrusted exclusively to the living teaching office of the Church, which in turn is bound to it: it is not superior to the Word of God but can teach 'only what has been handed on' (*Dei verbum* 10b). Hence none of the three realities, and that is, Scripture, tradition and Magisterium, can exist without the others; together, under the action of the Holy Spirit, they contribute effectively to the salvation of souls (cf. *Dei verbum* 10c).

Therefore, one goes from Revelation to the handing on of the deposit through Scripture and tradition, and so one reaches the mystery, as faithful interpreter and transmitter in turn of what the Church has received from God. But how was this teaching reached?

---

5 The text, on this very important and significant passage throughout the whole of the Council, refers back to the Council of Trent, Decree *De canonicis Scripturis*, DH 1501 [Collantes 2.006]. In the original Latin, the text of *Dei verbum* 9 states: 'Sacra Traditio ergo et Sacra Scriptura arcte inter se connectuntur atque communicant. Nam ambae, ex eadem divina scaturigine promanantes, in unum quodammodo coalescunt et in eundem finem tendunt. Etenim Sacra Scriptura est locutio Dei quatenus divino afflante Spiritu scripto consignatur; Sacra autem Traditio verbum Dei, a Christo Domino et a Spiritu Sancto Apostolis concreditum, successoribus eorum integre transmittit, ut illud, praelucente Spiritu veritatis, praeconio suo fideliter servent, exponant atque diffundant; quo fit ut Ecclesia certitudinem suam de omnibus revelatis non per solam Sacram Scripturam hauriat. Quapropter utraque pari pietatis affectu ac reverentia suscipienda et veneranda est'.

1.2 The schema *De fontibus revelationis*

In the second congregation of the Council's central preparatory Commission, 9 November 1961, the schema was proposed as drawn up by the Theological Commission, which included biblical teachers and theologians such as L. Cerfaux, D. Van den Eynde, L. Di Fonzo, E. Vogt, A. Kerrigan, G. Castellino. The schema was divided into five chapters. The first concerned *De duplici fonte Revelationis*, divided into five points.[6] For our analysis I will report on the most important. The fourth point was entitled *De duplici fonte revelationis*, and explained that the Church has always believed and believes that the whole revelation of Christ handed on by means of the Apostles, is contained in Scripture and Tradition, like a dual source:

> Christi itaque et Apostolorum mandatis et exemplis edocta, sancta mater Ecclesia semper credidit et credit integram revelationem non in sola Scriptura sed in Scriptura et Traditione tamquam in duplici fonte contineri (cf. Conc. Vat.: Const. *De Fide Catholica*, cap. 2: Denz. 1787; EB 77), alio tamen ac alio modo. Nam libri Veteris et Novi Testamenti praeterquam quod revelata continent, insuper Spiritu Sancto inspirante conscripti sunt, ita ut Deum habeant autore (*Ibid.*).
>
> Traditio autem vere divinam a Spiritu Sancto continua successione in Ecclesia consevata, in rebus fidei et morum ea continet omnia, quae Apostoli, sive ab ore Christi sive suggerente Spiritu Sancto, acceperunt atque Ecclesiae praetor Sacram Scripturam quasi per manus tradiderunt, ut in eadem per praedicationem ecclesiasticum transmitterentur (cf. *ibid.*, et Conc. Trid., Sess. IV: Denz. 783; EB 57). Quare quae divina Traditio ratione sui continent, non ex libris, sed ex vivo in Ecclesia praeconio, fidelium fide et Ecclesiae praxi hauriuntur. Quod autem et praeterita attinet, plerumque ex variis documentis scriptis, non tamen inspiratis, innotescunt.[7]

6 See the whole schema: AD II/2.1, pp. 523–532.

7 *Ibid.*, p. 524. As regards this last sentence it is interesting to note the clarification about the presence in the Tradition of written sources, too, even though

Paragraph 5 was entitled *De habitudine unius fontis ad alterum,* and underlined that apostolic Tradition alone was the certain criterion for interpreting and explaining the Scriptures, which, in their turn, as inspired, provided a divine tool to illustrate the truths of faith. With significant emphasis—which would give rise to a heated discussion—it was underlined that only Tradition is the path through which the revealed truths, *in primis* those inspired, are made known and clear to the Church:

> Nemo ergo Traditione exinde minoris facere aut ei fidem derogare audeat. Licet enim Sacra Scriptura, cum sit inspirata, ad enuntiandas et illustrandas veritates fidei instrumentum praebeat divinum, eius nihilominus sensus nonnisi Traditione apostolica certe et pleni intellegi vel etiam exponi potest; immo Traditio, eaque sola, via est qua quaedam veritates revelatae, eae imprimis quae ad inspirationem, canonicitatem et integritatem omnium et singolorum sacrorum librorum spectant, Ecclesiae innotescunt et clarescunt.[8]

Both, then, Scripture and Tradition, are in relation with the Magisterium, in that they constitute the one deposit of faith, authentically interpreted not by the individual faithful person but by the living Magisterium of the Church. It is interesting to note that the Magisterium, as living, interpreting Tradition, acts as a close and universal norm of belief. The emphasis of the attribute 'living' is placed not on Tradition (as would often be done afterwards) but on the Magisterium, which not only judges directly or indirectly what is in the deposit concerning faith and morals, but also illustrates and clarifies what is

---

not inspired by the Fathers, while the Tradition remains essentially oral transmission of Revelation. Ottaviani himself would clarify it in the *disceptatio schematis,* saying: 'Dicit de praecipuo medio quo Traditio intacta ad nos pervenit et deposito custoditum est; non est dubium quod medium praecipuum est ipsa praedicatio, sed sunt etiam alia, v. gr., scripta non ispirata Patrum' (*Ibid.,* p. 533). The said final sentence of n. 4 would be eliminated by the definitive schema presented at the Council, cf. AS I/3, pp. 15–16.

8 AD II/2.1, p. 524.

contained in an obscure or implicit manner in the sources, in Scripture and Tradition. It is paragraph 6 *De habitudine utriusque fontis ad Magisterium* which says:

> Ut autem ambo fontes revelationis concorditer et efficacius ad salute hominum concurrent, providus Dominus eos tamquam unum fidei depositum ad custodiendum et tuendum et authentice interpretandum non singulis fidelibus utcumque eruditis concredidit, sed soli vivo Ecclesiae Magisterio (cf. Enc. *Humani generis*, 12 aug. 1950: AAS 42 (1950) 567, 569: Denz. 2314; EB 611). Magisterii Ecclesiae ergo est, qua proximae et universalis credenda normae, non modo iudicare in iis, quae sive directe sive indirecte ad fidem et mores spectant, de sensu et interpretatione cum Scripturae Sacrae tum documentorum et monumentorum quibus temporis decursu Traditio consegnata est et manifestata, sed ea quoque illustrare et enucleare quae in utroque fonte nonnisi obscure ac velut implicite continentur (*Ibid.*, p. 569: Denz. 2314; EB 611).[9]

In what has been quoted up to now the condemnation of the free examination of the Scriptures proposed by Protestantism is notable. Since, then, it is about Sacred Scripture (chapters 2–5), the schema, against the unbalanced readings of *Formgeschichte*, solemnly affirms the personal inspiration of hagiography, from which it follows that all and the individual parts of the sacred books are inspired: all that is declared by hagiography is expressed by the Holy Spirit. Then by reason of divine inspiration, all Sacred Scripture is infallible and devoid of error: 'Ex divinae Inspirationis extensione ad omnia, directe et necessarie sequitur infallibilitas et inerrantia totius Sacrae Scripture',[10] taking into account, however, the human way of expressing the hagiography and therefore a 'fides historica sacrae Scripturae in narrandi modo'.[11] Alongside that, another aspect solemnly underlined

9 *Ibid.*, pp. 524–525.

10 *Ibid.*, p. 526.

11 *Ibid.*

by *De fontibus* was the historical truth of the facts about the life of Christ, as described in the Gospels, condemning those errors which threatened the historical truth of the infancy of Christ, the Redeemer's signs and miracles, his admirable death, resurrection and ascension to the Father.[12] Above all this second part, concerning the Sacred Scriptures, was believed, as we shall see, in the first analysis of the schema, to be an obstacle to exegetical progress, a warning rather than an exhortation to scholars. Then, later, the line of criticism would shift to the schema as such.

1.2.1 The discussion in the Central Commission

The said schema was presented to the central preparatory Commission with a report from Cardinal Ottaviani, who made sure of showing that *De fontibus*, compared to Trent and Vatican I, represented a homogenous development, bringing together the unanimous element of the Tradition. Ottaviani noted that in the numbers speaking about Tradition (4–6), its presentation differed in three ways from that of the two previous councils: 1) 'Traditio' was not used in the plural ('sine scripto traditionibus') but in the singular; 2) in place of the phrase 'sine scripto' there was reference to the inspired books ('inspiratis libris'); 3) 'traditionem per praedicationem ecclesiasticum usque ad nos pervenire' was added. Such modifications had been made with the aim of improving theological understanding of Tradition, and this again due to three things: 1) to better adapt the text to the current mode of expressing the Magisterium; 2) to remove the ambiguity of the phrase 'Traditionis in scripto'; and, 3) to show the essential link between the Tradition and the living Magisterium, as requested by many bishops. According to the hopeful Ottaviani, the text of the schema set out to offer the genuine teaching of the Church according to the needs of the time; the way the text progressed was neither scholastic nor merely parenthetic, but so as to unite two needs: to teach and to exhort.[13]

---

[12] Cf. n. 21, in *Ibid.*, p. 529.

[13] Cf. *Ibid.*, pp. 535–537.

The report from the President of the Theological Commission was followed by observations from the other Cardinal-members. According to Cardinal König, paragraph 5 of the schema set out in a very defensive way the importance of Tradition compared to Scripture. Scripture was not of the same value. The Church has cultivated and always cultivates the greatest veneration for Sacred Scripture, used as a principal source: 'tamquam fonte principali utitur'.[14] Experience taught that often the exegetes and the simple faithful, too, understood parts of Scripture even without recourse to Tradition, so according to Cardinal Döpfner it seemed very rigid to state that the certain and full meaning of the Scriptures can be gained solely with the help of Tradition,[15] and therefore he saw good reason to insert a clause for a correct scripture hermeneutic: 'non sine auxilio theologorum'.[16]

One of the strongest and most adverse observations to the schema was that of Cardinal Bea, who would rekindle his fervour in the council chamber. The schema was judged to be defensive with regard to the errors of a few exegetes, calling into question the probity of their intentions. There was not sufficient mention of the *munus* and the *ius* of Catholic exegetes, who have the task of investigating the sacred Books at a systematic level; of study and research, moreover, promoted by Popes Leo XIII and Pius XII. Bea suggested withdrawing the schema, which was contrary to the (scriptural) Magisterium of Leo XIII, Benedict XV, Pius XI and Pius XII,[17] and consulting the Pontifical Biblical Commission, as well as other exegetes at the international level, above all those in whose regions the denounced New Testament exegetical problems largely emerged (France, the United States, Germany and Austria). Ottaviani, on the other hand, let Bea know that it was not about the freedom of hostile research, but a serious concern about what was being taught in seminaries: how

14 *Ibid.*, p. 538.

15 *Ibid.*, p. 539.

16 *Ibid.*

17 Cf. *Ibid.*, pp. 547–548.

could one not be concerned and not act against such a tendency when, for example, it was believed that the first two chapters of Saint Luke were not historical?[18] Thus Ottaviani rejected Bea's proposal, so as not to postpone the Council indefinitely, but he did not foresee that, having seen the problem out the door, it would come back in through the window.

Finally, Cardinal Alfrink regretted the fact that the schema, in the first chapter, seemed to ignore modern studies on Revelation, Sacred Scripture and the Church. In fact, in his opinion, the position and function of Scripture in the Church and its relationship with the Magisterium had great importance in the discussions with the separated brethren.[19]

The disquisition on the schema with the subsequent final approval concluded with the words of Cardinal Ottaviani who, once again, defended the work done, redeeming it from the recurrent objection of being too defensive:

> I note, he said, that Councils are for this purpose: to defend dogma, to defend the truth. Councils are forced above all by the errors which proliferate. Therefore, if there is a defensive element there, too, I see that it corresponds fully with the aim of the Council.[20]

It would be precisely this vision which would be contested in the incipient Council. At the Council, taking its cue from the criticism of *De fontibus*, opposed to it would be another more pastoral, or rather more ecumenical vision, so as to indicate a fundamental change with respect to the established self-awareness of a council for the Church.[21]

---

18 Cf. *Ibid.*, pp. 549.

19 Cf. *Ibid.*, p. 551.

20 Ibid., p. 563.

21 Already in the preparatory phase, Fogarty commented, 'the topic of "the pastoral" was raised by a bloc of German, Dutch, and French bishops, with significant agreement from Latin American and from "missionary" bishops, the terms of the problem were not yet clear. It would be the Pope's opening

Vatican II could not be understood correctly leaving aside this new self-awareness.[22]

1.2.2 The discussion of De fontibus in the Council

The definitive text of the schema, approved by the central Commission and by the Holy Father, was presented in the Council for public discussion in the XIX General Congregation, on 14 November 1962,[23] introduced by a report from Cardinal Ottaviani, followed by that of Fr S. Garofalo, biblicist and to a large extent the creator of the schema. Ottaviani warned those present to suggest corrections and

---

speech, *Gaudet Mater Ecclesia,* that would provide reference for a common concept of "the pastoral", at least during the first period of the Council', G. Fogarty, 'The Council Gets Underway', in G. Alberigo (ed.), *History of Vatican II,* vol. II, *The Formation of the Council's Identity. First Period and Intersession. October 1962—September 1963* (Maryknoll / Leuven: Orbis / Peeters, 1997), p. 70, footnote 3.

22 A significant change with profound symbolic value would come about with the withdrawal of *De fontibus* and the creation of a mixed Commission (doctrinal and ecumenical) by the Pope. Burigana writes about this: 'The withdrawal of *De fontibus* was the sign of a change of perspective with regard to the preparation, the end of the uncertainties and misunderstandings about the meaning of the council which had dragged on since the announcement by John XXIII on 25 January 1959 until the opening of Vatican II on 11 October 1962. The Pope's decision had profound symbolic value, with immediate effect on the working of the council overall and not just for the editorial history of the schema', Burigana, *La Bibbia nel Concilio,* p. 11.

23 The week from 14–21 November 1962, along with the period from 14 November—8 December the same year, were really decisive for the future of the Council. In Ruggieri's opinion, these two periods 'represented a turning point that was decisive for the future of the Council and therefore for the future of the Catholic Church itself: the shift from the Church of Pius XII, which was still essentially hostile to modernity and in this respect heir to the nineteenth-century restoration, to a Church that is a friend to all human beings, even children of modern society, its culture and its history... It can be said that during the week of discussion of *De fontibus* the Council took possession of its purpose in the terms in which *Gaudet Mater Ecclesiae* had described it', Ruggieri, 'The First Doctrinal Clash', pp. 233, 253.

amendments to the schema the object of discussion, and not anything else. He was prophetic because many interventions did not suggest amendments to the text, but attested to the way the schema presented itself compared to the feelings of the separated brethren and people of today. Many accused the schema of an absence of any pastoral tone. According to Ottaviani, a view shared by other Fathers such as Cardinal Santos,[24] Cardinal Garibi y Rivera,[25] and the Master General of the Dominicans, Fr A. Fernandez,[26] 'the first office, the fundamental office is teaching: "Teacher". The Lord's mandate is of the utmost importance: "Teach all nations". Herein already lies the foundation of the pastoral. After all, compared to the form of language, once the style has been managed, greater pastoral expression can be given'.[27]

And subsequently, he thus responded to some requests which came to the presidency about the insufficient inspiration of the new theology in the schema: 'the inspiration of the conciliar phrase must be the inspiration of the centuries, not of a particular school, which today is present but perhaps tomorrow has fallen into oblivion'.[28]

24 Cf. AS I/3, pp. 76–79.

25 Cf. *Ibid.*, pp. 122–124.

26 Cf. *Ibid.*, pp. 236–237: '1. Verbum "pastorale" adiectivum est. Et nec intellegi nec explicari potest nisi per ordinem ad substantivum. Sunstantivum ergo hoc in casu duplex agnoscitur, et ne unum pro alio sumantur oportet; a) vel agitur de substantive, quod et pascua et cibus; b) vel agitur de substantive, quod est methodus administrandi cibum et pascua. 2) Iamvero munus pastorale Concilii principaliter ad substantivum, quod est pascua vel cibum, refertur. Concilium enim veritatem tuetur, veritatem proponit. Veritas clara, perspicua, est id quod ab ipso spectatur. Munus pastorale uniuscuiusque nostrum, principaliter, ad substantivum refertur, quod est methodus. Pastorum est doctrina concilarem, cibum sanum, omnibus ministrare attentibus conditionibus loci, temporis et personae. Rudis, rude; sapienter sapientibus... Non ita debemus indolem pastoralem quaerere ut sit obtinenda etiam cum detriment veritatis. Unde si inter duas formulas, una magis pastoralis sed minus clara et exacta et alia minus pastoralis sed magis clara et exacta, sine dubio in Concilio haec secunda est praeferenda. In praxi pastorali eligatur prima', *Ibid.*, p. 237.

27 AS I/3, p. 27.

In the wake of Ottaviani, Garofalo also presented the aim of the Council as the exposition of teaching, the primary and immediate goal of an ecumenical council, mainly in line with the extraordinary and ordinary church Magisterium and at the same time with the salvation of souls, the supreme law of the Church. Garofalo clarified the traditional position about the summoning of a council for the exercise of extraordinary Magisterium. In fact, he said, the constitutions of an ecumenical council are not the encyclical letters of a Pope, which instead belong to the ordinary Magisterium. Even less was it necessary to equate them to the homilies given by pastors in church for the instruction of the faithful. According to Vatican I, to the council belongs the exercise of a solemn doctrinal Magisterium about things to be believed and to be lived,[29] and for the definition of such matters the Divine Redeemer has guaranteed the charisma of infallibility.[30] Nor, concluded Garofalo, does a council perform its office if it rejects the condemnation of errors, in whatever form this might happen, therefore assuring the Fathers that the schema presented had provided, with an appropriate characteristic language, *ex iustitia et caritate*, to ensure that the separated brethren in a very clear way might be able to recognise the teaching of the Catholic Church.[31] This was the classic sense. The strong opposition to the schema would mean the emergence of a call for proper reform with regard to this common way of conceiving a council.

The first opposition came by means of Cardinal Liénart. The schema as presented was incomplete. He believed that it was true that Revelation came to us through two paths, Scripture and Tradition, like two rivulets. But the decree had omitted presenting the primary source from which these two rivulets emanated, that is, the Word of God, carefully stated by the Council of Trent when it referred to the holy Gospel. It was

28 *Ibid.*

29 Cf. chapter 3 of the Constitution *Dei Filius*: DH 3011.

30 Cf. chapter 4 of the Constitution *Pastor aeternus*: DH 3074.

31 Cf. *Ibid.*, pp. 28–32.

necessary, therefore, according to Liénart, to speak in the decree about the Word of God, as essential source of every revelation:[32]

> Would it not be very appropriate, he said, with the voice of this decree, to pay a solemn tribute to the Word of God in this sacred synod, particularly with regard to our separated brethren, who so love the Word of God, cultivate it and venerate it, so that they know well that on this matter our devotion is no less inferior to theirs.[33]

However, the risk was that of limiting the Word of God to Sacred Scripture, given this sole declination in Protestant circles. Cardinal Liénart concluded his intervention saying that our faith was not founded on scholastic arguments but on every word which comes from the mouth of God.[34]

Speaking next, Cardinal Frings observed that in the decree being examined the voice of *Mater et Magistra* could not be heard, that of the Good Shepherd who called the sheep by name, but that of scholastic, professorial language, which did not edify, nor give life. There was a desire instead for that pastoral note with which John XXIII wanted every part of the Council to be imbued. Considering then the problem of the two sources of Revelation, he said that the way to present this teaching ('modus loquendi de duobus fontibus revelationis')[35] was not ancient, it was unknown to the Fathers, to the scholastics and to St Thomas, foreign to every ecumenical council, introduced instead at the time of historicism. He then distinguished an *ordo essendi* and an *ordo cognoscendi*. In the *ordo essendi* there is one source of Revelation, the Word of God; in the *ordo cognoscendi*, with regard to us therefore, there are two ways through which we can know what God has revealed. In his ways of seeing things, therefore, it was

---

32 Cf. *Ibid.*, p. 33: 'Oportuit ergo de verbo Dei in hoc decreto tractari quasi de essentiali fonte revelationis omnis.

33 *Ibid.*

34 *Ibid.*, p. 34.

35 *Ibid.*, p. 35.

better to dissuade the Council from putting at the forefront such a controversial teaching between Catholics and non-Catholics, so as not to offend the separated brethren: today, that opportunity which was there four centuries ago is no longer there. According to Frings, the teaching on inspiration, too, seemed to coerce the freedom of research and therefore to be too rigid. Besides, the Council had not been summoned to solve school issues still challenged among Catholic theologians, nor to anathematize one school in favour of another, but simply to condemn heresies.[36] Cardinal König was also of the same opinion as Cardinal Frings:

> In truth, he said, in the schema is proposed a judgment which up to today is still disputed among the theologians and periti, and about which there is not the unanimous consent of Tradition.[37]

It is interesting in this regard to read a final report from Rahner about the preparatory schema, done for Cardinal König, for whom he was peritus, but known by a good number of the German episcopate and theologians.[38] In fact, Rahner suggested abandoning the schema *De fontibus* because it dug up again a question contested by theologians, especially between Geiselmann,[39] who attempted to reduce the sources to Scripture, and Lennerz[40], from the Gregorian, who instead defended the common position: Scripture and Tradition

---

36 Cf. *Ibid.*

37 *Ibid.*, p. 42: 'De habitudine inter Scripturam et Traditionem. Nam in schemate propugnatur sententia, de qua usque ad nostrum tempus inter theologos, revera peritos, adhuc disputatur et de qua ex Traditione consensus unanimis non habetur'.

38 Cf. Rahner, *Sehnsucht nach*, pp. 150–163. Report for Cardinal König dated 19.9.1962, from Innsbruck.

39 Geiselmann, *Die Heilige Schrift und die Tradition: zu den neuren Kontroversen über das Verhältnis der Heiligen Schrift zu den nichtgeschriebenen Traditionen.*

40 Cf. H. Lennerz, 'Scriptura sola', in *Gregorianum* 40 (1959), pp. 38–53; Id., 'Sine scripto traditiones', in *Ibid.*, pp. 624–635.

are two ways through which Revelation comes to us.[41] This highlights how much the German episcopate depended largely on Rahner.[42]

Tradition as a source of Revelation, was it therefore a problem of schools or rather did this problem serve as a 'pastoral path' in respect of the separated brethren, ignoring, therefore, what Tradition itself unanimously had received and handed on? These last interventions aroused an articulated and bright summing up from Mgr Parente, who spoke not as assessor from the Holy Office but as titular Archbishop of Tolemaide. Thus, starting from the Tridentine text: 'libris scriptis et sine scripto traditionibus', drawn up during the IV session and read without prejudice, Parente was able to conclude that truth and discipline were contained in the written books and non-written traditions; therefore, by way of conclusion, the Tridentine canon anathematized those who consciously did not accept either the inspired books contained in the canon, nor the oral traditions.[43]

---

41 Cf. for an analysis of the two positions A. Buckenmaier, *"Schrift und Tradition" seit dem Vatikanum II. Vorgeschichte und Rezeption* (Paderborn: Bonifatius, 1996), pp. 198–207.

42 Cf. Rahner, *Sehnsucht nach*, pp. 158–159. In his report Rahner wrote: 'In fact the whole discussion around Geiselmann, Lennerz, etc., should be eliminated here, because on the one hand this is not an issue with a mature theological decision, and this should be resolved by the Council, and on the other hand the obvious and indispensable role of Tradition and the oral proclamation of the Magisterium, even in the face of a pronounced Protestant Biblicist mode, can be defined, if one wants, without listening to the questions of Geiselmann. Stakemeier has strongly complained that Tromp had no knowledge especially about the wishes of the Commission-Bea. From a reading of the famous French theologian Laurentin, I know that in France, too, there is a desire to avoid a stance being taken on this controversy' (*Ibid.*, pp. 158–159). As regards the complaints about Tromp, Rahner was referring to the rejection by the Doctrinal Commission to make contact, in the preparatory phase, with the Secretariat for Promoting Christian Unity.

43 'Si quis autem libros ipsos integros cum omnibus suis partibus prout in ecclesia catholica legi consueverunt et in veteri vulgata Latina editione habentur pro sacris et canonicis non susceperit et traditiones praedictas sciens et prudens contempserit: anathema sit': DH 1504.

For Parente it was certain that the Gospel was the unique source of Revelation or the Revelation of Christ, of Christ himself the Incarnate Word, which comes to us through two rivulets to be held with the same honour and with the same respect of faith. Therefore he suggested not recourse to sophistry about the traditions rather than Tradition; this had already been overcome by historians and theologians: it was about *Traditio* and divine-apostolic *traditiones*. The Council of Trent had not defined the relationship between Scripture and Tradition, but affirmed, as is obvious, that between the two there was a real distinction: this need to distinguish was energetically affirmed.[44]

The significance of the *et et* which replaced *partim* was unanimously acknowledged from the time of Trent as the distinction between the two sources. All the theologians after the Council of Trent for four centuries up to our days agreed in acknowledging the duality of the sources of Revelation. Were they all wrong, asked Parente? The Church's Magisterium itself had shown that some dogmatically defined truths could be found in Tradition; and with some difficulty or sometimes not even with difficulty in Scripture, such as the Immaculate Conception of Mary and above all her Assumption into heaven, as resulted from the respective dogmatic Bulls.[45]

With Parente's report, the problem of the material sufficiency/insufficiency of Scripture was also elucidated. The fact that no-one could demonstrate that everything had been written by the Apostles, can be proved, said Parente, with this argument: if God had wanted his Revelation to be handed on just in writing, why did

---

[44] Cf. AS I/3, pp. 132–134: 'Non satis igitur est, *iuxta mentem Concilii Tridentini, non satis est* catholico suscipere libros scriptos tamquam fontem *revelationis divinae* [veritatis revelatae], sed debet pari fide amplecti "sine scripto traditiones". (*Neque sophisticeretur de traditionibus potiusquam de Traditione; iam historici et theologi hoc superarunt; est Traditio et traditiones, sed tamen divino-apostolica*). Concilium non definit quaenam sit habitude utriusque fontis, sed utriusque veram distinctionem et necessitate energice affirmat, uti patet', *Ibid.*, pp. 133–134.

[45] Cf. *Ibid.*, p. 134.

he allow some things therefore to be lost, as some Pauline epistles attest?[46] It is openly offensive, he went on, to say that for the Fathers of the Church and for the ancient theologians Scripture was sufficient from the material point of view. Parente quoted different witnesses in this regard, including Saint Irenaeus, Tertullian, Saint Basil, and Saint Augustine. Coming then to the scholastic theologians, he demonstrated that the question was known by these. For Saint Thomas, the things handed on orally by the apostles with the assistance of the Holy Spirit were preserved in the Church's observance by means of the succession of the faithful. Saint Bonaventure, too, attested to the existence of things not-written; and so on up to the modern theologians, such as Bellarmine, Franzelin, and Lennerz.[47]

46 Cf. *Ibid.*, pgs. 134–135.

47 Here is the original address in this key passage on the material insufficiency of the Scriptures in the Fathers and the theologians: '[Iam] saeculo II Irenaeus [(*Adv. Haer.* III, 3)] potiusquam ad Sacram Scripturam, ad traditiones orales Ecclesiarum, praesertim Romanae, provocat, ut pura veritas fidei inveniatur. Item Tertullianus in *Praescriptione haereticorum.* Quarto saeculo, [perspicue] Basilius, in *De Spiritu Sancto*, n. 27: "Ex asservatis in Ecclesia dogmatibus et praedicationibus, alia quidem habemus e doctrina scripto *tradita* [prodita], alia vero nobis in mysterio tradita recepimus ex traditione Apostolorum". [*Epiphanius* (*Panarion* 61): "Sed traditione quoque opus est: neque enim ex Scripturis peti possunt omnia; idcirco alia Scripturis, in traditionibus alia sancti Apostoli reliquerunt". *Augustinus*, De Baptismo, V, 23: "... sunt multa quae universa tenet Ecclesia et ob hoc Apostolis praecepta bene creduntur, quamquam scripta non reperiantur". Inter theologos scholasticos: *S. Bonaventura*, in III Sent., d. 9, a. 1: "Dicendum quod multa Apostoli tradiderunt, quae tamen non sunt scripta". *S. Thomas*, S. Th. III, q. 25, a. 3, ad 4: "Apostoli familiari instinctu Spiritus Sancti quaedam Ecclesiae tradiderunt servanda, quae non reliquerunt in scriptis, sed in observatione Ecclesiae per successionem fidelium". Angustia temporis sat multa alia omitto: si quis plura cupiat, adeat Bellarminum, Franzelin et Lennerz, qui de hac re ultimis diebus vitae suae consueto acumine et eruditione disseruit in *Gregorianum* (1959–60–61)]', (*Ibid.*, pp. 135–136). Parente was also referring, in his intervention, to the J. R. Geiselmann issue, about whom he said: 'textum tridentinum torturae subiciit ut faveat formulae lutheranae de Scriptura sola, quam Patribus Concilii tribuere audit, nescio qua fonte', *Ibid.*, p. 136.

He was then called to order because the time at his disposal had elapsed. And so Cardinal Frings was persuaded to apologise for not having expressed himself clearly in his previous intervention, due to poor sight, meaning he was forced to say many things from memory. He corrected himself saying that 'in the order of being there is one source, Revelation itself, from which arise two rivulets, Sacred Scripture and Tradition'.[48] Cardinal Caggiano (Archbishop of Buenos Aires), too, observed that the problem of the duality of the sources was not a disputed issue; it was unanimously accepted. The problem was not discussed among Catholics but among Christians. Now, if they, too, sought the truth and venerated it, it would be good to be clear out of love for charity, and this in obedience to the inaugural words of John XXIII, according to which there was a need to proclaim the teaching in a complete manner.[49] However, it was precisely the Pope's inaugural discourse which lent itself to diverse interpretations; above all it provided a large group of Council Fathers with an opportunity to renounce the prepared schema in the name of the Pope's request for a pastoral council. Thus with the Council began the first great hermeneutic problem of the Council.

What has been mapped out up to now was one of the most theological disputes about the prepared schema. However, more time was taken up by the *disceptatio*, concerning the acceptance or otherwise of the schema as such. Various Fathers, such as Cardinal Ruffini,[50] Cardinal Siri,[51] asked, in respect for the norms of the Council, that the schema be welcomed, and discussed and modified where necessary. Normally, those who were in favour of the schema

48 *Ibid.*, p. 139.

49 Cf. *Ibid.*, pp. 71–73. Cardinal Browne, on the other hand, underlined that the ordinary Magisterium of the Church was expressed in the same way by the extraordinary Magisterium: Scripture and Tradition were two sources of the transmission of Revelation. He quoted Leo XIII, *Providentissimus Deus*; Saint Pius X, in the anti-modernist oath; Pius XII, *Humani generis*, cf. *Ibid.*, p. 83.

50 Cf. *Ibid.*, p. 37.

51 Cf. *Ibid.*, p. 38.

were not against modifications being made, a sign of the will to dialogue. For example, Siri asked that more space be given to the treatment of Sacred Scripture, since the space devoted to Tradition was not proportional in comparison to that devoted to Scripture.[52] Caggiano and others had expressed a *placet iuxta modum*.[53] Archbishop Morcillo Gonzalez, while he defended the schema, redeeming it from the accusations of being insufficiently pastoral and ecumenical, suggested an improvement in style in order to be more responsive to the times and asked that the material insufficiency of Scripture not be defined: otherwise the contrary judgement which, with just freedom, was taught among Catholics, would be condemned.[54]

The most recurring and decisive objection to the schema came from different Fathers, who as a rule made recourse to John XXIII's address *Gaudet mater ecclesia*, as nullifying the real stakes: was a rigid schema like *De fontibus*, doctrinally too scholastic and insufficiently pastoral, appropriate for the times and the desire of the Pope?[55] Was not the so longed-for unity of Christians perhaps decisively compromised by this, favouring instead their estrangement? One of the most authoritative advocates of this vision was Cardinal Léger:

> It was contrary to the spirit of a positive renewal desired by the Supreme Pontiff for the present Council, to establish a consti-

---

52 Cf. *Ibid.*, p. 39.

53 Cf. *Ibid.*, p. 73.

54 Cf. *Ibid.*, pp. 59–62: 'Veniam nunc denique ad quosdam defectus particulares alicuis momenti. Et imprimis propositio secundum quam Traditio continet veritates revelata nullo modo in Scriptura contentas. Qua doctrina, si definiatur, damnaretur sententia, quae, aequa libertate, inter catholicos docetur; et hoc verum est. Unde oportet ut propositio ista emendatione mandaretur', *Ibid.*, p. 61.

55 Ruggieri, showing how some Fathers were inspired by the Pope's *Gaudet* even to the extent of paraphrasing it, notes: 'While a theologian might perhaps have some quarrel with the sharp distinction between the presentation of doctrine and doctrine itself, this was the position taken in *Gaudet Mater Ecclesia*", Ruggieri, 'The First Doctrinal Clash', p. 254.

> tution on the fear of errors… errors must not blind the Church. In fact nothing encourages the influence of evil so much as a negative position which reverberates over passive Catholics and restrains their fruitful action, weakening it… Contrary to that a clear and positive way of speaking helps Catholics, attracts non-Catholics and restores the audible teaching of the Church to all men.[56]

Cardinal Alfrink, too, was of the same opinion. The schema on the sources of Revelation did nothing but repeat what could be found in any manual of theology, hardly finding there any additional new study. Instead, then, this was the time to recall the words of John XXIII, according to whom there was no need to call a Council for such a discussion.[57] And he would put it thus:

> These are the moments more than ever to look to the unity of Christians, about which the Supreme Pontiff himself said many beautiful things in his allocution.[58]

According to Cardinal Bea the schema, as it was proposed, did not respond to the aim indicated by the Supreme Pontiff, which was not that of debating doctrinal issues, but rather that of presenting teaching in a way suitable for modern times. So the schema was lacking in that pastoral character. What was said was true, that the pastoral has its foundation in doctrine, but for Bea the foundation was not to be identified with the pastoral, it was simply a foundation. In the vision rejected by Bea, every manual of theology and exegesis could be defined as pastoral. But that is precisely what they lacked.[59]

---

56 AS I/3, pp. 41–42.

57 'Etenim ad huiusmodi tantum disputationes habendas non opus erat, ut Concilium Oecumenicum indiceretur', AS I/1, p. 172.

58 AS I/3, p. 44.

59 'Verum quidem est, ut antea dictum est, omnem doctrinam esse fundamentum doctrinae pastoralis et praxis pastoralis, sed fundamentum non est ipsa res, est fundamentum. Secus omnis tractatus theologicus, omne manual scripturisticum, posset dici sine ambiguitate tractatus pastoralis, quod certe non obtinet', *Ibid.*, p. 49.

So Bea formulated a vote: to replace the schema with a new one, 'shorter, clearer, less ambiguous, mainly pastoral and mainly ecumenical. If this is done, certainly the schema can be of great benefit for the modern world ...'[60]

The same Léger-Alfrink-Bea vision could be found in Cardinal J. Ch. Lefèbvre (Archbishop of Bourges),[61] in Cardinal Silva Henriquez[62] and in Archbishop Bengsch.[63] For Archbishop Seogijapranata, who spoke on behalf of the Indonesian bishops, the schema should be rejected because it did not respond to the aims of the Council, which he clarified in three points: 1) to preserve and promote the faith among the faithful of this time; 2) to renew the (Christian?) life and encourage the witness of the faithful; 3) to adapt the way of proposing Christian doctrine to the needs of this time, the era of scientific progress, as well as the age of atheism, materialism, non-religiosity and moral decadence.[64]

For the Melkite Patriarch, Maximos IV Saigh, who spoke in French, the Council had to remain outside what he described as a 'dispute between schools',[65] in relation to the discussion about two sources of Revelation. According to his judgement, there was no need to go ahead in the Council with formulating new definitions of faith. Here there was a major risk: to restate the Church's traditional views or to stop the harmonious development of dogma. On the ecumenical level the schema ran the risk of repeating the now outdated formula ('formules dépassées') of the Counter Reformation and Anti-modernism.[66] In a truly ambiguous speech, Saigh asked the Council to re-establish the balance between the head and the body, destabilised by the First Vatican Council. The Church—the clergy and the

[60] *Ibid.*, p. 51.
[61] *Ibid.*, pp. 75–76.
[62] *Ibid.*, pp. 80–81.
[63] *Ibid.*, pp. 87–89.
[64] Cf. *Ibid.*, pp. 58–59.
[65] *Ibid.*, p. 53.
[66] *Ibid.*, p. 54.

faithful—seemed to him like 'a dwarf deprived of its vital strength' ('un nain démuni de ses puissance vitales').[67] It was necessary to put aside a school classroom issue and give precedence to the schema on the Church and on the sacred hierarchy, moving on then to issues of a social and pastoral order. The whole world, in his words, was expecting this from the Council.[68]

Certainly the schema could be improved as regards pastoral style, but the insistence on disapproval did not focus on the style per se, but on the substance expressed in a manner which did not correspond to the aims of the Council, and was contrary to the Pope's wishes. The substance of the teaching was safe for the most part, but a new methodology was required, which linked the pastoral and the doctrine. This still somewhat nebulous discourse became clearer with the intervention of Bishop De Smedt, who spoke on behalf of the Secretariat for Promoting Christian Unity. He immediately went to the heart of the matter, asking: what is needed so that a doctrine and a specific style might serve to improve dialogue between Catholics and non-Catholics? We must all return to the one Christ. All accept Him, Catholics and non-Catholics. However, when reference is made to the *way* in which one gains access to Christ, that is where disharmony begins. For centuries the method of defence was used, which, in his judgment, produced no progress in reconciliation. So therefore it was time to present a new method, thus conceived by him:

> The characteristic of this method is that it is not just concerned about the truth (to be set out) but also the way (to use) through which doctrine is set out so that it can be correctly and precisely understood by others... This new method can now be used in the Council as the Supreme Pontiff wishes it. Our conciliar expositions will have the ecumenical spirit if we make them actions by which non-Catholics can clearly under-

---

67 *Ibid.*

68 *Ibid.*

> stand how the Catholic Church sees and lives the mystery of Christ.[69]

The proposed schema should be judged by this new methodology. Therefore it was not, as many complained, a matter of a scant ecumenical spirit in the text. According to De Smedt at stake was a true and proper conciliar and theologically new methodology. The new nature of this method was what was called 'ecumenical dialogue'.[70] It could be asked: why was this discourse on ecumenism not tackled at the appropriate time and place, in the scheduled *disceptatio* on the schema *De oecumenismo*? Didn't the whole Council want to show itself in a new way, that is, ecumenical, also in questions concerning the doctrine of the faith and morals? In my opinion, here it is appropriate to explain a key idea for reading the conciliar Magisterium in its totality and in relation to the teachings: a pastoral Magisterium which *per se* does not surpass the level of authentic ordinary Magisterium, and which therefore *per se* is not renunciatory of the preceding extraordinary Magisterium or separated from it, but which necessarily presupposes it so as not to fall into a possible ambiguity. I will return to this issue.

Cardinal Florit's intervention, in favour of *De fontibus*, was focussed precisely on the methodological issue. The problem, in fact, was this: a new methodology for doctrine or an updated doctrine according to the new methodology. Florit said:

> As regards doctrinal substance, I consider that we all agree, rather than widely dissent about the method for proposing fundamental things. The main question at the moment is that of the *method*; if in fact it is a matter of believing the scholastic method, *which moreover was very much lessened in the proposed schema: I repeat, if the scholastic method is to be believed,* up to

---

69 *Ibid.*, p. 184.

70 *Ibid.*, p. 186: 'oramus hos Patres ut velint examinare utrum sufficienter consideraverint veram naturam novae methodi quae vocatur dialogus oecumenicus eiusque conditiones ac sequelas'.

> now approved by the Church and by its nature more certain, but less suited to today's mentality (in that the modern mind is more historical and longs for experience and religious emotion), or if a method is to be chosen, which we call historical-positive, which in recent years has been connected with the biblical-liturgical-patristic culture, seeing it prevail where a dispute of theological ideas with the Protestants is in force.[71]

So Florit suggested finding a higher synthesis between the two Catholics tendencies, cautioning, however, against the danger of falling into a dangerous subjectivism, by following the historical-positive method, ultimately so widespread also among Catholic exegetes, that, for example, through the hermeneutical method of *Formgeschichte*, the words of Christ reported by the evangelists were attributed to the (creating) mind of an *unconscious* community:[72]

The doctrinal and pastoral anxiety in the work of those who defend the first tendency can be easily perceived, in that the other judgment, by its nature, if it is not proceeded with great caution, gradually and despite the correct aim of those applying it, can open the path to a *dangerous* subjectivism, much more in that today's society is devoid of a philosophy and a world vision (Weltanschauung), capable itself of interpreting the present realities, without falling into pessimism and an 'existentialist' anguish.[73] For Florit, just as for Parente,[74] for Browne[75] and others, it was necessary to distinguish substance from

[71] *Ibid.*, p. 101.

[72] Cf. *Ibid.*, p. 103.

[73] *Ibid.*, pp. 101–102.

[74] 'Opportunum censeo distinguere schematis substantiam, quae essentialis est, ab eius forma, quae est accidentalis. Imprimis et super omnia de substantia rerum disputandum *esset*, nempe de principiis quae in schemate proponuntur, ut consensus attingatur in re tanti momenti', *Ibid.*, p. 132.

[75] For example, concerning the scant ecumenicity of the schema *De fontibus*, Cardinal Browne suggested not reinterpreting the sacred doctrine, but using charity towards the Protestants, helping them to resolve their doubts, in that the greatest difficulty concerned precisely the Catholic teaching on the Church and the primacy of the Pope, (cf. *Ibid.*, p. 82). Cardinal McIntyre

its form. A different view, however, was held by Bea, Meyer[76] and De Smedt, for whom, when all was said and done, this distinction was still linked to a scholastic formula, no longer suitable for the time and for systematic and exegetical development.

Cardinal Florit was convinced that the 'task of the Good Shepherd is that of defending the flock from errors'.[77] Cardinal Ritter, on the other hand, was of a different opinion:

> If the Council has solutions to the current problems, he said, it should present them in a clear and distinct manner. If the solutions are missing, the Council should say this, too, or remain silent. If errors exist, it must show them and condemn them. However, the Council must abstain from saying things that are not helpful, which endanger unity and give rise to suspicion.[78]

These were two diametrically opposed visions, which often faced each other bitterly in the Council. For me, the second view, which I summarised in the interventions of Bea, De Smedt and Ritter, came off better. This, which would constitute a real pastoral principle of the Council, can be best indicated in the words of Cardinal Bea himself:

> It is not sufficient to simply propose Catholic teaching. It is necessary to propose it in a way in which our non-Catholic brothers can understand it and look to its foundation. If we speak about Sacred Scripture, it is not sufficient to repeat what has already been said, but what today expresses greatest difficulty for our separated brethren. Generally there is no mention of this in the schema.[79]

---

concurred with this view, cf. *Ibid.*, p. 70.

76 Cardinal Meyer suggested re-working the schema with the co-operation of theologians and exegetes from different countries and of varying tendencies, so that the outcome might demonstrate trust in Catholic exegetical work and thereby take into account the Popes' openings in this area, particularly that of Pius XII, cf. *Ibid.*, pp. 169–170.

77 *Ibid.*, p. 103.

78 *Ibid.*, p. 48.

79 *Ibid.*, p. 50: 'Non sufficit proponere simpliciter doctrinam catholicam. Oportet

1.2.3 A first evaluation

The discussion about *De fontibus,* which began the *disceptatio* on the schema prepared by the Central Commission and approved by the Pope, is of great importance for gathering the first signals—moreover programmatic—about the conciliar mind. Discussion about a specific text gradually widened out to a broader problem, that of the Council in its entirety, in its positioning itself with regard to the world of today, to culture, to the biblical-theological factors of the last century. John XXIII's address, *Gaudet mater ecclesia,* was the real trailblazer of the Council[80] and cause of a major dispute about the aim of the Council: what was the real meaning of a pastoral Magisterium? To present doctrine with clarity, condemning errors for the good and progress of faithful or to formulate the same teaching in a more optimistic way with regards to modern times? So the Council already began with the problem of its correct hermeneutic. Two schools emerged, two sides, two visions of Christianity and its ancient and venerable Tradition,

---

eam proponere eo modo ut nostri fratres non-catholici eam intelligere possint et eius fundamenta perspiciant. Si loquimur de Sacra Scriptura, non sufficit repetere ea quae iam dicta sunt, sed ea quae hodie respiciunt difficultates qua fratres nostri non-catholici habent. Et de hac re in schemate fere nihil habetur'.

80 According to Congar, this inaugural address was a 'discreet criticism' of the negative vision of the four preparatory dogmatic schema (*De fontibus, De ordine morali, De deposito fidei,* and the *Formula nuova Professionis Fidei*), whose sources were Trent, Vatican I, the Encyclicals *Pascendi, Mediator Dei, Humani generis,* and the anti-modernist decree *Lamentabili,* (cf. Y. Congar, 'Erinnerungen an eine Episode auf dem II. Vatikanischen Konzil', in Klinger—Wittstadt (eds.), *Glaube im Prozess,* p. 22; abbreviated: Y. Congar, *Erinnerungen*). According to P. Smulders, on the other hand, Pope John, during the preparatory period, in various addresses and above all in the opening address of the Council, let it be known that he was satisfied with the work of the Theological Commission. This would also emerge from a comparison of the Italian and Latin texts of the opening address. The Latin text did not give the sense of the Pope's hesitations, expressed with more emphasis in the Italian text, both published in *L'Osservatore Romano* on 12 October 1962, pp. 2–3, cf. P. Smulders, 'Zum Werdegang des Konzilskapitels "Die Offenbarung selbst"', in *Ibid.,* p. 105.

which we can summarise by describing one as conservative and the other progressive.

The opposition began with the problem of the relationship between Scripture and Tradition and unravelled also in the way of presenting the inspiration and historicity of the Gospels. The schema, with notable emphasis, underlined the priority of Tradition compared to Scripture, to the point of being, for some, a schema about Tradition. This would have enraged the Protestants, who, on top of all that, had also been invited to the Council. The arguments led to asking for its re-formulation, but they were almost all very weak. Tradition as a source of Revelation equal to Scripture, was not a question of theological schools and in addition still the subject of debate. It was a unanimous fact of the handing on itself of the deposit of faith, from the Apostles through the Fathers, the councils, right up to the preparatory schema itself on the sources of Revelation. The Christian faith had decided, through the Magisterium, that there were two paths through which the one Gospel of salvation was revealed: Sacred Scripture and Tradition. The term 'source', so suspicious to theologians dissenting from the schema, certainly did not want to express that Scripture or Tradition were the origin of Revelation. The origin, the *Ursprung,* was certainly God, in Revelation itself, in the Gospel. 'Source' alluded to the sources of Revelation as much as their handing on and consigning to the Church. It was suffice to explain it a bit more clearly, reading n. 4 of the schema *De fontibus* in the light of the first three paragraphs (on Revelation and its diffusion), rather than, as would be done, eliding completely the clear proposal, to the point of seriously endangering the very cogency of Tradition for the transmission of the *depositum fidei.* 'Tradition' then summed up the Tridentine sense of the 'unwritten traditions', understood both as 'traditions', that is to say cultic, liturgical customs, as well as 'Tradition', that is the unwritten handing on of Revelation. Here, consequently, is placed the material insufficiency of the Sacred Scriptures in the handing on of revealed truths.

The fundamental problem of the request for a particular emphasis to be placed on the Word of God to re-appraise ecumenically the significance of Tradition was easily found in making the Word of God equal to Sacred Scripture. To indicate the Word of God as sole source could only be corrected if oral preaching and written transmission could be verified in it. According to some experts, appointed by the Italian Bishops' Conference with the aim of providing their observations on the schema *De fontibus*, it was equivalent to stating that above the two sources of Revelation there was a sole source, the Word of God (in Latin *Verbum Dei*). Sacred Scripture is fixed in the whole of Christian Tradition through the *Verbum Dei*. The prophets proclaimed and wrote the *Verbum Dei*. In the New Testament the preaching of Christ and the Gospel are called *Verbum Dei* (cf. Mk 7:13; Lk 5:1; Ac 4:13; 2 Co. 2:17, etc.). Now, the *Verbum Dei* was only known by means of Scripture and Tradition. If these two were removed, consequently the means by which the Word of God could be known would be eliminated.[81]

---

81 AA.VV., *Osservazioni raccolte dagli esperti nominati dalla Conferenza Episcopale Italiana. In schema De Fontibus Revelationis Animadversiones* (a text comprising 15 pages including a Propositio: 'SUPER DUOS FONTES REVELATIONIS EST UNICA ORIGO, SCILICET VERBUM DEI'), in AEF, Folder 2, Schema 'De divina revelatione'. The judgment of the theologians of the Italian Bishops' Conference highlights the equivocal nature of the proposition as formulated above and the need to preserve Scripture and Tradition to know the Word of God. For Protestantism, Sacred Scripture is like a 'hand of God' in Christ, but the supreme, perfect and divine revelation is that made in Christ, in the events and figures about whom the Bible speaks: therefore not in the book, but outside the Bible, and by reason of it the Church and the Bible is judged. This errs of subjectivism, since the work of Christ and his person can only be known by means of Sacred Scripture and Tradition. Therefore, and this is the conclusion, if Sacred Scripture is not assumed as a 'source' of Revelation the possibility of knowing the Revelation of Christ is eliminated. Here is the text examining the Propositio:'Affirmatio est aequivoca. Nam unus fons Divinae Revelationis est et vocatur "Verbum Dei". Nam S. Scriptura ita in tota traditione hoc nomine designatur. Prophetae "Verbum Dei" loquuntur et scribunt. In N. T. praedicatio Christi et evangelium vocantur "Verbum Dei"

So it was necessary to distinguish the two sources—or better still, the two rivulets—even if the term in itself was not pleasing, needing to be replaced with a new, more appropriate one. But sometimes the brief conciliar interventions left no room for these in-depth examinations.

Another somewhat unambiguous and disconcerting fact should be underlined: reference was often made to the 'separated brethren' and to the ecumenical dialogue to be boosted, of which the incipient Council represented a great promise. But this was thinking, almost in one direction, about the Protestant brothers and their ecumenical difficulties. What about the separated brethren from the East? Concern was rarely given to their position with regard to Tradition, which in truth could be a help to resolving the issue, without needing to do all the work again. It was Bishop Franić who brought this deficiency to the attention of the Council, a somewhat embarrassing shortfall for a pastoral work which was taking great care to be ecumenical at all costs. Bringing his direct experience, he attested to the fact that the Orthodox Serbs considered Tradition as a second source of Revelation after Scripture.[82]

(Mk 7:13; Luke 5:1; Act 4:31; 2 Cor. 2:17 etc. etc.).Verbum Dei non cognoscitur nisi ex S. Scriptura et ex Traditione. Si igitur haec duo tolluntur, eliminantur ea ex quibus Verbum Dei cognosci potest.Propositio si intelligitur in sensu quod supra S. Scriptura et Traditionis auctoritatem sit aliquod Verbum Dei indeterminatum, redolet protestantismus. Nam protestantes retinent revelationem supremam, perfectam et divinam factam esse in Christo. Ergo non in libro; sed extra Biblia. Biblia tantummodo referent "manum Dei" fuisse in Christo et in eventibus et in personis de quibus ipsa agunt. In hoc est eius auctoritas. Igitur ex revelatione facta per Christum diiudicandum est de Ecclesia et de Bibliis. Haec theoria docetur, v.g., a H. H. Rowley, *The Authority of the Bible*, Birmingham 1949; W. Robinson, 'The Authority of the Bible', in *The Expository Times* 62, 1950, 76–79 etc. Sed peccat subiectivismus, quia opus Christi et eius persona non aliunde cognoscuntur quam ex Sacris scripturis et Traditione. Si itaque negatur earum auctoritas, neque doctrina de Christo ex illis deducta tuta esse potest. Quin immo si S. Scriptura non assumitur uti fons revelationis Christi, non daretur fons pro cognoscenda revelatione ipsius Christi. Ergo S. Scriptura fons necessarius pro revelatione cognoscenda statuenda est'.

Finally, the real problem was the *method*. However, there was even disagreement about its purpose. Method for the conservatives was to tell the truth in charity, without renouncing setting out doctrine according to a conciliar *canon*. Method for the progressives was to guide doctrine ecumenically; a charity, that is, not against the truth, but without its necessary payability. This was the reason for the compromises to which it was often necessary to turn for the final approval of a document. This schema would be a privileged testimony to this arduous expressive endeavour.

1.2.4 The decisive opinion of theologians

I have already outlined previously the significant influence of theologians in the preparation for the Council and its development. Here I will focus above all on the judgment of some theologians—who revealed themselves to be the most influential—on the schema *De fontibus*. It is a matter of reports, conferences and drafts of real and proper alternative schema, to be suggested to the Fathers. In fact, the reaction of a great number of Fathers, supported by their theologians, was to reject not just *De fontibus* but the first four dogmatic schema. For example, Rahner suggested starting the discussion in Council from the schema on the liturgy and on the unity of the Church in relation to ecumenism (schema V and VII). Both better expressed the pastoral reason for the Council desired by the Pope.

> Schema V, Rahner said, among all of them seems to be the most mature and balanced (*das reifste und ausgewogenste*); it is dealing with an issue which, unlike the dogmatic and moral themes of the first schema, can count on a positive understanding on the part of the faithful and an openness to the world, it offers more possibilities that the unity and love of the Council may be exercised with it, showing it to the world.[83]

---

82 Cf. AS I/3, p. 246.

83 Rahner, *Sehnsucht nach*, pp. 156–157. The same report from Rahner for Cardinal König, dated 19.9.1962 from Innsbruck.

The decision not to follow the order of business at the opening of the discussions on the schema, according to the schedule of the schema sent to the Fathers, was a dramatic turn of events. It began, in fact, on 22 October 1962, with the schema on the sacred liturgy. According to Küng, it was a tactic to take time and so organise the rejection of the dogmatic schema. E. Schillebeeckx, too, had made the same suggestion, in one of his judgments on the first four schema, prepared for the Dutch bishops.[84] Schillebeeckx's comment on the first dogmatic schema, translated into Latin (47 pages) and English (57 pages, not corresponding with the Latin text), was distributed first of all anonymously and reached almost 2,600 copies distributed among the Fathers, with the title *Animadversiones in primam seriem schematum constitutionum et decretorum de quibus disceptatur in Concilii sessionibus.*[85] It was a proposal to show how the Council needed a new theological leaning. Therefore it was necessary to take time to re-draft the schema, so that they might be fruit of the work of a pluralist theology and not just an echo of Roman theology. The only source of moral and religious values was the Gospel; for that reason Schillebeeckx suggested putting as a preamble to the schema *De fontibus* chapter IV of the schema *De deposito*, which spoke about Revelation. In particular, the Belgian Dominican spoke out against the language of the two sources of Revelation. In the English translation of his report, Schillebeeckx distinguished between 'revelation-in-reality' and 'revelation-in-word'. In his opinion, the schema *De fontibus* constituted a devaluation of 'revelation-in-reality' to the almost exclusive benefit of 'revelation-in-word'. Revelation through the word was

84 Cf. Congar, *My Journal of the Council*, p. 161.

85 Cf. Fogarty, 'The Council Gets Underway', pp. 73–74. The text was composed hurriedly. The *Animadversiones* were not even reviewed. Fogarty notes: 'This may be the reason why they are not "completely correct", as Semmelroth notes in his diary (November 11, 1962), probably referring to the statement that the encyclical Humani generis had followed Trent on the question of the "two sources". This is mistaken; the encyclical explicitly speaks of "sources of revelation" (DS 3883)', *Ibid.*, footnote 20.

manifestation of the revelation in its very essence as 'revelation-in-reality', because manifestation of something supernatural.[86] For Schillebeeckx, the theory of the two sources had been surpassed by the theology of the last thirty years. Starting from the fact that there were truths also present in the oral as well as written tradition, this theory was based 'on the presumption that revelation is other than the communication of a set of conceptual truths. This change in terminology is unfortunate' with the risk of forgetting revelation in itself, which he defined precisely as 'revelation-in-reality'.[87] This theological judgment would be very influential in the passage to the new theology of Revelation.

In his theological work aimed at re-directing the work of the schema on the sources of Revelation, Ratzinger also distinguished himself according to a renewed theology in the very concept of 'revelation'. Ratzinger supported an important passage: the problem would be shifted from Tradition to Revelation itself and this would also indicate the path of the new schema *De divina revelatione*.[88] On

86 Cf. B. J. Cahill, *The renewal of Revelation Theology (1960–1962). The development and responses to the fourth chapter of the preparatory schema De deposito fidei* (Rome: Pontificia Università Gregoriana, 1999, doctoral thesis), pp. 152–157; Cf. also Montaldi, *In fide ipsa essentia revelationis*, pp. 216–217. Montaldi, in appendix L of his book, published an extract of the English version of Schillebeeckx's report. The entire English text of Schillebeeckx's comments on the 'first series' of conciliar schema is in ASV, Envelope 759, folder 247, published in KT 2/2, pp. 948–991: *Commentary on the "prima series" of the "Schemata Constitutionum Decretorum de quibus disceptabitur in concilii sessionibus"*.

87 KT 2/2, pp. 949.

88 In his comment on *Dei verbum*, Ratzinger would say, with regard to chapter I *De ipsa revelatione*, that the text of *De fontibus*, not having a chapter on Revelation, had limited its teaching to the theme of the two sources, a teaching 'from the time of historicism' with its 'fixation on seeing the "positive" characteristic, which here freely, unconsciously, is presented in the guise of ecclesial traditionalism. To the more important processes in the struggle for the Constitution on Revelation without doubt belongs the breach (Durchbruch) through which this restricted view (Blickverengung), the counter-

10 October 1962 Ratzinger gave a conference to the German Fathers on the schema *De fontibus*. Here he distinguished three main problems arising from the schema: the relationship between Scripture and Tradition, the problem of inspiration, and the relationship between the Old and New Testaments. In his opinion, to present Scripture and Tradition as two sources was ambiguous, because both were quite the same Revelation. The Revelation of God is the source, from which, like two rivulets, flow Scripture and Tradition. For Ratzinger, the Council should not be seen as a battle against some theological schools, but against those who rejected the core of faith. The world was waiting for the answer of faith in the hour of unbelief.[89]

Ratzinger, along with Rahner, then collaborated in the draft of a new schema, an alternative to *De fontibus*, entitled *De revelatione Dei et hominis in Jesu Christi facta*. A study group had in fact been created, gathered around the Bishop of Mainz, H. Volk.[90] In the schema the

---

question on what happens for all the things fixed in the positive sources, when God "reveals" himself, and so a new awareness above all of the essence and foundation of Christian existence' (LThK[2], *Das Zweite Vatikanische Konzil*, II, p. 506). For Ratzinger, the discourse on *sources* was based fundamentally on a falsification of the concept of 'revelation', through an identification with its historical manifestations. Returning to the original concept of 'revelation', one could better connect Scripture and Tradition, so as not to present them more mechanically alongside each other, but in another (Ineinander), more organic fashion. Thus Scripture acts as a 'measure' (Maßstab) and verification for Tradition and Tradition 'preserves' Scripture, cf. *Ibid.*, pp. 518–526.

89 Cf. Montaldi, *In fide ipsa essentia revelationis*, pp. 215–216.

90 To H. Schauf, this group of German theologians, in which he also took part, gave the impression of being a political group rather than a study meeting. On 14 November 1962, Schauf noted in his *Diario*: 'In the afternoon I was at the meeting of the German theologians. It was more a conspiracy (Verschwörung) and a political meeting than a theological dialogue. When once again the delay did not make the whole schema collapse, then a unique criticism should be made, continually, by those most able, to achieve what is longed for. I openly said to Lengeling, to Bishop Pohlschneider, to Archbishop Schäufele, that I was not happy with the way of doing things', H. Schauf, 'Auf dem Wege zu der Aussage der dogmatischen Konstitution über die göttliche Offenbarung

different minds of the two theologians can be identified. The first part was edited by Rahner: this can be recognised from the teaching and style (even the somewhat-tangled Latin conveys the complexity of the author's thought), while the second, on the relationship between Scripture and Tradition, was Ratzinger's.

Congar, in his introduction to the text, informs us that the classical theses of Rahner were easily recognisable in it. In fact, he says:

> The thesis 'Hörer des Wortes' of the supernatural 'existential', when not even that of the 'anonymous Christians', were in this text to be clearly perceived as a background.[91]

One thing immediately surprises the reader: in a writing on divine Revelation (with the title 'La rivelazione di Dio e dell'uomo fatta in Gesù Cristo'),[92] the author immediately begins by speaking about the human person, made in the image of God, and of his vocation to be assimilated to God, participating in divine charity, without hiding a reference to his 'anonymous Christianity'.

"Dei verbum" n. 9 "Quo fit ut Ecclesia certitudinem suam de omnibus revelationis non per solam Sacram Scripturam hauriat"', in Klinger—Wittstadt (eds.), *Glaube im Prozess*, p. 67 (henceforth abbreviated as: Schauf, 'Auf dem Wege'). This is an important contribution from Schauf, especially because of some unpublished parts of his diary and for some acts of the Council's Theological Commission in reference to *Dei verbum* published here.

91 Cf. Congar, 'Erinnerungen', p. 28. As appendix to these memories of Congar (reported in *My Journal of the Council*) was published the Latin-German text of *De revelatione Dei et hominis in Jesu Christi facta* (pp. 35–50) and an alternative text of *De fontibus* by Congar himself, suggested as a preamble to the Rahner-Ratzinger schema (pp. 51–64), to which I will return.

92 According to H. Sauer, *Erfahrung und Glaube*, p. 121, who offers a comment on the Rahner-Ratzinger schema, the genitive form of the title: in Latin 'Dei et hominis', in German 'Gottes und Menschen', allows the interpretation in the sense of an objective and subjective genitive. In the first meaning, God himself becomes object of human knowledge, where 'God' is no longer an object of external and material knowledge, but above all foundation and horizon of all knowledge, therefore, in an excellent way, foundation and horizon of the same human consciousness. The whole comment is on pp. 121–136.

The human person, Rahner says, is ineluctably ('unausweichlich') in relation with God, both whether he or she knows it or not, or implicitly, when secretly he / she lives in his will, or preserves truth in injustice. The human person experiences always being provided with such breadth of spirit and will, which with truth can be said to be capable of the infinite, so as never to rest in the finite. Here is a key point of Rahner's thought: the human person at least implicitly[93] is in relation with such an ineffable mystery, in whose immeasurable depths every finite being has his or her origin, God.[94] In the Incarnate Word, says Rahner, is revealed both the truth about the human person and that about God.[95] And so chapter II sees an explanation of the hidden presence of God in the history of humanity. Again the concept of natural 'instinct' appears, open to the supernatural. Since the human person was created by God, it cannot not come about that at least in a hidden manner, as if by instinct, the person turns to the true God and that there disappears from the earthly orb the explicit

---

93 Is there in Rahner an implicit consciousness without it *already* being perception, even if still athematic, of the mystery, of God, understood as foundational concept of being as existence? Evidently not, otherwise implicit consciousness would have no reason to be. Due to the indissolubility in Rahner between being-existence and supernatural knowledge, profoundly linked through the supernatural existential, so as to devalue grace and demand it for nature, there is a real ambiguity in this thought, founding the anonymous Christian. Cf. my work, S. M. Lanzetta, 'Il caso Rahner: una critica eccesiva o teologicamente scorretta', in *Fides Catholica* 2 (2009) pp. 549–560.

94 Cf. Congar, 'Erinnerungen', pp. 34–35. The Latin text is as follows: 'Quapropter credidi nomine ineluctabiliter ad Deum referri, sive explicite iam cognoscat et agnoscat hanc suam ad Deum habitudinem, sive implicite occultis secundum Dei dispositionem modis tantum in ea vivat, sive veritatem in iniustitia detineat (cf. Rom. 1:29). Experitur enim homo semper sese tali mentis et voluntatis amplitudine praeditum, ut infini capax recte appellari possit et sic in finitis numquam quiescens saltem implicite ad illud ineffabile referatur mysterium, in cuius infinito abysso finite omnia sua habet originem, Deum', *Ibid.*

95 'In ipso Verbo Dei incarnato revelatur veritas tam hominis quam Dei. Revelatur quis sit homo', *Ibid.*, p. 36.

profession and worship of God. So the Church, according to the German Jesuit, mindful of the explicit salvific will of God, knows that no-one who has already reached the age of reason can perish, if not through their own fault, and that no one can save themselves unless through means of grace and faith in God.[96] Rahner omits the question of limbo for children who die without baptism and those without the use of reason.[97]

---

[96] The Latin texts states: 'Homo, ergo, cum ita ad Deum creates sit, numquam potest efficere, ne saltem arcano quasi instinctu referatur ad Deum verum, numquam, ne professio explicita et cultus Dei in orbe terrarium penitus evanescat. Saepe homines, ignorantes Deum verum, tamen eum coluerunt et colent et numquam cessarunt nec cessabunt quaerere, "Si forte attrectent eum aut inveniant" (Act 17:23, 27). Quapropter Ecclesia memor semper universalis voluntatis salvificae divinae scit neminem, qui ad usum rationis pervenerit, posse perire, nisi sua propria formali culpa, neminem salvari nisi gratia et fide in Deum (cf. Hebr 11:6)', *Ibid.*, p. 40.

[97] Rahner was very averse to the insertion of the question of limbo into chapter X of the preparatory schema *De deposito*. This can be deduced from his report, in which he revealed to Cardinal König that he was terrified by such a proposal. Rahner wrote: 'From where do the authors know what they assert "cum autem infantes ex sese sint huius voti incapaces" "since children are per se incapable of such a request" (3.9f.)? It this a statement of faith? Is it a certain knowledge of experience and metaphysics? Neither one nor the other... Why does this obscure question need to be defined? Why does this need to be done as we knew more than what God has revealed to us?' (Rahner, *Sehnsucht nach,*. pp. 105–106). In fact, Rahner questioned also the truth of 'monogenism', supported, in continuity with *Humani generis*, by *De deposito*. Was it not absolutely clear, if you were to ask the Jesuit, that biblical Adam was not instead the figure of an original group of parents, morally representative then of their descendants as regards original sin? How could only one constitute the beginning? (cf. *Ibid.*, pp. 101–103). Finally, Rahner questioned church celibacy, too. Celibacy was not directly and clearly of divine law, as it was instead guaranteeing the Church priests for sacred ministry. Therefore, according to Rahner, where it did not succeed in having a sufficient number of priests, such as in Latin America, the Church must have the courage, without fear of suffering any spiritual pain, of no longer requiring celibacy (cf. *Ibid.*, pp. 143–146). These three positions are part of the same report for Cardinal König, which

Chapter III is entitled *De revelata presentia Dei in praedicatione Ecclesiae*. The author is different, and Ratzinger's hand can be identified. Here are tackled in a more *ex professo* manner the themes of Scripture and Tradition. The emphasis moves to the Church, in which the Lord Jesus is present, and to the proclamation of the Gospel. In fact, the individual revealed truths, it is said, which can be read both in the Old and New Testaments and which are explained in the Church's teaching and preaching, can all be reduced to just one truth, Jesus Christ, God-man.[98] Through the testimony and preaching of this truth, Christ has established his Church, entrusting to her the office of an infallible Magisterium. Tradition is conceived in this ecclesial perspective by the spreading of the Gospel and its teaching. In fact, Tradition is

> The preaching, understood as action and preached reality, exercised by the legitimate successors of the apostles… This as a way of the actual presence of Christ revealed in the Church is to be venerated. But since the words of the Lord are 'spirit and life' (Jn. 6:64) this Tradition is not exercised solely by means of the legitimate preaching of the Word, but by means of the entire life of the Church, in primis through the use of the sacraments instituted by himself and among these above all the celebration of the Holy Eucharist.[99]

---

bears the date of 4 January 1962 and amounts to 36 type-written pages.

98 Cf. *Ibid.*, p. 43.

99 *Ibid.*, pp. 43–44: 'Haec praedicatio, ut actio et ut res praedicata, a legitimis successoribus apostolorum exercita, traditio vocari solet. Hac igitur traditione, quam Ecclesia secundum mandatum Domini administrat, sermo Dei currit per saecula (cf. 2 Thess. 3:1); haec ut modus praesentiae actualis Christi revelati in Ecclesia veneranda est. Sed quia Verbum Domini "spiritus et vita" sunt (Jn. 6:64), haec traditio non solum praedicatione legitima verbi, sed tota vita Ecclesiae exercetur, in primis usu sacramentorum ab ipso institutorum et inter ea prae ceteris celebratione Sacrae Eucharistiae, sub cuius signis Christus sese tradit hominibus et homines tradit Patri per corpus suum crucifixum, resuscitatum, vivens in Gloria Dei'.

The Church claims its full right over Sacred Scripture, both for the New and the Old Testament, due to the fact that, in no other way if not by means of faith, they have been received by the Tradition of the Church, and by it they can be known with some certainty. Therefore,

> Scripture alone is not sufficient, but only in the living Tradition of the Church is the Word of God, which from our scattering calls us to be one new man (cf. Eph. 2:15), made live for us.[100]

So, for Ratzinger, the relationship between Scripture and the Church was dual. On the one hand the Church was bound to Scripture: the Church was not the owner but its handmaid. On the other hand, Scripture needed the Church which has the mandate of preaching and by the mandate of the Lord explains the Scriptures.

The schema closes with a preface which recalls the pastoral care which moves the Church in the present moment: it neither suggests a theological system, nor formulates new dogmas, but simply puts on the lamp-stand the light of the Gospel, so that its light may shine for all people.[101] Thus a notable emphasis and significant re-centering can be perceived: Tradition is conceived as the handing on of this Word of life which enlightens all people, of which the Church is the depository. The path for the new schema was thus to a great extent already marked out.

One of the most influential theologians during the whole span of the Council and moreover mainly hostile to the preparatory schema, in particular to *De deposito* and *De fontibus*, was certainly K. Rahner. Important in this regard is the testimony of Cardinal König, who wanted him as his theologian at the Council, until his promotion as peritus and member of the Theological Commission. König said:

> I myself was a member of the Theological Commission and so I can attest to Rahner's intense collaboration. Many of his

[100] *Ibid.*, p. 47: 'Numquam ergo Scriptura sola sufficit, sed in vita tantum traditione Ecclesiae fit pro nobis illud vivum Dei verbum, quod vocat nos ex dispersione nostra in unum novum hominem (cf. Eph. 2:15)'.

[101] *Ibid.*, p. 50.

> proposed formula were made their own by members of the Commission and of the Secretariat and inserted into the new texts which were being drawn up.[102]

However, Rahner did not hide his concern, when, before the start of the Council, he received the bad news of a censure from Rome to which his writings had to be subjected before publication. With a concerned tone about his enormous amount of work already planned, he said: 'No one can order me that under such circumstances something might come to mind in my poor brain'.[103] He would write nothing more. So he asked Cardinal König to take up his cause directly with John XXIII, concerned, too, about his reputation among young theologians. König, on 12 July 1962, wrote to the President of the German Bishops' Conference, Cardinal Frings, asking him to

---

102 F. König, 'Rahners theologisches Denken im Vergleich mit ausgewählten Textstellen der dogmatischen Konstitution "Lumen Gentium"', in Klinger—Wittstadt (eds.), *Glaube im Prozess*, p. 123. R. Laurentin also praised his presence at the Council, and said that Rahner, along with Frs Congar and de Lubac, was 'one of those people who during the pontificate of Pius XII was troubled. A few years before it would have been unthinkable that he would sit on a Roman Commission. That was a testimony to the forgiveness and broad dialogue which John XXIII had opened', (R. Laurentin, 'Ein Eindruck vom Konzil', in *Ibid.*, p. 65). See also the interview with K. Rahner, carried out by H. Sauer on 8 January 1982, at the Jesuit College in Innsbruck, about Rahner's work at the Council, particularly about the Constitution on Divine Revelation, cf. Sauer, *Erfahrung und Glaube*, pp. 762–769.

103 This is correspondence with Cardinal König, published, along with some of his (partial) conciliar reports, in *Entschluß* 43/6 (1988) 29. *Entschluß* is a monthly journal from the Austrian Jesuits. From the introduction to the publication we learn that Fr Georg Sporschill asked Cardinal König to make available Rahner's material on the Council and his correspondence with König. The choice of texts and comments was edited by H. Vorgrimler, who would re-publish them in 1990 (omitting the correspondence) in the already cited text, *Sehnsucht nach dem geheimnisvollen Gott*. Georg Sporschill, an Austrian Jesuit, recently published, with Cardinal Martini, *Conversazioni notturne a Gerusalemme. Sul rischio della fede* (Milan: Mondadori, 2008): a somewhat ambiguous book.

intervene with John XXIII, with Cardinal Alfrink also united to the cause. A letter signed by all three was given directly to John XXIII by Cardinal Bea. About a month later the problem was resolved. König wrote again to Rahner, on 25 August 1962, asking him to be his conciliar theologian, as well as for the whole of the Austrian Bishops' Conference. And so Rahner, without further concerns, was able to go to Rome with König to take part in the work of the Council.[104]

His general judgment on the first four schema was very negative. In a report about *De fontibus* dated 19 September 1962, Rahner criticised the title, symptomatic of its content: it should not talk about 'sources', but rather 'revelation' or the 'Word of God' (*de Verbo Dei*).[105] As well as writing with Ratzinger a text on revelation alternative to the schema, as we have already seen, he personally wrote a fuller report on *De fontibus*, entitled *Dissertatio brevis de schemate "De fontibus revelationis"*.[106] Here, Rahner demonstrated his concern for the diriment position of the text with regard to some of the still unresolved issues in the field of theology. In his opinion, the schema was barely pastoral, lacking in an ecumenical spirit and the assertions lacked a theological qualification. This last judgment is present in the report quoted above. Rahner asked at what level the Magisterium of *De fontibus* lay. It had always been said right from the outset that the Council did not want to define any new dogma. So would there be different levels of magisterial authority from what had existed previously? Was the defining magisterial authority of the Council only involved in the re-confirma-

---

104 Cf. *Entschluß* 43/6 (1988) 29–31. For further information on this difficult situation in which Rahner found himself and his getting overheated with those whom he described as 'terrible bigwigs' (members of the Roman Curia), see H. Vorgrimler, *Understanding Karl Rahner. An Introduction to his Life and Thought* (London: SCM Press Ltd, 1986), p. 150, (German original, *Karl Rahner verstehen. Eine Einführung in sein Leben und Deken*, [Freiburg im B.: Herder, 1985]).

105 Cf. Rahner, *Sehnsucht nach*, p. 158.

106 The text was published in the original Latin by Sauer, *Erfahrung und Glaube*, pp. 657–668.

tion of errors? These issues were to be resolved, and the preparatory text, in his opinion, did not offer a clear response.[107] A manifestation of the old conciliar style was pressed into a new pastoral framework. Unfortunately, still today Rahner's questions have not had a definitive response. The Council would refer to the theological interpretation and theologians would refer to the Council.

However, the *Dissertatio brevis* focussed its criticism above all on the absence of unanimity between theologians about the problem of the sufficiency / insufficiency of Scripture, but always having as an exegetical mirror the thesis of J. R. Geiselmann. According to Rahner, there was disagreement among theologians, verifiable in two assertions:

1. according to some, some truths of faith cannot be explained through the Scriptures, not even with an implicit reference and under the guidance of the Magisterium;
2. according to others, some truths implicitly or explicitly contained in Scripture cannot be explained through oral Tradition alone, with the testimonies of the first centuries. For example, the dogma of the Assumption has Scripture as its ultimate foundation. Therefore, according to Rahner, the Council could not resolve the question by proposing a constituent Tradition. Better instead to see the ultimate foundation of every revealed truth in Scripture. The truths of faith, even when not easily explained by the oral Tradition of the early centuries, however always spring from Sacred Scripture.[108] According to Rahner, thus another age-old problem was resolved: Geiselmann was not condemned and the Protestants would not have been scandalised.[109]

In the footsteps of Rahner, Y. Congar also busied himself so that the preparatory schema might be rejected, regarded as being barely

107 Cf. Rahner, *Sehnsucht nach*, pp. 157–158.

108 Sauer, *Erfahrung und Glaube*, pp. 663–664.

109 Cf. *Ibid.*, pp. 664–665.

pastoral and ecumenical.[110] Congar also wanted to propose an alternative text to *De fontibus*, focused entirely on divine Revelation with a marked ecumenical character.[111] The fact which emerges and which confirms the thesis I support is interesting: the desire to pursue the ecumenical goal especially in teaching and right from the outset; from the beginning, which is Revelation, thought had been given to the separated brethren. Of course Congar was not the whole Council, but is important to see reflected in him that *mens* which gradually developed more and more strongly. The theme of Tradition only appears in the Congar schema in passing and in a paragraph which, I think, could also be omitted.[112] The schema proceeds as follows: from Christ revelation of God to the Church, his body and people of God, into which one is incorporated through Baptism. The Church, unique bride of Christ, has the aim of gathering together into one all those

---

110 For an overall vision of Congar at the Council see W. Henn, 'Y. Congar al Vaticano II', in *Communio* 42 (1995), pp. 59–68. For his judgment on the schema see Congar's *My Journal of the Council*, pp. 151ff.

111 The text was published by Congar himself as an appendix to one of his writings and following on from the Rahner-Ratzinger text. Cf. Congar, *Erinnerungen*, pp. 51–64. In one of Congar's reports on *De fontibus*, an idea similar to that of Schillebeeckx's returns about Revelation: it is defined in an implicit manner and not only as *locutio formalis*, that is not just as manifestation of a word in the strict sense of the word, but of a word which leads to a series of statements of a propositional or thesis manual types. Thus one forgot the revealing God; the Revealing One and the act of revelation were forgotten in favour of a Revelation conceived as a certain supply of sentences, in which each went to make up a small bundle in the Church's basket. Biblical renewal had highlighted the biblical notion of 'Word', having a noetic and dynamic value, while philosophical reflection had placed the emphasis on the aspect of the *personal* revelation which the revealing of God and the faith which responds to him establish between us and the living God. These two orders of reflection, exegetical and philosophical, had a very certain ecumenical and spiritual value. Congar criticised a 'notion atomisée de la Révélation', no longer with an organic link with its scholastic teachings or life, cf. Y. Congar, 'Le Schema "De Revelatione"', in *Études et Documents*, n. 14, 11 July 1963, pp. 1–2.

112 Cf. Congar, *Erinnerungen*, p. 59.

who are in Christ: on the one hand all those who have received the baptismal purification, on the other hand all those who, outside the body of Christ, in an illegitimate manner, constitute ecclesial communions. The Church is called not so much to confirm unity in itself, but rather with all those who bear the name Christian.[113]

The theological reports were not without influence, they did not leave the situation as it was before. John XXIII established a Mixed Commission, which made provision for the longed-for collaboration between the Theological Commission and the Secretariat for Promoting Christian Unity: thus the schema could be re-drafted according to the favoured new theological leanings.

Before moving to an analysis of the new schema on Divine Revelation it is appropriate to draw attention in this circumstance to the initiative of 19 Cardinal signatories who, on 24 November 1962, addressed a letter directly to the Supreme Pontiff, manifesting to him their appreciation at his decision to transfer the schema *De fontibus* to a Mixed Commission and at the same time making clear that it was necessary for the Council to clearly state some doctrinal principles against arising deviations, especially in the exegetical field. According to these Fathers, concerned and saddened above all for the priests and seminary students, it was ever more widespread to read about doubts and even explicit denials of historical and objective truths of some Old and New Testament passages, the work of professors who furthermore benefitted from a diocesan *imprimatur*. So they wrote to the Pope:

> Most Holy Father,
>
> the undersigned Cardinals thank Your Holiness for the decision taken to transfer the schema on the Dogmatic Constitution 'De fontibus Revelationis' to a mixed Commission with the task of correcting the text, making it briefer, more precise and more in conformity with the aim of the Sacred Ecumenical Council.

[113] Cf. *Ibid.*, pp. 61–62.

At the same time, however, as Pastors of souls, with total submission, we wish to make it clear how necessary it is that the Ecumenical Council state clearly some doctrinal principles to assure the Catholic faith against the errors and diversions of our times, scattered a bit everywhere.

In some way it should be especially declared:

1. that divine Revelation (*locutio Dei ad homines*) is an external and public fact, historically ascertainable;
2. that the divine-Catholic Tradition is, as well as Sacred Scripture, means of divine Revelation;
3. that the divine-Catholic Tradition is necessary to guarantee the value itself of Sacred Scripture, and to interpret with clarity the obscure biblical texts, in matters of faith and morals;
4. that both Sacred Scripture and divine-Catholic Tradition are a remote rule of divine Revelation; the proximate rule is the living and unfailing Magisterium—ordinary and extraordinary—of the Holy Church, which sets out what is to be believed as divinely revealed truth that which is contained in the 'Depositum Fidei';
5. that Sacred Scripture must be interpreted with rational and therefore also literary criteria, but above all with the criteria of Catholic hermeneutics, which are principally:
    a) Sensus Ecclesiae, that is, 'sensus quem tenuit et tenet Sancta Mater Ecclesia';
    b) Interpretatio unanimis (morally 'unanimis') SS. Patrum;
    c) Analogia fidei.
6. that scientific, philological and historical studies are to be encouraged, for a broader and more precise knowledge of the Word of God, encouraging and fomenting in particular true progress in studies regarding the Semitic languages,

> archaeology and Ancient Eastern history, according to the papal Encyclicals 'Providentissimus Deus', 'Divino afflante Spiritu' and 'Humani generis'.
>
> We are particularly saddened and very concerned—above all for Priests and Seminarians—to notice that in authoritative publications, furnished with a regular ecclesiastical Imprimatur, it is dared to doubt or even deny the historical and objective historicity of important passages of the Old and New Testaments always believed to be true and real, with wonderment, and almost as a scandal, by the Jews themselves and various of the separated brethren, which seems positive to us'.[114]

On 4 December 1962, the Cardinal Secretary of State Cicognani wrote to Cardinal Ottaviani to bring him up-to-date about this petition about the schema 'De Fontibus Revelationis', and as President of the Mixed Commission sent him a copy of the text.[115]

2. *From the new schema to the Dogmatic Constitution De divina revelatione*

The clash over the text of *De fontibus* was very heated. The Fathers were divided. Therefore it was difficult to proceed. So it was proposed to vote on whether or not to interrupt the disquisition on the schema. However, the voting did not achieve the necessary two-thirds in favour of the interruption, as the presidency Council wanted. On 21 November 1962 there was a communiqué from the Secretary of the

114 AEF, Folder 2, Schema 'De divina revelatione'. The letter runs to five pages. The text continues in explaining some heterodox positions about the historicity of some of the pericopes of the Old and New Testaments, including the Annunciation itself. Recognisable among the signatories are the following Cardinals: G. Godfrey, G. T. Heard, A. Bacci, G. Câmara, A. Caggiano, S. Wyszynski, L. Traglia, F. Quiroga y Palacios, R. Santos, L. Concha, G. Siri, G. P. Agagianian, B. de Arriba y Castro, E. Ruffini.

115 Cf. ASV, Envelope 760, Folder 258 and AEF, Folder 2, Schema 'De divina revelatione'; Letter from the Secretary of State n. 94678, of Cardinal Cicognani to Cardinal Ottaviani with insert.

Council, Fr Felici, who expressed the Pope's desire to create a Mixed Commission for the study of a new schema on Revelation. The commission was chaired by the respective Cardinals of the Theological Commission and the Secretariat for Promoting Christian Unity, Ottaviani and Bea, with Fr Tromp and Mgr Willebrands as secretaries. Called to be part of the Mixed Commission from the College of Cardinals were Cardinals Liénart, Frings, Ruffini, Meyer, Lefèbvre and Brown. Thus began a long work of revision which would last as long as the Council. It was a unique case. The text, which then became *Dei verbum*, went through a bristly and thorny path: often it was necessary to proceed by agreements reached only after numerous discussions and reshuffles, and finally, as we shall see, to reach a significant (ecumenical) compromise. In the meetings from 25 November to 7 December 1962 the Mixed Commission proceeded with the revision of the structure of the schema, formulating a new title which omitted the problem of the duality of the sources: *De divina revelatione*. The work which followed, as Ratzinger confessed in his introduction to the Constitution, was always subject to a key problem, which remained with the text right up to the end: that *plus* of the Tradition compared to Scripture, that is to say, the problem of the material insufficiency of the Sacred Scriptures.[116]

---

[116] Cf. LThK², *Das Zweite Vatikanische Konzil*, II, p. 501. It is interesting what Tromp reports in his diary about the meeting of the *de Fontibus Revelationis* Mixed Commission, Session V, held on the afternoon of 7 December 1962, KT 2/1, pp. 163–165. The verbal typescript of the meeting is in ASV, Envelope 760, folder 260, published in KT 2/2 [Protokolle n. 12], pp. 871–881. There was opposition between Bea, according to whom a question about the distinction of the two sources should not be raised, and Ottaviani, Browne and Ruffini, who objected since it was a serious matter of faith at stake, *de re fidei*. According to Charrière and Griffiths the silence of the sub-commission on such a point, afterwards would not have had a negative but positive value and probably would have been explained mistakenly to the faithful. For the Secretary, especially in matters to do with the sacraments, not everything could be proved from Scripture alone. Rahner, on the other hand, defended the fact that *other truths*, excluding the canon, were implied in Sacred Scrip-

A decisive step forward was made on 23 February 1963, when it was agreed to leave the matter open: the Council was not called on to resolve it.[117] So the new formula adopted towards the end of February gained the approval of the President of the Co-ordinating Commission as well as that of the Pope himself.[118]

---

ture. A new formula was drafted to combine Scripture and Tradition, proposed by Parente and made his own by Bea: 'Divinae Revelationis thesaurus non solum in S. Script., sed etiam in S. Traditione asservatur, quae quidem ab Apostolis, sive a Christo sive a Sp. Sto edoctis profluens ad nos usque pervenit (Conc. Trid. S. IV; C. Vat s. III). Immo quaedam veritates revelatae praesertim quae ad singulorum librorum inspirationem, canonicitatem et integritatem Librorum Sacrorum spectant, non nisi ex Traditioni innotescunt vel clarescunt'. Put to the vote, there were 19 in favour of this formula, 16 against, and 6 abstentions. There is also a brief report with an explanatory note (cf. ASV, Envelope 760, folder 259, published in KT 2/2 [Dokumente 19.], pp. 1056–1058). In the note, inter alia, it says: 'Under pressure from ecumenism some modern theologians have tried to bring the Catholic position closer to the Protestant one, exalting Sacred Scripture, source of the whole of Revelation, and reducing Tradition to an explanation and illustration of Sacred Scripture. Hence the struggle, within the heart of the Council, against the expression "De Duplici Fonte Revelationis", which, for at least four centuries, has been in use in the schools and documents of the papal Magisterium. Mgr Parente had prepared a temporary formula which said: "S. Traditio latius patet quam S. Scriptura". Not having been accepted by the majority, he presented another which affirmed the presence of revealed truths in Tradition, which are not found in Sacred Scripture. This second formula was made his own by Cardinal Bea and was thus proposed for voting', KT 2/2, p. 1058.

117 According to Tromp's report, the Mixed Commission, on 23 February 1962, with 29 votes in favour, 8 against, and one abstention, agreed on the following choice: 'In textu componendo vitandas esse omnes expressiones insinuantes vel dicentes vel nagantes traditionem latius patere quam Scripturam, aut quibus Scriptura et Traditio separai videtur', KT 2/2, p. 663.

118 Cf. Betti, 'Storia della Costituzione', pp. 34–36; Ratzinger, *Einleitung*, in LThK^2, *Das Zweite Vatikanische Konzil*, II, p. 501.

The Mixed Commission proposed and examined five formulae.[119] This is also gleaned from Schauf's *Diario*,[120] which also reveals to us

[119] For an overall vision of the work of the Mixed Commission see the whole of the Minutes drawn up by Tromp, *De reformando Schemate De Fontibus Revelationis*, including the reports of the Plenary Session of the Commission de doctrina fidei et morum, 22 February 1963, and of the Plenary Sessions of the Mixed Commission, from 23 February 1963 to 4 March 1963, in ASV, Envelope 763, folder 281, published in KT 2/2, pp. 657–669. See also Tromp's *Diario*, KT 2/1, pp. 235–263.

[120] This is how Schauf reports the proposed formulae:

'1. Revelatio oretenus facta item ab Apostolis primario oretenus transmissa est, quae transmissio Traditio oralis vocatur. Praeterea predicatio, ab Apostolis facta, *partim scripto quoque*, Spiritu Sancto inspirante, consignata est. Quaenam scripta inspirata sint, ex sola Traditione orali innotescit, quae insuper haec scripta integra conservat et authentice explicat. Hinc ut Revelatio adaequate audiatur, ad Scripturam et Traditionem tamquam fontes, ex quibus Revelatio cognoscatur, Magisterium Ecclesiae et fideles attendant oportet.

2. Christi itaque et Apostolorum mandatis et exemplis edocta, Sancta Mater Ecclesia semper credidit et credit integram revelationem seu puritatem ipsam Evangelii quod fons est omnis et salutaris veritatis atque morum disciplinae, contineri *in libris scriptis et sine scripto traditionibus*. Unde et libros inspiratos et traditiones tum ad fidem tum ad mores pertinentes, pari pietatis affectu ac reverentia suscipit et veneratur Ecclesia (In the margin is written in my hand: 'Charue').

3. Certum est *Traditionem oralem*, ab Apostolis profluentem, sive a Christo Domino sive a Spiritu Sancto edoctis, in quantum continet omnem et salutarem veritatem et morum disciplinam, *latius patere quam S. Scripturam* (In the margin in my hand: 'Parente').

4. Christus Evangelium suum, fontem omnius veritatis salutaris et morum disciplinae primum promulgavit. Deinde iussit Apostolos ut illud omni creaturae praedicarent: quod et fecerunt, *sive* per scripta Spiritu Sancto inspirante exarata, *sive* per doctrinam a Christi ore aut a Spiritu Sancto acceptam, et oretenus tradendam, quae et fidei depositum constituunt et fiunt fontes cognitionis Revelationis Christianae, pari pietatis affectu et reverentia ab Ecclesia suscipienda. (In the margin, the note: 'Browne').

5. (Ad mentem Conc. Vatic. I) Sacrum Revelationis Depositum *vel* in verbo Dei scripto *vel* in verbo Dei tradito invenitur. Ex alterutru Magisterium

an 'explosive episode', which took place in the Mixed Commission to get to the said neutral formula: an act of sabotage orchestrated by Bea against Ottaviani. In his *Diario* entry for 28 February 1963, Schauf notes that the Theological Commission was concerned with five formulae *De insufficientia Scripturae* or *De Traditione*. Balić spoke first of all, then Rahner, then Schauf ,whose book in the meantime had also been published: *Die Lehre der Kirche über Schrift und Tradition in den Katechismen* (Essen 1963), on the teaching of the catechisms,[121]

Ecclesiae ea haurit quae definire vult et christifidelibus fide divina credenda proponere. Unde S. Scriptura et S. Traditio pari pietatis affectu et reverentia suscipienda et veneranda sunt', Schauf, 'Auf dem Wege', pp. 69–71.

[121] In his book on the teaching of the Church about the Scripture and Tradition relationship in the Catechisms, a book which Schauf had praised saying that it would have opened the eyes of some bishops, while Rahner had asked the author if he had prepared any other bombs (cf. Schauf, 'Auf dem Wege', p. 79: *Diario* of 1 October 1963), Schauf reached the following conclusions, summarised by him as follows:

'1. Doctrina catechismorum, luce clarius expressa, hisce verbis reddi potest: dantur veritates revelate quae in sacra scriptura non habentur. Statuitur principium tali modo ut admissio unius tantum casus, puta inspirationis etc., non sufficiat.

2. Catechismi non obiter, sed ex professo doctrinam de qua agitur saepe saepius tractant. Inculcant doctrinam uti omnino tenendam. Eam uti doctrinam distinguentem catholicos a protestantibus habent.

3. Catechismi ab episcopis approbati sunt, immo aliquando officiales non tantum sunt, sed ut adhibendi, et quidem aliquando exclusive, in institutione iuventutis necnon populi catholici proponuntur. Agitur ergo de actu eminenti magisterii ordinarii episcoporum.

4. Si hoc in casu catechismi errarent tali unanimitate per longissimum tempus clare et fortiter docentes actum est de magisterio ordinario episcoporum, non tantum temporis praeteritis, sed etiam praesentis et future, actum est de auctoritate catechismorum, etiam future temporis. Episcopi ipsi induxissent positive fideles et populum catholicum in errorem invincibilem.

5. Tenere ergo debet doctrina unanimis catechismorum, si illa doctrina a) proponitur uti certa tenenda, b) uti distinguens catholics a protestantibus,

then Trapé, then van den Eynde and Tromp. There was a major disagreement about the formulae. In fact, on 23 February 1963 at 4.00

---

c) si per varias regiones per longissimum tempus a multis episcopis unanimiter proponuntur.

6. Doctrina eo sensu tenenda est quo eam catechismi intellexerunt et expresserunt. Si ergo hodie ab aliquibus theologis, sicut etiam in tempore antetridentino illud, "contineri in sacra scriptura" latius accipitur—quod in se fieri potest—tamen omnino dici nequit doctrinam catechismorum falsa esse, e contra eo in sensu quo catechismi dicunt veritates non contineri sacra scriptura veritas stet maneatque necesse est.
7. Illud, "in scriptura non contineri" a catechismis intellegitur eo sensu ut veritates revelatae agnoscenda sint quae neque explicite neque implicite in scriptura habentur ut inde argumentando valide et licite deduci possint', (*Ibid.*, pp. 71–71).

Interesting, in this regard, are some considerations, too, reached by the Franciscan van den Eynde on the modern controversy of *partim-partim*: the common opinion which said that not all truths are contained in Scripture does not deny that in some way they can be reached with the help of Tradition. Therefore, if the common consent to the Tridentine decree was caused by an erroneous interpretation of the decree or by simple opposition to the Protestants, the fact remains, and it is worthy of note, that the Church, for four centuries, professed that not all the truths are contained in Scripture. In the words of Schauf, it is a doctrine of the ordinary Magisterium of the bishops. This would be an effective response, which however Rahner, along with other followers of Geiselmann, did not want to hear. Van den Eynde said:'Theoria de sufficientia materiali Scripturae, si pressius examinatur, non videtur opinioni communi directe contraria. Nam asserendo omnes veritates revelatas in Scriptura esse contentas, non affirmat omnes ex sola Scriptura demonstrari vel vere cognosce possi; opinio communis autem, licet proclamet quasdam veritates in Scriptura non contineri, non negat eas aliquo modo ad Scripturam reducibiles esse. Diversus ergo usus vocabulari *contineri* aliqualem spem affert ut nova formula inveniatur quae utrique parti satisfaciat.... Etiam dato, non concesso, illum consensum ab erronea interpretatione Decreti Concilii Tridentini, sess. IV obortum esse et per oppositionem ad Reformationem propagatum, manet semper factum, summe attendendum, quod per quatuor secula tota Ecclesia professa est, non omnes veritates vere et proprie in libris sacris contineri, proindeque Scripturam materialiter insufficientem esse', *De Scriptura et Traditione*, cit. in *Ibid.*, pp. 74–75.

p.m. there was a meeting of the Mixed Commission. First of all there was a report from Ramirez OP, while Feiner reported on behalf of the Secretariat. At the end, the *disputatio de formulis.*[122] 'It was delegated to Florit, Charue, Garrone and De Smedt to find a formula, which had to be absolutely neutral. *So after the proposal of Bea; since Ottaviani was still present another question was posed...*',[123] that 'caused an explosion'.[124] In fact, on 28 February 1963 Schauf wrote in his *Diario*:

> At the session on 25 February 1963 discussion on my letter to the Bishop of Aachen. Enclosed is the letter of 27 February 1963: the major subsequent session was held on 23 February as a session of the Mixed Commission de Revelatione respectively de Fontibus... Ottaviani left the meeting early, since he had to attend a function. Bea assumed the first presidency, Brown trusts Ottaviani. When Ottaviani was still present, a question was put to the vote.[125] When Ottaviani was absent Bea changed the question for voting, so the agreement was to be that nothing was to be said about insufficiency, nothing in favour or against. Instead the vote was 29/9 along the lines of abstention. Browne had already protested that this issue was being supported. The certainly dramatic subsequent session, which alas I witnessed, was on 25 February 1963. Ottaviani had drawn up a text, which he read out loud. He formally protested against the change in the question, criticised the legal validity of the vote, explained that he would have recourse to the tribunal if necessary (in spirit I can already see him here), since, by means of the vote according to Bea's question, the *status quo* had changed; the doctrine which had been taught by the ordinary Magisterium up until now, was now placed only as *quaestio disputa*, but in fact it was a matter of the foundation of faith... Ottaviani presented a new question for voting: are there revealed truths which are not contained in

122 Cf. Schauf, 'Auf dem Wege', p. 69.

123 *Ibid.*

124 *Ibid.*

125 In a note Schauf adds: 'As far as I remember, it was put along the lines of Parente's form', *Ibid.*, p. 76, footnote 5.

Sacred Scripture neither explicitly nor implicitly? The opposition and others asked for half an hour to think. What was to come out came out. On behalf of the Secretariat Bea rejected the vote. The session literally blew up. The Co-ordinating Commission had to decide. Ottaviani: I reject a decision in the sense that this Commission can make decisions of faith… Surely the ship of the Council was never so firmly berthed as in this session … How should one proceed? It was said that the two Eminences should talk. In any case the matter should go to the Pope as well. Browne explained, what he always wanted to happen, that this matter was so important it should be brought to the Council. The whole of the Holy Office indicated it was willing, with all its resolute authority, to insist on this matter … This should be added, too: Franić explained that in Orthodox circles there was some concern that the Catholic Church might question the teaching it had held up to now about Scripture and Tradition, which was also the teaching of Orthodoxy. Spannedda emphasised the problem; he wanted to know what to teach the people and if the teaching given up to now was erroneous along with all the doctrinal books, etc. The Spanish gave glory to their name, Fernandez, Mag. generalis OP and Barbado… Without doubt Ottaviani proceeded tactically and methodically and created great opposition. With difficulty he will regain this lost ground. In fact, as regards the question, Ottaviani was not wrong. The *status quo* is at risk if nothing is said. This is his concern. Why not say: *eo in sensu, probativo quoad nos non omnia in Scriptura?* Why discuss the question at more length and compare the *status quaestionis* from before and today and at the same time the answers?[126]

---

[126] *Ibid.*, pp. 76–77. In more detail, the quarrel between Ottaviani and Bea developed along the following lines: Ottaviani reprimanded his colleague that the Secretariat for Promoting Christian Unity had prejudiced the issue of the material insufficiency of Scripture and thus encouraged the neutrality of the Mixed Commission. Ottaviani wanted a new vote to take place, after the one the previous Saturday when he was absent, and be on the Acta of the Commission: it was necessary to declare if in Tradition there are revealed truths not contained in Scripture. Bea and the members of the Secretariat replied that such

Another important piece of information given to us by Schauf is dated 1 March 1963, when he noted in his *Diario*:

> Today's session at 4.30 p.m. was relatively calm, here Ottaviani communicated that in the Secretariat of State the formula sub. 3 was approved by the Pope in substantia. Browne (and Parente) presented this formula. How will it be interpreted? Probably by each side in their own way.[127]

---

a question was already contained in the approved resolution, appealing to the co-ordinating Commission of the conciliar work (cf. Bea's *Letter* to Cicognani, President of the Commission 'de coordinandis laboribus Concilii', in ASV, Envelope 763, folder 274 and the enclosure in ASV, Envelope 760, folder 258, published in KT 2/2, pp. 1107–1109). For Ottaviani traditional doctrine could not remain silent. 'Tacere propter opportunitatem postea esse dolendum'. Bea immediately replied with five arguments: 'Non fuisse rem praeiudicatam sessione praevia Secretariatus: idem enim fecisse Commissionem doctrinalem cum hac differentia, quod membra Secretariatus erant concordes, membra Commissionis e contra; 2) In formula ultima a se proposita non agi de opportunitate sed de re videlicet de quo affirmaretur vel negaretur Traditionem latius patere quam S. Scripturam, vel statueretur separatio inter S. Scripturam et S. Traditionem; 3) Non esse unum theologum qui recedat a doctrina traditionali, sed plures inde a Tridentino: mutatum esse statum quaestionis; 4) In formula a se proposita nil affirmari vel negari, sed silcri; 5) Agi de valorizatione Traditionis respectu Orientalium et simul de invenienda formula apta pro dialogo cum protestantibus', KT 2/2, p. 661.

127 Schauf, 'Auf dem Wege', p. 78. The formula drafted by Browne and reviewed by Parente, which pleased the Holy Father (see the letter Cicognani sent to Ottaviani on 27 February 1963, confirming the Pope's positive opinion with his own words: 'It is truly acceptable', KT 2/2, p. 1186), said: 'Christus Dei Filius Evangelium suum fontem omnis veritatis et morum disciplinae, primum promulgavit. Deinde iussit Apostolos, ut illud omni creaturae praedicarent, quod ipsi fecerunt et per scripta Spiritu Sancto inspirante exarata, et oretenus tradendo, quae ex ipso ore Christi vel a Spiritu Sancto dictante [Conc. Trid. et Vat. I] acceperant. Hoc autem verbum Dei, sive scriptum sive traditum, unum Depositum fidei constituit, ex quo Ecclesiae Magisterium haurit ea omnia, quae fide divina credenda proponit tamquam divinitus revelata', KT 2/2, p.663.

On 27 March 1963 the schema was approved by the co-ordinating Commission and in May was handed over to the General Secretary to the Fathers, without, however, being discussed. In his address closing the Second Session of the Council, on 8 December 1963, Paul VI alluded to the schema on Divine Revelation, submitting it to the work of the Third Session. According to Ratzinger, with hindsight this choice was prudent, because it succeeded in liberating the schema from the pitfalls of an 'ecclesio-monism', while the Church was called to transcend itself to move towards the Lord.[128]

So on 3 January 1964 it was announced that the text had to be put forward in the third period of the Council, reviewed according to the written observations sent in in the meantime by the Fathers. There were two groups of *animadversiones Patrum*: those which arrived prior to 10 July 1964 and those which arrived after this date. Once again the debate about Tradition was heated. For some, the schema succeeded in resolving the complex problem of the material sufficiency / insufficiency of Scripture in a neutral manner. For others, instead, the schema was silent about the dogmatic fact of Tradition as indispensable vehicle of faith alongside Scripture. Unlike before, however, the Fathers, accepting the schema, proposed amendments, which in their eyes were right and proper.

The next text (form D or schema II) on the theme of the material insufficiency of Scripture was in fact elusive. After an introduction came the first chapter, entitled *De Verbo Dei revelato*. The whole schema amounted to five chapters, four of which examined Sacred Scripture.[129] Paragraph 7 contained the proposal to reduce the sources of Revelation to only one, the Gospel of Christ, stating:

> Christus Dominus mandatum dedit Apostolis, ut Evangelium suum, id est ea quae per totam suam vitam fecerat ed docuerat, tamquam fontem omnis et salutaris veritatis et morum disciplinae omni creaturae praedicarent. Quod quidem

[128] Cf. Ratzinger, *Einleitung*, in LThK², *Das Zweite Vatikanische Konzil*, II, p. 501.

[129] Cf. AS III/3, pp. 785–791.

> Apostoli fecerunt cum per scripta Spiritu Sancto inspirata, cum oretenus tradendo ea, quae ex ipso Christi ore vel a Spiritu Sancto dictante acceperant. Hoc autem verbum Dei, scriptum vel traditum, unum Depositum Fidei constituit, ex quo Ecclesiae Magisterium haurit ea omnia, quae fide divina tamquam divinitus revelata credenda proponit.[130]

In paragraph 8 the mutual relationship between Scripture and Tradition was described as follows:

> S. Scriptura et S. Traditio ita mutuo se habent, ut altera alteri extranea non sit. Imo arcte inter se connectuntur atque communicant. Nam ambae ex eadem scaturigine promanantes, in unum quodammodo coalescunt et in eundem finem tendunt. Quapropter utraque pari pietatis affect ac reverentia suscipienda ac veneranda est.[131]

Finally, paragraph 9 studied the relationship of Scripture and Tradition with the Magisterium, teaching that ecclesiastical Magisterium was the *regola fidei proxima,* while the *remota* was the Sacred Deposit itself.[132]

2.1 The *animadversiones* on schema II

At this point it is good to focus somewhat on the Fathers' observations on the new schema sent to them, which in fact re-wrote the previous one prepared by the Central Commission, since it was based essentially on the theme of the duality of the sources of Revelation.

The German-language council Fathers and those of the Scandinavian Bishops' Conference were in favour of the new schema. They approved the 'doctrinam cautam' which manifested the mutual connection between Scripture and Tradition, and asked that its form be retained, expressed after so much effort.

> We explicitly believe, the said Fathers wrote, that nothing more than what has already been said should be said about this

[130] *Ibid.*, p. 784.

[131] *Ibid.*

[132] Cf. *Ibid.*, pp. 784–785.

> issue, but the consensus achieved in the Mixed Commission after so much disquisition should be retained.[133]

In addition, they asked for a change in the way of expression as regards the term 'source',[134] which in the Latin described more the water than the spring from which it emanates. The problem was about the spring itself. So it was better to say that Scripture and Tradition did not emanate 'ex eadem scaturigine', but 'ex eodem fonte',[135] so as to maintain indisputably the uniqueness of the source of Revelation, a theme, as has been seen, much discussed right from the first assemblies and dear to the German-speaking Fathers.[136]

The Indonesian Bishops' Conference spoke along the same lines, praising the text because it highlighted the place which Scripture and

---

[133] Cf. AS III/3, p. 905.

[134] Cf. n. 8, line 14: 'ex eadem scaturigine promanantes': Hellín, *Dei verbum*, p. 70.

[135] Cf. AS III/3, p. 908. The final text did not accept this proposal but retained the original concept of *scaturigine*: 'Nam ambae, ex eadem divina scarturigine promanantes, in unum coalescunt et in eundem finem tendunt', cf. Hellín, *Dei verbum*, p. 71.

[136] Cardinal Florit in his report on paragraph 9 ('from my first conciliar report': an addition in pen, in the header of the typewritten paper), explaining the mutual relationship between Scripture and Tradition, wrote as follows in reference to the term 'scaturigo': 'So that again it is clear in this Constitution there is no intention to lean towards one solution over another, in the proposition it was avoided saying "emanating from the same divine FONT', and it was preferred to say 'emanating from the same divine SOURCE'. The reason was this: so that by applying the term 'FONT' to God himself, in no way was the application of the same term in favour of Tradition and Scripture precluded. So the famous question remains open; and precisely not only as regards the substance, but also as regards the terminology used up to now', AEF, Folder 2, Schema 'De divina revelatione', page Mutua Relatione, no. 9 (Dalla mia prima relaz. concil.) f. 3. The whole folder contains: La prima relazione conciliare, al n. 8 e al n. 9 (3 ff.) and the Relatio circa Cap. I et Cap. II Schematis Constitutionis dogmaticae "De Divina Revelatione" (25 September 1964), (6 ff. with the addition of a page Cap. I et II Historia Delineatio). The whole binder is composed of ten folders.

Tradition have in the life of the faithful; positively it indicated the path along which Catholic exegesis advanced and in a balanced way reflected the Church's true devotion in the area of the Word of God. It was then suggested that it should be added that the Gospel of Christ comes to us not only through Scripture alone but also by Tradition through the preaching of the Gospel and by means of Christian customs, *in primis* the liturgy.[137]

Much more enthusiastic, on the other hand, were Patriarch Maximos IV[138] Saigh and Cardinal Richaud.[139]

Others, however, in a greater number, manifested their perplexity, concerning above all the notable stylistic device used to neutralise the theme of the material insufficiency of the Scriptures: there was a danger in making the teaching on Tradition barely comprehensible, having had to tone it down for prudential reasons. For example, Bishop A. Jacq (Titular Bishop of Cerasenus), let it be known that the discourse on 'integral Tradition' was missing, that he understood there to be unity between *traditio realis* (transmitted reality) and *traditio verbalis* (the act of transmitting). The *traditio realis* was almost absent. It had to include the handing on of the whole of Christianity, that is to say, the faith, Christian practices, the institutions, the disciplinary and sacramental traditions and above all the liturgy. This was important from an ecumenical point of view because for the Orthodox, Tradition, as well as being doctrine of the faith, also incorporated the law of God, the sacraments, the liturgical rites. For the Eastern Christians, the liturgy expresses the faith of the Church and is the 'place' of knowledge of the Scriptures. This had to be talked about in the schema, in such a way that an integral Tradition became a living tradition.[140] The Armenian Patriarch of Cilicia, Pierre XVI Batanian, said that the text reduced to a minimum the doctrine on

137 Cf. AS III/3, pp. 913–915.

138 Cf. *Ibid.*, p. 872.

139 Cf. *Ibid.*, p. 793.

140 Cf. *Ibid.*, pp. 840–842.

Tradition, which for many centuries, especially since the sixteenth century, the Catholic Church, by means of its ordinary Magisterium, its theologians, and its 'auctores probatos', had proposed. It was a *Traditio constitutiva* of faith. So the Patriarch manifested his hesitation over some expressions found in the schema, saying:

> These words 'S. Scriptura et s. traditio ita mutuo se habent ut altera alteri extranea non sit'[141] are very obscure, and can be understood in various ways. They can mean that Sacred Scipture and Sacred Tradition contain the same truths and that Tradition does not surpass Sacred Scripture in anything, and contains nothing more: this is nothing but giving in placidly to the Protestants and rejecting what the Catholic Church has taught up to now. Page 7 n. 10 says: 'S. Scripturam, s. traditionem ac Ecclesiae Magisterium ita inter se internecti et consociari, ut unum sine aliis consistere non possint'.[142] Is this true? Is it true that Tradition and Magisterium of the Church do not have substance without Scripture? Must it not be admitted that the oral Magisterium of the time of the apostles and the time of the subsequent generations was the one source of faith?[143]

Bishop Carli also manifested his profound perplexity at a schema he defined as 'minimalist', saying with a touch of humour:

> Our schema is called 'de divina revelatione', but more accurately it should be 'de Sacra Scriptura', since in the schema Sacred Tradition (which by means of the same right belongs to divine revelation) has the figure of a certain *'Cinderella'*, as the Italians say.[144]

Bishop Tabera Araoz (Bishop of Albacete, Spain), demonstrating himself to be generally in favour of the schema, enlightened his

141 Cf. Hellín, *Dei verbum*, p. 70.

142 Cf. *Ibid.*, p. 80.

143 AS III/3, p. 804.

144 Cf. *Ibid.*, p. 817.

peacemaking character, aimed at calming souls not against the separated brethren, but between the different theological opinions. The good intentions of minimalism and irenicism encountered in the teaching displayed were unable, however, in his opinion, to be a motive for further theological examination.[145] This vision would be very important because subsequently it would open the path to a renewed theological in-depth examination of the concept of 'tradition'; the problem in fact would shift from its effective and real substance in ordinary Magisterium to its renewed theological understanding.

Bishop Builes (Bishop of S. Rosa de Osos), echoing the common doctrine accepted by the Church about Tradition, confirmed that, according to Catholic teaching,

> Not all the divinely revealed truths can be found in Sacred Scripture; and some divinely revealed truths can only be found in *divine Tradition*... Therefore it should be established in a *clear* manner in the decree of this Second Vatican Council the dual moment of divine Tradition, that is to say: 1. the Divine Tradition is required to understand the meaning of Sacred Scripture in a certain and full way. 2. The Divine Tradition is the *only way and source* to find some divinely revealed truths. In the schema on the divine Tradition the moment certainly remains as if in shadow.[146]

Finally, also worthy of note is the written intervention of Cardinal Siri, according to whom saying that Tradition not only explains Scripture but also complements it could not be omitted. In the new draft the desire to prepare a text suitable for dialogue with the separated brethren had prevailed and it did not sufficiently provide the reason for the Catholic faith.[147] So in twelve points Siri listed the deficiencies of the text as regards Catholic teaching in this area, held definitively by the Church. It would be a bad example if a Council had

---

145 Cf. *Ibid.*, p. 881.

146 *Ibid.*, pp. 809–810.

147 Cf. *Ibid.*, p. 800.

offered just a minimum of the dogmatic *res* of the traditional teaching of the Church, what's more already approved at previous councils. If it were said that Catholic biblical knowledge can prove all truths with the Bible alone, that would force an insincere exegesis: if one thinks, for example, of the teaching of the seven sacraments. Also the historical facts at the start of the Church concerning specific truths of the New Testament belong solely to Tradition. Finally, Siri made his own the same anguish of Paul VI, who, in his address closing the Second Session of the Council, wanted the question about Revelation to be developed so as to defend the deposit of faith from all errors, abuse and doubt. And he concluded: the very sufficiency of Scripture is in no way taught by Scripture itself.[148]

In such a way the problem of doctrine and its pastoral presentation had resurfaced. It could now be better seen that, in the first instance, the supporters of 'doctrinal pastorality' had not reflected well: it was becoming ever easier to silence doctrine to support the pastoral approach. If the two dimensions were not cautiously distinct, each with its own object and goal would run the risk of silencing, in an ecumenical council, what was instead the patrimony of the Church's faith. Two elements would now come together: the compromise formula on the theme 'Scripture-Tradition' and the effort to keep open the field of systematic-theological in-depth examination of Tradition, seen no longer as a *per se* but in relation to Revelation and to Sacred Scripture. Somehow the council axis would move from the Magisterium to theology.

---

[148] Cf. *Ibid.*, p. 800. Other Fathers were of the same opinion. For example the Bishops of the Apostolic Region of Bordeaux (cf. *Ibid.*, pp. 898–899); the Rector of the Society of the Catholic Apostolate, Fr Moehler (cf. *Ibid.*, p. 855); the Bishop of Palma (Brasil), Mgr Bandeira de Mello (cf. *Ibid.*, p. 871).

2.2 The theological sub-commissions come to grips with the problem of Tradition

The Theological Commission began to study the Fathers' observations. The work was hard and complex. On 7 March 1964 a sub-commission was created, whose President was Charue, and as members Florit, Barbado, Pellettier, van Dodewaard, Heuschen and the English Abbot Butler. The periti included Betti, who became the secretary, Castellino, Cerfaux, Congar, Rahner, Gagnebet, Garofalo, Ratzinger, Grillmeier, Semmelroth, Smulders, Schauf, etc.[149] The sub-commission itself was then divided again into two groups. It was Bishop Charue, in effect, who suggested the creation of two sub-commissions. Florit, on the other hand, suggested three. Two were established, with Charue chairing the first and Florit the second. Both sub-commissions had as their theme: 1) *De revelatione* and 2) *De Traditione*. Taking part in the latter, *De Traditione*, as periti, were Betti, Congar, Rahner and Schauf, who at a first meeting was concerned directly about these issues: 1) *Traditio in sua natura et momentum traditionis*: Congar had to report on this; 2) *Traditio et Scriptura*: Rahner and Schauf had to report on this, and 3) *Traditio et Scriptura relate ad Ecclesiam et Magisterium*: here again, Congar. Betti, on the other hand, had to prepare a general report on these partial reports.[150] 'The greatest difficulty', said Ratzinger, 'remained here, too, the problem of the material sufficiency of Scripture'.[151] During one of the sessions, Schauf informs us of an interesting fact:

> Before today's meeting (12 March 1964) a great disagreement with Rahner, who now wants to hear nothing about the insufficiency of Scripture. About a formulation, which offers revealed things, which could not be proved by Scripture, he

---

149 Cf. Ratzinger, *Einleitung*, p. 501.

150 Cf. Schauf, 'Auf dem Wege', pp. 79–80, notes from his *Diario* for 12 March 1964.

151 Ratzinger, *Einleitung*, p. 501.

said: what does to prove, to demonstrate mean? Who stops me from finding it in Scripture?[152]

The next day Schauf met Betti, who was leaning towards Florit's formulation on the relationship between Scripture and Tradition, 'which roughly said: Etsi Verbum Dei ex scripturis non patet, constatare tamen ex traditione potest ... In addition to Florit's text Betti formulated: Etsi ex S. Scriptura veritas rei non costat, Traditio tamen Scripturae interpretatio, which to me', said Schauf, 'does not seem sufficient. Surely it is better as follows: Etsi veritas aliqua revelata ex Scriptura cum certitudine erui non potest, Traditio tamen eam certe testificare potest (vel simile quid) ... '.[153]

The sub-commissions worked from 20–25 April 1964 on two burning issues. As well as the normal report on chapter II, two periti were delegated, one to represent the majority, K. Rahner, and the other the minority, H. Schauf, so as to be able to report within the Commission on the Fathers' observations about the relationship between Sacred Scripture and Tradition. The Theological Commission, in fact, was divided: there was a majority of theologians who supported a neutral formulation of the Scripture-Tradition relationship, which left open the question, opting, in any case, for an at least implicit sufficiency of the Scriptures; and a minority which, instead, did not want to reduce the Scripture-Tradition relationship to a *quaestio disputata*, but, con-

[152] *Ibid.*, p. 80.

[153] Schauf, 'Auf dem Wege', p. 80 (*Diario* of 13 March 1964). In his observations on schema II Florit had also suggested the formula to better express the relationship between Sacred Scripture and Tradition to be added to paragraph 8. The precise formula was: '*Quod si in aliquibus s. traditionem a S. Scriptura profluere non constat, semper tamen in S. Scriptura ipsa reflectitur eamque illuminat*' (AS III/3, p. 837). In effect, Florit's endeavours to mediate between those who affirmed the sufficiency and those who instead affirmed the material insufficiency of the Scriptures can be seen. In fact, Florit would have an indispensable mediating role at the heart of the Commission and therefore in the Council, so that the new text might be approved precisely on this sensitive issue.

firming the cogency of the material insufficiency of the Scriptures, at least from Trent onwards, asked to pronounce in favour of an integral concept of *Traditio*, thus believing in shaping ecumenical dialogue on the clear dogmagtic formulation. The problem would present itself under a new theological guise, but new in these terms: dialogue starting from dogmatic truth or dialogue without necessarily disturbing dogmatic truth? Here, however, one clearly sees the passage which, in a certain sense, we can call *from the Council to theology*. The Council cannot be understood without taking into account this change, too: from the Magisterium to a more appropriate theological choice, considering the time, the sciences, the new world.

H. Schauf reported the conclusion Rahner reached on behalf of the theological majority and, in addition, his report on behalf of the minority.[154] There were two theological conceptions which compare and contrast. Two approaches to dogma, two theologies, which will also contend for the magisterial tenor of Vatican II.

To Rahner was assigned the *Relatio de Animadversionibus Patrum circa Proemium et Caput I Schematis "De Divina Revelatione"*.[155] Rahner concluded with the suggestion of a new ten-page text *De Traditione*. The most important conclusions of Rahner's position, and therefore that of the majority, were the following:[156]

---

[154] Schauf, 'Auf dem Wege', pp. 81–97.

[155] See K. Rahner, *Relatio de Animadversionibus Patrum circa Proemium et Caput I Schematis "De Divina Revelatione"* (Sub-commission "De Divina Revelatione"), a six-page text in AEF, Folder 2, Schema "De divina revelatione".

[156] In a letter dated 4 April 1964, Rahner gave his Report to Betti and a draft of the text on the relationship between Scripture and Tradition. Inter alia, Rahner wrote: 'In uno puncto prorsus dissentio a sententia, quam propugnat Schauf. Nullatenus censeo litem de insufficientia Scripturae comparative ad traditionem esse denuo instaurandam. Satis de hac re disceptatum est. Nec relationes Patrum, si aeque ponderantur, ad talem renovationem istius litis cogunt. Sufficienter de pondere et momento traditionis in schemate sermo esse potest ad omnium satisfactionem, quin haec quaestio iterum tangatur', Betti, *Diario*, p. 35.

In no way was it asked (*expedit*) that the schema might teach a positive and unlimited material sufficiency of the Scriptures compared to Tradition. Rahner suggested some reasons to refrain from engaging with this problem:

1. the Theological and the Mixed Commissions, after a lot of discussion, had reached a way of proceeding.
2. It is wrong that silence on this issue can harm and lessen the dignity and situation of Tradition. It is obvious that the living Tradition also leads to Scripture and contains all that is taught in Scripture; it is the constitutive source of our knowledge of Revelation and the norm of an authentic scripture interpretation; it is to be held with equal piety and affection compared to Scripture.[157]
3. In fact it is a disputed issue and the theologians' discord must not be resolved by the Council. It is not evidenced by the Tridentine mindset. Many testimonies in favour of the insufficiency of the Scriptures say nothing more than what is admitted by all, and that is the need of Tradition for every Catholic teaching. This, according to Rahner, was to be noted above all against Siri[158] and Florit.[159] It is not sufficient, as

---

[157] 'Evidens est vivam traditionem ipsam Scripturam portare, continere omnia, quae in scriptura docentur, esse eatenus etiam fontem constitutivum nostrae cognitionis de divina revelatione, esse normam authenticate explicationis doctrinae scripturisticae et pari pietatis affectu ac reverentia suscipiendam esse ac Scriptura. Haec si dicuntur (et fusius dicuntur quam in schemate recepto) nullum est periculum damni pro traditione eiusque aestimatione', Schauf, 'Auf dem Wege', p. 82.

[158] Cf. AS III/3, p. 800.

[159] Cf. *Ibid.*, p. 831. Florit also suggested improving and expanding the dogmatic import concerning Tradition. He said that it was necessary to speak about Tradition in a truly traditional manner even if the language was appropriate to adapt it to the modern theology and the mentality of the time. The Council had to maintain the doctrine of the independence of Tradition with respect to the Scriptures with regard to the transmission of Revelation for three

Bishop Builes referred only to Lennerz,[160] to confirm the Tridentine mindset. If reference is made to the Catechisms (as Siri did), these do not provide an *ad hominem* argument to prove the need of Tradition. If it is said that Tradition is necessary as source material and in a certain limitless and distinct manner, one can respond by saying that Tradition is not necessary only for the truths not contained in Scripture. If it is said that it is dogmatically and historically evident, and perhaps known that the first supposition is true, one can respond saying that it is not at all easy to derive some dogmatic truth from the tradition of the first three centuries, since for the dogmatic theologian it is not easy to discern a (necessary) historic argument from Scripture, if this truth has a distinct Tradition and material source. Perhaps there is a dogmatic theologian who maintains that a specific truth not contained implicitly in the Scriptures has an explicit testimony in the Fathers of the early centuries?[161]

reasons: 1) it was largely confirmed by the ordinary Magisterium; 2) it is not subject to any doubt among the clergy and the people of God; 3) it is indispensable so that dialogue with the separated brethren might not become fruitless. And here Florit quoted the words of Pius X: 'You open wide the doors to welcome those who are outside, and in the meantime, you make those who are inside go out' (cf. Sacra Rituum Congregatio: Sectio historica, n. 77: *Romanae Beatificationis et Canonizationis Servi Dei Pii X*... Typis Polyglottis Vaticanis 1950, XX-VIII). Cf. *Ibid.*, pp. 832–833 (the very careful entire intervention is on pp. 831–837).

160 Cf. *Ibid.*, p. 807.

161 '*Quidnam* enim ex his catechismis allatis exemplis ut obiective verum ab unoque dogmatice admitti debet? Si diceretur traditionem esse necessariam ut fontem materialiter et quidem illimitate distinctam respondendum est questione, numquid traditio sit solum necessaria pro veritatibus, quae dicuntur non contineri in Scriptura. Si dicitur esse evidens quaedam ista evidentia sit dogmatica an humano-historica tantum, et num constet priorem suppositionem esse veram, et insuper respondendum est nullatenus facilius esse derivare quaedam dogmata ex traditione trium primorum seculorum quam ex Scriptura et hinc argumentationem historicam (necessariam) pro

4. If it is said that many things are not contained in Scripture but are nevertheless dogmatic teachings of the Church, is that excluding they may be *implicitly* contained in Scripture? If the dogma itself of the Assumption of the Blessed Virgin into heaven has its ultimate foundation in Scripture and such foundation cannot be merely not loathsome to Scripture, who can exclude from Scripture *every* kind of presence of the truth in some way? Can one exclude every type of implication before knowing what kind can be debated? If one lists the truths which cannot be found in Scripture in a *clear* way is it already confirmed that they are not contained therein in an objective manner?[162]

5. What are the cases in which the axiom about the material insufficiency of Scripture should be applied *ex fide*? From the defenders of this axiom comes the example of the truth of infant baptism, sacramental character, etc. But what in these cases can force me to admit (*tamquam de fide*) if this axiom is supposed as true? In no way can I affirm that from Scripture I can prove infant baptism, the seven-fold number of the sacraments and more? If in no concrete and specific case I am obliged to apply this axiom *ex fide*, what is its purpose when there is nothing as certain and even less a binding obligation?[163]

---

theologo dogmatico reapse non evadere facilior, si traditionem habet ut fontem materialiter distinctam (!). Numquid enim habentur pro dogmatibus, quae dicuntur nullatenus, ne implicite quidem, in Scriptura, testimonia explicita in Patribus pro eorum origine Aspostolico ex primis saeculis?', Schauf, 'Auf dem Wege', p. 83.

162 'Si ipsum dogma Assumptionis BM Virginis, "ultimum fundamentum" in Scriptura habet et tale fundamentum non potest esse mere non-repugnantia cum Scriptura, quis *omnes* speciem continentiae huismodi veritatis in Scriptura excludere potest? Potestne omnis species implicationis excludi, antequam sciatur quales species tales omnio in quaestionem venire possint?', *Ibid.*, p. 85.

163 'Si abstrahimus a testimonio, quod traditio reddere debet ipsi Scripturae, quinam sunt *determinati* casus, quibus applicari *ex fide debet* axioma de

6. Where does knowledge of such an axiom come from? From the divine-apostolic Tradition of revealed realities? Are there concrete and specific cases? If there is a *human* (even if universal) persuasion must such persuasion be taught by a council? Why?[164]

This was Rahner's position. Fundamentally, however, it was a reduction of Tradition to the Fathers of the first three centuries, demonstrating that the axiom of the material insufficiency of the Scriptures was impossible to prove, and therefore could be left out of the concilar declaration. In effect, one cannot demonstrate, with an *ad extra* proof of the transmission of Revelation, the foundation of faith and its uninterrupted transmission. This is a *petitio principii*, in which the Scriptures are absolutized. The proof of Tradition is Tradition itself and its ecclesial reception, not up to the third century, but up to today, without interruption, from which one infers what is not contained (directly and explicitly) in Scripture. What is then recognised, at least implicitly, to be present in Scripture, that is not by means of Scripture but by means of Tradition, which thus finds therein its ultimate and canonical rule. Rahner, as Schauf pointed out to him, was confusing historical tradition with dogmatic Tradition. And this due to his

---

insufficientia materiali Scripturae? Utique afferentur talia exempla a defensoribus huius axiomatis (paedobaptismus, character sacramentalis, etc. etc.). Sed quosnam ex istis casibus *cogor* admittere (tamquam de fide), si istud axioma ut verum supponitur? Possumne nihilomnius affirmare me ex Scriptura eruere posse paedobaptismum, septenarium numerum sacramentorum et ita porro? Sed si ad nullum casum concretum et determinatum illud axioma certo et ex fide (et non tantum ex mea probate persuasione humana) applicare obligor, ad quid valet istud axioma generale, quod nullam habet certam et obligatem applicationem?', *Ibid.*, pp. 85–86.

164 '*Undenam* habetur cognitio huius axiomatis? Habeturne de eo traditio divino-apostolica de re ut revelata? Habeturne talis de axiomate hoc ut generali? Ubinam? ... Quinam sunt isti casus, quod ipsa revelatio exhibet? An habetur persuasio *humana* (esto vera et satis universalis) quaedam dogmata non posse iuxta privatam singulorum (etsi multorum) evidentiam erui ex Scriptura? Debetne et potest talis persuasio doceri a Concilio? Cur?', *Ibid.*, p. 86.

philosophical-speculative and not positive method, based, that is, on the sources of faith.

H. Schauf gave the report representing the minority, entitled *Relatio de Animadversionibus Patrum circa Relationem inter Traditione et S. Scriptura*, comprising 27 pages.[165] It was a reasoned response to the official position summarised by Rahner. He had said that it was a Theological Commission decision to put to one side the burning issue of the material insufficiency of the Scriptures. Schauf retorted: shouldn't the Commission instead take into account the requests of the Fathers, leaving them to discuss the pros and cons in the council chamber?[166]

The salient points of Schauf's report can be summarised as follows:

1. Concerning the doubt raised by Siri and criticised by Rahner, in relation to the constant magisterial teaching of that dogmatic *plus* given to Tradition, in reality the arguments counted for little. In fact: what can be said about the words of John

---

[165] Cf. H. Schauf, *De relatione inter Traditionem et S. Scripturam relatio* (Subcommissio "De Divina Revelatione"), Aachen 31 March 1964, in AEF, Folder 2, Schema "De divina revelatione". Schauf wrote in his *Diario* on 20 May 1964 that the day before he had sent about 100 copies of two pages of observations about Rahner to Tromp. A copy was also sent to Florit, which I found in his archive: (Id., *Observationes ad Conclusionem Relationis R. P. Rahner de Cap. I Schematis "De Divina Revelatione" [pag. 6 ad pag. 9]*, Aachen 15 May 1964 [ff. 2], in AEF, Folder 2, Schema "De divina revelatione"). He also sent Tromp a re-drafted article with a prayer to be placed eventually in the *Gregorianum* or *Antonianum*. It was an article or more precisely news about 'Religionsgespräch' of Düsseldorf and on 'Latomus', and observations, taking a stance then in the journal *Theologische Quartalschrift*, on Geiselmann's attack on Backes and himself, cf. Schauf, 'Auf dem Wege', p. 80.

[166] On 27 March 1964 Schauf had already written a letter to the secretary of the Commission, Fr Betti, enclosed with his Report on the Scripture-Tradition relationship. Schauf was concerned that the balance of the Commission was weighted too easily towards the majority. He wrote: 'Mihi in eo insistendum videtur ut Commissio Theologica argumenta allata ex utraque parte vere examinet, et quidem methodo theologico (!) serio (!)'. And in the PS he cautioned: 'Teneatis, quaeso, lineam! Petatis argumenta!', Betti, *Diario*, p. 35.

XXIII himself, who in the Encyclical *Ad Petri cathedram*, had reiterated the duality of the transmission of Revelation? And likewise the provincial Councils approved by the Holy See, the catechisms, the very interpretation of the Tridentine Council about the axiom *sine scripto traditionibus*?

2. One cannot deny the doctrine affirmed for centuries in the catechisms themselves, in an apodictic and universal manner, that not everything which God has revealed can be known thanks to Sacred Scripture alone. Therefore the material insufficiency of the Scriptures cannot be restricted to the inspiration of the sacred books and to the canon.[167]

3. Geiselmann openly admits the insufficiency of Scripture as regards customs and morals.[168] However, Rahner does not

[167] Schauf listed a series of possible formulae of the doctrinal tradition, some inferred from the *animadversiones* of the Council Fathers: 'a) Formula Florit (supra 3, b: already set out); b) 'Non omnia quae Deus revelaverit ex sola Scriptura, seposita Traditione, sufficienter colliguntur', vel: 'Credenda sunt quae in Traditione divino-apsotolica habentur, etiam si non expresse in Scriptura leguntur nec inde per bonam consequentiam deduci queunt'. (Cf. Colloquium Ratisbonense anno 1601). c) 'Latius patere fidem et verbum Dei quam Scriptura' (Stapleton). d) Non solum sunt credenda et servanda quae expressa in divinis litteris habentur, aut probantur ex ipsis, verum etiam quae sancta mater Ecclesia ut in Traditione contenta credit et observat' (cf. J. Eck). e) 'Omnia fidei mysteria ceteraque creditu necessaria in corde Ecclesiae inveniuntur, in membranis tamen S. Scripturae non omnia expresse haberi vel inde certe cognosci posse' (cf. Coster). f) 'Quemadmodum S. Scriptura non est unicus modus Traditionis ita nec est modus revelationis (materialiter) omni numero adaequatus vel exhaustivus' (Möhler, cf. AS III/3, p. 855). g) 'Traditio, eaque sola, via est qua veritates quaedam revelatae, inter quas ipse SS. Librorum Canon, Ecclesia innotescunt' (Nicodemo, cf. AS III/3, p. 824). h) 'S. Scripturam per Traditionem non solum explicari, sed etiam compleri' (Siri, cf. AS III/3, p. 800)', Schauf, 'Auf dem Wege', pp. 90–91.

[168] As well as the literature already cited, see J. Geiselmann, 'Tradizione', in *Dizionario teologico*, edited by H. Fries, Brescia: Queriniana, 1968, vol. III, pp. 521–532 (especially 521, 529–532; German original, *Handbuch theologischer Grundbegriff*, [Muncih: Kösel, 1962–1963]).

mention this. J. Beumer who in 1962 wrote 'Die mündliche Überliferung als Glaubensquelle' (in Handbuch der Dogmengeschichte I/4), in the review of Schauf's book (Essen 1963) in *Scholastik* 39 (1964) 122, contrary to Rahner admits that in the catechisms the same ordinary Magisterium is proclaimed. Approving the conclusion which Schauf reached, Beumer, too, stated that 'non omnia in scriptura sic continentur ut etiam inde probari possint'. The interpretation of the catechisms offered by Rahner is not sustainable. In discussion it is necessary to start from what is taught unanimously by the ordinary Magisterium. One cannot compare, as Rahner does, the proof of Scripture with the proof of *historical* tradition (and this of the first centuries); instead it is necessary to compare the proof of Scripture (which does not exist) and the proof with dogmatic Tradition, which necessarily refers to the constitutive Tradition. Willingly it can be conceded that certain proof from historical tradition is not possible. However, that is not an aporia of the truth, but of theology as knowledge.[169]

4. Rahner's method does not respond to the rules of positive theology. It is necessary to start not from theory or theological speculation but from positive sources.
5. Finally of note: Vatican II in dogmatic issues does not wish to pronounce in an absolute and definitive manner. What is said to be infallible is not, unless a teaching consists of infallibility.

169 'Non agitur ut Rahner supponere videtur de comparatione inter probationem ex scriptura et inter probationem ex traditione *historica* (e. gr. primorum saeculorum), sed de comparatione inter probationem ex scriptura quae fieri nequit et probationem ex traditionem quae dogmatica vocatur et sic ad traditionem constitutivam impellit. Libenter conceditur aliquando probationem ex traditione historica forsan, possibilem non esse. Hoc autem non est aporia veritatis, sed theologiae ut scientia est… Methodus Rahner observare non videtur regulas theologiae positiviae… Iterum ergo dicendum est insipiendum esse non a theoria vel speculatione theologica, sed ex fontibus positivis', Schauf, 'Auf dem Wege', pp. 94–96.

Therefore if the schema remains as such, an obvious argument is raised: either the Council did not want to teach anything about this issue or it left it in doubt or left it open. On the other hand, for four centuries the ordinary Magisterium has proposed insufficiency in a clear and definitive manner. Therefore, a conclusion in which it might be said that the ordinary Magisterium can prevail over that of the Council would not be a terribly honorary conclusion for the Council. If what for four centuries has been professed clearly in the catechisms is rejected, there will be a great scandal, which is greater than what is called, justly or unjustly, the Galileo scandal.[170]

6. So the conclusion: it is necessary to remain within the teaching of the ordinary Magisterium.

The text bears the date of 15 May 1964, written in Aachen. The Doctrinal Commission, however, had a different opinion. The majority sided with Rahner's thesis. Betti accused Schauf's text of being polemical towards Rahner.[171] At the vote, 17 Fathers were against, 7

---

170 'Denique notandum: Conc. Vat. II in dogmaticis generatim non absolute et definitive loqui vult. Quae dicuntur ergo infallibiliter vera non sunt, neque aliunde de infallibiliter vera doctrina constet. Ideo, si schema remanet, argumentum obvium habetur: Concilium aut nihil de quaestione docuisse aut quaestionem ut dubiam habuisse ut apertam etc. Alia ex parte autem Magisterium ordinarium per 4 saecula in catechismis aperte professa sunt, habetur scandalum maximum quod maius est quam vocatur, iuste, vel iniuste, transeat, Galilei. Conclusio: standum est in doctrina magisterii ordinarii!', *Ibid.*, pp. 96–97.

171 Betti, *Diario*, pp. 44–45: Schauf, wrote Betti, 'accuses [Rahner] of not observing the rules of positive theology, and of sustaining the fundamental sufficiency of Scripture alone with speculative arguments… For the Schema *De divina Revelatione* there will be this glitch, too, just as there was for the teaching on collegiality in n. 22 of *De Ecclesia*, the piece by Cardinal Browne on 12 February (1964)'. Rahner, in donating two of his books to Betti translated into French, wrote this dedication: 'To Rev. Fr. Betti OFM *grato animo d.d.d.*', where the three letters 'd', as Betti himself explains, were not referring to a death, but were indicating him as a triple *doctor*, due to the fact

in favour of overlooking the problem of the material insufficiency of the Scriptures without adding formulae which would have overloaded the text in paragraph 8.[172] It was impossible to reach any unity

---

that he had 'not fallen into the flattery of the *Dominus et Praelatus* Schauf concerning the issue of Scripture and Tradition', *Ibid.*, p. 44.

172 The background to this very frenzied day, 3 June 1964, which culminated in the vote of 17 placet and 7 non placet, was described by Fr Betti with some ironic comments about what he believed to be an 'unrepetant minority'. There was a 'muttering thick with plotters'. The fires were stoked precisely on paragraph 8 about Tradition. Betti wrote: 'Examination of the new Chapter II *De divina Revelationis transmissione*. As rapporteur on the text and secretary of the Sub-commission which had drafted it, I illustrated the main points. I emphasised the rationale which had dissuaded [us] from reviving the question of whether Tradition has an excess of quantative content compared to Scripture ... . Around about 5.30 p.m. paragraph 8 on Tradition was tackled. For an unrepentant minority it still seemed absurd and almost offensive (cf. 1 Cor 1:23f.). The fires were stoked by Mgr Franić, and especially by Schauf who churned out the heated parts of his *Animadversiones* of 15 May. They believe, and want it said, that Tradition allows us to know not just the truths about Scripture, inspiration, the canon, the exact meaning, etc., but also others equally belonging to the faith. At the request of Cardinal König, Rahner, Schauf's favourite target, replied. But it was like screaming at the deaf. Mgr Charue referred back to the authority of Mgr Florit, who, as President of the Sub-commission, had had some import in the approval of the text at that session. But Cardinal Ottaviani appealed to an intervention of Mgr Florit with the Italian bishops, who, also because of his influence, would have declared themselves en masse in favour of the limitless constitutive Tradition. And Mgr Florit, singled out twice, could not himself say what he thought because he was absent, hospitalised. During the break, from 6.00 p.m. to 6.15 p.m., hardly anyone rested. In the different groups there was a muttering thick with plotters. Everywhere could be perceived the heavy presence of the shadow cast by Cardinal Ottaviani over Mgr Florit: a shadow of sadistic opportunism, which had led him to behaving in one way with the Italian bishops and in another way within the Sub-commission responsible for the text... When the meeting began again, the war continued. Not even the easy-going quip of Abbot Butler on the innocuity of the text which, as regards the quantative "more" of Tradition, did not deny or affirm but was only silent on the matter, was worth silencing the small group of complainants. At this point Mgr Philips

between the sides. The only possibility left was the choice of two relators, Florit as representing the majority but also of the Roman School, without whom, as Ratzinger implied, a final outcome would not have been achieved, just as without Parente collegiality would not have been approved,[173] and Franić as representing the minority. Florit's clear and persuasive words[174] succeeded in gaining from the council chamber that consent necessary for the schema to be approved. In fact, the Archbishop of Florence attested to the fact that, as regards the individual moment of Tradition as regards its objective content which exceeds Scripture, that among the testimonies *de integro* with certainty that is manifested through the canon and the inspired books. On this question a limit was reached beyond which it was not necessary to go any further. The Magisterium has never declared what is without foundation in Scripture, nor has it defined what is contained solely in Tradition. It leaves freedom to find the foundation both in Scripture and Tradition. From the ordinary Magisterium it is not clearly known what is the relationship between

---

and I, who by now were seated as spectators *ut viderunt finem,* limited ourselves to saying *videant consules,* with the Fathers deciding by voting. The vote was taken at 6.35 p.m.: 17 *placet* and 7 *non placet.* The text was finally approved. The dissatisfied were able to prolong their dissent with *an hoc* report in the council chamber', *Ibid.,* pp. 46–47.

173 Cf. Ratzinger, *Einleitung,* p. 502.

174 Florit had given Betti a statement to be read at the Doctrinal Commission, in which he responded to Cardinal Ottaviani about his leaning in favour of constitutive Tradition among the Italian bishops. Florit said: 'The reservations, to which Cardinal Ottaviani alluded yesterday evening, date back to a time prior to the composition of the new text; giving priority to the conscience of the council Fathers compared to what could be his personal point of view, he approved the new text and strongly recommended it'. After the text was read in the Commission, Betti added: 'Cardinal Ottaviani, who was oozing a black humour, was thankful for this chronological clarification' (Betti, *Diario,* pp. 47–48). It should not be forgotten that Betti had taught Florit that the Council was a school of theology 'which was worth more than any other attended or taught up to now', *Ibid.,* p. 28.

Scripture and Tradition: hence it was possible to solve the numerous appeals to the ordinary Magisterium, nor could the suspicion of diplomatic silence on the part of the Commission creep in.[175] If the quantative object of Scripture and Tradition were identical it was neither affirmed nor denied. The most significant issue about the material insufficiency of Scripture was therefore left open, not just as regards the substance, but also as regards the terminology.[176]

---

175 However, it must also be asked of Florit how the ordinary Magisterium of at least four centuries can prove just by a clear statement about the issue of the relationship between Scripture and Tradition, given that, among the many magisterial statements, there was still no clear expression about the aforesaid relationship: instead isn't it necessary to confirm the cogency of the teaching and its reiteration? Is 'not-saying-anything' justified according to a new theological methodology?

176 Cf. AS III/3, pp. 137–140: 'Per hanc ultima affirmationem, singulare Traditionis momentum asseritur, quod in eo est ut saltem in uno Scripturam, quoad contentum obiectivum, ipsa excedat: in testimonio nempe, de integro [dico de integro] canone et inspiratione librorum sacrorum exhibendo. Et ita in hac quaestione limite attingimus, ultra quos progredi non oportere videtur. Equidem Patres non desunt qui vellent ut, praetor dictam de Scriptura attestationem Traditioni propriam, aliarum quoque revelatarum veritatum transmissio uni Traditioni tribueretur. Advertere tamen iidem Patres velint ad istam affirmationem faciendam rationes non adesse cogentes. Cum enim agatur de quaestioni facti, id quod de veritatibus Scripturam respicientibus Traditioni ascribitur, ad nullam aliam veritatem in concreto applicare astringimur. Pro nulla enim Magisterium hucusque declaravit omni carere in Scriptura fundamento, nullamque uti sola Traditione contentam umquam definivit. Cuique igitur libertas relinquitur cuiusvis veritatis divinitus revelatae fundamentum sive in Scriptura sive in Traditione inveniendi. Haec libertas, quae in modo agendi Magisterii innititur, in Schemate quoque nostro partier servatur [Nota n. 10: Quod Magisterium ordinarium, tam frequenter invocatum, iuxta recentiora ac graviora studia,—ego ipse fortasse progressus sum hac in re consulendo illa opera—iuxta recentiora ac graviora studia clare non constat ex locutionibus variis a magistero adhibitis, quaenam sit relation inter Scripturam et traditionem… cum ergo ex magisterio ordinario certa haberi nequeat doctrina in quaestione, ratio non datur suspicandi aliquod diplomaticum silentium ex parte commissionis nostrae, neque ratio adest

Franić, on the other hand, proposing again the teaching that numerous Fathers had set out, about the deposit of faith consigned to the Church by Scripture and Tradition, with the latter having a formal and material breadth greater than the former, submitted to the Council Fathers some burning problems: the breadth of Tradition set out in the schema did not fully express the Catholic mindset. It was about a question of truth, which could not be silenced. The schema did not contain an error, but a '*defectum notabilem*'.[177]

Discussion of the text occupied the Council from 30 September until 6 October 1964. In the Fathers' speeches on the schema two sides could still be perceived, just as at the start: the one symbolised by Ruffini,[178] who complained about the fact that constitutive Tradition was passed over in silence, and that symbolised by Döpfner, who instead supported the text because it succeeded in solving a burning issue, leaving the matter open.[179] A question of method, as planned at the outset, but which necessarily impacted upon the doctrine of the faith or better sought not to commit it too much, preferring a broader consensus. The Doctrinal Commission re-examined the text

quidquam timendi. Etenim si illud quod a nonnullis circa hoc putatur verum est, verum manebit]... Utrum autem hoc commune obiectum etiam quantitative idem sit, neque affirmatur neque negatur... Notissima igitur quaestio aperta relinquitur: et quidem non solum, quoad substantiam, verum etiam quoad hucusque usitatam terminologia'.

177 Cf. *Ibid.*, pp. 124–129. Franić also suggested two formulae to summarise the long-standing problem of insufficiency: 'Per eandem Traditionem non solum quaedam veritates revelatae verum etiam ipsae Scripturae nobis certe innotescunt...', or a longer text on behalf of the minority of the Doctrinal Commission: 'Per eandem Traditionem quaedam veritates revelatae quae in Sacra Scriptura vel expresse non leguntur vel ex ea per se sola, etiam adhibita interpretatione ex Traditione desumpta, probari ac erui non possunt, quamvis forsan in ea fundamentum habeant, immo Sacrae Litterae absoluta certitudine Ecclesiae innotescunt in eaque indesinenter actuosae redduntur', *Ibid.*, pp. 128–129.

178 Cf. AS III/3, p. 142–145.

179 Cf. *Ibid.*, p. 145.

from 10–11 November 1964. Then on 20 November the schema amended for the *suffragatio* and *expensio modorum* was redistributed in the council chamber, but due to the prolonging of time up to the IV Session, and due to confusion in the aula about other schema, only towards the end of the Council, on 18 November 1965,[180] was it possible to proceed to a definitive vote, which was divided as follows: 2,350 voters, of whom 2,344 placet, and 6 non placet. Thus was the text of *Dei verbum* promulgated in the same session.[181]

2.3 '...non solam sacram Scripuram hauriat': winning back the axiom left aside?

Meanwhile the schema amended after the Fathers' amendments (form E), presented on 14 June 1964, added a new paragraph to the previous schema, paragraph 8, entitled *De Sacra Traditione*. The first

180 Many Fathers were still dissatisfied with the text, however. The *Coetus Internationalis Patrum*, established between the Second and Third Sessions and made up of conservative bishops, produced a ten-page printed text, in which they highlighted all the *animadversiones* to the schema *De Revelatione*. It was circulated among the Fathers, asking them to sign the observations indicated there and send them to the Secretary of the Council as soon as possible, no later than 31 January 1965. The text was in Betti's hands on 16 February 1965, and he peremptorily said: 'I read it with disgust. I will report to Mgr Florit and to Mgr Charue, after a careful examination' (Betti, *Diario*, p. 63). On the other hand, Mgr Carli along with Mgr de Proença Sigaud and Mgr Lefebvre, in a letter to the Pope on 25 July 1965, requested, inter alia, there be a new discussion on *De divina Revelatione* and a new report from the minority. Betti noted that the reply to Mgr Carli was 'tit-for-tat. The Secretary of State Cardinal Cicognani, in a letter on 11 August, replied to him that the existence of the Committee as such could not be approved, and his endeavours were to be condemned' (Betti, *Diario*, p. 68). For the historian De Mattei, this response is blatant hypocrisy, because the very Rule of the Council, in article 57, encouraged the formation of groups of conciliar Fathers, who shared the same point of view. Above all, the response pretended to ignore the de facto existence of various conciliar sides and a real progressive Alliance, cf. De Mattei, *Il Concilio Vaticano II*, p. 455.

181 Cf. Ratzinger, *Einleitung*, pp. 502–503.

sentence read as follows: 'Itaque praedicatio apostolica quae in inspiratis libris speciali modo exprimitur, continua successione usque ad consummationem temporum conservari debeat',[182] where the first phrase as far as 'speciali modo exprimitur' had been added to avoid the most thorny question, taking up the debate of a whole Council, about the material sufficiency of the Scriptures.[183] On 20 November 1964, to the schema *Constitutionis Dogmaticae de Divina Revelatione,* distributed in the aula for the *expensio modorum,* 154 Fathers proposed adding (paragraph 8, page 15, line 34) a sentence to explain the insufficiency of the Scriptures, as follows: 'atque ea veritates quae per solam Scripturam cognosci non possent, ut verbum Dei nobis innotescunt'. 8 Fathers suggested a longer formula:

> Per eandem Traditionem quaedam veritates revelatae, quae in Sacra Scriptura vel expresse non leguntur, vel ex ea per se sola, etiam adhibita interpretatione ex traditione desumpta, probari ac erui non possunt, quamvis forsan in ea fundamentum habeant, immo et ipsae Sacrae Litterae absoluta certitudine Ecclesiae innotescunt.[184]

Paragraph 9 studied the mutual relationship between Sacred Scripture and Sacred Tradition and from the outset stated:

> S. Traditio ergo S. Scriptura arcte inter se connectuntur atque communicant. Nam ambae, ex eadem divina scaturigine promanantes, in unum quodammodo coalescunt et in eundem finem tendunt. Quapropter utraque pari pietatis affect ac reverentia suscipienda et veneranda est.[185]

[182] Cf. Hellín, *Dei verbum,* p. 60. Again in this synopsis of the four subsequent drafts of the Constitution on Divine Revelation (indicated by A. Grillmeier also as form D, E, F, G: 'Die Wahrheit der Heiligen Schrift und ihre Erschließung. Zum dritten Kapitel der Dogmatischen Konstitution "Dei "Verbum" des Vatikanum II', *Scholastik* 41 [1966], pp. 161–187), see the whole development of the text, on pp. 2–175.

[183] Cf. Hellín, *Dei verbum,* p. 60.

[184] Modus 36, cf. AS IV/5, pp. 698–699; *Ibid.,* p. 69.

[185] *Ibid.,* pp. 71–73.

Two Fathers regretted that the *munus* of Tradition (cf. no. 9, p. 16. lin. 3–13), '*prout a Scriptura distinguitur*', was not sufficiently affirmed. The apostolic *paradosis*, they said, was handed on both through oral preaching and Scripture.[186] 111 Fathers suggested, with a slightly different formula, an addition to line 13: '*quo fit ut non omnis doctrina catholica ex (sola) Scriptura (directe) probari queat*'.[187]

The responses to the last two measures were as follows: 'De paradosis apostolica in genere actum est explicite sub n. 7 Traditio et Scriptura variis modis inter se implicantur, neque in subtilitates hic intrare oportet'.[188] In fact, the majority position of the Commission—which was then that of the Council itself—represented by Florit, worked on precisely not entering into details: this problem reached a threshold beyond which it was good not to go, leaving room for eventual in-depth examinations by theologians.

Furthermore, the *modus* was welcomed and the proposed formula added, but expressed with a small revision: '*quo fit ut Ecclesia certitudinem suam de omnibus revelatis non per solam Sacram Scripturam hauriat*'.[189] For the last time the problem of the scriptural insufficiency was presented and was also resolved.[190] In a very general way, room

186 Modus 40/C, cf. AS IV/5, p. 700; *Ibid.*, pp. 71–72.

187 Modus 40/D, cf. AS IV/5, p. 700; *Ibid.*, p. 73.

188 R. *Ad C*, AS IV/5, p. 700.

189 R. *Ad D*, AS IV/5, p. 700.

190 The theological background to arriving at this addition was also difficult. The *Modus* of the 111 Fathers, in fact, suggested an important modification in *directe*; '*quo fit ut non omnis doctrina catholica ex (sola) Scriptura (directe) probari queat*'. Tromp aimed for the adoption of this modification, *directe probari queat*, because it would have called into play again the value of the additional Tradition. That *directe* could be understood in two ways: 1) nothing would be changed in the text if *directe* meant everything could not be proved directly by Sacred Scripture, but the help of Tradition was necessary; 2) on the other hand it would have been a dirty trick to the whole text if by that *directe* it was meant that every truth can be demonstrated by Scripture indirectly, attesting at the same time to the existence of an infallible Magisterium and the indefectibility of the Church, in such a way that the Magisterium

was also left open to the other possibility of knowledge of Revelation, that offered by Tradition. However, this way of speaking did not allude in an unambiguous manner to the constitutive Tradition and could also be understood as a reference solely to apostolic or post-apostolic preaching. It required a necessary hermeneutic, which however was susceptible to different interpretations, as it would be. So therefore I ask once again: was it the Council which posted the hermeneutic problem of the Council?

Once again the Doctrinal Commission had to tackle a sensitive problem. On behalf of the Pope, the Secretary of State, Cardinal Cicognani, on 18 October 1965 handed over a note to Cardinal Ottaviani asking the Theological Commission to choose from the seven proposed formulae the one which had the majority support: '*qui in maiore Consilii parte pollent*'. Formula n. 3 was chosen, that of C. Colombo, and inserted into the definitive text. The formula immediately received ecumenical support.[191] H. Ott explained that

---

could also define a truth of faith without reference to Scripture, even while dealing with a divinely revealed truth. Tromp, as Betti attests (*Diario*, pp. 70–72), was inclined towards this second meaning. In the Doctrinal Commission, Fr Fernández, Fr Gallagher, and Mgr Parente all spoke out along the same lines as Tromp, with Mgr Parente saying that Catholic teaching was not contained *totaliter* in Scripture. According to Betti, 'once again it was all getting involved with the question *de duplici fonte*... Myself and Cardinal Florit insisted that the question was resolved in paragraph 9, with the formula already introduced, but freed from the obstacle of *directe*; that in fact was to conveniently explain the text, but without changing it... Therefore the vote was taken (3 October 1965): 15 against, 10 said not to make any addition' (*Ibid.*, pp. 72–73). The subsequent vote on 6 October, too, after some disagreement, confirmed there was to be no addition to the text, overlooking a suggestion from Philips. So the formula in paragraph 9 was left somewhat vague, according to Colombo's proposal. According to Fr Betti, this formula, even if understood by him in a slightly different way from Colombo, 'while in fact it recognises the insufficiency of Scripture on a gnosiological level, leaves open the question of insufficiency or otherwise on the constitutive level', *Ibid.*, p. 74.

191 The IV World Ecumenical Conference on Faith and Order had been held in

it was certainly well-founded for a Protestant, too, who had not forgotten its foundation: not just Scripture but also the preaching and interior testimony of the Holy Spirit.[192]

The problem of the material insufficiency of the Scriptures was thus resolved, quarantined, or was a much bigger problem in fact created: its correct interpretation? Florit, nevertheless, in his *Relatio de modis* proposed by the Fathers and resolved by the Commission (22 October 1965), indicated three reasons for the latest insertion:

1. On the one hand the addition '*quo fit ut Ecclesia certitudine suam...*' provided an explanation of the preceding words, according to which Tradition transmits wholly the Word of God; on the other hand, it links well with what follows, and that is, that the Church venerates with equal feeling of reverence both Scripture and Tradition.[193]

Montreal in 1963 and it had tackled the question of Tradition. It distinguished between Tradition (the Gospel itself) and traditions (the different forms of expression and the different denominational traditions), with the desire to offer a more united concept between Tradition and Church, highlighting its ecclesiological understanding (cf. G. G. Blum, *Offenbarung und Überlieferung. Die dogmatische Konstitution Dei verbum des II. Vaticanums im Lichte altkirchlicher und moderner Theologie* [Göttingen: Vandenhoeck & Ruprecht, 1971], pp. 70–74). In this sense *Dei verbum* was praised by M. Thurian ('Un acte oecuménique du Concile: le vote de la Constitution dogmatique sur la revelation', in *Verbum Caro* 76 [1965], pp. 6–10). According to Blum, the vision of the Orthodox theologians was very similar, as a vision of Tradition as intimate charismatic or mystical thought of the Church and dynamic moment of the manifestation of God in Christ in the Holy Spirit, cf. Blum, *Offenbarung und Überlieferung*, pp. 75–82.

192 Cf. Ratzinger, *Einleitung*, p. 526. Here Ratzinger quotes H. Ott through Hampe, *Die Autorität*: 'Übrigens steht es doch wohl auch für einen Protestanten, der das Fundament der Reformation nicht vergessen hat, fest: daß wir Gewißheit über Gottes Offenbarung nicht aus der Schrift allein schöpfen, sondern daß sie uns durch die Predigt und das innere Zeugnis des Heiligen Geistes zuteil wird'.

193 On this see also *Modus* 41, p. 16, lines 13–15: in place of the 'pari pietatis affectu' 15 Fathers suggested 'uno pietatis affectu', concerned that the *pari*

2. The Catholic teaching constantly sanctioned by praxis was being highlighted, according to which the Church draws certainty of the things revealed from Scripture as linked to Tradition and that therefore Scripture alone is not sufficient, but Tradition can offer a decisive argument.
3. The meaning of the statement is to be judged from the tenor of the schema, from which it emerges that: there was no desire to present Tradition as a quantitative supplement to Scripture, nor to present Scripture as an integral codification of Revelation.[194]

---

prejudiced the distinction between Scripture and Tradition, one inspired, the other not. The response was: 'Expressio Tridentini "*pari* affectu" aptius indicat, Traditionem et Scripturam eandem habere divinam originem, sed nos easdem esse quoad communicationem, scilicet inspiratam vel non. Praeterea non praeiudicat quaestionem de earum respective contento', (AS IV/5, p. 701). It was appropriate to leave the Tridentine expression, which while attesting to the same divine origin of Scripture and Tradition, distinguished its mode of communication. So the nature of their respective content was not prejudiced. Thus was there a return to the distinction, even though somewhat veiled, of the two sources of Revelation? The Council would not renounce the received teaching, but would seek to present it generally in a more congenial manner. And this would give rise to the main problem.

194 'Altera additio facta est in n. 9, pag. 16, lin. 13 hisce verbis: "*quo fit ut Ecclesia certitudinem suam de omnibus revelatis non per solam Sacram Scripturam hauriat*" (cf. Mod. 36, 40-D, 56). Quoad huius additionis significatione, haec tria adnotanda sunt: Attengo integro n. 9 contextu, ubi de mutua inter Scriptura et Traditionem relatione, per addita verba duo obtinentur, nempe: ex una parte, aliqua datur explicatio verborum quibus paulo ante dicitur Traditionem verbum Dei *integre transmitter* (cf. pag. 16 linn. 8–11); ex altera autem parte, ulterior praebetur iustificatio verborum quae immediate sequuntur, quibus affirmatur Scripturam et Traditionem pari pietatis affectu ac reverentia suscipiendas et venerandas esse (cf. pag. 16 linn. 13–15). In tuto ponitur doctrina catholica, constant Ecclesiae praxi sancita, iuxta quam Ecclesia certitudinem suam de revelatis haurit per sacram Scripturam nonnisi cum Traditione coniunctam; quapropter, ubi ad illam certitudine assequendum Scriptura sola non sufficit. Traditio decisivam afferre potest argumentum. Sensus huiusmodi affirmationis ulterius diiudicandus est atque circumscribendus ex Schematis tenore. Ex quo quidem patet: nec Traditionem praesentari veluti quantitativum S. Scripturae

So Florit called for consideration of the tenor of the schema. The most decisive argument seemed to be the last one: the Theological Commission had considered things well not to present Tradition simply as a quantitative supplement to Scripture and Scripture as an integral codification of Revelation. Material insufficiency had led Tradition to be a materially cognitive supplement of truth not contained in Scripture. The choice was for the formal complementarity of Tradition, so as to support, too, the many ecumenical hopes placed in the Council. But a Tradition deprived of the importance of its content could obviously be limited to a mere auxiliary functionality compared to Scripture, to its simple interpretation, with the possibility remaining, however, that in limited cases Tradition might offer decisive elements. That, to us, appears to be the general conciliar tenor of the Scripture-Tradition relationship. There should be no surprise therefore that in the reception of the Council Tradition is often perceived simply as an interpretative tool, as if that *plus* which it offers to faith by reason of its revelatory unity with the Scriptures had almost been forgotten. I will return to this issue in a more systematic fashion.

After all, the Council seemed to have spoken. Is there any need to do more than the Council? In our opinion, knowing *why* the Council spoke thus, the theological concept of the communication of Revelation, through Sacred Scripture and Sacred Tradition, highlighting the latter, both the material and formal element, could also be improved. If the substance of something is lost, the form is impacted, too. Only from the unity of the two is there a subject with precise identity.

2.4 A 'significant compromise' alongside a new theological development

In the report on the schema *De Divina Revelatione*, amended by the Commission after the observations of the Fathers, Florit, presenting in the aula, said:

---

supplementum; nec S. Scripturam praesentari veluti integrae revelationis codificationem', AS IV/5, pp. 740–741.

> The amended text is and remains a human work: therefore, by its nature, it can be further improved. The imperfections which perhaps remain there all the same, we believe, without presumption, to be able to overcome them qualitatively in a way more than sufficient.[195]

A human work, undoubtedly assisted by the Holy Spirit, who protects against errors, but not *per se* sanctifies and inspires the text. A work which has seen the interaction of many theological and also disparate minds; which at the same time united a faithfulness to the original inspiration of the Council: pastorality and ecumenicity with a renewed theological endeavour, which in the meantime was always increasing. For example, it is not difficult to glimpse behind *Dei verbum* 8 the hand of Y. Congar and the concept of the 'dynamic-organic' tradition of the Tübingen theological school of the nineteenth century.[196] This theological endeavour, born out of seeing *Traditio* not as source of Revelation, because there is only one source, the Gospel, the Word of God incarnate, was careful to highlight the same Tradition in a wider vision, that of Revelation. It was a move from the sources of Revelation to Revelation itself[197] and in it—a new chapter is also added, *De ipsa revelatione*—can be seen the intertwining between Scripture and Tradition, privileging, without doubt, the written moment of Revelation, and related to this one sees the oral [Tradition]. Preaching was seen as preparatory to Scripture and Scripture as the moment of the fullness of the oral transmission of

---

195 'Textus emendatus opus humanum est et manet; quod propterea, ipsa natura sua, ulterius perfici potest. Attamen imperfectiones, quae fortasse ibidem permanent qualitatibus abunde superari, sine praesumptione, putamus', AS IV/1, pp. 379–380.

196 Cf. Ratzinger, *Einleitung*, p. 519.

197 H. Sauer, 'Von den "Quellen der Offenbarung" zur "Offenbarung selbst". Zum theologischen Hintergrund der Auseindersetzung um das Schema "Über die göttliche Offenbarung" beim II. Vatikanischen Konzil', in Klinger—Wittstadt (eds.), *Glaube im Prozess*, pp. 514–545, where the theological work of Rahner is indicated as a *turning point*.

Revelation. This would balance the too traditional tenor of theology, with the danger of falling into *'sola traditio'*. The first schema, *De fontibus*, had given rise in many people precisely to this suspicion. In the passage from this schema to schema II and right up to the end of the drafting of *Dei verbum*, one nagging question remained: what is it about the material insufficiency of Scripture, in other words, of the constitutive Tradition of Revelation? In the attempt to explain the relationship between Scripture and Tradition in a new, more pastoral manner, the fact was raised that we find ourselves faced with a still debatable academic question. In reality, the insufficiency of the Scriptures was not a *quaestio disputata*: it was unanimous among theologians, with the exception of a few, to consider the contribution of Tradition to be indispensable for some revealed truths not contained in Scripture;[198] it became so to justify the choice of a more

[198] The bibliography on this is substantial. Above all in the years immediately prior to Vatican II there was an increasing number of studies on 'Scripture and Tradition' Here are some: see the accurate bibliography provided by G. Baraúna in the appendix to his work *Quaenam Sacrae Scripturae sufficientia in Ecclesia catholica teneatur*, in Pontifical International Marian Academy, *De Scriptura et Traditione*, Rome 1963, pp. 73–111, Appendix 85–111, and the forty authors who have written in the aforesaid *De Scriptura et Traditione*; K. J. Becker, 'Das Denken Domingo De Soto über Schrift und Tradition vor und nach Trient. Ein theologiegeschichtlicher Beitrag zum Verständnis das Trienter Dekretes', in *Scholastik* 30 (1964), pp. 343–373; C. Pozo, 'Escritura y Tradición. A propóito de las recientes monografías de J. R. Geiselmann y J. Beumer', in *ATG* 28 (1965), pp. 179–198; M. Schmaus, 'Animadversiones ad opus recens historiam Traditionis non scriptam tractans', in *Divinitas* 8 (1964), pp. 131–141; H. Schauf, 'Die Lehre der Kirche über Schrift und Tradition in den Katechismen, cit.; Id., Schrift und Tradition', in *Antonianum* 39 (1964), pp. 200–209; A. Trapé, 'De Traditionis Relatione ad S. Scripturam iuxta Concilium Tridentinum', in *Augustinianum* 3 (1963), pp. 253–289. On the other hand, some theologians have put forward the idea that Trent had left open the question about the material insufficiency of the Scriptures. See also this contribution from J. R. Geiselmann, 'Das Missverständnis über das Verhältnis von Schrift und Tradition und seine Überwindung in der katholischen Theologie', in *Una Sancta* 11 (1956), pp. 132–139; J. Beumer, 'Katho-

neutral formulation. The key arguments to cause the shift to a more bland and evasive text as regards the relationship between Scripture and Tradition with the emphasis on content rather than form were those of Rahner and Florit, one relying on the Fathers and the other on the Magisterium. Rahner believed that the material insufficiency of the Scriptures could not be proved, due to the absence of a sure testimony, too, besides that in Scripture and the Tradition of the first three centuries. As I noted, this also caused a reduction of dogmatic Tradition to its historical verifiability of the early centuries, ignoring its homogenous development up to the threshold of Vatican II. The presence, even if at least implicit, of a truth in Scripture does not avoid posing the problem of constitutive Tradition. Just as one can search for a foundation in Scripture, so the same truth is believed by the Church's credo. There is always first the oral Tradition and then the written one. Florit, on the other hand, attested to the fact that among the many magisterial locutions there was not one clear one which verified the precise identity of the material insufficiency of the Scriptures. He, too, moved to a new theological assessment: rather than a positive *locutio*, which confirmed the cogency of the fact in the reiteration of the magisterial teaching, one which expressed its quasi-definition at a specific moment. Two very similar arguments, expressive of an identical theological mindset, which moved the outcomes of the Council. *Dei verbum*, in a certain sense, was 'symbol' of the Council and its changes. Burigana wrote in this regard:

> The Council was dominated by the struggle to remove the idea that it was not possible to formulate in an orthodox fashion Catholic teaching on revelation without an explicit declaration of the superiority of the magisterial Tradition compared to

---

lisches und protestantisches Schriftprinzip im Urteil des Trienter Konzils', in *Scholastik* 34 (1959), pp. 249–258; Y. Congar, *La tradition et les traditions: Essais historique* (Paris: Fayard, 1960), pp. 207–232; Id., 'Le débat sur la question du rapport entre Écriture et Tradition, au point du vue de leur contenu materiel', in *Revue des sciences philosohiques et théologiques* 48 (1964), pp. 645–657.

> Scripture in the transmission of revelation... A complex reconstruction of the drafting of *Dei verbum* enables one to grasp the importance of the constitution for the Catholic Church; in the Council the shift took place from a theology founded essentially on papal Magisterium, to a reflection in which was central the in-depth examination of the Word of God, to whose understanding the traditions of the primitive Church, the Fathers of the Church, and the declarations of the Magisterium had to contribute. It was a theology in which ecumenism and the pastoral were not accidental, but essential dimensions in a process of recovery of the centrality of Scripture. In the Council the idea of uniformity in the forms of expression of Catholic teaching was abandoned to accept the existence of a plurality of schools, which appeal to the common patrimony of the Roman Church; with *Dei verbum* the perspective expressed in *De fontibus revelationis,* which identified the Roman School as unique depository of orthodoxy, denying the legitimacy of other interperetations of the mystery of revelation, was abandoned.[199]

The text of *Dei verbum* in the condensed formula of paragraph 9:

> Consequently it is not from Sacred Scripture alone that the Church draws her certainty about everything which has been revealed. Therefore both Sacred Tradition and Sacred Scripture are to be accepted and venerated with the same sense of loyalty and reverence

was soon greeted by some periti and theologians as a 'compromise', even if a compromise theologically open to science and new acquisitions. In fact, Rahner said that the text definitively approved by Paul VI bore the traces of its laborious path:

> It is an expression of a manifold compromise, which however is more than a compromise: it is a synthesis of a greater significance: the text binds faithfulness to ecclesial Tradition with the yes to critical science, and opens in a new way a path

[199] Burigana, *La Bibbia nel Concilio,* pp. 8, 17.

> to faith today. It praises neither Trent nor Vatican I, but nor does it mummify the things of the past, since one knows that faithfulness in spiritual things can be achieved only through ever new complete acquisitions.[200]

Writing to Cardinal König on 29 April 1964, Rahner rejoiced that improvements had been made to the text, even if not so exciting: 'the important theme had won', that is, that of the relationship between Scripture and Tradition, so that 'now', Rahner said, 'the impression is no longer given of being a wretched compromise like before'.[201]

A compromise, therefore, but which led to a new theological opening, and to a new study of Revelation itself. Thus *Dei verbum* was able to enlighten a new concept of Revelation: not positive, but rather historico-salvific and dialogical.[202] God communicates himself to the human person, and this communication happens not just through *words*—God is not just the one who speaks—but also through *signs*, through his gestures; a supernatural manifestation made up of *verba*

---

200 Ratzinger, *Einleitung*, p. 503: '… er ist [der Text] ein Ausdrück vielfältiger Kompromisse. Aber der grundlegende Kompromiß, der ihn trägt, ist doch mehr als ein Kompromiß, er ist eine Synthese von großer Bedeutung: der Text verbindet die Treue zur kirchlichen Überlieferung mit dem Ja zur kritischen Wissenschaft und eröffnet damit neu dem Glauben den Weg ins Heute. Er gibt Trient und das Vatikanum nicht preis, aber er mumifiziert auch das Damalige nicht, weil er weiß, daß Treue im Geistigen nur durch die immer neu vollzogene Aneignung verwirklicht warden kann'.

201 From Munich Rahner wrote to Cardinal König: 'Verangenen Sonntag bin ich von Rom nach einer Woche von Kommissionsizungen wieder zurückgekommen. Es tagte eine kleine Kommission, um das Schema über die Offenbarung unter dem Vorsitz von Exzellenz Charue nach den Verbesserungswünschen, die in Rom unterdessen eingegangen waren, zu verbessern. Wenn auch keine aufregenden Änderungen vorgenommen worden sind, so glaube ich doch, daß das Thema erheblich gewonnen hat und nun nicht mehr so sehr den Eindruck eines dürftigen Kompromisses macht wie vorher. Wie Eminenz wissen, war ich auch Ende Februar/Anfang März bei den Kommissionssitzungen der theologischen Plenarkommission dabei', in *Entschluß* 43/6 (1988), p. 36.

202 Cf. Blum, *Offenbarung und Überlieferung*, pp. 16–37.

et signa. With Vatican II is fulfilled 'the passage from an *intellectualistic conception* to an *historico-salvific personalistic conception* of revelation'.[203] So there was a major re-evaluation of biblical history and the revelatory progress which, in the fullness of time, encounters Christ, Word and event of God. A theology of Tradition, as it developed after the Marian dogmas of 1854 and 1950, risked causing a de-historicisation of theology with the consequent reduction or even exclusion of the Fathers of the Church. That was due to the fact that it followed this hypothesis: to verify a fact of faith it was necessary, in a longitudinal fashion, to go back to the beginning, but it was sufficient, in transverse fashion, to verify the knowledge of the faith of the Church at any moment in its history.[204] So it was necessary to re-instate a more historical-patristic method. Theology was no longer crystallised on what could be known from Tradition, which was not contained in Scripture, explicitly or implicitly. The emphasis on the historico-salvific dynamism of Revelation shifted the centre of gravity of the problem: with the passing of the intellectualistic conception of Revelation, as handed on by Vatican I, the problem of constitutive Tradition also gradually lost its edge.[205] 'The problem of "Scripture

---

203 G. Pozzo, 'La nozione di rivelazione nella "Dei verbum" e gli sviluppi nella teologia post-conciliare', in AA.VV, *Ripensare il Concilio* (Casale Monferrato: Collana Cultura e Teologia 2, Piemme, 1986), p. 31. See also Buckenmaier, *"Schrift und Tradition"*, pp. 208–281.

204 Cf. J. Ratzinger, *The Nature and Mission of Theology: essays to orient theology in today's debates* (Milan: Jaka Book, 1995), pp. 148–149 (German original, *Wesen und Aufgabe der Theologie* [Freiburg im B.: Einsiedeln, 1992]).

205 Pozzo explains that 'the intellectualistic conception (of Vatican I) understands divine revelation as communication of truth by God to the human intellect, sustained by freedom and illuminated by grace. The historico-salvific perception (of Vatican II) understands revelation as self-manifestation of God himself to and in the history of humanity, through the mission of Jesus and the Spirit. There is obviously no opposition between the two conceptions, since the second does not exclude, but integrates the first. The self-revelation of God in fact also implies a communication of truth at the intellectual level and recognisable from the noetic point of view' (Pozzo, 'La nozione di rivelazione', p. 31). For

and Tradition" remains unresolvable', wrote Ratzinger, 'until it is extended and becomes the problem of "Revelation and Tradition" and therefore becomes integrated into the wider context to which it belongs'.[206] There was a preference, then, for a new historical-speculative theological method, and the more positive one based on the 'sources' of Revelation was overlooked.[207]

This move which took place in the Council, precisely in the Theological Commission, and through which the conciliar document was arrived at, is very important: it characterises the *novum* of the teaching of Vatican II and at the same time offers us a hermeneutical interpretation. The Council wanted to leave its magisterial discourse in the channel of the ordinary, proposing the teaching again in pastoral and ecumenical terms and re-launching theological discourse, so there was a shift from a scholastic-metaphysical method to a speculative and historical-salvific method, open to the new exegetical-theological gains and to the new problems of the modern world,

---

Ratzinger, the fact that Tradition exists is based on the non-identity of Revelation and Scripture. The problem of the sufficiency or otherwise of the Scriptures must be transferred to another problem: Scripture does not exhaust Revelation; the latter is broader according to ecclesial faith as the living 'place' of its reception. This establishes the otherness between Scripture and Tradition, in which the latter also has a dogmatic value concerning faith and morals, according to a correct interpretation of the Tridentine decree. For Ratzinger, therefore, Tradition is rule of faith in a formal manner. '... if therefore', he says, 'there is alongside Scripture a second and, right from the outset, independent material principle, it becomes in comparison to that absolutely secondary; probably, one would have to respond rather with a no', Ratzinger, 'Un tentativo', p. 48. The whole study is pp. 27–73.

206 *Ibid.*, p. 35.

207 For an overall view of the reception of *Dei verbum*, see R. Latourelle, *Theology of Revelation* (New York: Alba House, 1966), pp. 453–490 (French original, *Théologie de la Révelation* [Paris: Studia 15, Desclée de Brouver, 1963]). For its reception in the post-conciliar period, see Pozzo 'La nozione di rivelazione', pp. 29–49. For the reception of the conciliar teaching on 'Scripture and Tradition' among German theologians, see Buckenmaier, *"Schrift und Tradition"*, pp. 282–483 (from K. Rahner up to E. Drewermann).

in primis the pressing secularisation and atheism which were appearing on the horizon.

However, the question remains, to which it is important to respond, so as to give reason to our magisterial-hermeutical goal: did *Dei verbum* change the meaning of the traditional teaching on the 'Scripture and Tradition' relationship? It did not change it, but it did not even want to define it, because that lay outside its original resolution. It deliberately left the question still open to new gains, at the same time supporting its pastoral and above all ecumenical goal. It did not deny what the ordinary Magisterium had unanimously asserted: Tradition is constitutive of the faith of the Church like Scripture itself, but it tried to translate it into theological-pastoral terms for the modern times with which the Council was calling for dialogue. Confirmed was what H. Schauf already feared, that a Council would pronounce at an inferior or at least equal level compared to the already acquired ordinary Magisterium. This means that Vatican II, *per se*, that is, by reason of the level of authority exercised, was incapable of solving the problem of the material insufficiency of Scripture. Vatican II cannot be used to deny preceding doctrinal patrimony, but only starting from the preceding patrimony and with the Council can new ways be sought to examine the patrimony in-depth, comparing it with the new modern language and the new culture. Without the previous teaching the Council itself would be incomprehensible. So to set up Vatican II as judge of the whole Tradition of the Church, starting from our given, seems to be a mistaken and above all prejudicial act. Instead, for a correct conciliar hermeneutic, in this context, the opposite is necessary: to judge the new by reason of the already acquired teaching. This method, which seems to us to be the only one capable of solving the 'Vatican II problem'—except for the case of wanting to see Tradition in the light of the Council for the teaching on the sacramentality of the episcopate—attesting to the Council itself, what it was and what it did, tells us that Vatican II, when it teaches about the relationship between

Scripture and Tradition, favours a rather practical, ecumenical approach (even if moved by a speculative one), which remains at the ordinary level, thus expressed *in a new* (and *neutral*) way for the first time by the Magisterium, and therefore not infallible, open to a subsequent increased understanding, improvement and a possible dogmatic definition. 'Scripture and Tradition' is a teaching with ordinary magisterial value, even though taught by an Ecumenical Council. An advantageous work could show, starting from Trent and Vatican I through Vatican II, the inter-locking of the *non-written traditions* with the centrality of Revelation.

3. Interesting correspondence on the eve of the approval of De Divina Revelatione

From archival research of ASV there emerged a whole file devoted to the theme of Divine Revelation,[208] from which, on the one hand, there emerges Paul VI's great concern about the imminent approval of the text, asking Ottaviani to check all the modifications before it was brought to the council chamber, and expressing the explicit desire that the role of the constitutive Tradition of the faith be underlined; and on the other, the intervention of some Cardinals who wrote directly to the Pope: some manifesting perplexity at the formula adopted about the Scripture and Tradition relationship, others instead encouraging the Pope to welcome the text as it had been formulated according to the pastoral and ecumenical goal desired by John XXIII. Finally, a report from Mgr Ugo Lattanzi, handed to Ottaviani with the request to deliver it to the Supreme Pontiff, about the ambiguity of the formula chosen about the *Traditio constitutiva* problem as different from the Scriptures.

On 24 September 1965, Pericles Felici wrote to Ottaviani, expressing the Pope's wish that the constitutive nature of Tradition be expressly stated. Felici wrote:

---

[208] Cf. ASV, Envelope 797, file 424.

> Your Most Reverend Eminence,
> in relation to the examination of the Modi which this Commission will carry out, following the vote which recently took place in the Council Chamber on the schema *Constitutionis dogmaticae de divina Revelatione*, I am honoured to inform your Most Reverend Eminence that it is the will of the HOLY FATHER that in the most appropriate place in the schema it be stated clearly and most explicitly about the *constitutive* nature of Tradition, as Source of Revelation.
> To that end the SUPREME PONTIFF himself has kindly indicated the following quotation from St Augustine: 'Sunt multa quae universa tenet Ecclesia, et ob hoc ab Apostolis praecepta bene creduntur, quamquam scripta non reperiantur' (*De baptismo c. Donat.*, V, 23, 31: PL. 43, 192).
> Kissing the sacred purple and with sentiments of profound respect,
> I remain
> Obedient and devoted
> To your Most Reverend Eminence,
> Pericles Felici.

It is interesting to note the return to the idea of the 'sources' of Revelation, after a long discussion between the Fathers and the periti and that, what's more, the text of St Augustine cited by the Pope did not appear in the approved text. On 27 September 1965, Cardinal Ottaviani wrote to the Pope in these terms:

> Most Holy Father,
> The central sub-commission composed of His Eminence Cardinal Florit, His Grace Mgr Charue and His Grace Mgr (name illegible), assisted by the Secretaries Tromp and Philips and by the Rapporteur of the Text Fr Betti, and which was entrusted with the task of giving the opinion of the Doctrinal Commission on the text of the Decree on Revelation, agreed on the following terms about the sources of Revelation.

> In n. 12, 2 line 37, after the word proponit, suggests 'non autem ex S. Scriptura omnis doctrina catholica directe demonstrari potest'.
> The text continues 'patet igitur S. Traditionem et S. Scripturam et Ecclesiae Magisterium ... inter se connecti et consociari ut unum sine aliis non consistat'.
> In a footnote the term 'directe' is explained as follows:
> 'In oppositione ad indirecte, qui in ipsa S. Scriptura docetur Sacrum Magisterium Ecclesiae'.
> In this way the constitutive value of Tradition would be guaranteed, in fact, from the terms used it appears clear that the deposit of Faith is not contained in Scripture alone.
> Fr Tromp is of the opinion that other requests could cause interminable discussion and controversies.
> If such a formula were still believed to be unsatisfactory, I would ask that instructions be given about the matter.
> Prostrated in kissing the Holy Foot, I implore the Apostolic Blessing.[209]

In a handwritten letter, 10 October 1965, Paul VI wrote to Cardinal Ottaviani, manifesting again his careful attention about the text on Revelation:

> My Lord Cardinal,
> I would be grateful if you would let me know the amended text of the Schema 'de divina Revelatione', before it is printed and distributed to the Council Fathers, since I wish to assure myself that I can give my approval to such a text.
> With respectful greetings, I thank you and bless you
> Paulus PP. VI

On 11 October 1965, Cardinal Ottaviani acknowledged receipt of the Holy Father's letter, and wrote in these terms:

> Most Holy Father,
> I have just received the august letter of Your Holiness dated yesterday and I hasten to assure you that, as soon as possible,

[209] In red pen in brackets is added the name 'Cardinal Ottaviani'.

> I will send Your Holiness the complete text de DIVINA REVELATIONE.
> I have written 'as soon as possible', because the examination of the 'modi' has still not been completed, but will be in the Commission meeting this afternoon.
> I am very happy to note that Your Holiness intends to satisfy yourself so, with a sure conscience, you can give approval to the text that will be proposed. I say that because I trust that the personal intervention of Your Holiness will be able to correct any serious defects which might be found in the draft of the text: defects which turn out to be approved by the majority of the Commission, after serious discussion which sometimes ended with voting from which it can clearly be seen what sort of Commission I had to chair and over which I could not impose my views, supported only by a tenuous minority.
> I also believe that the Constitution DE REVELATIONE will need an intervention similar to that of the 'nota praevia' for De Ecclesia. But if this should happen, it is better that it comes to the Commission, in such a way that in the Assembly of the Fathers a text be proposed already perfected by the august suggestions of Your Holiness. To save time, as soon as the drafts are corrected, I will send them to Your Holiness, maybe chapter by chapter, as they are ready.
> Forgive me, then, Your Holiness, if I raise another matter, but I do not wish to delay in expressing to Your Holiness my great gratitude for your direct intervention in saving celibacy, the jewel and dignity of priesthood.
> Bowing to kiss the Holy Foot, I implore the Apostolic Blessing.[210]

Here there is a split in the Doctrinal Commission: according to Ottaviani a *nota praevia* should be introduced to *De Divina Revelatione,* too, to explain the correct meaning of some easily deceptive expressions approved by the majority. Just a day later, Ottaviani wrote to the Supreme Pontiff once again, manifesting a certain disappointment at the fact that the majority had not succeeded in paragraphs 9

210 In closing is added in red pen the name 'Cardinal Ottaviani'.

and 10 in highlighting more the constitutive role of Tradition. On 12 October 1965, Ottaviani wrote:

> Most Holy Father,
> Yesterday evening, at the Doctrinal Commission, the examination of the 'modi' on DE REVELATIONE came to an end and the Reports which Cardinal Florit and Mgr van Doddeward, Bishop of Harlem, will give in the Council Chamber to present the resolutions adopted about the 'modi' themselves, were approved...
> The minority on the Commission did not succeed in ensuring that in paragraphs 9 and 10 the 'constitutive' role of Tradition, too, in the entirety of the deposit of Revelation, might be highlighted more clearly and explicitly. Mgr Philipps (Philips), however, said that it was sufficiently expressed.
> If Your Holiness wishes the Commission to return to the issue before it is brought to the General Congregation in St Peter's I am willing to summon it for a new Meeting, so that a possible intervention by Your Holiness might be adopted as its own by the Commission, so that (in) St Peter's the thing might be judged not as imposed from on high, but as proposed by the Commission.
> In expectation of Your Holiness' revered commands, I implore the Apostolic Blessing.[211]

At this point the exchange of letters between the Pope and Ottaviani is interrupted. However, we know from a letter of the Substitute of the Secretary of State, A. Dell'Acqua, sent to Ottaviani on 18 October 1965, and from documents in ASV,[212] that Cardinals Ruffini, Dante, Döpfner and Journet, had ensured the Pope received their own comments concerning the text 'De Divina Revelatione'. Dell'Acqua handed them on to Ottaviani. I have chosen two of the interventions of these eminent prelates, since I believe they are more significant and

---

211 In red pen is added the name 'Cardinal OTTAVIANI'.

212 In ASV Envelope 787, file 424, there are the notes of four prelates mentioned by Dell'Acqua.

reflective of the position of the Doctrinal Commission and then of the Council.

3.1 The observations of Döpfner

On 14 October 1965 Cardinal Döpfner sent to the Pope some observations on the conciliar Schema 'De Divina Revelatione'. Fundamentally there were two, one regarding the theme of inspiration and the other the Scripture and Tradition relationship. The German prelate observed that, if one says that Sacred Scripture 'propter Inspirationem veritatem salutarem sine errore docere' then there is a material distinction between the saving truths, for which inerrancy is shown, and the profane truths, which instead can be always and continuously false. The time of Modernism called for modifying this distinction, in which profane things were not subsumed under the formal reason of what was said. Now there was no longer time to restore such a state of the problem, which even though it had not been contradicted, had experienced theological progress. The exegetes were strongly in disagreement over this way of banishing possible errors to the 'profane'.[213] The most important point for our theme is the Cardinal's position on the relationship between Scripture and Tradition. In his opinion, the Catholic faith's need for Tradition and Magisterium was clearly stated in the schema. It is clearly taught that Tradition has an original priority, that it also supports Scripture. It is clearly said that without it the canon of the inspired books cannot be known. The 'material insufficiency' of Sacred Scripture in comparison to Tradition is also explicitly stated. Here the existence of a constitutive Tradition and not just explicative co-related to the deposit of faith appears clearly. The schema is silent (but decided nothing) only about 'quaestionem ulterioris "insufficientiae materialis" S. Scriptu-

[213] Cf. J. Döpfner, *Lettera inviata al Sommo Pontefice contenente alcune osservazioni sullo Schema De Divina Revelatione,* 14 October 1965, 4 pages (here pages 1–2), to which is attached a one-page letter sent by Döpfner to Mgr Angelo dell'Acqua, Substitute of the Secretary of State, in which he asks him to hand over the letter to the Pope.

rae'. And legitimately so due to the fact that the issue is disputed among theologians, that is, such further insufficiency can or must be truly affirmed as divinely revealed. This silence was of great ecumenical value, as appears from the very fact that John XXIII wanted to transfer the question to a Mixed Commission. Such a Commission, after lengthy discussion, decreed that nothing should be said about this question. In fact, the question implied other supremely difficult questions, which it was not appropriate to examine at the Council. Tradition and Magisterium were not to be confused and together they do not create the truths to be defined, but they are drawn from Scripture and Tradition. If something more were to be said to placate souls about this, the Cardinal added, something could be said. According to Döpfner, 'not every Catholic truth can be derived from Scripture alone without the help of Tradition and Magisteum'. The path of the Council, which left open the disputed question while leaving it intact, remained nevertheless open to other gains.[214] So it

[214] Here are the salient points in the original: 'Clare exhibetur in Schemate necessitas Traditionis et Magisterii pro fide catholica certo stabilienda. Clare docetur Traditionem originariam prioritatem habere et sustinere etiam S. Scriptura. Clare indicator sine hac Traditione ambitum canonis et hinc S. Scripturae libros, prouti sunt inspirati, cognosci non posse. Hinc etiam explicite quoad rem docetur aliqua sic dicta "materialis insufficientia" S. Scripturae comparative ad Traditionem. Hinc etiam patet clare natura et existentia alicuius Traditionis constitutivae et non tantum explicativae relatae ad depositum fidei. Traditionis Schema silet (sed nihil decidit) circa quaestionem ulterioris "insufficientia materialis" S. Scripturae. Et legitime quidem. Nam disputatur inter theologos, num talis ulterior insufficientia et quidem (quod notandum est) tamquam divinitus revelata vere asseri possit aut debeat. Hoc silentium magni momenti oecumenici est, uti iam elucet ex facto quod Joannes XXIII papa fel. reg. hanc quaestionem Commissioni mixtae ex Commissione Theologica et Secretariatu pro Unione Christianorum fovenda discutienda commisit et haec Commissio Mixta post longas discussiones magna maioritate qualificata decrevit de hac quaestione in Schemate nihil esse decidendum... Talis quaestio insuper multiplices quaestiones ulteriores summe difficiles implicaret (si quaestio solvi deberet), quae a Concilio opportunis non tractantur. Praeterea conceptus Traditionis non confunden-

seems that for Döpfner the material insufficiency of Scripture was there simply for the definition of the canon. Further insufficiency is debatable. But precisely the 'silence of great ecumenical value' confirms my thesis.

3.2 The observations of Ruffini and Lattanzi

Cardinal Ruffini also wrote to the Holy Father. His position was opposite to that of Döpfner. Unlike the latter he did not send lengthy observations, but wrote a letter to the Pope on 17 October 1965:

> Most Holy Father,
> From the first moments of your election to the Chair of St Peter, Your Holiness has encouraged me to help you and be close to you.
> Encouraged by this august kindness, from time to time I dare to humble my own doctrinal concern.
> I was assured that Your Holiness would have seen to it that the Schema 'De Divina Revelatione' would explicitly state that Sacred Tradition, as well as being declarative of Sacred Scripture, is also constitutive, that is, that it can constitute alone—sine Sacra Scriptura—as a constitutive fact, a source or a means of the truth of faith.
> I have come to learn that the Theological Commission has discussed at length, demonstrating once again, in its majority, aversion to admitting an explicit statement in the sense set out.

---

dus est cum conceptus Magisterii, cum Magisterium non creet veritates definiendas, sed eas ex Scriptura et Traditione haurire debeat sicut in Constitutione "Lumen Gentium" iterum clare inculcatur... Si censeretur aliquid plus dici debere ad placandos animos, posset dici, sine dubio non omnem veritam catholicam ex sola Scriptura sine adiutorio Traditionis et Magisterii certo hauri posse. Et hoc modo quoad rem posset reiici doctrina Protestantium de "sola Scriptura", quin tamen quaestio illa inter catholicos disputata et a Concilio ipso intacta relicta tangeretur. Prudenti vero equilibrio inter sententias catholicas iam nunc in Schemate statuto ulteriori indagationi theologicae via aperta manet, praesertim cum nemo neget fautores ulteriors insufficientiae S. Scripturae etiam in postero stare posse suae sententiae', *Ibid*. pp. 2–4.

> I cannot hide my displeasure, taking into account—in the matter—the constant teaching of the Holy Church, repeated up to today in all the Catholic Schools.[215]

I will not focus on the reports of Cardinals Dante[216] and Journet[217] but focus my attention on another report written on 11 November 1965 by Mgr Ugo Lattanzi from the Lateran, also a conciliar peritus, and sent to Cardinal Ottaviani, so that he might present it as soon as possible to the Pope.[218] It is an analysis of the final formula approved by the conciliar majority to describe the relationship between Scripture and Tradition, leaving open, as has been repeated, the problem of constitutive Tradition. It is printed below almost in its entirety, given the clarity with which the theological problems were seen, problems which to many other periti seemed to have been resolved or at least not inconveniced. Lattanzi wrote:

> The formula to which I refer is the following: 'quo fit ut Ecclesia certitudinem suam de omnibus revelatis non per solam Scripturam hauriat' (Cap. II n. 9 p. 16 line 13).
> Now it seems to me that such a formula is either ambiguous or false or dangerous and false together, in relation to the 3 different interpretations which could be given to the fundamental word "certitudo" (.)
> And in fact such a word could mean 3 different things:

215 In red pen is added the name: 'Cardinal Ruffini'. Also in pencil above the header.

216 It developed as follows: 'Punctum I. Sacra Scriptura et Traditio. Earum mutua relatio', composed of three pages; followed by: 'Adnexum I. De relatione inter Sacram Scripturam et Traditionem', 2 pages; 'Punctum II. Inerrantia Sacrae Scripturae in actuali Schemate Constitutionis dogmaticae de divina revelatione', 2 pages, with 'Adnexum II. De restrictio inerrantiae Sacrae Scripturae introducta in textum actualem Schematis Constitutionis dogmaticae de divina revelatione', 4 pages (undated, in 1965), in *Ibid.*

217 Cf. C. Journet, *Schema Constitutionis Dogmaticae de Divine Revelatione*, 5 pages (undated, 1965), in *Ibid.*

218 The letter is 2 pages on notepaper headed 'Pontificia Universitatis Lateranensis', in *Ibid.*

1) Revealed doctrine;
2) Certain faith of revealed things;
3) Certain information of revealed truths.

1. Now if the word certitudo means revealed doctrine, the formula is ambiguous as well as tautological, as it is easy to observe.
2. If the word certitudo means instead certain faith about revealed things, the formula is false: since the Church does not draw the certainty of its faith from Scripture, but from the authority of God who reveals it.
3. Finally, if the word certitudo means (and this meaning is the most obvious) certain information of revealed truths, the formula is dangerous or false, depending on whether the Schema acknowledges (but is quiet about) the existence of a divine constitutive Traditio, that is a Traditio which is obiecto dicitor quam Scripturam, or which denies it.

And in fact:

a. if on the one hand the Schema acknowledges such a Traditio and on the other omits clearly teaching its existence, the silence of the Schema and I will say also of the Constitution once promulgated, could be easily interpreted as tacit consent to the opinions which are spread more and more and which draw ever closer to the Protestant positions about sola Scriptura (And I underline that to demonstrate that the Schema, by remaining silent, does not conform to the advice of His Holiness Paul VI, which was even quoted in the preceding edition of the Const. De divina Revel., on page 53).
b. If then the Schema denies the existence of the constitutive divine Traditio, it is easy to infer that it offers the non-Catholics the proven logical and irrefutable proof that the Church has defined numerous dogmas (for example, the need for infant baptism, the seven-fold number of the Holy Sacraments instituted by the Lord, the Immaculate Conception, the Assumption of Our Blessed Lady into heaven, etc.)

> without having any certain information about them. This is a consequence as logical as it is absurd.
>
> And in fact the Church does not draw certain information about these truths from Scripture, since they are dogmas which are not there, not even implicitly contained therein; and the Church does not draw it from divinely constitutive Traditio, since that is a denied source (because non-existent!).
>
> To that end I believe highly significant to be the declaration which the newspaper 'Le Monde' made on 31 October—1 November 1965, page 6, attributed to Fr Martelet SJ and of which I enclose a photocopy. In conclusion, it seems to me, Your Most Reverend Eminence, that the formula of the Schema should be thus amended: 'quo fit ut Ecclesia non omnes veritates revelatas e sola Scriptura hauriat'.
>
> Obviously this formula is totally different from the other: 'quo fit ut Ecclesia omnes veritates revelatas non e sola Scriptura hauriat'.
>
> I hope, Your Eminence, that the Lord might grant you the immediate opportunity to be able to bring these pages to the Throne of His Holiness; and in this hope I kiss the sacred purple and confirm, Your Most Reverend Eminence, to be yours devoted in Christ
>
> (Mgr Ugo Lattanzi, peritus of the Council).

We cannot say that Mgr Lattanzi was wrong in highlighting that the silence of the Council on such a sensitive point would have caused—at least implicitly—an erroneous interpretation in those who note that in Vatican II there is 'tacit consent' to absorb constitutive Tradition into the Scriptures. Above all, what is more surprising, is that the very will of the Supreme Pontiff, manifested accurately to Ottaviani, was in some way eclipsed in the definitive choice of the 'compromise formula' The representative stance of Döpfner had won the day.

4. 'Scripture and Tradition' in the other documents of Vatican II

Another hermeneutical path which could be of help in confirming that the Council, while not foregoing common teaching in *Dei verbum*, had as a goal a significant effort at pastoral and ecumenical renewal, is the examination of the concept of Tradition in the other conciliar documents. The choice of the teaching of *Dei verbum* was motivated by a precise goal. From an analysis of the other areas of the Council where this concept emerges, an interesting fact can be clarified: the Church is preserving her everlasting teaching and above all it can be seen that she is obliged to have recourse to Tradition when speaking in an indisputable manner on specific aspects of the deposit of faith.

4.1 'Scripture and Tradition' in *Lumen Gentium*

I will begin my analysis with *Lumen Gentium* before moving on to other constitutions, decrees and some of the declarations. I will examine only the most significant and most salient passages for this hermeneutical examination. One of the most important recourses of *Lumen Gentium* to Scripture and Tradition is where it teaches about the salvific necessity of the Church. Through his teaching Christ unique Saviour has instilled this salvific necessity. In n. 14 it is stated:

> This Sacred Council wishes to turn its attention firstly to the Catholic faithful. Basing itself upon Sacred Scripture and Tradition, it teaches that the Church, now sojourning on earth as an exile, is necessary for salvation.

The Tradition of the Catholic Church attests, along with Scripture (cf. Jn 3:5), that,

> Whosoever, therefore, knowing that the Catholic Church was made necessary by Christ, would refuse to enter or to remain in it, could not be saved (*Ibid.*).

In n. 20 reference is made to Tradition to confirm that among the ministries exercised in the Church, the primary position is occupied by the office of bishops, constituted as successors of the Apostles through the imposition of hands: this generates the transmission of the 'apostolic seed'. In fact, St Irenaeus[219] said that precisely through this uninterrupted succession the apostolic Tradition is 'manifested and preserved'.

The place of Tradition which manifests the faith of the Church and its own intimate constitution is the liturgy, from which it appears, both in the East and the West, that through the imposition of hands is conferred the grace of the Holy Spirit and the sacred character of the sacrament of Orders is impressed,[220] so that the Bishops possess the office of Christ, teacher, shepherd and high priest (cf. *Lumen Gentium* 21, in which the sacramentality of the episcopate is taught).

Lumen Gentium 25 explains the teaching role of the Bishops, referring to the prerogative of infallibility which belongs to the Roman Pontiff and to the body of Bishops united to him. Referring then to Vatican I, it says that in their teaching the Bishops express a judgment according to Revelation, handed down in writing or by Tradition and preserved by apostolic succession:

> But when either the Roman Pontiff or the Body of Bishops together with him defines a judgment, they pronounce it in accordance with Revelation itself, which all are obliged to abide by and be in conformity with, that is, the Revelation which as written or orally handed down (*scripta vel tradita*) is transmitted in its entirety through the legitimate succession of bishops and especially in care of the Roman Pontiff himself,

219 Cf. St Irenaeus, *Adv. Haer.* III, 3, 1: PG 7, 848A and *Adv. Haer.* III, 2, 2: PG 7, 847. Cf. *Lumen Gentium* footnotes 45 and 46.

220 In footnote 57 reference is made to the Council of Trent, 'which in Session 23, chapter 4 teaches that the sacrament of Orders impresses an indelible character: DH 1767 [Collantes 9.291]. Cf. John XXIII, *Iubilate Deo,* 8 May 1960, AAS 52 (1960), p. 446. Paul VI, Homily in the Vatican Basilica, 20 October 1963, AAS 55 (1963), p. 1014'.

> and which under the guiding light of the Spirit of truth is religiously preserved and faithfully expounded in the Church.

Here the footnote refers to Gasser's explanation of Vatican I.[221] *Lumen Gentium* 55 refers to the Scriptures and 'ancient Tradition', in as far as from both can be inferred the unique place of the Virgin Mary in the economy of salvation:

The Sacred Scriptures of both the Old and the New Testament, as well as ancient Tradition show the role of the Mother of the Saviour in the economy of salvation in an ever clearer light and draw attention to it.

In the *Nota explicativa praevia* reference is made to Tradition to explain that even though the 'college' has always existed, is not always active, however. The magisterial acts of the college of bishops are such when they are done in union and with the 'consent' of the Head of the college, the Pope. In fact, n. 4 says:

> Though it is always in existence, the College is not as a result permanently engaged in strictly collegial activity; the Church's Tradition makes this clear.

What is certainly firmly established in Tradition is the 'hierarchical communion of all the bishops with the Supreme Pontiff' (*Ibid.*), and not the Bishops acting always collegially.

4.2 'Scripture and Tradition' in the other conciliar documents

A significant recourse to Tradition is found in *Sacrosanctum Concilium,* to establish a correct reform as homogenous progress of the forms of worship already recognised by the Church's two thousand year-old Tradition, paying particular attention to the need of the current times. For example, *Sacrosanctum Concilium* n. 4 states that

> In faithful obedience to Tradition, the sacred Council declares that holy Mother Church holds all lawfully acknowledged rites to be of equal right and dignity; that she wishes to preserve them

[221] Mansi 1215CD, 1216–1217A.

> in the future and to foster them in every way. The Council also desires that, where necessary, the rites be revised carefully in the light of sound tradition, and that they be given new vigour to meet the circumstances and needs of modern times.

Sound tradition is wed to legitimate progress. To encourage legitimate progress, *Sacrosanctum Concilium* urges careful theological, historical and pastoral study before the introduction of any new form, so that 'care must be taken that any new forms adopted should in some way grow organically from forms already existing' (n. 23). *Sacrosanctum Concilium* then asks that where there had been useless additions or duplications to rites, there should be some simplification or additions, where appropriate, of particular elements according to the traditions of the Fathers (n. 50). The Divine Office is structured according to Christian Tradition so as to sanctify the whole course of the day and night (n. 84); reform is recommended taking into account 'the entire Tradition of the Latin Church' (n. 91), and Latin in the Divine Office to be retained by clerics according to the 'centuries-old tradition of the Latin rite' (n. 101). The Church, then, celebrates the paschal mystery of Christ every eighth day, the 'Lord's day', according to the Tradition handed down from the apostles, beginning from the very day of Christ's resurrection (n. 106). The Church venerates the Saints, their relics and their images according to its tradition (n. 111) and is also enriched by a sacred musical patrimony, coming from the Church's musical tradition (n. 112), which excels among all the expressions of Christian art due to the fact that it is an integral part of liturgical prayer. In short: in its liturgy, the Church cannot but refer in an indispensable way to its two-thousand year-old liturgical and artistic-musical tradition.

We then find an important reference to the Church's Tradition in *Dignitatis humanae,* where, alongside recourse to it, the aim of the Council is also specified, according to the programmatic indications of John XXIII. The Council, in fact, 'searches into the sacred Tradition and doctrine of the Church—the treasury out of which the

Church continually brings forth new things that are in harmony with the things that are old' (*Dignitatis humanae* 1).

In the decree *Ad Gentes* reference is made to Tradition in two significant points: 1) for the promotion of the religious life in the young Churches (while there is no reference to Tradition in the renewal of religious life according to *Perfectae caritatis*), and 2) for a vital link between the young Churches and the one Church.

The religious who work in the establishment of a new Church in mission lands, must also hand on the rich patrimony with which religious tradition is filled, taking into account the heritage and specific nature of each nation (*Ad gentes* 18). The young Churches, then, must know how to link with their cultural experience all elements of the Church's Tradition, so as to remain in strong communion with it (*Ad gentes* 19). The particular traditions must be integrated into the unity of the Church. To do that, *Ad gentes* promotes

> Such theological speculation should be encouraged, in the light of the universal Church's Tradition, as may submit to a new scrutiny the words and deeds which God has revealed, and which have been set down in Sacred Scripture and explained by the Fathers and by the Magisterium.

Presbyterorum ordinis calls on the sacred minister to cultivate a knowledge which is also sacred. As well as assiduous study and meditation on the Sacred Scriptures, a fruitful source of nourishment for the presbyterate 'is also study of the Holy Fathers and other Doctors and documents or Tradition' (n. 19).

Optatam totius, on the other hand, teaches that among seminary students 'those practices of piety that are commended by the long usage of the Church should be zealously cultivated' (8). In n. 10 it refers to the 'venerable tradition of celibacy' 'according to the holy and fixed laws' of the Latin Rite.

In *Christus Dominus* there is only one reference to Tradition, speaking about the pastoral mission of the bishop. In n. 14 bishops are exhorted to have zealous care for the teaching of the catechism, not just to children and young people, but to adults, too. The catechism, then, must be 'based on Sacred Scripture, Tradition, the liturgy, Magisterium, and life of the Church'.

An important doctrinal reference to Tradition is found in the Decree on Ecumenism, *Unitatis redintegratio*. In very clear terms, n. 3 states that the separated brethren, as attested by the Tradition of the Church, do not benefit from that unity from which instead the Catholic Church is indefectibly constituted. It is said:

> Nevertheless, our separated brethren, whether considered as individuals or as Communities and Churches, are not blessed with that unity which Jesus Christ wished to bestow on all those who through Him were born again into one body, and with Him quickened to newness of life—that unity which the Holy Scriptures and the ancient Tradition of the Church proclaim. For it is only through Christ's Catholic Church, which is 'the all-embracing means of salvation', that they can benefit fully from the means of salvation.

The Catholic Church looks with profound reverence to the Eastern Churches, by reason of their liturgical and spiritual Tradition:

> The very rich liturgical and spiritual heritage of the Eastern Churches should be known, venerated, preserved and cherished by all. They must recognize that this is of supreme importance for the faithful preservation of the fullness of Christian Tradition, and for bringing about reconciliation between Eastern and Western Christians (*Unitatis Redintegratio* 15).

As regards authentic theological tradition, too, the Catholic Church sees in the Eastern Church the living reflection of Tradition itself, attesting to the handing on of the mysteries of the faith. The patrimony of the Eastern tradition of the sons of the Catholic Church belongs to the full Catholicity and apostolicity of the Church.

> Where the authentic theological traditions of the Eastern Church are concerned, we must recognize the admirable way

> in which they have their roots in Holy Scripture, and how they are nurtured and given expression in the life of the liturgy. They derive their strength too from the living Tradition of the apostles and from the works of the Fathers and spiritual writers of the Eastern Churches. Thus they promote the right ordering of Christian life and, indeed, pave the way to a full vision of Christian truth. All this heritage of spirituality and liturgy, of discipline and theology, in its various traditions, this holy synod declares to belong to the full Catholic and apostolic character of the Church. We thank God that many Eastern children of the Catholic Church, who preserve this heritage, and wish to express it more faithfully and completely in their lives, are already living in full communion with their brethren who follow the tradition of the West (*Unitatis Redintegratio* 15).

Therefore faithfulness to the two-thousand year-old Tradition of the East and the West is a source of true ecumenism and recovery of the unity of Christians in the one Church of Christ. Finally, in line with all of that, we find another important reference to Tradition in the Decree on the Catholic Eastern Churches, *Orientalium ecclesiarum*. The Council has a special care for the Eastern Churches, due to the fact that they are 'living witnesses' of the Tradition of the Church (*Orientalium ecclesiarum* 1). Therefore,

> The Catholic Church holds in high esteem the institutions, liturgical rites, ecclesiastical traditions and the established standards of the Christian life of the Eastern Churches, for in them, distinguished as they are for their venerable antiquity, there remains conspicuous the Tradition that has been handed down from the Apostles through the Fathers[222] and that forms part of the divinely revealed and undivided heritage of the universal Church.

The Council, recognising 'by the most ancient tradition of the Church' (*Orientalium ecclesiarum* 9), the special honour to be given

[222] Cf. Leo XIII, Apostolic Letter *Orientalium dignitas,* 30 November 1894, in 'Leonis XIII Acta', vol. XIV, pp. 201–202.

to the Patriarchates, 'determines that their rights and privileges should be re-established in accordance with the ancient tradition of each of the Churches and the decrees of the ecumenical councils' (*Ibid.*).[223]

In conclusion, from the examination of these conciliar texts, in which is manifest doctrinal recourse to the Church's Tradition, an important fact emerges: while in *Dei verbum*, to respect the prearranged aims, Vatican II avoided teaching the theological concept of Tradition in an integral manner, that concept, as affirmed in the development of the Magisterium itself, and while nevertheless determining its cogency alongside Scripture, is regularly turned to in order to teach some of the doctrines of the faith recognised by the Church: the truth of the unity and unicity of the Church, the Church as unique way of salvation, the liturgy as normative norm of the Church's prayer, the presence of the living liturgical and theological tradition in the Eastern Churches, manifesting their Catholicity. These conciliar documents of course do not resolve the problem—deliberately left open by *Dei verbum*—of additive Tradition, due to the fact that was outside their competence. De facto, however, they highlight the constitutive importance of Tradition for the faith of the Church, so as to justify the recourse to it as regards the correct ability to decipher the truths of the faith and the unity of the Church. In the mind of the Council, Tradition, as well as being an indispensable hermeneutic resource for Scripture, is at the same time the 'place' where the Revelation of God is manifested and channel through which it comes to us, together with Sacred Scripture.

---

[223] Cf. Council of Nicaea I, canon 6; of Constantinople I, canons 2 and 3; Chalcedon, canon 28; canon 9; Constantinople IV, canon 17; canon 21 [DH 600–661]; Lateran IV, canon 5 [DH 811]; Florence, *Decr. Pro Graecis* [DH 1307–08; Collantes 7.159–60]; etc.

5. *'Scripture and Tradition' in the Catechism of the Catholic Church*

A final reference to the 're-gaining' of the dyadic relationship between 'Scripture and Tradition' is found in the *Catechism of the Catholic Church.* The *Catechism* devotes *ex professo* nn. 74–83 to the matter. From the study of apostolic Tradition it gets to the relationship between Tradition and Sacred Scripture. N. 83 is very precise, distinguishing between apostolic Tradition and church traditions. It says:

> The Tradition here in question comes from the apostles and hands on what they received from Jesus' teaching and example and what they learned from the Holy Spirit. The first generation of Christians did not yet have a written New Testament, and the New Testament itself demonstrates the process of living Tradition.
>
> Tradition is to be distinguished from the various theological, disciplinary, liturgical or devotional traditions, born in the local churches over time. These are the particular forms, adapted to different places and times, in which the great Tradition is expressed. In the light of Tradition, these traditions can be retained, modified or even abandoned under the guidance of the Church's Magisterium.

Therefore the provision of apostolic Tradition must not be confused with the traditions as church or simply devotional practice. The oral Tradition bears a *normative* provision for the faith as much as Sacred Scripture. In fact, immediately afterwards, the *Catechism of the Catholic Church,* in n. 84, explains that the deposit of faith (cf. 1 Tm. 6:20) was entrusted to the whole Church, and is contained 'in Sacred Scripture and Tradition'. As such it was entrusted by 'the apostles ... to the whole of the Church'. After all, only thus, is that '*utraque*' in reference to Sacred Scripture and Tradition understandable: '*Quapropter utraque pari pietatis affect ac reverentia suscipienda et veneranda est*' (*Dei verbum* 9, with reference to Trent and Vatican I).[224]

[224] Another important example for verifying recourse to the Church's Tradition was the magisterial intervention aimed at correcting some points of the Dutch Catechism. Precisely this was to do with the virginal conception of Jesus by Mary, attested to by Tradition based on Scripture, and the problem of polygenism, which, in fact, does not resolve the problems for which monogenism was rebuked, but increases them (cf. *Dichiarazione della Commissione Cardinalizia sul Nuovo Catechsimo ['Die Nieuwe Katechismus']*, 15 October 1968, in AAS 60 [1968] 685–691 and *Supplemento al Nuovo Catechismo* [with the edited modifications according to the Cardinals' Commission], in *Il Nuovo Catechismo Olandese* (Turin: Elle Di Ci, 1975[6]), pp. 15–91 [Appendix]). As regards monogenism, in the *Supplemento al Nuovo Catechismo* it is said: 'formulae whose obvious meaning is monogenist are used concerning original sin by Saint Paul, by the Tradition of the Church, especially by the Council of Trent, and also by the Second Vatican Council. It is evident that in one way or another they contain the revealed truth; they cannot be abandoned lightly', *Ibid.*, p. 39.

IV

PASTORAL EPIPHANIES OF VATICAN II

IN THE INTENTIONS AND FORMATION OF THE CONCILIAR TEACHING ON THE CHURCH

IN THIS CHAPTER I will focus on the Church at the Second Vatican Council. Without doubt it was the central theme of the whole Assembly. Paul VI, in his address at the start of the Second Session of the Council, wanted to re-launch it with great inspiration. According to the Pope, the Church desired a complete definition of herself.[1] John Paul II, then, would define *Lumen Gentium* as the '*Magna Charta* of the Council ... so that with renewed and invigorating zeal we may meditate on the nature and function of the Church, its way of being and acting'.[2] The 1985 Synod of Bishops saw the ecclesiology of communion as the pivotal point of the whole magisterial importance of Vatican II: 'The ecclesiology of communion', it stated, 'is the central and fundamental idea of the Council's documents'.[3] This was certainly also to balance the excessive emphasis put on the concept of Church as people of God, to the point of declining into a vision of a democratic Church or Church from below.[4] How-

---

1 Cf. AS II/I, p. 189.

2 *Insegnamenti di Giovanni Paolo II*, II/2 (1978) 14.

3 ESV, I (1965–1988) 2379.

4 The critical voices raised in this sense include J. Ratzinger, O. Semmelroth, Y. Congar, J. Hamer. Cf. J. A. Domínguez, 'Le interpretazioni postconciliari', in P. Rodriguez (ed.), *L'ecclesiologia trent'anni dopo la "Lumen Gentium"* (Rome:

ever, various interpretations of the question remained: what is the implied key to the ecclesiology of Vatican II? For many, it is the concept of *communio*.[5] For others, instead, that would just be a cliché referring to the concept of Church as communion, what's more linked to the mediation of preceding ecclesiological acquisitions, while the real peculiarity of the conciliar ecclesiology remained that which saw in the Church the new people of God: not a people *from* peoples but a people *among* the peoples, thus manifesting its Catholicity.[6] Given the complexities in the field of post-conciliar ecclesiology[7] some authors therefore prefer to speak about 'ecclesiological perspectives' rather than the ecclesiology of Vatican II, distinguishing at least three of them: the Church as sacrament of salvation, the Church as people of God and the Church as communion.[8]

There was in fact a renewed theological and doctrinal reflection on the Church, which over a broad range accompanied the conciliar work on *De Ecclesia*. The specific causes of the ecclesiological renewal can be divided into four:[9]

Armando Editore, 1996), pp. 42–43.

5 See for example J. M. Tillard, *Chiesa di chiese. L'ecclesiologia di comunione* (Brescia: Queriniana, 1989) (French original, *Église d'Églises. L'ecclésiologie de communion* [Paris: Cerf, 1987); W. Kasper, *Theology and Church* (London: SCM Press, 1989) (German original, *Theologie und Kirche* [Ostfildern: Grünewald, 1987); M. Semeraro, *Mistero, comunione e missione. Manuale di ecclesiologia* (Bologna: EDB, 1996); R. Marangoni, *La Chiesa mistero di comunione. Il contributo di Paolo VI nell'elaborazione dell'ecclesiologia di comunione (1963–1978)*, (Analecta Gregoriana, 282), Rome: Pontificia Università Gregoriana, 2001.

6 Cf. G. Canobbio, 'L'ecclesiologia successiva al Vaticano II', in AA.VV, *La primavera della Chiesa. A quarant'anni dal Concilio Vaticano II*, edited by P. Ciardella (Milan: Paoline, 2005), pp. 44–51.

7 See A. Anton, *El misterio de la Iglesia. Evolución historica de las ideas eclesiológicas*, II vols., (Madrid: Editorial Católica, 1986).

8 This is the proposal of Routhier, 'La recezione dell'ecclesiologia conciliare', pp. 3–18.

9 Cf. G. Vadopivec, 'Chiesa', in *Dizionario del Concilio Ecumenico Vaticano II*,

1. The *Liturgical Movement,* with the rediscovery of the ancient liturgy and the need for greater participation by the faithful in the mystery, highlighted the common priesthood of the faithful, as well as the sacramentality and collegiality of the Episcopate, as resulted from the ancient liturgical texts (including the *Traditio apostolica* of St Hippolytus of Rome);
2. The *biblical and patristic movement,* with the 'return to the sources' or *ressourcement*: not simply a going backwards but reflection on the origins, keeping the view open to the present and the past. Thus was highlighted the concept of Church *people* of God, and *body* of Christ, charismatic and eschatological. In the Fathers, the Church was always the mystery of Christ and the mystery of our communion in Christ;
3. The *movement of the apostolate of the laity,* with a great influence on the development of the theology of the laity and the apostolate of the laity, tied to the exercise of a baptismal priesthood; and finally,
4. The *ecumenical movement,* which according to many was the main influence in the ecclesiological renewal. There was a shift from an atmosphere of controversy to one of discussion and fraternal encounter. If before what was spoken about was only what was missing in the communions separated from Rome, what the Church or Communion lacked, now instead what they have and are was the focus. Ecumenical contact encouraged the re-evaluation of the *Eastern tradition,* with the consequent rediscovery of the local Church, of sacramental and eucharistic ecclesiology, of the heavenly Church united with the pilgrim Church.

According to G. Vadopivec, editor of the 'Church' entry in the *Dizionario del Concilio Ecumenico Vaticano II,* there were two opposing tendencies in theology in these years: one more conceptual and

---

ed. by S. Garofalo (Rome: Unedi, 1969), cols. 713–716.

abstract, tending to consider more the truth per se, and another more concrete and personal, aimed at reaching things and people, the true and ultimate object of faith. This latter tendency insisted more on the difference between notional expression and expressed reality.[10] Two tendencies which we can also characterise as one being more dogmatic and the other more pastoral: tendencies which run through the whole of the Council; the triumphant, if we can call it that, would be the latter, with a considerable consequent theological shift.

The original schema, precisely due to the difficulty of finding the right path for a renewed ecclesiological sense, preserving faithfulness to the received teaching, was re-worked, widely amended, right up to the definitive promulgation of the Dogmatic Constitution on the Church on 21 November 1964, according to the needs laid down by John XXIII in the opening address and then by Paul VI. There was a desire to put aside the theological issues still being debated and at the same time offer a more 'living' teaching, which would go beyond a merely legal vision of Church, a simple identification of the mystical Body of Christ with the Roman Catholic Church.

> The intention, explained Tangorra, was to provide ecclesiology with a standing more theological and less juridical, more communion-based and less hierarchical, more diaconal and less self-referential, more pilgrim and less triumphant.[11]

In clarification of a new element which did not want to and does not reject the old, the Church militant was seen above all and better perceived as pilgrim, at times problematic and passionate—we will see the intense dispute about collegiality—at times calm and confident. In spite of everything, problems exist. The broadly majority agreement reached in the Council did not impose itself in the subsequent period, especially as regards the unambiguous and peaceful reception of this additional element.[12]

---

10 Cf. *Ibid.*, cols. 716–717.

11 G. Tangorra, 'Ecclesiologia del Concilio Vaticano II', in G. Calabrese et al. (eds.), *Dizionario di Ecclesiologia* (Rome: Città Nuova, 2010), p. 494.

In the work of the Assembly there was a very precise intention in presenting the new ecclesiological issue: to deepen the Church as mystery, as people of God on the march, the Church as hierarchical communion, and at the same time to make it more comprehensible to the 'other Christians' as Paul VI said,[13] encouraging and facilitating ecumenical unity. A great ideal, which however was unable to free itself from some significant magisterial choices: at times it preferred not to say, at other times to say a bit more, precisely to extend a hand. In the analysis of the ecclesiological teaching of the Dogmatic Constitution *Lumen Gentium* we cannot escape consideration of these theologically very important consequences, with the aim of evaluating correctly the dogmatic teaching of Vatican II in terms of ecclesiology. I will try to do this in the subsequent pages, studying above all the various processes which led to the promulgation of the Constitution on the Church, and then some of the ecclesiological issues of significant importance. Thus I aim to contribute to a calm interpretation of *Lumen Gentium* and the dogmatic teaching of the Council, according to the *intentio Patrum*, in the wake of the uninterrupted *Traditio*, without exaggeration and prejudice.

1. The schema De Ecclesia

The text on the Church was distributed to the Fathers in the XXV General Congregation, 23 November 1962, along with the schema *De B. Maria Virgine*. In its entirety the schema comprised 11 chapters, opening with *De Ecclesia militantis natura* and concluding with *De oecumenismo*.[14] Subsequently I will report the salient points of the schema, that is, those which would be the main focus of debate in the council chamber. In this way it will also be easier to have a rather

---

12 Cf. *Ibid.*, p. 495.

13 AS II/1, p. 193.

14 Cf. AS I/4, pp. 12–91.

synoptic vision of the corrections or sometimes the substantial modifications produced in the prior text.

Chapter I presented teaching on the Church focused on its forms, particularly that of the 'body'. In n. 6 the teaching of Pius XII was taken up again, stating that the Church-society is the mystical Body of Christ. In n. 7 it was stated in tune with *Mystici Corporis* that uniquely the Roman Catholic Church *is* the mystical Body of Christ:

> Docet igitur Sacra Synodus et solemniter profitetur non esse nisi unicam veram Iesu Christi Ecclesiam, eam nempe quam in Symbolo unam, sanctam, catholicam et apostolicam celebramus, quam Salvator sibi in Cruce acquisivit sibique tamquam corpus capiti et sponsam sponso coniunxit, quamque post resurrectionem suam S. Petro et Successoribus, qui sunt Romani Pontifices, tradidit gubernandam; ideoque sola iure Catholica Romana nuncupatur Ecclesia.[15]

Chapter II was devoted to the members of the Church (n. 9). Those who preserve the three bonds of unity: the profession of faith, the sacraments, and the jurisdiction of the Roman Pontiff, are real and proper members of the Church. Those instead who ignore that the Roman Catholic Church is the true and one Church of Christ, but preserve by means of grace an implicit desire to belong to it, or are governed by a sincere desire and want what Christ wants, or even not knowing Christ, sincerely desire to fulfil the will of the Creator, these are related to the Church in *voto*, as well as catechumens themselves:

> Ii igitur vere et proprie membra Ecclesiae dicendi sunt qui, regenerationis lavacro abluti, veram fidem catholicam profitentes et Ecclesiae auctoritatem agnoscentes, in compagine visibili eiusdem cum Capite eius, Christo videlicet eam regente per Vicarium suum, iunguntur, nec ob gravissima delicta a Corporis Mystici compage seiuncti sunt. Voto autem ad Ecclesiam ordinantur non catechumeni dumtaxat, qui, Spiritu Sancto movente, conscio et explicito desiderio ad Ecclesiam

---

[15] *Ibid.*, p. 15.

> aspirant, sed ii quoque, qui etsi ignorantes Ecclesiam catholicam esse veram et unicam Christi Ecclesiam, tamen, gratia Dei implicito et inscio desiderio simile praestant, sive quod sincera voluntate id volunt quod vult ipse Christus, sive quod etsi ignorantes Christum, sincere adimplere desiderant volutatem Dei et Creatoris sui.[16]

N. 10 examined the union of the Catholic Church with the separated brethren. The Church, it is said, knows she is united with them for various reasons. The grace of Christ, not excluding sanctifying grace, also works outside the visible confines of the Church, so that the separated brethren can be incorporated into her, in the way that Christ knows. So the separated brethren were also exhorted to unite themselves to the one Church of Christ, since outside her they lacked those heavenly gifts necessary for salvation, enjoyed solely by those who truly and objectively, were members of the Church. The most important paragraphs state:

> Cum omnibus autem, qui veram fidei vel unitatem communionis sub Romano Pontifice non profitentur, tamen desiderio, etsi inscio, ea cupiunt, pia Mater Ecclesia semetipsam scit plures ob rationes coniunctam,[17] singulari modo si baptizati christiano nomine gloriantur, et, quamquam non credunt fide catholica, tamen amanter in Christum credunt Deum et Salvatorem, imprimis autem si fide et devotione erga Sanctissimam Eucharistiam et amore erga Deiparam eminent. Nam fidei illi communi in Christum accedit eiusdem consecrationis baptismalis participatio; orationum, expiationum et beneficiorum spiritualium aliqua saltem communio; immo aliqua in Spiritu Sancto coniunctio, quippe qui non solum donis et gratiis in ipso mystico corpore operatur, sed sua virtute, non exclusa gratia sanctificante, etiam extra venerandum illud

---

16 *Ibid.*, pp. 18–19.

17 Here the text refers back to Leo XIII, Apostolic Letter *Praeclara gratulationis*, 20 June 1894, in ASS 26 (1893–94) 707.

> Corpus agit, ut fratres separati, modo a Christo statuto, eidem incorporentur.[18]

In chapter III was presented, without further doubts, the Episcopate as the supreme rank of the sacrament of Orders, in other words as belonging to the sacrament of Orders and at the same time as the highest rank. Consequently, the Episcopate bestowed the character of the sacrament of Orders, conferring on the elect the specificity of validly administering the sacrament of Confirmation and ordaining the Church's ministers.[19]

Chapter IV, on the other hand, was devoted to the residential bishops. Within this chapter the question of the relationship between the Pope and the Episcopate was examined, a question which would then become Primacy and Collegiality. Episcopal ordination conferred on the candidate the three *munera Christi*: to sanctify, to teach and to govern, where, however, the exercise of the jurisdiction does not happen due to the ordination itself, but by virtue of a *mission* received from the one who exercises the supreme governance of the Church, the Pope. The schema guarded against the danger of believing such a mission as coming from the Church understood as congregation of the faithful or also from the faithful or from a civil authority, clarifying that it comes solely from the successor of the apostle Peter. Here the document quoted St Leo the Great, who said about the blessed Peter the apostle:

> Ab ipso omnium charismatum fonte (*Iesu Christo*) tam copiosis est irrigationibus inundates, ut, cum multa solus acceperit, nihil in quemquam sine ipsius participation transierit.[20]

---

[18] *Ibid.*, p. 19. Here a footnote (n. 17) referred back to the well-known distinction of St Augustine: '*Ducere in via et ad viam;* ducere *in Christo* et *ad Christum*'. Cf. *In Ps.* 85, 15: PL 37, 1092. Clement VIII, Instr. *Magnus Dominus*: '§ 1. Divina Spiritus Sancti luce eorum corda collustrante, coeperunt ipsi secum cogitari se et greges quos pascerent non esse membra Corporis Christi, quod est Ecclesia'.

[19] Cf. AS I/4, p. 23.

The schema was also responding to some errors concerning the conferring of the exercise of governance on individual bishops. It was not in conformity with the truth, it said, to affirm that bishops have only a power of delegated jurisdiction and not true and proper and ordinary jurisdiction, joined to the episcopal office itself; or to say that by means of the supreme power of the Roman Pontiff that of the bishops could be abolished, absorbed or increased, or that it was not of divine right and reality, or finally that it did not belong to the very constitution of the Church, but could be changed to another. Only barely could the authority of the Pope diminish the right of Bishops, which, in reality, is strengthened by the same supreme authority, as St Gregory the Great says:

> Meus honor est honor universalis Ecclesiae. Meus honor est fratrum meorum solidus vigor. Tum ego vere honoratus sum, cum singulis quibusque honor debitus non negatur.[21]

N. 16 examined the theme of the episcopal College, which succeeds the apostolic College as regards teaching authority and pastoral governance. With reference above all to an ecumenical council, the schema affirmed that the College, one with its Head, the Roman Pontiff, and never without him, is one subject with full and supreme power over the whole of the Church. Such power, even though ordinary, in that it is inherent in the office, is exercised only in an extraordinary manner and in faithful subordination to the Vicar of Jesus Christ on earth, and is legitimate, when, as and to what extent, he deems it appropriate:

> Una cum capite suo, Romano Pontifice et numquam sine hoc capite, unum subiectum plenae et supremae potestatis in universam Ecclesiam creditor.[22] Potestas tamen huius Collegii,

---

[20] St Leo, *Sermo 4 de natali ipsius*: PL 54, 149. Cf. Id. *Epist.* 10: PL 54, 629, cit. in *Ibid.*, p. 26, footnote 8.

[21] St Gregory, Epist. *Ad Eulogium epis. Alexandrinum*, l. 8, c. 30: PL 77, 933, cit. in *Ibid.*, p. 26, footnote 11.

[22] A footnote explains: 'Doctrina habetur in theologia De Conciliis Oecumenicis et in

> etsi ordinaria, utpote officio inhaerens, nonnisi modo extraordinario[23] et in devota subordinatione Iesu Christi Vicario in terris quando, quomodo et quousque eidem in Domino videtur expedire, legitime exercetur.[24]

Finally, chapter XI, examining ecumenism, added another important block to the ecclesiological picture, upheld and explained in more depth subsequently: the 'elementa quaedam Ecclesiae', existing in the communities separated from the Catholic Church. Principally Sacred Scripture and the Sacraments, which, as means and signs of unity, can produce mutual union in Christ, and, by their nature, as 'res Ecclesiae Christi propriae', drive towards Catholic unity. The firm conviction remains, however, that the fullness of the Revelation of Christ was handed on only to the Catholic Church. In n. 51, entitled *De habitudine Ecclesiae Catholicae ad communitates christianas separatas,* it is explained that in the separated communities

> Enim elementa quaedam Ecclesiae exsistunt ut potissimum Scriptura Sacra et Sacramenta, quae, ut media et signa unitatis efficacia unionem mutuam in Christo producere possunt et natura sua, ut res Ecclesiae Christi propriae, ad unitatem catholicam impellunt... Sacra Synodus, dum elementa ab his communitatibus servata, ibi quoque salutifera esse atque fructus vitae spiritualis christianae producere posse non den-

---

doctrina de successione Apostolorum eorumque Collegii' (*Ibid.*, n. 16, p. 33). It also refers to the *Schema Const. Dogm. Secundae de Eccl. Christi* (c. 4: Mansi 53, 310) in which it is explained that, even though the bishops are not bestowed with the *munus* of teaching in the universal Church and governing it, however to them, too, has the Lord given the power of binding and releasing (cf. Mt. 18:18), exercised in the ecumenical councils, right from the outset (cf. *Ibid., Relatio Kleutgen de schemate reformato*, pp. 321–322). It was also said: '*N. B.*: Corpus seu collegium per se ab hoc praescindit utrum sit subiectum potestatis iurisdictionis tantum an etiam aliarum potestatum', *Ibid*, n. 16, p. 34.

23 The footnote states: 'Dicitur "modo extraordinario"; hoc sequitur ex eo quad Concilia Oecumenica assolute loquendo non necessaria sunt; ergo *actio* Corporis Episcoporum, in quantum agitur de actione *iuridica,* non est ex institutione divina permanens in Ecclesia', *Ibid.*, n. 17, p. 34.

24 *Ibid.*, p. 27.

> egat, firmiter tamen docet plenitudinem Revelationis a Christo soli Ecclesiae Catholicae commissam esse eamque dividi non posse, atque proinde ab omnibus christianis ibi agnoscendam esse.[25]

Thus were set out the essential elements for the ecclesiological discussion, on which the debate in the aula would focus, moving on two perspectives: on the one hand, the schema as such, and on the other the problem of the ecclesiological doctrine, especially with a view to ecumenism. One of the key issues which would emerge significantly would be the question about being a member of the Church in the full and not full sense. For some, this was a teaching still to be discussed at the theological level and still to be left open to discussion.

2. The objections to the schema: towards a new and manifold redaction

The schema *De Ecclesia* was distributed to the Fathers on 23 November 1962. Discussion about the schema took place from 1–7 December 1962, from the XXI to the XXXVI General Congregation, up to the end of the First Session of the Council. The debate saw the intervention of a very large number of Council Fathers, to which were added equally numerous *Animadversiones scriptae de Ecclesia*. This time, too, there was preference for re-drafting the schema, largely due to the same reasons which led to the rejection of *De fontibus*. Once again two tendencies could be perceived, which we could indicate as that of the 'conservatives', in the sense of preferring to 'conserve' the schema, even if it required some improvements, and that of the 'progressives', who wanted a re-arrangement of the teaching to respond to the pastoral and above all ecumenical needs. Here, too, those who appreciated the schema in substance were not opposed to revision of its form, as would be said by Cardinal Bacci[26] (and in a

---

[25] *Ibid.*, pp. 82–83.

similar vein, Ruffini,[27] Siri,[28] and Browne).[29] The other line, instead, raised objections with the aim of demonstrating the only way out: an overall re-drafting of the schema. Along these lines, for example, worked König,[30] Alfrink,[31] De Smedt,[32] Döpfner,[33] Suenens,[34] Maximos IV Saigh, according to whom the demand for a total re-working of the schema 'should not be read as an act of hostility and even less a deviation from sound doctrine. Rather, it is a testimony of the interest there is in the text and the importance attributed to it'.[35] For some Fathers, the re-working of the schema was appropriate according to faithfulness to the inaugural address of John XXIII. These included, for example, Cardinal Tatsuo Doi (Archbishop of Tokyo),[36] Archbishop De Provenchères (Archbishop of Aix, France),[37] De Smedt[38] and Cardinal Bea.[39]

In presenting the schema, Cardinal Ottaviani was 'prophetic', pre-empting the criticisms and saying that the text had been prepared so as to be largely pastoral, biblical and accessible to the multitude, not scholastic but with a form comprehensible by everyone. 'I would say this', he added, 'since I expect to hear the usual litany from the

26 Cf. *Ibid.*, pp. 230–232.

27 Cf. *Ibid.*, pp. 127–129.

28 Cf. *Ibid.*, p. 174.

29 Cf. *Ibid.*, pp. 232–233.

30 Cf. *Ibid.*, p. 132.

31 Cf. *Ibid.*, p. 136. He asked that the schema be re-drafted by a new Mixed Commission appointed by the Pope.

32 Cf. *Ibid.*, p. 144.

33 Cf. Ibid., p. 186.

34 Cf. *Ibid.*, p. 223.

35 *Ibid.*, p. 295.

36 Cf. *Ibid.*, p. 397.

37 Cf. *Ibid.*, p. 459. According to this Archbishop the schema should be re-worked in such a way that it might be more biblical, pastoral and ecumenical, cf. *Ibid.*, pp. 459–461.

38 Cf. *Ibid.*, p. 144, footnote 25.

39 Cf. *Ibid.*, p. 229.

Council Fathers: it is not ecumenical, it is scholastic, it is not pastoral, it is negative and so on'.[40] But he also announced an unpleasant episode: in order to make the schema on the Church fall, even before it was presented to the Fathers some theologians had already set to work drafting alternative texts: 'Igitur ante praevisa merita iam iudicatum est'.[41] This was confirmed by Rahner, who, on 5 November 1962, writing from Rome to his disciple Vorgrimler, told him:

> [to overthrow the official schemata] Philips of Louvain had produced a similar schema on the church and Congar a kind of preface in the form of a confession of faith. Daniélou has attempted to tailor a new garment from scraps of the official schemata. I'm impatient to how things will develop. We still don't know what is coming after the schema on the liturgy. But the inclination after that to begin on the *Ecclesia* schema seems to be growing. It is said that already ten cardinals are in favour. That would be good, and in that case there would be an increasing prospect of certain other schemata of a theological kind being consigned to the silence of the tomb.[42]

And a month later, on 5 December 1962, writing again to his friend and disciple, Vorgrimler, Rahner said:

> At present they're discussing *De Ecclesia* in the Plenum. I've made a commentary on it which is being circulated in an edition of 1300 copies. I've already sent it to you. It is still uncertain whether we shall secure a rejection of the schema as in the case of *De fontibus revelationis*. More uncertain than in the case of the first schema. Today I'm at last to go with König to a session of the commission which is to make a new schema to replace the one that has fallen through ... D. went away

40 *Ibid.*, p. 121.

41 *Ibid.*

42 H. Vorgrimler, *Understanding Karl Rahner. An Introduction to his Life and Thought* (London: SCM Press Ltd, 1986), p. 158 (German original, *Karl Rahner verstehen. Eine Einführung in sein Leben und Denken* [Freiburg im Br.: Herder, 1985]).

> again today. He was there a very long time. That was very good for me, because he wrote both the opinion on *De BMV* and the counter-opinion against *De Ecclesia* on matrices so I don't have to go begging round the German speakers who saw to producing the thing. All in all we have printed about 50,000 sheets with all the equipment here. When we add the Ratzinger-Rahner schema to that it will be even more.[43]

The schema *De Ecclesia* was presented in the council chamber with a report from Bishop Franić, who was careful to draw attention to the fact that, after many days of discussion in the plenary sessions of the Theological Commission, it had been decided to adopt the teaching contained in Pius XII's Encyclical *Mystici corporis*. In chapter III the solution disputed for centuries between the schools, that is, the question of the sacramentality of the episcopate, finally reached a definitive solution ('definitive dirimitur'),[44] and so proclaimed in a solemn manner that the episcopate was the supreme rank of the sacrament of Orders. There had been no objection to this choice in the Theological Commission. Then practical questions about governance of the Church, and episcopal Conferences, too, had been omitted, since the Commission had judged that such a problem did not belong to the channel of teaching and immutable questions, but to those commissions dealing with disciplinary issues. The chapter which examined ecumenism (chapter XI) had been strictly set out along dogmatic principles, a chapter which differed from the constitution *De oecumenismo* composed by the Secretariat for Promoting Christian Unity. In fact,

> In the Secretariat's constitution some practical norms are given, according to which, in the judgment of the Secretariat, ecumenical action is exercised. In our commission certain issues which belong to the dogmatic principles of this issue, *which* is very current for our times, were sufficiently discussed.[45]

---

43 Vorgrimler, *Understanding Karl Rahner*, p. 159.

44 *Ibid.*

Criticisms of the schema were immediate.[46] Cardinal Liénart opened the debate in the chamber. His criticism was based essentially on the formulae and the manner of speaking used, so as to run the risk of corrupting the mystery. In his judgment there was no need to express the relationship between the mystical Body and the Roman Church so as to make an identity emerge,

> As if the mystical Body were totally included within the confines of the Roman Church. The Roman Church is in fact the true Body of Christ, but it does not exhaust it. To the mystical Body of Christ belong those who are justified; as grace is not given to people which is not the grace of Christ, likewise no-one who is not incorporated into Christ is justified. In fact they do not belong to the Roman Church if not those who, having received the sacrament of Baptism, are united with those who do not refuse the bonds of faith and communion. The mystical Body of Christ is extended much more broadly than the Roman Church militant, embracing also the Church which is suffering in purgatory and the Church in triumph in heaven… I regret that those separated from the Roman Church do not benefit with us from all the supernatural gifts, which the Church bestows; but it is not given to us to say that in no way do those who are not incorporated into the Catholic Church not adhere to the mystical Body of Christ. Hence it appears that our Church, even though it is the visible manifestation of the mystical Body of Christ, cannot identify itself with it in the absolute sense.[47]

45 AS I/4, p. 204..

46 For an overall vision see also the *Relatio de Observationibus factis a Patribus Concilii circa primum Schema constitutionis de Ecclesia*, by the Secretary of the Commission Con. de doctrina fidei et morum, Fr S. Tromp. The report is dated Romae, 5–26 m. iulii 1963, in ASV, Envelope 755, folder 242, published in KT 2/2, pp. 620–653.

47 'Summe vere cavendum est ne formulae modusque loquendi de Ecclesia, illud mysterium corrumpant; ne taliter enuntietur relatio Ecclesiae romanae ad Corpus Mysticum eorumque identitas, quasi Corpus Mysticum intra fines Ecclesiae romanae totaliter includeretur. Est enim Ecclesia romana verum Christi Corpus quin tamen

And so Liénart asked that the article which supported this absolute identification between the Catholic Church and the mystical Body of Christ (article 7, chapter I) be removed, and that, at the same time, the treatment on the Church appear in a less juridical and more mystical fashion, according to her nature. Here one can already glimpse the choice that would be made about introducing a distinction between Church of Christ and Catholic Church, so as to combine the identity and unicity of the Church (historical aspect) and its not-total absorption in the Roman Church (mystical aspect), leaving aside the too legal aspect of the concept of the mystical Body, and opting for a prevalence of other themes of the Church, more theological, more biblical and more mystical. Were the two aspects of the Church, historical and mystical, in opposition in the previous Magisterium? When Jesus established the Church, had he already taken into account this possible conflict? As we will have the opportunity to see later, this bipartition—which would become a sort of dilemma—while it arose following the fact of the division of Christians, seeks to provide a doctrinal basis for ecumenical endeavour.

As far as this study is concerned, a very interesting question was raised in the intervention of Cardinal Bueno y Monreal, Archbishop of Seville. The question of the Church mystical Body of Christ was propitious for raising a more fundamental and important question for the whole of the conciliar teaching:

> What is the value, he asked, that the Council wishes to give to its doctrinal declarations? Two things can be inferred from the ordinary Magisterium: the Spirit as soul of the mystical Body

illud exhauriat. Ad Corpus etenim Christi Mysticum pertinent quotquot iustificentur, cum nulla detur hominibus gratia quae non sit Christi gratia, cumque nemo iustificetur quin Christo incorporetur. Ad Ecclesiam vero romanam non pertinent nisi qui baptismi sacramento rite suscepto, ei sunt aggregati, quique fidei communionisque vincula non abnuerunt. Corpus ergo Mysticum multo latius extenditur quam Ecclesia romanamilitans. Amplectitur etiam Ecclesiam in purgatorio dolentem et Ecclesiam in caelo triumphantem. ... apparet quod Ecclesia nostra, quamvis sit visibilis manifestatio Corporis Mystici Iesu Christi, non possit cum eo absolute, sensu dicto, identificari', AS I/4, pp. 126–127.

> and the Roman Church as mystical Body. The first statement has been taught by Leo XIII and by Pius XII; the second by Pius XII, in the Encyclical *Mystici Corporis* and also in the Encyclical *Humani generis,* so that contrary judgments might be rejected. Is the approval of the formulae in the Council an act of the solemn Magisterium?[48]

Cardinal König, instead, highlighted the fact that the questions presented in the schema were legitimately still disputed among theologians, others, instead, would be treated by other future schema. Since, then, the Church transcends the national communities and since the nations at this time were ever closer (today we would talk of globalisation), destined to live side-by-side in a united world scenario, it was not of great benefit to the Church's teaching to take advantage of a right, rather than her much more noble *munus,* which is that of bringing the Gospel to all peoples, thus also encouraging other benefits to the whole of humanity. The schema could not but speak of the sincere will of the non-Christian peoples. In a more doctrinal fashion, König highlighted another problem: quite a few theologians today considered the Church as radical sacrament of humanity, a consequence of which was that the non-baptised were related to the Church not so much with a merely subjective *voto* (desire), but also by objective reasons, as, for example, the participation in the very human nature assumed by Christ.[49] Here one sees the influence of Rahner in this very radical way of conceiving the relating of the non-baptised to the Church.

For Cardinal Alfrink, too, the schema needed to be done again, since it spoke in a vague and minimalist way about the participation of the baptised in the life of grace, as well as their relationship to the

---

48 *Ibid.,* pp. 130–131.

49 Cf. *Ibid.,* pp. 132–133: 'Theologi non pauci Ecclesiam *hodie* tamquam sacramentum radicale humani generis considerant, ex quo sequeretur, quod non-baptizati non tantum voto mere subiectivo sed etiam rationibus obiectivis ad Ecclesiam ordinantur, v. g. participatione eiusdem naturae humanae, quam Christus assumpsit', *Ibid.,* p. 133.

Church. In addition, what was set out in chapter IV about the episcopal College was expressed in fairly negative terms. Alfrink noted some fundamental difficulties:

> It is said in n. 16 that the College of bishops—'one with its head and never without him'—is constituted as 'one subject with full and supreme power over the whole of the Church'; but immediately it is added that this power in the universal Church is not exercised 'unless in an extraordinary fashion'... What about the ordinary Magisterium of the episcopal body which is exercised outside the ecumenical Council, treated widely in chapter VII? So therefore there is some irreconcilability between chapter IV and chapter VII.[50]

With Cardinal Ritter the criticism moved towards a more general and methodological consideration of the schema: the defect was not to be found in some shortcoming, for which it would have been easy to compensate, but in the very method or system according to which the schema progressed. For Ritter, the Church was the same mystical Christ who lives and works through all its members, in whom the Holy Spirit lives and works, too, the Spirit of Christ. By means of this concept one can understand the Church and 'the work according to each member' by which the Church grows in 'its building up in charity'. Indeed each member of the Church has a part to play in these activities and this life, each according to their own measure. Thus Ritter now addressed the whole Assembly asking them to pronounce gently on itself, on what the Church is in herself:

> The job of this Council—if not the biggest, at least one of the major tasks—is to indicate in a gratifying, clear and appropriate way what the Church feels herself to be, what the Church is saying about herself. And we must point out what the Church *today* feels; we cannot, going back to a partial Tridentine or Vatican concept, leave aside the theological work of

[50] *Ibid.*, p. 135.

> recent times which gave so much perfection to the concept and understanding of the Church, mystical Body of Christ.[51]

Then it was the turn of Bishop De Smedt. In his address he used arguments similar to those used previously, but now more elaborated with theological precision. He began by saying that the schema appeared to him on the one hand lacking in ecumenical spirit and on the other far from the doctrine presented by the Doctors and preachers of the Church. De Smedt asked the Council Fathers: 'Shouldn't a certain triumphalism, a certain clericalism and a certain legalism be altered in this schema? In three areas'.[52] *Triumphalism* with regard to the manner of speaking, the pompous and romantic style, to which, according to the Bishop of Bruges, *L'Osservatore Romano* and other Roman documents had already become accustomed. *Clericalism,* because there prevailed a traditional image of the Church, in the form of a pyramid: Pope, bishops and priests and at the base the Christian people seen in a receptive light. In reality, he observed,

> What is permanent is the people of God; what passes is the ministry of the hierarchy. In the people of God we are linked to each other and we have the same rights and fundamental offices. We all participate in the royal priesthood of the people of God. The Pope is one of the (ex fidelis) faithful; bishops, priests, lay people, religious, we are all faithful. We access the same sacraments, we need forgiveness of sins, Eucharistic bread and the Word of God, and we reach out for the same homeland, through the mercy of God... We must be careful, in speaking about the Church, not to fall into some hierarchism, *some clericalism, some episcopal idolatry or Pope idolatry.*[53]

Finally, *legalism,* because the real characteristic of the Church, her motherhood, the centre of primitive Christian ecclesiology, had not been highlighted. 'Mater Ecclesia' tells us that all the baptised are

51 *Ibid.,* p. 138.

52 *Ibid.,* p. 142.

53 *Ibid.,* p. 143.

children of the Church. All Christians are generated by the Church through valid Baptism. In whatever Christian class they may find themselves, they are all children of the Church and will always remain as such. Even if some are separated, they are always brothers and sisters: the bond of generation never ceases. The solution offered by De Smedt was to speak about the Mother. In the way adopted, on the other hand, to speak rather about a judge and to proceed in that way not only was it not good theology, but in addition it was not the way a good Mother would allow speaking about herself.[54] De Smedt's 'ecumenical methodology' was now coloured by a new feature: it had to be maternal. A theology like that which emerged from the schema did not speak of mercy, which the Pope had spoken about in his inaugural sermon.[55]

What resulted in the council chamber to be above all a problem of methodology was also recognised by Bishop M. Lefebvre, who put forward a proposal shared also by Cardinal Ruffini.[56] The main difficulty, in his opinion, arose from the fact that, due to the circumstances of the day and at the explicit request of the Supreme Pontiff, it was necessary to speak directly to the world and to all people, a concern sensed much more today than in previous councils. The means of social communication increased day-by-day the zeal for the preaching of the truth and the desire for unity. How to link two compelling needs: 1) to teach doctrine in an unambiguous manner, and 2) to make oneself understood by all people? Lefebvre suggested two documents, one dogmatic, to be reserved for the representatives at the work of the Council, and one more pastoral, for the use of everyone, both Catholics and non-Catholics, as well as non-Christians. Thus would be avoided the long-standing problem of not being able to publish a dogmatically pastoral document, rigorous in teaching

54 Cf. *Ibid.*, pp. 142–143.

55 Cf. *Ibid.*, p. 144, footnote n. 25.

56 Cf. *Ibid.*, p. 291.

and understandable by everyone. A very intelligent solution, but which unfortunately was not met with very much enthusiasm.[57]

In his address Bishop Carli di Segni seemed to want to respond directly to De Smedt's strong words. In fact, he drew attention to the fact that while there was a pressing request for the Council to give a more ecumenical slant to the document on the Church, unfortunately the 'union or ecumenical concern' was not felt in the same way by all the Fathers. Some even exaggerated this concern. Therefore, in Carli's judgement:

a. it was not sufficient to see everything in the light of the highly desired ecumenical union, but it was necessary to respect the hierarchy of the aims established by the Pope;

b. the ecumenical concern should not exercise a greater influence than necessary over the work of the Council. The danger was that of saying: let us remain silent on doctrine so as not to hurt the feelings of Protestants and declare the death of ecumenism. It was commonplace, according to Carli, to hear it said that issues not spoken about were:

> Tradition, the Blessed Virgin Mary, so as not to upset the Protestants, nor the primacy of the Supreme Pontiff so as not to upset the Easterners; nothing was said about atheistic Communism or materialism, so as not to see the Church mixed up in political affairs, nor anything about the Church militant which smacks of militarism; nor is the ordinary Magisterium of the Church cited in the Council, I don't know for what reason.[58]

And with a very prophetic intuition, Carli exhorted the Council to declare its *mens*:

> If it intends to define something or *just* propose in a solemn manner. In this and in other schema this barely appears. It is

---

[57] Cf. *Ibid.*, pp. 144–146.

[58] *Ibid.*, pp. 159–160.

essential that this question is resolved by the Fathers, so that after the Council theologians don't introduce an endless dispute.[59]

---

59 *Ibid.*, p. 161. In his report on the observations on the schema on the Church, Fr Tromp informs us that 'gravissima est quaestio de qualificatione doctrinali, quam directe vel indirecte in prima Concilii Sessione moverunt plures Patres, et in discussionibus de Ecclesia Em.mus Bueno y Monreal, Exc.mi Carli, Ibanez, Jubany, Lamont, Plaza. Commissio Theologica processit e principio in exponendis materiis doctrinalibus omnia quoad substantia debere esse absolute certa ideoque irreformabilia, quippe cum agatur de decretis factis a magisterio Ecclesiae universali in sua universalitate solemniter congregato. Hoc autem minime significat omnia etiam esse fide divina credenda et tenenda [Denz. 1839]; et etsi conclusio stricte dicta theologica sit absolute certa et irreformabilis, tamen semper fuerunt, qui negarent eandem proponi posse tamquam credendam fide proprie divina. Ad quam distinctionem Exc.mus Tinivella in Concilio attentionem movit. Et etiam si Rom. Pontifex, suprema sua auctoritate explicat legem naturalem, quin provocet ad revelationem, huismodi decreta per se non credenda sed tenenda sunt, attamen ut infallibilia et immutabilia. Quare as mentem Commissionis Theologicae minime necesse erat ad omnia et singular addere qualificationes, cum semper et ubique adsit minima qualificatio: "saltem absolute certum et irreformabiliter tenendum". Nec Concilia anteacta ad omnia et singular dederunt qualificationem. Ut autem aliqua doctrina retineatur de fide definite, id ex modo speciali dicendi clare appareat necesse est'. Up to here one can deduce the *mens* of the Theological Commission, according to which what is doctrinal material, as regards the substance, must be absolutely certain and irreformable, which, however, does not mean that everything must be taken with faith *credenda* or everything with faith *tenenda*. It was not necessary to add a theological qualification for every statement, just as indeed the previous Councils had not done so, however there always remaining a minimal qualification. Hence, then, the specificity of Vatican II: according to many Fathers it was not about proposing what was disputed, although no Father explained clearly what was still a matter of dispute. However, one could not deprive of its certainty a question which a well-known theologian had begun to dispute. The Fathers did not express themselves clearly on this specific issue. It simply appears that, according to Bea and some others, the theological unrest of those years was healthy; others, instead, saw an imminent danger in this unrest. Here is Tromp's Latin text on this second passage:'Cum principio super exposito [the theological qualification of doctrines], saltem si sibi constant, omnes ii consentire videtur, qui ut Em.mi Montini et König necnon Exc.mi Charue,

From the German side arrived another very significant criticism, aimed at rejecting the schema. The strong voice of Cardinal Döpfner was raised, indicating a substantial defect which pervaded the entire document. Like Alfrink, Döpfner, too, focused his comments on the concept of 'members' of the Church. Its legal significance prevailed over the theological. It originated in the Pauline epistles, where it illuminated principally being baptised in Christ by means of the Holy Spirit, signifying the effect of grace. Instead in the schema, it was understood in a merely legal sense, applying it to the Church as (external) society, as visible Catholic Church. Furthermore, according to Döpfner, it was easy to show that the episcopate was an institution of divine right and that the joint teaching of the ordinary Magisterium of the episcopal College, one with the Roman Pontiff, was infallible, even if the individual bishops were not infallible. What's more, it was not appropriate to define a *quaestio disputata*, that is, if a bishop appointed by the Roman Pontiff also had jurisdictional power through the appointment, derived from the Pope, or whether, according to the opposite judgment, he has designation of the person and the consequent *cooptatio* in the episcopal College, which makes the bishop, by divine right therefore, participant in power. In conclusion, Döpfner also expressed a possible council agenda about the way to proceed, now inevitably aimed at the reworking of the preparatory documents.[60] He proposed the following stages:

Jubany, Philbin, Rodriguez, Weber at Rev.mus P. Butler dicunt quaestiones disputatas proponi non esse. Id enim implicate a sola posse proponi de quibus disputari nequeat, i.e. quae absolute certitudine gaudeant. Quid autem sit quaestio disputata, nemo Patrem clare edixit. Constat autem veritatem aliquam hucusque indubitatam non privari sua certitudine eo quod theologus quidam etiam notabilis de ea disputare incipiat. Ceterum Patres singua hac in re nihil clare enutiaverunt. Id solum apparuit, quod nonnulli, ut Em.mus Bea at Exc.mus Hurley una cum Abbate Butler putant fermentationem hodiernam theologiam esse salutarem ideoque sat facile considerari osse aliquam quaestionem ut disputabilem; alii autem, ut Exc.mi Hervas, Fares, Franić, Martinez, Philbin et Plaza in eadem hac fermentatione etiam existimant imminere periculum', KT 2/2, pp. 634–635.

a. in the remaining days of the first Session disquisitions on the schema should continue;
b. there should then be a vote to see if the schema was satisfactory or not;
c. there should be a break (until 15 February) so that further comments could be passed on to the competent commission;
d. up to the start of the new period the commission would examine the new schema corresponding to the Fathers' wishes, helped by the periti competent in this field.[61]

---

60 Interesting is the position of Bishop D. Hurley (Archbishop of Durban) about the need to create between the first and second conciliar sessions 'alicuius commissionis vere centralis, et—sit venia verbo—centralizantis, cui munus sit finem Concilii ad mentem Summi Pontificis clare exponere, necnon curare ut media necessaria ad illum finem attingendum adhibeantur, *ut iam hoc mane dixit em.mus car. Léger*' (*Ibid.*, p. 197). Hurley reiterated that the goal to be achieved was renewed pastoral care. The Council had been summoned not to define new truths, but to renew the Church's pastoral activity. It was necessary to be concerned about the *way* of speaking about doctrine and not largely doctrine. In fact, the way 'non in mera adaptatione verborum et locutionum consistit, sed in genere loquendi, non scholari, nec oratorio, sed plano et communi, simul et praeciso, non iuridico nec desiccato, sed in quo percipiatur unctio quaedam amorque Dei et hominum' (*Ibid.*, p. 198). In this pastoral concern true teaching *per se* was as important as teaching *pro hominibus*, to whom we have been sent (cf. *Ibid.*). Cardinal Bea spoke along similar lines (cf. *Ibid.*, p. 229). This position seems to us to be truly emblematic of the hermeneutical problem of Vatican II.

61 Cf. *Ibid.*, pp. 183–186. The salient points of the text are as follows: 'Ita facilius monstrari potuisse, quod episcopatus est institutio iuris divini, vel quod communis doctrina magisterii ordinarii collegii episcopalis una cum Romano Pontifice est infallibilis, licet singuli episcopi infallibiles non sint; uno verbo: doctrina de episcopatu, tam ardenter desiderata, facilius et cohaerentius dari potuisset. ... ne conciliariter definiri videatur quaestio disputata, utrum nominatio episcopi per Romanum Pontificem habenda sit collatio potestatis a potestate Papae derivanda. Nam sententia opposita, secundum quam est designatio personae eiusque cooptatio in collegium episcopale, ita ut particeps fiat potestatis collegii huius iure divino ei inhaerentis, bonis rationibus fulcitur' (*Ibid.*, p.185). The problem encountered here is this: of course the episcopate is of divine right, but not the College likewise, an institution derived from that of the Twelve. Therefore to insist on the episcopate as divine institution is not sufficient for resolving the question of the College as equal to the institution.

Cardinal Frings intervened indicating what was for him a prejudicial omission: the schema ignored the integral Tradition of the Church because it had chosen only that of the last one hundred years. There was no mention of Greek and Latin Tradition.[62]

Cardinal Suenens proposed an 'overall plan', in other words a 'ratio ipsius Concilii',[63] which up until then had been lacking. A rationale which proposed to examine in an appropriate manner the magisterial heart of the Council itself, the ecclesiological theme. It would comprise two parts: *de Ecclesia ad intra* and *de Ecclesia ad extra*. It was essential to look at the Church in herself, as mystery of the living Christ and his mystical Body, and at the Church as establisher of dialogue with the world. The world was waiting for the Church to resolve the most binding social questions. Dialogue then had to be undertaken with three interlocutors: 1) with the Catholic faithful; 2) with those not in communion with the Catholic Church; and, 3) with today's world. Suenens was so enthusiastic about this dialogue with the world that he thought about a real and proper *secretarium pro problematis mundi hodierni*.[64]

For Cardinal Bea, too, and for Cardinal Montini as well,[65] the theme of the Church was the major issue to be examined, and so it was right and proper to tackle such a problem with the greatest awareness. For Bea, as well, it was inappropriate to insert into a conciliar constitution an issue still debated among the theologians about being a member of the Church in the true and proper sense.[66]

---

62 Cf. *Ibid.*, p. 219.

63 *Ibid.*, p. 223.

64 Cf. *Ibid.*, pp. 221–225.

65 Cf. *Ibid.*, p. 292. For Montini the most important question to be examined in the ecclesiological theme was that of the episcopate, to be proposed according to the schema of Vatican I: 1) the institution of the college of the apostles; 2) the succession of the episcopal body to the apostolic body; 3) the *munus* and the faculty of each bishop and therefore the sacramental foundation of the episcopal *munus*, cf. *Ibid.*, p. 293.

66 In his report (cit.), Tromp, in summarising, draws attention to the following

The question for Bea was still not mature, while Pius XII, even if in the ordinary magisterial form, had clearly taught it, even condemning the contrary errors in *Humani generis*. So was it necessary to ignore the recent Magisterium to go back to more ancient teaching, as Frings had suggested? Yes, in fact Bea explicitly cited Frings' objection.[67] In reality, Tradition went forward, not backwards.

Bishop Volk agreed with the analysis of Bea and added an ecumenical argument in a theological fashion: the separated brethren were waiting for real evangelical teaching on the Church. It was essential to present the Church not just as *medium salutis* but also as *fructus salutis*, and that is to say, as a community of those redeemed by the grace of Christ. This aspect also enlightened the reference to the Kingdom of God. The Council should propose the teaching of the Church as *euangelion*: 'thus is dogmatic teaching in itself truly pastoral'.[68]

The intervention of Cardinal Lercaro, entirely focused on the Church of the poor, had great resonance. In his opinion, the mystery of the Church had to be proposed to the people of our time as the 'magnum Sacramentum' of Christ the Word of God who works in the midst of men and women, and since today the mystery of the Church is mainly in the poor, as John XXIII believed, too, the Church itself

---

observations on such a problem: '1. Melius non adhibetur vox membrum (Suenens, Doi et Epp. Japon). 2. Doctrina de membris est quaestio disputata (Bea, Charue). 3. Separetur quaestio de membris a quaestione de necessitate salutis (Alfrink c. s.). 4. Melis est incipere a Christo Capite influente gratiam quam a membris (Ancel, Hengsbach). 5. In schemate membra tantum iuridice considerantur (60 Epp. Galliae). 6. Distinguantur varii gradus membrorum (Bougon, Reetz). 7. Fortius urgeatur nexus qui restat cum separatis (Bergonzini). 8. Magis urgeatur necessitas credenda ad salute obtinendam (Beck). 9. Necessitas Ecclesiae ad salute non solum consideretur individualiter, sed etiam collective (König, Vairo). 10. Non placet parallelismus inter baptismum et Ecclesiam, ad salute quod spectat (Alfrink c. s.). 11. Doctrina antiquissima et traditionalis de necessitate ad salute est dura: numquam nude fidelibus exponatur (Olano)', KT 2/2, pp. 638–639.

67 Cf. *Ibid.*, p. 229.

68 Cf. *Ibid.*, p. 388.

today is an 'Ecclesia pauperum'. It could well be said that, in Lercaro's ecclesiology, the poor functioned as architectural principle. The Council had to sketch out a true doctrine of the 'Church of the poor', starting from evangelical poverty, from its dignity and highlighting the ontological relationship between the presence of Christ in the poor and the presence of Christ in the Eucharistic action and in the sacred hierarchy. In short, what had to be more at the heart of the Council was the evangelisation of the poor. His intervention was greeted with applause.[69]

While Lercaro was concerned about the poor, another bishop, S. Méndez Arceo, struggled to convince the Council Fathers that the origins of Freemasonry were not anti-Christian. In his opinion, non-Catholic ministers and Christians found few differences between Masonic groups and a community union with the Church, but they themselves would represent a valid leaven to eliminate from masonry itself what is anti-Christian and anti-Catholic, if they knew the Catholic Church better, if they understood and loved it.[70]

From what has been set out up to now it seems clear that a large number of Fathers were inclined towards a re-working of the Schema, producing very similar arguments. However, from the *orationes Patrum* there emerged a series of theological elements which clashed against each other. One among all and the most important concerned the Church: the legal aspect or the pastoral-spiritual? In my opinion, this question is invalidated from the outset, for a fundamental reason: Catholic teaching had never known *aut aut* but always an *et et.*

The difficulties were underlined by the intervention of Bishop Ancel (Auxiliary of Lyons). In the disquisition, he said, there was nearly always an opposition between the legal and the spiritual character of the Church, between the potestative aspect and that of the service of the hierarchical authority or between the collegial authority of the bishops and the primacy of the Supreme Pontiff.

---

69 Cf. *Ibid.*, pp. 327–330.

70 Cf. *Ibid.*, pp. 340–341.

According to Ancel, the opposition was not merely obvious but significant and therefore demanded a solution. Where did it lie? In the Gospel, said Ancel. There it can be clearly read that Peter is not separate from the college of the apostles, but that the primacy is a gift for the college itself. Therefore, in revising the text, it is necessary to give a central place to the study of the Gospel.[71]

3. *The schema on the Church*

On 22 February 1963 the Co-ordinating Commission proposed a new order of themes to be treated in *De Ecclesia*. It was to follow the key concept that the Church is *Lumen Gentium,* so it was necessary therefore that everything to do with dogmatic issues was shown to be in connection and unity with the pastoral decrees and with discipline. On 21 February, in a plenary session, the Commission *De doctrina fidei et morum* had created a Sub-commission 'de Ecclesia', chaired by Browne and with members Leger, König, Parente, Schröffer, Charue, and Garrone. This Sub-commission examined some alternative schema. There were five most important ones: that of Parente, that of the German bishops, the Chilean bishops, the French, and that of Mgr Philips, which was the structure of *Lumen Gentium*.[72]

3.1 Parente's schema

It was Cardinal Ottaviani who asked Parente to draft a schema on the Church, taking into account the indications of the Council's Co-ordinating Commission.[73] It was finished in February 1963 and bore the title *De Ecclesiae Corpore Christi Mystico ac Lumen Gentium*. Parente began by saying that Vatican II, with its authority, confirmed the doctrine contained both in Scripture and Tradition and in the documents of the Magisterium or defined by previous Councils. The

---

71 Cf. *Ibid.*, pp. 379–381.

72 Cf. Hellín, *Lumen Gentium*, p. XXV.

73 Cf. *Ibid.*, pp. 681–693.

schema was divided into three chapters, which substantially took up again the teaching of the previous schema: *De Ecclesiae Mysterio, De Constitutione hierarchica Ecclesiae, speciatim de Episcopis* and *De Ecclesiae principiis et actione in bonum humanae societatis.*

In n. 2 Parente illustrated the teaching of the Church as means of salvation necessary for everyone, reiterating the teaching of Pius XII about belonging *reapse* to the Church for those who, re-born through sacramental washing, profess the true Catholic faith and recognise the visible authority, and who are not separated from it by most serious sin. Instead, related to the Church in *voto* are not just catechumens who are moved by the Holy Spirit, but also those unaware that the Catholic Church is the one true Church, and all other people of goodwill, taking up again the distinctions of the previous schema. Parente also affirmed the action of the Holy Spirit outside the Catholic Church, which by its virtue acts in the separated brethren, by reason of the *elementa,* so all may become one flock under one shepherd.

3.2 The Philips schema

Mgr Philips' schema was the basic tool for the drafting of the future *Lumen Gentium.* On 1 October 1962, while *De Ecclesia* was being discussed in the council chamber, the votes on the overall acceptance of the schema were announced. According to Melloni, this was 'a plebiscite on what had until this point been the "Philips schema"..., but would now become the base text (or "*textus receptus*", in conciliar Latin): of 2301 fathers present, there were 27 invalid votes, 43 against, and 2231 in favour'.[74]

74 A. Melloni, 'The Beginning of the Second Period: The Great Debate on the Church', in G. Alberigo (ed.), *History of Vatican II,* vol. 3, *The Formation of the Council's Identity. First Period and Intersession. October 1962—September 1963* (Maryknoll / Leuven: Orbis / Peeters, 2000), p. 45: 'On the one hand, the vote on 1 October had forever buried the preparatory schema, and it would be impossible now to turn back. Vatican II, the vote said, would write neither a treatise on the nature of the Church nor one of those scholastic reviews that the preparatory schema contained; the only things that would remain in the

In truth this schema had two versions: the first appeared already in November 1962, when the schema was discussed, and was redrafted with the aim of responding to the demands contained in John XXIII's inaugural address;[75] the second, entitled *Lumen Gentium*, was proposed in the first days of February the following year. This was accepted by the Doctrinal Commission as the basic working resource on 6 March 1963.

In the first schema, Philips, having set out the question *De nonchristianis ad Ecclesiam adducendis,* added a very interesting note, which, however, was not to be inserted in the text of the schema. In this note it was said that it was better to abstain—as desired for the previous schema—from questions still disputed by theologians. Here it was not the case that the Council pronounced on the thorny issue about whether Catholics must declare themselves imperfect, inchoative or in part hindered members. There was a difference of judgment among theologians: for some the question of 'members' was not per

---

schema were the things that Philips had taken over from the theses of Lattanzi and Gagnebet. On the other hand, the vote accepted the "new" schema as the measure of what was possible; ... While Philip's cautious and politically astute work of weaving together the new schema had broken down the prejudice (invoked to defeat the preparatory schema) that no change could be made, his work also still bore the mark of the original schema in its uncertainties, ambiguities, compromises and juxtapositions', p. 46.

75 Cf. Hellín, *Lumen Gentium*, p. 706. That is explained in the *Intentum* of the first Philips' schema: '1) Expositio non sit mera repetito doctrinae vulgatae et velut classicae, sed talis ut, secundum emolumenta recentioris studii exegetici, patristici et speculativae reflexiones, breviter exponatur *placita principaliora* pro intensiore vita Ecclesiae catholicae, eo modo ut omnem animam bene dispositam intime commoveant. 2) Orientatio schematis sit *positive et constructive,* non pure defensiva et reprobativa. Firme servata omnium errorum condemnatio in praesenti tempore magis misericordiae medicina adhibenda est, et vis doctrinae catholicae pro hodiernis necessitatibus uberius explananda, ut errantes, vel acatholici ad Ecclesiam iam respicientes non removeantur, sed ad meliorem intelligentiam adducantur. 3) Declaratio ita conficiatur ut Ecclesiae, religiosae veritatis facem attollens, appareat ut *amantissima omnium mater ...*', *Ibid.*

se necessary, nor could different ranks of membership be admitted; for others, it was essential to pose the question to state the difference between non-Catholic Christians and well-disposed pagans, who were largely spoken of as imperfect members; finally, for others still it was necessary to be wary of saying something which might undermine the mystery of Christ and by reference and proportionately the Church, too. So, according to Philips, it was not appropriate that the Council should solve such an issue; besides, the concept of 'members' was to be thought of as compared to the human body.[76] So the question of being a perfect or imperfect member of the Body of Christ vanished. Melloni says that from this point of view the schema was not innovative, even if the paragraph on 'members'

> Had led people to judge that the proposals of the preparatory commission were incompatible with the ecumenical expectations aroused by the Council. The new text included neither the tripartite division of catechumens, baptized non-Catholics, and 'people of good will', which had been in Philips's proposal of the year before, nor Vagaggini's formula, which distinguished between the intention of complete and visible membership, and the action of grace, which 'by its power' makes members even of those outside the institutional boundaries of Roman Catholicism.[77]

---

[76] Cf. *Ibid.*, p. 710: 'In praecedente textu cunsulto abstineatur a quaestione, inter theologos controversa,utrum christiani acatholici simpliciter dicendi sint non-membra Ecclesiae an membra imperfect, incoative vel partim impedite, cum ea unita. De placitis obiectivis omnes concordant. Quidam autem aestimant rationem membri dividi non posse, neque varios gradus admittere. Alii autem, qui magis ad efficacitatem ecclesialem baptismum attendant, et distinctionem efferre volunt inter acatholicum baptizatum et paganum etiam bene dispositum, potius de membro imperfect loquuntur. Ceterum cavendum est, ne dicatur aliquem ad Christum pertinere posse, quin eodem proportionali modo ad Ecclesiam pertineat. Videtur autem Concilium hanc controversiam de modo proponendi doctrinam dirimere non oportere, eo minus quod vocabulum "membri" funditus nititur in quadam comparatione, nempe cum organismo humano'.

I will now examine the most important passages of Philips' second proposal, which we will then find again in the Dogmatic Constitution.[78] The whole schema was organised into two chapters: *De Ecclesiae Mysterio* and *De constitutione hierarchica Ecclesiae et in specie de Episcopatu*. In the first chapter Philips distinguished Catholics being in the Church, the union of the Church with non-Catholics and the duty to lead non-Christians to the Church. Those who recognised in the Church all the means of salvation instituted in her, and make up part of the visible whole in union with the Supreme Pontiff and the bishops, preserving the bonds of Baptism, of the profession of faith and of ecclesiastical communion, belong to the Church 'reapse et sine restrictione'. While related to the Church in *voto* are catechumens, those who do not know that the Catholic Church is the one Church of Christ, but sincerely want to carry out the will of Christ, and those who, unaware of Christ, want to carry out the will of their Creator.[79] As regards the union of the Church with non-Catholics, Philips presented again the teaching already seen in the schema *De Ecclesia*, proposed by Parente. The second chapter examined the issue, which became more thorny, but also typical of *Lumen Gentium*, of collegiality. In n. 5 Philips looked at the collegial nature of the Episcopate. Just as Saint Peter together with the apostles constituted one college, so, in apostolic succession, the Roman Pontiff constitutes one college with the bishops. The college, however, is not authentic without the Pope, who, as successor

77 Melloni, 'The Beginning of the Second Period', p. 49. Melloni goes on to say that the victorious thesis was that of Schauf, borrowed from Tromp ('Zur Frage der Kirchengliedschaft', in *Theologische Revue* 58 [1962], pp. 217–224), even though the concluding sections try to show how Catholics, Christians in general, and non-Christians are related to the Church, cf. *Ibid.*

78 The schema is reported in Hellín, *Lumen Gentium*, pp. 694–705.

79 In the footnote Philips stated: 'Doctrina, in hac ultima paragrapho expressa (concerning belonging to the Church in *voto*) ab omnibus peritis admittitur. Plures tamen eorum aestimant hanc explicationem proprie theologicam (scilicet de modo quo necessitas Ecclesiae cum voluntate salvifica universali cohareat) non esse a Concilio imponendam' (*Ibid.*, p. 697). Hence we can understand how this vision came to be overlooked.

of Peter, is the Head. Then, echoing the initial schema, he recalled the meaning in which college should be understood: one with the Roman Pontiff and never without the Head, it was the subject of full and supreme power in the universal Church. Such supreme collegial power was exercised solemnly and in an extraordinary manner in an ecumenical council. Equally it was the business of the Pope to determine the norms and method according to which the college, with its Head, has supreme power in the Church to be exercised in practice and *pro temporum.*[80] Finally, significant, too, is the explanation Philips gave about the *munus docendi* of the bishops, taken up almost literally by *Lumen Gentium* 25:

> Imo, licet singuli praesules infallibilitatis praerogativa non polleant, quando tamen, etiam per orbem dispersi, sed collegialem nexum servantes, authentice docentes una cum Romano Pontifice ut testes fidei in revelata fide tradenda in unam sententiam conveniunt, tunc doctrina Christi infallibiliter enunciant. Quod adhuc manifestius obtinetur, quando in Concilio Oecumenico adunati, cum Romano Pontifice et sub eius suprema auctoritate, sunt pro universa Ecclesia fidei et morum doctores et iudices, quorum definitions ab omnibus sincere animo accipi debent. Quae definitiones infallibiles erunt, si ex tenore verborum vel contextus constat Concilium plenitudinem suae potestatis ad statuendam doctrinam irreformabilem, adhimplere voluisse.[81]

3.3 The German schema

During the interval between the First and Second Session of the Council, the German-language Fathers met in Munich to agree on a course of action in the Council, critically examining the various schemata, including, in particular, the one on the Church. Writing to the Holy Father, where they presented their critical observations about the schema and suggesting an alternative, they attested to the

80 Cf. Leo XIII, *Satis cognitum,* DH 3307.

81 Hellín, *Lumen Gentium,* p. 703.

work undertaken by the group in the days 5 and 6 February 1963.[82] On 21 February 1963, at a meeting of the Commission *de Doctrina fidei et morum,* Bishop Schröffer spoke about the 'de conventu Monacensi', that is, the meeting of the German-speaking Fathers which had taken place on the dates mentioned in Munich.[83] Schröffer explained their position,[84] reporting principally on *De Ecclesia*: the objections of the Protestants had always been borne in mind. The ecclesiology had been examined in such a way as to be understood by non-Catholics. Therefore the intention was to hold to a *via media* between the different tendencies which had appeared in the conciliar discussions. Finally, in summary, the rapporteur explained the reasons for the choices about the various images of the Church, the Church as universal, fundamental and eschatological sacrament, the members of the Church, the ministry of the bishops and the episcopal college. Schauf, too, refers to this meeting held in Munich in a report addressed to Tromp on 8 February 1963.[85] He was almost the only

---

82 Cf. AS I/4, p. 601.

83 Cf. Tromp's *Diario,* 21 February 1963, in KT 2/1, p. 229.

84 Cf. the *Relatio lecta ab Ecc.mo D. Schröffer in sessione plen. 21 Febr. [1963],* in ASV, Envelope 761, folder 229, published in KT 2/2, pp. 773–776.

85 Cf. ASV, Envelope 761, folder 268, published in KT 2/2, pp. 1163–1170. In this report Schauf says that he was preparing an 18-page critical response to the observations of Fr. Semmelroth on *De Ecclesia* (see O. Semmelroth, *Adnotationes criticae ad schema De ecclesia,* 5–6 February 1963, ff. 6, in ASV, Envelope 761, folder 268; H. Schauf, *Bemerkungen zu den Adnotationes zum Schema De Ecclesia* [written in response to Semmelroth], in ASV, Envelope 761, folder 268, published in KT 2/2, pp. 1090–1105). He was aware of the criticisms of Fr Schillebeeckx on the same theme and had also drafted for the occasion a critical response to these observations, comprising 13 pages (see E. Schillebeeckx, *Animadversiones in "Secundum Seriem" Schematum Constitutionum et Decretorum de quibus disceptabitur in Concilii sessionibus. De Ecclesia et De Beata Maria Virgine,* 30 November 1962, in ASV, Envelope 749, folder 249, published in KT 2/2, pp. 1119–1130). Schauf wanted the observations of Schillebeeckx and Philips to be known in the Munich meeting, but it was not possible to send Semmelroth's criticisms to Rome, due to the many false assumptions to which they gave rise (cf. KT 2/2, p. 1165). Schauf also notes

one to rebut the *Übermacht* of the others. With regret, however, he also wrote about the theological superficiality with which some eminent periti rejected the theology of the schema *De ecclesia*. The heaviest criticisms came from Semmelroth, who had not examined the acta of the Preparatory Commission and had been chosen as adviser. He did not even know about Gagnebet's conference.[86] Rahner had reported on the theme *De membris Ecclesiae*. That could also be talked about, but, according to Schauf, that was not the concept of Church membership, since it was not expressed in such a manner in any of the few Church documents. Schauf asked ironically: had Rahner become a Saul from Paul? He replied that he wanted to write this before, but that would have been too hasty. For Schauf the

the participants at the meeting: all the German bishops, with the exception of Archbishop Schäufele of Freiburg and the Auxiliary Bishops Tenhumberg and Sedlmeier, because they were ill. The Austrian and Swiss bishops, the Bishop of Stockholm, the Auxiliary Bishop of Namur in Belgium and the Auxiliary Bishop of Strasbourg, Elchinger, who seemed to be in close agreement with the majority of the French episcopate. There were various German and Austrian abbots and a priest from Bologna as Lercaro's observer. Then the following theologians: Rahner SJ, Ratzinger (Bonn), Semmelroth SJ, Wulf SJ, Hirschmann SJ, Schmaus (Munich), Grillmeier SJ, Schnackenburg, Stakemeier (Paderborn), Betz (Luxembourg) and the writer Schauf. Three Cardinals chaired the meeting: Frings, König and Döpfner. The latter guided the work (cf. *Ibid.*, p. 1164). See also the observations of H. Volk (et alii), *De Ecclesia*, 5–6 February 1963, ff. 36, in ASV, Envelope 761, folder 268.

86 Cf. KT 2/2, p. 1167. The conference of Fr Gagnebet OP, presenting the schema *De ecclesia*, was held in Rome on 2 December 1962 and the text sent to Ottaviani on 3 December 1962. It can be found in ASV, Envelope 759, folder 249, published in KT 2/2, pp. 1021–1-33. Inter alia, the Dominican wrote that the main aim of the schema was to insist on the true identity between the mystical Body such as it exists on earth and the Roman Catholic Church; between the Church of charity and the juridically organised visible society. The majority of bishops had expressed the formal desire that 'l'admirable enseignement de "CORPORIS MYSTICI" sur ce point' be taken up again. 'La Conférence épiscopale allemande de Fulda a insisté sur la valeur pastorale et œcuménique de cette doctrine et qui unifie dans une synthèse complète l'aspect visible et l'aspect invisible de l'Eglise', KT 2/2, p. 1025.

concept of 'membership' could not be silenced in the first schema. One had to respond with a legitimate question, since such a concept was an unequal and profound statement about the Church.[87] Grillmeier reported on *De episcopis*. The whole was presented like a ride across Lake Constance ('ein Ritt am Bodensee'), however not in such a cold winter, where everything was definitely frozen. In the Magisterium, said Schauf speaking in the aula, it is necessary to distinguish the *munus testium, iudicium et doctorum imponentium doctrinam*. This was important also for the teaching of the bishops outside their dioceses, important for the preaching of an auxiliary bishop and for the infallibility of the College of bishops. There was great amazement among the listeners. They were convinced that the *Commissio praeparatoria* was not so stupid.[88] Finally, according to the Fathers, from what is said in Schauf's letter, there was a need to strengthen the relationship not just with the separated brethren, but also with those of no faith. And at the end, some humour from Schauf: we could serve at table with the image of the *Ecclesia manducans*.[89]

So what can be inferred from the German-speaking Fathers themselves? Among the critical annotations of the schema *De Ecclesia*,[90] the Fathers from Germany and Austria stated that among the many reasons why they were unhappy with the schema was the fact that what they desired most was missing: a positive, ecumenical and pastoral aspect. The schema said nothing of theological value about the individual statements: that would create major hermeneutical difficulties about the way to interpret the propositions. It was not

87 Cf. *Ibid.*, pp. 1166–1167: 'Auch könne die in dem alten Schema ausgesprochene Gliedschaft nicht verschwiegen warden, weil auf eine legitime Frage geantwortet werde, weil diese Gliedschaft eine ungleich tiefere Aussage über die Kirche sei usw'. (p.1166).

88 Cf. *Ibid.*, p. 1167.

89 Cf. *Ibid.*, pp. 1169–1170: 'Der Bezug nicht nur auf die fratres separate, sonder auch die infidels möge stärker betont warden. (Wir können hier mit dem Bild der Ecclesia manducans aufwarten)'.

90 Cf. AS I/4, pp. 602–608.

clear if their authority derived from being proposed as dogma or with the authority of the other statements of ordinary Magisterium. Among the various images taken from Scripture, only that of the 'body' was considered, to the point of becoming a logical concept and no longer just an image. The question of the fate of children who died without Baptism should be left open. Then there was a need to be careful in speaking about members of the Church. The language used seemed exclusive: or one was a member of the Church in the full sense or otherwise one was not really a member. According to the German-language Fathers, it was essential to correct the manner of expression: if a Christian does not have one of the three bonds he or she is nevertheless member of the Church, even if not in the full sense, and therefore in an imperfect manner. So, they suggested accompanying the term 'members' with the specification 'vero et proprio sensu' or 'pleno et perfectu sensu' or simply it was necessary to avoid using it.[91] Then important criticism about the teaching regarding the college of bishops, which should be put at the front and not almost at the end. The relationship between the Roman Pontiff and the bishops should not be described in a negative fashion, that is by determining the limits of episcopal power, but rather in such a way as to demonstrate mutual inter-dependence: neither could the college be separated from the Pope, nor the Pope from the college. It was not sufficient to say that the ordinary power of the college was exercised only in an extraordinary manner. Instead, there does exist a real collegiality even outside the Council and in a way antecedent to the express will of the Pope.[92]

---

91 'Quae dicuntur de membris Ecclesiae, cautius dici debent. Estne ratio membri in indivisibili, quasi aut homo sit sensu pleno membrum Ecclesiae aut omnino non realiter sit eius membrum? Alternativa talis non videtur poni posse: nam etsi quidam non omnia tria vincula habet, sed tantum unum vel alterum, tamen pro sua parte realiter, etsi non sensu pleno et perfecta ad Ecclesiam pertinet et imperfecte dici potest eius membrum. Ergo: aut dicatur 15, 18 et 20 loco "vero et proprio sensu" "pleno et perfecta sensu" aut simpliciter evitetur terminus "membrum" et describantur tantum concrete diversi casus, qui diversimodam relationem hominis ad Ecclesiam determinant', *Ibid.*, pp. 604–605.

92 'Non sufficit dicere potestatem collegii ordinariam solummodo modo extraordinario

Finally, among the corrections suggested to individual sentences, the German and Austrian Fathers wanted the Church, in place of 'catholica romana', to be better referred to as 'catholica', for the following reasons: *romanitas* did not belong to the traditional characteristics of the Church and it is not even, as such, of divine right. They then suggested saying 'pascendi' instead of 'governandi', in reference to bishops, because this is better suited to the episcopal *munus*.[93]

The new German schema[94] was thus modified due to the main objections made to that approved by the Central Commission. The whole schema comprised five chapters, in which the laity and religious were included. Significant emphasis was given to chapter II, *De membris Ecclesiae*. Two forms were drafted: one in which the term 'member' did not appear, making reference exclusively to '*de coniunctionem* cum Ecclesiam', and the other, an alternative, in which the distinction between 'membrum perfectum Ecclesiae' and 'membrum imperfectum' was made, due to the 'imperfectae coniunctiones cum Ecclesia'. In explaining *De necessaria cum Ecclesia coniunctione*, the schema adopted the distinction between membership *in re* and membership *in voto*. To understand the effectiveness of this, the following reasons were put forward: the salvific universality of the will of God, the unity of humankind and its history (with reference to Ac 17:26–28), the real unity of Christ with humanity by means of the Incarnation (justified with reference to Rm 8:29 and Heb 2:1–15) and the objective redemption of each person. Somewhat exuberant reasons. What's more, in a completely unusual fashion, in explaining the three bonds of belonging to the Church, as regards the Sacraments, the phrase 'legitima coena Domini' is introduced, justified with reference to Ep 4:5 and to Denzinger 686, 864, 2202 and to the Code of Canon Law, canon 87.[95] In none of these references, however, is

exerceri. Existit realis collegialitas etiam extra Concilium et antecedenter ad explicitam voluntatem Summi Pontificis', *Ibid.*, p. 606.

93 Cf. *Ibid.*, p. 607.

94 Cf. *Ibid.*, pp. 610–632.

95 Cf. *Ibid.*, p. 616.

mention made of the Eucharist as 'legitima coena Domini'(the first two numbers of Denzinger do not exist).

In the alternative there was acknowledgement, due to the three bonds, of a 'different rank of union with the Church, and therefore the name members in the language of the Church today must not simply reject those who are united to the Church only imperfectly'.[96] Thus was distinguished a 'coniunctio perfecta cum Ecclesia' to which corresponded those who were 'membra perfecta Ecclesiae' and an 'imperfecta coniunctio cum Ecclesia' to which corresponded those who were 'membra imperfecta'. The novelty of the German schema was precisely the distinction of a different rank of belonging to the Church, of perfection and imperfection, where, however, imperfect belonging was to be appreciated due to the cogency of the existing bonds. In other words, it was the bonds of unity themselves which admitted a gradation per se. In fact,

> Since the sacramental bond and the hierarchical bond can be verified with a different rank, just like the real Lord's supper and other sacraments, above all baptism, whether apostolic succession is missing or not, unity with the Church on this dual aspect, too, can be greater or less.[97]

Therefore,

> Whoever has received valid Baptism, without also being united to the Church with the perfect symbolic bond and with the hierarchical bond, on the other hand certainly is not united to the Church in a perfect way, but on the other hand the eminent bond is not lacking, which truly unites to the Church.[98]

---

96 *Ibid.* 'Secundum positivam necessitudinem ad haec tria elementa aliam et aliam homines diverso gradu Ecclesiae *uniuntur,* adeo ut nomen membri in lingua Ecclesiae hodiernae non simpliciter denegari debeat iis, qui imperfecte tantum Ecclesiae uniuntur'.

97 'Cum etiam vinculum sacramentale et vinculum hierarchicum diverso gradu verificari possint, prout vera coena dominica aliaque sacramenta praeter baptisma et aliquid successionis apostolicae habentur aut deficiunt, coniunctio cum Ecclesia etiam sub hoc duplici respect maior aut minor evadit', *Ibid.,* p. 618.

Finally, still in this chapter, reference was made to the *elementa* of the Church, already seen in the first schema. In precise terms it was speaking about *De Ecclesiae elementis extra Ecclesiam datis*, by means of which the Christian communities, by preserving them, can gain access to the Church of Christ. 'The Church of Christ is not only one but also unifying (*uniens*), and therefore those elements of the Church which are outside its visible whole, are not only recognised sincerely as gifts of Christ, but a lot will be done so that they may be united to her, so that such elements may not only find their own perfection, but also that

[98] 'Qui baptisma valido suscepit, quin etiam iungatur Ecclesiae vinculo symbolico perfecto et vinculo hierarchico, ex una parte non perfecte, sicut oportet, Ecclesiae unitur, ex altera parte non caret vinculo eximio, quo Ecclesiae vere adstringitur' (*Ibid.*, pp. 617–618). To justify the excellence of Baptism compared to the other bonds, the text had cited just before the Code of Canon Law, canon 87 (cf. also canon 86 of the 1983 Code of Canon Law), which said: 'Baptismate homo constituitur in Ecclesia Christi persona cum omnibus christianorum iuribus et officiis, nisi, ad iura quod attinet, obstet obex, ecclesiasticae communionis vinculum impediens, vel lata ab Ecclesia censura'. It is Baptism, in fact, which establishes the Christian person in the Church of Christ, with all the other rights and offices. However, the new Code, in canon 11, clarifies the purely ecclesiastical laws binding on Catholics alone: 'The canon represents one of the most important innovations of the Code of Canon Law, compared to previous legislation. It is the fruit of the new ecclesial spirit which prevailed at the Second Vatican Council, above all in the ecumenical sphere' (L. Chiappetta, *Il Codice di Diritto Canonico. Commento giuridico-pastorale,* I (Naples: Dehoniane, 1988), p. 23). So, in what sense, if it exists, is to be perceived a (legal) gradation between the three bonds of communion with the Church with regard to non-Catholics? *Lumen Gentium* would opt for this solution with *plene,* which would be taken up by the 1983 Code of Canon Law, canon 205: 'Plene in communione Ecclesiae catholicae his in terris sunt illi baptizati, qui in eius compage visibili cum Christo iunguntur, vinculis nempe professionis fidei, sacramentorum et ecclesiastici regiminis'. In both the Codes the three bonds remain foundational to belonging to the Church. The problem, however, must be studied at a theological level.

the Church herself may grow and be enriched'.[99] Here the emphasis is placed on 'journeying together' towards ecclesiological perfection.

I will make one last reference to chapter III, where episcopal collegiality is explained, looking first at the Roman Pontiff, his primacy and his infallibility. Let us recall that the German-speaking Fathers were unable to accept that kind of limit placed on the ordinary power of the College to be exercised in an extraordinary manner. Power which ended up being only in name. Here, in the schema, they proposed a widening of its exercise, highlighting the infallibility of the ordinary collegial Magisterium, taking into account the necessary conditions. In fact,

> While such infallibility does not stem from the ordinary Magisterium of the many individual bishops fallible in themselves, and without prejudice to the infallibility of the whole Church believing in the order of the execution placed on the infallibility of the teaching and binding Church and not vice versa, the infallibility which this teaching examines can only stem from the quality of the *collegial* action of the bishops as such.[100]

Nevertheless, it fell to the Pope to determine the norms and method for such an (ordinary) exercise.

---

99 'Quo magis variae communitates religiosae christianae retinent elementa, quibus Ecclesia ut signum constituitur, fidem scilicet, sacramenta et successionem apostolicam, eo magis etiam accedunt ad Ecclesiam Christi. Cum insuper vera Christi Ecclesia non tantum sit una, sed etiam uniens, haec elementa Ecclesiae extra compagem visibilem suam data, non tantum sincere ut dona Christi agnoscit, sed etiam satagit, ut sibi ipsi uniantur, cum ita non solum illa perfectionem propriam inveniant, sed etiam Ecclesia ipsa augeatur et ditescat', *Ibid.*, pp. 618–619.

100 'Certum enim est collegium episcoporum fungi magisterio ordinario debitis sub conditionibus infallibili. Cum talis infallibilitas non componi possit ex multis magisteriis singulorum episcoporum de se fallibilium computatis, cumque infallibilitas totius Ecclesiae credentis in ordine exsecutionis nitatur infallibilitate Ecclesiae docentis et obligantis et non vice versa, infallibilitas, quae huic doctrinae convenit, non potest provenire nisi ex eo, quod sit qualitas actus *collegii* episcoporum qua talis', *Ibid.*, p. 623.

3.4 The French schema

The French theologians, too, had been at work.[101] Philips, in one of his written notes for the Belgian episcopate and then seen by many other Council Fathers,[102] gave some very important indications. 'The Constitution', he said, 'is an act of the extraordinary and universal Magisterium, but only intends to impose an infallible and irreformable doctrine in the parts where this intention is manifest. It is extremely important to know if this is the position of the Council'.[103] The orientation of the presentation had to be pastoral, which did not mean neglecting dogmatic substance. Simply to present the truth in a clear language, capable of obtaining the adherence of the intellect and the heart. The formulation had to be positive and constructive, not purely apologetic and defensive. Maintaining the condemnation of errors, the Church was now hurrying to ensure mercy prevailed and provide

---

[101] On 28 November 1962, in the plenary gathering of the French bishops, after the presentation of the schema *De ecclesia* by Fr Gagnebet, Fr Congar set out the working programme for the Constitution. He set out the opinions of recent exegetes, according to whom, for St Paul 'mystical body' did not designate a social body but rather the union with the Body of Christ of all those who live in his grace. From this derives a new notion of 'member'. Collegiality was seen to be better and the formula of papal infallibility, in the new Constitution, was to be presented more perfectly than in Vatican I. This information is from the *Nota Patris Gagnebet de actuositate R. Patris Congar O.P. et aliorum ad emendandum Schema de Ecclesia,* in ASV, Envelope 759, folder 249, published in KT 2/2, p. 947.

[102] This note, entitled *Ce que nous attendons et espérons de la constitution dogmatique sur l'Église,* was prepared by a group of theologians from different nations (Germany, Austria, Belgium, France, Italy, etc.), at the request of a number of Council Fathers. It was drafted by Philips in French for the first applicants from the Belgian episcopate and was given to Tromp by Philips on 29 November 1962, in ASV, Envelope 759, folder 249, published in KT 2/2, pp. 994–1013.

[103] KT 2/2, pp. 994–995: 'La Constitution est une acte du magistère extraordinaire et universel, mais elle n'etend imposer <u>une doctrine infaillible</u> et irréformable que pour les parties de l'exposé où cette intention est manifeste. Il est extrêmement important de savoir si telle est bien la position du Concile'.

suitable explanations for a more precise and rich knowledge of dogma. The text had to take account of ecumenical repercussions, too.[104]

So a schema on the Church was prepared and sent by sixty bishops on 21 February 1963.[105] The schema comprised three chapters, which illuminated the mystery of the Church (*Ecclesia ut finis salutis* and *ut instrumentum salutis*), the hierarchy of the Church and the states of evangelical perfection. In the explanation of the Church as instrument of salvation, the manifold elements which constituted the visible Church, but which can exist in an incomplete way even outside the Church, were highlighted. The Church then is not just effective instrument of the grace of Christ, but also the 'sign' raised up among the peoples. As regards belonging to the Church, the schema spoke of 'reapse et sine restrictione' for Catholics (not hit by censures), while for non-Catholics were set out those 'plure rationes' by which the Church was joined to them. The text did not speak about membership *in voto*, nor 'members' of the Church. Notable (and also new) emphasis was placed on the theme of the episcopal College. The French bishops believed that

> The Supreme Pontiff can only carry out his *munus* of universal governance by means of the College of bishops, since alone it has been instituted by divine right to help the successor of Peter in this service. According to the Catholic faith, to the College of all the bishops united to the successor of Peter is integrated in an ordinary way the power of the supreme and full governance in the universal Church (cf. Mansi, 52, 1109). This power is exercised in a different way and collegially differently, both by the bishops where they are scattered, and when they are gathered in an Ecumenical Council with the Supreme Pontiff.[106]

---

104 Cf. *Ibid.*, p. 995.

105 Cf. Hellín, *Lumen Gentium*, pp. 751–761.

106 'Ex altera parte Summus Pontifex non potest munus suum regendi universalem Ecclesiam adimplere nisi per collegium Episcoporum, quippe quod solum sit iure divino institutum ad successorem Petri in hoc munere adiuvandum. Secundum catholican fidem in Collegio universorum Episcoporum Petri

Thus the power of the College was placed as an exercise of ordinary and universal governance of the bishops dispersed throughout the world in union with the Supreme Pontiff, alongside the rare summoning of a council. The text of Vatican I, to which the French bishops referred, while effectively confirming that in the Church there is a supreme and full power united only to its Head, not in Council but also when the bishops are dispersed throughout the world, concludes by stating that, even though the promise of such supreme power was made by Christ only to Peter and his successors, then it can be inferred that the full and supreme power has been handed on by Peter to his successors, independently from the joint action with the other bishops.[107] However, the expression according to which the Supreme Pontiff can only exercise his universal *munus regendi* by means of the College remains also problematic. This would open the path to a heated debate in the council chamber: the College, it must be asked, is it per se of divine institution? And therefore one subject with the Pope in the exercise of the power of jurisdiction or rather a subject subordinate to the Pope as regards the exercise of that power? Is the College's power of jurisdiction always on-going or set in motion by the Supreme Pontiff?[108]

---

successor unitorum ordinarie inest suprema et plena potestas regiminis in Ecclesiam universalem (cf. Mansi, 52, 1109). Quae potestas tamen aliter et aliter collegialiter exercetur, sive episcopi disperse sint sive in Concilio Oecumenico una cum Summo Pontifice coadunati', *Ibid.*, p. 756.

107 It is the *Relatio* of Bishop M. Zinelli (Bishop of Treviso): 'Igitur Episcopi congregate cum capite in concilio oecumenico, quo in casu totam ecclesiam repaesentant, aut disperse, sed cum suo capite, quo casu sunt ipsa ecclesia, vere plenam potestatem habent. At verba Christi omnia consistere debent. Si ex eo cum apostoli cum Petro et successoribus futurum se esse promisit, aliaque concessit, apparet hanc vere plenam et supremam potestatem esse in ecclesia cum suo capite coniuncta, eadem prorsus ratione, ex eo quod similes promissiones factae sunt Petro soli et eius successoribus, concludendum est, vere plenam et supremam potestatem traditam esse Petro et eius successoribus, etiam independenter ab actione communi cum aliis episcopis', Mansi, 52, 1109.

108 These problems emerged in effect at the First Vatican Council and the

3.5 The Chilean schema

Cardinal Silva Henriquez, on behalf of a number of Latin American bishops, handed over to the Co-ordinating Commission a schema on the Church,[109] presented rather under the form of *Adnotationes genericae*. The text arrived on 21 February 1963. The main notes appeal to the fact that the schema should be re-worked according to John XXIII's discourse *Gaudet mater ecclesia*, giving a pastoral aim to the constitution itself, demanded by our times, in other words a *living* doctrine, proposed in a clear, perspicuous and friendly manner. The constitution itself had to illuminate three ideals: offer pastoral teaching, enlighten the missionary aim of the Church (a vitality *ad extra*) and the ecumenical aim, in such a way that the separated brethren, through the presentation of a teaching with common elements, might more easily join the Church.[110] According to the Latin American bishops, the schema drafted by the Central Commission offered a too legal view of the Church and did not allow the dimension of Church-mother to emerge much. It was essential to present the Church as Bride of Christ, as the second Eve who regenerates everyone to salvation with the second Adam. The passage on bishops did not satisfy theological needs; 'since the style of the Second Vatican Council must be pastoral, missionary and ecumenical, it is better to constantly find in the schema the scriptural and patristic foundation',[111] not by way of adoption, but deduction: the teaching must be derived from Scripture and from the Fathers. At times non-Catholics were called 'separated brethren', at other times it was said they were not members. How, the Latin American Fathers asked, can they be

---

response was that the full and supreme power cannot be in a Body separated from the Head; for such power to be also in the Body, it had to receive it from the one who has it per se, the Roman Pontiff, independently from the bishops, cf. Mansi, 52, 1109–1010.

[109] Cf. Hellín, *Lumen Gentium*, pp. 762–845.

[110] Cf. *Ibid.*, pp. 763–764.

[111] *Ibid.*, p. 769.

brethren and non-members? So it was necessary to amend the schema according to the calm traditional teaching so as to highlight also the new teaching and theology subject to it.[112]

These were the main objections. As regards the suggested alternative schema, the Chilean bishops were more ambitious than a simple plan of annotations. In fact, they drew up a new schema comprising thirteen chapters, in the last of which featured the treatise on the Blessed Virgin Mary mother of God and humanity, exactly the schema *De B. V. Maria*, proposed now as part of that on the Church and stripped of elements in opposition to ecumenical dialogue, such as mediation and co-redemption. The schema was also furnished with a rich set of notes and bibliography at the start of each chapter, with expansive references to modern theology.

The Church was presented in a Trinitarian fashion and with rich Mariological referencing, linked to Mary the new Eve, prefiguring the one who on the Cross was taken from the side of the new Adam. The Chilean schema insisted on the need to provide a Mariological foundation to the treatise on the Church, for its ecumenical implications. The theme of the new Eve could highlight the Church as body, being a biblical and patristic theme. This theme recapped the following elements: 1) the union between Christ and the Church: only one flesh; 2) Christ's love for the Church; 3) the Church's total submission to Christ; 4) the origin of the Church from the side of Christ; 5) the theology of the Sacred Heart; 6) the indefectibility of the Church; 7) the holiness of the Church; 8) the motherhood of the Church. In this way the Marian devotion of the Latin-American Church shone out. In fact, such teaching, according to the new schema, also had pastoral value: it manifested the holiness of marriage, together with the theme of Church-spouse, like Mary.[113] Alongside the Mariological element of the Church, also underlined was the pneumatological aspect: the Holy Spirit soul of the Church. And that, too, was for the

[112] Cf. *Ibid.*, pp. 768–770.

[113] Cf. *Ibid.*, p. 775.

great ecumenical implications of such teaching, particularly for the dialogue with Orthodoxy and Protestantism.[114] As regards the theme of Christians members of the Church, the Chilean schema abandoned the terminology 'membra sensu proprio et vero' because it was unreal. They argued: a new-born baptised Protestant up to the age of reason is member 'proprie et vere', but if that person commits no positive act contrary to the truths of faith or to the Church, remains so even afterwards. A sort of de facto anonymous Catholicism. But, according to the Chilean bishops, the original schema demanded much more than *Mystici Corporis* to belong to the Church and much more than the ancient tradition: what do you say to newly-born Catholic children about the profession of the true faith? And to those non-Catholic Christians, who barely know that the Pope exists, about the juridical bond of communion? Questions which led these Fathers to abandon, however, de facto, the very teaching of *Mystici Corporis* and of the ancient tradition, simply overlooking the question.[115]

As regards collegiality, the Chilean schema affirmed that this was a key issue at the Council:

> Everything depends on this issue. To put it more precisely: everything depends on an inversion: either to start from the presentation of the individual bishop as in the suggested schema. This is equivalent to the *status quo* in the Church of tomorrow. Nothing changes. Or to start from the episcopate as college and everything is possible in the Church of tomorrow.[116]

They offered three main reasons about collegiality, like three goals of the constitution itself: a pastoral reason, according to which collegiality contributed to creating a network of bishops to act together at the international level, too; an apostolic reason, starting not from the individual bishop but from the bishops in collective mode, so as to demonstrate their 'strength' before the world; and an ecumenical goal,

114 Cf. *Ibid.*, p. 781.

115 Cf. *Ibid.*, p. 788.

116 *Ibid.*, p. 791.

giving strength and value to the episcopal body, referring to a more ancient and more traditional teaching. It was not about reducing the power of the Supreme Pontiff, even though it was necessary to complete Vatican I, but to give him more strength and authority, with a better episcopal organisation alongside him.[117] For the Chilean Fathers this theology of collegiality was indispensable, and in their schema they also proposed the establishment of a central Commission of bishops, appointed by the Pope, so as to encourage the universal mission of the Church and to increase communion between all the bishops; an international body more suitable also to the renewed world needs of the Church, as well, obviously, as those of the national and regional episcopal Conferences.[118]

At the start I referred also to the prophetic proposal to insert the Marian schema as the last chapter of the schema on the Church. In fact, the Chilean schema not only promoted this move, but also that of avoiding those sensitive issues in ecumenical dialogue. For example, the central interest for the Marian schema seemed to focus around the question of Mary's mediation. Here instead a more biblical and more patristic Mariology of the motherhood of Mary with respect to Christ and to the Church was suggested. Moreover, entering into issues still debated by theologians was avoided: for example, if the Virgin was unaware of the real identity of the Son at the moment of the Annunciation and the understanding of *virginitas in partu*. The schema depended largely on the theology of R. Laurentin.[119]

The five schema outlined above, each in their own way, ultimately produced a fundamental contribution to the re-drafting of the Dogmatic Constitution on the Church, of which Philips was the leader.

---

[117] Cf. *Ibid.*, p. 792.

[118] Cf. *Ibid.*, pp. 798–799.

[119] Cf. *Ibid.*, p. 840.

4. An initial analysis

I will now try to gather the salient points which have emerged so far from the debate on the Church. They are valuable elements at the hermeneutical level because they help us to understand not only the teaching per se in the magisterial intentions of the Council Fathers, but at the same time they offer us a light to understand the stance of the Council as such on such a doctrinally central issue. Once again a problem appears, similar to that encountered about the material insufficiency of the Scriptures, and of which many Fathers took advantage (Bea, Frings, De Smedt, the Germanic schema, the Chilean schema, etc.): the question about being a member of Christ in a true and proper way was still debated among theologians, and so it was not appropriate that the Council pronounce on the matter. Moreover, the language 'member in the full and perfect sense' and 'member in a not full and perfect sense', therefore 'imperfect', lent itself to ambiguity, while, according to the German-language Fathers, belonging to the Church acknowledged an intrinsic graduality by reason of the graduality of the *tria vincula* themselves. It was best also to abandon the classical language and replace it with a more up-to-date language, omitting the problem *sic et simpliciter*, or absorbing it into that of the *coniunctio* of the non-Catholics with the Church (*coniunctio imperfecta*, objectively different from the *perfecta*). As well as the Germanic scheme, the support of Philips was decisive, too, who, while raising the problem in his first schema, ignored it in the second. *Lumen Gentium* 15 would do the same. *Lumen Gentium* 16 would speak of the relation of non-Christians to the Church, as Philips had done, distinguishing non-Christians from non-Catholics, and the duty of the Church (different, by reason of the fact that they are indeed *related* to the mystical Body) of leading them back to the flock.

Was it really the same to examine or leave aside the question of members of the Church? Here, too, it is right to doubt the argument according to which it was an issue still under discussion. Instead, as attested by *Mystici Corporis,* it had already been calmly accepted by the Magisterium.[120] Pius XII, taking up again the ecclesiological theology systematised by St Robert Bellarmine[121] and improved in the Catechism of St Pius X,[122] distinguished a belonging '*reapse*' to the Church, in other words a real belonging, for those who, having received Baptism, profess the true faith and are not separated from the visible whole of the Church, nor excluded by the legitimate authority for their faults (thus remaining united to the Sacred hierarchy), from a belonging understood as direction ('*ordinatur*'), moved by even an unaware desire or vow, '*inscio quodam desiderio ac voto*', for those who lack even one of the three aforesaid requirements, available only in the Catholic Church. Thus was outlined in this second case a subjective direction by reason of the desire represented in various ways.[123] One of the most frequent objections to this

120 Pius XII, Encyclical Letter *Mystici Corporis,* in AAS 35 (1943) 242–243; Epist. C. S. Officii ad Archiep. Boston, 8 aug. 1949.

121 Cf. R. Bellarmine, *Disputationes de controversis christianae fidei adversus huius temporis haereticos,* Parisiis 1613, t. II, contr. 1, libr. 3: *De Ecclesia militante,* cap. 2: *De definitione Ecclesiae,* pp. 106–109. Explaining the three bonds which make of the Church one supernatural *coetum hominum,* Bellarmine, with the help of Saint Augustine (collat. 3), distinguishes a soul and a body in the *corpus vivum* of the Church. The soul is the interior gifts of the Holy Spirit, faith, hope and charity. The Body, on the other hand, is the external profession of faith and communion of the Sacraments, united to the obedience to the legitimate pastor, the Roman Pontiff. In his dispute about the Church militant, moreover, Bellarmine is careful essentially to respond to three objections from heretics: 1) the true Church is invisible; 2) sometimes the visible Church falls into error concerning faith and morals and does not repent; 3) the true Church, which is invisible, cannot fail, cf. *Ibid.,* capp. XI-XVII, pp. 142–159.

122 Pius X, *Catechismo della Dottrina Cristiana* (Rome, 1913), n. 132.

123 Pius XII, Encyclical Letter *Mystici Corporis,* in AAS 35 (1943) 202, 243. Among the various commentaries on the Encyclical see A. Liegè, 'L'appartenence à l'Église et l.Enc. "Mystici Corporis"', in *Revue de science philosophique et théologique* 32 (1948), pp. 703–726; K. Rahner, 'Membership of the Church according to the teaching of Pius XII's Encyclical 'Mystici Corporis Christi', in Id., *Theological Investigations,* II (London: Darton,

traditional position was that of grouping together pagans, catechumens and all the other non-Catholic Christians. This doctrine of belonging to the Church was defined *sententia certa,* while *de fide* belonging to the Church as a necessary means of salvation for all peoples.[124] The debate got carried away on the eve of the Council, in the preparatory Doctrinal Commission itself. Tromp noted in his diary that, in a conversation with Fr Witte, he had suggested if it would not be better instead of '*reapse membra sunt*' of *Mystici Corporis,* to say '*sensu proprio membra sunt*'. Witte agreed and was sure that the 'ecumenicals' would have no problem either.[125] On 14 May 1962, in a discussion with Mgr Felici, Fr Tromp explained how the question about belonging to the Church was connected to the question of the infallibility of the Church. Felici would speak to the Pope about it.[126] Cardinal Bea had intervened on a number of occasions about the issue, open to a theology which could be described as 'plural membership';[127] he also wrote in *L'Osservatore Romano,* leaving a number

Longman & Todd Ltd., 1963), pp. 1–88 (German original, 'Die Gliedschaft in der Kirche nach der Lehre der Enzyklika Pius XII. "Mystici Corporis Christi"', in Id., *Schriften der Theologie,* II [Einsiedeln: Benziger, 1964], pp. 7–94). Here Rahner defends the fact that if it is said that only the baptised Catholics belong to the Church this does not mean that outside the Catholic Church there is nothing Christian: 'Wenn in dieser Lehre gesagt wird, daß nur die getauften Katholiken zur Kirche gehören, so ist damit nicht behauptet, daß es *außerhalb der katholischen Kirche* nichts Christliches gebe', *Ibid.,* p. 30.

124 Cf. Ott, *Grundriss der katholischen,* p. 373 and 376.

125 Sunday 13 May 1962, KT 1/1, p. 439.

126 KT 1/1, p. 441. John XXIII had written a *Letter* to the Chinese people, addressed also to Cardinal Tien-Chen-Sin entitled *Quotiescumque Nobis,* on the question of the true worship offered to God through Jesus Christ in the Church and by means of the Church, his mystical body, to which one can only belong through the Bishops successors of the Apostles, joined with the supreme Pastor who is the successor of Peter. The *Letter* was published in *L'Osservatore Romano* on 29 June 1961. However, Fr Hürt was not in agreement and wrote to Cardinal Bea about this teaching expressed by the Pope about members of the Church. Bea did not reply. Cf. KT 1/1, p. 257.

127 In *La Civilità Cattolica* 4 (1960), pp. 561–568: the separated Protestants are

of people perplexed.[128] In short, he affirmed that all the baptised simply are members of the Church. Ottaviani reported to Tromp who, in a conversation with Bea, told him that in matters of *De membris* he was following the judgment of *Divini Redemptoris*, while the Secretary of the Theological Commission was following that of *Mystici Corporis*. In return, Tromp told Ottaviani that the opposition between the two encyclicals was only in Bea's mind. This drove Cardinal Ottaviani to ask Tromp for a report on the matter.[129] So Tromp wrote an 11-page *Memorandum de Membris Corporis Christi Mystici*, dated 2 February 1961.[130] Within the preparatory Doctrinal Commission the discus-

our brothers by reason of what is stated in *Mediator Dei* about those who, validly baptised, 'become, as by common right, members of the priestly mystical Body of Christ (AAS 38 [1947] 555). In *La Civilità Cattolica* 1 (1961), pp. 113–129, Bea intervened on the theme of a Catholic faced with the problem of Christian unity. According to Bea, Pius XII, through *Mystici Corporis*, intended to exclude from membership of the Church only the formal heretics and schismatics. Tromp attested that on 30 September 1960 Fr Hürt, according to what was reported by *Basler Nachrichten*, told him that for Bea all the baptised were members of the Church. Cf. KT 1/1, p. 85.

128 *L'Osservatore Romano* of 27 January 1961 reported Bea's talk at the *Angelicum* about the separated brethren. Here he took up the argument about their membership of the Church by virtue of Baptism. Schism and heresy separated from the Church, but this was true for those who consciously separate themselves from the mystical Body of Christ and not for those who are in good faith, finding themselves inheriting a personally not chosen reality. These latter are subjects and members of the Church although not in a full sense. Another article appeared in *L'Osservatore Romano* on 1 February 1961.

129 Cf. KT 1/1, p. 177.

130 ASV, Envelope 739, folder 117. The entire text, along with Tromp's first brief draft (which we will look at it in the subsequent paragraph), the record of Leclerq of 25 May 1961, with the general observations on Tromp's report, and Salaverri's report to Tromp about the members of the Church dated 22 May 1961, was published in KT 1/2, pp. 855–863. Here Tromp responds essentially to Bea's position. According to Tromp, abstracting from the question of the good faith of Protestants, per se *Mystici Corporis* denies membership of the Church to the schismatics and heretics only in the full sense in which it can be affirmed of Catholics, but does not exclude any other

sion on the theme began on 11 July 1961, with a report from the secretary and various *animadversiones.*[131] On 29 September 1961 there was strong opposition from Fenton, who even asked for the whole constitution to be cancelled.[132] Schauf noted in his diary that Fenton's problem lay in the fact that, from his perspective, whoever did not belong to the Church could not be saved. In reality, those making a profession of Catholic faith belonged to the Church. But Fenton did not want to hear anything about the Catholic faith, because for him it was identical to divine faith: whoever had faith consequently also had Catholic faith.[133]

Now in the Council it was a matter of giving to this doctrine a form of extraordinary teaching, also with further in-depth examination and

---

membership and the influence of the grace of Christ. Tromp draws attention again to the fact that non-membership *reapse* of the schismatics and heretics to the Church is not a question of percentages but purity of faith and of essence. In fact, if we say that schismatics and heretics, who represent more or less 45% of Christianity, are members of the Church, then Vatican I would not be ecumenical without mentioning them, too, and the Pope himself would not benefit from infallibility over the whole Church without them. But the Church remains the unblemished Spouse only in the purity of her faith. Where is the purity if the heretics are members of the Church? Of those who are not subjects of the Church in the full sense it can only be said that they are *membra voto* (cf. *Ibid.*, pp. 861–862). The one-page votum of J. Salaverri on members of the Church (*De Mystico Christi Corpore in sua ratione ad Ecclesiae membra,* Comillas, 20 January 1961), can be found in ASV, Envelope 732, folder 57. S. Tromp, on 12 May 1961, wrote by hand a new 20-page *votum De Membris Ecclesiae* [Subcommissio de Ecclesia: Caput: de membris], in ASV Envelope 734, folder 48. In ASV Envelope 739, folder 117, there are other interventions of Tromp as voti on *De membris Ecclesiae.* See then ASV Envelope 793, folder 434/3, where there are a number of voti of important theologians on *De membris Ecclesiae,* including Schmaus, Lecuyer, Backes, Brinktrine, Philips, Congar, etc.

131 Cf. KT 1/2, p. 243.

132 Cf. *Ibid.*, p. 289. Fenton's report on members of the Church can be found in ASV, Envelope 733, folder 45.

133 *Diario* of 27 September 1961, cit. in KT 1/1, p. 542, footnote 464.

improvements, but considering that it was common teaching. However, since it was a very sensitive issue from an ecumenical point of view, it was preferred to still leave it to theological debate. I believe, therefore, that the only truly cogent reason which justifies such a choice is that of ecumenical dialogue. Precisely these reasons cannot be ignored then in the analysis of the teaching of membership of the Church taught by *Lumen Gentium*.

With *De Ecclesia* Vatican II had to complete the teaching of Vatican I about the primacy of the Roman Pontiff, so as to highlight the mystery of the infallibility of the universal Church in the systematic picture of the pastoral service of the hierarchy. So spoke, for example, Maximos IV Saigh,[134] Montini,[135] etc. In this context the teaching of a doctrine which illuminated collegiality in the Church, as characteristic of the bishops understood as a body, was pressing. Now the Council had to invert the priority: it had to overlook the traditional tendency, which started from the individual bishop, studying his essence and his *munus* in the light of the sacrament of Orders, and focus instead on the episcopal College, that is on the bishops as a body, in relation to their Head, the Roman Pontiff. It was the French who brought this question to its most heated debate at the Council: Pope and bishops—two or just one subject with jurisdictional power? And it was the Chileans who invoked the cogency of such a teaching for the Church's tomorrow.

Finally, the demand for a more ecumenical, missionary and pastoral teaching (cf. the Chilean schema) also had as a goal the magisterial acquisition of new theological proposals, with which to 'up-date' the traditional ones.

---

[134] Cf. AS I/4, p. 295.

[135] Cf. *Ibid.*, p. 293.

4.1 The question *De membris Ecclesiae* in the preparatory phase of the Council

Let us return to the question of members of the Church in more detail. In the session of the *De Ecclesia* Sub-commission, on 6 February 1961, during the preparatory phase of the Council, Fr Tromp informs us that a conclusion was reached in the dispute about the *De membris voto*: on the one hand the doctrine of *Mystici Corporis* was to be preserved, and on the other the spiritual bonds with the separated brethren were expressed.[136] So, on 14 April 1961, Tromp drafted the (brief) text which brought together the outcomes of the discussions and the relative position of the Sub-commission. I will focus now at greater length precisely on this text, which, even though brief, frames the problem very clearly, raising the observations from valuable periti. From it all we will be able to obtain an analysis of the problem.

The text was entitled *De membris Ecclesiae et de eius necessitatem ad salutem.*[137] It was divided into two points: 1) the need of the Church for salvation; and, 2) spiritual union with the separated brethren.

As regards the first point the text poses a parallel: just as the Church is necessary for salvation, so no one can be saved by themselves if, while knowing that the Catholic Church has been instituted by God by means of Jesus Christ, refuses to enter therein, so no one can save themselves unless by means of Baptism received in *re* or in *voto*, by which means, not setting any obstacles, one becomes a member of the Church. Therefore, no one can save themselves unless they become a member of the Church, in *re* or in *voto*. Taking up the provisions of *Mystici Corporis,* the text goes on to explain who belongs to the Church. However, for salvation it is not sufficient to be a member of the Church

136 S. Tromp, *De Membris Ecclesiae et de eius necessitatem ad salutem,* C. T. 5/61: 31, 14 April 1961, ff. 3, footnote 1, in ASV, Envelope 739, folder 117. Text published in KT 1/2, pp. 855–856. Cf. also Tromp's *Diario,* where however the drafting of the schema is fixed on 13 April 1961: 'Mane in officio confeci notas ad caput: "de membris Ecclesiae"', in KT 1/1, p. 207.

137 S. Tromp, *De Membris Ecclesiae et de eius necessitatem ad salutem,* cit.

reapse or in *voto*, but it is nevertheless necessary to remain in a state of grace, joined to God through faith, hope and charity.

As regards the second point, the text clarifies the spiritual value of the union of the Church with the separated brethren. So, the Church is joined spiritually with those who are members of the Church only in *voto* and therefore in *re* separated from her; largely if they are baptised, who, lacking in the Catholic faith, however believe in God and in the Saviour. To their joint faith in Christ is added, in some way, the communion of prayers, of penance and spiritual assistance. The very participation in baptismal grace is aimed above all at realising the union of new members with this mystical Body. Finally, the text warns Catholics not to consider their position almost as a privilege, due to their merits, but simply a benevolent choice of Christ, and to live with fear because they will be judged more severely.[138]

---

[138] Cf. *Ibid.* The original states (omitting the footnotes): '1. (Necessitas Ecclesiae ad salutem). Docet S. Synodus, sicut semper docuit Sancta Dei Ecclesia, Ecclesiam esse necessarium ad salute, ideoque nemine salvari posse, qui sciens Ecclesiam Catholicam a Deo per Iesum Christum esse conditam, tamen eam renuat intrare. Sicut autem nemo salvari potest nisi sive re sive voto recipiat Baptismum, quo quis non ponens obicem, fit membrum Ecclesiae, sic nemo salute obtinere valet, nisi membrum Ecclesiae existat sive re sive voto. Sunt autem ii solum reapse membra Ecclesiae, qui regenerationis lavacro receptor veram fidem profitentur, neque a Corporis Mystici compage semetipsos separarunt vel ob gravissima admissa a legitima auctoritate seicunti sunt. Solo autem voto membra Ecclesiae sunt non catechumeni dumtaxat, qui conscio et explicito voto ad Ecclesiam aspirant, sed ii quoque, qui etsi ignorantes Ecclesiam Catholicam esse veram Christi Ecclesiam, tamen inscio et implicito desiderio ad eandem ordinantur, sive quod sincera voluntate volunt quod vult ipse Christus, sive quod ignorantes Christum, sincere implere desiderant voluntatem Dei Creatoris et Domini. Ut autem salute quis acquirat non sufficit, ut sit vel reapse vel voto membrum Ecclesiae, sed etiam moriatur in statu gratiae, fide, spe et caritate cum Deo coniunctus.2. (Unio spiritualis cum fratribus separatis). Licet ii qui voto dumtaxat sint membra Ecclesiae, ab eadem reapse separate existant, tamen Ecclesia scit sese cum iis spiritualiter coniunctam, maxime si baptizati, etsi carentes fides catholica, nihilominus amanter in Christum, accredit quoque orationum, expiationum et beneficio-

4.2 The observations of the periti about Tromp's text

Noteworthy among the *Animadversiones* on Tromp's text about the members of the Church is that of Fr Carlo Balić.[139] In his opinion, Tromp decided on the necessary phrase 'membra in voto' for baptised Christians but not in communion with the Church. For Balić, it was better to avoid the expression 'membra in voto' due to the fact that it was not used directly by *Mystici Corporis*. In fact, Pius XII's Encyclical referred only to 'membra reapse', that is to say, those who kept the *tria vincula,* while for non-Catholics it spoke of belonging *voto* to the Church. It was better to retain the term 'member' for Catholics alone. For non-Catholics it would have been better, according to Fr Balić, to use a more generic formula, thus imitating Vatican I, for example: '*nullus potest salvari qui nullatenus pertinet ad Christi Ecclesiam*'. Balić was conscious of the fact that this was a very thorny and burning issue for ecumenism. However, he did not want to propose a schema of his own on this point, nor sing from a different hymn sheet if everyone was in agreement about using the term 'membra voto' for the separated brethren.

---

rum spiritualium communio; eiusdem gratiae baptismalis participatio, immo quaedam in Spiritu Sancto coniunctio, quippe non solum donis et gratis in ipso Mystico Corpore operantur, sed iisdem etiam extra Corpus illud venerandum agit, ut nova membra Corpori adsimulet. Ut autem illa Spiritus Christi ad Corporis Mystici augmentum operatio uberiorem consequatur effectum, Ecclesia precari numquam desinit, ut fratres separati internis divinae gratiae impulsionibus ultro libenterque concedentes, ab eo statu se eripere student, in quo de sempiterna salute non excluduntur quidem, tamen vere secure esse nequeunt: nam etiamsi inscio desiderio ac voto ad mysticum Redemptoris Corpus ordinentur, tot tamen tantisque coelestibus muneribus adiumentisque carent, quibus iis solummodo frui licet, qui reapse sunt membra Ecclesiae. Memores igitur sint omnes Ecclesiae filii conditionis suae eximiae non propriis meritis, sed electioni peculiari Christi adscribendae, cui si cogitatione verbo et opera non correspondent, nedum salvantur, severius iudicabuntur'.

139 C. Balić, *Circa "membra in voto" Ecclesia Christi,* die Pentecostes 1961, ff. 11, in ASV, Envelope 739, folder 117.

The report of Y. Congar is interesting, too, in this regard.[140] The Fathers and the ancient writers did not start out from the Church but from Christ. For St Thomas Aquinas, too, the question to be formulated was not: 'Quin sunt membra Ecclesiae?', but 'Utrum Christus sit caput Ecclesiae?', 'Utrum sit caput omnium hominum?' For Congar, the question was of a Christological nature. So, in his opinion, 'not just all people are potentially members of Christ, but also many non-Catholics effectively and actually receive a certain influence of the grace of Christ and so, in this sense, are to be included among the members of Christ'.[141] *Mystici Corporis* realises a synthesis between the idea of Church as mystical Body and the idea of Church as juridical society. So Congar summarises the teaching of this Encyclical implied in the theme of membership, clearly expressing the magisterial intention, without adding any personal comments:

> The mystical Body of Christ and the Society organised juridically are identical; for wayfarers, after Christ, the mystical Body of Christ is the Roman Church.[142]

G. Philips also intervened on this issue. In his opinion the teaching about members of the Church was clear and precise but the way of presenting it had some flaws. In his *Animadversiones* to Tromp's text, Philips reported a certain friction between the spiritual reality, according to which Christ can be united to someone—after all affirmed by the schema—and instead the legal, more drastic and exclusive reality. What stopped him from signing the text, unless it was obligatory to do so, was the theological systematisation, which found other dissenters. Here are his observations in the easily understandable original Latin:

140 Y. Congar, *Nota De Membris*, C. T. 5/61: 104, ff. 2, in *Ibid.*

141 'non solum omnes homines membra Christi in potentia esse, sed etiam multos Acatholicos effective et actualiter aliquam influxum gratiae a Christo accipere et sic, in hoc sensu, inter membra Christi computandos esse', *Ibid.*

142 'Corpus Christi mysticum et Societas iuridica organizata idem sunt; Viatoribus, post Christum, Corpus Christi mysticum est Ecclesia Romana', *Ibid.*

> Difficultas mea non est doctrina, sed de eius praesentatione theologica.
> Doctrina concrete propositam sincere admitto et profiteor.
> Prasentatio autem non placet propter sequentes praesertim rationes:
>
> 1) statua conditione membri et non-membri, nulla agnoscitur categoria illorum qui imperfect adhaerent.
> 2) insufficienter mihi videtur efferri realitas sacramentorum, quae apud dissidentes diverso gradu adest.
> 3) praecipua ratio est quod in altera parte schematis statuitur aliquem Christo coniungi posse, quin eodem gradu ad Corpus eius adhaereat; ita ut realitas spiritualis a iuridica conditione nimis seiugantur.
>
> Quaestio non est de doctrina fidei sed de modo theologicae cogitationis. In perspectiva theologica quae in schemate supponitur, textus clare, logice et concinne procedit. Quae theologica systematizatio a pluribus non admittitur, et quamdiu non imponatur, ei subscribere non possum. Si autem imponitur, admittam.
> Aricciae, d. 11ª m. Iulii 1961
> G. PHILIPS.[143]

So we are at the eve of the Council. On the question of members the preparatory position was clear and the teaching could be said to be common: members of the Church were those who professed entirely the Faith received from Christ and handed on by the Apostles, who kept the seven sacraments and were under the ecclesiastical hierarchy. The problem was in defining non-Catholics 'membra voto': that seemed more logical to Tromp but to Balić less faithful to *Mystici Corporis,* or to avoid this term, while underlying another possible formulation, maybe more generic. Philips recognised the quality of

---

[143] G. Philips, *Animadversiones in Cap. De Membris* [cf. C. T. 5/61: 63], C. T. 5/61: 101, f. 1, in *Ibid.* See also Philips' more extensive *Nota*: *De Membris Ecclesiae,* 7 April 1961, ff. 7 (f. 7: Addendum of 16 May 1961), in *Ibid.*

the teaching. It was the way it was presented which did not convince him, certainly for pastoral but largely ecumenical reasons. On this aspect, as I have underlined on a number of occasions, the dispute in the Council was very heated. Congar, on the other hand, outlined the theological line which would have more resonance: to set out the question on Christ more than on the Church. It was not sufficient to see a spiritual communion with non-Catholics, but already their *reapse* belonging to the Church by reason of the influence of the grace of Christ. In this way, however, new problems emerged, which remain unresolved today. However, everyone conformed to the dictates of Pius XII's Encyclical.

A new more communion-based theological approach to *De membris*, however, could mean above all a shift of the same problem, or even its silencing. The question took another turn, largely due to the authoritative interventions of Cardinal Bea, who stated that all the baptised were members of Christ. And therefore it is totally legitimate to recover its *status* on the eve of the Council.

5. *Doctrinal elements in the making in Lumen Gentium*

The new schema (schema II) of the *De Ecclesia* Sub-commission, drawn up on the basis of the theologians' schema, then presented to the Fathers and by them to the conciliar Commission, was tabled for discussion in the chamber on 22 April 1963.[144] A long discussion began, in which, however, some Fathers revealed themselves still to be dissatisfied for reasons which in my opinion go back to what is central to Vatican II: ecumenical, pastoral issues. For example, Bishop Léon-Arthur Elchinger (Auxiliary Bishop of Strasbourg) had something to say about the relationship which the new schema established between the Church and non-Christians. It seemed to him to be a clearly insufficient draft. From the theological point of view, the text remained individualistic and extrinsic, since it did not mention, in his opinion,

---

[144] Cf. AS II/1, pp. 215.281.

> Either the solidarity of the whole of humanity with the Son of God, so strongly affirmed by the Greek tradition, nor the positive preparatory role of the cosmic religions. From the pastoral point of view, this text does not lay the foundations too much of the Church's missionary activity and does not sufficiently guide the dialogue of Christians with pagans, a dialogue which, in our pluralist world, is becoming ever more urgent.[145]

For Elchinger the evangelical preparations were different. In his way of seeing things, the people of Israel 'was the Christian Church in the flesh', which, even though it still did not recognise the fulfilment of its vocation in Christ, nevertheless remained chosen. Israel preserved the essential Christian values: faith in the living God and in the promises, Scripture, etc. This new way of seeing would signify in the Council a real turning point in the theology of salvation, according to the different orderings of the People of God.[146]

But among all Cardinal Bea must be highlighted, since, as the representative for ecumenism, this issue was dear to his heart, still recognising some faults in the new ecclesiological schema. For example, speaking about the one Church of Christ, nothing was said about its scriptural foundation, which for ecumenical dialogue was instead a central argument. Thus it was also said that the Church 'pillar and support of truth' was built on Peter and the apostles and their successors. Bea noted there was a mixing-up of scriptural texts, because Scripture did not say that the Church was built 'on Peter and the apostles'. That is, the schema arranged some scriptural texts in an anti-ecumenical fashion. Therefore, according to Bea, it was necessary to discuss and arrange to suit today's conditions and needs what was cogent ('quae hodie praestanda sunt') so that it might serve dialogue with the separated brethren.[147] And he added:

---

145 *Ibid.*, p. 657.

146 Cf. *Ibid.*, pp. 657–658.

147 Cf. AS II/2, pp. 20–22.

> I am not saying that new arguments need to be set out, but from those emerging (extant), and there are many, can be suggested those which are largely appropriate to today's needs.[148]

This was generally the atmosphere which animated the drafting of teaching on the Church. There was no lack of Fathers, like Ruffini and Siri, for example, who thought first about setting out a clear and theologically precise teaching, and only afterwards about its pastoral dissemination. There could not be a contradiction between the two aspects: the second arose from the first. For others, the majority which imposed itself, the two dimensions, one subordinate to the other, could be problematic: that is why the practical is of major concern to us.

In the pages that follow, I will try to illustrate some of the theological elements of the ecclesiological teaching of *Lumen Gentium*, taking into account the status of the question being illustrated, so as to examine some significant doctrinal shifts which took place in the Council, in obedience to the pastoral priority which John XXIII had recommended.

5.1 The new text does not use the term 'members' of the Church

As already we have had the opportunity to see, the question of 'members' of the Church was judged to be an academic question and left to theological discussion. To use it in the Council would have meant not just resolving it—the Council was not a school—but also compromising dialogue: between being baptised and not being Catholic was not a vacuum. The first schema, according to various Fathers, risked simply excluding non-Catholics from the Church, seeing their relation to the visible Church as *voto*, thus compromising the reality of Baptism. Baptism per se incorporated the Christian into the Church at an initial level. But to define a non-Catholic as an 'imperfect member' or member 'not in the true and full sense', nevertheless meant to preclude any type of ecumenical dialogue. From the second schema up until the final one

148 AS II/2, p. 22.

this term no longer appeared. The reason was given by the Maronite Patriarch of Antioch, Pierre-Paul Meouchi. In his particular considerations of the second schema, he said:

> The text does not use the term *membra*. It simply describes the situations where a relationship with the Church can be found: full belonging, *voto* belonging, different bonds which exist between non-Catholic Christians and the Church. This stance of the authors of the schema comes, it seems to me, from the widening they have rightly given to the Pauline doctrine of the 'Body of Christ which is the Church'; otherwise if there was a continuation to identify purely and simply the Body of Christ and the visible, hierarchical Church, without any distinction of elements, it would not have been able to call other equally justified people and the Saints 'members' of the visible Roman Church. Again due to this, the schema leaves the question open on this chapter, and thus gains ecumenical value. In every way, it seems better to me to keep all these parts concerning the *members* of the Church in this dogmatic schema and not to put them in the schema on Ecumenism.[149]

Shortly afterwards the same Patriarch would add that the term 'membra' was rightly not used, because it was a term taken from the human body, and so insufficient for having to define the relationship between Christians and their Head.[150] A dual problem arises from the Patriarch's words:

1. the teaching about 'members' of the Church was linked to an identification of the ecclesial Body with the visible Church, so, from a widening of the Pauline vision one could infer that non-Catholics, too, were incorporated into the Church (which advisedly should be understood as visible);
2. the restriction of the term 'members' to Catholics denied just non-Catholics the possibility of being so.

149 AS II/1, pp. 693–694.

150 Cf. *Ibid.*, p. 694.

Here in fact should be underlined a misunderstanding which occurs frequently: confusing *de facto* belonging to the Church, for which neither Baptism alone nor sanctifying grace alone are sufficient, with the also extraordinary work of the grace of the Holy Spirit, which makes people just, but does not incorporate them into the Church *per se,* even though placing the just person in a relationship with the mystery of the Church. Such a connection in the Church, then, since sometimes it is originated and nourished only by Baptism, is initial and not perfect with respect to the visible Church, linked, in good faith, primarily to the dimension of the invisible Church, which, in turn, is the mystery which acts in the visible, hierarchically ordered Church, always moving towards it. The two ecclesial dimensions cannot therefore be separated, even though the two theological questions remain distinct: on the one hand we have salvation also outside the visible confines of the Church, and on the other the question of belonging to the Church. In remaining silent about the question of 'members', was there a risk in separating the visible aspect of the Church from the mystery of the Church? It is also true that a renewed ecclesiological theology strongly wanted to recover the aspect of *communio,* sometimes highlighting the permanence of a strong tension in *Lumen Gentium* between legal Church and Church as communion.[151] Was there really a wish to go beyond the societal and legal aspect of the Church?[152] But at what price? However, the

[151] Cf. A. Acerbi, *Due ecclesiologiche. Ecclesiologia giuridica ed ecclesilogia di comunione nella "Lumen Gentium"* (Bologna: EDB, 1975).

[152] According to G. Calabrese, yes, and he says: 'The decision to highlight in the first chapter of LG the reality of the mystery of the Church and to follow it with not just the chronological but also the logical and theological consequentiality in the second chapter on the people of God and the third chapter on the hierarchical constitution of the Church and in particular the episcopate, manifests, in an obvious and cogent manner, the Council's desire to overcome any ecclesiological legal-societal tendency and any danger of a simple visible and ecclesio-centric definition of the Church of Christ', 'Chiesa come "popolo di Dio" o Chiesa "comunione"?', in Associazione Teologica Italiana, *La Chiesa e il Vaticano II,* p. 69; also p. 109. Cf. also, Domínguez, 'Le interpretazioni

theological sacrifice of the theme of 'members' of the Church was a gain at the ecumenical level. There were good and respectable reasons to table a new discourse with non-Catholics. However, there was also a significant risk, as reported by Bishop Tabera Azoz: considering as *one* and *identical* the work of the Holy Spirit, outside just as inside the Church, clashed with the principal of the universal salvific mediation of the Church.[153] A good part of the post-conciliar period would be concerned in fact about this aspect: a work of the Holy Spirit, parallel, if not alternative to Christ and to the Church. The definitive position of *Lumen Gentium* on this matter can be found starting from n. 13, in which it is said that 'all ... are called to belong to the new people of God':

> All men are called to be part of this catholic unity of the people of God which in promoting universal peace presages it. And there belong to or are related to it in various ways, the Catholic faithful, all who believe in Christ, and indeed the whole of mankind, for all men are called by the grace of God to salvation (*Ibid.*).

From this it follows, in an initial and general way, that Christians belong in various ways (which will be *full* or *not full*) to the Church, here defined as catholic unity of the people of God, and this due to the fact that they are more or less Catholics, while only non-Christians are put at the level of being related to the people of God (as results from the subsequent paragraphs). However, here there is a risk—at least initial—of relativising the *elementa Ecclesiae*, for which the Council would prefer *subsistit in* to *est* to better explain the identity of the one Church of Christ 'governed by the successor of Peter and

---

postconciliari', pp. 35–75. Other theologians wanted to compare *Mystici Corporis* with *Lumen Gentium* or show a substantial moving on. Cf., for example, G. Baum, 'La réalité ecclésiale des autres Églises', in *Concilium* 4 (1965), especially pp. 65–69; C. Moeller, 'Il fermento delle idee nella elaborazione della Costituzione', in Baraúna (ed.), *La Chiesa del Vaticano II*, p. 174.

153 Cf. AS II/1, p. 732.

by the Bishops in communion with him' and at the same time the presence, outside its visible structure, of 'many elements of sanctification and of truth [which] as gifts belonging to the Church of Christ, are forces impelling toward catholic unity' (*Lumen Gentium* 8).[154] In other words, can there be on-going belonging to the Church, but not full and therefore imperfect?[155] If the answer is yes, then the solution

[154] The reading of '*subsistit in*', in line with the whole of the Tradition of the Church and with the intention of affirming one subsistence of the Church of Christ, confirming at the same time the presence of elements of sanctification and truth outside its visible structure, is made by the Magisterium in the following documents: Congregation for the Doctrine of the Faith, *Notification on the book 'Church: Charism and Power' by Father Leonardo Boff OFM*, 11 March 1985, in AAS 77 (1985) 756–762; Id., *Declaration 'Dominus Iesus' on the unicity and salvific universality of Jesus Christ and the Church*, 6 August 2000 (n. 16 and footnote 56), in AAS 92 (2000) 742–765. Subsequently I will return to the reasons for the choice in the Doctrinal Commission.

[155] Here one distinguishes between the thesis of Cardinal Journet, according to whose theory of the co-existence of the soul and body (where the soul is, the body is, too), a belonging to the soul of the Church on the part of just non-Catholics must be extended also to the Body. Therefore, in this case, there would be invisible belonging to the visible Church, since the desire would already be belonging to the Church indivisibly composed of soul and body (cf. C. Journet, *L'Église du Verbe Incarné*, t. II, (Paris: Desclée de Brouwer, 1951), p. 574 and 953. This thesis was repeated to explain the position of *Lumen Gentium*: Id., *Il mistero della Chiesa secondo il Concilio Vaticano II* (Brescia: Queriniana, 1967) (French original, 'Le mystère de l'Eglise selon le Concile du Vatican', in *Revue Thomiste* 65 (1965), pp. 9–14). However, I share S. Carusi's criticism of this thesis, which what's more refers to St Thomas: how could there be an on-going but imperfect member, in our case by reason of charity or perhaps faith or Baptism? What is on-going implies only perfection. Imperfection lies on the side of power. So Carusi suggests, to avoid confusion or real and proper errors of faith, taking up again the distinction of act and potential and to refer again to the theory of being directed to the Church, as goal which admits a graduality and a diversity of subjects towards their one finalising principle, the Catholic Church, cf. S. Carusi, 'I giusti acattolici sono membri della Chiesa cattolica secondo il Magistero?', in *Divinitas* 2 (2012), pp. 249–268.

seems to be that stated by H. Fries on the eve of the Council: the one who is saved belongs to the visible Church, even if not belonging visibly to the Church.[156] However, the question remains: is a visible belonging, which, however, is not perfectly *in re*, possible? So, while the Church 'recognizes that in many ways she is linked' with non-Catholics (*Lumen Gentium* 15: the invisible or visible Church? It is also true, however, there should not be any juxtaposition between the two, since it is the same and one Church), for non-Christians it is said that they 'are related in various ways to the people of God' (*Lumen Gentium* 16). Did the problem re-surface that many Fathers wanted to overcome, but which was unanimous in theologies up to the Council, of the full identity between the mystical Body of Christ and the Catholic Church and the solution given about the belonging of just non-Catholics to the Church?[157] If it were not specified about how non-Catholics can be 'members' of the ecclesial Body, that is, how their 'union' with the Church is to be understood, is there the risk of separating the invisible Church, *fructus salutis*, from the visible,

---

[156] 'Wer gerettet wird, gehört deshalb zur sichtbaren Kirche, auch wenn er nicht sichtbar zur Kirche gehört', H. Fries, in *Handbuch theologischer Grundbegriffe*, Id. (ed.) (Munich: Kösel, 1962), pp. 821–822.

[157] For a *status quaestionis* see J. Salaverri, *De Ecclesia Christi* (Madrid: B.A.C., 1952²); T. Zapelena, *De Ecclesia Christi* (Rome: Pontificia Università Gregoriana, 1950⁵); (Roma 1954⁶); R. Brunet, 'Le dissidents de bonne foi sont'ils membres de l'Église', in *Analecta Gregoriana* 58 (1954), pp. 199–218; S. Tromp, 'De Ecclesiae membris', in *Divinitas* 6 (1962), pp. 481–492. According to Fr Tromp, the definition of Church as *Corpus Christi Mysticum* could be taken in a dual manner, if the adjective *mysticum* was understood in a reduplicative or non reduplicative way. If not in a reduplicative way, then the mystical Body of Christ is simply the Roman Catholic Church. If in a reduplicative manner, on the other hand, the mystical Body of Christ is the Church in that it possesses an internal, immediate and invisible aspect. In a mediated manner, however, one sees the influence of the Holy Spirit in the divine works of the Church, (cf. S. Tromp, *Corpus Christi quod est Ecclesia*, I, [Introductio generalis] Pontificia Università Gregoriana, Romae 1946, p. 169). In many cases, where the appropriate logical distinctions are missing, often the Catholic Church is placed as an alternative to the Church of Christ.

medium salutis?[158] Therefore, a risk of reading the distinction between Church of Christ and Catholic Church as real, to the point of justifying an effective incorporation of non-Catholics in the Church of Christ, even though still not full (which could also become no longer necessary) in the Catholic Church? This could not be, nor was it the intention of *Lumen Gentium*, which instead states in an inequivocal manner, that the Church of Christ is the one Church which the Lord wanted to build on Peter, entrusting to him and the other Apostles the dissemination and governance (cf. *Lumen Gentium* 8). And that *this* pilgrim Church (therefore visible or hierarchical) is necessary for salvation (cf. *Lumen Gentium* 14). Meanwhile, what is here of concern in the Constitution on the Church is to highlight the ecclesiogical description of 'people of God', open to the accession of all other peoples, effecting a significant passage from *De membris* or *De personis* to *De populo Dei*.[159] Hence one can also begin to understand the relationship of non-Catholics to the Church. Here one sees an 'opening', which, however, if left in a generic way, provokes a certain confusion, if not a real and proper ignorance about the matter, in the interpretation and consideration of the traditional teaching of the relation of non-Catholics to the Catholic Church.

---

158 Meanwhile Philips' position on this burning issue of ecclesiology is clear: '... in no place [in the Magisterium] is reference made to a distinction proposed for some time by some theologians, according to which someone could belong to the soul of the Church, through their internal disposition, without being a member of its visible body, with an external confession. The Magisterium has never separated a soul from the body in the Church. This unhappy solution, conceived to find an exit, has found almost no defenders in the Council' (G. Philips, *La Chiesa e il suo mistero. Storia, testo e commento della Lumen Gentium* (Milan: Jaka Book, 1982²), p. 175 [French original, *L'Église et son mystère*, Paris: Desclée & Cie, 1967]). The fact is, however, that the distinction *reapse* and *voto* translates the theology of the mystical Body of Christ gifted with a soul and a body. As we will see subsequently, however, this position would lead Philips to believe that baptised non-Catholics are members of the Church, cf. *Ibid.*, p. 180.

159 Cf. Routhier, 'La recezione dell'ecclesiologia conciliare', p. 12.

The theme of belonging to the Church, however, is really decisive for a correct interpretation of the Council, intimately linked to the theme of the visible boundaries of the Church and its ability to operate beyond these, too. Besides, the one salvific Subject is never confused. Absurdly, if so there could not be salvation outside the confines of the Church, for the simple fact that there would be no Church, which is both present outside, and first and above all in herself. It can be clearly seen, subsequently, too, that the interpretation of the ecclesiology of Vatican II cannot start from the Council and stop at the Council itself: it requires the faith of the Church and the reading Tradition has done, above all as regards the unanimous certainty of the Catholic Church about being *the* Church of Christ and the *one* Church of Christ. Only from here can a correct hermeneutical approach emanate, when a true unity of Christians in the one Body of Christ is desired. This unity has never been lost, despite the divisions. It has been preserved without interruption by the Church of Christ which is the Catholic Church. The *subsistit in* of *Lumen Gentium* is to be read in the light of the *est* of *Mystici Corporis*[160] and as a homogenous development of the theology of the unity of the Church in the plurality of the particular Churches, from which derives the plurality of the ecclesifying elements, patrimony of the Church, but which, due to the divisions, now find themselves in a fragmented fashion present also outside the visible structure of the Church. It is necessary to underline, in the theology of the 'elements of sanctification and of truth' (*Lumen Gentium* 8), the prevalent historical dimension according to which one looks at them as goods of the Church distinct and feasible even outside of it. They must be seen in their unity and in their fullness according to the Church: in the Church we can distinguish what

[160] 'Iamvero ad definiendam describendamque hanc veracem Christi Ecclesiam—quae sancta, catholica, apostolica, Romana Ecclesia est—(cf. Con. Vat. I, *Const, de. fid. cath.* cap. I) nihil nobilius, nihil praestantius, nihil denique divinius invenitur sententia illa, qua eadem nuncupatur "mysticum Iesu Christi Corpus"', Pius XII, Encyclical Letter *Mystici Corporis Christi,* 29 June 1943, in AAS 35 (1943) 199.

characterises them and specifies them. They can be contemplated, too, separately from the Church by reason of the historical separations which happened within Christianity. Hence the cogency of ecumenism and the reconstruction of Catholic unity, which is effective when there is movement from the historical level of divisions to the metaphysical level of the one Church of Christ, precisely according to those elements which cannot endure separated from unity.

Therefore, in the correct hermeneutic of the full incorporation into the Church, it is necessary to take the following into account:

> The Council does not dwell on the *vexata quaestio*, speaks about it subtly, but decisively... The term 'member' was omitted deliberately. The new formulation is less cutting and is not exclusive, because it obviously admits the graduality of incorporation into the Church... Also, it is expressly asked of a member of the Church, as well as the visible bonds, first of all that they 'have the Spirit of Christ', which is the principal bond, incomparable, beyond all other bonds. However, the other three traditional bonds are re-confirmed: faith, the sacraments and communion with the ecclesiastical regime.[161]

5.2 Only catechumens belong to the Church *in voto*

The theme of 'members' of the Church was not therefore irrelevant. The absence is seen in a spectacular way, when, from the second schema onwards, only catechumens would be inserted by *desire* into the Church. And non-Catholic Christians?

Let us look at the various passages which follow in the drafting of the schema, up to the approval of the Constitution.[162] The schema of the preparatory Commission, as we have seen, presented the united by *in voto* membership of the catechumens, non-Catholic Christians, who were unaware that the Catholic Church was the true and one Church of Christ, and the non-Christians, who, unaware of Christ,

---

[161] Vadopivec, 'Chiesa', col. 784.

[162] For an overall vision of the four texts and the appropriate modifications, see Hellín, *Lumen Gentium*, pp. 120–121.

sincerely desire to fulfil the will of their Creator. The second schema would give rise to a modification subject to misunderstanding, as Cardinal Siri would note:[163] after having spoken of catechumens, who, moved by the grace of God, explicitly desire to become members of the Church, it introduced the discourse on non-Catholics and non-Christians with a 'suo modo iem valet et illis…',[164] that is, for those who are unaware that the Catholic Church is the one true, etc. 'Suo modo', but in what way?, and 'idem valet', what does it mean? This expression was not kept by the Commission. In fact, in the schema amended by the Sub-commission, according to the *animadversiones Patrum* (schema III), this expression no longer figured, but the reference to the Christians separated from the Catholic Church and to the non-Christians did not figure either. The intention was very clear: there was no need to confuse the *voto* of Baptism with the sacrament of Baptism, and therefore, it was not the same to speak of catehcumens and Christians, even though non-Catholics. The *discrimen* was Baptism.[165] The salvific necessity of the Church was in fact closely linked to the salvific need of the sacrament of Baptism, without however any more being described as *essential means*, as some Fathers demanded, but only need (of obligation), by reason of Christ's will, sole necessary mediator. The Commission responded to the various proposals of defining the Church as *necessitas medii*[166] or simply of

[163] Cf. AS II/1, p. 610.

[164] *Ibid.*, p. 220.

[165] Bishop Antonio Jannucci (Bishop of Penne-Pescara) said, in Italian: 'Out of respect for the rich encyclical *Mystici Corporis* the concept of "*member of the Church*" must be expressed better in the schema. Of course the Bellarmine concept is respected, justified by the Protestant dispute, which highlights the visible, social and legal element of the Church, as unequivocal sign for the full and true incorporation to the Church. At the same time, however, today one must make the ontological element, which really makes 'member of the Church' (and that is, valid baptism, however received) stand out more', AS II/2, p. 176.

[166] It was Bishop Arturo Tabera Araoz (cf. AS II/1, p. 731). Bishop Van der Burgt, too, speaking on behalf of the Indonesian bishops, said: '… quae dicuntur de

obligation,[167] or demonstrated *ex necessitate Christi*,[168] stating that the means was derived uniquely 'ex unico Mediatore Christo'.[169] Therefore, in the definitive text, there is a 'necessitatem fidei et baptismi expressi verbis inculcando (cf. Mc. 16:16; Io 3:5)' and a 'necessitatem Ecclesiae, in quam homines tamquam per ianuam intrant...' (*Lumen Gentium* 14), without qualificative specifications.

All that sheds light on the reason for the omission, in the third schema, of the reference to non-Catholics (and to non-Christians) as regards the *voto*. A number of Fathers also complained about a focus in the second schema on a too subjective aspect of the *voto*, and silence about the real and objective relating of everyone to the Church, by reason of objective redemption. It was the Dutch bishops who denounced it. And it was they who concluded their *animadversiones* as follows:

> It is astonishing that the schema, speaking about the need of the Church, does it solely in the sense of individual salvation, and remaining silent in truth on the Church as 'sacramentum mundi'.[170]

necessitate Ecclesiae ad salute non sufficient. Nodus quo necessitas affirmatur suggerit potius necessitate praecepti quam medii, dum tota traditio docet necessitate medii. Haec necessitas medii in textu intenditur, sed non bene exprimitur' (AS II/2, p. 60). Bishop Joseph Attipetty (Archbishop of Verapoly, Malabar-India), also spoke along these lines: 'Doctrina a maioribus accepta docet Ecclesiam necessariam esse non solum necessitate praecepti, sed etiam necessitate medii' (AS II/2, p. 140).

167 Bishop Vladimir Malanczuk, whose argument was that, since grace is at work also outside the confines of the Church and also through extra-sacramental means, the essential means of the Church as regards salvation could not be presumed, intending by that an identification of the mystical Body of Christ with the Roman Catholic and visible Church, but only a positive divine institution. The unicity of the Church was, in his opinion, the centripetal path, while Catholicity was the centrifugal path, cf. AS II/2, pp. 176–177.

168 Cardinal Silva Henriquez, President of the Chilean Bishops' Conference, and 44 other episcopal signatories, cf. AS II/2, pp. 137–138, cf. also AS II/2, pp. 216–218 (Venezuelan Bishops' Conference).

169 Cf. AS III/1, p. 202.

The text (schema III) was therefore modified.[171] Such modifications were adopted into the definitive text, which thus stated:

> Catechumens who, moved by the Holy Spirit, seek with explicit intention to be incorporated into the Church are by that very intention joined with her. With love and solicitude Mother Church already embraces them as her own (*Lumen Gentium* 14).

If, on the one hand, it is true that non-Catholic Christians do not have the *voto* of Baptism but the sacrament, therefore they cannot be in the same position as the non-baptised (both catechumens and non-Christians), and the *prior* schema absorbed everyone into one (catechumens, non-Catholics and non-Christians); on the other hand, however, how can non-Catholics be part of the Church? *Lumen Gentium* 15 only speaks of 'many ways' in which the Catholic Church is linked to non-Catholics, but does not explain their status:

> The Church recognizes that in many ways she is linked with those who, being baptized, are honoured with the name of Christian, though they do not profess the faith in its entirety or do not preserve unity of communion with the successor of Peter.

Lumen Gentium 16 speaks about non-Christians, who instead are related to the People of God in various ways: first of all the Jews, then Muslims, those who seek the unknown God, and finally all people of good will who live in an honest way, according to the precepts of natural law.

From this there arises an objective difficulty with regard to the precise definition of the ecclesial *status* of the separated brethren. A certain ecumenical euphoria would try to align everyone by virtue of Baptism. This would generate some confusion in the post-conciliar period, with the attempt to get away from a membership defined within

170 'Mirum est quod schema, loquens de necessitate Ecclesiae, loquatur de ea tantum sub respectu salutis individualis, sileat vero de Ecclesia ut "sacramentum mundi"' (AS II/1, p. 592). By stating this, the Dutch Bishops' Conference was clearly expressing its own theological dependency.

171 Cf. AS III/1, p. 188.

certain limits, and source of continual divisions, and to move together towards a super-church, a common home, beyond historical differences. History—above all the historical divisions, as it is said —would thus be absorbed in a certain theology of ecclesiological pluralism.

5.3 From '*reapse et simpliciter*' to '*illi plene*', and no longer with '*tantum*'

Here I will focus again on the theme of incorporation into the Church, introduced now from what we have seen about the omission of the term 'members' and the re-designation of the *status* of the *voto*. Comparing the four schema on the Church, another substantial ecclesiological shift can be detected: from members 'vere et proprie'[172] of schema I, to the 'reapse et simpliciter loquendo Ecclesiae societati incorporantur illi tantum, qui ... '[173] of schema II, and up to the 'Illi plene Ecclesiae societati incorporantur qui Spiritum Christum habentes ... '[174] of schema III, where the adverb 'tantum' disappeared. This third modification would be kept in the promulgated Constitution.[175]

What was the reason for this significant development? We have already seen the opposition to 'membra vere et proprie'. But things went further. First of all, it must be noted that the expression 'reapse et simpliciter' was considered by many Fathers to be obscure or incorrect[176] or still discussed by theologians.[177] Bishop Gerard Van

[172] AS I/4, p. 18.

[173] AS II/1, p. 220.

[174] AS III/1, p. 188.

[175] For a synoptic vision cf. Hellín, *Lumen Gentium*, pp. 114–117.

[176] It was Bishop Van der Burgt, according to whom 'voce "reapse" omnes baptizati non catholici omnino excluduntur ab hac incorporatione. Hoc falsum videtur, ut iam discussione primae sessionis huius Concilii clare et saepius dictum est. Quomodo enim christiani non catholici vere Christo incorporari dici possunt, nempe baptismo, fide, spe et caritate, si non etiam modo reali Ecclesiae incorporantur?', AS II/2, p. 60.

[177] See for example Cardinal De Barros Câmara, who spoke on behalf of 153 Brazilian bishops, and according to whom the teaching brought by this expression, like similar ones, 'voto', 'tantum', was the object of discussion, and,

Velsen (Kroonstad, South Africa), who presented himself as a missionary and not very familiar with the Latin language, said that this terminology was dogmatic and technical. It would be better to describe the problem simply from the pastoral point of view. Above all, with regard to n. 9 of the text (the Church's link with non-Catholic Christians), Van Velsen, who had missionary experience and contact with Protestants, said that this was a paragraph of significant importance for ecumenical matters. It was best to reformulate it.[178]

Against this, some Fathers asked that 'reapse et simpliciter' be modified with 'sensu plenu et perfecto Ecclesiae societati incorporantur'.[179] Bishop Van Dodewaard referred to the words of John XXIII, who in his inaugural address put the emphasis on the 'vinculo perfectae unitatis',[180] while it was Paul VI himself who in his *Allocutio ad Concilium* on 29 September 1963,[181] spoke about this matter, speaking of a 'bond of perfect unity of Christ' by which non-Catholics are united to us ('qui sunt Nobiscum vincula perfectae unitatis Christi coniuncti');[182] a bond of unity which only the Catholic Church can offer, even though, per se, it is demanded by the strength of Baptism.[183] In reference to ecumenism, Paul VI then invited the Fathers

---

furthermore, did not contribute to clarifying the problem, cf. AS II/1, p. 423.

178 Cf. AS II/2, pp. 57–58.

179 Cf. the request of Bishop Jean Julien Weber (Archbishop of Strasbourg) (AS II/1, p. 745); the position of Bishop Bartholomew Evangelisti (Bishop of Meerut, India) (AS II/1, p. 661); etc. Cf. also Hellín, *Lumen Gentium*, p. 116.

180 Bishop Jean van Dodewaard (Bishop of Haarlem, Holland), asked that reference be made to the inaugural words of John XXIII: 'Vinculo perfectae unitatis Ecclesiae societati incorporantur illi tantum, etc.' (AS II/1, p. 434).

181 AS II/1, pp. 183–199 and in AAS 55 (1963) 841–859.

182 AS II/1, p. 193.

183 'Haec unitas quam per se vi Baptismatis ipsi participare deberent, ab una catholica Ecclesia illis offerri potest, et ab iis vi naturaque sua percupitur' (*Ibid.*). As we have seen, the ecclesiological-ecumenical structure, as regards the bond of unity of the separated brethren, would be constructed precisely on the foundation of the sacrament of Baptism, avoiding reference to the problem of *imperfecta* or *non plena* belonging to the Church. It is therefore

to provide the theological teaching on the Church with a clear explanation which could also be examined by the separated brethren, with the aim of being able to easily reach unity of agreement.[184]

In truth, the 'reapse' sounded like an exclusion of the non-Christians from the Church, and, as we saw before, if Baptism was necessary to enter into the Church, consequently it was Baptism which incorporated into the Church,[185] unless some obstacle had been put in place on purpose, such as, for example, a heresy, or schism. The problem of the identification of the mystical Body with the visible Church returned, an identification which had to be overcome to avoid the Roman spirit becoming exclusivity and an impediment to true unity. So it is legitimate to ask: are Catholicity-the Roman spirit really in opposition to unity? Is the Church ultimately divided in its visible and invisible aspects, or are both necessary to have that 'Christus totus'? In reality, the Commission in its *Relatio* on n. 8, *De Ecclesia*

---

legitimate to ask: is Baptism sufficient to be fully Christian? Is there a hierarchy of importance between the *tria vincula*: faith, sacraments and hierarchical communion, or do they have to be simultaneously in order for there to be the fullness of Christian identity? It was Paul VI who responded in that discourse, adding: 'Ecclesiam Christi unam esse et unam esse debere; et arcanam hanc et aspectabilem unitatem in rem deduci non posse nisi una fide, nisi participatione eorundem Sacramentorum, nisi apta cohaerentia unici ecclesiastici regiminis' (*Ibid.*). Unfortunately, however, two visions regarding the ecumenical movement in the Church would unravel.

184 'Potest inde teologica doctrina magnificas accipere explicationes plane dignas, quae etiam a seiunctis Fratribus attenta consideratione perpendantur; quae quidem explicationes, ut flagrantibus exoptamus votis, ipsis facilius usque iter demonstrent ad consensionum unitatem efficiendam' (*Ibid.*, p. 190). This seems to us to be a key passage for understanding a sort of 'ecumenical shift' which took place at the Council, and, in our case, in the doctrine concerning the Church.

185 Cf. what Bishop Alexandre Poncet said (titular Bishop of Basilinopoli), AS II/1, p. 701. Along the same lines, Cardinal Silva Henriquez (cf. AS II/3, pp. 400–403), according to whom it was necessary to consider the Church not as individuals but as communion.

visibili simul ac spirituali (antiquus n. 7), had already explained that the mystery of the Church,

> Is present and manifests itself in concrete society. Visible class and spiritual element are not two realities, but a complex reality, which unites the divine and the human, means of salvation and fruit of salvation. That is illustrated similarly with the mystery of the Word incarnate.[186]

In schema III, corrected by the Doctrinal Commission, we come to 'Illi plene', with 'tantum' present no longer. The motive put forward was so as not to exclude from full incorporation children who had not yet reached the age of reason and simple Christians, who were incapable of recognising all the conditions of membership. This had been suggested, inter alia, by Bishop Cesare Francesco Benedetti.[187]

---

186 'Mysterium Ecclesiae adest et manifestetur *in concreta societate*. Coetus autem visibilis et elementum spirituale *non sunt duae res*, sed una realitas complexa, complectens divina et humana, media salutis et fructus salutis. Quod per analogiam cum Verbo incarnato illustratur' (AS III/1, p. 176). N. 8 of schema III is very important because it has another significant modification: from the *est* by which one discerns the identity between the Church of Christ and the Catholic Church to *subsistit in*, shifting the emphasis onto subsitence and, as would be explained by the Doctrinal Commission itself, this was to better ensure that this agreed with what followed, the affirmation of 'elements of sanctification and of the truth', 'outside its whole' (cf. *Ibid.*, p. 177). A lot has been written on this matter and so I will not dwell on it in a systematic manner. It has also been shown that with this change in language the Church did not lose her self-awareness of being the one true Church of Christ (cf. A. Von Teuffenbach, *Die Bedeutung des subsistit in [LG 8]: zum Selbstverständnis der katholischen Kirche*, Utz, Wiss, Munich 2002). I will simply note that right from the first schema, in the chapter devoted to ecumenism, there was talk of elements of truth present outside the visible confines of the Church and there was no need to change the *est*. The Commission would opt for the change with the aim of indicating a middle way between those who wanted *est* and those who wanted instead a form of subsistence (one of *consistenza*) close to *est*, such as, for example, 'subsistit integro modo in Ecclesia catholica' or 'iure divino subsistit'. All those present in the Commission adhered to the solution, cf. AS III/6, p. 81.

It was not said, however, if the 'tantum' had been removed for non-Catholics, too. Since they did not possess that 'full' incorporation, what sort of incorporation into the Church did they possess? There was no response to the question, but clearly a not-full communion was to be understood. However, it remained difficult to specify its limits and furthermore in the post-conciliar period this fact lent itself to various interpretations, to the point of creating a certain confusion about who does and doesn't belong to the Church, or not yet belongs. I will return to this argument in examining the development of post-conciliar Magisterium.

5.4 From '*cuisdam collegii*' to '*collegium seu coetus stabilis*'

Finally, I will concentrate on another ecclesiological element of significant importance, the 'college'.[188] Here, however, unlike what has been studied up to now, a change is noticed in modifying not by removing, but adding and explaining better, in order to avoid misunderstandings. The teaching on collegiality was a very sensitive point in the conciliar discussion. Suffice to note that 360 lines of text were

---

187 Cf. AS II/1, p. 626; for the statements from the Commission AS III/1, pp. 202–203.

188 For an overall view of the problem see Ratzinger, 'La collegialità episcopale: spiegazione teologica del testo conciliare', in *La Chiesa del Vaticano II*, pp. 733–760; U. Betti, 'Relazioni tra il Papa e gli altri membri del Collegio Episcopale', in *Ibid.*, pp. 761–771. Betti is inclined towards two inadequately distinct subjects, the Pope and the College, and adds: 'The difficulty which someone would encounter in trying to infer from the defining words of Vatican I, which attribute to the Roman Pontiff not just "potiores partes", but "totam plenitudinem supremae potestatis", almost as if he had a greater power than that of the whole college, is without doubt outside the historical and doctrinal context in which the statement was made; and even in open contrast with what the dogma of papal primacy forces us to believe' (*Ibid.*, p. 766). But it is not about a greater or lesser power, because, as Betti rightly says, the power is one, it comes from Christ and is over the universal Church. But it is 'all the fullness of the supreme power', thus, as the *Nota explicativa* clarifies, there is no College without the Roman Pontiff.

discussed in nine General Congregations, with 119 speeches and 56 written interventions.[189] Nor was there a lack of Fathers who revealed themselves to be clearly against collegiality,[190] and those like H. Jedin who considered it to be 'a new and unusual expression', without, however, having 'identified a reason to explicitly oppose it'.[191]

Among Florit's personal papers I found a text on the crucial point of chapter III of *Lumen Gentium*, referring to the theme of collegiality. The handwritten note headed 'The Crucial Point of the famous chapter III' bears the title 'Non diarchia' and as sub-title 'How to reconcile the full and supreme power attributed to the college of bishops with the likewise full and supreme personal power of the

---

[189] Cf. AS II/2, pp. 82–124, 222–914; Melloni, 'The Beginning of the Second Period', p. 64.

[190] Cf. AS II/2, pp. 82–89.

[191] H. Jedin. *Storia della mia vita* (Brescia: Morcelliana, 1987), p. 313 (German original, *Lebensbericht* [Mainz: Matthias-Grünewald Verlag, 1984]). He adds: 'I was deeply convinced that the authority by virtue of which bishops take part in the general council, does not derive wholly from the Pope who transmits to them their jurisdiction over a given diocese, but from the consecration itself as bishops; the usual distinction, clear in Canon Law, between consecration and jurisdiction does not correspond in my opinion to the state of things based on the liturgical texts and practice in the ancient Church. So I would definitely side with those who consider the Pope and bishops together as holders of the apostolic office and of apostolic responsibility, despite the definitions of the First Vatican Council, which were not completed in their day with a decree on the authority of the bishops' (*Ibid.*). Jedin himself, envisaging what would happen after the end of the Council (he was not very happy about both the approval of *Gaudium et spes* as a pastoral constitution and the poor way to entrust to almost exclusively French laity the reporting of the Council: 'It was a demonstration and as such a concession to the era of the masses and to the *mass media'*, *Ibid.*, p. 321) said with regard to synodality, for which he himself had fought: 'It could be easily understood that the constitution on the Church was a "spectacular event" in Church history, but one could not envisage the consequences which would stem from the concept of the episcopal college for a "synodalisation", and from that of the church as "people of God" for its democratisation', *Ibid.*, p. 322.

Roman Pontiff'.[192] To this is added another document composed of two type-written sheets, with the title '3) Unity of Regime'.[193]

J. Ratzinger also raised doubts about this, and saw the main problem as lying in having misunderstood the historical development which underpinned the doctrine of collegiality, as reference and rediscovery of the local Church and its hierarchy, and not as a juxtaposition of the bishops to the Petrine primacy. The motions of the non-Catholic observers at the Council, which always needed to aim at the pastoral and ecumenical goal of the gathering, could be a source of inspiration to understand this teaching correctly, reading it in a very circumscribed context.[194]

The alternative schema, we have seen, presented somewhat 'over-abundant' ideas. The Chilean schema saw in collegiality a manifestation of the pastoral aim of the Council. The German and French schema always saw it as on-going. For the French, the Pope was unable to exercise his power of jurisdiction over the whole of the Church unless through the College. The discussion about n. 12 of schema II, which integrated the institution of the twelve apostles 'cuisdam collegii', began indicating an elevated emphasis, alongside a certain confusion.[195]

---

192 AEF, folder n. 5: Concilio Ecumenico Vaticano II. Schema "De Ecclesia", 4 ff.

193 *Ibid.*, 2 ff.

194 Cf. J. Ratzinger, 'Problemi e risultati del Concilio Vaticano II', *Giornale di Teologia* 8, Queriniana, Brescia 1966, pp. 10, 57–79. See the original text in Id., *Zur Lehre Zweiten Vatikanischen Konzils*, I (Gesammelte Schriften 7/1), cit., pp. 377–381. See also my own contribution, S. M. Lanzetta, 'La valutazione del Concilio Vaticano II in Joseph Ratzinger poi Benedetto XVI', in *Fides Catholica* 1 (2012), pp. 87–120.

195 Among the points proposed by the Cardinal moderators at the Council for a 'guiding vote', subject to an audience with Paul VI (acclaimed that day as 'lived collegiality'), there was also this: the episcopal college, presented as subject of divine right, having full and supreme power over the universal Church. The five points were revised by Carlo Colombo and the vote scheduled for 17 October 1963 (cf. AS II/3, pp. 574–575), and already announced with great

The *status* of the problem was excellently set out by Cardinal Siri. He noted that there were fundamentally two positions:

1. a *co-gubernatio,* in which some participate in the governance of the head in a fitting way as college, that is to say under the Roman Pontiff, as it was and is in the Church's Tradition;
2. a *co-gubernatio,* in which a certain right to participate in the universal governance of the Supreme Pontiff, *quamvis 'sub' eius regimine,* is presumed.

Obviously, it was said, the first position was acceptable and traditional, the second erroneous and could not be sustained. If one can be admitted to the participation in the same office of the Pope no longer could any difference between the bishop and the Pope be seen. To participate in the office of the Pope is the right of the primacy itself. The institution of the primacy desires that the Pope alone can do everything, and that no-one can be obliged or limited in the exercise of his universal governance. This second concept of collegiality could in no way be traced back to *Pastor Aeternus* of the First Vatican Council.[196]

To Bishop Seitz, the expression 'cuiusdam collegii' sounded vague and seemed minimising, while the conciliar line was aimed at strongly

emphasis by *L'Avvenire d'Italia*. Voting was deferred and Paul VI asked for the voting slips to be burned. In the meantime the parallel operation of the Moderators was obvious, helped by Dossetti's procedural experience. Dossetti was removed as secretary of the college of Moderators (cf. Melloni, 'The Beginning of the Second Period', pp. 306–307). It is interesting to see what Schillebeeckx wrote in his Notes on 29 October 1963: '*Collegiality as ius divinum!* Such a markedly unanimous declaration by the Council is *in fact a dogma. By virtue of divine right, the collegial leadership of the Church is the doctrinal fundament of pastoral aggiornamento in our days. All the rest ensues from this*' (Schillebeeckx, *The Council notes*, p. 37). If the vote on the *ius divino* of collegiality had passed in the Council for Schillebeeckx it would have been a dogma ('not pastoral'?, one asks). In his judgement, however, the collegial leadership of the Church, understood as decentralisation, is the fundament of pastoral aggiornamento, cf. *Ibid.*, p. 36.

[196] Cf. AS II/1, p. 611.

emphasising the note of collegiality. In his opinion, it was necessary to define *collegiality* and base it on Tradition.[197] Bishop Carli, on the other hand, denounced that wish, foreign to Tradition, wanting to affirm an ordinary always on-going collegiality.[198]

The text in its iter experienced a very ponderous path comprising significant changes: from 'cuisdam collegii'[199] of schema I to 'ad modum collegii instituit'[200] of schema III, to arrive at 'ad modum collegii seu coetus stabilis instituit'[201] of the promulgated text (cf. *Lumen Gentium* 19), after having been modified according to the Fathers' procedures, adding finally the *Nota explicativa praevia*.[202]

---

197 Cf. *Ibid.*, p. 712.

198 Cf. *Ibid.*, p. 449.

199 *Ibid.*, p. 232.

200 AS III/1, p. 212, explaining already that 'vocabulum *collegium* non sensu iuridico de coetu perfecte aequalium intelligitur; sed de coetu stabili, a Dominio instituto, ut patet iam ex Mc 3:14 et 16: "epoièsen dôdeka...kai epoièsen toùs Dôdeka"' (*Ibid.*, p. 234), as had been noted by Cardinal Ruffini (cf. AS II/2, pp. 855–86), by Fr Aniceto Fernandez (cf. *Ibid.*, pp. 422–423), by Bishop Costantini (cf. *Ibid.*, p. 447), and by many others: cf. Hellín, *Lumen Gentium*, p. 158.

201 AS III/8, p. 57: 'Loco expressionis: "*ad modum collegii* instituit", 99 Patres proponunt ut dicatur: "ad modum collegii *seu coetus stabilis* instituit". 10 Patres suggerunt formulam: "ad modum *cuisdam* collegii", dum 9 alii diversas variantes minores eiusdem formulae inducere vellent. 10 denique Patres formulam ipsam delendam esse aestimant'. And this was the response: 'Secundum illa quae dicuntur in Relatione, pag. 81, C, scribatur: "ad modum collegii *seu coetus stabilis* instituit"'.

202 *Ibid.*, pp. 11–13. Some were not in agreement about the *Nota explicativa* at the end. These included Ratzinger (cf. LthK^2, *Das Zweite Vatikanische Konzil*, I, p. 349: it was gesture which directed at the minority who were opposed to collegiality, which in the light of the *Nota*, recognised the lack of foundation of the opposition ['das Gegenstandlose ihrer Opposition'], feeling encouraged by the acceptance of the text) and Jedin, who however then said: 'During the crisis of November 1964 I was on the side of those to whom the *Nota explicativa* of *Lumen Gentium* seemed superfluous, since the First Vatican Council had been quoted on a number of occasions. However, the events following the Council have proved the Pope to be right, where he—we must

The *Nota* was inserted at the behest of the Pope, and provided the correct interpretation of the college, seen not in a legal sense of a group of equals, but in a theological sense of a stable class of unequals, in which there was no transmission of the extraordinary power from the Apostles to their successors, nor equality between the Head and the members of the College. What's more, one became a member of the College through episcopal consecration and hierarchical communion with the Roman Pontiff and with the bishops dispersed throughout the world.

Now, it was about explaining correctly the participation of the bishops in the power of the universal jurisdiction of the Roman Pontiff. Precisely this judgement was not always unanimous and still today sees theology in dialogue to understand if it is a dual inadequately distinct subject which acts or just one subject. Inclined towards the first solution was the Prior General of the Dominicans, Fr Fernandez. He distinguished two subjects having supreme power in the Church: a) the Roman Pontiff and b) the episcopal Body always united with the Head. This second supreme power, however, should not be seen as an alternative to the first, almost as if it lessened it. It was effective only by reason of the first. The power then was exercised in a solemn way in the ecumenical councils and in an ordinary fashion in various ways at the invitation of the Roman Pontiff or for moral benefit with his tacit consent.[203]

Parente, on the other hand, explained that the question about the unity or plurality of the subjects remained open, even if, according to his way of seeing things, it was about two subjects, 'inadequate quidem distincta, unica manet potestas'.[204] Nor should the adjective 'plena' referring only to the Roman Pontiff or to the Roman Pontiff with the bishops create problems. The difficulty vanished if one considered

recognise, in a rather unusual form—underlined and interpreted once again the doctrine defined in his time', Jedin, *Storia della mia vita*, p. 319.

203 Cf. AS II/2, pp. 422–424.

204 AS III/2, p. 206.

that power in the Church was not dual, but one, that which Christ conferred on the whole college (Peter and the Apostles).[205] Thus Parente succeeded in preparing souls for the future majority vote on collegiality. Philips, too, would explain that the question was under debate: two subjects *inadequately distinct?*[206]

So the problems remained.[207] The Council was divided on this issue. Mgr Franić drew attention to this in his report on chapter III. First of all the schema declared that new teaching on the episcopal College has 'quoque iure divino' supreme power throughout the Church. Then, the teaching on the supreme power of the College of bishops 'ex institutione divina' could not be proved from Scripture or from Tradition. Everyone was agreed on the fact, then, that there was not a collegial action of the bishops without the Pope and that such actions can only be with the Pope and under the Pope. Conciliar disagreement then focused on the theoretical question of whether the collegial power of the bishops always comes from Christ by means of the Pope or from Christ to the bishops without the Pope. Franić concluded: if this question, strongly disputed among theologians, is left open there, we can achieve conciliar unanimity and great peace will reign among us.[208]

205 *Ibid.*, p. 207.

206 Cf. Philips, *La Chiesa e il suo mistero*, pp. 262–263.

207 In a note strictly reserved for the Holy Father, signed by 25 Cardinals, by a Patriarch, a bishop and 4 superiors of religious Congregations, chapter III of the schema on the Church was severely criticised, and especially the new teaching of collegiality which, while in the pre-conciliar era was only a theological thesis, was now becoming a common teaching, unexpectedly passing over the truly common teaching supported by the Magisterium. In reality, the new teaching on collegiality was less common and less probable than that attested to up to to the Council (cf. AS VI/3, pp. 322–329). The letter is accompanied by some very interesting theological *adnexa* (pp. 330–338).

208 Cf. AS III/2, pp. 193–200.

5.4.1 The personal interest of Paul VI in chapter III of Lumen Gentium

The Holy Father participated with considerable interest and apprehension in the discussions about chapter III of the re-drafted schema on the Church. There are two very interesting letters which testify to his watchful care so that the truth about collegiality might be stated without obscuring or trying to correct Vatican I and his determined desire about the *Nota praevia,* after a theological report requested from the Jesuit Fr Guglielmo Bertrams.[209] On 5 November 1964, Cardinal Cicognani wrote to Cardinal Ottaviani:

> Most Reverend Eminence,
>
> I have the honour of communicating to your Reverend Eminence that the Holy Father wants to know as soon as possible of the modified text of Chapter III of the Schema 'De Ecclesia' and, in any case, before such a text is presented to the Congregation of the Council Fathers; and that is so that He can be aware that the suggested doctrinal formulae are such that His Holiness can accept and promulgate them.
> As is obvious, it is completely desirable that the conclusions of that Commission might merit the acceptance of the August Pontiff; that if He considered it appropriate to make some changes, the Commission would have prior knowledge of them, so that it could be done as soon as possible to bring the text to a satisfactory formula.
> In making your Eminence aware of what is stated above, I am delighted to take this opportunity to humbly kiss the hands and confirm my sense of deep respect
> Your Most Reverend Eminence's
> Humble and Obedient True Servant
>
> G. Card. Cicognani.[210]

---

209 See the account of the work of Paul VI on this issue made by Fr Giovanni Caprile SJ, reported in extracts in *L'Osservatore Romano* on 20 February 1965, p. 5.

210 In ASV Envelope 785, folder 400.

In fact, the suggestions proposed by the Theological Commission on 10 November 1964 were not accepted. In their place was the *Nota explicativa praevia*. On the same day a new letter from Cicognani, with a more pregnant theological tenor, was addressed to Cardinal Ottaviani. The Cardinal Secretary of State wrote:

> Most Reverend Eminence,
>
> I am fulfilling the esteemed task of sending back to you the volume of the Schema of the conciliar Constitution 'De Ecclesia', with the attached booklet of the 'Addenda' which Your Eminence, in a gesture of sensitive thoughtfulness, deeply appreciated by the Holy Father, had recently submitted for His august examination. With the two booklets are some observations for the most precise formulation of the proposed text.
>
> The Vicar of Christ, having to do his duty and promulgate the new text, has expressed, therefore, the wish that it be preceded by an explanatory Note from the Doctrinal Commission on the significance and value of the modifications made to the text and for such an explanation it might be appropriate to bear in mind the procedure followed in the First Vatican Council (cf. Mansi, vol. 52, Congregatio Generalis octogesima quarta, 11 iulii 1870, coll. 1218–1230).
>
> In this way the Commission might want to use the charity of formulating an appropriate response to the difficulties raised about the issue, so that that might assuage the mind of many Council Fathers, and make possible a greater and more internally convincing acceptance in the council chamber. In fact, the Commission, which has good reasons for maintaining its own thoughts, must also have good reasons with which to unravel the difficulties.
>
> In addition, it is the will of the August Pontiff that some points of the Schema be clarified, as indicated in the enclosed pages; and, in particular, that the constitutive dependency of the collegial Authority of the bishops on the consent of the Roman Pontiff be expressed. I refer also to the text of an opinion,

which was requested about the matter from Fr Guglielmo Bertrams SJ. The Holy Father, while he expresses His gratitude, wishes to formulate for the work of Your Eminence and of the whole Theological Commission His most cordial greetings, supported by the comforting Apostolic Blessing.
I willingly take this opportunity to most humbly kiss the hands and express my profound respect for
Your Most Reverend Eminence
Your Humble and Obedient Servant

G. Card. Cicognani.[211]

Also very interesting are the observations made by Fr Bertrams in his theological report on chapter III of the Constitution De Ecclesia, dated 12 November 1964, most probably asked for directly by the Holy Father.[212]

---

[211] *Ibid.* In the same envelope and folder there is a handwritten note from the Holy Father, dated 13 November 1964, addressed to Cardinal Ottaviani, thanking him 'for the work undertaken in the Commission "De doctrina fidei et morum', which you have chaired'.

[212] G. Bertrams, *Notae quod capitulum tertium schematis De Ecclesia,* in *Ibid.* See also the *Relatio De Suggestionibus Commissioni Doctrinali propositis,* 5–6 June 1964, ff. 6, 7 June 1964, in ASV, Envelope 787, folder 424. As it says at the start of the report, these are observations from the Doctrinal Commission on the examination of suggestions made about chapter III of the Schema De Ecclesia: 'Commissio Doctrinalis gratum suum animum expressit pro libertate qua in examinandis suggestionibus sibi propositis uti protulit ad perficiendum textum Capitis III Schematis de Ecclesia'. Inter alia, some Fathers suggested 'ut supprimatur Collegii Episcoporum Caput, et ut addatur postea: Romanus Pontifex, ut supremus omnium christianorum pastor…' Suppressio de Capite Collegii Commissioni non videtur opportuna: ex una parte non habet valorem restrictivum: consulto enim non dicitur "ut" vel "quatenus" caput collegii; ex altera parte ordo idearum exigit hanc incisam, quia explicat quare in textu qui de munere docendi Episcoporum agit, tam fuse de potestate docendi Romani Pontificis fiat sermo. Cetero statim postea, scilicet lin. 24, explicite dicitur de Romano Pontifice: "ut universalis Ecclesiae magister supremus". Admittitur autem additio "omnium christianorum" sed potius scribatur "christifidelium". Protestantes et Orthodoxi unum se "christianos" dicunt, sed generatim vocem

The Jesuit responded to two questions. The first: 'Is it not necessary to modify the text so that the rights of primacy be saved?' And the second: 'It is appropriate to amend the text?' With the first question he wanted to respond to the perplexity of many Council Fathers who had strong suspicions about the theology of collegiality, which could undermine Petrine primacy. Bertrams argued saying that precisely the primacy of the Pope was mentioned at the start of the chapter and there was no reason to interpret Vatican II as a correction of Vatican I. This statement could be of help today, too. Rather, the doctrine of collegiality appeared as a supplement to that. Various prelates were suspicious that the new collegial teaching was inclined towards an 'episcopal council'. Bertrams replied saying that the schema on the Church did not change the doctrine on the Church, but rather set it out in a more systematic way. So the whole of chaper III was not to be rejected, but rather it was necessary to modify some passages, with the aim of enabling there to be an almost unanimous vote on the text and for an ecumenical end, too: if the discussion on collegiality collapsed *in toto*, the Easterners would be disillusioned. So Fr Bertrams concluded his close examination indicating some amendments. In short, he stated that episcopal jurisdictional power was promoted, directly and approved by the Roman Pontiff, while the *munus docendi e regendi*, according to the ontological reality, was conferred by the sacrament of Orders. Here is the original text of the report in full:

> I. Estne omnino necessarium textum emendare, ut salva sint iura primatus?
> Responsum: Patres Concilii, qui hoc affirmant, sine dubio moti sunt sincero zelo salvandi iura primatus. Attamen ratio habenda est:
> 1) Initio capitis fit relatio ad Conc. Vat. I et expresse dicitur firmiter credenda esse omnia illa, quae ad primatum spectant. Hic obiective non potest esse ulla ratio interpretandi Conc. Vat. II tamquam correctura Conc. Vat. I. Potius doctrina huius

"christifidelium" non adhibent", *Ibid.*, f. 6.

capitis clare apparet tamquam supplementum ad illa, quae in Conc. Vat. I dicta sunt, id est: salvis omnibus, quae in Conc. Vat. I proposita sunt. Haec ratio, a—nisi fallor multis—Patribus Concilii sufficiens habetur, ut in hoc capite—praeter relationem ad Conc. Vat. I—non sit sermo de primatu.
2) Revera autem saepius in hoc capite iura primatus explicite referuntur. Si simul considerantur illa, quae initio de doctrina Conc. Vat. I dicuntur, necnon illa, quae saepius in ipso capite explicite de primatu dicuntur, non iam habetur ratio vera probata affirmandi iura primatus non esse salva.
3) Positive constat plures praelatos et officiales vere timere 'consilium episcopalem', de quo sermo fuit. Hic timor videtur influere, non modo reflexo, sed de facto, in iudicium quoad collegialitatem corporis Episcoporum. Accedit ratio, quod doctrina, quam aliquis tenendam habebat, non facile mutatur. Hac ratione autem notandum est schema de Ecclesia non mutare doctrinam Ecclesiae; potius ipsa doctrina Ecclesiae magis organice proponitur.
Ratione habitis omnibus dictis respondendum censeo: negative.
II: Estne opportunum ut aliqui textus emendentur?
Responsum: Semper habentur—saltem inter theologos et publicistas—tendentiae minus favorabiles iuribus primatus. Hac ratione negari nequit, ut textus, qui non sunt ex toto praecisi, forte afferuntur—nunc et in futurum—tamquam argumentum Conc. Vat. I correctum esse per Conc. Vat. II. Porro negari nequit haberi Patres in Concilio, qui sincere iudicant se textus ex toto non praecisos approbare non posse. Ratione habita horum dictorum opportunum esse censeo, et fere moraliter necessarium, ut aliqui textus emendentur.
III. Necessitas talis emendationis iustificare potest eo, quod in re tam magni momenti pro Ecclesia omnia fieri debent, quae, in quantum hoc sit possibile, omnibus Patribus permittunt, ut textum approbent.
Porro ipse Sanctus Pater facilius approbare potest textum, qui secundum eius iudicium ab omnibus approbari possit.

Vere hisce emendationibus suppositis difficultates propositae videntur sufficienter esse solutae, ut omnes Patres voto maioritatis se associari possint. Accedit ratio oecumenica: Si enim doctrina capitis non approbatur, Orientales se delusos habent.

Altera ex parte Patres maioritatis ob rationes allatas non possunt aegre ferre emendationes applicatas, eo vel minus, quod doctrina in hoc capite contenta per ipsas non modificatur, nec asserta restringuntur; potius illa, quae implicite dicta sunt et aliunde constant, explicite dicuntur.
Emendationes proponendae
Pag. 62, 41 et 63, 1: natura sua nonnisi in hierarchica communione cum Collegii Capite et membris exerceri possunt, qua deficiente potestas authentice docendi et regendi in Ecclesia constituta non est. Et addatur nota: Documenta Ecclesiae quae affirmant potestatem iursidictionis conferri a Summo Pontifice, referuntur ad potestatem iuridice in Ecclesiam constitutam; mentione non faciunt munera docendi et regendi, quatenus haec secundum realitatem ontologicam, sacramentalem conferuntur per consecrationem episcopalem.
Pag. 64, 11: quae quidem potestas nonnisi consentiente Romano Pontifice exerceri potest, qui quoad tale exercitium promovendum, dirigendum,[213] approbandum bonum Ecclesiae respiciens secundum propriam discretionem procedit.
Pag (g). 66, 24: qui, salva fidei unitate et unica divina constituione universalis Ecclesiae super Petrum fundatae,
Pag. 72, 18: Christus, quem Pater sanctificavit et misit in mundum (Jo. 10:36), consecrationis missionisque suae Episcopos participes per Apostolos effecit, qui munus ministerii sui (here the phrase is interrupted).
Pag. 75, Nota explicativa tertia: de consensu Romani Pontificis diaconatus conferri potest viris matures uxoratis.

[213] 'aut: ordinandum; aut etiam omittatur et dicatur: promovendum, approbandum'. I refer back to the text.

> Illa quae dicuntur in Nota ad: Addenda ad Relationem generalem, necnon illa, quae dicuntur in: Osservazioni sul Capitolo III 'De Ecclesia', le Relazioni e le risposte ai 'modi' mihi videntur fundata; omnia illa etiam ex parte mea dicere possum.[214]

5.4.2 Unresolved problems

The Council laid great emphasis on collegiality. In my opinion, there was a fundamental problem, which was put in an ambiguous manner and which caused great difficulty: is the college of apostles of divine institution?[215] From here the path was open to justify collegiality *ex*

---

214 At the end in red ink is written the name of the author: P. Bertams, S.I.

215 The difficulty arose on 11 March 1963, right from the Plenary Session of the Commission, which was working on the reform of the first part of the schema *De ecclesia*. At 5.00 p.m. a discussion began about the meaning of the apostolic college. Browne raised a doubt 'de asserto Apostolos institutos fuisse ut collegium. Exc.mus Franić putat nimium extolli collegium apostolicum: historice forsan praecedere Collegium, sed ontologice prius esse primatum, quod incipit ab ipso Christo, cuius Petrus est vicarius. Respondet Mons. Philips vocem collegium non sumi senso iuridico sed sensu historico. Nec expedire ut hac in re procedamus cum timore laedendi iura Pontificis: talem intentionem longe abesse. Observat Em.mus Ottaviani non agi de intentione, sed de re, scilicet utrum Apostoli reapse constituent fundamentum Ecclesiae. Intercedit Exc.mus Charue et redit ad dicta in sessione praecedenti. Dicit Apoc. 21:14 non esse mere eschatologicum et in epistola ad Eph. Apostolos dici fundamentum ratione praedicationis, quae includat munus docendi, regendi, sanctificandi. Exc.mus Parente etiam regreditur ad antea discussa de Petro rupe et Apostolis fundamento: nil obstare, quin sermo fiat de collegio apostolico, sed hodie huic voci subicii ideas falsas. Quare in capite primo melius dici ad instar collegii; cui solutio adhaerent Em.mus Browne, Exc.mus Florit et ipse relator'. Others spoke, too, but in the end all agreed that 'in capite primo scribendum esse: ad instar collegii' (ASV, Envelope 763, folder 281, in KT 2/2, pp. 681–682. Cf. also Tromp's *Diario*, KT 2/1, pp. 299–303, with other interventions on the theme). More subtle was the question if the Apostles were *reapse* the foundation of the Church (rather than the Churches?) or just Peter. What was clear, however, but which then went through further variations, was the fact that Christ established the Apostles *in the form of* or *in the way of a college* and not the college as such. For a correct hermeneutic it is necessary to go back to the historical and not legal meaning

integro, and hence the practical need for episcopal Conferences.[216] According to some, including the French schema,[217] and the German one,[218] definitely so. But according to Ruffini, justified by Scripture itself, no. Christ did not institute the College of Apostles, but the Apostles, called by the collective name the 'Twelve' (*tôn dôdeka*, cf. Mt 10:1, Mk 3:16), who lived with Jesus, gathered by him in the manner of *societas*. Ruffini doubted they were then also instituted as a properly called college (a stable class) for a historical faith reason: the Apostles were dispersed throughout the world from the year AD 42 until about the year AD 67, and never acted in a collegial manner, unless at the Council of Jerusalem (cf. Ac 15), the first ecumenical council.[219] The Minister General of the Friars Minor, Fr Sépinski, was also not convinced of the *ius divinum* of the collegial doctrine.[220]

---

of this term, as Philips had already said.

216 In 1980 K. Walf reported on the omissions and ambiguities of Vatican II in ecclesiological matters in the following terms: 'It is beyond doubt that in Vatican II's teaching about the episcopal college there are positive possibilities. However, it is legitimate to state that the risk of misrepresentation about the origins of episcopal power in the local church is very high. It is likely that in the final analysis it is about an unneccesary complication of the pope-bishop relationship. Furthermore, if one takes into account the exegetical and historical information, it is impossible to consider the episcopal college as the collective successor of the apostolic college. This aspect has been rightly pointed out by Barion and—a long time before him and independently of the problem raised by Vatican II—by Rudolf Sohm', K. Walf, 'Lacune e ambiguità nell'ecclesiologia del Vaticano II', in *Cristianesimo nella storia* 2/1 (1981), p. 195. Cf. H. Barion, 'Das Zweite Vatikanische Konzil-Kanonistischer Bericht (II)', in *Der Staat* 4 (1965), p. 347.

217 Cf. Hellín, *Lumen Gentium*, p. 756.

218 AS I/4, p. 262.

219 Cf. AS II/2, pp. 85–86.

220 'Doctrina de collegialitate episcopali a schemate proposita, non plene convincit, speciatim si schema huic doctrinae chrisma *iuris divini* vindicare intendit. ... sed fundaretur, secundum meum submissum iudicium, in iure mere ecclesiastico' (*Ibid.*, p. 882). Sépinski was one of the signatories of a very critical letter on chapter III of the schema *Lumen Gentium* sent to the Holy

I believe that the reason for the misunderstanding was in having exchanged 'episcopate' with 'college'. The episcopate is of divine institution by reason of the institution of the Apostles (as would be recognised also in the Council, in a definitive manner, with the sacramentality of the episcopate, and by reason of a homogenous development of teaching) but the college is not, with instead the power of jurisdiction (like the *munus sanctificandi* and *docendi*) being of divine institution, conferred by Christ on Peter and the bishops in communion with him. If from Christ to Peter and by means of Peter to the apostles, this is discussed today. However, the Council was not afraid this time of willingly setting out along the path of theological discussion, which, at other times, it had discouraged for other teachings. Obviously, there was a more forward-looking desire which drove the Fathers.

Inter-related to this was another question: sometimes the teaching of the college, as subject of supreme and full power over the Church, *cum et sub Petro*, was explained with the *munus docendi* of the bishops, who, as Vatican I said,[221] exercise their power both in a solemn manner in council and in an ordinary and universal way dispersed throughout the world. Preserving their bond of unity with Peter, even in the case of an ordinary Magisterium (teaching in a definitive manner), they are infallible teachers. By reason of that, Bishop Narciso Jubany Arnau (Bishop of Barcelona)—and with him ten other bishops—proved episcopal collegiality through Vatican I and Pius XII's *Munificientissimus Deus*, another example of collegial Magisterium as regards the preparation for the dogma of the Assumption.[222] The German-language Fathers, too, in the schema they

Father, stating, inter alia, this point: 'The Church is becoming *da monarchica, episcopaliana e collegiale*; and this by divine right and by virtue of episcopal consecration', AS VI/3, p. 325.

221 Dogmatic Constitution *Dei Filius*: 'Further, by divine and Catholic faith, all those things must be believed which are contained in the written word of God and in tradition, and those which are proposed by the Church, either in a solemn pronouncement or in her ordinary and universal teaching power, to be believed as divinely revealed', DH 3011, a teaching already set out by Blessed Pius IX in *Tuas libenter* on 21 December 1863.

presented, as a result of the meeting in Fulda, had placed episcopal collegiality alongside the supreme Magisterium, exercised in the Church by the Pope and by the bishops united to him, and they explained it as a function of the latter.[223]

In truth, episcopal collegiality as regards the exercise of the *munus regendi*—the theme of collegiality at the Council was addressing this—and magisterial collegiality are two distinct things and it is not right to use one to justify the other. One cannot speak of collegiality in the Magisterium, rather than universal Magisterium, in which the guarantee of the universality is the gathering of the bishops *cum Petro*. If it was about the universal Magisterium in the Church and common pastoral praxis, what was the need to suggest a doctrine of collegiality, when this had always been there? This in fact was how Bishop Giuseppe Fenocchio (Bishop of Pontremoli) responded, inviting the Council to clarify its intention.[224]

The relationship between primacy and episcopate is still problematic today. What is certain is that Vatican II did not resolve all the problems about it, it even opened new ones. According to Walf,[225] the only significant change brought about by the Council about this relationship lies in having added the adjective *plena* to the *potestas* of the ecumenical council (cf. *Lumen Gentium* 22). While the Code of Canon Law states that the Pope has 'suprema ac plena potestas

[222] Cf. AS II/2, pp. 581–582.

[223] Cf. AS I/4, p. 623.

[224] 'Si autem qui collegialitatem propugnant intendat adserere: *a)* quod potestas quo Romanus Pontifex Ecclesiam gubernat simul sit potestas collegii episcoporum, *b)* vel quod Romanus Pontifex debeat Ecclesiam regere in forma permanenter collegiali, *c)* vel quod missio primaria singulorum episcoporum sit regimen totius Ecclesiae cum Romano Pontifice: haec omnia cum doctrina Vaticani I de primatu nullo modo conciliari possunt. Si autem hoc non intendunt, quid volunt nisi quod semper factum est, etsi melius id fieri possit?' (AS II/2, p. 742 [741]). Bishop Carlos E. de Sabóia Bandeira Melo (Bishop of Palmas, Brasil) was also against the doctrine of collegiality as proposed at the Council, cf. *Ibid.*, p. 121–123.

[225] Cf. Walf, 'Lacune e ambiguità', pp. 191–196.

iurisdictionis' (canon 218) over the whole Church and the Council just has 'suprema potestas' (canon 228), for the Constitution on the Church the *ordo episcoporum* also has 'suprema ac plena potestas'. That of the Pope differs from that of the college by the addition of the adjective *universalis*. However, in the same document, *Lumen Gentium*, the authority of the Pope is never said to be *episcopal*; while that of the diocesan bishop with respect to the diocese is (cf. 27: *propria ordinaria* and *episcopal*). Only in the decree *Christus Dominus* is the adjective *episcopal* recovered to define the *potestas* of the Pope (cf. nn. 2 and 9). Perhaps it is from this sort of friction between the Pope and bishop in *Lumen Gentium* that a certain competition between the two often arises? The central problem is that there is an absence of unambiguous and clear theological and legal language. Often, one is faced with compromise formulations.

There is another element: the primacy of the Roman Pontiff is not defined in *Lumen Gentium*, as already in Vatican I, as 'primatus iurisdictionis' but only as 'sacer primatus' (n. 18), to which the jurisdiction is subject (when it is seen in continuity with Vatican I), but obviously the two expressions are not equivalent, nor do they have the same weight in a dogmatic constitution, with the risk of being open to modifications of the subject itself. Finally, another problem to be underlined concerns the emphasis on collegiality in the episcopal Conferences. In reality what is their legal status and what is the legal value of their decisions? Are they an intermediary body between the Pope and the bishop? In fact that is the case, but the Constitution on the Church does not provide the reason for the nature and collegial value of the decisions of the episcopal Conferences. So, what is their power of autonomous jurisdiction outside the Council? *Lumen Gentium* 22 simply states: 'This same collegiate power can be exercised together with the pope by the bishops living in all parts of the world, provided that the head of the college calls them to collegiate action, or at least approves of or freely accepts the united action of the scattered bishops, so that it is thereby made a collegiate act'. Isn't the habitualness of the exercise of collegial power of the Bishops' Conferences somewhat established? In a very general way, *Lumen Gentium* 23 adds: 'This variety of local churches with one common aspiration is splendid evidence of the catholicity of the undivided Church. In like manner the Episcopal bodies of today are in a position to render a manifold and fruitful assistance, so that this collegiate feeling may be put into practical application'. Thus is left to the work of the Bishops' Conferences the task of manifesting and realising concretely the collegiality of the Church, as if the operation itself had to describe the being.[226] In fact, there is an omission here:

---

[226] Paul VI, with the Letter *Apostolica sollicitudo* of 15 September 1965, established the Synod of Bishops as a permanent council of the bishops of the universal Church and in support of it, manifesting the episcopal collegiality taught by the Council. From 11–28 October 1969 the First Extraordinary General Assembly of the Synod of Bishops took place on the theme: *The Co-operation between the Holy See and the Episcopal Conferences.* The agenda focused on the study of ways to put into practice 1) the collegiality of the Bishops with the Pope and 2) the study of the Bishops' Conferences in their relationship with the Pope and with the individual bishops. In the fundamental preparatory Schema for the discussion, drafted according to the motions of the Bishops' Conferences (30 August 1969), the 'essentially pastoral proposition' of the Synod of Bishops was underlined, 'of great importance in truth for the life of the Church in today's world' (ESV no. 603). Furthermore, in its doctrinal introduction it distinguished 'different ways of collegial unity of the bishops with the Supreme Pastor of the Church': essentially a 'collegial sentiment' ('affectus collegialis') and a 'strictly collegial activity'. 'The exercise of this collegial sentiment appears much broader than the strictly collegial activity' (*Ibid.*, no. 599). Hence: 'The episcopal Conferences are the fruit of collegial sentiment and of the common care of each bishop beyond the confines of his own local Church … .' (*Ibid.*, n. 601). In the Report *Elapso oecumenico Concilio* (3 October 1969), the option was for a solution about the two subjects, Pope and College: 'Therefore it is false to infer from this teaching that the Roman Pontiff acts alone and that he himself carries out actions in an exclusive manner, such as the appeal of the bishops to collegial action, or the approval of their joint action; just as it is false to deduce that he acts separated or disassociated from the college of bishops, as if there could be a distinction between these two complementary and equal subjects of the supreme author-

> Nothing significant is said about the legal aspect as far as the competence of the Bishops' Conference is concerned, although just here more than at any other point of the conciliar texts it would have been able—and should have been—to make some statement about the way of realising the so-called collegial action of the episcopal college.[227]

6. *The Church of* Lumen Gentium*: a multi-layered teaching to be accepted correctly*

At Vatican II, the doctrine of collegiality—in a more visible manner—like that of the Church in general, far from being definitive or at least unanimously received, opened itself to many still unresolved questions, which makes the theological debate lively and calls on us to ascertain why fifty years after the Council the theologial renewal surrounding the mystery-Church, alongside laudable enrichments, still presents significant difficulties.[228] Above all it is about a change

---

ity of the Church' (*Ibid.*, no. 656. The Latin runs differently, however, in one very important aspect: '... veluti si distinctio inter haec duo subiecta auctoritatis supremae in Ecclesia mutua et adaequata esse posset'. The Latin puts the emphasis on the distinction, which is not mutual and adequate, and not on the two complementary and equal subjects). The 1985 Synod of Bishops also underlined the 'pastoral usefulness' of the Bishops' Conferences, linked to the 'current situation', cf. *Ibid.*, nn. 2744, 2748.

227 Walf, 'Lacune e ambiguità', p. 196.

228 A first analysis of the problem was made fifteen years after the Council, with a Conference in Bologna in 1980 on the *Ecclesiology of Vatican II: dynamisms and perspectives*. About forty international experts spoke about the situation. There were differing judgements. See (*Cristianesimo nella storia* 2/1 [1981]). The conclusion of the meeting was entrusted to J. M. R. Tillard (*Vatican II and the post-conciliar period: hopes and fears*, pp. 311–324) according to whom Vatican II did not want to substitute Vatican I but re-read it in the light of episcopal collegiality. For Tillard, the problem concerns 'the status of infallibility linked to some conciliar declarations which, considered in the dynamism of ecclesial life, are re-read by another motion of the same type and having the same authority. The obstacle encountered by legislators of the new institu-

of ecclesiological perspective, more missionary and open to the world compared to the previous one, summarised in the first schema. The move to a broader vision, however, did not meet with an easy and univocal reception. The analysis of J. Ratzinger, testimony to this shift and ecclesiological progress generated by the Council, not without new problems opening up, is very objective, starting from his reflection on the second session of the Council. In it can be seen the improvements, the bias given to the text, and also its limitations. For Ratzinger, the ecclesiology which the first schema preserved, referring to the *tria vincula* and so to the question of members of the Church, therefore relegating the position of non-Catholics with regard to their integration into the Church to a 'debatable notion of *votum ecclesiae*',[229] was insufficient. He made the following objection to this

tional norms is constituted, in my opinion, more by what I have just described than the ambiguity of the texts of Vatican II or by the obscure desire to sweeten their impact. But the problem must also be examined from another point of view: the re-examination of the notion of *plena potestas*. Each *munus* needs the power which allows it to be fulfilled. However, the power is proportional to the *munus*, and not the other way round' (*Ibid.*, pp. 319–320). This would enable Tillard to understand the *munus* of the bishop of Rome in the light of the *munus* of the episcopal college, so as to no longer be a totalising power and not even the source of the power of the college, by reason of the recognition of the sacramentality of the episcopate (cf. *Ibid.*). Therefore, in his opinion, the problem of the reception of this teaching is fundamentally based on friction between pope and college, rooted and resolved in the line of the primacy of jurisdiction of the Pontiff, returning in some way to Vatican I. However, in my opinion, this highlights the lack of precision, which could lend itself to misunderstanding, with which terms such as *potestas* and *munus* are used in Vatican II and the shelving of the classic distinction between *potestas ordinis* and *potestas iurisdictionis*. In fact precisely the *potestas iurisdictionis* seems to have something missing compared to an elevated theology of Orders. This has a strong impact in the governance of the Church in the framework of the particular Churches.

229 J. Ratzinger, *Mon Concile Vatican II. Enjeux et perspective* (Perpignan: Artège Spiritualité, 2011), p. 121. See the complete original text in Id., *Zur Lehre des Zweiten Vatikanischen Konzils*, I (Gesammelte Schriften 7/1), cit., pp. 394–

magisterial position: 'Everything here is considered starting from a purely individualistic point of view', in other words, Christians see their relationship to the Church to be equal to that of non-Christians, to whom was also attributed a secret *voto* of belonging to the Church. The reconstruction of the text on the Church and its various modifications took into account the motions of the Protestant observers, to whom their churches now seemed to be split into so many separate pieces, and therefore felt unappreciated. With the move to the new schema it was strongly affirmed that these Christians did not exist solely as *isolated individuals* but as *Christian communities,* whose positive Christian significance and ecclesial character was recognised.[230] Ratzinger confronted the non-Catholic observers' criticism of the Roman Curia's preparatory schema, which above all reproached the consideration of other Christians as individuals. At the same time he highlighted a methodological problem about the text on the Church. It was definitely important to pay attention, in the text on the Church, to ecumenism. The new schema on the Church without doubt presented the advantages, but since it left in ecclesiological-ecumenical discourse 'an area of uncertainty of this sort that it is solely by the addition of the text on ecumenism that it reflects current thought',[231] there was also posed the problem of an open but incomplete vision. Allowing for this completion with another text, the schema on the Church recognised by itself, therefore,

> Its incompleteness and its need for completion. In simple terms, by the juxtaposition of the two texts where the second develops what is not indicated in the first, the Council shows that this first text—the doctrinal text on the Church—is an open text and not at all exhaustive. It seems to me that this

---

396 (report on the schema on the Church with ecumenism), pp. 396–398 (limitations of the schema on the Church), pp. 398–402 (outline of the problem).

230 Cf. Ratzinger, *Mon Concile Vatican II,* pp. 123–124.

231 *Ibid.,* p. 124.

> point of view was not taken sufficiently into consideration. The doctrinal text of the Council on the Church is not a theological treatise, nor a complete presentation on the Church, but a signpost… It seems to me there is a risk of profoundly failing to appreciate the value of a conciliar text if we force ourselves at all costs to find therein the totality of the questions treated theologically in detail.[232]

Therefore Ratzinger called for recognition of the limit the schema on the Church put on the ecumenical problem itself, having to obtain from another text those principles only outlined in the text, and which only in their unity provide an open and systematic ecclesiological framework. In some way, the limit and problem derived from the position of the Protestant observers and at the same time from the more adequate response which the Church wanted to give to the ecumenical problem. *Unitatis redintegratio* (cf. 1, Introduction) became, in a certain sense, the fulfilment (limit) of *Lumen Gentium,* having to read the former alongside and in the light of the latter, with reference to ecumenical endeavour. In my opinion, from this arises also the problem of the different magisterial level of the two documents with a different nature: one a dogmatic constitution compared to a decree.

Ratzinger then arrived at the heart of the ecumenical problem, confirming the position of one of the most representative experts of the ecumenical proposal at the time of the Council, Professor E. Schlink, lecturer at the University of Heidelberg. On 23 October 1963, Schlink, at a news conference in Rome, explained his perception of the state of the ecumenical problem in the documents of the Second Vatican Council.[233] Schlink started from the idea that the 'Roman Church' (instead of Roman Catholic) wanted to identify itself in an exclusive way with the one, holy, Catholic and apostolic

232 *Ibid.*, pp. 124–125.

233 For the text of the interview on *De oecumenismo,* Ratzinger refers to J. C. Hampe, *Ende der Gegenreformation?* (Stuttgart-Berlin: Kreuz Verlag, 1964), pp. 393–396. For a dossier about all the statements of the most important Protestants in reference to the Council, see *Una Lauda* 19 (1964), pp. 185–189.

Church. If the Church grants non-Catholic Christians some bond with the Church, it does so in reference to the Roman Church. Instead for Schlink it was appropriate to state that these non-Catholic Christians, by grace and with a view to salvation, are *membra* of their Church and not instead of the Roman Church. So, what then would be the significance of ecumenism for the Roman Church if not a continuation of the Counter-Reformation by other methods and a much more accommodating fashion? Thus, in opposition to Roman ecumenism, as denounced by him, Schlink set up another model which did not forsee the absorption of the separated brethren into an existing Church but considered a communion of separated Churches. Ratzinger acknowledged that Schlink's starting point was just: the Roman Catholic Church does identify itself with the Church of Christ.[234] In his opinion what could then be stated about the theses of the Protestant professor was as follows: 1) the Catholic Church could never accept Schlink's theses, developed starting from the principle that the existence of all the Churches was justified in itself; 2) however, despite the Catholic Church considering herself as the Church of Christ, it also recognised her historic deficiencies, and that the plurality of the Churches, which as such should exist in the Catholic Church, *de facto* find themselves to exist outside the Catholic Church, and that, perhaps, can only exist outside her.[235]

From this Ratzinger reaches the tendency of the Council. Vatican II, faced with the historical situation which characterises Christianity today, recognises the existence of the Churches in the plural, even outside the one Church: the Church acknowledges that the name of Church can be predicated, under precise conditions, even of non-Catholic Christian communities (cf. *Lumen Gentium* 15: 'Churches or ecclesiastical communities', in which there is allusion to both Protestants and Orthodox, who have kept 'the episcopate, celebrate the Holy Eucharist and cultivate devotion toward the Virgin Mother of God').

---

[234] Cf. J. Ratzinger, *Mon Concile Vatican II*, cit., p. 128.

[235] Cf. *Ibid.*, pp. 131–132.

These Christian communities outside the Catholic Church are certainly not the Church but of the Churches.[236] In this way the Constitution on the Church opened itself to a new ecumenical idea, thus rediscovering principally the local or particular Church, but at the same time there also emerged new questions about the incorporation of Christians into the one Church: what is the difference between the Orthodox and the Protestants as regards their not full incorporation into the one Church, or, as *Unitatis redintegratio* 3 states, 'even though this communion is imperfect' with the Church? ('in quadam cum Ecclesia catholica communione, etsi non perfecta, constituuntur'). It is clear that for the Decree on Ecumenism that all Christians, who already in some way (at least through Baptism) are part of the People of God, must be 'fully incorporated' into the Church led by Peter.[237] But leaving the ecumenical discourse to the endeavour to restore unity and appealing to working on the *elementa Ecclesiae,* by means of which outside the visible confines of the Catholic Church there was not a vacuum and by means of which the Churches or Christian communities are not deprived of value and significance (cf. *Unitatis redintegratio* 3), is there not also the risk in some way that the dogmatic fact of salvation *only* in the Church might be obscured? And in return the need to be fully incorporated into it, in other words the need to become Catholics for a true ecumenism aimed at re-establishing the unity of Christians in the one Church? It seems there endures a sort of friction between invisible and visible Church. The discourse about the *tria vincula* of belonging to the Church—bonds of 'professionis fidei, sacramentorum et ecclesiastici regiminis ac communionis' (*Lumen Gentium* 14)—recalled by *Lumen Gentium* for Catholics, are presented in *Unitatis redintegratio* in a more generic way:

[236] Cf. *Ibid.,* p. 132.

[237] 'Uni nempe Collegio apostolico cui Petrus praeest credimus Dominum commisisse omnia bona Foederis Novi, ad constituendum unum Christi corpus in terris, cui plene incorporentur oportet omnes, qui ad populum Dei iam aliquo modo pertinent' (*Unitatis redintegratio* 3). The *credimus* in this case reiterates a given from the Church's Tradition.

> Jesus Christ, then, willed that the apostles and their successors—the bishops with Peter's successor at their head—should preach the Gospel faithfully, administer the sacraments, and rule the Church in love. It is thus, under the action of the Holy Spirit, that Christ wills His people to increase, and He perfects His people's fellowship in unity: in their confessing the one faith, celebrating divine worship in common, and keeping the fraternal harmony of the family of God (*Unitatis redintegratio* 2).

Here, however, to underline the cogency of ecumenism, there is emphasis on the initial incorporation into Christ of the separated brethren through Baptism (cf. *Unitatis redintegratio* 3), who are rightly recognised as brothers and sisters in the Lord by Catholics. Baptism, therefore, as the Decree on Ecumenism recalls, stating more clearly the three bonds of membership of the Church,

> Is only a beginning, an inauguration wholly directed toward the fullness of life in Christ. Baptism, therefore, envisages a complete profession of faith, complete incorporation in the system of salvation such as Christ willed it to be, and finally complete ingrafting in eucharistic communion (*Unitatis redintegratio* 22).

'Baptism therefore establishes a sacramental bond of unity' (*Ibid.*), but does not exhaust the unity itself of Christians in the one Church of Christ, and this by reason of the not full or even only initial incorporation of non-Catholics into the Church of Christ. From the comparison between the Constitution on the Church and the Decree on Ecumenism can be seen on the one hand the opening of the concept of Churches or ecclesial communities—communities because they lack the sacrament of Orders and therefore the genuine and substantial Eucharistic presence (cf. *Ibid.*)—and this is so fundamentally due to Baptism, and on the other hand the unclear status of membership of the Church for the ecclesial communities, which distance themselves from the local Churches due to an even more deficient incorporation compared to the one Church. In other words, we can ask ourselves: are the particular Churches not in (full) communion with the Catholic

Church incorporated into the Church of Christ? And are the ecclesial communities also incorporated (like the local Churches? differently from them?) into the Church of Christ? Of course the real distinction between Church of Christ and Catholic Church is not right for affirming an initial incorporation of the two ecclesiological manifestations outside the Catholic Church into the Church of Christ, in view then of incorporation into the Catholic Church. If that was the case the one Church would multiply, assuming the provision of *Lumen Gentium* 8 as a division between Catholic Church and Church of Christ. *Subsistit in* is to be read—as we have already seen—along the lines of the substantial identity of the Church of Christ with the Catholic Church and the formal distinction between the two to ascertain the presence of ecclesial elements outside the visible whole, too. The point is the different incorporation into the Church of the separated Churches and Protestant communities. For the latter, Baptism is inserted into Christ but not into the Church, rather into the respective Protestant communities. On the other hand, for the particular Churches separated from the Church, Baptism and the other sacraments, particularly Eucharist and Orders, giving them the ecclesiological status of Churches, constitute the faithful in them as reborn through Baptism in a communion although imperfect with the one Church, while meaning that 'their existence as particular Churches is wounded',[238] by reason of their non-communion with the Roman Pontiff. In fact, the document *Communionis notio* (1992) would state 'the ministry of the Successor of Peter as something *interior* to each particular Church is a necessary expression of that fundamental *mutual interiority* between universal Church and particular Church'.[239]

The problem which Vatican II wanted to overcome with respect to a more closed ecclesiological vision remains as regards the absence

238 Congregation for the Doctrine of the Faith, *Letter to the Bishops of the Catholic Church on some aspects of the Church understood as Communion*, 28 May 1992, n. 17, in AAS 85 (1993) 849.

239 *Ibid.*, n. 13, in AAS 85 (1993) 846.

of a precise distinction of the concept of incorporation into the Church (linked to the fact of the *tria vincula*), between those for whom it is on-going and therefore in a full or perfect way and those for whom it is on-going but only potentially or in other words gradually, and therefore in an imperfect way and not full. There also remains a certain ecclesiological indistinction between Churches and communities, while a valid contribution is given to an ecclesiological reconsideration of the Churches and communities of the baptised outside the visible confines of the Catholic Church, who certainly do not constitute an ecclesial vacuum (*Unitatis redintegratio* 3 and 4).

In the final analysis there is the problem of the correct relationship between the universal Church and the particular Churches, between the universal Church and the ecclesial communities. The Declaration from the Congregation for the Doctrine of the Faith, *Mysterium Ecclesiae* (1973), focused the problem, and responded initially to a hermeneutical pitfall which was developing about the correct co-relation between Church and Churches or ecclesial communities, indicating the ecumenical endeavour as reunification of Christians in the one Church, which was not to be confused. In one passage it stated:

> The followers of Christ are therefore not permitted to imagine that Christ's Church is nothing more than a collection (divided, but still possessing a certain unity) of Churches and ecclesial communities. Nor are they free to hold that Christ's Church nowhere really exists today and that it is to be considered only as an end which all Churches and ecclesial communities must strive to reach.[240]

240 Congregation for the Doctrine of the Faith, Declaration *Mysterium Ecclesiae* in defence of the Catholic doctrine on the Church against certain errors of the present day, 24 June 1973, in AAS 65 (1973) 398. Already, Cardinal Ottaviani's 1966 letter to all the Presidents of the Bishops' Conferences about some errors concerning the interpretation of the conciliar decrees, underlined the liberty with which some erroneous conclusions about the mystery of the Church and the desire for unity with the separated brethren were being deferred from *Unitatis redintegratio*. N. 10 of the emerging errors denounced

With the Declaration *Dominus Iesus* (2000) came a more precise picture of ecclesiological incorporation.[241] The Churches which have kept the Eucharist and apostolic succession are true particular Churches and therefore at work in them is the Church of Christ, even if full communion with the Catholic Church is missing, due to the fact that they do not accept the Catholic doctrine of the Primacy.[242] From this it would seem that the Orthodox faithful are incorporated into the Church of Christ by reason of their being a true particular Church, while not yet being in full communion with the Catholic Church. *Dominus Iesus* says that the 'Church of Christ is present and operative also in these Churches'.[243] It is also necessary to be carfeful absolutising the insertion into the Church of Christ so as not to once again create a fracture between the visible and invisible Church. So, it would be better to say that such faithful are members (de facto) of their particular Church, and in imperfect communion with the one and holy Church. Are they then *in voto* members of the Church by reason of their membership to the mystical Body of Christ? The salvific reason of the particular Churches is nevertheless and always drawn from the universal Church,[244] unique salvific mediation in Christ. Therefore being true

this fact: 'In addition, it is necessary to comment about ecumenism. The Apostolic See praises, undoubtedly, those who promote initiatives, in the spirit of the conciliar Decree on Ecumenism, that foster charity toward our separated brothers and to draw them to unity in the Church. However, it is regrettable that some interpret the conciliar Decree in their own terms, proposing an ecumenical action that offends the truth about the unity of the faith and of the Church, fostering a pernicious irenicism [the error of creating a false unity among different Churches] and an indifferentism entirely alien to the mind of the Council', in AAS (1966) 661.

241 A reading of incorporation into the Church in the light of recent Magisterium has been done, with the claim to solve the associated problems, by P. Goyret, *L'unzione nello Spirito. Il Battesimo e la Cresima* (Vatican City: LEV, 2004), pp. 57–61.

242 Cf. *Dominus Iesus*, n. 17, in AAS 92 (2000) 758.

243 *Ibid.*

244 Cf. *Ibid.*, n. 16, in AAS 92 (2000) 757: 'Quocirca, in conexione cum unicitate

particular Churches and being truly inserted into the Church of Christ (invisible aspect), does not mean being incorporated to all effects into the one Church. The imperfect communion with the Catholic Church demands the effort of the Church itself so that the faithful not in communion with the Catholic Church become *membra* of it. On the other hand, the ecclesiological status of the ecclesial communities is different. *Dominis Iesus,* taking up the teaching of *Unitatis redintegratio,* recalls that 'those who are baptized in these communities are, by Baptism, incorporated in Christ and thus are in a certain communion, albeit imperfect, with the Church'.[245] They are inserted into Christ and therefore in an initial communion with the Church, which urges to become full and perfect communion by reason of Baptism which, per se, is tension towards 'the integral profession of faith, the Eucharist, and full communion in the Church'.[246] What is largely lacking here is full or perfect insertion into the Church of Christ. That happens fully in their own ecclesial communities and imperfect communion with the Church is enjoyable, as well as by reason of Baptism and faith (not the whole) and also through other ecclesial elements, such as the Word of God, the presence of the Holy Spirit with its grace, etc. The ecumenical endeavour is greater and must be aimed above all at making these Communities Churches and therefore building up full communion with and in the one Church of Christ.

While the ecclesiological-ecumenical panorama has fortunately expanded with the conciliar vision, there remains however the

---

et universalitate mediationis salvificae Iesu Christi, tamquam veritas fidei catholicae *firmiter credenda est* unicitas Ecclesiae ab ipso conditae'.

245 *Ibid.*, n. 17, in AAS 92 (2000) 758–759. Philips, on the other hand, in this regard believed that 'whoever has received valid baptism in a dissident community, becomes a member of the Church; but the fact of belonging to a "separate" denomination stops the person from exercising his fundamental quality as member of the Catholic [Church]', Philips, *La Chiesa e il suo mistero,* p. 180.

246 *Dominus Iesus,* n. 17, in AAS 92 (2000) 759. Here it refers back to *Unitatis redintegratio* 22.

problem of a clearer definition of incorporation into the Church. Being visible Church cannot be simply absorbed into the invisible, with the risk of favouring a sort of anonymous belonging, privileged by being in imperfect communion with the Church. A 'not full' (contrary to the 'Illi plene' of *Lumen Gentium* 14) or 'imperfect communion' (of *Unitatis redintegratio* 3) while not explaining precisely the ordinary condition of the Christian for salvation, at the same times does not exempt from the duty of bringing to everyone the one Church of Christ, or viceversa of bringing everyone to the one Church of Christ. *Lumen Gentium* leaves a lot of room for non-Catholics belonging to the Church (cf. n. 15), limiting itself to listing the reasons why the Church is linked to them. That has necessitated another document on ecumenism and then various other clarificatory magisterial documents have appeared in time. In my opinion, precisely all of that is a sign of an ecclesiological and ecumenical doctrine, set out by a Council but needful of development, clarification and in-depth examination, with the appropriate rebuttal of errors often found, precisely due to a very open vision, encouraging ecumenical endeavour at the pastoral level, but not always as clear and definitive at the dogmatic level. An absence of appropriate incontrovertible scholastic-metaphysical distinctions gives rise to interpretations completely abusive and contrary to dogma.

The emphasis on the ecclesial elements present outside the confines of the visible Church, if not always leading back to the clear placement in the one-Church, risks encouraging an ecumenical vision concentrated solely on a certain de facto unity rather than the truly ecumenical aim: to reach a full and visible unity, edifying the Church in all peoples, a Church made up of the unity and identity of the Church of Christ, the Catholic Church: this was really the desire of Vatican II, thus read in its entirety.

A more historical or pastoral vision of the division of the brethren runs the risk of stopping at the contingent historical fact and losing from sight that transcendence of the mystery-Church. The value of the open vision of *Lumen Gentium*, which provides a way of starting a careful reflection on the concept of local or particular Church, does not at the same time resolve the limitation that the same Constitution on the Church brings with it with regard to an exhaustive or definitive ecclesiological vision. It is not enough to recognise that *Lumen Gentium* moves to a vision of 'open Church', even against that 'closed' one of the preceding Magisterium and the old theology. The development is also problematic and demands a reflection which, emanating from the Church as conceived at the Council, opens even more to a full universality. That is due to a broader reflection emanating from the post-conciliar theological reception itself and from pastoral experiences in the parishes.

Encountered in *Lumen Gentium* are a variety of magisterial levels and numerous ecclesiological facts, which do not always presuppose or complement each other. For example, the so fundamental clarificatory distinction between *potestas* and *munus* occurs only in the *Nota praevia*. Who does not give to that *Nota* its correct hermeneutic importance as directed? After all, other facts per se necessary to the discourse are missing or are mentioned only in passing.

Now, we will try to ask ourselves a posteriori and with our eyes fixed on today: what does it mean to say that outside the Church there is no salvation? The theologies are conflicting. Above all preaching, which sometimes represents a great danger for misorientating the faithful. Has the shift from a Church 'ark of salvation', or to use the words of St Augustine 'huius arcae mysterium',[247] to a Church 'sacramentum totiusque humani generis unitatis' (*Lumen Gentium* 1; cf. *Lumen Gentium* 9),[248] perhaps signified setting aside the necessary salvific-sacramental incorporation into the one Church of Christ, the Catholic

[247] St Augustine, *De baptismo contra Donatistas*, V, 28.39: PL 43.196.

[248] In a footnote the text refers to St Cyprian, *Epis*. 69.6: PL 3.1142B; Hartel 3B, p. 754: 'Denique quam sit inseparabile unitatis sacramentum et quam sine spe sint et perditionem sibi maximam de indignatione Dei adquirant qui schisma faciunt et relicto episcopo alium sibi foris pseudoepiscopum constituunt, declarat in libris Regum scriptura divina'.

Church, to make room for a broader ecumenical vision, less rigidly rooted in what was handed down by the perennial Tradition of faith? In the immediate post-conciliar period the screeching between the *adagium* 'outside the Church there is no salvation' and the new teaching of *Lumen Gentium* was perceived, to the point of needing, according to the opinion of some, a drastic solution: simply to set aside the old phrase, despite the fact that Pius XII in *Humani generis* had already bitterly criticised some contemporary theological tendencies: 'Some', he said, 'reduce to a meaningless formula the necessity of belonging to the true Church in order to gain eternal salvation'.[249]

In this regard and about the 'strident discrepancy', G. Vodopivec commented:

> The Council did not aim to take or resolve the complex theological problems which the development of the interpretations of the *investigation* imagines, but, faithful to its pastoral aim, of uniting the living problems which today assail believers and the conscience of the Church, the very context of the Constitution indicates the fundamental formulation of the whole problem: the Church as People of God is open to all humanity. Therefore it first speaks of the Catholic faithful (n. 14), then of non-Catholic Christians (n. 15), of non-Christians (n. 16) and finally of the missionary character of the Church (n. 17). The guiding idea throughout is the Church as universal sacrament of salvation, the background is the *theology of communion*. From here new vistas open out onto problems old and new. If a definitive and comprehensive solution is not given, which perhaps humanly it is not even possible to reach, it proves to be an important theological renewal and re-thinking.[250]

---

[249] Pius XII, Encyclical Letter *Humani generis*, 12 August 1950: EE 6, no. 727. Prior to this he had also recalled: 'Some say they are not bound by the doctrine, explained in Our Encyclical Letter of a few years ago, and based on the Sources of Revelation, which teaches that the Mystical Body of Christ and the Roman Catholic Church are one and the same thing', *Ibid.* Cf. also Pius XII, Encyclical Letter *Mystici Corporis Christi*, 29 June 1943: AAS 35 (1943) 193ff.

[250] Vadopivec, 'Chiesa', coll. 780–781.

In fact, however, an increasing and rather pluralistic vision of salvation, led the Congregation for the Doctrine of the Faith to publish *Dominus Iesus*, whose ecclesiological emphases we have already seen, to reiterate the correct significance of that *extra Ecclesiam nulla salus* of St Cyprian memory: outside the universal salvific mediation of Christ and of the Church (by means of the Church, understood as means and obligation) there is no salvation, even if it can be verified outside its visible confines, with an at least implicit desire.[251] The mystery-Church transcends the confines of the geographic *hic et nunc* but always remains the identical Church of Christ. Isn't there to be read here the Church 'sacramentum universalis' only along the lines of the Church 'ark of salvation' for all peoples, for every person of goodwill? But in a renewed and broader fashion, dependent on the great missionary increase at the end of the nineteenth and subsequent century? There was missionary progress, a new flowering, to which one must look with dogmatic faith, from which to deduce the new pastoral efforts. The fact is that the missionary tension of the Church after Vatican II terrifyingly weakened. The strong ecumenical concern was able to divert attention from the recognised facts. Was there no need to deepen in a renewed manner the bond between Church and sacraments, since today it is precisely these which seem to experience in our parishes moments of massive desertion and superficial discovery only at times of family or community celebrations? Perhaps confusion or secularisation arises from the significant emphasis on the Word to the detriment of the sacraments?

---

[251] Cf. nn. 13–22, in AAS 92 (2000) 754–764. Cf. also the Letter from the Holy Office to the Archbishop of Boston, *De necessitate Ecclesiae ad salutem*, 8 August 1949: DH 3866–3873, responding to the salvific rigourism in taking literally *extra Ecclesiam nulla salus* by St Benedict's Center and Boston College. For a historical-patristic and magisterial *excursus* on this saying see Philips, *La Chiesa e il suo mistero*, pp. 169–175. I distance myself from Philips, however, when he, like Rahner, defines just non-Christians as 'anonymous Christians' (cf. *Ibid.*, p. 173). One becomes a Christian solely by means of the sacrament of Baptism.

However, it is essential to shed light on a prior element: how to read the new factor of the Church 'sacramentum'? Cardinal A. Dulles, commenting on the nature and structure of the Church, highlights that the idea of Church as sacrament in *Lumen Gentium* is 'of foundational importance', and signifies the great mystery of grace and salvation centered in Jesus Christ.[252] However, the perplexities of the American theologian J. Clifford Fenton at the Council, who attributed this expression to the Modernist G. Tyrrell,[253] and who was able to have an incorrect interpretation: the Church would institute the sacraments and could abolish them at its discretion, were not totally unfounded according to Dulles.[254] He wrote: 'the idea of Church as general sacrament did not imply her temporal priority over the individual sacraments. If it is true that the Church makes the sacraments, it is no less true that the sacraments make the Church. She does not have creative power over them'.[255] According to Witte, too, very careful attention had to be paid to the expression Church 'veluti sacramentum':

> In fact, such an expression presents at least an apparent ambiguity. Isn't the Church already the sacramental sign of the unity of the faithful and the Eucharist the 'sacrament of unity and peace'? ... If the term 'sacrament of unity' can equally indicate an inner reality of the Church, is it not at first sight paradoxical to want to make it the characteristic of the new perspective of the Constitution?[256]

[252] A. Dulles, 'Nature, Mission and Structure of the Church', in M. L. Lamb—M. Levering, *Vatican II: renewal within tradition* (Oxford: Oxford University Press, 2008), p. 26.

[253] See the controversy generated between Fenton and Semmelroth (who would then speak about the Church as *Ursakrament*) in G. Wassilowsky, *Universales Heilssakrament Kirche* (Innsbruck: Tyrolia, 2001), pp. 390–397.

[254] See *De ecclesia: Observationes D. Fenton circa usum verbi "Sacramentum" tamquam designationem Ecclesiae Catholicae,* Rome 18 November 1963, ff. 2, in ASV, Envelope 766, folder 296.

[255] Dulles, 'Nature, Mission and Structure of the Church', p. 27.

[256] J. L. Witte, 'La Chiesa "sacramentum unitatis" del cosmo e del genere umano', in Baraúna (ed.) *La Chiesa del Vaticano II*, p. 494. Witte notes that the term

The Church realises the salvation of every man and woman and therefore the unity of the whole of humanity *ex opere operato* through her sacraments. Salvation can come about also in an extraordinary manner, but it is analogous to the work of the sacraments—Baptism by desire can be such only if there is sacramental Baptism—according to the universal salvific will of God. Obviously to the Church as a whole is given a value analogic to the seven sacraments, which can only mediate and cause salvation. Among these par excellence is placed the Eucharist, true sacrament of unity (cf. *Lumen Gentium* 3 and 11). Only where there is Eucharist and therefore the sacramental priesthood is the (particular) Church, in other words the salvific presence of the mystical Body of Christ, of Christ himself, Head, who acts in his members and on their behalf. The real hermeutical endeavour would be that of holding always as identical the mystery of the Church—where *Lumen Gentium* is generic it is good to fill the gap referring expressly to the centuries-old reality of the Church—while considering the changed historical and social circumstances, which give rise to

'sacrament of unity' did not appear in the preparatory schema *De Ecclesia*; only in the chapter *De oecumenismo* was the Church considered as a sign of unity without, however, using the phrase 'sacramentum unitatis'. In *Lumen Gentium,* on the other hand, it constitutes one of the dominant motives enabling the emphasis to be put on the sacramental character of the Church and consequently to underline its strong aspiration to lead back to unity the world in which it is committed. According to Witte this paradox is one of the real features of the Catholic Church: its fullness of grace in Christ and its being everything to the world (cf. *Ibid.*, p. 495). So therefore we ask ourselves, why in a dogmatic constitution was there a desire to put such an emphasis, to the point of making it a sort of *Leitmotiv,* on the Church as 'sign and ... instrument of intimate union with God and of unity with the whole of humanity'? Perhaps right from the outset of the dogmatic discussion there was a concern to set the pastoral emphasis, or better still place it right from the dogmatic discussion? This represents a hermeneutical danger, because at the reference to humanity thus understood globally, a theological-dogmatic treatment of it does not follow, but only the raised emphasis on the Church as 'sign and instrument'. About the 'world', then, *Gaudium et Spes* would speak, here too with emphases of great optimism, which often lose from sight, however, its dual biblical valence.

numerous and new pastoral challenges. Among these *in primis* a new inspiration towards unity, as a demand and opportunity arising also from the new globalised society. To these only the Church as she is in herself can respond. Carrying unity within herself, without ever having lost it: it is one of her ontological features, by reason of which, in her sacraments, she becomes visible *sign* of unity for all people of goodwill, when they become the body of Christ, in the one faith and the one Baptism (cf. Ep. 4:4–5), in other words, in the sacraments themselves. There could never be a Church alongside the world, functionary of its unity. It is the world which must be saved by the Church. The new perspective vision of the conciliar Constitution on the Church—as besides attested to right from n. 1, in contintuity with all the other councils—must teach us that the mystery of 'Catholic' always comes before the facts and before every solution: it is rooted in the Most Holy Trinity, it reaches us in time in Christ the Word humanly and sacramentally present in the midst of his own to lead us back again to God, in the Lord's Trinitarian embrace. Thus it can be seen that first there is the *Traditio Ecclesiae* and then the understanding of the new fact of the Council. If, instead, the path of experience is favoured, then beyond the text and the conciliar event itself is placed the perception of the Church at a historical moment, which would allow the development of the doctrinal and pastoral fact of the Council in the light of church life itself, that 'concretized, deepened lived experience expressed in a language bestowed with meaning'.[257] Along the same lines is the ecclesiological reception of Vatican II as understood by G. Routhier in the wake of Y. Congar:[258] a living reception which grows in time according to the current experience of the Church. In that way when will the reception itself come to an end? So therefore it would seem the most opportune way to overcome the hermeneutical difficulties encountered from time to time.

[257] Routhier, 'La recezione dell'ecclesiologia conciliare', p.22.

[258] Y. Congar, 'Vie de l'Église et conscience de la catholicité', in *Esquisse du mystère de l'Église* (Paris: Cerf, 1953^{2}).

For others, instead, the very difficulties about the calm reception of the dogmatic text on the Church are symptomatic of a still incomplete work, which must be done above all analysing the oldest information about the Church in the light of the new of *Lumen Gentium*. For example, for H. J. Pottmeyer, since *Lumen Gentium* overcame the ecclesio-centric perspective of Vatican I, it is appropriate to read Vatican I in the light of Vatican II.[259] Only in this perspective can one have a true and new reception and a reconciled understanding of the category of communion as complex reality but suited to the mystery of the Church.[260]

In my opinion, however, the pre-conciliar teaching on the Church, far from being an impediment to a more open ecclesiological reflection, is instead a preparation and its necessary presupposition. Moreover, it cannot simply be overcome by the fact that the teaching of *De Ecclesia* at Vatican I is *defined*, therefore of the Catholic faith, while that of Vatican II is not, but *proposed* in an authoritiative and solemn manner. Therefore I believe that a truly Catholic ecclesiological vision must take into account what had already been recognised by faith and at the same time broaden its ecumenical horizons, explaining in a more accurate and metaphysical manner the different states of incorporation into the Church, the concept of apostolic college, of collegiality and that of 'quasi-sacrament' applied to the Church, so as to avoid arbitrary interpretations or incomplete receptions. All that however convinces me of the fact that

> Vatican II did not have the last word about the Church, it spoke the word which seemed appropriate for our time, unquestionably recovering the living tradition of the Church, and it wanted to underline, above all, its pilgrim dimension.[261]

---

[259] H. J. Pottmeyer, 'Continuità e innovazione nell'ecclesiologia del Vaticano II e la ricezione del Vaticano I alla luce del Vaticano II', in *Cristianesimo nella storia* 2 (1981), pp. 71–95.

[260] Cf. Calabrese, 'Chiesa come "popolo di Dio" o Chiesa "comunione"?', p. 96, who did his thesis on Pottmeyer.

[261] Canobbio, 'L'ecclesiologia successiva al Vaticano II', p. 54.

V

PASTORAL EPIPHANIES OF VATICAN II

IN THE INTENTIONS AND FORMATION OF THE CONCILIAR TEACHING ON THE BLESSED VIRGIN MARY

IN THE PHASE immediately prior to the Second Vatican Council, there was a great deal of attention focused on the Mother of the Lord. Mariology had a very well defined epistemological foundation. There was no seminary or theology faculty where scrupulous study about the Virgin Mary did not take place. Even in the ante-preparatory phase of the Council, when the bishops were charged with sending to Rome their suggestions about the themes to be discussed, a significant number mentioned the Mother of God. Suffice to recall that from the Italian bishops alone—as can be inferred from the research of S. Perrella—out of 311 *vota* sent to the ante-preparatory Commission, 205 observations and requests concerned the Madonna. Among these of further note is the fact that there were 16 *vota* about the co-redemption of Mary and 8 bishops asking for its dogmatic definition.[1]

Of no lesser interest is noted, again in Italian circles, the mediation of Mary linked to her dispensation of all graces. There were 100 *vota*

---

1 Cf. S. Perrella, *I "vota" e i "consilia" dei vescovi italiani sulla mariologia e sulla corredenzione nella fase antipreparatoria del Concilio Vaticano II* (Rome: Marianum, 1994). According to Perrella, the vote on the dogmatic definition of co-redemption was not welcomed for two reasons: 1) the pastoral nature of the Council, and 2) its ecumenical direction, cf. *Ibid.*, p. 206.

concerning the *mediatio universalis* or *mediatio omnium gratiarum*, of which 84 concerned its solemn dogmatic definition and the remaining 16 requested a clear and authoritative conciliar teaching on mediation.[2] To have an idea instead of the global *consilia et vota* which reached the Council concerning the Madonna, we can say, according to the research of A. Escudero Cabello, that there were 714 texts which concerned either Mariology or the debate on Marian mediation, also starting from other theological issues.[3]

As E. M. Toniolo reports, right from 'the first counting of the *vota* of the Bishops, classified according to the order proposed by the schema *De deposito fidei*, emerged the importance of a treatise on the Blessed Virgin Mary, primarily under the aspect of *universal mediation*'.[4] That would be entrusted to Fr Carlo Balić, who in the drafting of the first schema *De Beata*—a schema which would see eight editions due to the subsequent revisions until the presentation of the text at the Council—would say in the *De Ecclesia* Sub-commission (2 June 1961) that he had strove to make all the bishops happy in the light of their petitions: both those who asked for a *sermo magnus* on the Madonna, and those who opposed new definitions.[5]

---

2 Cf. *Ibid.*, pp. 172–208.

3 Cf. A. Escudero Cabello, *La cuestión de la mediación mariana en la preparación del Vaticano II. Elementos para una evaluación de los trabajos preconciliares* (Rome: LAS, 1997), p. 55.

4 E. M. Toniolo, *La Beata Maria Vergine nel Concilio Vaticano II*, Centro di Cultura Mariana 'Madre della Chiesa', Rome 2004, pp. 36–37. On the Marian theme inserted by the Theological Commission into the concise schema *De deposito fidei pure custodiendo*, as the last theme to be treated, only three members made any observations: V. Scherer, G. Philips and A. Michel. Philips' objection concerned the lack of any opportunity for a new definition of Marian co-redemption, until the theological dispute had not further developed. Then he asked, adding it by hand: 'Perhaps it was appropriate to treat the perpetual virginity of Mary?', cf. *Ibid.*, p. 35, footnote 24.

5 *Ibid.*, p. 62. See the dossier edited by Fr Balić on the Madonna, about the *consilia et vota*, the *proposita* and the *studia* sent by the bishops, by the Roman Congregations and theology Faculties in the ante-prepatatory phase of the

As we will see, the Council would abandon the idea of a dogmatic definition in the area of Marian soteriology, also carefully avoiding any implied terminology. Right from the ante-preparatory phase, from 28–29 October 1960 when the *De Ecclesia* Sub-commission met, the doctrinal themes were chosen which would then go to make up the drafting schema. On 30 November the Sub-commission established the general criteria for the drafting of the documents: a) to avoid systematic treatises, in order to see better the real needs of the Church; b) to omit what was not of undisputed ownership or considered not current; c) not to condemn personal errors, except in the case of danger for the faith; d) to refer to what had emerged in the preparatory consultations; e) to avoid repetitions and long-winded structures; f) to omit still disputed questions.[6]

At the Council a great dispute took shape, new under many aspects. While initially the at times passionate prevailing emphasis was on how to define, for example, co-redemption: immediate or mediated, direct or indirect, Mary co-operating with salvation with *de congruo* or *de condigno relative* merit, it now seemed that Mariology was entering into a more 'political' phase: at stake were not the high-flying distinctions of the dispute, in other words the way of perfecting a theological judgment, but whether it was appropriate or not to discuss the Madonna, whether to have a substantial and hefty discourse in its own right or to insert it, for more ecumenical and pastoral reasons, into the totality of the mystery of the Church. For some it was precisely the subtle Mariological issues which had engendered a crisis in Mariology, which applied to other areas of theology, too. Hence the so-called 'Marian question' was born.[7] The

Council. The typewritten dossier comprises 66 pages, and is kept at PAMI, in the *Archivio Balić*, year 1961.

6 Cf. G. M. Besutti, *Lo schema mariano al Concilio Vaticano II. Documentazione e note di cronaca* (Rome: Marianum, 1966), p. 19; Toniolo, *La Beata Maria Vergine*, p. 39.

7 During the conciliar work R. Laurentin published a book *Mary's Place in the Church* (London: Compass Books, 1965; French original, *La question mariale*

Council, while it was driven, according to Laurentin, to tackling *ex professo* the problem of the Mariological crisis with a 'serious effort ... to come to a better understanding', it was also 'the hour of frankness, becoming clearly conscious on the eve of commitments which will guide the Church perhaps for centuries'.[8] Mary Most Holy had become a problem of positioning in theology and of Mariology itself in the field of theological discourse as such. To the point that in the conciliar discussions, the Mariological question, like that about collegiality, became defined as a 'banner' question.[9] What would then become chapter VIII of the Dogmatic Constitution *Lumen Gentium*, 'The Blessed Virgin Mary, Mother of God, in the Mystery of Christ and the Church', according to G. Baraúna, 'has its history littered with ups and downs'.[10]

[Paris: Ed. du Seuil, 1963]), in which he was at pains to take stock of the situation: the crisis (or crest for others) which Mariology was experiencing, provoking the genesis of a 'Marian question', was not just of an ecumenical order, but even before that internal to Catholicism. On the eve of the Council, Mariology appeared separated from the body of faith and from the whole of revelation. Speculation over the subtle questions had in some way encouraged a loss of the vision of the Christological foundation. For example, Laurentin asks himself 'whether the attacks against the notion of the *debitum peccati*, irritating because reifying, have not gone so far that they compromise the fundamental dogmatic truth contained in the definition of the Immaculate Conception: that Mary was redeemed by Christ' (*Ibid.*, p. 24). The French Mariologist proposed finding a 'result' between the maximalist and minimalist Mariology to highlight ecumenism, too: to return to the sources and focus on the function of the already defined dogmas, placing them within the humble condition of Mary, rather than on the accentuation and multiplication of Marian privileges (cf. *Ibid.*, pp. 91–100). G. M. Roschini responded to Laurentin on the Mariological issues, in *La cosidetta "questione mariana"*. Risposta ai rilievi critici del Prof. R. Laurentin, di S. E. Mons. P. Rusch e del Prof. A. Mueller (Vicenza: Tip. S. Giuseppe, 1963). See also J. A. De Aldama, *De quaestione mariali in hodierna vita Ecclesiae* (Rome: PAMI, 1964).

8 R. Laurentin, *Mary's Place in the Church*.

9 Melloni, 'The Beginning of the Second Period', p. 95.

10 G. Baraúna, 'La SS. Vergine al servizio dell'economia della salvezza', in

1. The schema De Beata Maria Virgine

On 23 November 1962, in the XXV General Congregation, the schema on the Blessed Virgin Mary, entitled *De Beata Maria Virgine Matre Dei et Matre hominum*, was distributed to the Fathers along with the schema on the Church.[11] The difficulties concerning Marian

---

Baraúna (ed.) *La Chiesa del Vaticano II*, p. 1137. For a careful historical reconstruction of the discussion of the Mariological schema, besides the work of E. M. Toniolo, see particularly G. Besutti, 'Note di cronaca sul Concilio Vaticano II e lo schema "De Beata Maria Virgine"', in *Marianum* 26 (1964), pp. 1–42; Id., *Lo schema mariano al Concilio Vaticano II. Documentazione e note di cronaca*; C. Antonelli, *Il dibattito su Maria nel Concilio Vaticano II. Percorso redazionale sulla base di nuovi documenti di archivio* (Padua: Messaggero, 2009); the recent doctoral thesis of A. Greco, *"Madre dei viventi". La cooperazione salvifica di Maria nella "Lumen Gentium": una sfida per oggi* (Lugano: Eupress FTL, 2011 (1st part)).

11 As well as the eight subsequent drafts of this schema following the first text of Balić, it is appropriate to recall the starting points of this text. First of all the schema of the Holy Office, whose Mariological passage, drafted by Balić (21 February 1960), was inserted into the proposed dogmatic constitution *De Ecclesia*. The title was *De Maria, Matre Christi Capitis et Ecclesiae*. Inter alia, Balić noted Mary's real participation in the redemption of humanity: a subjective and objective co-operation. The schema also examined the universal mediation of Mary as regards the graces, both in the acquisition thereof and their distribution; it also focused on the perpetual virginity and bodily death of Mary. At the suggestion of the secretary of the Doctrinal Commission, Fr Sebastian Tromp, this schema was then moved as the last question to be treated in the proposed constitution *De deposito fidei pure custodiendo*. As a result of that the Marian presentation, according to Fr Tromp, had a second-rate value compared to other questions to be put to the Council. Finally, Fr Luigi Ciappi, a theologian in the Apostolic Palace, was entrusted with the task of developing in a series of points the schema *De depositio fidei*. The part concerning the Madonna was paragraph 5. Inter alia, Ciappi noted that Mary Most Holy was not to be placed on the margins but at the centre of Christianity. He then treated Mary Associate of Christ the Saviour, her universal Mediation, perpetual Virginity, the Marian veneration of hyperdulia, Mary cause of the unity of Church, and the spiritual priesthood of the Virgin. In a meeting with Fr Tromp, and at his suggestion, Ciappi cancelled in pen the

teaching, integral and open at the same time to ecumenical dialogue, had already been predicted, so much so that the preparatory Commission believed it appropriate to insert a section 'Praenotanda' as an introduction to the schema, where the intentions which had guided the preparation of the text on the Madonna were explained.[12] First of all it was noted that the preparatory Commission had received about 600 *voti*, asking for a treatise on the Blessed Virgin Mary ('sermo fiat').[13] It would have been a highly flawed act on the part of the Church if a Council did not speak also about the Madonna, especially in these times where there was a major conflict between the faithful and Satan.[14] In order to avoid theological controversies about the origin, the authority and the meaning of the sources used, the schema was careful to refer to the Magisterium of the Church, by which Scripture and the Fathers were to be interpreted. So in the schema: a) nothing was taught that had not been declared by the Magisterium; b) various errors about the Blessed Virgin Mary were rejected and erroneous opinions corrected. More precisely: b.1 that the virginity in childbirth was unambiguous, identical with the virginity before childbirth; b.2 that the Most Blessed Virgin at the time of the

themes regarding Marian veneration, Christian unity and Mary's spiritual priesthood. Finally, as I have already said, thanks to the Mariological denseness of the bishops' *consilia et vota*, it was decided to have a separate schema about Marian issues. So it was in the sixth draft of the preparatory schema, in the meeting of 2 March 1962, that Fr Balić heard from the Sub-commission that *De Beata* was autonomous from *De Ecclesia*. At the same meeting there was a lengthy discussion about whether the Madonna could be called *Mediatrix omnium gratiarum, solo titulo intercessionis*. The Secretary intervened in the debate saying that the doubts about the mediation of all graces could be resolved if it were true that Mary, as was stated in the final number of *Mystici Corporis*, offered to the Father on Golgotha the divine victim for the salvation of the whole of humanity. Cf. Toniolo, *La Beata Maria Vergine*, pp. 22–40, 75–77.

12 AS I/4, pp. 98–100.

13 AD I, II/1 pp. 131–142.

14 *Ibid.*, II/5, p. 103.

Annunciation was not aware that the Son whom she conceived was God; b.3 rejected were both the error of the maximalists, who spoke as if the Virgin acted in the redemption as Christ or said that Mary did not die, or was not redeemed, and that of the minimalists, who spoke as if Mary was at the same level as all the other members of the Church, like all the other children of Adam; c) in the arguments treated 'tota et integra doctrina catholica est proposita et exposita'.[15] Omitted, then, were those expressions and words which, even though used by Supreme Pontiffs, and very true in themselves, could be understood with difficulty by the separated brethren, in this case by the Protestants. Among these the following were to be listed: 'Corredemptrix humani generis' (St Pius X); 'Reparatrix totius orbis' (Leo XIII); 'materna in Filium iura pro hominum salute abdicavit' (Benedict XV; Pius XII); 'merito dici queat Ipsam cum Christo humanum genus redemisse' (Benedict XV). Furthermore, it was explained how the mediation of the Blessed Virgin did not undermine the mediation of Christ but exalted and honoured it. For the same reason Marian veneration in no way was to the detriment of the worship of Christ.

With these premises, the schema, concise and very dense in its system of notes—a real Mariological treatise in the footnotes—developed through six points.[16] First of all, the schema underlined in n. 1 the indissoluble union between Christ and the Virgin Mary: *De arcta necessitudine intra Christum et Mariam iuxta Dei beneplacitum*. Mary 'alma Parens, quae cooperata est caritate ut fideles in Ecclesia nascerentur',[17] not just in a super-eminent and complete (*prorsusque*) fashion,[18] is an individual member of the Church, rather is its very exemplar,[19] and what is more is also called Mother.

15 Instructio S. C. S. Officii, *De motu oecumenico:* AAS 42 (1950) 144.

16 Cf. AS I/4, pp. 92–97.

17 St Augustine, *De sancta virginitate*, VI, 6: PL 40, 399.

18 Here the text refers again to St Augustine who said: 'Maria portio est Ecclesiae, sanctum membrum, excellens membrum, supreminens membrum, sed tamen totius corporis membrum', *Sermo 25, De Verbis Evangelii Matthei XII*, 41–50, 7: PL 46, 938.

N. 2 studied the salvific *munus* of the Madonna in the work of salvation: *De munere beatissimae Virginis Mariae in oeconomia salutis.* The Virgin persevered in her consent given at the Annunciation, thus perfecting her collaboration in the work of redemption, from the time of the virginal conception of Christ until his death. She remained beneath the Cross not without divine counsel, suffering in an overwhelming manner with her Only-Begotten, offering Him with a heavy soul as the price of our redemption and this through and in Him.[20] Thus she was given to us by Christ as our mother (cf. Jn 19:26–27). Providence disposes that here on earth Mary was generous associate in the acquisition of grace for humanity, and was saluted by right and merit also as 'heavenly minister and dispenser of graces':

> Cum itaque beatissima Virgo ab aeterno praedestinata ut esset Dei hominumque mater, divina Providentia sic disponente hisce in terris Christi passibilis fuerit generosa socia in gratia pro hominibus acquirenda, caelestium quoque gratiarum administra et dispensatrix iure meritoque salutatur.[21]

Mary, who has a part in the mystical Body of Christ, assumed into heaven was constituted Queen and Our Lady, by means of the Son has obtained a certain primacy over all things ('quemdam primatus'):

---

19 Here the reference is to St Ambrose, with the same text that would be taken up by *Lumen Gentium* 64: Mary 'bene desponsata, sed virgo quia est Ecclesiae typos', *In Lucam,* II, 7: PL 15, 1555 (1635–1636).

20 In a foootenote it is explained that Mary, renouncing her rights in the offering of the maternal sacrifice of the Son, became our spiritual mother. The compassion had strong links with redemption, since Mary rightly can be called our *Co-Redemptrix*: 'Summi Pontifices loquendo de Maria sub cruce dicunt quod Maria exercebat actus fidei, spei et caritatis, ita unita amore doloribus Christi ut sit connexio inter compassionem Mariae et redemptionem; ipsa renuntiat iuribus maternis et offert sacrificium maternum, fitque nostra mater spiritualis. Pauci verbis: compassio Mariae connexionem habet cum redemptione, talique modo ut ipsa inde merito dici possit *corredemptrix,* et per modum unius recensentur fructus redemptionis Christi et compassionis Mariae', AS I/4, footnote 11, p. 104.

21 AS I/4, p. 93.

therefore not as some believe 'in peripheria[22] sed in ipsomet "centro" Ecclesiae sub Christo collocari'.[23]

N. 3 explained the titles of the association of Mary *cum Christo: De titulis quibus conosciatio Beatae Virginis Mariae cum Christo in oeconomia nostrae salutis exprimi solet.* Mary, as the new Eve, in fulfilling with the Son the work of redemption, is called by different titles, coming from venerable Tradition and from the full sense of the faithful.[24] Not

---

22 In the footnote it is explained that this marginal tendency of Mariology is to be subscribed to minimalism, which takes the name of 'ecclesiological path', or 'ecclesio-typical', while Pius XII provided the correct relationship between Mary and the members of the Church: 'De tendentia "minimalistica" inter ipsos quosdam catholicos viros sparsa, qui potissimum sic dictam viam "ecclesiologicam" tenant, cf. e.g. Pinsk J., *Grundsätzliche und praktische Erwägungen zur christlichen Verkündigung im Marianischen Jahr,* Berlin 1954; Geiselmann J. R., 'Marien-Mythos und Marien-Glaube', in *Maria in Glaube und Frömmigkeit,* 1954, pp. 39–91. Pius XII, *Nuntius Radiophonicus Lis qui interfuerunt conventui internationali mariologico-marino,* Romae habitat, 24 oct. 1954: AAS (1954) 679: "Etsi verum est Beatissimam Virginem quoque, uti nos, Ecclesiae esse membrum, tamen non minus verum est eam esse Corporis Christi Mystici membrum PLANE SINGULARE"', *Ibid.,* footnote 15, p. 107.

23 AS I/4, p. 93.

24 Footnote 16 is a rich summary of the Marian titles, starting from the principle of the recirculation of the apostolic Fathers, and therefore of the role of Mary as new Eve. After the Fathers, the Marian titles experienced a fertile increase thanks to theologians and Popes. Among the most important are: *Mater spiritualis hominem, Regina caeli et terrae, Nova Heva, Mediatrix, Dispensatrix omnium gratiarum, Corredemptrix.* Already from the fourteenth century the title *Redemptrix* could be found. Then when in the 15th and 16th centuries this title became unusual, however with the Church already having placidly acknowledged the teaching of the immediate co-operation of Mary in our redemption, to the word 'Redemptrix' was added the particle 'co-', so that Mary was called Co-redemptrix, while Christ was the Redeemer. From the seventeenth century this title was very common not only in pious books but also in various theological treatises (cf. J. Carol, *De corredemptione Beatae Virginis Mariae,* Rome 1950, p. 482). Then there is the use of the word by the Popes and more generally the doctrine of the immediate co-operation of Mary in the papal Magisterium, from Pius VII to Pius XII, who preferred the title

without merit she is called 'Virgo gratiarum Mediatrix'.[25] If Saint Paul prayed continually here on earth, without ceasing, for his children born in faith, how much more must we trust in the prayers and the intercession of the Blessed Virgin Mary, our mother. Among the mediators subordinate to the work of redemption, one cannot think of one greater than the Mother of God. Being Handmaid of the Lord, she is called Mediatrix of all graces, for the acquisition of which she was associated to Christ, so much so as to be called our advocate and mother of mercy. Now, while remaining glorious associate of Christ in heaven, she intercedes for us all, so that in all the graces conferred on humanity the maternal charity of Mary is present, in no way obscured or lessened by the unique mediation of Christ. Mary's mediation does not stem from any other need but from divine approval and the super-abundance of the merits of Christ. As regards the manner of mediation, the texts states:

> Quoniam etiam nunc Christi gloriosi in coelis socia manens, pro omnibus per Christum intercedit, ita ut in omnibus gratiis hominibus conferendis adsit materna caritas B. Virginis.[26]

Socia to *Corredemptrix*, cf. *Ibid.*, pp. 107–108.

25 *Ibid.*, p. 94. Footnote 17 reports that more than 500 Fathers from all the continents had called for a solemn definition of a social *munus* of the Virgin Mary, particularly her universal mediation of the graces. After having explained with De Aldama (*Sacrae Teologicae Summa*, III, Matriti 1956, p. 149) that the mediation of all the graces is a truth *de fide ex magisterio ordinario*, all the testimonies of the Popes, from Pius XI up to Pius XII, are reported, cf. *Ibid.*, pp. 108–109.

26 *Ibid.*, p. 94. Here the text deliberately tones down the problem of maternal causality in the distribution of all the graces by speaking in very general tones, with St Augustine, that the mediation of Mary is fruit of her maternal charity. In fact, in the footnote it is said that 'Dum non est difficultas admittendi Mariam esse mediatricem omnium gratiarum quatenus associata fuit Christo in illis acquirendis (utique abstractione facta a quaestione an *immediate* vel *mediate, directe* vel *indirecte*, in *actu primo active* recipiendo vel alio modo ...), variae quaestiones surgunt si gressum faciamus ad Mediatricem quatenus *distribuit* gratias, idque potissimum quoad earum *universalitatem*. Quod Maria potest nobis omnes gratias impetrare, clarum est. Quod autem *nulla gratia datur nisi interveniat* Maria, alia est res: venit enim quaestio de interventu

N. 4 examined *De singularibus privilegiis Dei hominumque Matris.* It was stated that, with the most ancient and doctrinal tradition, the Madonna experienced temporal death, as fully assimiliated to the Son in the mystery of the Redemption,[27] after which she was assumed body and soul into heaven. She was incorrupt in bringing her Son to light and remained pure afterwards.

N. 5 dealt with veneration of Mary in a very succinct manner: *De culto erga beatissimam Virginem Mariam,* and finally n. 6 was a strong ecumenical appeal: *Maria Sanctissima Fautrix unitatis christianae.* Mary who on Calvary bore all men and women in her maternal heart, ardently desires that everyone, not just those who have been reborn in Baptism and are led by the Spirit, but also those who do not know Christ, be united in faith and charity to the divine Saviour. The Synod said that it was certain that Mary, who interceded at Cana on behalf of the spouses so that her Son might perform the first miracle (cf. Jn 2:3–11), was also now able to implore from God for the reunification of everyone into one flock under one shepherd (cf. Jn 10:16).

2. *The written observations to the Marian schema*

The schema on the Blessed Virgin Mary was not discussed in the Council hall in the general sessions which took place at the start of

---

directo et *indirecto, de Veteri Testamento* et de gratiis quae conferuntur in Sacramentis' (*Ibid.*, no. 21), p. 111). With the mediation of all the graces confirmed, all the other issues were still freely debated among theologians.

27 The schema arranged among the oldest testimonies in the West of the death of Mary the Gregorian Sacramentary, which Adrian I sent to Charlemagne between the years 784–790. In the prayer of the day for the Assumption it was expressly stated that Mary experienced temporal death. Only in recent years, a footnote in the Schema said, had the view about the translation of Mary into heaven without death become disseminated, *abiisse et non obiisse.* It then quoted Cardinal Ottaviani (in *Acta Pontificiae Academiae Marianae Internationalis,* I, Romae 1961, p. 63), who confirmed the *mens* of Pius XII was rather inclined towards the temporal death of Mary, for a theological rather than merely historical motive, cf. *Ibid.*, footnote 26, pp. 112–113.

December 1962. However, in the discussion on the ecclesiological schema, seven Fathers had made reference to the Marian question and had proposed uniting the schema on the Madonna into that on the Church. The Fathers from Central-Eastern Africa concurred with this view, as did the German-speaking Fathers, the Scandinavians, and the western French Fathers. At the end of the First Session of the Council, the Fathers were informed that all those who wished could present observations on the Marian schema up to the last day of February the next year. About 85 Fathers did so, 42 in person, others collectively.[28]

The real problem was that of whether or not to insert the schema on the Madonna into that on the Church. A problem, however, which recalled another more acute one which had already, in some way, divided the opinion of theologians about Mary: the relationship between the Christo-typical and the ecclesio-typical vision of Mariology. A relationship which, in turn, was also understood as the balance between minimalist and maximalist Mariologists: the former, as we have already seen from the preparatory schema, were ecclesio-typical, while the latter were Christo-typical.

I have already mentioned that in the debate on the Church there emerged on the part of some Fathers the desire to re-appraise Mariology and Marian devotion, and thus favour the ecumenical problem in the Council.

The Chilean Cardinal, Silva Henriquez, one of the supporters and co-ordinators of the alternative *De Ecclesia* schema, along with others (Garrone,[29] Elchinger,[30] Mendez Arceo),[31] 'took the occasion (of this general debate on the Church) to plead that the schema on the Virgin Mary be incorporated into the Constitution on the Church, a proposal that was aimed at reducing the danger of anti-ecumenical manipulation use of Mariology'.[32]

---

28 Cf. AS II/3, p. 300.

29 AS II/1, pp. 366–368.

30 *Ibid.*, pp. 378–380.

31 *Ibid.*, pp. 385–387.

It was a real 'battle'. Many were saying that ecumenical success or otherwise depended on the Council's Mariological position. Fr Balić raised some doubts about Congar's Catholic honesty.[33] Rahner in turn reported to Vorgrimler:

> A Ukrainian bishop distributed pamphlets in front of the Aula; the Spaniards distributed printed leaflets everywhere; Roschini produced a brochure; people were talking of a battle for and against the Madonna; Balić distributed a lengthy booklet printed by the Vatican Press in the form of a schema.[34]

What happened? Like the other schema, the Mariological schema presented a problem of the general positioning of the Council and only afterwards, as a consequence, a more doctrinal problem in reference to the pastoral and ecumenical aim of the Assembly. The written observations were produced by the Fathers from 1 June—24 September 1963. Meanwhile the title of the Marian schema had been changed by the Council's Co-ordinating Commission: from *De Beata Maria Virgine Matre Dei et Matre hominum* it had become *De beata Maria Virgine, Mater Ecclesiae*. This new title, too, the first effort aimed at underlining the ecclesiological component of Mariology, would find many in disagreement, even while keeping the treatment of the subject separate.[35]

---

32 Melloni, 'The Beginning of the Second Period', p. 45.

33 D. Aračić, *La dottrina mariologica negli scritti di Carlo Balić* (Rome: PAMI, 1980), pp. 106–119.

34 Vorgrimler, *Understanding Karl Rahner*, pp. 177–178.

35 See also the Commissio de Doctrina Fidei et Morum, *Il Relatio Secretarii circa observationes factas ad Schema Constitutionis de B. M. Virgine* (1 Iunii-15 Sempt. 1963), ASV, Envelope 765, folder 294, in KT 2/2, pp. 754–762. The question of the theological qualification of the doctrine was presented again. The Fathers from Central-Eastern Africa and Eastern Africa asked for a clear qualification of the Mariological teaching. The German-speaking and Scandinavian bishops also asked for a theological qualification, in other words that at the start it should be stated that it was teaching the common doctrine of the Church but not a new dogma ('ut in initio dicatur doceri doctrinam

Illustrative of all the stances was that of a bishop, who in the month of December 1962, asked that the Blessed Virgin be treated in a separate document, that the mediation of all graces by Mary be defined, and that the feast of the Mediatrix of all graces be inserted into the Church's official calendar. February the following year he literally changed his ideas: he wanted Marian teaching to be inserted into the schema on the Church, that the Mariological issues raised remain under discussion, that it be stated clearly that Mary is not in place as an intermediary between God and humanity and that therefore the words *Mediatrix* and *corredemptrix* be expunged.[36] Instead, among those who approved the schema, only two did not appreciate the Blessed Virgin being invoked as Mediatrix of all graces.[37]

Noteworthy above all among the opponents of the Marian schema were the bishops of Western France, who accused the schema of legalism, rationalism, Latinism and Westernism. They wanted a more biblical and pastoral schema: the schema prepared by Balić did not respond to the problems of the day, neither of the Catholic world nor ecumenism. It was necessary to read a sort of perichoresis between the Church and Mary: Mary is in the Church (because she is the eminent member) and the Church in Mary (because it is the cause and root).[38] In his report on the Marian schema *De. B.M.V. Matre Ecclesiae*, R. Laurentin considered it, even with a new title, a simple re-printing of the previous one.[39] The French Mariologist, cautioning against making a constitution on Our Lady a major point of discussion between Mariological schools of thought, perhaps choosing the most influential—hence his criticism of the phrase on which depended the

Ecclesiae commune, non autem fieri novum dogma'), especially in reference to the mediation of Mary, cf. KT 2/2, p. 755.

36 Cf. AS II/3, p. 301.

37 Cf. *Ibid.*, p. 302.

38 Cf. *Ibid.*, pp. 302, 835–836.

39 Cf. R. Laurentin, *De Beata Maria Virgine Matre Ecclesiae. Note sur le Schéma Marial de Mai 1963* (4 numbered pages in the handwriting of Florit with letters from A to D), in AEF, Folder 5, Schema "De Ecclesia".

whole direction of the schema: the predestination of Mary *uno eodemque decreto,* dating back to Carlo del Moral, founder of the doctrine of the merit *de condigno,* 'the key point to be discussed'[40] —instead invited the Council and theologians to return to the common sources, finding a communion in the tendencies and in a fundamental teaching, so as to present to the separated Christians a plan inclined to facilitate the discovery of the Holy Virgin.[41]

To these fundamental objections others added more accidental things: superfluous repetitions, very complicated ways of speaking and a widespread apologetic tendency.[42]

2.1 A strong ecumenical concern

However, the greatest difficulty 'derived from ecumenical concern'.[43] The insertion of the discourse about Mary into that on the Church, was able to 'avoid more easily those Marian thorny questions unrewarding for the separated brethren'.[44] Some Fathers wanted the Mother of God to be presented as the first redeemed, mother of believers and example. The Japanese bishops, on other hand, pro-

---

40 *Ibid.*, f. A.

41 'The fundamental question which the revision of the Marian schema poses is therefore the following: is the object to provide support to the theses of the most engaged Mariological Schools, or to promote essential and unquestionable leanings which would lead to so many divergent Schools, so many theories, to go back to the common sources, communion without direction and a fundamental doctrine, finally to present to the separated Christians a plan inclined to facilitate their discovery of the Virgin?', *Ibid.*, f. D.

42 Cf. AS II/3, p. 302.

43 *Ibid.*

44 *Ibid*, p. 303: '... quod tali modo procedendi facilius evitari possint quaedam queastiones mariales spinosae et separatis ingratae'. E. Schillebeeckx in his cited report of 30 November 1962 on the Marian schema united with the ecclesiological one advised introducing the discourse on Mary as the last chapter of *De ecclesia* which examined the eschatological nature of the Church, so as to present Mary as an eschatological figure of the Church and in a way as not to have a separate schema. Cf. KT 2/2, pp. 1078–1079.

posed Mary as a type or figure of the Chuch, also because, as another Father said, it was a traditional and ecumenical title.[45] Of the 85 Fathers who had sent their written observations only a few were in favour of the *votum* expressed by 280 bishops to define the dogma of the universal mediation of Mary, while about 500 bishops and prelates were substantially in favour of the fact of Mary's universal mediation.[46]

The heaviest criticisms about the scant ecumenical inspiration of the Marian text came from Cardinal Bea and the German-speaking Fathers, in union with the Scandinavians. According to Bea, the schema did not respond to the aims of the Council. It was necessary to set out in substance the Church's Marian teaching starting out from Sacred Scripture and from the most ancient tradition. For example, the Councils which had spoken most about the Madonna, Ephesus and Trent, had done it in a very indirect and oblique manner. One should not start from the teaching of the last century but from Scripture and ancient tradition. It was not enough to omit the expressions which could be misunderstood: instead, it was right and proper to bear in mind the reasons of the separated brethren, both the Easterners, and, even more, the Protestants, as much as was possible. If the teaching of the Supreme Pontiffs of the last hundred years was set out the impression was given that Marian teaching was a certain novelty, without roots in the Bible nor the ancient traditions.[47] So the real problem was to establish what were the 'ancient traditions' and how they could be recognised discarding the recent Magisterium of the Church. Bea had a fairly personal idea of the Magisterium: the recent Magisterium, of the last Pontiffs, in his opinion, *today* was no longer living. Only the traditions of the first

---

45 Cf. AS II/3, p. 303.

46 For a careful classification of the research about this see Greco, *"Madre dei viventi"*, pp. 31–39.

47 Cf. AS II/3, p. 677: '...oportet potius *rationem habere eorum mentis*, in quantum possibile est' (Bea's italics).

centuries were living.[48] Pius XII had defined this vision another face of 'archaeologism'.

For the German-speaking Fathers, who were in very close contact with the Protestants, weren't the things said in the schema perhaps a source of obstacles to ecumenical unity? Why was there now a desire to teach what Pius XII had deliberately avoided? The risk of failure lay in the fact, according to the Protestant Bishop Dibelius, that the major obstacle to unity was represented precisely by the Catholic Church's Mariology.[49]

For his part, the Antiochene Patriarch Meouchi proposed removing n. 6 entirely from the schema, about *Mary Most Holy advocate of Christian unity*, or re-writing it.The conclusion of the schema should refer to Christ the one Redeemer and Mediator: which would give Mariology an effective sign of ecumenical consideration.[50]

---

48 In his particular observations about the schema, he would comment about page 7, line 24, as follows: 'Quid sunt "superiora documenta"? item quid intelligitur "Magisterium vivum Ecclesiae"? Auctores videntur potissimum cogitare de "supremo magisterio Ecclesiae" et quidem potissimum Summorum Pontificum inde a Leone XIII (cf. pag. 14, V, 1). Iamvero dicendum videtur Magisterium omnium horum Pontificum *hodie* iam non esse "vivum". Agitur ergo de documentis recentioribus *traditionis*. Si ita est, non intelligitur cur maxime his documentis insisti debeat et non *toti* traditioni atque maximae antiquae. Utique haec documenta, quia sunt supremi magisterii, maiorem auctoritatem habent; sed ipsa quoque in traditione antiqua fundantur et ad hanc traditionem appellant. Unde fortasse dicedum esset: documentis traditionis, speciatim supremi magisterii Ecclesiae, interpretum depositi revelatum', *Ibid.*, p. 679.

49 It was the sermon for the anniversary of the day of the Reformation in 1962, in a similar way to the *Deutsches Pfarrerblatt*, 15 January 1963, cf. *Ibid.*, p. 840.

50 Cf. *Ibid.*, p. 754. Meouchi did not even share the idea of the co-redemption of Mary. In his opinion, the Virgin did not offer the 'pretium redemptionis'. He said: 'Would the Virgin's offering be a true sacrifice? Would this offering by the Virgin be for her part a free adherence to the oblation of Christ which can only be called true sacrifice? Is it a new acceptance of the Redemption of Christ by which the Virgin herself was redeemed? All this alludes to "co-redemption". But this teaching is still obscure, not yet mature. There is no need to make it

The new Chilean Mariological schema, in fact, focussed on a greater use of Scripture and on the trinomial Mary-Church-Christ, also derived from a heightened ecumenical concern. There were 9 chapters set out as follows: 1. Maria Mater Iesu et mater Ecclesiae; 2. Maria Virgo, typus Ecclesiae; 3. Maria in Ecclesia et Ecclesia in Maria; 4. Mariae Virginis maternitas fecunda; 5. Nova Eva subiecta novo Adamo; 6. Virgo assumpta, imago Ecclesiae consummatae; 7. Mariae actuosa maternitas; 8. Cultus erga Mariam Matrem; 9. Maria, mater unitatis christianae. According to the Chilean bishops, the theme of co-redemption and mediation should not be put at the centre. Mary, they said, at the foot of the Cross was united with all her heart to the sacrifice of her Son; in faith Mary was said to be a type of the Church.[51]

One of the important reasons which König highlighted in his address for the insertion of the schema on the Madonna into the ecclesiological schema was the predominant ecumenical motive: an ecclesio-typical Mariology would have made possible the encounter both with the Eastern and the Protestant traditions.

Later, on 25 October 1963, it would instead be some Eastern bishops who would take up a postion in favour of a Mariological schema separated precisely for ecumenical reasons.

2.2 The real theological problem: the mediation of Mary

'The major ecumenical concern came to light when the question of mediation and co-redemption was touched upon ... '.[52] Precisely on this issue the disagreement between the Fathers persisted.[53] In the

a matter for Council discussion. Rather, it is necessary to withdraw it from our discussion and leave open the exchange between theologians', *Ibid.*, p. 753.

51 Cf. *Ibid.*, pp. 304–305, 824–829 (825).

52 'Maxime autem praeoccupatio oecumenical in lucem prodit, quando tangitur quaestio mediationis et corredemptionis ... ', *Ibid.*, p. 303.

53 For an introduction to the issue see M. Hauke, 'Maria als mütterliche Mittlerin in Christus. Ein systematischer Durchblick', in *Sedes Sapientiae. Mariologisches Jahrbuch* 2 (2008), pp. 13–53 (Italian translation, *La mediazione materna di Maria in Cristo: una riflessione sistematica,* in AA.VV., *Maria Corredentrice.*

close examination of the observations in their entirety, a fact stood out: it was necessary to distinguish the *title* from the *teaching*. As regards the title, *Mediatrix of all graces*, only a few seriously rejected it. These included those who said to ascribe it solely to Christ, for others it was better to talk of Mary as 'advocate' rather than Mediatrix; there were those who said such a title needed careful explanation or it would be better to omit it. The German Fathers, as we will see in more detail, did not reject the title *Mediatrix* in itself but its long version, *Mediatrix of all graces*, because, in their opinion, it was not co-extensive with *all graces*, such as, for example, sacramental grace: Mary could not be described as Mediatrix of sacramental grace. As regards instead the teaching, according to the opinion of some, it was not stated in a satisfactory manner. Others stated: if 500 Fathers had asked for a solemn definition of the title, it was essential to speak about such things in an affirmative and not defensive manner. A few then said that the schema exaggerated by default, two that the teaching of co-redemption and mediation had been introduced in a veiled and covert manner. There were those opposed to the request of the 500 Fathers, due to the danger of the teaching of mediation, opting for a petition, *de facienda definitione*, of 600 bishops, with the aim of proving there were a greater number of bishops who did not want it. The bishops of Central-Eastern Africa asked solely that the mediation of the Virgin be more clearly explained.[54]

The main opposition to the mediation of Mary came from the German-speaking Fathers, along with the Scandinavian Fathers. They met in Fulda in August 1963 with the aim of discussing and organising work for the Second Session of the Council. The action and above all

Storia e teologia, vol. XIII, [Frigento: Casa Mariana Editrice, 2011], 71–130); Id., *La mediazione materna di Maria secondo Papa Giovanni Paolo II*, in AA.VV., *Maria Corredentrice. Storia e teologia*, vol. VII, (Frigento: Casa Mariana Editrice, 2005), pp. 35–91; A. M. Apollonio, 'Maria mediatrice di tutte le grazie. La natura dell'influsso della Beata Vergine Maria nell'applicazione della Redenzione', in *Immaculata Mediatrix*, 7 (2007), pp. 157–181.

54 Cf. AS II/3, pp. 309–310.

the theological opposition to the presented schemata, including the Mariological schema, had to be planned. Of particular note in the Fulda meeting was the theological work of K. Rahner.[55] In the archive of Cardinal Florit, Archbishop of Florence and member of the Theological Commission, I rediscovered the papers from the theological report of the Fathers gathered in Fulda: the report of the German-speaking Fathers and that of the Scandinavian Bishops' Conference, with attached the personal report of Bishop H. Volk. Both were published among the observations of the Fathers to the Marian schema.[56] What is interesting is an indication in the original papers which states as follows after the letterhead: '(quas Secretariatui Generali Oecumenici Vaticani II transmittandas decreverunt Patres iidem in Conferentia Fuldensi diebus 26 et 27 Augusti 1963)'.[57]

The observations on the schema were therefore drawn up in the Fulda meeting on the days indicated above and then transmitted to Rome. The first observation was focussed on the way of setting out Mariological teaching. From a passage in the original schema, which said: 'clarum verbum ex quo patet, quid reapse Ecclesia catholica qua talis de munere, privilegiis et cultu mariali *credit*, tenet docetque', it could be inferred that the Council wanted to proceed to some dogmatic definition. There was a major conciliar discrepancy—between the aim and the documents—as had already been seen in the schema *De fontibus*.[58] This difficulty, along with a contradiction, appeared in the schema with regard to the teaching about mediation

---

55 Cf. De Mattei, *Il Concilio Vaticano II*, pp. 303–305, 320–322. Rahner's influence here is documented by Wiltgen.

56 Cf. AS II/3, pp. 837–853.

57 The *Propositiones circa schema De Beate Maria Virgine Matre Ecclesiae a Patribus Conciliaribus linguae germanicae et Conferentiae Episcoporum Scandinaviae exarartae*, amounting to 22 pages (here is page 1), to which seven are added as *Appendix*, contains the report of Volk, in AEF, Folder 5, Schema "De Ecclesia". Both were published in full in the AS, where there is no reference, however, to the venue and dates I reported above.

58 Cf. AS II/3, p. 837.

and co-redemption. These two truths were taught: the first through explicit words, the second only as regards the substance, avoiding the term *co-redemption*. But neither of the truths was a dogma of the Church, so they could not be analysed among those which the Church believed without any shadow of doubt, and what's more the *meaning* of the mediation and co-redemption of Mary did not sit clearly with the other taught truths, nor was a clear delineation of it offered.[59]

In addition it was necessary to consider very carefully the words of a professor from the Gregorian University, Roberto Lieber, about the magisterial choice of Pius XII: for the Angelic Shepherd, as stated a few days before his death and at the end of the Marian Congress in Lourdes, the truths of the mediation and co-redemption were still unclear and not greatly developed, to the point that he had deliberately avoided them. According to Leiber, Pius XII had no intention of changing this attitude.[60]

---

59 'Haec difficultas et apparens saltem contradictio in schemate (declarat sese non velle condere nova dogmata, sed ea profferre, quae *ab Ecclesia creduntur*) maxime apparet in doctrina de mediatione et corredemptione Beatae Virginis. Haec explicite docentur, primum explicitis verbis, alterum saltem quoad rem, etsi verbum corredemptionis ipsum evitetur. Attamen haec duo *non* sunt dogmata Ecclesiae; non debent nec possunt recenseri inter ea, quae Ecclesia hodie iam incunctanter *credit*, preaesertim cum de *sensu* mediationis et corredemptionis B. M. V. non clare inter omnes constet, nec certa et clara delineatio huius sensu exhibeatur in schemate ipso', (*Ibid*, pp. 837–838). Here one sees that while raising objections to the teaching, the correct meaning of the uninterrupted *traditio* about the truth of mediation and co-remption is ignored. If the Popes of the last hundred years and more had reiterated it constantly, it was a sign that it now belonged to the deposit of the truths *de fide* (believed and definitive even if not defined). The one strong point here lay in 'what the Church today already believes without hesitation'. Translated into theological terms, that adverb 'incunctanter' says very little and in many ways is superfluous: it is not about what the Church believes 'without doubt', but what the Church believes: either because it is an already-defined truth or because it is in any case definitive. The Council should not have set aside the censures and the levels of the theological affirmations of the teachings.

60 'Was die Fragen der "Mediatrix" und "Corredemptrix" anghet, hat Pius XII

According to the German-speaking Fathers, the schema fell foul of another danger. Fr Balić wrote that the Virgin 'con-acquisisse gratias cum Christo, obtulisse Deo victimam ut est pretium nostrae Redemptionis'.[61] If this is true, it is also claimed that in the Virgin the last principle of merit (indeed grace) is similar to the immediate object of merit itself, which is false, something not understood by the simple faithful, rejected by many theologians, and a contradiction for the Protestants.[62] Here the real painful point was the association of Mary to Christ in the acquisition of redeeming grace, which for the German and Scandinavian Fathers should be rejected.[63] Bea, too, manifested some fear in this regard, even though his reasoning was the other way round.[64] So, the Fathers gathered in Fulda were asking

---

noch wenige Wochen vor seinem Tod in den Tagen gleich nach Beendigung des Mariologischen Kongresses in Lourdes geäussert, die beiden Fragen sein zu ungeklärt und zu unreif, er habe in seinem ganzen Pontifikat bewusst und absichtlich vermieden, Stellung zu ihnen zu nehmen, sie vielmehr der freien theologischen Auseinandersetzung überlassen. Er danke nich daran, diese Haltung zu ändern' (*Stimmen der Zeit* 163 [1958–59], p. 86), in *Ibid.*, p. 839.

61 AS II/3, p. 840: 'Similiter schema ipsum: 8, 24s et 9, 32: "socia in *gratia* pro hominibus *acquirenda*", quae assertio multum excedit formulam 8, 7s.: "operam consociari in humani generis redemptione peragenda"'.

62 *Ibid.*

63 In the amendments to the schema, on p. 8, lines 24–25, they suggested: 'Scribatur: "generosa socia in opera redemptionis", non vero: "in gratia pro hominibus acquirenda". Insinuari in hoc textu videtur Maria ipsas has gratias suo merito acquisivisse. Iamvero its non tantum doceri videtur "corredemptio", quae doctrina ultra sensum generalem non tangi debet a Concilio, sed alia incommode accedunt. Gratia enim complete spectant nullius meriti aut meritoriae acquisitionis a parte purae creaturae opus est. Id valet etiam de B. Maria Virgine. Insuper a fortiori non potest illlas gratias sibi acquirere, quae sibi propriae sunt, quaeque nullius praecedentibus meritis ex pura benevolentia Dei ei donari debent, ut mereri omnino posset' (*Ibid.*, p. 845). As can be seen, the concept of active co-operation in redemption is completely missing.

64 'Etiam haec de gratia per Beatam Virginem acquisita saltem aliquot argumento probari deberent; item ex eo quod B. V. M. in terra fuit Christi "passibilis" socia, non sequitur immediate, quo denim nunc est "gratiarum administra et

not so much for the avoidance of the term 'Co-Redemptrix' but the avoidance of all that which, in reference to the doctrine of the mediation and co-redemption, was not generally acknowledged in a satisfactory manner. What's more, to the Council Fathers—as was specified—from Austria, Germany, Sweden and Scandinavia, the term *Mediatrix* or the derivation *mediation* presented no problems, it could even be retained, rather than the title *Mediatrix omnium gratiarum*, due to the fact that it would have suggested the idea that the Madonna was also the Mediatrix of the grace of the sacraments *ex opere operato*: a question to be omitted due to the different meanings of the term 'grace', not highlighting in such a way its personal character, but leading to a complicated conception of the heavenly mediation of Mary, almost as if the Virgin became in some way minister of grace.[65] Finally, one other element. The Fathers gathered in Fulda asked that the aside about the minimalists (as we have seen, in note 15 of the schema some German authors, Pinsk and Geiselmann, were quoted) be removed from the schema: they should not be libelled, just as the names of the maximalists were not cited.[66]

The observations of the above-mentioned Fathers were also accompanied by an appendix, which included the notes of the Bishop of Mainz, H. Volk. His first reservation was about the title itself of the schema: 'Maria Mater Ecclesiae' was not correct because 'mother' signified a certain separation between Mary and the Church, not implying that Mary is its example or figure. What's more, 'mother' also indicated the presence of a 'father', completely unusual in applying a paternity to the Church. Volk suggested the title 'Maria Matris fidelium'. He, too, was opposed to the title 'Mary, Mediatrix of all graces', and for the following reasons:

dispensatrix"', *Ibid.*, p. 679.

65 *Ibid.*, p. 841.

66 *Ibid.*, p. 846. The bishops of Central-East Africa, too, said there was no need to mention these two extremes, maximalist and minimalist, in a doctrinal schema. Other bishops also had somethings to say about this, cf. in summary *Ibid.*, p. 309.

1. the notion 'Mediatrix' was obscure. The schema ended up uniting two different species: Mary's imploring prayer and her participation, administration and dispensation of grace. It was possible to understand the prayerful intercession, but the other element seemed difficult;
2. in fact the expression 'administra e dispensatrix' of all grace was not believed by the faithful, and the very notion of 'grace' was not sufficient to explain the mystery;
3. the teaching pertinent to the mediation of all graces by Mary belonged to the teaching of the mediation of the Church, because Mary is a figure and exemplar of the Church. Mary, in an excellent and specific manner, participates in the mediation of the Church, of which she is also a most excellent member. So there was no need to oppose Mary to the Church, because the Virgin is a figure of it: 'since Mary belongs intimately to the Church, the teaching of the mediation of the Church and of Mary complement each other and an in-depth examination is necessary',[67] Mary was therefore to be counted among the people of God and described as a member of the Church, so that her pre-eminence compared to other members of the people of God stems from it.[68]

However, on the contrary there were those who asked that the link between Mary and the Church should be more clearly stated, that the truths about Mary's mediation and co-redemption should be set out with more clarity. It was a serious matter that Reparatrix and Co-redemptrix, terms used by the Popes, should be omitted: it was the primary duty of the Council to speak to those who were in the Church. The Protestants and those who had a false concept of redemption were unable to understand the role of associate applied to the Virgin. The Catholic use now sanctioned by the term *Co-Redemptrix* was able to explain why the Madonna is Mediatrix of all graces. The Protestants were not expecting diffidence and limitations, but the measure [of

67 'Quia Maria penitus ad Ecclesiam pertinent, doctrinam mediationis Ecclesiae et Mariae vicissim inter se supplere at augere necesse est', *Ibid.*, p. 851.

68 Cf. *Ibid.*, p. 852.

the Church's teaching].[69] Noteworthy among those who did not accept the restriction of the teaching for ecumenical ends was Blessed Giacomo Alberione. He said: 'If we want the Blessed Virgin Mary to truly be the Mother of the Church, we must solemnly proclaim her Mediatrix of all graces'.[70]

It can be seen, he continued, that the major objection to such a definition derives from the fear of misunderstanding by the separated brethren. This objection, if it really exists, is not new. What the Council must do is rather set out the truth of the *Blessed Virgin Mary Mother of the Church* in a perfectly logical manner, without fear of reaching the ultimate logical conclusion, that is to say, arriving at the definition of the universal mediation of the Virgin as regards grace. Such a definition would certainly be more acceptable to the separated brethren than the dogma of the Immaculate Conception or Mary's bodily Assumption.[71] So we can say that the Saints are always more forward-looking. With their intuition and their theology they overcome fear and closure, which are often only human.

2.3 Theologians and the co-redemption of Mary

The most debated question in Mariological circles was certainly that of the co-redemption of Mary, as a pressing backdrop to mediation. Normally these two dimensions of Marian soteriology go together.[72]

---

69 Cf. *ibid.*, p. 304.

70 *Ibid.*, p. 684.

71 Cf. *Ibid.*

72 It is interesting to note that in the stance of the Belgian episcopate led by Cardinal Mercier, about the petition for the dogmatic definition of 'Mary Mediatrix of all graces', the backdrop of the Marian mediation of graces is always co-redemption, as active and immediate participation by Mary in the work of Redemption, which was then an obstacle in the Holy Office for a dogmatic definition. On this see M. Hauke, 'Riscoperta: la petizione del Cardinal Mercier e dei Vescovi belgi a Papa Benedetto XV per la definizione dogmatica della mediazione universale delle grazie da parte di Maria (1915)', in AA.VV., *Maria Corredentrice. Storia e teologia*, vol. XIII (Frigento 2011), pp. 183–244 (with an Italian translation of the petition; Id., 'Riscoperta: la

The debate among theologians took on new vigour, especially in 1904, when the fiftieth anniversary of the definition of the dogma of the Immaculate Conception was being celebrated. One of the greatest Italian Mariologists, G. M. Roschini, in the 1950s highlighted the difficulties about having an unambiguous theological judgment due to different nuances, for example about the merit of Mary, and principally the three ways of relating to it, while failing, however, to understand the reason for the rejection of the title 'Co-redemptrix': the adopted reasons did not stand up. The title had also appeared in papal Magisterium.[73]

Mary truly contributed with Jesus, in an active and personal manner, in our salvation. Her *fiat* at the Annunciation (cf. Lk 1:38) and the *stabat* at Calvary (cf. Jn 19:25) were the two solemn moments of her offertorial association with the Redeemer. She alone, with the unique title of mother, associate, companion, spouse, intervenes in making herself salvific object of the work of Christ her Son. Consequently, Mary has truly *offered* the Son as sacrifice; *with* and *in* the Son she has offered herself to the Father, 'as a living sacrifice, pleasing

---

petizione del Cardinal Mercier e dei Vescovi belgi a Papa Benedetto XV per la definizione dogmatica della Mediazione universale delle grazie da parte di Maria (1915). Introduzione teologica e testo originale francese', in *Immaculata Mediatrix* 3 (2010), pp. 305–338; See also Id., 'Maria, "Mediatrice di tutte le Grazie" nell'Archivio Segreto Vaticano del Pontificato di Pio XI. Rapporto intermedio sulle tracce trovate', in *Immaculata Mediatrix* 7 (2007), pp. 118–129 (German original, 'Maria, "Mittlerin aller Gnaden", im Vatikanischen Geheimarchiv aus der Zeit Pius' XI.—Zwischenbericht einer Spurensicherung', in *Theologisches* 36 (2006), pp. 381–392); Id., *Maria, "mediatrice di tutte le grazie". La mediazione universale di Maria nelle iniziative teologiche e pastorali del Cardinale Mercier* (1851–1926) (Collana di Mariologia 6) (Lugano: Eupress FTL, 2005) (German original, *Maria, "Mittlerin aller Gnaden". Die universale Gnadenmittlerschaft Mariens im theologischen und seelsorglichen Schaffen von Kardinal Mercier* [Mariologische Studien 17], Regensburg 2004).

[73] Cf. G. M. Roschini, *La Madonna secondo la fede e la teologia*, vol. II, (Rome: F. Ferrari, 1953), p. 14.

to God' (cf. Rm 12:1). Therefore, with good reason, the Virgin has become the deposit of the grace of salvation and the dispenser of grace, of all those graces which the faithful beseech from Her.

The active co-operation of Mary in the work of salvation was acknowledged almost unanimously by theologians, and three paths or ways of understanding it could be distinguished:

a. *immediate* or *proximate* co-redemption: a direct and personal participation on the part of Mary in objective redemption, with an active maternal role in the acquisition with Christ of salvific merit. Mary, through generosity, or through justice relative however to the mercy of Christ, has truly helped the Redeemer. Of note among the theologians supporting this thesis were A. M. Lépicier,[74] E. Campana,[75] D. Bertetto,[76] and G. M. Roschini.[77] More recently, M. Hauke,[78] Stefano M. Manelli,[79] A. Apollonio,[80] P. D. Fehlner,[81] and B. Gherardini.[82]

---

[74] A. Lépicier, *L'Immacolata Madre di Dio Corredentrice del genere umano* (Frascati: Stabilmento Tipografico Tuscolano, 1905), pp. 15–16.

[75] E. Campana, *Maria nel dogma cattolico* (Turin: Marietti, 1945), pp. 170–177.

[76] D. Bertetto, *Maria nel dogma cattolico* (Turin: SEI, 1950), pp. 392–450.

[77] Roschini, *La Madonna*, pp. 311–406.

[78] M. Hauke, 'Maria compagna del Redentore. La cooperazione di Maria alla salvezza come pista di ricerca', in *Rivista teologica di Lugano* 7 (2002), pp. 47–70; Id., 'La cooperazione attiva di Maria alla Redenzione. Prospettiva storica (patristica, medievale, moderna, contemporanea)', in Telesphore Cardinale Toppo et al. (ed.), *Maria, unica cooperatrice alla Redenzione.* Atti del Simposio sul Mistero della Cooredenzione Mariana, Fatima, Portugal, 3–7 May 2005, New Bedford, MA 2005, 171–219 and in *Immaculata Mediatrix* 2 (2006), pp. 157–189; Id., 'La mediazione materna di Maria in Cristo: una riflessione sistematica', in AA.VV., *Maria Corredentrice. Storia e teologia,* XIII (Frigento 2011), 71–130.

[79] S. M. Manelli, 'Maria Corredentrice. Nuovi saggi di soteriologia mariana', in *Divinitas* 44 (2001), pp. 73–90; Id., 'Maria Corredentrice nel pensiero del beato Giacomo Alberione', in *Immaculata Mediatrix* 2 (2003), pp. 189–207; Id., 'Il mistero di Maria corredentrice negli scritti di Madre Costanza Zauli', in *Immaculata Mediatrix* 3 (2003), pp. 361–378; Id., 'Maria a titolo unico è corredentrice', in AA.VV., *Maria Corredentrice. Storia e teologia,* vol. V

Some monographic series contribute to deepening teaching along this line;[83]

b. *mediated* or *remote* co-redemption: only an indirect participation on the part of Mary in redemption, through her *fiat* at the Annunciation, by which she co-operates, even if only remotely, in the salvation of humanity realised by Christ alone. Here the emphasis is on the sufficiency of Christ as unique and absolute redeemer. The theologians of note here were W. Goossens[84] and H. Lennerz;[85]

(Frigento: Casa Mariana Editrice, 2002), pp. 7–31.

80 A. Apollonio, 'I "punti fermi" della Cooperazione mariana', in AA.VV., *Maria Corredentrice. Storia e teologia*, vol. I (Frigento: Casa Mariana Editrice, 1998), pp. 17–35; Id., 'The Holy Spirit and Mary Coredemptrix', in AA.VV., *Mary at the foot of the Cross.* Acts of the International Symposium on Marian Coredemption, Academy of the Immaculate, New Bedford 2001, pp. 61–91; Id., 'Maria mediatrice', cit.

81 P. D. M. Fehlner, 'Il cammino delle verità di Maria Corredentrice', in AA.VV., *Maria Corredentrice. Storia e teologia*, vol. V (Frigento: Casa Mariana Editrice, 2002), pp. 33–119; Id., 'Immaculata Mediatrix: Towards a Dogmatic Definition of the Coredemption', in *Mary Coredemptrix, Mediatrix, Advocate, Theological Foundation, II. Papal, Pneumatological, Ecumenical*, ed. M. Miravalle (Santa Barbara 1997), pp. 259–329; Id., 'The Coredemptrix: Key to Mystery of Christian Life', in AA.VV., *Mary at the foot of the Cross*, pp. 361–385.

82 B. Gherardini, 'Corredenzione: i termini del problema', in *Divinitas* 40 (1996), pp. 117–146; Id., *La Corredenzione nel mistero di Cristo e della Chiesa* (Rome: Vivere in, 1998); Id., 'La Corredenzione di Maria. Dottrina della Chiesa', in *Immaculata Mediatrix* 1 (2001), pp. 97–105.

83 There are two series managed by the Franciscans of the Immaculate: 15 volumes of the work AA.VV., *Maria Corredentrice. Storia e teologia* (Frigento: Casa Mariana Editrice, 1998–2013), and nine volumes of AA.VV., *Mary at the foot of the Cross*, Acts of the International Symposium on Marian Coredemption, Academy of the Immaculate (New Bedford (MA) 2001–2010).

84 W. Goossens, *De cooperatione immediata Matris Redemptoris ad redemptionem obiectivam, quaestionis controversae perpensatio* (Paris: Typis Desclée de Brouver, 1939).

85 H. Lennerz, 'De redemptione et cooperatione in opera redemptionis', in *Gregorianum* 22 (1941), pp. 301–324.

c. between the two is a somewhat middle solution, *immediate passive* co-redemption: by her *fiat* Mary co-operates directly in redemption on behalf of humanity, which however is received totally from Christ. Mary declares her yes freely, but is a figure of the saved Church. Once again Christ is the absolute redeemer. The leader of this school of thought was H. M. Köster,[86] then K. Rahner,[87] O. Semmelroth,[88] etc.

However, the meaning of the co-redemptionist teaching which we re-discover in the papal Magisterium tends towards the first solution: Mary's active and immediate co-operation in redemption.[89] *Lumen Gentium* must be read in the same vein, with a strong emphasis also on the offertorial role of Mary, as true maternal priestly ministeriality. What's more, with Perrella we notice that

> Catholic theologians, whatever their theological opinion, ensured that Marian co-redemption derived from divine approval: if a 'co-redemption' on the part of Jesus' Mother exists, it is because God in his goodness and freedom has wanted to associate the action of the Mother with that of the Redeemer Son, always safeguarding the unicity and absolute and independent efficacy of Christ's work. In this light, Mary's co-redemption, in whatever form it might be understood, was always presented as secondary, by itself insufficient, dependent or subordinate, only hypothetically necessary.[90]

86 H. M. Köster, *Die Magd des Hernn* (Limburg: Lahn, 1947).

87 K. Rahner, *Probleme heutiger Mariologie,* in *Aus der Theologie der Zeit* (Regensburg 1948), pp. 85–113.

88 O. Semmelroth, *Urbild der Kirche. Organischer Aufban des Mariengeheimnisses* (Würburg: Echter, 1950).

89 Cf. Roschini, *La Madonna*, pp. 381–387.

90 Perrella, *I "vota" e I "consili"*, p. 160. In a footnote Perrella confesses that to extricate himself from the complex pre-conciliar Mariological vocabulary, by now no longer used—'a language so far from and foreign to contemporary theology and vocabulary'—he had to have recourse to the expositive clarity of G. Roschini ('Mediazione di Maria', in *Dizionario di Mariologia* (Rome: Studium, 1961), pp. 325–329; 340–344), cf. *Ibid.*, footnote 38.

Co-redemption constituted teaching proximate to the faith, that is, a teaching definable because resulting from the ordinary Magisterium. However, with John XXIII the Council had chosen a different path. This path was confirmed in the subsequent debate.

3. *Two positions, two discourses and a paradigmatic vote*

By the now the debate on the Marian schema signalled more and more a clear division among the Fathers. There was a very notable confrontation on the most pressing issues, the mediation of all graces and co-redemption, the cogency of the current Magisterium or just the most ancient traditions, Mary Mother of the Church, because associated with Christ in redemption and therefore Mediatrix of all the graces, or just an eminent member of the Church, her part being an exemplary figure of it. The debate about the insertion or otherwise of the Marian schema into that on the Church was also very close: to speak about Mary as part of the discourse on the Church, while it could be a significant ecumenical device, also re-appraised in some way the Marian fervour of a more Mediteranean theology. One discourse on Mary in its own right, on the other hand, would highlight, in the continuity of the great Marian tradition, the unique and singular role of Mary in redemption, and therefore in the Church: unique co-operator with the Redeemer, Mediatrix of *all* the graces, therefore Mother of the Church, that is, mother of all its members, a member Herself depending solely on the Head, Christ, because subordinate to Him[91]. On 24 October 1963, while the dispute was in full swing—from which the Council would take a decisive direction—the college of Cardinal moderators announced that at the will of the Pontiff they had to choose from within the Doctrinal Commis-

[91] On 25 October 1963, Alfonso M. Montà OSM wrote to Cardinal Ottaviani, saddened at the 'proposal to merge the Constitution De Beata Maria Virgine with the Constitution De ecclesia' and asked the Cardinal's opinion about the possibility of presenting a petition directly to the Holy Father, so that his personal intervention might solve the issue, in ASV, Envelope 766, folder 300.

sion two speakers who would present to the Assembly respectively, the reasons for the merging of the texts, and the reasons for their separation. Cardinal Santos, who would speak on behalf of the supporters of a separate schema, was chosen, and Cardinal König, who would speak on behalf of those in favour of incorporation.

3.1 The report of Cardinal Santos

Santos began by making reference to Mary's place in the mystery of God: daughter of the Father, mother of the Son, Spouse of the Holy Spirit, salvation of the People of God, Queen and Teacher of the Apostles, exemplar of the perfection and auxiliary of Christians called to holiness. Undoubtedly, the Blessed Virgin belongs to the People of God and is a super-eminent and singular member of the Church, but before every other redeemed person she received in full measure the fruit of the mystery of the Church, salvation. Mary was redeemed in a singular fashion, in a preservative manner: from this derives her singularity compared to other members. Therefore, she was also a free instrument and thus cause of the mystical Body which is the Church, and so she became mother of the People of God. For that reason the text on the Blessed Virgin Mary could not be inserted into the one about the People of God. It was necessary to distinguish first and foremost those who in the Church belong to the People of God, and among these highlight the distinctiveness of Mary Most Holy, which in turn distinguishes her from all the other members, both from the sacred hierarchy and the faithful. To Mary belongs a place of her own: she is the *exemplar* of sanctification and the author of the sanctification of all the members, because beneath the cross she merited with Christ the grace of our redemption; therefore she has also become its dispenser in its application. Mary is a member of the Church but is above the Church. Echoing St Bernard, Santos stated that Mary 'stat inter Christum et Ecclesiam'. The other members are incorporated by reason of passive participation in redemption. Mary, on the other hand, is active in the objective redemption of Christ and her own passive redemption was, unlike the others, preservative and not liberative. From this derives the soteriological function of the Bleesed Virgin, who was associated to objective redemption itself, essentially differing from the function of the other members. We could say, as *Lumen Gentium* would then re-state, that Mary in title only is co-operating with Christ. Therefore it was not correct to reduce Mariology to Ecclesiology. Instead, Mariology had a vital link with Christology and Soteriology. If Mary is acknowledged one can penetrate maximally into the mystery of the incarnation and thus highlight her christological link; the soteriological link is instead inferred from the subordinate co-operation of Mary with Christ. For such reasons, Santos asked to have a document on Mary in its own right, nor was it appropriate that a Council should resolve the controversies between Catholics about the Christo-typical or ecclesio-typical positions.[92] A separate Mariological treatise would probably unite souls, highlighting Mary in Christ and therefore in the Church: Co-Redemptrix and therefore Mediatrix on behalf of the Church, of all members, of which she is mother. Nuancing the emphases, chapter VIII of *Lumen Gentium* would try to do this, remaining nevertheless 'the first document of the extraordinary and solemn Magisterium dealing "ex professo" with the salvific role of Mary'.[93]

---

[92] Cf. AS II/3, pp. 338–342.

[93] Baraúna, 'La SS. Vergine', p. 1139. And he adds: 'Does this document represent real progress, is it right to expect it from a text which requires the supreme authority of the Church, residing within the Episcopal College? The answer can only be affirmative. With this one does not want to say naturally that the outcome achieved after so many debates and compromises could not be more brilliant' (*Ibid.*). According to Baraúna, one should not expect from *Lumen Gentium quantitative* progress about Marian doctrine (new dogmas) but *qualitative* progress: rooting the Mariological discipline, and therefore the person and work of Mary, in God's salvific plan, in the history of salvation, highlighting its biblical and patristic foundation. Cf. *Ibid.*, pp. 1140–1141.

3.2 The report of Cardinal König

König began with a somewhat different tone compared to the text drawn up in Fulda. He immediately referred to the speaker who had preceded him. He did not wish in the slightest to contradict him in what he said: 'I am contradicting', he said, 'neither the teaching nor the piety of what has been said, rather from my heart I agree to it most willingly'.[94] So the objections were not to do with the doctrinal content or devotion. Rather, the problem lay in the fact that in the Doctrinal Commission, on 9 October, the majority of the Fathers had voted that teaching about the Blessed Viring Mary should be set out in the schema on the Church: such teaching should be integrated into the constitution on the Church. The Viennese Cardinal set out three reasons for this. First and foremost a *theological* reason. It was not appropriate to separate the teaching on the Mother of God from other parts of dogmatic theology: if a caesura was created between Mariology and the other subjects, the path was being opened to unfounded and false theological exaggerations. A separate schema could be interpreted as if the Council had in mind new Marian dogmas, which in truth was not the Council's intention. Again, if the Church was conceived solely as *institutum salutis*, the Blessed Virgin would have remained extraneous to it. But if the Church is also People of God and communion of Saints, then the Blessed Virgin Mary is an eminent member of it. This integration would signify with clarity the relationship of Mary to Christ the one mediator, and the Church herself would better perceive the value of the teaching about the Blessed Virgin. The Church understood as fruit of the redemption highlighted Mary as eminent and typical member, as means of salvation, and that Mary received everything from Christ, and by his grace became *cooperatrix* in the work of salvation.

Then there was an *historical* reason for the merging of the texts. All the litanies which preach about Mary are all derived from consideration of the Church as mother, just like devotion to Mary in general.

---

94 AS II/3, p. 342.

In chapter 12 of the Book of Revelation the presence of Mary is deduced only as passing for that of the woman-Church. The Marian privileges are unique but contain an ecclesiological significance: in the Church and for the Church. Mary is a type of the Church, therefore the precedence of the Church over Mary was to be preferred. Then there was a *pastoral* reason: to teach people correct faith in the incarnation and Mary's proper place therein; finally, there was an *ecumenical* reason. An ecclesiological treatment of Mary would have facilitated among Easterners the easy recognition of the *Theotòkos* and in non-Catholic Christians the rediscovery of the veneration of Mary testified to by the Scriptures and the ancient traditions. The theme 'Mary—People of Israel—Church' was favoured at that time not just by Catholic theologians but also by non-Catholics. A number of Protestants, it was said, claimed that in Luke (1:28), in John (19:25) and in the Book of Revelation (12) is veiled Mary figure of the Church.[95]

So Mary and the Church referred one to another: one discourse on both would, for theological, historical, pastoral and above ecumenical reasons, be more fruitful. Max Thurian, still a Protestant, was in agreement with this, as noted by Wenger:

> While Cardinal König was speaking, I looked over at Brother Max Thurian, who was opposite me. His whole being was engrossed as he leaned over the banister of the tribune toward the speaker. What Cardinal König was saying about Protestant Mariology corresponded exactly to the thought of Brother Thurian, as expressed in his book, *Marie, mère du Seigneur, figure de l'Eglise* (Taizé Press 1962).[96]

3.3 A vote which divided the Council

The vote followed at the end of the speeches. The question to which they had to respond *placet* or *non placet* was the following: 'Are the

95 Cf. *Ibid.*, pp. 342–345.

96 Quoted in Melloni, 'The Beginning of the Second Period', p. 97, footnote 386.

Fathers content that the schema De Beata Maria Virgine Matre Ecclesiae be adapted to become chapter VI of the schema on the Church?'[97] The vote resulted in a very narrow victory for the ecclesio-typicists: of the 2,193 voting, 1,114 wanted the unification of the schema and 1,074 voted against.[98] The majority was very narrow: only by 40 votes did the Council go down a Mariological route with a strong ecumenical emphasis, which would also mark the trend of the subsequent work. Here a question presented itself again: the pastoral and the ecumenical, up to what point can they condition the teaching on the Blessed Virgin Mary, which König, too, recognised as true and Catholic? It is demonstrated by that almost insignificant majority, but which in reality was an indicator of a Council divided in two, divided over two Mariological-theological visions. It was the first time that had happened. Mariology, or rather a Mariological vision, divided souls. The Dogmatic Constitution on the Church itself would take on this new stance. Meanwhile, from now on the Council would choose more decisively the path of ecumenical dialogue. For this reason, I believe that the same chapter VIII of *Lumen Gentium* does not exhaust all the treatment on the Mother of God, which in truth seems rather subject to this new pastoral direction.

4. *A first analysis of an* in fieri *Mariology*

The Mariologists were already divided before the Council on the Christo-typical or ecclesio-typical vision of Mary. The former placed the emphasis on union with Christ in the work of redemption, underlining Mary's unique place in the Church. The latter, on the other hand, underlined the role of Mary in the Church, preferring to emphasise Mary as a member of the Church. A strong ecumenical desire, united with an ecclesio-typical vision of Mariology, led a great number of Fathers to prefer the insertion of the text on Mary into the

---

97 Cf. AS II/3, p. 345.

98 Cf. *Ibid.*, p. 627.

dogmatic discourse on the Church. Mary and the Church were presented in an inter-dependent manner, with the first emphasis on the Church, in the light of which the role of Mary was then considered. The Christo-typical vision ran the risk of forgetting the goal of redemption: to build the Church as place of salvation, and a Mariology markedly such was accused of placing the emphasis more on the Marian prerogatives than on Christological faith. The ecclesio-typical vision endorsed the mystery of the Church *fructus salutis* and therefore that of the Church *medium salutis,* with a greater emphasis on the characteristic of Church as People of God. Mary was seen in this people, not outside, nor above nor beneath. Therefore neither one nor the other Mariological tendency was sufficient taken in itself. However, with a predominantly ecclesio-typical Mariological formulation, which indicated, even by a small amount, the official entry, because conciliar, of Mary into the mystery of the Church, Marian teaching was not always set out in all its richness and tradition. The desire to refer to the most ancient traditions prevailed, judging the recent Magisterium of the Popes rather to be in contradiction with those traditions. Here another typical post-conciliar problem arises: whether to refer to the great traditions (of the Fathers or of the first centuries?) against a somewhat fragmented tradition of the recent Magisterium, subject to developing in history? What did the Council mean by ancient tradition? In truth, was not the Magisterium organ of the living tradition, vouching for its vivacity, in so far as it reiterated it, enriching what had been received? However, very often the reasons inclined towards an ecumenical choice.

Mary's mediation of all the graces was the real Mariological crux and at the same time—as many believed—the glitch in a Council of ecumenism, because coupled with the teaching of the unique and singular participation of Mary in the objective redemption in *actu primo*. Fundamentally, the idea, isolated and dear only to a few theologians, that Mary could not be Mediatrix of graces because she was unable to merit grace—no-one can merit the principle of merit—unique gift of the Redeemer, prevailed, and this would therefore have excluded a direct, active and immediate intervention on the part of Mary in the acquired redemption. Mediatrix, yes, but not in a co-redemptive sense, but rather in the sense of the Virgin's prayerful intercession at God's side on our behalf. This good was married with a rather reductive ecclesiological conception: Mary would be in some way inferior to the Church, because its member and its figure. Consequently also the title of Mother of the Church would not be theologically correct, because referring definitively to the cognitive co-operation of Mary with Christ as the new Eve.

Co-redemption, which in the original schema was taught in the way of a fundamental teaching, even if the term was avoided, was in reality the *discrimen* of the subsequent position: to set it aside had to be a *conditio sine qua non* for a Mariology circumscribed (to the Church) and not all-embracing, avoiding the heightened risk of annoying the separated brethren even more. For a moment it is forgotten, or it is deliberately overlooked, that the separated brethren have in fact no concept of active and free co-operation with God in grace. How useful was it to choose a path of dialogue encouraging deep down a more pessimistic vision of human co-operation in salvation? We see its influence in recent Mariological-ecumenical dialogues, too. How influential this attitude has been, too, in post-conciliar Mariology, to the point of it becoming an 'ectoplasm': Mary absorbed into the Church to the point of disappearing or merging with the faithful, among the sinners and the ignorant? What did the vote on 29 Ocotber 1963 mean for subsequent Mariology and deep down for Catholic theology?

The journey of chapter VIII on the schema on the Church would still be fraught. There was an attempt to mediate between two positions, to reach compromises, to express teaching on Mary in a somewhat placid and consensual manner. The questions about co-redemption and mediation would not be set aside: they would be presented with an emphasis on content,[99] but that *turning point* would then lead many theologians to see Vatican II as a sort of caesura between pre- and post-conciliar Mariology. Vatican II would be the *Anfang* of a new way of perceiving the Mary question. In theological terms is this vision valid, or does it risk encouraging a fragmented Mariology? Mariology cannot and must not forget its roots.

5. Two Mariological visions, Balić and Philips, in a difficult synthesis

On 19 November 1963 the Commission of four Fathers led by Cardinal König decided that the adaptation of the schema and its insertion into De Ecclesia should be done by Mgr Philips, general relatore of the schema on the Church along with the author of the already existing schema on Mary, Fr. Balić.

However, to understand the fraught path which then led to the promulgation of chapter VIII of the Constitution on the Church, it is good to go back momentarily and recall a sudden decision taken by John XXIII to block the text of the Constitution on Mary, so that it would not be handed on to the Central Commission and therefore to the Council. It was 25 April 1962 when Mgr Pericle Felici communicated this decision, disconcerting and motiveless according to Fr Tromp, who in turn asked Cardinal Ottaviani to make the Pope aware of the beneficial reasons for a Marian constitution in an ecumenical council. The Pope had probably already perceived the ecumenical risks of Mariological teaching. Ottaviani drew up in his hand a *Memorandum* to submit to the Pope, the fundamental points of which are set out below:

---

[99] Cf. Perrella, *I "vota" e i "consilia"*, p. 209: 'The rejection to proceed to a dogmatic definition of the teaching on co-redemption and the negation of a certain terminology did not signify the Council's disinterest in the question of the Virgin's co-operation in Christ's work of salvation, but in fact that question would be one of the salient points of chapter VIII of the constitution *Lumen Gentium*'.

1. There are many *vota* from the Fathers, 250 of which are calling for the definition of Mary Mediatrix of all graces.
2. The Constitution has been approved by fifty members and consultors, even by those who are inclined towards an irenic ecumenism.
3. It is an essential Constitution, because an ecumenical council which does not look at the BVM would be a scandal to many, or at least a great surprise.
4. It is an essential Constitution so that the Protestants might understand that the Catholic teaching on the mediation of the BVM does not contradict the teaching on Christ as sole Mediator and the precepts of Sacred Scripture.
5. Without this Constitution, the Constitution on the Church would remain incomplete. Due to the errors widespread everywhere today, it is appropriate that it be clearly set out that in the Mystical Body the BVM does not have a marginal place, but totally a central one due to the will of God and of Christ.
6. And the separated Easterners must not be forgotten: they must not be given the opportunity to say that the Council, in order not to offend the Protestants, remained silent about the Deipara, considering it to be an obstacle for an ecumenical Council.
7. Forming the opinion that the Council is under the influence of the Protestants must be absolutely avoided.
8. So it is totally desirable that the Constitution is proposed *more solito* to the discussion of the Central Commission.[100]

[100] The *Memorandum* is dated 26 April 1962, in ASV, Envelope 750, folder 222. The text was published in Toniolo, *La Beata Maria Vergine*, p. 85 and in KT 1/2, p. 870. Tromp also wrote a version by hand in Latin *De Beata Maria Virgine Mediatrice*, 10 April 1962, in the same Envelope and folder in ASV, cf. KT 1/2, p. 871: Mary intercedes with her continual love with God and Christ on our behalf. Since her intercession has all her strength and efficacy from the bloody sacrifice of her blessed Son, her mediation does not harm the fact that Christ is the sole mediator between God and humanity, just as participating goodness does not stop the sole good, God, remaining the source of all goods.

The Pope replied favourably, welcoming the requests of Ottaviani's *Memorandum*, and ordered that the process proceed *more solito* in the discussion on the prepared Marian schema; thus the first stage was already reached, as we saw, of that 'profound Council division on the issue: a Council truly at the crossroads, in seeking the difficult solution of universal consensus, integrating as the last chapter of *De Ecclesia*—but not as a simple epilogue!—the dogmatic and religious treatment of the Virgin Mary'.[101] Some of the problems listed by Ottaviani were still the *punctum dolens* of the subsequent dispute. We will see that a compromise solution was necessary in order to satisfy everyone: on the one hand we have a Balić who sought to mediate, accepting the *animadversiones* of the German and Scandinavian Fathers with the Butler, Spanish and Chilean schema, and the Philips draft, having as its base a soteriological approach to the mystery of Mary and the preparatory schema as reference; on the other hand, Philips, in his work as main author of the new chapter VIII of the being-promulgated Constitution *De Ecclesia*, would seek to replace the soteriological approach with a more biblical and ecclesiological approach, allowing his reticence for the co-redemption of Mary and particularly the mediation, to shine through almost to the end. Mary had to belong, especially in the time of the Church and eschatological time, more to the Church than to Christ.

5.1 The two paths

Meanwhile, the question was how to proceed after the vote, in fact, had split into two the Fathers' wishes. Was it necessary to re-draft a new schema integrated into that on the Church or still have a separate one? In the meantime, already different material was circulating as alternative proposals to the original text. Was it necessary, therefore, to integrate all the proposals into a broader text? The solution was not easy. At the suggestion of Charue, it was decided first of all to form a restricted Sub-commission entrusted with the task of drawing up

---

101 Toniolo, *La Beata Maria Vergine*, p. 194.

the new Marian schema. Its members, as well as including the two Commission relators, König and Santos, would be Bishops Doumith and Théas of Lourdes. König was President of the Sub-commission. Initially, on 12 November 1963, Fr Balić was asked to draw up a new text of Mary, but having refused, the text was drawn up by Mgr Philips and then sent by König to Balić for his opinion.[102] In a letter in German addressed to him, König asked Balić to give his point of view about easily reaching a *consensus universalis*; a lot depended on his decision.[103] Balić was inclined towards a solution which aimed at agreement between the different sides, whereas Philips was convinced of the impossibility of reconciling the different positions.

The new text drawn up by Philips and forwarded to Balić for a response, in fact, was concerned not so much with examining the suggestions coming from the Fathers, but rather offering a new draft with a clear ecclesiological imprint. That was due to the fact that the previous schema had been drafted largely with a logic foreign to ecclesiology; its main idea, Mary's association with the Redeemer, in turn was rooted in the vision of an anterior predestination of Mary compared to the Church and independent from it.[104] Instead, the new text followed a biblical and ecclesiological line which Mgr Philips had already had the opportunity to set out in his work a few years' earlier, *Le mystère de Marie dans les sources de la Révélation*: this provided him with the interpretation then preserved in the then promulgated text.[105] Philips' text was thought of as chapter VI or the Epilogue to the schema on the Church and was entitled *De loco et munere B. Virginis Deiparae in mysterio Christi et Ecclesiae*. The whole text was divided into ten points:[106] 1. Outline of the general principles; 2. Mary

---

102 Cf. C. Balić, *Relatio circa compositionem capituli octavi const. Dogmaticae De Ecclesia*, in ASV, Envelope 766, folder 203.

103 Cf. ASV, Envelope 773, folder 325.

104 Cf. E. M. Toniolo, *La Beata Maria Vergine nel Concilio Vaticano II*, cit., p. 216.

105 G. Philips, 'Le mystère de Marie dans les sources de la Révélation. Essai bibliographique 1959–1961', in *Marianum* 24 (1962), pp. 1–64.

106 See the whole text in Toniolo, *La Beata Maria Vergine*, pp. 219–228, accom-

in the Old Testament; 3. Mary at the Annunciation; 4. Mary and the Child Jesus; 5. Mary in Jesus' public life (Cana, Capernaum and the Cross); 6. Mary's glorious ending (presence in the Upper Room and the Assumption); 7. Mary in the time of the Church (the intercession of the Blessed Virgin in heaven and mediation with regard to lasting grace in heaven under Christ the sole Mediator); 8. Mary as type of the Church; 9. The worship of Mary; 10. Conclusion.

A synoptic view of this text alongside the official schema highlights the significant biblical focus of the discourse about Mary, which went towards replacing the *munus* of Mary in the economy of salvation. The sacrificial offering of the Son, the price of our redemption, was strongly toned down. It went from 'vehementer cum Unigenito suo condoluit; eum ut pretium redemptionis nostrae, cum Ipso et per Ipsum magno animo obtulit' of the original schema, to 'vehementer cum Unigenito suo condoluit, Eius sacrificio seipsam cum Ipso et per ipsum magno animo consociavit'. In this way Philips intended to exclude from magisterial teaching the not-yet defined truths of mediation and co-redemption, especially in nn. 7 and 8 which 'move the axis from Balić's Christocentrism to Philips' Ecclesiocentrism'.[107]

As regards the Marian titles, Philips, sharing the criticisms of the German and Scandinavian Fathers about the impossibility of Mary being Mediatrix of *all* the graces (otherwise she would have to be Mediatrix of the sacramental graces, too), in the new section *Maria in tempore Ecclesiae* (n. 7), had preferred to the 'omnium gratiarum Mediatrix' of the official schema the phrase 'eius generosa in ordine gratiae meditatio indesinenter perdurat': Mary's mediation, inserted into that of the Church, was attributed to the mediation of grace (and not of the graces), remaining as a foundation the gift of Christ source of grace through her. N. 8 highlighted Mary 'type of the Church', where with St Augustine and St Ambrose the participation of the

panied also by the sources: 1) the official schema and 2) Philips' French theological paper.

107 *Ibid.*, p. 232.

Church in the mystery of Mary virgin and mother was indicated. Finally, the theme of Mary advocate of Christian unity, so dear to Balić, was erased, but the faithful were simply encouraged to pray that peace and harmony might be achieved, recognising everyone as children of Mary.

Philips was convinced that his schema, unlike the new one prepared by Balić, could avoid the compromise of 'cut and paste' with a view to combining all the Mariological proposals. In reality,

> He too had performed a 'compromise', even with himself: because the biblical development which was progressing in a linear fashion in his study contained in the journal *Marianum*—and that he had sent to König as an attachment to this elementary proposal of a Marian schema—got stuck when it was amalgamated with the elements taken from the official schema.[108]

In a meeting of the Sub-commission held on 18 November 1963 in the sacristy of St Peter's, it was nevertheless decided that Balić and Philips should work together to prepare a new draft of the Marian text.[109] At that meeting, Balić, who had refused to prepare a text, nevertheless presented copies of a 15-page text divided into 3 points:[110] 1. Praenotanda; 2. Text of the official schema and that corrected text according to the amendments from the German-speaking Fathers and those of the Scandinavian Bishops' Conference; and, 3. Further considerations. The text had already been composed on 7 September 1963 (as can be deduced from the dates placed next to the parts). What is interesting in this text is the addition of a redactional and hermeneutical criterion: it was re-stated that the Council did not intend to define dogma, but only to propose solid

108 *Ibid.*, p. 228.

109 Cf. *Ibid.*, p. 197.

110 Cf. ASV, Envelope 766, folder 203. Toniolo offers a synoptic comparison with the official text, reporting in capital letters the corrections according to the amendments from the German-speaking and Scandinavian Fathers (cf. *Ibid.*, pp. 201–210).

and sound teaching *common to Catholics*, requiring from the faithful, for the individual teachings, that assent due to the teaching of the ordinary Magisterium.[111] The text was entitled *De Beata Maria Virgine Matre Christifidelium*. A significant change could also be seen here with regard to the mediation of all the graces. Balić accepted the observations of the German Bishops and reduced the mediation of all the graces, acquired by her association with Christ on earth, to the mediation of grace: from 'caelestium quoque gratiarum administra et dispensatrix iure meritoque salutatur' to 'in opere redemptionis, eo ipso caelestis quoque gratiae mediatrix et advocata nostra iure meritoque salutatur'. The reason was the same: 'hisce in terris Christi passibilis fuerit generosa socia', now the text said that Mary in heaven is Mediatrix *of grace* and our advocate.[112] A passage in n. 3 about the titles of Mary's association with Christ in the economy of salvation was also changed: from 'ut in omnibus gratis hominibus conferendis adsit materna caritas B. Virginis' to 'ita ut quae olim cooperata est fide et caritate ut fideles in Ecclesia nascerentur, sit etiam nunc nostrae salutis media et sequestra'. Mary, by reason of faith and charity (an Augustinian theme), is defined Mediatrix in heaven 'of our salvation', while the role of her maternal charity in giving grace to all people remains in the shade.[113]

5.2 Towards chapter VIII of *Lumen Gentium*

We have seen that the Mariological approaches of Balić and Philips were different. In the meeting on 18 November 1963 it was decided that the two Mariologists should work together: both were appointed official editors of the Marian text. Philips, as first editor, Balić as co-editor. The major problem was the following: from which text

[111] 'Itaque sacra Synodus doctrinam solidam et sanam et inter catholicos communem denuo fidelibus proponit; quin novum inde dogma definiatur, sed singula, quae dicuntur, cum eo assensu fideli recipiantur oportet, qualis ex magisterii doctrina ordinaria singulis convenire noscitur', *Ibid.*, pp. 201–202.

[112] Cf. *Ibid.*, p. 203.

[113] Cf. *Ibid.*, p. 205.

should the work of drafting a final text begin? Balić was not giving up. At all costs he wanted a fundamental path to be traced from the preparatory Marian schema, therefore the assumption of a Christological-soteriological vision opening out to the Church. On 21 November, writing to Philips, he offered two solutions: 1) to unite elments of the Philips text and the official schema amended according to the more decisive observations of the German and Scandinavian Fathers. This position would have satisfied those who wanted to insert the schema on Mary into that on the Church; or, 2) to integrate the official text, already corrected by Balić with the amendments from the German and Scandinavian Fathers, with the other Mariological proposals, in other words, with the other four schema: Philips, the Spanish one, the Chilean one, and Butler's. This solution would have satisfied those who instead wanted an autonomous schema. Meanwhile Balić himself had already done this merging of the four schema with his first published composition, starting out from the original schema.[114] Philips sharply did not accept being involved in this project and with Balić's Mariological vision. The reason for his dissent was doctrinal, which for Balić was rather a certain theology. This theology could not use a schema where only truths *de fide credenda* were to be proposed.[115] The two positions: that of Balić, referring above all to the ordinary Magisterium of the Popes on co-redemption and mediation, and that of Philips, more rooted in the historico-salvific provision in the light of ecclesiology, seemed irreconciliable.

The decisive turning point came on 26 November when, in an act of Franciscan humility, Balić accepted the assumption of Philips' schema as the basic text of the future chapter VIII, despite the fact there was 'magna dissentiones inter peritos'.[116] In fact, in a purely

[114] There is a typewritten copy of this schema, 21 November 1963, at PAMI, *Archivio Balić*, 1963. The text is also offered by Toniolo as an appendix indicating the different parts of the composition, in *La Beata Maria Vergine*, pp. 341–346.

[115] Testimony provided by Tromp's *Diario*, VII, 4 December 1963, cit., in *Ibid.*, p. 235.

consultative meeting of the periti of the Sub-commission, eight (Schmaus, Bélanger, Grillmeier, Ciappi, Llamera, Balić, García, and Di Fonzo) were in favour of using the official text as a basis for the amendments and only four (Laurentin, Moeller, Ochagabía and Philips) were in favour of a completely new text.[117]

From here there was a succession of eight subsequent drafts of the text, until its promulgation in *Lumen Gentium* on 21 November 1964.

I do not intend to reconstruct all the stages of a still elaborate process, stages moreover already well and widely studied.[118] In this context it is important simply to highlight some passages I believe to be significant, with a view to glimpsing the hermeneutical elements suitable for our goal. Again we find a very cautious Philips as regards Balić's soteriological insertions / suggestions. For example, in the third draft of the text, Philips changed the term *consociatio* to *unita* and then *coniunctio* about the union of the Mother with the Son from the Annunciation to Golgotha. In I.2 on the Exposition of the general principles, Balić's 'cum Eo indivulse consociatur' became in Philips 'eique fidelissime unita'. In the promulgated text there would be a slight modification, underlining the bond of unity: 'Eique arcto et indissolubili vinculo unita' (*Lumen Gentium* 53).[119] In II.3, *De Maria in Annuntiatione,* Balić suggested 'sub ipso et cum ipso, potenti Dei gratia, mysterio redemptionis sociata', while Philips eliminated the concept of association with the Redemption, changing it to *service*: 'sub Ipso e cum Ipso, potenti Dei gratia, mysterio redemptionis inserviens', as would be stated in the promulgated text, too (cf. *Lumen Gentium* 56).[120]

---

116 ASV, Envelope 773, folder 325.

117 The Minutes and the transcription of the official record of this private meeting of the periti are preserved: *Ibid.* and PAMI, *Archivio Balić,* 1963.

118 See especially the synopsis of the eight drafts in Toniolo, *La Beata Maria Vergine,* pp. 347–427; Greco, *"Madre dei viventi"*, pp. 177–233.

119 Cf. *Ibid.*, pp. 352–353.

120 Cf. *Ibid.*, pp. 366–367. In the *Iustificatio emendationum,* Philips explained the reason for this choice: Mary was preserved from sin because thus it was better

In II.4, with regard to *De munere B. Virginis in oeconomia salutis*, there is this change: from 'Haec autem Novae veluti Hevae cum Novo Adamo *consociatio* in redemptionis opere' to 'Haec autem Matris cum opere salutari Filii sui *coniunctio* a tempore virginalis conceptionis Christi ad Eius usque mortem manifestatur', remaining unchanged until the promulgated text (cf. *Lumen Gentium* 57).[121] Still in this section, speaking about the Presentation of Jesus in the Temple, Philips did not share the oblative vision of Mary, casting a shadow over the offering of Calvary, and eliminated the following pericope: 'sub luce Simeonis prophetica, una cum Filio, salutaris illius hostiae oblationem inchoavit, aeterno Patri summe acceptam, quam sub cruce erat consummatura', while he added that Mary accepted the dual prophecy of Simeon, that which exhibits the Son to contradiction and the sword which pierces her own soul, a text accepted definitively even if slightly modified (cf. *Lumen Gentium* 57).[122]

In II.8 Philips accepted Balić's insertion on the predestination of Mary and her association with the Redeemer: 'his in terris Christi Redemptoris fuerit generosa Socia' for which she became 'ob causam mater gratiae', compared to Balić's 'ob causam gratiae'. However, he removed Balić's reference to Mary 'Mediatrix et Advocata nostra'. The text was then modified by the Doctrinal Commission, up to its definitive placement in *Lumen Gentium* 61, where the 'generosa socia' remains; Mary becomes our Mother in the order of grace:[123]

> Beata Virgo, ab aeterno una cum divini Verbi incarnatione tamquam Mater Dei praedestinata, divinae Providentiae consilio, his in terris exstitit alma divini Redemptoris Mater, singulariter prae aliis generosa socia, et humilis ancilla Domini.

---

to serve the mystery of the Redemption. He says: 'Praeservata est ab omni peccato praecise ut melius mysterio redemptionis inserviat. Ponitur vero *inserviens*, loco "*sociata*", ut appareat modus quo exercetur haec consociatio', *ibid.*, p. 254.

121 Cf. *Ibid.*, pp. 368–371.

122 Cf. *Ibid.*, p. 372.

123 Cf. *Ibid.*, pp. 382–383.

> Christum concipiens, generans, alens, in templo Patri sistens, Filioque suo in cruce morienti compatiens, operi Salvatoris singulari prorsus modo cooperata est, oboedientia, fide, spe et flagrante caritate, ad vitam animarum supernaturalem restaurandam. Quam ob causam mater nobis in ordine gratiae exstitit.

Finally, one last comment. Philips perfected Balić's expression: 'mediatio indesinenter perdurat', with 'cooperatio et mediatio indesinenter perdurat', but deleted the *compassion* of Mary united to the *passion* of the Son, underlining that Mary is *ancilla Domini*, who remains resolute in her consent also on Calvary, until the eternal reunification of all the elect.[124]

Up to the fifth draft our two Mariologists proceeded in this alternation of cuts and additions. The sixth draft of the schema was that of the Doctrinal Commission, which on 25 February received from the Sub-commission edits III, IV and V. Now it was the job of the Commission itself to make the amendments. Once again there arose the problem of Mary's mediation. Garrone, against Parente, believed that this teaching was still not mature. Fernández, against Henriquez, wanted the text not to talk just about the one Mediator, but that it should also state clearly that Mary was Mediatrix. According to Philips the co-operation of Mary could be spoken about without mentioning the word 'Mediatrix'. In turn Charue suggested proceeding in this way: a. leaving the old text as a base; b. changing the order as Henriquez wanted, starting from Christ the mediator; c. highlighting clearly in the text the main points of Mary's co-operation in salvation: the consent at the Annunciation and under the Cross; d. adding as a secondary formula that if in the Church the faithful honour the Blessed Virgin as Mediatrix, such mediation is to be understood as totally subject to Christ.[125]

---

[124] Cf. *Ibid.*, pp. 384–385.

[125] This is the *Relatio* of Fr Sebastian Tromp: ASV, Envelope 758, unnumbered folder, entitled *Relatio Secretarii de laboribus 15 Martii—16 Iulii 1964*, pp. 4–8.

On 3 June, the Sub-commission decided that Philips should prepare a new text on the mediation of Mary, having as a basis the text already approved, and, in addition, highlighting, as Parente asked, the co-operation of Mary in salvation at the two central moments, the Annunication and the Cross. The problem which concerned the periti in the Sub-commission was precisely and once again the relationship of Mary's mediation with Christ and compared to the whole mystical Body.[126] However, two days later, in the plenary session of the Doctrinal Commission, there was an unpleasant incident: Parente complained that Philips had not carried out the wishes of the Sub-commission, once again omitting the title 'Mediatrix' as well as that of 'generosa socia'. Parente asked, as Fr Tromp's report tells us, that it should be clearly stated that the Church recognised the Mother of God as Mediatrix.[127] So Philips was asked again to draft a new text according to the points listed above by Charue. In the last text of 9 June 1964, Philips amended the paragraph *De Maria ut ancilla Domini Redemptoris,* adding the title 'Mediatrix': 'Propterea B. Maria Virgo

[126] See the summary of the Sub-commission meeting made by Congar, Wednesday 3 June 1964, in his *My Journal of the Council,* pp. 537–538. Congar was against Parente's proposal and described Balić as a clown. He summed up his own position as follows: '.... Mediation: we have shown (earlier) how the Virgin was associated with the work of salvation on earth; with regard to her mediation in heaven, I learnt that she does not intervene in the communication of *SACRAMENTAL* graces. I have also heard it said that the Pope is AGAINST 'mediation'' (*Ibid.,* pp. 537–538). Ancel's proposal, shared by Philips, was the following: '... two difficulties with Parente's text: 1) the idea of *particeps mediationis Christi* [participant in the mediation of Christ]; 2) one cannot put forward in a conciliar text a doctrine that is not accepted by ALL. Nothing should be said about mediation, either for or against it' (*Ibid.,* p. 537). The point of the problem set by Parente was if there was something more than just intercession (cf. *Ibid*). Moeller wanted to avoid the title *Mediatrix,* because 'our separated brethren are waiting for us here...' (*Ibid.,* p. 539).

[127] Cf. ASV, Envelope 779, folder 351. Cf. Toniolo, *La Beata Maria Vergine,* p. 290, footnote 44, about the page in Tromp's *Diario,* which is used to write this account. Nevertheless the decision was taken by an absolute majority.

in Ecclesia, praeterquam aliis, etiam titulo Mediatricis condecorari consuevit'.[128] However, this pericope containing the title 'Mediatrix' in the amendments of the Council Fathers was still hotly debated. The proposals could be divided into three positions: 1. a first group wanted the title to be retained or expressed more strongly;[129] 2. others asked that it be removed;[130] 3. others asked that other titles, such as Advocate, Auxiliatrix, of Succour, be put alongside Mediatrix,[131] a position which was then accepted by the Commission established to make the choice.[132] So n. 62 finally read: 'Propterea B. Virgo in Ecclesia titulis Advocatae, Auxiliatricis, Adiutricis, Mediatricis invocatur'.

With Philips' prior amendment the word 'Mediatrix' entered the Marian text, even if with great effort and reticence. In any case, however, it was not a theological goal of the text but a description, as is clear from the final text, of the titles of Our Lady. Toniolo would say:

> At last—good or bad?—the title '*Mediatrix*' has also entered into the chapter on the B. V. M., not with theological terminology, but as bestowed on her by the Church, in the sense

---

[128] See the synopsis of the redaction of n. 50: *De B. Virgine et Ecclesia,* paragraph *De Maria ut ancilla Domini Redemptoris,* in *Ibid.*, pp. 291–293.

[129] This group included Ruffini (E 2721), De Castro Mayer (E 2727), Van Lierde (E 2728), Battistelli (E 2817), Olazar Muruaga (E 2771), etc. Cf. AS III/6, p. 30.

[130] These included Meouchi (E 2518), Janssens (E 2620), Volk (E 2935), Alfrink (E 2884), Willebrands (E 2936), etc. Cf. *Ibid.*, pp. 30–31.

[131] These included Aldegunde Dorrego (E 2668), Silva Henriquez (E 2822), Doumith (E 2816), Weber (E 2519), etc. Cf. *Ibid.*, p. 31.

[132] The choice of the *third suggestion* was justified as follows: 'Haec autem ultima expressio "*invocatur*", ab omnibus libenter accipitur loco vocabuli "*condecoratur*", quod nimis ad decorationem exteriorem videtur alludere. Similiter longe maior pars Commissionis statuit inserendam esse explicationem: "Nulla creatura ex unico fonte cooperationem". Ita autem, ut patet, in materiam inter theologos controversam non intratur, sed simpliciter clarificatur idea secundum analogiam fidei, scilicet comparatione facta cum uno sacerdotio Christi et una bonitate Dei', *Ibid.*, p. 32.

> explained of total dependence on the sole mediation of Christ, and with the precise goal of uniting the faithful directly and more intimately to their Mediator and Saviour.[133]

Chapter VIII, now in its complete form and as the final part of *De Ecclesia,* was presented in the council chamber by Archbishop Maurice Roy on 29 September 1964. From his report[134] some significant facts emerge for our hermeneutical discourse. First and foremost, the Council did not want to impose a solution on the controversy between the two Mariological tendencies, the Christo-typical and the ecclesio-typical. In an absolute manner, the type of every perfection is Christ, to which Mary in a singular way is compliant, so that, according to an ancient tradition, she can well be called *Typus Ecclesiae.* The two dimensions, the Christo-typical and the ecclesio-typical, do not exclude but complement each other. The Council, then, 'according to its universal method, did not enter into the controversies between Catholic theologians, but everywhere set out for the faithful the calm foundations of Catholic teaching, about which all the Fathers agreed, so that pastoral preaching might be supported in a solid manner and the piety of the Christian people might be greatly enthused by it'.[135]

Roy had divided his intervention, highlighting the three parts of chapter VIII. In the first, he said, was set out the *munus* of the Blessed Virgin in the economy of salvation, according to the *clear* ('placida') things contained in Sacred Scripture and Tradition. Tradition, then, follows an order, observed in the sacred books themselves, in reference particularly to the words which show the dignity of the Mother of God, also not ignoring those texts which according to the non-Catholics presented some difficulties.

The second part, concerning the relationship of Mary with the Church, first and foremost insisted on the *co-operation* of the Blessed

133 Toniolo, *La Beata Maria Vergine,* p. 294.
134 Cf. AS III/1, pp. 435–438.
135 *Ibid.,* p. 436.

Virgin Mary in universal salvation ('imprimis insistit super cooperationem B. Virginis ad salutem universalem'): in the initial consent at the incarnation of the Redeemer, in the oblation of the sacrifice on the cross ('in oblatione sacrificii in cruce peracta') and in perpetual heavenly intercession. In that context the title *Mediatrix* was cited, 'which did not please many members of the Commission', but explained in a way that the excellence of the one mediator was in no way overshadowed. The third part, finally, concerned practical teaching on worship and preaching.

Thus Roy, too, confirmed the reticence about Mary's mediation, starting from the objection about its extension: to *all* the graces, to the point of arriving at the very concept of mediation in itself, considered to be a disputed question. Consequently, the Council assumed the title but did not pronounce—as had happened elsewhere about the constituive Tradition and members of the Church—on the teaching, on its being common or definitive, nor did it resolve therefore the potential misunderstandings. Without doubt, the criticism of the German and Scandinavian Bishops, united to the theological vision of Philips, had to a large extent dictated the theological line of the document itself and an obvious ecumenical goal in the Mariology of Vatican II. An ecumenism which aimed at interest in a new dialogue, above all with the Protestant brethren, seeking more consent on common beliefs than dogmatic clarification on what separates us. Vatican II wanted precisely this.

But we must ask ourselves: does this reticence about Mary's mediation, presented now in a more descriptive than argumentative way so as not to get mixed up—according to the Commission—in a theme still under discussion, indicate *per se* (due to the fact that it is conciliar teaching) progress in Mariological teaching as regards the soteriological aspect of Mary, or, as I believe, at least a (pastoral) impasse, if not also a regression, compared to the ordinary Magisterium of the Popes and the teachings of the Church Fathers?[136] The

[136] Cf. L. Gambero, *Maria nel pensiero dei Padri della Chiesa* (Cinisello Balsamo:

important point to glimpse a hermeneutical key in Mariological teaching in this case (but generally for the other teachings, too, as Archbishop M. Roy said) is this: how much has the Council's pastoral decision influenced teaching about the role of Mary in the mystery of Christ? In the post-conciliar period, has the theme of the co-redemption and mediation been perhaps silenced rather out of suspicion, and consequently to a large extent put to one side by reason of the will of Vatican II? However, the issue has continued to be studied and clarified by many theologians. So a bigger problem is unravelled, which fifty years on from the Council gathering impacts upon us: what type of ecumenism is it appropriate to encourage? The dogmatic, that is, the one which roots its horizon in revealed doctrine (not just *de fide credenda* but also *de fide tenenda*) and from here draws the motives for the comparison with the separated brethren, aiming at the whole *Traditio Ecclesiae*,[137] or the pastoral—which largely was desired by

Paoline, 1991).

137 Within this perspective lay the ecumenical Magisterium of Benedict XVI. See in particular his address to the plenary meeting of the Congregation for the Doctrine of the Faith, 27 January 2012, in *L'Osservatore Romano* of 28 January 2012, p. 8: 'Today, moreover, one of the fundamental questions is the problem of the methods adopted in the various ecumenical dialogues. These too must reflect the priority of faith. Knowing the truth is a right of the conversation partner in every true dialogue. It is a requirement of love for one's brother or sister. In this sense, it is necessary to face controversial issues courageously, always in a spirit of brotherhood and in reciprocal respect. It is also important to offer a correct interpretation of that order or "hierarchy" which exists in Catholic doctrine', observed in the Decree on Ecumenism, *Unitatis Redintegratio* (n. 11), which in no way means reducing the deposit of the faith but rather bringing out its internal structure, the organic nature of this unique structure'. And again, with regard to an ecumenism of truth in the one Church: 'The crucial problem which marks ecumenical dialogue transversally is therefore the question of the structure of revelation—the relationship between Sacred Scripture, the living Tradition in Holy Church and the Ministry of the Successors of the Apostles as a witness of true faith. And in this case the problem of ecclesiology which is part of this problem is implicit: how God's truth reaches us. Fundamental here is the discernment between

many Council Fathers—which starts out from the historic and pragmatic fact, and on behalf of this aims at a possible dialogue, without changing teaching, but de facto neither improving understanding of it, but even with the risk of altering its significance by virtue of the dialogue method chosen, if it doesn't in fact also change the judgment? Is ecumenism in Vatican II a dogmatic fact or by and in itself pastoral? Does *Unitatis redintegratio* draw its ecumenical provision from *Lumen Gentium* or set itself as 'praxis' in some parallel fashion?[138] These are questions to which I believe a response is necessary. In my most modest opinion, to leave them unanswered would mean simply putting off the problem.

Despite all that, however, chapter VIII of the Dogmatic Constitution on the Church is a sign of great Mariological progress, and besides a significant concentration on Mary's co-operation in

---

Tradition with a capital "T" and traditions. I do not want to go into detail but merely to make an observation. An important step in this discernment was made in the preparation and application of the provisions for groups of the Anglican Communion who wish to enter into full communion with the Church, in the unity of our common and essential divine Tradition, maintaining their own spiritual, liturgical and pastoral traditions which are in conformity with the Catholic faith (cf. Constitution *Anglicanorum Coetibus*, art. III). Indeed, a spiritual richness exists in the different Christian denominations which is an expression of the one faith and a gift to share and to seek together in the Tradition of the Church'.

138 The hermeneutic of *Unitatis redintegratio* itself is conflicting, cf. O. Morerod, 'Unitatis redintegratio entre deux herméneutiques, in AA.VV., *Vatican II: rupture ou continuité? Les herméneutiques en presence*, Actes du colloque organisé par l'ISTA, Toulouse 15–16 mai 2009, in *Revue Thomiste* 110 (2010), pp. 52–70. Does the decree have a dogmatic enforceability as Kasper would like or just pastoral, as Kolfhaus prefers? See the *status quaestionis* in Kolfhaus, *Pastorale Lehrverkündigung*, pp. 82–123. The points of *Unitatis redeintegratio* which leave themselves most open to misunderstanding are in *Unitatis redintegratio* n. 11 in relation to that 'order or "hierarchy" which exists in Catholic doctrine' (as I have said) and in *Unitatis redintegratio* n. 9 with regard to the '*par cum pari*' to be respected in dialogue with the separated brethren. This latter text was also read as doctrinal parity.

Redemption, rightly believed '*the centre of the conciliar Marian teaching*'.[139] Precisely thanks to the Marian treatise of *Lumen Gentium* the minimalism of Mary's co-operation in Redemption is overcome: her uniquely indirect and passive participation, and thus the disputed question of co-redemption, receives a valid magisterial clarification, along the lines of the active co-operation and listening to the classical Mariological vision.

In Parente's words, 'despite the contrary tendencies, the conciliar text preserved the substance of traditional Mariology, as regards Mary's soteriological participation, too'.[140] Whoever cannot see this must be short-sighted. Suffice to report the texts cited in the footnotes to be aware of the riches of the magisterial and theological sources which speak about the mediation of Mary in the area of grace (cf. *Lumen Gentium* 62).[141]

The comments above are certainly not a rejection of the new which is encountered, nor is it a desire to ignore that for the first time an Ecumenical Council devoted to the Most Holy Virgin such an expansive Mariological treatise, in a systematic synthesis, which perhaps went far beyond the very expectations of those Fathers who, initially, concerned at the reductionist insertion of *De Beata* into *De Ecclesia*, asked that the Mother of God not be ignored. The conciliar teaching on the Madonna chose, in a forward-looking manner, a middle way, reflecting the theological positions which were beginning to settle down, when they weren't clashing: Mary is placed in Christ and in the Church, operating thus that necessary mediation between the Christological and the Ecclesiological-Anthropological aspects.

139 A. Escudero Cabello, 'Approcci attuali e proposte teologiche sul tema della cooperazione mariana', in *Marianum* 61 (1999), p. 177.

140 P. Parente, *Teologia di Cristo, alfa e omega del mondo e dell'uomo*, I, (Rome: Città Nuova, 1970), p. 622. See also by the same author 'Il punto sulla mediazione di Maria', in *Scripta de Maria* 4 (1981), pp. 625–643.

141 Cf. also M. Hauke, 'Maria als mütterliche Mittlerin in Christus. Ein systematischer Durchblick', in *Sedes Sapientiae Mariologisches Jahrbuch* 2 (2008) 53.

The more Mary is in Christ the more she is of the Church and each of us. In my doctoral thesis, I treasured this positioning of the mystery-Mary, because it is the most suitable for highlighting another Mariological theme so dear to me, the priesthood of Mary.[142]

However, the critical comments are necessary—they emerge particularly in the Mariological branch of theology, because Mary is the 'nexus mysterium', using an expression dear to Ratzinger—to find a homogenous hermeneutic path and above all responding to the Council, and objective, which helps not to make of the Second Vatican Council—as is often the temptation—the only council in the history of the Church, as if theology only began fifty years ago. In the Mariological text of *Lumen Gentium,* an important synthesis is also present with several limitations. According to S. Perrella such a synthesis is not devoid, just like the rest of human discourse, of limitations, gaps, compromises, insights missed even though stated at the start (in *Lumen Gentium* 54).[143] There was like a *neutrality* in the Council, dictated by guiding criteria outlined in the ante-preparatory phase, 30 November 1960, which asked, in summary, to omit debated issues and avoid apologetic objectives for a greater faithfulness to the pastoral needs of the Church. 'Precisely these factors, permeated by the pastoral and ecumenical spirit, directed the reflection of the Council Fathers within a pre-constituted furrow, to the point of crystallising and assuming the character of a real DNA of chapter VIII'. This has determined 'a missed validation of the pre-existing theological models, but that did not stop the editors adapting them as valid references, indications nevertheless integrated by a reference to theological research for the questions not completely thematised'.[144] There are Mariological questions which still remain

142 See S. M. Lanzetta, *Il sacerdozio di Maria nella teologia cattolica del XX secolo. Analisi storico-teologica* (Frigento (AV): Casa Mariana Editrice, 2006).

143 Cf. S. M. Perrella, 'La B. V. Maria nel capitolo VIII della "Lumen Gentium". Contenuti—valutazione—recezione,' in Id. (ed.), *La Madre di Gesù nella coscienza ecclesiale contemporanea. Saggi di teologia* (Vatican City: PAMI, 2005), pp. 123–124.

open and certainly their *status* can only refer to the theological moment from which Vatican II also had to necessarily start out. However, it is different if the theme in question was still debated or had already risen to level of common opinion, of *opinio certa*.

For a subsequent in-depth 'integral' and theological Mariological examination in the broader sense, I believe it necessary to evaluate and in some way get into the right perspective the very reasons which gave rise to the limitations and compromises. I believe that the most opportune theological work today is that of *contextualising* the Second Vatican Council, evaluating it for what it is, and according to what corresponds to the truth. From the historico-theological contextualisation arises the correct hermeneutic of the facts and magisterial teachings.

Our Lady, Mother of the Church, is certainly a great help to us and the story of her schema is encouragement in this undertaking.

[144] Greco, *"Madre dei viventi"*, pp. 390–391. For other limitations inherent in chapter VIII of *Lumen Gentium*, with the aim of illustrating a 'perfectable' and 'perspective' conciliar Mariology, see *Ibid.*, pp. 393–412.

CONCLUSION

THE SECOND VATICAN COUNCIL FOR THE UNITY OF THE CHURCH

At the end of our hermeneutic journey through Vatican II, choosing some of its more emblematic texts and teachings, and at the same time significant for perceiving the novelty of Vatican II compared to the preceding Magisterium, novelty which we hope is registered in the uniqueness and indefectibility of the Church, I wish by way of summary to highlight the facts which have gradually emerged as paths for a further and more specific reflection. It is unquestionable that the last Council, perhaps in a way never before seen in the history of the Church, has been the object of the most disparate hermeneutics and judgments of the most varied kind. Continuity or rupture with the Church can both be attested to, and so it is today. Even if the rupture is developed in a different fashion, with a more historic or more theological edge: one minute as impact of the dogmatic pastorality of the Council, the next as new ecclesial phase inaugurated by the last gathering, and the next just as '*Anfang des Anfangs*', it is nevertheless rupture with the Church and, as we saw, with the theology attested to up until the dawn of 1962. Did the Council really want to inaugurate above all a new theological phase? A theology with a more pastoral face? In which, however, necessarily metaphysical theology was embellished with a dark, intransigent face, by now unacceptable? Hence the reasons for this work, about which I now wish to point out some fundamental features.

1. A problem about the hermeneutic applied to the Council

Often the category 'event' is preferred over and above the text or the decisions, and this is intimately linked to the 'experience'. The text would encourage this unity, remaining almost in the middle, due to its expansive conversational nature. Going down this route, however, it is obvious that in the hermeneutical category applied to Vatican II one ends up positioning the Council before the Church and understanding the Church from the Council and not vice-versa. Instead, first there is the Church and then its councils. I believe this problem had already been perceived very well by St Robert Bellarmine, who, even though with polemical and apologetic verve, in his dispute *De Conciliis et Ecclesia* explained that the Church can be seen in two ways: either as gathered in council or as spread throughout the whole world. In his work he starts off with the treatise on the councils rather on the Church, despite contravening the order of nature, due to the fact that the question of the councils was connected more to that of the Roman Pontiff—which indeed comes first—than to the disputation itself on the Church.[1] An apologetic-doctrinal necessity, but the order of nature, however, remains unchanged, and must: first the Church as mystery and sacrament, as mystical body and people of God—people to be led to the body and not vice-versa, with the risk of confusing it with a *Volkskirche*—then a council, or the twenty-one councils to illuminate the foundation of the Church and express its mystery with magisterial teaching. Now, fifty years after Vatican II, are we (still) to accept the Council, or its teaching? And if its teaching, must we not necessarily contextualise it with a view to seeing its magisterial positioning, the novelty it brought and at the same time the necessary harmonious marrying with the teaching attested to up to the dawn of the ecumenical gathering?

In this work I asked questions above all about the two main constitutions and axes bearing the whole of the conciliar Magisterium, *Lumen Gentium* and *Dei verbum*. And in them I only examined some doctrinal

1 'Praeponimus autem disputationem de Conciliis, disputationi de Ecclesia, licet, ordo naturae contra suadere videretur, quoniam disputatio de Conciliis magis connexa est cum disputatione de Summo Pontifice, quae iam praecessit, quam disputatio de Ecclesia'. R. Bellarmine, *Disputationes de controversis christianae fidei adversus huius temporis haereticos*, cit, t. II, contr. 1, I. 1, cap. 1, p. 2.

issues—one cannot even see a dogmatic constitution as conciliar *unicum*, given the different magisterial levels which occur in it: in *Lumen Gentium* there is the sacramentality of the episcopate, collegiality or the doctrine of membership of the Church—with a view to analysing in depth its genesis and the hostilities, highlighting the intentions of the Fathers so as to be able to come to a most trustworthy judgment about the level of assent which such Magisterium requires and the respective theological qualification of the teachings I examined. Here we encountered a problem which returns, almost as a *Leitmotiv* of Vatican II: the choice by the Council Fathers to leave open some theological issues and to debate others, guided roughly by the ecumenical and generally more pastoral aim of the Council. Hence the *status quaestionis* of the teachings left open by the Council and entrusted again to theological discussion, or instead those that were taught, at times with *parresìa*, even if their doctrinal tradition was a lot younger. This is our hermeneutical thesis: the pastoral aim of the Council played such a decisive role in guiding even the conciliar Magisterium towards a general authentic ordinary level, while giving itself therein other layers such as infallibility itself in the *fides credenda*. There would be something definitive, at least from what has emerged, only about the sacramentality of the episcopate, but the theological position is not unanimous. I will look at these issues in more detail.

2. The Council's position about the theological qualification of the teachings

There are two official responses from the General Secretariat of the Council about the theological qualification of the conciliar teaching, the last of which, reporting the opinion of the Theological Commission, was applied to the Dogmatic Constitution on the Church and the Dogmatic Constitution on Divine Revelation. The first statement dates back to 29 November 1963, in the 78th General Congregation.

At the start of the Congregation, the secretary of the Council, Bishop Pericle Felici, said:

> Taking into consideration conciliar practice and the unique aim of this council, which is principally pastoral, this Sacred Synod defines in an infallible manner only the things of faith and morals which are believed by the universal Church, which are as such indicated openly by the Synod itself. At the same time the other things on which Council does not declare that in an open manner, are not defined by it infallibly, but manifested by the authentic Magisterium as Church doctrine. Therefore in the case of a definition of faith the council Fathers are to be forewarned and will be forewarned and in the text it will be necessary to designate the expressions, which explicitly manifest the desire that something be defined.[2]

It is important to note in this first response that, to the unique aim of the Council, which is principally pastoral, corresponds *normally*, that is, when there is not a conciliar declaration which openly defines an infallible doctrine, an authentic ordinary Magisterium which sets out a Church doctrine.

The second response is that reported in the appendix to *Lumen Gentium* and then applied also to *Dei verbum*. As I already said in the first chapter, it is a notification made by the General Secretariat of the Council in the 123rd General Congregation, on 16 November 1964, which reports the opinion of the Doctrinal Commission and therefore its doctrinal declaration of 6 March 1964 about the theological

---

2 AS II/6, p. 305: 'Ratione habita, tum moris conciliaris, tum finis peculiaris huius Concilii, qui est principaliter pastoralis, haec Sacra Synodus ea tantum de fide vel de moribus, ab universa Ecclesia tenenda, definit modo infallibili, quae uti talia ipsa Synodus aperte indicaverit. Ideo cetera de quibus Concilium hoc aperte non declarat, non sunt ab ipsa infallibiliter definita, sed authentico magisterio exposita tamquam Ecclesiae doctrina. Quapropter, in casu alicuius definitionis de fide, Patres conciliares praemonendi sunt et praemonebuntur atque in textu expressiones adhibendae erunt, quae explicite ostendant voluntatem aliquid sic definiendi'.

qualification of the teaching on the Church. The fundamental rule is this: 'As is self-evident, the Council's text must always be interpreted in accordance with the general rules that are known to all'. The text of the declaration, which I note in full, states:

> Taking conciliar custom into consideration and also the pastoral purpose of the present Council, the sacred Council defines as binding (*tenenda definit*) on the Church only those things in matters of faith and morals which it shall openly declare to be binding. The rest of the things which the sacred Council sets forth, inasmuch as they are the teaching of the Church's supreme Magisterium, ought to be accepted and embraced by each and every one of Christ's faithful according to the mind of the sacred Council. The mind of the Council becomes known either from the matter treated or from its manner of speaking, in accordance with the norms of theological interpretation.[3]

In this response of the Doctrinal Commission we note the passage from the reference to the authentic ordinary Magisterium of the Council to the *mind* of the Council, recognisable from the 'matter treated' ('ex subiecta materia') and 'its manner of speaking' ('ex dicendi ratione'), for those teachings which, taught by the supreme Magisterium of the Church, do not benefit from an open declaration of a definitive nature (or infallibility). Nevertheless, the formula is not very clear.[4]

Pope Paul VI, in his homiletic address at the last public session of the Council, on 7 December 1965, returned to the theme of the qualification of the conciliar teaching, confirming the fontal pastoral status of the Council, which nevertheless did not impede the path to doctrinal in-depth analysis:

---

3 AS III/8, p. 10: 'Ratione habita moris conciliaris ac praesentis Concilii finis pastoralis, haec S. Synodus ea tantum de rebus fidei vel morum ab Ecclesia tenenda definit, quae ut talia aperte ipsa declaraverit. Cetera autem, quae S. Synodus proponit, utpote Supremi Ecclesiae Magisterii doctrinam, omnes ac singuli christifideles excipere et amplecti debent iuxta ipsius S. Synodi mentem, quae sive ex subiecta materia sive ex dicendi ratione innotescit, secundum normas theologicae interpretationis'.

4 Cf. Ratzinger, LThK^2, *Das Zweite Vatikanische Konzil*, I, p. 349.

> But one thing must be noted here, namely, that the teaching authority of the Church, even though not wishing to issue extraordinary dogmatic pronouncements, has made thoroughly known its authoritative teaching on a number of questions which today weigh upon man's conscience and activity, descending, so to speak, into a dialogue with him, but ever preserving its own authority and force; it has spoken with the accommodating friendly voice of pastoral charity; its desire has been to be heard and understood by everyone; it has not merely concentrated on intellectual understanding but has also sought to express itself in simple, up-to-date, conversational style, derived from actual experience and a cordial approach which make it more vital, attractive and persuasive; it has spoken to modern man as he is.[5]

The same Pope again at the General Audience on 12 January 1966 said:

> There are those who ask what authority, what theological qualification the Council intended to give to its teachings, knowing that it avoided issuing solemn dogmatic definitions engaging the infallibility of the ecclesiastical Magisterium. The answer is known by whoever remembers the conciliar declaration of March 6, 1964, repeated on November 16, 1964: given the Council's pastoral character, it avoided pronouncing, in an extraordinary manner, dogmas endowed with the note of infallibility; but it still provided its teaching with the authority of the supreme ordinary Magisterium. This ordinary Magisterium, which is so obviously authentic, has to be accepted with docility, and sincerity by all the faithful, in accordance with the mind of the Council on the nature and aims of the individual documents.[6]

The question emerged during the work of the Council, especially during the First Session. Many Fathers raised it both directly and

---

5 In AAS 58 (1966) 57.

6 In *Encicliche e Discorsi di Paolo VI*, vol. IX, 1966 (Rome: Paoline, 1966), pp. 511–52.

indirectly. This is referred to in the Doctrinal Commission by Fr Tromp in his *Relatio de Observationibus factis a Patribus Concilii circa primum Schema Constitutionis de Ecclesia,* which bears the date 5–26 July 1963.[7] Tromp said 'gravissima est quaestio de qualificationi doctrinali'. According to the mind of the Commission 'minime necesse erat' to add the respective qualification to every proposition, the minimal qualification remaining everywhere and always: 'saltem absolute certum et irreformabiliter tenendum'. With this principle set out, 'saltem si sibi constant', everyone was satisfied. The most eminent Fathers, Montini and König, as well their Graces Charue, Jubany, Philbin, Rodriguez, Weber and Fr Butler added that the disputed questions should not be proposed, but only those which had an absolute certainty should be examined ('dicunt quaestiones disputate proponi non posse. Id enim implicat ea sola posse proponi de quibus disputari nequeat, i.e., quae absoluta certitudine gaudeant'). However, Tromp noted that none of the Fathers said clearly what questions were disputed ('Quid autem sit quaestio disputata, nemo

[7] In ASV, Envelope 755, folder 242, published in KT 2/2 pp. 620653, here pp. 634–635. Cf. also AS I/4, p. 161. The same question was also presented in the Fathers' observations on the first Mariological schema: what was the theological qualification of the Marian teaching? (Cf. KT 2/2, p. 755). Again, the question about the theological qualification of the teachings was put by Tromp in one of his handwritten notes, in which he complained about the lack of a comparison in the discussion about the two dogmatic Constitutions, *De Revelatione* and *De Ecclesia* with the introduction of the Dogmatic Constitution *De Fide Catholica* of the First Vatican Council: (*Nota Secretarii Commissionis,* 17 December 1963, ff. 4, in ASV, Envelope 762, folder 272). Towards the end (f. 4), Tromp, writing about what Vatican I meant by 'de doctrinae qualificatione theologica', stated: 'Id quod Concilium Vaticanum primum intendebat, erat propositio veritatis catholicae, propositio doctrinae prout ab Ecclesiae catholica, sancte custodia et exposita accipitur seu salutaris Christi doctrinae. Quare secundum Concilium Vaticanum primum in omni Constitutione dogmatica omnis expositio doctrinalis debet gaudere saltem illa qualificatione quae technice exprimitur verbis: doctrina catholica'. Therefore, according to Vatican I, the doctrinal teaching of a dogmatic Constitution must enjoy at least the level of 'Catholic doctrine'.

Patrem clare edixit'). He also noted some truths, up to now considered to be certain, could not improperly be deprived of their certainty, when a well-known theologian began to dispute it. On this subject, however, the rest of the Fathers said nothing of any clarity ('Constant autem veritatem aliquam hucusque indubitatam non privari sua certitudine eo quod theologus quidam etiam notabilis de ea disputare incipiat. Ceterum Patres singula hac nihil clare enuntiaverunt').

Again Tromp reported that it seemed according to the judgment of Bea, Hurley and Abbot Butler that the phenomenon of today's theology was healthy and that, by reason of that, more appropriate for considering disputable questions. Others instead, such as Hervas, Fares, Franić, Martinez, Philbin and Plaza, saw an imminent danger in this turmoil.

This absence of clarity about what was disputed and what instead enjoyed consensus among even representative theologians in fact lasted right until the end. Recourse was often made to theology and how it was to be the main teacher of the Council and of the Fathers: if there was a certain theological disagreement there, as, for example, on the question of the material sufficiency of the Scriptures, perhaps only because some representative theologian such as Geiselmann had proposed a different way from the common path, then the question was believed to be 'disputed' by some Fathers and periti, with notable courage, and therefore, if not avoided, at least left in suspense.

Given its importance, an *Observatio* of Fr Tromp about the theological qualification offered by the Doctrinal Commission on 29 November 1963, preceded on 29 October the same year by another similar formula prepared by an ad hoc Sub-commission, must be noted.[8] The Secretary of the Doctrinal Commission raises some questions about the official formula, presented in the Council by the General Secretary. For Tromp the text of the Doctrinal Commission

---

8 Cf. S. Tromp, *Observatio Secretarii Commissionis doctrinalis de Qualificatione Theologica*, 25 December 1963/16 January 1964, ff. 8 (handwritten), Rome 16 January 1963, in ASV, Envelope 762, folder 272.

'should not be berated', but, in his opinion, needed some amendments, which he was careful to underline. In the first sentence he was not happy with the use of the words: 'ea tantum de fide vel de moribus… tenenda definit'. The word 'de fide' on the one hand and 'de moribus' on the other were not correctly placed. 'De fide' in the ordinary sense of the word indicates the virtue of faith, while the juxtaposed word 'de moribus' indicates the subject matter. It would be better to write: 'ea tantum in re fidei vel morum tenenda definit'.[9] In the other sentence, 'Ideoque etc.', the unsatisfactory words were: 'sed authentico magisterio exposita tamquam Ecclesiae doctrina'. The difficulty stemmed from the fact that these words were explained by a number of theologians as 'maxima qualificatio', against which there is a minimum. So those things which were not defined solemnly in the Council, are or can be believed, as some things already were, either '"de fide catholica" simpliciter' or also 'de fide catholica definita', as clearly contained in Sacred Scripture and in Sacred Tradition, or even solemnly proclaimed as a dogma of faith in another Council.[10]

Finally, another interesting comment from Fr Tromp, prophetic about what in fact would happen among theologians. As regards the other sentence: 'Ideoque cetera… non sunt ab ipso (Concilio) defi-

---

9 Cf. *Ibid.*, f. 2: 'a) In prima periodo non placent verba: "ea tantum de fide vel de moribus… tenenda definit". Et hac quidem de causa, quia verba de fide ex una parte et verba de moribus ex altera, non recte iuxta ponuntur. Dum enim verbis de fide, saltem secundum modum ordinarium dicendi, indicatur virtus fidei, verbis iuxtapositis de moribus, indicatur materia. Scribendum potius erit: "ea tantum in re fidei vel morum tenenda definit"'.

10 Cf. *Ibid.*, ff. 2–3: 'b) In periodo autem altera: "Ideoque etc." non satisfaciunt verba: "sed authentico magisterio exposita tamquam Ecclesiae doctrina". Difficultas ex eo provenit quod haec verba a pluribus theologis explicabuntur ut maxima qualificatio, dum et contra agitur de minima. Etenim etiam in iis, quam a Concilio non solemniter definiuntur, multa sunt, vel saltem in esse possunt, quae iam aliunde sive "de fide catholica" simpliciter, sive "de fide catholica" definita, sunt credenda, puta quia claris verbis in S. Scriptura vel in S. Traditione continentur, vel iam in alio Concilio tamquam fidei dogma solemniter proclamata sunt'.

nite, sed authentico magisterio exposita tamquam Ecclesiae doctrina', this gives rise, Tromp commented, to many disputes. The question is whether the things which are taught in the Council 'tamquam Ecclesiae doctrina' are absolutely certain and of irreformable subject matter, or whether there may be errors there ('errori obnoxia'). The discussion will probably never end.[11]

Tromp said that if it wanted the Council could adopt a different formula, prepared by himself in these terms, which stated in the original:

> Dicatur S. Synodus nullam velle veritatem definire tamquam de fide catholica credendam, nisi ex verbis adhibitis id clare constat: omnia autem alia a se in rebus fidei et morum proposita, retinenda esse saltem ut doctrina catholicam.[12]

But immediately afterwards he added that perhaps it would be better to make no distinction between things defined and those to be believed at least to be Catholic teaching, as did Vatican I in the introduction:

> S. Synodus, innixam verbo Dei scripto vel tradito, prout illud ab Ecclesia Catholica sancte custoditum ad genuine expositum accepit, salutarem Christi doctrinam profiteri et declarare constituisse, adversis erroribus reiectis.[13]

However, this second suggestion, very useful though it is, distanced itself from the goal Vatican II had set itself of not condemning errors which were opposed to doctrine. And this, too, played a significant role as regards the difficulties in the discernment of the teachings. What

---

11 Cf. *Ibid.*, f. 3: 'c) Accedit quod secunda periodus: "Ideoque cetera non sunt ab ipso (Concilio) definita, sed authentico magisterio exposita tamquam Ecclesiae doctrina" dabit ansam multis disputationibus. Etenim movebitur quaestio, utrum ea quae in Concilio Oecuemnico tamquam Ecclesiae doctrina exponuntur, sint absolute certa, ideoque quoad rem irreformabilia, an potius possint esse errori obnoxia. Et probabiliter disputationum non erit finis'.

12 *Ibid.*, p. 7.

13 *Ibid.*

emerges from the Council overall, in an unequivocal manner, is precisely the minimum theological qualification: 'at least what is believed unequivocally by it', because declared as such by the Council. The question set by Fr Tromp remains open, 'if the things which the conciliar Magisterium declares as doctrine of the Church are absolutely certain and irreformable or susceptible to new more precise formulations due to possible errors' ('errori obnoxia'). I believe the second possibility to be the more probable. For the rest the general norm was re-stated, in other words conforming to the spirit of the Council, which according to the common rules of theology emerges from three aspects (cf. *Lumen Gentium* 25): from the character of the documents, from the insistence in suggesting a certain teaching, and from the way of expression. In the teachings examined by us, that is, a) the relationship between 'Scripture and Tradition' with the connected problem of Tradition as a source distinct from the Scriptures for the transmission of divine Revelation, b) teaching concerning the Church: specifically the question of membership and therefore belonging to the Church, collegiality and its general sacramentality, etc., c) the Mariological teaching in its general location, avoiding the question of Mary's mediation tied inseparably to that of co-redemption, the Council testifies to the effective exercise of the authentic ordinary Magisterium, even though the form is that of the extraordinary or solemn Magisterium, because it is the teaching of an ecumenical council. Therefore such Magisterium demands a religious deference of the intellect and the will in the field of an adherence which is not of faith, neither *credenda* nor *tenenda,* but is a 'probable' adherence, which nevertheless always moves towards the logic of the obedience of faith. There is nothing to stop the Magisterium itself from declaring the definitive nature of one of these doctrines and at the same time there is nothing to stop them from being 'a defectibus immunia', but in a healthy and fruitful co-operation between Magisterium and theology, as desired by *Donum veritatis,* something could be refined, especially with regard to the necessary and more frequent magisterial reference to what exists before the Council.

The Magisterium itself should show this unity between before and after more frequently.

Finally, in my opinion the most suitable theological qualification for the teachings examined by us, *salvo meliore iudicio,* seems to be that of *sententiae theologicae ad fidem pertinentes*: questions on which the Magisterium has still not pronounced definitively, whose denial could lead to endangering other truths of faith and whose truth is guaranteed by their intimate link with Revelation.

3. *The neutral magisterial position about the material sufficiency/insufficiency of the Scriptures*

Another fact to be borne in mind in evaluating the *mens* of the Council in its totality and the intersection of its aim with the teaching it proposed, is the question thus formulated about which we also saw the intense debates in the Theological Commission and the Sub-commission: 'not all the truths are contained in Sacred Scripture' ('non omnes veritates esse in S. Scripturam'), or as formulated by Ottaviani in the form of a question to put to the vote (on which the Secretariat for Unity placed its veto): 'Is Sacred Tradition more manifest than Sacred Scripture?' ('S. Traditio latius patet quam S. Scriptura?'). The final decision of the Council was to leave the question open: not to express itself, that is, neither in favour of the material sufficiency nor the insufficiency of the Scriptures, leaving instead its formal insufficiency strengthened. Could the question really be said to be in dispute before the Council? In my opinion, no, but there was a desire to state it to encourage ecumenism. We have seen the quarrel between Ottaviani and Bea. For the former, to be silent because of an opportunity could be painful ('tacere propter opportunitatem postea esse dolendum'). For the latter, on the other hand, it was not an opportunity but a changed *status quaestionis*: from Trent up to that moment it was not just the occasional theologian who called into question the constitutive Tradition. The problem was that they did not want two equal and almost parallel sources of Revelation. There was a re-evaluation of Sacred Scripture, but leading back often to the one revelation of the Word of God. Without doubt there is a theological improvement of *Dei verbum* with regards to the greater focus on the question of the sources than on God's Revelation itself, but the question of the constitutive Tradition remains a common teaching as it emerges from the authentic ordinary Magisterium of the Catechisms. Ratzinger in his *Milestones* shows clearly that that of Geiselmann was rather an 'alleged discovery':[14] Revelation would be enough *and* in Scripture *and* in Tradition, which left itself open, for subsequent theologians, to liberating themselves from Tradition to refer to Scripture alone, considering itself to be materially sufficient. There was talk of a material completeness of the Bible in questions of faith. Geiselmann's thesis and the abuse made of it by theologians such as Küng arose in reality at an historic moment in which there was like an empire of the historical-critical method, to which all the achievements which wanted to be the proud holders of a systematic nature, and the great and ideological hope of finally having found the point of ecumenical contact with Luther's reform, necessarily had to be attributed. Geiselmann's thesis, whose implications were unknown by the author himself, had, according to Ratzinger, 'cruder versions ... in the Council's increasingly heated atmosphere', to the point of forgetting the Catholic starting point: Scripture needs oral Tradition to be interpreted and at the same time only thanks to it are unwritten truths handed down to us. Moreover as Paul VI himself had indicated to the Council, reporting, through his Secretary of State, the quote from St Augustine: 'Sunt multa quae universa tenet Ecclesia, et ob hoc ab Apostolis praecepta bene

---

[14] Cf. J. Ratzinger, *Milestones. Memoirs: 1927–1977* (San Francisco: Ignatius Press, 1997) p. 124 (German original, *Aus meinem Lebel. Erinnerungen 1927–1977* [Stuttgart: Deutsche Verlags-Anstalt, 1998]).

creduntur, quamquam scripta non reperiantur'.[15] However, this suggestion was ignored.

To understand the real issue at stake on the theme of the sources of Revelation, what Ottaviani wrote to Felici on 17 November 1962 still seems to me to be very topical:

> Today's edition of *L'Osservatore Romano*, Saturday 17 November, publishes on the front page a report on this morning's council session, highlighting the disagreement among the Fathers about the Schema on the two sources of Revelation. It says, inter alia: 'A difference of opinion was noted above all about the opportunity to clarify in a solemn form in the Council the doctrine concerning the Sources of Revelation, with the theological studies on this argument not being sufficiently mature. In fact, the problem of whether Revelation has two distinct sources, Scripture and Tradition, or just one with two different expressions, is still being discussed'. I note the following about this report: that it is imprudent and inappropriate that an organ of the Holy See and the Press Office of the Secretary of the Council should highlight the discord among the Fathers about the foundations of the Faith; it gives unnecessary scandal; that in the last sentence, siding with the audacious opinion of a few modern ecumenists, it affirms what is false, first of all because it is not true that theological studies on this theme are not mature and then because it states that the problem of whether Revelation has two distinct sources is under discussion. This statement borders on heresy, because both the Council of Trent and that of Vatican I clearly defined that there are two distinct sources: a truth repeated and illustrated by all the theologians, after the Council of Trent, and already present in the Fathers of the Church and in the Scholastics, including St Thomas. Against Luther, who acknowledged Scripture alone as Source of Revelation, the Council of Trent defined (Session IV) that there were two

15 St Augustine, *De baptismo c. Donat.*, V, 23, 31: PL 43, 192. Cf. ASV, Envelope 787, folder 424.

> Sources, Scripture and Tradition, to be accepted 'pari pietatis affectu ac reverentia' under pain of anathema (See Denzinger n. 783). In recent times the Protestants themselves have begun to recognise Tradition distinct from Sacred Scripture. A few of our theologians, who, in recent times, prompted by impulsive ecumenism, have raised doubts about this argument, are effectively contested by serious theologians, such as Fr Lennerz and Fr Boyer, both Jesuits. I deplore *L'Osservatore Romano*'s report not just for the lack of prudence, but also for the lack of doctrinal and historical truth.[16]

The most important arguments to achieve the passage to a more bland and ambiguous text in the matter of placing the emphasis on content in the relationship between Scripture and Tradition were those of Rahner and Florit, one based on the Fathers and the other on the Magisterium. However, neither of them wanted to deny *expressis verbis* the cogency of the constitutive Tradition, but simply to explain it in such a way as to find a conciliar agreement and encourage ecumenical debate. But with Vatican II the question of the *Traditio constitutiva* lost its edge and the problem shifted to the 'Revelation and Tradition' relationship, with the risk, however, of seeing it solely and as interpretative, because by now it was free of a more or less revelatory relationship at the quantum level. Rightly, there was no desire to reduce the question to a relationship of quantity. The attention was focussed on the passage from a conceptual revelation of Vatican I to a more experiential or historico-salvific revelation, as communication of the Revealing itself through events and words, having its culminating moment in Christ, and no longer as communication of a totality of truth. The two aspects of Vatican I and Vatican II must and can be seen in unity. Without doubt with *Dei verbum* there was progress from this point of view: Revelation is analysed in-depth in it being a vital and life-giving mystery, in its establishing a *covenant* between God and man which has in Christ and finally in the Eucharist

16 In ASV, Envelope 758, folder 245, published in KT 2/2, pp. 1145–1146.

its eternal seal. That notable criticism made by some Council periti about Revelation understood as conceptualisation of the faith and the scholastic way of presenting it, however, had a preponderant and almost unilateral repercussion in the post-conciliar period: the faith and therefore its catechetical proclamation, are more and more presented, and at times solely, as *experience* of Christ, than as communication of his truth; more and more, or solely, as *encounter* with the Lord rather than communication of infallible dogmas, carried by the Church in its unchanging credo. In faith the subjective act of believing would be more important than the objective knowledge of the truths of faith. Thus one sees a displacement of the dynamic aspect of revelation to the detriment of the noetic. At the basis of this vision is found the criticism of faith as knowledge of God and therefore the Logos itself as Truth and Love. Today there is a gap between truth and love. Only their reconciliation in the truth of the Word Incarnate can give back to faith its vitality and can truly lead the human person to the encounter with God in Christ, preventing the human person from stopping at a dogmatic nominalism, apparently believing.[17] Today a strong dogmatic subjectivism reigns in the Church. I believe that the problem lies precisely in the correct relationship between Scripture and Tradition, which needs to be re-illustrated in Revelation, a relationship between the noetic and dynamic aspect of the Word of God, in the end between *fides qua* and *fides quae*. So the question remains uppermost: does faith draw from Scripture alone or also and jointly from the Church's Tradition? And just at a formal level or that of content, too?

In my opinion there is still an urgent need today to recover the sense of Catholic identity, to re-think and give full status to the genuine and theological concept of the living Tradition, which, while

[17] On this question I would refer the reader to my own Editorial text: S. M. Lanzetta, 'Quel dissidio tra la fede e il suo annuncio', in *Fides Catholica* 1 (2012), pp. 5–22; see also A. Livi, *Vera e falsa teologia. Come distinguere l'autentica "scienza della fede" da un'equivoca "filosofoa religiosa"* (Rome: Leonardo da Vinci, 2012), especially pp. 198–225.

it transmits the faith, also gives it that *plus* which Scripture alone cannot offer. It is that certainty of always remaining within the Church and to learn in a new way, in every time, the ancient being Christian. The concept of '*Traditio*' is suffering a serious crisis: it is being identified with a political and sociological connotation and therefore responds, in the collective imagination, to a sort of attempt at restoration or simply revolutionary in the post-Conciliar Church. Tradition would immediately indicate its opposite in progressivism and would simply exacerbate the deep wound which the Church is experiencing after Vatican II. On the other hand, only if full status is given back to the life-giving content of *Traditio fidei* in the theological universe is it possible to raise up the Church again, to see it in its uninterrupted unity.

It is not necessary to bring back the debate to a crystallisation on the quantitative *plus* offered by the oral Tradition. To overcome this impasse and restore to the oral Tradition its constitutive cogency for the faith it is appropriate to note that the truth, God, always surpasses us. The projection of the Tradition over Scripture, which refers back to a broader source, divine Revelation—so it is clear that there can only be one source, Revelation itself—is deep down admissible by the same projection of Truth over Tradition, and therefore Revelation. God while revealing himself, always remains other. This explains the superiority of the mystery compared to history and the need to gradually draw close to it through an evermore more profound knowledge: what the living Tradition offers to the faith of the Church. The cross-reference to Sacred Scripture is always necessary, but it is possible solely according to Tradition and not Sacred Scripture. Sacred Scripture is the *regola* of the faith in so far as it is divinely inspired; Tradition, instead, divinely assisted, not only allows the Scriptures to be always contemporary for humanity and not to become a Word spoken in the past, but also enables faith to be able to have in itself a solid basis for those truths which it bears in itself embryonically and which mature in the path of the Church's faith. Scriptures alone do not speak to us.

A route on which to embark in the in-depth analysis of the concept of Tradition united to Scripture as channels of faith (of course Revelation remains the source), could be that of the Eucharist: to better highlight the concept of Tradition in its Eucharistic meaning to *give* what has been *received* and so to increase the faith in and understanding of what one has to that extent that it is faithfully handed on according to the canon of the Church. I will just sketch out a draft. There is great affinity between Tradition and the Eucharist, which comes from Sacred Scripture along with Tradition, as for it being understood as *mysterium fidei* par excellence, to the point of becoming like the 'heart of the Church', to use an expression from de Lubac, acknowledged then by John Paul II in *Ecclesia de Eucharistia*: the Eucharistic *makes* the Church and in turn the Church makes the Eucharist.[18] In 1 Co 11:23 St Paul *transmits* what he has *received,* and that is, that on the night he was *betrayed* the Lord took some bread, gave thanks, and said: 'This is my body'. He then did the same with the chalice, saying: 'This is my blood'. It is interesting to note in this pericope the construction with the same verb *paradídomi*. This verb, which follows on immediately from to receive, 'what I received' (*parélabon*: from *paralambàno*), used by the Apostle to indicate to transmit, 'this I handed on to you' (*parédoka*: from *paradídomi,* an indicative active aorist), is the same which is then found again in the handing over of the Lord as 'betrayal' and 'gift of Self' in the eucharistic sacrifice, which draws intimately on the sacrifice of Calvary. The content of *tradere,* which initially was an *accepi,* is this: when the Lord on that night handed himself over (*paredídeto*: an imperfect indicative), he offered his Body and his Blood. In the light of this St Paul, writing to the Galatians (2:20), was able to remind them, with the

---

[18] John Paul II, Encyclical Letter *Ecclesia de Eucharistia,* 17 April 2003, especially chapter II 'The Eucharist Builds the Church', nn. 21–25, in AAS 95/7 (2003) 447–450.

same verb, that 'Christ loved me and gave himself for me' ('*paradóntos eautòn*'), and to the Ephesians (5:25) that Christ loved the Church with this offertorial love, 'and gave himself up for her' ('*eautòn parédoken upèr autês*'). See also Mark 14:21: 'But woe to that one by whom the Son of Man is betrayed!' (*paradídotai*: a passive present indicative). *Tradere,* which is always initially an *accipere,* is then repeated by St Paul in 1 Co 15:3 to announce the paschal mystery of Christ, who suffered, died and rose according to the Scriptures and finally appeared to Cephas and to the Twelve. The Church proclaims this faith in the died and risen Lord when she celebrates the divine mysteries. The Tradition of the Church is brought to life precisely by this sacramental connection in the living sacrifice of the Lord, made present every day by the Church, right up until the end of time.

Of course this does not resolve the problem of whether Tradition brings something which is not already present at least indirectly in Scripture. But it is not for this reason that one seeks to ascertain the need for Tradition, which in no way can be separated from Scripture to understand the faith. In this sense Tradition cannot be reduced to a purely material aspect. However, it remains clear that Scripture would not be sufficient to transmit the faith without Tradition, whose *proprium* is to bring orally, like in a maternal womb which is the Church, those truths which, taught and confirmed by the Magisterium, can climb to the level of infallible truths, or because they are held definitively or declared as such by a solemn act, alongside one of its other prerogatives of being the sole valid interpreter of the Scriptures themselves.

The transmission of the faith in the Eucharist constitutes the today of the Church, its being living presence in the world. So it is impossible to look just at the Gospel to understand what the Church believes when she professes her faith and her eucharistic faith. It is necessary to read the Gospel in the perspective of the oral proclamation of that faith which preceded its written drafting and in the perspective of the life of the Church which follows the Gospel. Therefore it is necessary to look at the liturgy, with which the Church has believed and transmitted the faith in the Eucharist and therefore the mystery itself. The transmission of the mystery of the Eucharist highlights the *actus tradendi* and the *obiectum traditum*. Prayer as *lex orandi* proclaims the *lex credendi* and this establishes prayer. The *lex credendi* is given always by Scripture and Tradition together as can be inferred in the *lex orandi*.

4. *Members of the Church and the co-extensivity of the mystical Body and of the Roman Catholic Church*

In *Lumen Gentium*'s study of the Church we met with considerable insistence the theme of members of the Church, tied then to the broader question of belonging to the Church. In itself the theme assumes great significance at the dogmatic level: from its correct positioning it highlights the need for the means of the Church and her call to gather all peoples together into unity for salvation. The conciliar Constitution on the Church overlooked the specific theme of members, which in the conciliar debate saw a tormented dispute among the Fathers: to speak about members meant either excluding who was not a member or defining them as 'imperfect members'. That would have clearly clashed with the raised emphasis of optimism desired by the Holy Father in the programmatic address. Moreover, there was a desire to go beyond the proximity of the mystical Body of Christ with the visible Roman Catholic Church, pointing to the Church invisible mystery which transcends her historical and juridical boundaries. According to various Fathers, the mystery of the Church was broader than her earthly and hierarchical manifestation. Therefore all those who were baptised already belonged to the Church (mystery), although, at a visible level, there was not a full communion with the Catholic Church, unique mystical Body of the Lord.

But now the question which still remains open is as follows: *have baptised non-Catholics been incorporated as members of the Catholic*

Church? Lumen Gentium speaks of not fully belonging, while belonging fully is for Catholics only, who, as well as Baptism, keep the Sacraments and communion with the hierarchy. So, is not fully belonging visible? If it were we would be in communion with non-Catholics. *Lumen Gentium* 15 says that the Church is with them 'plures ob rationes coniunctam', while *Unitatis redintegratio* 3 speaks about a certain communion, even though not perfect: 'in quadam cum Ecclesia catholica communione, etsi non perfecta, constituuntur'. Only with *Dominus Iesus* (17) was it clarified that those who believe in Christ and are baptised are incorporated in Christ and are constituted in a certain communion, albeit imperfect, with the Church. A communion which admits a perfectibility in view of the subject that is related to it but which still remains in imperfection, therefore in *being oriented* fully to incorporation (on account of *Lumen Gentium* 16 it seems not: only non-Christians are *related* to the Church), which, *in re*, de facto, is imperfect. This seems to be the most persuasive solution, which, however, bears in itself a certain friction: how can one *already* be incorporated into the Church without having full communion with it, save incurring heresy or schism? Above all, how can that be considered without reference to appropriate philosophical-metaphysical categories? In any case is there a certain opposition being outlined between members as subjects and the communities as a totality? There are two approaches to the question: one more canonical (cf. can. 87/1917), according to which one is a member of the Church (or constituted 'people') by virtue of Baptism, therefore everything that is Christian is in relation to the Church, and a more theological approach, which instead judges 'communion' with the Church, according to which Baptism alone would constitute the Christian as an initial or imperfect member.[19] In the words of Ratzinger, it is unnecessary to develop

19 However, as I noted, the fact remains that the new Code of Canon Law, canon 11, indicates a decisive shift compared to that of 1917: since ecclesiastical laws are binding solely on Catholics, canon 18/1917, taken up however by canon 96/1983, loses its cogency in a problem which is difficult to tackle and resolve on a typically theological level. In this sense the discrepancy between the legal

beyond (*entfalten*) this distinct approach of belonging to the Church, especially in reference to the question of members. In this way separated brethren being Christians is recognised and at the same time the wound of their separation is not hidden.[20]

Unfortunately, on this point there is not unanimity among theologians, and very often confusion is generated; it seems rather that the question has not lost its urgency. From our way of looking at the theme of *plene* or *non plene* belonging the most important point of the question is left vague: the visible aspect of the Church, that is, the corporate and hierarchical, which seems to be included in the invisible and mystical. Another question is the possibility of salvation outside the visible confines of the Church, another is being a member of the one Body of Christ, which as an historic and sacramental given is salvific. Ecumenism in fact aims at the visible union of Christians in the one mystical Body. The theme is therefore very sensitive, left in part unresolved. Moreover, Cardinal Bea, for example, wanting to broaden the question of members to a more ecumenical perspective and therefore wanting in some way to show the Church as broader than the visible Church, included in it the purgative and triumphant Church. In reality, at an ecumenical and theological level in general it is not the purgative or triumphant Church to be the necessary means of salvation, but solely the Church militant or pilgrim Church. It is the Church as visible body to be the mystery of salvation. In this regard Fr Tromp's *Observationes De Ecclesia militantis natura,* about chapter I of the schema De Ecclesia (which I found in AEF and present also in ASV),[21] dated 10 February

---

level of belonging to the Church and the theological level is alleviated, having to distinguish the ecclesial statute of the real particular non-Catholic Churches from the simple Christian communities, through the declaration *Dominus Iesus* (cf. nn. 16–17, in AAS 92 [2000] 757–759).

20 J. Ratzinger, 'Der Kirchenbegriff und die Frage nach der Gliedschaft in der Kirche', in Id., *Kirche-Zeichen unter den Völkern* (Gesammelte Schriften 8/1) (Freiburg im B.: Herder, 2010), pp. 302–305.

21 Cf. S. Tromp, *Observationes ad Caput I: De Ecclesia militantis natura* (CFM 3/63: 1. De Ecclesia), 10 February 1963 (ff. 5), in AEF, Folder 5, Schema 'De

1963, are very interesting, explaining the cogency of the theme of members and at the same time it seems to us highly prophetic about the theological risk which was building up, and had in fact had shown itself, about its exclusion or simply being put to one side. I would like to present its key passages, in which Tromp, having reported the thought of Bea to which I have just referred, and that of Frings and Liénart, gave his opinion, indicating the real theological problem that was being hidden in the discussion.

According to Tromp, the Council, in a singular if not exclusive way, was able to consider the Church with regard to the correctly named mystery, by reason of the theandric action of the Incarnate Word, which instils grace and supernatural gifts in every member. But in so doing it would propose a very unilateral doctrine, which would not satisfy the pastoral and ecumenical needs. That is to say, there was the risk of absorbing the visible aspect of the Church in the invisible. Of course, Tromp said, the divinity of Christ infinitely surpasses his humanity; sacramental grace infinitely surpasses the visible signs; the mystical bonds surpass the social ones, but in this order of salvation, the humanity of Christ, the eucharistic sacrifice, the sacramental signs and the legal structure of the Church occupy a completely singular place and the nativity, the preaching, the death, resurrection and ascension of Christ in the flesh, the material and form of the sacraments, the social character of the Church determined by its very founder, must be set out clearly for the faithful. There was contempt for a certain 'supernatural existentialism'. A healthy ecumenism, on the other hand, demands that the social character of the Church be presented in a clear way if there is a desire for visible and not just mystical unity. In this economy salvation is given only by means of the visible Church of Christ, in which the Roman Pontiff happily reigns. The ecumenical problem is not resolved—Tromp added again by way of conclusion—if the regime and Magisterium as Christ has

---

Ecclesia'; ASV, Envelope 763, folder 273: an 8-page manuscript, dated 9–10 February 1963, and another 5-page text, dated 10 February 1063.

determined them and which are found only in the Roman Catholic Church are not accepted.

The theological endeavour, then, should be that of not separating drastically the visible and hierarchical aspect of the Church from the mystical and communion aspects, the Church sacrament and people of God from the Church mystical body united as a society, according to the Pauline theology of the Body of Christ (cf. Ep 4:4–6; 1 Co 12:12–30). Pius XII had already denounced the danger of an unreal gap between Church as a 'juridical body' and Church 'as a union of charity': this visible and juridical Church is the Church of Christ, the Church of charity and the universal family of Christians.[22] There is no true communion without hierarchy: it would only be an autocracy or confusion of roles. Hierarchy, then, is to be understood in its meaning of *ieros archê*, of sacred or divine origin: a divine principle which comes from on high and descends towards us to gather us as *ekklesía*, which by itself is at the same time *summons* and *congregation*, *Ecclesia convocans et congregans—Ecclesia convocata et congregata*. First there is the active sense of summons but the second is no less necessary nor less important, as noted by H. de Lubac.[23] The Fathers with St Augustine,[24] St Isidore of Seville,[25] St Ildefonsus,[26] etc., indicate the two dimensions of the one body which is the Church: the divine convocation and the community of the convoked. The Church in itself is she who gives baptism and receives it; a hierarchical society and a community of grace; it is dual mystery of communication and of communion, and this by the communication of sacred things through the sacraments and the communion of Saints, which

22 Cf. Pius XII, *Address to the seminary students of Rome*, 24 June 1939.

23 H. De Lubac, *The Splendour of the Church* (London and New York: Sheed and Ward, 1956), p. 70 (French original, *Méditation sur l'Église* [Paris: Desclée de Brouwer, 1985]).

24 St Augustine, *Contra Faustum*, 1. XII, c. 16: PL 42, 263.

25 St Isidore of Seville, *De ecclesiasticis officiis*, 1. I, c. 1: PL 83, 739–740; *Etymologiae*, 1. VIII, c. 1: PL 82, 293–295.

26 St Ildefonsus, *De cognitio baptismi*, c. 73: PL 96, 138C.

constitutes it mystery of grace. With De Lubac I am convinced that there is no need to state that the Church is composed of a visible and social aspect as a hierarchical society and a mystical aspect as Body of Christ; there is always the danger of dividing itself:

> We must look for the multiple elements of which she is composed and the many aspects under which she may be considered, in the interior of the Church herself considered in her unimpairable unity—that is, in the interior of the Mystical Body. ... It is this twofold aspect of the one Church in her present state which is, precisely, called up by the Pauline doctrine of the 'body of Christ'.[27]

It is the Church sacramental and life-giving *Body* of the risen Lord which is in itself mystery and hierarchical order. When St Paul defines the Church 'Body of Christ' he is not creating anything new, says Ratzinger, but is offering simply a brief formula to describe a reality which has impressed itself from the outset in the becoming of the Church. It is therefore totally false to presume that the Apostle had borrowed one of the widespread allegories from the historical philosophy of his time and applied it to the Church.[28]

Certainly the concept of 'Church' illustrated by *Lumen Gentium* in the broadest sense was notable theological progress, seeking to examine its mystery from within, highlighting her communion and sacramental aspect. 'The concept of communion has the advantage of expressing the reality of the Church, while the notion of sacrament[29] highlights above all the external-institutional aspect'.[30] The

---

27 De Lubac, *The Splendour of the Church*, pp. 69, 82.

28 J. Ratzinger, 'Ursprung und Wesen der Kirche', in Id., *Kirche-Zeichen unter den Völkern* (Gesammelte Schriften 8/1) (Freiburg im B.: Herder, 2010), p. 233: 'So hat Paulus in der Sache gar nichts Neues geschaffen, wenn er die Kirche "Leib Christi" nennt; er bietet nur eine Kurzformel für das, was von Anfang an das Wesen der Kirche prägt. Es ist vollkommen falsch, wenn immer wieder behauptet wird, dass Paulus nur eine in der stoischen Philosophie seiner Zeit verbreitete Allegorie auf die Kirche angewendet habe'.

29 In the sense of *sacramentum tantum* distinct from *res et sacramentum* and from

Church, through the Council, in the words of St John Paul II, 'did not at all want to close in on herself, refer to herself alone (the so-called "ecclesiocentrism"), but, on the contrary, wanted to open out further'.[31] In fact, this is the notable ecclesiological emphasis of *Lumen Gentium*: an open vision, for a highly pastoral goal, to invoke the unity of the whole of humankind with God by means of the Church, its sign and instrument. Perhaps precisely the notable emphasis, mixed with an emotional drive, overcame the theological confines of the preconciliar Church. The strongly hopeful opening united to a superfluous and discursive theological exertion lent themselves to misunderstanding or embarrassment for the Church which was already there.

On closer inspection, in an over-excited post-conciliar period, this was only the beginning in putting the concept of the Church into perspective, opposing to the institution, the charism; to the visible Church, the invisible; to the earthly Church, the heavenly one. In the 1985 Synod of Bishops, twenty years after the Council, reflecting on the effects produced by it, it would be said: 'We cannot replace a false unilateral vision of the Church as purely hierarchical with a new sociological conception which is also unilateral. Jesus Christ is ever present in his Church and lives in her as risen'.[32]

Broadly speaking the Council re-discovered the local Church, and this is a factor of major ecclesiological in-depth examination. In this sense the emphasis should also be placed on collegiality, seen in the light of the very norms given by John XXIII to the Council, that is to say, pastorality and ecumenism, as Ratzinger would point out.[33]

---

res tantum.

30 A. Favale, 'Genesi della Costituzione', in AA.VV., *La Costituzione dogmatica sulla Chiesa* (Turin: Elle Di Ci, 1967[4]), p. 22.

31 John Paul II, Address *Deo gratias*, at the end of the II Extraordinary Assembly of the Synod of Bishops, 7 December 1985: ESV n. 2767.

32 ESV, n. 2729.

33 Cf. J. Ratzinger, 'Problemi e risultati del Concilio Vaticano II', *Giornale di Teologia* 8, Queriniana, Brescia 1966 (on the third and fourth sessions of the Council), p. 58. The complete original text can be found in Id., *Zur Lehre des*

Instead, it served to encourage a more democratic vision of Church. On the contrary, according to Ratzinger, episcopal collegiality, as taught by the Council, did not have as its aim that

> Of transforming the bishops into small popes and strengthening the clericalisation of the Church; its aim was rather to correct the unilaterality of an exaggerated practice of the primacy through a new accentuation of the multiplicity and fullness represented in the bishops. On the basis of this goal must its pronouncements be interpreted; then the positive ecumenical meaning of them automatically comes to light.[34]

The 1985 Synod was also very clear on this point:

> On the other hand, the one and unique spirit works with many and varied spiritual gifts and charisma (1 Cor. 12:4ff), the one Eucharist is celebrated in various places. For this reason, the unique and universal Church is truly present in all the particular Churches (*Christus Dominus* n. 11: EV 1/593), and these are formed in the image of the universal Church in such a way that the one and unique Catholic Church exists in and through the particular Churches (*Lumen Gentium* n. 23: EV 1/338). Here we have the true theological principal of variety and pluriformity in unity but it is necessary to distinguish pluriformity from pure pluralism. When pluriformity is true richness and carries with it fullness, this is true catholicity. The pluralism of fundamentally opposed positions instead leads to dissolution, destruction and the loss of identity.[35]

5. *A new 'form' of Magisterium?*

A final question must be considered by way of an overall view of the work done and at the Council overall. The question to be posed is as follows: was progress made at Vatican II about a new form of Magis-

Zweiten Vatikanischen Konzils, I, pp. 417–472; 527–575.

[34] *Ibid.*, p. 79.

[35] ESV, n. 2740.

terium for the Church? Some authors have already begun to raise this question,[36] which, however, in the theologians at the Council and in the immediate post-conciliar period, was already present as awareness of a change: the theological character of the magisterial *aggiornamento* had encouraged a way of teaching which was no longer condemnation of errors and in return definition of truth—by condemning errors one states what alone is true—but rather an affirmation or declaration of truth in a way which could also encourage its perception in others and finally unity. The real substance of original sin in every human person should instead be an impetus to be more careful in this aspect. The ministry of truth, which belongs properly to the Church because Christ is the truth (cf. Jn 14:6), is the greatest act of love which the Church from the outset has always manifested towards her children and towards every person of goodwill. Today, above all, in a confusion of ideas and opinions, the Church must and can shine out once again as unique teacher of truth and of life, therefore of love.

So, did a predicative or declarative Magisterium make any progress in the Council as a new form of the *munus docendi*?

It is important to remember that it was John XXIII, in his inaugural address at the start of the Council, who indicated a new magisterial form to be adopted to set out the truth. Paul VI, in his address at the start of the Second Session of the Council, on 29 September 1963, took up his predecessor's desire, saying:

> Hence we shall ever keep in mind the norms which you, the first Father of this Council, have wisely laid down and which

36 Cf. Kolfhaus, *Paatorale Lehrverkündigung*, pp. 213–219, in which he states that Vatican II, through *Unitatis redintegratio, Dignitatis humanae* and *Nostra Aetate,* wanted to use a *munus praedicandi* rather than *docendi* because it was teaching orientated towards praxis and not exercised as *munus determinandi.* I believe here a theological concept to define the pastoral magisterium of Vatican II is lacking. See also T. Citrini, 'A proposito dell'indole pastorale del magistero', in *Teologia* 15 (1990), pp. 130–149; E. Vilanova, 'Magistero "pastorale" nel post-concilio', in *Revista Catalana de teologia* 17/1–2 (1992), pp. 105.132.

> we may profitably repeat here: 'Our task is not merely to guard this precious treasure, namely our Faith, as if we were only concerned with antiquity, but to dedicate ourselves with an earnest will and without fear to that work which our era demands of us, pursuing thus the path which the Church has followed for nearly 20 centuries'. Hence, 'that method of presenting the truth must be used which is more in conformity with a Magisterium prevalently pastoral in character' (AAS 54 [1962], pp. 791–792 [p. 1101–1103]).[37]

Again, the Holy Father Paul VI, in the same address *Salvete fratres* at the Second Session of the Council, pointed out this need to express in a more consonant manner what the Church believes and thinks about herself. In this case, the Magisterium is presented more as a *declarative* form of teaching (in reflexive mode):

> The time has now come, we believe, when the truth regarding the Church of Christ should be examined, coordinated and expressed more deeply. The expression should not, perhaps, take the form of a solemn dogmatic definition, but of declarations making known by means of the Church's Magisterium, in a more explicit and authoritative form, what the Church considers herself to be.[38]

There is also a new indication of this new form of ecclesiastical Magisterium in the First Ordinary General Assembly of the Synod of Bishops, which was held from 29 September to 29 October 1967, and where among the different topics on the agenda there was also the problem of the spread of atheism. It was in that Synod that a suggestion was made to the Holy Father, and then approved, about the establishment of an International Theological Commission, under the Congre-

37 In AAS 55 (1963) 845.

38 *Ibid.*, pp. 848–849: 'Nobis prorsus videtur advenisse nunc tempus, quo circa Ecclesiam Christi veritas magis magisque explorari, digeri, exprimi debeat, fortasse non sollemnibus illis enuntiationibus, quas definitiones dogmaticas vocant, sed potius declarationibus adhibitis, quibus Ecclesia clariore et graviore magisterio sibi declarat quid de seipsa sentiat'.

gation for the Doctrine of the Faith, which would be able to help the Holy See in the examination of theological problems of greatest significance. In the 24 October 1967 Report *Ratione habita* from the Synodal Commission, for a further examination *On Dangerous Opinions and on Atheism,* two years after the closure of the Council, the actual dangers to faith and Catholic doctrine were highlighted.

> It does not seem surprising, it may be noted, that the opportune and fruitful renewal which the Second Vatican Council brought to the Church, changing at it did many seemingly permanent customs and ways of thinking, and giving a strong impulse to new thought and to the beginning of a new manner of Christian life, has aroused difficulty and even uncertainty.[39]

The report again complained that despite the effort to follow the pastoral direction given to the Council by John XXIII, it was no longer a question of

> Sound and fruitful investigation, or legitimate efforts to adapt the expression of traditional doctrine to new needs and to the ways of modern human culture, but rather of unwarranted innovations, false opinions, and even errors in the Faith. For truths of the Faith are falsely understood or explained, and in the developing process of understanding doctrine its essential continuity is neglected.[40]

Already 'a certain arbitrary and false interpretation of the spirit of the Council'[41] was spreading. Despite everything, the bishops were encouraged to maintain a pastoral attitude in the exercise of their Magisterium, without neglecting vigilance in keeping the pressing doctrinal dangers at a distance from their faithful:

> In fulfilling their office of teaching, the bishops must be concerned both with faithfully preserving the deposit of faith

---

39 EDS 1, n. 452.

40 *Ibid.*

41 *Ibid.*, n. 454.

> and with protecting their flocks from the dangers that threaten them. But a positive way of setting forth the truth will usually be more fitting than a mere negative condemnation of error.[42]

However, the problem which emerges from this new pastoral attitude is the following: was not the Magisterium of the preceding councils and preceding Popes pastoral in condemning errors? Does not the greatest charity consist in distinguishing error from truth, like the darnel from the good seed? Would perhaps this new way of facing the revealed truth lead the Magisterium itself in some way to become liberated at a practical level from the previous Magisterium? The *munus* is not under question, but its form. So it does not mean that the Magisterium, choosing a form more in tune with today, is freeing itself from the very *munus docendi* and renouncing teaching. But simply that the teaching, with a more pastoral form, which however by reason of its object is always dogmatic or moral teaching, proves to be for the believer and for the theologian to be hermeneutically more confused: it would mean distinguishing in it the reasoning and the way of presentation from what it is to be believed in faith and morals; more often it means discovering in the same reasoning the properly dogmatic given which there is a desire to teach. So it is not just a matter of condemning errors as above all stating the truth in an unequivocal manner. Therefore I believe that even if a more declarative form of Magisterium, that is to say, more pastoral, is both useful and necessary to reach the heart of the human person, to question minds, and more in tune with the modern spirit of the search for a greater self-determination, there is no need, however, to neglect the proper dogmatic form which is definitive and infallible teaching.

In conclusion, I believe it can be said that from the Second Vatican Council there are various questions which still remain open. As we saw in the discourse about Our Lady, their status as open questions can only testify to the moment when the Council itself, due to a choice of field, wanted to leave it still open to theological debate. The open

---

42 *Ibid.*, n. 458.

questions are verifiable, besides Mariology (as regards a more in-depth and precise explanation of the soteriological mystery of Mary, and in particular with regard to Mary's co-operation in redemption, declinable precisely as co-redemption and mediation of all the graces), also in the dogmatic texts concerning the mystery of the transmission of divine Revelation and the mystery of the Church in her expanse. Ecumenical endeavour had led a drive towards the formulation of a teaching more current with the present time. Making use in a more abundant manner of biblical and patristic studies, consequently the novelty of the Council does not necessarily contain the 'entire' development subsequent to the Fathers and therefore to the whole of Tradition. Scripture does not provide us, for example, with a treatise on the Trinity: for this it was necessary to wait for the Fathers, and the Fathers, for example, do not teach us about the infallibility of the Pope: for this it was necessary to wait for the First Vatican Council, even if the doctrine was already mature from before and was logically connected with Revelation. If the conciliar plea is exclusively a 'return to the sources', a consequence of this, per se, is that Vatican II does not recapture the whole of Church doctrine, but a part of it and sometimes only an initial part. If, on the other hand, 'return to the sources' were to mean an homogenous development of them according to the canon of the Church's living Tradition, then it would be possible to exit from a road which up to now seemed to have no way out. Between the sources and Vatican II there seems to us to be like a vacuum, which, alas, robs the faith. I hope, through this work, to have contributed to shedding light on the Second Vatican Council as part of a whole, a whole which is much greater: the Church.

I am delighted to conclude this work expressing a great desire, which surpasses our narrowness but which allows us to look further ahead, beyond the impasse in which we seem to have come to halt. I would see in a desirable dogmatic definition of the mediation of Mary Most Holy a major remedy for the climate of theological agitation which we are experiencing and for the diffidence towards the dogma and towards faith itself, as a gift from on high to be welcomed and to which one should adjust one's life. I believe that great advantages could stem from infallibly defining that Mary is Mediatrix and therefore our true Mother because she is our Co-Redemptrix:

1. the Magisterium would give full status to its most specific dogmatic *munus*;
2. the Second Vatican Council would no longer be misunderstood and welcomed as a new theological era for a Church which no longer needed to define dogmas, because her faith, being almost confused with praxis, would have, in some way, through action, deposed belief according to the *regula fidei* and according to the Symbol;
3. would have re-evaluated the concept of the constitutive Tradition of the faith, by an ecumenism in the truth of the deposit received and faithfully transmitted;
4. Mariology would shine out once again from its prophetic *munus* for theology;
5. there would be a wave of salutary grace for the whole of the Church.

These are points, however, which would merit a further treatise. May the Mother of the Church watch over all her children and over the whole Church, of which her Son is the living mystical Body, present in the world for the salvation of all peoples.

BIBLIOGRAPHY

Sources

a) Acta

Acta et documenta Concilio Oecumenico Vaticano II apparando. Series antepraeparatoria, 4 tomes in 15 vols., Rome: Typis Polyglottis Vaticanis, 1960–1961.

Acta et documenta Concilio Oecumenico Vaticano II apparando. Series praeparatoria, 4 tomes in 11 vols., Rome: Typis Polyglottis Vaticanis, 1960–1995.

Acta Synodalia sacrosancti Concilii Oecumenici Vaticani II 1970–1980, Vatican City: Typis Vaticani, 1970–1999.

Concilium Vaticanum II, *Constitutiones. Declarationes, Decreta,* Vatican City: LEV, 1993.

b) Diaries

Betti U., *Diario del Concilio: 11 ottobre 1962-Natale 1978,* Bologna: Dehoniane, 2003.

Chenu M. D., *Notes quotidiennes au Concilie. Journal de Vatican II 1962–1963,* Paris: Cerf, 1995.

Congar Y., *My Journal of the Council,* Collegville MN: Liturgical Press, 2012.

De Lubac H., *Carnets du Concile,* II tomes, Paris: Cerf, 2007.

Jedin H., *Lebensbericht,* Mainz: Matthias-Grünewald, 1984.

Schillebeeckx E., *The Council notes of Edward Schillebeeckx 1962–1963,* Leuven: Peters, 2011 (edited by K. Schelkens).

Tromp S., *Konzilstagebuch mit Erläuterungen und Akten aus der Arbeit der Theologischen Kommission,* Band I/1 e Band I/2 (1960–1962), Herausgegeben von A. von Teuffenbach, Rome: PUG, 2006.

Tromp S., *Konzilstagebuch mit Erläuterungen und Akten aus der Arbeit der Theologischen Kommission,* Band 2/1 e Band 2/2 (1962–1963), Herausgegeben von A. von Teuffenbach, Nordhausen: Bautz, 2011.

c) Magisterium

John XXIII, Address *Gaudet Mater Ecclesia,* 11 October 1962, in AAS 54 (1962) 785–795.

John XXIII, Address *Singulari prorsus,* 8 December 1962, in AAS 55 (1962) 39.

Paul VI, Address *Salvete fratres,* 29 September 1963, in AAS 55 (1963) 841–859.

Paul VI, Encyclical Letter *Ecclesiam suam,* 6 August 1964, in AAS 56 (1964) 611–614.

Paul VI, Address *Publica haec,* 18 November 1965, in AAS 57 (1965) 978–984.

Paul VI, Homily *Hodie Concilium,* 7 December 1965, in AAS 58 (1966) 51–59.

Paul VI, General Audience *Inseriti nel patrimonio della Chiesa gli insegnamenti del Concilio,* 12 January 1966, in *Encicliche e Discorsi di Paolo VI,* vol. IX, 1966, Rome: Paoline, 1966, pp. 49–52.

John Paul II, Address *Ad gravissimum munus,* 27 August 1978, in AAS 70 (1978) 694–696.

John Paul II, Address *Unum solummodo,* 17 October 1978, in AAS 70 (1978) 920–922.

John Paul II, Encyclical Letter *Ecclesia de Eucharistia,* 17 April 2003, in AAS 95 (2003) 433–475.

Benedict XVI, Address *Expergiscere, homo,* 22 December 2005, in AAS 98 (2006) 40–53.

Benedict XVI, Motu proprio *De usu extraordinario antiquae formae Ritus Romani,* 7 July 2007, in AAS 99 (2007) 777–781.

Benedict XVI, Letter *Ad Episcopos Catholicae Ecclesiae Ritus Romani* (on the occasion of the publication of the Apostolic Letter 'Motu Proprio Data' *Summorum Pontificum* on the use of the Roman Liturgy prior to the reform of 1970), 7 July 2007, in AAS 99 (2007) 795–799.

Benedict XVI, Letter *Ad Episcopos Ecclesiae Catholicae* (concerning the remission of the excommunication of the four bishops consecrated by Archbishop Lefebvre), 10 March 2009, in AAS 101 (2009) 270–276.

Benedict XVI, Address to the Plenary Session of the Congregation for Clergy, 16 March 2009, in AAS 101 (2009) 293–296.

Benedict XVI, Address to the Plenary Session of the Congregation for the Doctrine of the Faith, 27 January 2012, in *L'Osservatore Romano* of 28 January 2012, p. 8.

Benedict XVI, Meeting with the clergy of Rome, *Al concilio pieno di entusiasmo e di speranza*, 14 February 2013, in *L'Osservatore Romano* of 16 February 2013, pp. 4–5.

Congregation for the Doctrine of the Faith, *Circular Letter to the Presidents of Episcopal Conferences regarding some sentences and errors arising from the interpretation of the decrees of the Second Vatican Council*, 24 July 1966, in AAS 58 (1966) 659–661.

Congregation for the Doctrine of the Faith, Declaration *Mysterium Ecclesiae* in defense of the Catholic doctrine on the Church against certain errors of the present day, 24 June 1973, in AAS 65 (1973) 396–408.

Congregation for the Doctrine of the Faith, *Notification on the book 'Church: Charism and Power' by Father Leonardo Boff O.F.M.*, 11 March 1985, in *AAS* 77 (1985) 756–762.

Congregation for the Doctrine of the Faith, *Letter to the Bishops of the Catholic Church on some aspects of the Church understood as communion*, 28 May 1992, in AAS 85 (1993) 838–850.

Congregation for the Doctrine of the Faith, *Declaration 'Dominius Iesus' on the unicity and salvific universality of Jesus Christ and the Church*, 6 August 2000, in AAS 92 (2000) 742–765.

Congregation for the Doctrine of the Faith, *Responses to some questions regarding certain aspects of the doctrine on the Church*, 29 June 2007, in AAS 99 (2007) 604–608.

Congregation for the Doctrine of the Faith, *Note with pastoral recommendations for the Year of Faith*, 6 January 2012, in *L'Osservatore Romano* of 7–8 January 2012, pp. 4–5.

d) Theological works

AAVV., *Propositiones circa schema De Beata Maria Virgine Matre Ecclesiae a Patribus Conciliaribus linguae germanicae et Conferentiae Episcoporum Scandinaviae exaratae*, 22 pages, to which are added a further 7 pages which, as an *Appendix*, contain the Mariological evaluation of H. Volk, in AEF, Foldedr 5, Schema "De Ecclesia, published in AS II/3, pp. 837–853.

AAVV., *Osservazioni raccolte dagli esperti nominati dalla Conferenza Episcopale Italiana. In schema De Fontibus Revelationis Animadversiones* (a text comprising 15 pages including the analysis of a Propositio: "SUPER DUOS FONTES REVELATIONIS EST UNICA ORIGO, SCILICET VERBUM DEI"), in AEF, Folder 2, Schema "De divina revelatione".

AAVV., *Esposto di 19 Cardinali al Sommo Pontefice riguardante lo schema della Costituzione Dogmatica "De Fontibus Revelationis"*, 24.11.1962, (a text comprising 5 pages), in AEF, Folder 2, Schema "De divina revelatione".

Balić C., *Relatio circa compositionem capituli octavi const. Dogmaticae De Ecclesia, in* ASV, Envelope 766, Folder 203.

Balić C., *Circa "membra in voto" Ecclesiae Christi*, die Pentecostes 1961, 11 pages, in ASV, Envelope 739, Folder 117.

Balić C., *Pro-memoria circa vota ac consilia de B. V. Maria ab Episcopis et Praelatis pro Concilio Vaticano II apparando*, 26.4.1962, in ASV, Envelope 750, Folder 222.

Balić C., *De Beata Maria Virgine Matre Christifidelium*, 7.9.1963 (a text comprising 15 pages), in ASV, Envelope 766, Folder 203.

Bertams G., *Notae quoad capitulum tertium schematis De Ecclesia* [a report requested by the Secretary of State, on the basis of which Paul VI was assured of the soundness of the teaching of Chapter III of *Lumen gentium*, and given information about some important amendments to be made in order to arrive at the *Nota explicativa praevia*] in ASV, Envelope 785, Folder 400.

Commissio de Doctrina Fidei et Morum, *Relatio De Suggestionibus Commissioni Doctrinali propositis*, 5–6 June 1964, 6 pages, 7 giugno 1964, in ASV, Envelope 787, Folder 424 [report on the observations made to the Doctrinal Commission about Chapter III of the schema de Ecclesia].

Congar Y., *Erinnerungen an eine Episode auf dem II. Vatikanischen Konzil*, in E. Klinger—K. Wittstadt [eds.], *Glaube im Prozess. Christ nach dem II. Vatikanum*, Herder, Freiburg im B. 1984, pp. 51–64 [alternative text to *De fontibus* proposed as an introduction to the Rahner-Ratzinger schema, *De revelatione Dei et hominis in Jesu Christo facta*].

Congar Y., *Nota De Membris*, C.T. 5/61: 104, 2 pages, in ASV, Envelope 739, Folder 117.

Congar Y., 'Le Schema 'De Revelatione'', in *Études et Documents*, n. 14, 11 July 1963, pp. 1–8 [Congar's report for the French bishops on Schema II or Form D, particularly concerning Tradition].

Congar Y., 'Le texte révise du 'De Revelatione'', in *Études et Documents*, n. 13, 30 June 1964, pp. 1–12 [Congar's report for the French bishops on Schema II modified by the Sub-commissions and approved by the Theological Commission from 1 June 1964].

Congar Y., 'Textus propositus 'De Traditione'' (Subcommisio 'De Divina Revelatione'), [a text comprising two parts, each of four pages: a) *Traditio Populo Dei*; b) *De Traditione et Scriptura*], in AEF, Folder 2, Schema 'De divina revelatione'; *De Traditione et Scriptura*, Rome, November 1963, ff. 5–6, in ASV, Envelope 729, Folder 5.

Congar Y., 'La collégialité de l'épiscopat', in *Études et Documents*, 15 January 1963, n. 1; photocopy in ASV, Envelope 729, Folder 5, 7 pages.

Dante E., *Osservazioni sullo Schema De Divina Revelatione*, 1965, 11 pages [a report sent to the Holy Father], in ASV, Envelope 787, Folder 424.

Döpfner J., *Lettera inviata al Sommo Pontefice contenente alcune osservazioni sullo Schema De Divina Revelatione*, 14 October 1965, 4 pages, in ASV, Envelope 787, Folder 424.

Fenton J. C., *De ecclesia: Observationes D. Fenton circa usum verbi "Sacramentum" tamquam designationem Ecclesiae Catholicae*, Rome, 18 November 1963, 2 pages, in ASV, Envelope 766, Folder 296.

Gagnebet M. R., *Nota Patris Gagnebet de actuositate R.Patris Congar O.P. et aliorum ad emendandum Schema de Ecclesia,* Manuscript. Ex Civitate Vaticana, 30 November1962, 3 pages, in ASV, Envelope 759, Folder 249, published in KT 2/2, p. 947.

Gagnebet M. R., *Conférence de presentation du schéma De Ecclesia,* 3.12.1962, in ASV, Envelope 759, Folder 249, published in KT 2/2, pp.1021–1033.

Journet C., *Schema Constitutionis Dogmaticae de Divina Revelatione,* (1965), 5 pages [report on the Schema De Divina Revelatione, sent to the Holy Father], in ASV, Envelope 787, Folder 424.

Laurentin R., *De Beata Maria Virgine Matre Ecclesiae. Note sur le Schéma Marial de Mai 1963* (4 pages marked in pen by Florit with the letters A-D), in AEF, Folder 5, Schema "De Ecclesia".

Laurentin R., 'Le schéma 'de Beata Maria Virgine'', in *Études et Documents,* n. 5, 11 February 1963; photocopy in ASV, Envelope 729, Folder 5, pages 40–49.

Ottaviani A., 'Memorandum intorno alla Costituzione de B.M. Virgine', 26.4.1962, in ASV, Envelope 750, Folder 222, published in E. M. Toniolo, *La Beata Maria Vergine nel Concilio Vaticano II,* p. 85 and in TK 1/2, p. 870.

Philips G., *Ce que nous attendons et espérons de la constitution dogmatique sur l'Eglise,* in ASV, Envelope 759, Folder 249, published in KT 2/2, pp. 994–1013.

Philips G., *Animadversiones in Cap. De Membris* [cf. C.T. 5/61: 63], C.T. 5/61: 101, f. 1, in ASV, Envelope 739, Folder 117.

Philips G., *De Membris Ecclesiae,* 7 April 1961, 7 pages (page 7: Addendum of 16 May 1961), in Ibid.

Rahner K.—Ratzinger J., *De revelatione Dei et hominis in Jesu Christo facta,* as an appendix to Y. Congar, *Erinnerungen an eine Episode auf dem II. Vatikanischen Konzil,* in E. Klinger—K. Wittstadt [eds.], *Glaube im Prozess. Christ nach dem II. Vatikanum,* Herder, Freiburg im B. 1984, pp. 33–50. There are two copies of this text in ASV: *De revelatione Dei et hominis in Iesu Christo facta,* edited by the Presidents of the Bishops' Conferences of Austria, Belgium, France, Germany and Holland, (13–14 November 1962), one of 12 pages and the othere of 10, Envelope 759, Folder 256.

Rahner K., *Sehnsucht nach dem geheimnisvollen Gott. Profil-Bilder-Texte,* edited by H. Vorgrimler, Herder, Freiburg im B. 1990.

Rahner K., *Relatio de Animadversionibus Patrum circa Proemium et Caput I Schematis 'De Divina Revelatione'* (Subcommissio 'De Divina Revelatione') (6 pages), in AEF, Folder 2, Schema 'De divina revelatione'.

Rahner K.—Semmelroth O.—Ratzinger J., *De collegio episcoporum ejusque potestate in Ecclesia. Osservazioni,* 7 ottobre 1963, ff. 4, in ASV, Envelope 729, Folder 7.

Schauf H., *Anmerkungen zu den Adnotationes Schillebeeckx,* in ASV, Envelope 761, Folder 268, published in KT 2/2, pp. 1119–1130.

Schauf H., *Bemerkungen zu den Adnotationes zum Schema De Ecclesia,* [written in response to Semmelroth], in ASV, Envelope 761, Folder 268 [4], published in KT 2/2, pp. 1090–1105.

Schauf H., *De relatione inter Traditionem et S. Scripturam relatio* (Subcommissio 'De Divina Revelatione'), Acquisgrana 31 March 1964 (27 pages), in AEF, Folder 2, Schema 'De divina revelatione'.

Schauf H., *Observationes ad Conclusionem Relationis R.P. Rahner de Cap. I Schematis 'De Divina Revelatione' (pag. 6 ad pag. 9),* Acquisgrana 15 May 1964 (2 pages), in AEF, Folder 2, Schema 'De divina revelatione'.

Schillebeeckx E., *Commentary on the 'prima series' of the 'Schemata Constitutionum Decretorum de quibus disceptabitur in concilii sessionibus'. Memorandum prepared by Fr. Edward Schillebeeckx, OP at the request of the Dutch Bishops. Issued by the Secretariate of the Dutch Hierarchy,* 13 July 1962, pp. 56, in ASV, Envelope 759, Folder 247, published in KT 2/2, pp. 948–991.

Schillebeeckx E., *Animadversiones in 'Secundam Seriem' Schematum Constitutionum et Decretorum de quibus disceptabitur in Concilii sessionibus. De Ecclesia et De Beata Maria Virgine,* 30 November 1962, 10 pages, in ASV, Envelope 749, Folder 249, published in KT 2/2, pp. 1066–1081.

Semmelroth O., *Adnotationes criticae ad schema De ecclesia,* 5–6 February 1963, 6 pages, in ASV, Envelope 761, Folder 268.

Tromp S., *Memorandum de membris Corporis Christi Mystici,* Manuscript, 2 February 1961, 11 pages, in ASV, Envelope 739, Folder 117, published in KT 1/2, pp. 858–862 [pp. 855–863 contain Tromp's first draft of *De membris,* Leclerq's Protocol of 25 May 1961, with general observations on Tromp's report and on Salaverri's for Tromp on members of the Church, 22 May 1961. Envelope 739, Folder 117, also contains two dossiers from the De Ecclesia Sub-commission, 25 May 1961, with a good number of reports on the theme *De membris Ecclesiae*].

Tromp S., *De Membris Ecclesiae,* Manuscript, 11–12 May 1961, 20 pages, in ASV, Envelope 734, Folder 48 (see also Envelope 739, Folder 117 for further interventions on the same theme).

Tromp S., *De Membris Ecclesiae et de eius necessitatem ad salutem,* C.T. 5/61: 31, 14 April 1961, 3 pages, note 1, in ASV, Envelope 739, Folder 117.

Tromp S., *Observatio Secretarii Commissionis doctrinalis de Qualificatione Theologica,* 25 December 1963/16 January 1964, 8 pages, Rome 16 January 1963, in ASV, Envelope 762, Folder 272.

Tromp S., *Observationes ad Caput I: De Ecclesiae militantis natura* (CFM 3/63: 1. De Ecclesia), 10 February 1963 (5 pages), in AEF, Folder 5, Schema 'De Ecclesia' and in ASV, Envelope 763, Folder 273, where there are two exemplars: an 8-page manscript, dated 9–10 February 1963, and a 5-page text, dated 10 February 1963.

Tromp S., *II Relatio Secretarii circa observationes factas ad Schema Constitutionis de B.M. Virgine* (1 Iunii-15 Sempt. 1963), ASV, Envelope 765, Folder 294, in KT 2/2, pp. 754–762.

Tromp S., *Nota Secretarii Commissionis,* 17 December 1963, 4 pages [about the lack of a comparison in the discussion on *De Revelatione* and *De Ecclesia* with the introduction to Vatican I's Dogmatic Constitution De Fide Catholica], in ASV, Envelope 762, Folder 272.

Tromp S., *De Beata Maria Virgine Mediatrice,* in ASV Envelope 750, Folder 222, published in KT 1/2, p. 871.

Tromp S., *Relatio de Observationibus acceptis super Schema Constitutionis dogmaticae de Revelatione,* 10 January—7 February 1964, ff. 17, in ASV, Envelope 762, Folder 272.

Tromp S., *Relatio Secretarii de laboribus 15 Martii—16 Iulii 1964,* pp. 4–8 [report on the amendments made by the Doctrinal Commission on the Mariological text] in ASV, Envelope 758, Folder with no number.

Volk H. (et alii), *De Ecclesia,* 5–6 February 1963, ff. 36, in ASV, Envelope 761, Folder 268.

Authors

a) The Council and conciliar teachings

a.1) Status quaestionis

AAVV., 'Vatican II: rupture ou continuité? Les herméneutiques en présence', Actes du colloque organisé par l'ISTA, Toulouse 15–16 mai 2009, in *Revue Thomiste* 110 (2010) [Part One] and in *Revue Thomiste* 111 (2010) [Part Two].

AAVV., 'Vatican II', in *Concilium* 3 (2012) [special issue].

Beinert W., *Dogmatik studieren. Einführung in dogmatisches Denken und Arbeiten,* Regensburg: F. Pustet, 1985.

Berger D., 'Gegen die Tradition oder im Licht der Tradition? Zur neueren Interpretation des Zweiten Vatikanischen Konzils', in *Divinitas* 3 (2005), pp. 294–316.

Bordeyne P.—Villemin L. (eds.), *Vatican II et la théologie. Perspectives pour le XXIe siècle,* Paris: Cerf, 2006.

Brandmüller W., 'Il Concilio e i Concili. Il Vaticano II nel contesto della storia conciliare', in Brandmüller W. et al., *Le "Chiavi" di Benedetto XVI per interpretare il Vaticano II*, Siena: Cantagalli, 2012, pp. 43–65.

Brandmüller W. et al., *Le "Chiavi" di Benedetto XVI per interpretare il Vaticano II*, Siena: Cantagalli, 2012.

Bredeck M., *Das Zweite Vatikanum als Konzil des Aggiornamento. Zur hermeneutischen Grundlegung einer theologischen Konzilsinterpretation*, Paderbon: Schöningh, 2007.

Cantoni P., *Riforma nella continuità. Vaticano II e anticonciliarismo*, Milan: Sugarco, 2011.

Cavalcoli G., *Progresso nella continuità. La questione del Concilio Vaticano II e del post-concilio*, Verona: Fede & Cultura, 2011.

Delhaye P., 'L'autorité théologique des textes de Vatican II', in *Communio* 4 (1971), pp. 193–227.

Dumont B., 'Le conflit irrésolu', editorial in *Catholica* 117 (2012), pp. 4–11.

Faggioli M., *Vatican II. The Battle for Meaning*, New York/Mahwah (NJ): Paulist Press, 2012.

Frings H-J., *Aufbruch oder Betriebsunfall? Das II. Vatikanische Konzil und seine Folgen*, Ostfildern: Patmos, 2010.

Gherardini B., *Concilio Ecumenico Vaticano II. Un discorso da fare*, Frigento: Casa Mariana Editrice, 2009.

Gherardini B., *Concilio Vaticano II. Il discorso mancato*, Turin: Lindau, 2011.

Gherardini B., *Il Vaticano II. Alle radici di un equivoco*, Turin: Lindau, 2012.

Guarini M., *La Chiesa e la sua continuità. Ermeneutica e istanza dogmatica dopo il Vaticano II*, Rieti: DEUI, 2012.

Indelicato A., *Difendere la dottrina o annunciare il Vangelo. Il dibattito nella Commissione centrale preparatoria del Vaticano II* (Istituto per le Scienze Religiose di Bologna. Testi e ricerche di scienze religiose, N.s. 8), Genoa: Marietti, 1992.

Kasper W., 'Die bleibende Herausforderung durch das II. Vatikanische Konzil. Zur Hermeneutik der Konzilsaussagen', in Id., *Theologie und Kirche*, Mainz: Matthias-Grünewald, 1987.

Kasper W., '"Unitatis redintegratio". Il carattere teologicamente vincolante del Decreto sull'ecumenismo del concilio Vaticano II', in *Rivista Liturgica* 91 (2004), pp. 19–27.

Kolfhaus F., *Pastorale Lehrverkündigung—Grundmotiv des Zweiten Vatikanischen Konzils. Untersuchungen zu "Unitatis Redintegratio", "Dignitatis Humanae" und "Nostra Aetate"*, Berlin: LIT, 2010.

Jestin L., 'L'impasse des herméneutique', in *Catholica* 117 (2012), pp. 74–82.

Lamb M.L.—Levering M., *Vatican II: renewal within tradition*, Oxford: Oxford University Press, 2008.

Lanzetta S.M., *Iuxta modum. Il Vaticano II riletto alla luce della Tradizione della Chiesa*, Siena: Cantagalli, 2012.

Lavalette H., 'Reflexion sur la portée doctrinale et pastorale des documents de Vatican II', in *Etudes* 323 (1966), pp. 258–269.

Lucien B., 'L'autorité magistérielle de Vatican II. Contribution à un debat actuel', in *Sedes Sapientiae* 119 (2012), pp. 9–80.

Manelli S. M.—Lanzetta S. M. (eds), *Concilio Ecumenico Vaticano II: un concilio pastorale. Analisi storico-filosofico-teologica*, Frigento (AV): Casa Mariana Editrice, 2011.

Montaldi G., *In fide ipsa essentia revelationis completur. Il tema della fede nell'evolversi del Concilio Vaticano II: la genesi di DV 5–6 e i suoi riflessi su ulteriori ambiti conciliari*, Rome: PUG, 2005.

Pesch O. H., *Das Zweite Vatikanische Konzil: Vorgeschichte-Verlauf-Ergebnisse-Nachgeschichte*, Würzburg: Echter, 2001.

Sullivan F., 'Evaluation and Interpretation of the Documents of Vatican II', in *Creative Fidelity: Weighing and Interpreting Documents of the Magisterium*, New York: Paulist Press, 1996.

Sullivan F., *Magisterium. Teaching authority in the Catholic Church*, New York: Paulist Press, 1983.

Scheffczyk L., *Aspekte der Kirche in der Krise. Um die Entscheidung für das authentische Konzil*, Siegburg: Franz Schmitt, 1993.

Semmelroth O., 'Zur Frage nach der Verbindlichkeit der dogmatischen Aussagen des II. Vatikanischen Konzils', in *Theologie und Philosophie* 42 (1967), pp. 236–246.

Sauer H., *Erfahrung und Glaube. Die Begründung des pastoralen Prinzips durch die Offenbarungskonstitution des II. Vatikanischen Konzils*, Frankfurt am Main: Peter Lang, 1993.

Tück J.-H., *'Ein "reines Pastoralkonzil"? Zur Verbindlichkeit des Vatikanum II'*, in *Communio* 41 (2012), pp. 441–457.

a.2) Fathers and periti on the Council

Betti U., *La dottrina dell'episcopato nel capitolo III della 'Lumen gentium'*, Rome: Città nuova, 1968.

Betti U., 'De Sacra Traditione in Concilio Vaticano II', address for the inauguration of the Academic Year at the Theological Athenaeum in Florence, 15 November 1965, in *Antonianum* 41 (1966), pp. 3–15.

Betti U., 'La Tradizione è fonte di rivelazione?', in *Antonianum* 38 (1963), pp. 31–49.

Betti U., *La Rivelazione divina nella Chiesa*, Rome: Città nuova, 1970.

Betti U., *La dottrina del Concilio Vaticano II sulla trasmissione della rivelazione*, Spicilegium Pontifici Athenaei Antoniani, Rome 1985.

Küng H., *The Council and Reunion*, London and New York: Sheed and Ward, 1961.

Küng H., 'Was hat das Konzil erreicht?', in Universitas 21 (1966), pp. 171–186.

Küng H.—N. Greinacher (eds.), *Katholische Kirche—whoin? Wieder der Verrat am Konzil*, München: Piper, 1986.

Küng H., 'Das Zweite Vatikanische Konzil: Erbe und Auftrag', in Ökumene und Weltethos 3 (2004) pp. 28–41.

Küng H., 'Is the Second Vatican Council Forgotten?', in *Concilium* 41 (2005), pp. 108–117.

Küng H., *Erkämpfte Freiheit. Erinnerungen*, München-Zürig: Piper, 2002.

Küng H., *Ist die Kirche noch zu retten?*, München-Zürich: Piper, 2011.

Parente P., *A vent'anni dal Concilio Vaticano II. Esperienze e prospettive*, Rome: Città Nuova, 1985.

Parente P., *Il prossimo Concilio ecumenico tra il passato e l'avvenire: discorso pronunciato a Roma, il 18 maggio 1961, nella sede del Banco di Roma, sotto gli auspici del Centro italiano di studi per la riconciliazione internazionale*; with a presentation from the Permanent General Secretary of the Centro Tomaso Sillani, Rome 1961.

Parente P., *La crisi della verità e il concilio Vaticano II*, Rovigo: Istituto padano di arti grafiche, 1983.

Parente P., *Proposte, interventi e osservazioni nel Concilio Vaticano II*, edited by His Grace Mgr Michele di Ruberto, Vatican City: LEV, 2010.

Rahner K., *Das Konzil—ein neuer Beginn*, Wien-Freiburg-Basel: Herder, 1966 (conference held to mark the solemn closure of the Second Vatican Council in the Herkules-Saal of the Residence in Munich on 12 December 1965).

Rahner K., 'Lehramt und Theologie nach dem Konzil', in *Stimmen der Zeit* 178 (1966), pp. 404–420.

Rahner K. (ed.), *Reformation aus Rom. Die Katholische Kirche nach dem Konzil*, Tübingen: Wunderlich, 1967.

Rahner K., 'Die bleibende Bedeutung des II. Vatikanischen Konzils', in *Stimme der Zeit* 12 (1979), pp. 795–806.

Rahner K., 'Basic Theological Interpretation of the Second Vatican Council', in Id., *Theological Investigations*, vol. XX, London: Darton, Longman & Todd, 1981, pp. 77–89.

Rahner K., 'On the theology of the Council', in Id., *Theological Investigations*, vol. V, Baltimore and London: Helion Press and Darton, Longman & Todd, 1966, pp. 244–267.

Rahner K., 'The Second Vatican Council's challenge to theology', in Id., *Theological Investigations*, vol. IX, London: Darton, Longman & Todd, 1972, pp. 3–27.

Rahner K., 'On the theological problems entailed in a "Pastoral Constitution"', in Id., *Theological Investigations*, vol. X, London: Darton, Longman & Todd, 1973, pp. 293–317.

Rahner K., 'The new claims which pastoral theology makes upon theology as a whole', in Id., *Theological Investigations*, vol. XI, London and New York: Darton, Longman & Todd and The Seabury Press, 1974, pp. 115–136.

Rahner K.—H. Vorgrimler (eds.), *Kleines Konzilskompendium. Sämtliche Texte des Zweiten Vatikanischen Konzils*, Allgemeine Einleitung—16 spezielle Einführungen—ausführliches Sachregister, Freiburg im Br.: Herder, 2008.

Ratzinger J., *Die erste Sitzungsperiode des Zweiten Vatikanischen Konzils: ein Rückblick*, Köln: Bachem, 1963.

Ratzinger J., *Das Konzil auf dem Weg: Rückblick auf die zweite Sitzungsperiode des Zweiten Vatikanischen Konzils*, Köln: Bachem, 1964.

Ratzinger J., *Ergebnisse und Probleme der dritten Sitzungsperiode*, Köln: Bachem, 1965.

Ratzinger J., *Die letzte Sitzungsperiode des Konzils*, Köln: Bachem, 1966.

Ratzinger J., 'Problemi e risultati del Concilio Vaticano II', *Giornale di Teologia* 8, Brescia: Queriniana, 1966.

Ratzinger J., *Mon Concile Vatican II. Enjeux et perspectives*, Perpignan: Artège Spiritualité, 2011.

Ratzinger J., *Zur Lehre des Zweiten Vatikanischen Konzils* (Gesammelte Schriften 7/1–7/2), Freiburg im B.: Herder, 2012.

Ratzinger J., 'Papst Johannes Paul II. und das Vatikanische Konzil', in *L'Osservatore Romano* (weekly German edition), 22/45 (1992), pp. 9–10.

Siri G., *Informazione vera sul Concilio, Ecumenismo cattolico: due discorsi del cardinale Giuseppe Siri*, Diocesan Liturgical Catechectical Office, Genoa 1964.

Siri G., *La giovinezza della Chiesa: testimonianze, documenti e studi sul Concilio Vaticano II*, Pisa: Giardini, 1983.

a.3) On periti and theologians at the Council

Burigana R., 'Progetto dogmatico del Vaticano II: la commissione teologica preparatoria (1960–1962)', in G. Alberigo—A. Melloni (eds.), Verso il concilio Vaticano II (1960–1962). Passaggi e problemi della preparazione conciliare, Genoa: Marietti, 1993, pp. 141- 206.

Fattori M. T., 'Per una ricostruzione della partecipazione italiana al concilio Vaticano II: una mappa delle fonti personali', Rivista di storia della Chiesa in Italia, 49 (1995), pp. 103–125.

Grohe J.—Leal J.—Reale V. (eds.), *I Padri e le scuole teologiche nei concili.* Atti del VII Simposio internazionale della Facoltà di teologia, Rome, 6–7 March 2003, Vatican City: LEV, 2006.

Müller W. W., 'Yves Congar und Karl Rahner auf dem II. Vatikanischen Konzil. Über das Zusammenspiel von Lehramt und Theologie', in M. Belok-U. Kropač (eds.), *Volk Gottes im Aufbruch. 40 Jahre II. Vatikanisches Konzil*, Zürich: TVZ, 2005, pp. 101–136 (with bibliography).

Küng H.—Südbeck-baur W. (eds.), '"Ich hatte das Gefühl ich hätte endlos Zeit": mit dem Zweiten Vatikanischen Konzil begann sein rasanter Aufstieg zum weltbekannten Theologen. Doch Rom brach mit ihm. Fragen an Hans Küng', in *Zeitungen kritischer Christen* 5 (2008), pp. 44–45.

Lanzetta S.M., 'La recezione teologica del Vaticano II. Status quaestionis', in *Fides Catholica* 1 (2011) 121–158 and in Id.—S.M. Manelli (eds.), *Concilio Ecumenico Vaticano II: un concilio pastorale. Analisi storico-filosofico-teologica*, Frigento (AV): Casa Mariana Editrice, 2011, pp. 189–230.

Lanzetta S. M., 'La valutazione del Concilio Vaticano II in Joseph Ratzinger poi Benedetto XVI', in *Fides Catholica* 1 (2012), pp. 87–120.

Madrigal Terrazas S., *Karl Rahner y Joseph Ratzinger: tras las huellas del Concilio*, Santander: Sal Terrae, 2006.

Neufeld K. H., 'In the Service of the Council: Bishops and Theologians at the Second Vatican Council', in R. Latourelle (ed.), *Vatican II: Assessment and Perspectives Twenty Five Years After (1962–1987)*, vol. I, Mahwah, NJ: Paulist Press, 1998, pp. 74–105.

Semeraro M., 'L'influenza dei teologi nei lavori del Vaticano II', in *Nicolaus*, 29 (2002), pp. 89–99.

Wicks J., 'I teologi al Vaticano II: Momenti e modalità del loro contributo al Concilio', in *Humanitas*, 59/5 (2004), pp. 1012–1038.

Wicks J., 'Yves Congar's Doctrinal Service of the People of God', in *Gregorianum* 84/ 3 (2003), pp. 499–550.

Stacpoole A. (ed.), *Vatican II Revisited by Those Who Where There*, Minneapolis: Winston, 1985.

b) Historical questions about the Councils

b.1) General

Alberigo G. (ed.), *History of Vatican II*, 5 vols., Maryknoll / Leuven: Orbis / Peeters 1995–2006.

Burigana R., *Storia del Concilio Vaticano II*, Turin: Lindau 2012.

Chenaux P., *Il Concilio Vaticano II*, Rome: Carrocci, 2012.

De Mattei R., *Il Concilio Vaticano II. Una storia mai scritta*, Turin: Lindau, 2010.

Jedin H., *Storia del Concilio di Trento*, 4 vols., Brescia: Morcelliana, 1973–1979.

Schatz K., *Allgemeine Konzilien. Brennpunkte der Kirchengeschichte*, Paderborn: Schöningh, 1997.

Schatz K., *Vatikanum* I: 1869–1870, 3 vols., Paderborn: Schöningh, 1992–1994.

Zambarbieri A., *I concili del Vaticano* (Storia della Chiesa, Saggi 10), Cinisello Balsamo: San Paolo, 1995.

b.2) Development of the conciliar idea and evolution of the formal authority of the ecumenical council

Sieben H. J., *Die Konzilsidee der Alten Kirche*, Paderbon: Schöningh, 1979.

Sieben H. J., *Traktate und Theorien zum Konzil. Vom Beginn des Großen Schismas bis zum Vorabend der Reformation 1378–1521*, Frankfurt 1983.

Sieben H. J., *Die katholische Konzilsidee von der Reformation bis zur Aufklärung*, Paderbon: Schöningh, 1988.

Sieben H. J., *Die katholische Konzilsidee im 19. und 20. Jahrhundert*, Paderbon: Schöningh, 1993.

Sieben H. J., *Vom Apostelkonzil zum Ersten Vatikanum. Studien zur Geschichte der Konzilsidee*, Paderbon: Schöningh, 1996.

Sieben H. J., *Studien zur Gestalt und überlieferung der Konzilien, Paderbon: F. Schöningh, 2005.*

c) Theological issues: reception and hermeneutic

Angelini G., 'Dibattito—Vaticano II: la recezione del Concilio. Sul conflitto delle interpretazioni', in *Il Regno*, 53/10 (2008), pp. 297–303.

Alberigo G., 'Fedeltà e creatività nella ricezione del concilio Vaticano II', in *Cristianesimo nella storia* 2 (2000), pp. 395–397.

Alberigo G., 'Le ragioni dell'opzione pastorale del Vaticano II', in *Synaxis* 3 (2002), pp. 489–509.

Alberigo G., 'Vatican II and its History', in *Concilium* 4 (2005), pp. 9–20.

Alberigo G., *Transizione epocale. Studi sul Concilio Vaticano II*, Bologna: Il Mulino, 2009.

Alberigo G.—A. Melloni (eds.), *Passaggi e problemi della preparazione conciliare*, (Istituto per le Scienze Religiose di Bologna. Testi e ricerche di scienze religiose, N.s. 11) Genoa: Marietti, 1993.

Brancozzi E., 'La ricezione magisteriale del Vaticano II a cinquant'anni dalla convocazione', in *Sacramentaria e Scienze Religiose*, 18 (2009), pp. 51–68.

Bredeck M., *Das Zweite Vatikanum als Konzil des Aggiornamento. Zur hermeneutischen Grundlegung einer theologischen Konzilsinterpretation*, Paderborn: Schöningh, 2007.

Burigana R., 'Quale tradizione? Riflessioni e definizioni tra la IV Conferenza di Fede e Costituzione (Montreal, 12–26 luglio 1963) e la Costituzione Dei Verbum del Vaticano II', in *Studi Ecumenici* 1–2 (2009), pp. 121–147.

Canobbio G., 'Il Vaticano II e la sua recezione', in *Esperienza e teologia* 11 (2005), pp. 9–23.

Capovilla L. F., 'Dall'aurora del Vaticano II ai nostri giorni', in *Jesus Caritas* 4 (2009), pp. 7–15.

Caprile G., *Contributo alla storia della 'Nota explicativa praevia'. Documentazione inedita*, in *Paolo VI e i problemi ecclesiologici al concilio*. Colloquio internazionale di studio, Brescia, 19–20–21 settembre 1986 (Pubblicazioni dell'Istituto Paolo VI, 7), Brescia-Roma, Istituto Paolo VI—Studium, 1989, pp. 587–681, 587–697.

Casale U., *Il Concilio Vaticano II alle soglie del 2000*, Leumann (TO): Elle Di Ci, 1992.

Chenaux P., 'Recensione storiografica circa le prospettive di lettura del Vaticano II', in *Lateranum* 1 (2006), pp. 161–175.

Coppa G., *Problemi del concilio*, Alba: Edizioni domenicane, 1966.

Fattori M. T.—Melloni A. (eds.), *L'evento e le decisioni. Studi sulla dinamica del concilio Vaticano II*, Bologna: Il Mulino, 1997.

Fisichella R. (ed.), *Il Concilio Vaticano II. Recezione e attualità alla luce del Giubileo*, Cinisello Balsamo: San Paolo, 2000.

Forte B. (ed.), *Fedeltà e rinnovamento. Il Concilio Vaticano II 40 anni dopo*, Cinisello Balsamo: San Paolo, 2005.

Hünermann P., 'The Ignored "Text": On the Hermeceutics of the Second Vatican Council', in *Concilium* 4 (2005), pp. 118–136.

Komonchak J. A., 'Ecclesiologia—Ermeneutiche del Concilio: novità nella continuità. Benedetto XVI e il Vaticano II', in *Il Regno*, 54/4 (2009), pp. 80–83.

Lanzetta S., 'Il Concilio Vaticano II tra "fedeltà e dinamica"', in *Fides Catholica* 1 (2006), pp. 79–109.

Latourelle R. (ed.), *Vatican II, Assessment and Perspective Twenty-five Years After (1962–1987)*, 3 vols., Mahwah, NJ: Paulist Press, 1988–1989.

Laurentin R., *Bilan du Concile Vatican II*, Paris: Edition du Seuil, 1967.

Melloni A.—Ruggieri G., *Chi ha paura del Vaticano II?*, Rome: Carrocci, 2009.

O' Malley J. W., 'Vatican II: Historical Perspectives on its Uniqueness and Interpretation', in L. Richard—D.J. Harrington—J.W. O'Malley (eds.), *Vatican II, The Unfinished Agenda: A Look to the Future,* New York: Paulist Press, 1987, pp. 22–32.

O' Malley J. W., *What Happened at Vatican II,* Harvard: Harvard University Press, 2008.

O'Malley J. W., 'Erasmus and Vatican II: Interpreting the Council', in A. Melloni (ed.), *Cristianesimo nella storia. Saggi in onore di Giuseppe Alberigo,* Bologna: Il Mulino, 1996, pp. 195–211.

O'Malley J. W., 'Official Norms: On Interpreting the Council, with a Response to Cardinal Avery Dulles', in *America* 188/11 (2003), pp. 11–14.

O'Malley J. W., 'Reform, Historical Consciousness, and Vatican II's Aggiornamento', in Id., *Tradition and Transition: Historical Perspectives on Vatican II,* Wilmington: M. Glazier, 1989, pp. 44–81.

O' Malley J. W., 'The Style of Vatican II. The "How" of the Church changed during the Council', in *America* 188/6 (2003), pp. 12–15.

Marchetto A., *Il Concilio Ecumenico Vaticano II. Contrappunto per la sua storia,* Vatican City: LEV, 2005.

Marchetto A., *Il Concilio Vaticano II. Per la sua corretta ermeneutica,* Vatican City: LEV, 2012.

Pottmeyer H. J., 'Una nuova fase della ricezione del Vaticano II. Vent'anni di ermeneutica del concilio', in G. Alberigo—J.P. Jossua (eds.), *Il Vaticano II e la Chiesa,* Brescia: Paidea, 1985.

Pottmeyer H.J.—G. Alberigo—J.P. Jossua (eds.), *Die Rezeption des Zweiten Vatikanischen Konzils,* Düsseldorf: Patmos, 1986.

Rusch O., *Still interpreting Vatican II. Some Hermeneutical Principles,* New York: Paulist Press, 2004.

Routhier G., *Vatican II. Herméneutique et réception,* Montréal: Fides, 2006.

Routhier G., 'Bilan historiographique de la recherche francophone récente sur Vatican II', in *Rivista di Storia della Chiesa in Italia,* 54 (2000), pp. 443–468.

Routhier G., 'A 40 anni dal Concilio Vaticano II. Un lungo tirocinio verso un nuovo tipo di cattolicesimo', in *La Scuola Cattolica* 133 (2005), pp. 19–52.

Routhier G., 'Il Vaticano II come stile', in *La Scuola Cattolica* 136 (2008), pp. 5–32.

Routhier G.—P. Roy—K. Schelkens (eds.), *La théologie catholique entre intransigeance et renouveau. La réception des mouvements préconciliaires à Vatican II* (Bibliothèque de la Revue d'histoire ecclésiastique, 95), Turnhout: Brepols, 2011.

Ruggieri G., 'Towards a hermeneutic of Vatican II', in *Concilium* 1 (1999), pp. 1–13.

Ruggieri G., 'Ricezione e interpretazione del Vaticano II. La ragioni di un dibattito', in A. Melloni—G. Ruggieri, *Chi ha paura del Vaticano II?*, Rome: Carrocci, 2009, pp. 17–44.

Ruggieri G., *Ritrovare il concilio*, Turin: Einaudi, 2012.

Tagliaferri M., 'La ricezione del concilio Vaticano II: il recente dibattito tra teologia e storia' in *Rivista di Teologia dell'Evangelizzazione* 10 (2006), pp. 401–427.

Theobald C., *La réception du concile Vatican II, I, Accéder à la source*, Paris: Cerf, 2009.

Theobald C., 'Le devenir de la théologie catholique depuis le concile Vatican II', in J.M. Mayeur (ed.), *Historie du christianisme, 13: Crises et renouveau (de 1958 à nous jours)*, Paris: Desclée de Brouwer, 2000, pp. 169–271.

Theobald C., 'Enjeux herméneutiques du débat sur l'historie du concile Vatican II', in *Cristianesimo nella Storia* 18 (1997), pp. 359–380.

Theobald C., 'The Theological Options of Vatican II: Seeking an "Internal" Principle of Interpretation', in *Concilium* 4 (2005), pp. 87–107.

Tillard J. M. R., 'L'esprit du Concile dans la pastorale', in *Évangéliser* 18 (1964), pp. 502–518.

Tillard J. M. R., 'Il Concilio fermento della pastorale', in *Digest cattolico* 4 (1965), pp. 39–46.

Torresin A., 'Cosa è successo al Vaticano II. Un libro e un convegno', in *Il Regno* 55/8 (2010), pp. 248–250.

Venuto F. S., *La recezione del Concilio Vaticano II nel dibattito storiografico dal 1965 al 1985. Riforma o discontinuità* [Studia taurinensia 34], Cantalupa (TO): Effatà, 2011 (with bibliography).

d) Special theolgical issues (before, during and after Vatican II)

d.1) Relationship between Scripture and Tradition

AAVV., *La Révélation divine,* II tomi, Paris: Cerf, 1968.

Ardusso F. 'La Parola di Dio nella S. Scrittura e nella Tradizione', in *Archivio Teologico Torinese* 2/VI (2000), pp. 7–24.

Bacht H.—Fries H.—Geiselmann J. R., *Die mündliche Überlieferung. Beiträge zum Begriff der Tradition,* München: Hueber, 1957.

Betti U., *La dottrina del Concilio Vaticano II sulla trasmissione della Rivelazione,* Rome: Antonianum, 1985.

Blum G. G., *Offenbarung und überlieferung. Die dogmatische Konstitution Dei Verbum des II. Vaticanums im Lichte altkirchlicher und moderner Theologie,* Göttingen: Vandenhoeck & Ruprecht, 1971.

Buckenmaier A., *'Schrift und Tradition' seit dem Vatikanum II. Vorgeschichte und Rezeption,* Paderborn: Bonifatius, 1996.

Geiselmann J. R., *Die Heilige Schrift und die Tradition: zu den neueren Kontroversen über das Verhältnis der Heiligen Schrift zu den nichtgeschriebenen Traditionen,* Freiburg im B.: Herder, 1962.

Geiselmann J. R., *'Das Konzil von Trient über das Verhältnis der Heiligen Schrift und die nichtgeschriebenen Traditionen', in* M. Schmaus (ed.), *Die mündliche Überlieferung,* München: Hueber, 1957.

Geiselmann J. R., 'Tradizione', in *Dizionario teologico,* directed by H. Fries, Brescia: Queriniana, 1968, vol. III, pp. 521–532.

Gherardini B., 'Sul concetto teologico di tradizione', in AAVV., *Tradizione e Rivoluzione,* Atti del XXVII Convegno del Centro di Studi Filosofici tra professori universitari, Gallarate 1972, Brescia: Morcelliana, 1973, pp. 70–89.

Gherardini B., *Quod et tradidi vobis. La Tradizione vita e giovinezza della Chiesa*, Frigento: Casa Mariana Editrice, 2010.

Gherardini B., *Quæcumque dixero vobis. Parola di Dio e Tradizione a confronto con la storia e la teologia*, Turin: Lindau, 2011.

Hellín F. G., *Concilii Vaticani II Synopsis in ordinem redigens schemata cum relationibus necnon Patrum orationes atque animadversiones. Constitutio dogmatica De divina revelatione Dei Verbum*, Rome: LEV, 1993.

Latourelle R., *Theology of Revelation*, Staten Island, New York: Alba House, 1966: pp. 453–490.

Pozzo G., 'La nozione di rivelazione nella "Dei Verbum" e gli sviluppi nella teologia post-conciliare', in AAVV., *Ripensare il Concilio*, Collana Cultura e Teologia 2, Casale Monferrato: Piemme, 1986, pp. 29–49.

Rahner K., 'Scripture and Tradition', in Id., *Theological Investigations*, vol. VI, London and New York: Darton, Longman & Todd and The Seabury Press, 1974, pp. 98–112.

Ratzinger J., 'Un tentativo circa il problema del concetto di tradizione', in K. Rahner—J. Ratzinger, *Rivelazione e Tradizione*, Brescia: Morcelliana, 2006², pp. 27–73.

Sauer H., 'Von den "Quellen der Offenbarung" zur "Offenbarung selbst". Zum theologischen Hintergrund der Auseinandersetzung um das Schema "Über die göttliche Offenbarung" beim II. Vatikanische Konzil', in E. Klinger—K. Wittstadt (eds.), *Glaube im Prozess. Christ nach dem II. Vatikanum*, Freiburg im B.: Herder, 1984, pp. 514–545.

Schauf H., *Die Lehre der Kirche über Schrift und Tradition in den Katechismen*, Essen: Driewer, 1963.

Schauf H., 'Schrift und Tradition', in *Antonianum* 39 (1964), pp. 200–209.

Stakemeier E., *Die Konzilskonstitution über die göttliche Offenbarung. Werden, Inhalt und theologische Bedeutung*, Paderbon: Bonifacius-Druckerei, 1967².

Van den Eynde D., *De Sacra Scriptura et Traditione*, s.l.d., ff. 15, in ASV, Envelope 760, Folder 263.

Waldenfels H., 'Die Lehre von der Offenbarung in der tridentinischen Ära', in Id.—L. Scheffczyk, *Die Offenbarung von der Reformation bis zur Gegenwart,* (Handbuch der Dogmengeschichte, I/1 b), Freiburg im B.: Herder, 1977, pp. 5–53 (5–20).

d.2) Conciliar teaching on the Church (belonging to the Church, sacramentality and collegiality)

AAVV., *La Costituzione dogmatica sulla Chiesa.* Introduzione storico-dottrinale, testo latino e traduzione italiana, commento, Turin: Elle Di Ci, 1967[4].

AAVV., *La primavera della Chiesa. A quarant'anni dal Concilio Vaticano II,* P. Ciardella (ed.), Milan: Paoline, 2005.

Acerbi A., *Due ecclesiologie. Ecclesiologia giuridica ed ecclesiologia di comunione nella 'Lumen gentium'*, Bologna: EDB, 1975.

Associazione Teologica Italiana, *La Chiesa e il Vaticano II. Problemi di ermeneutica e recezione conciliare,* M. Vergottini (ed.), Milan: Glossa, 2006.

Baraúna G. (ed.), *La Chiesa del Vaticano II. Studi e commenti intorno alla Costituzione dogmatica 'Lumen gentium'*, Florence: Vallecchi, 1967[3].

Barion H., 'Das Zweite Vatikanische Konzil-Kanonistischer Bericht (II)', in *Der Staat* 4 (1965), pp. 341–359.

Betti U., 'Cronistoria della Costituzione', in G. Baraúna (ed.), *La Chiesa del Vaticano II: studi intorno alla costituzione dogmatica Lumen gentium,* Florence: Vallecchi, 1967[3], pp. 131–154.

Brunet R., 'Le dissidents de bonne foi sont'ils membres de l'èglise?', in *Analecta Gregoriana,* 58 (1954), pp. 199–218.

Canobbio G., 'L'ecclesiologia successiva al Vaticano II', in AAVV., *La primavera della Chiesa. A quarant'anni dal Concilio Vaticano II,* P. Ciardella (ed.), Milan: Paoline, 2005, pp. 44–51.

Carusi S., 'I giusti acattolici sono membri della Chiesa cattolica secondo il Magistero?', in *Divinitas* 2 (2012), pp. 249–268.

Congar Y., *Vie de l'èglise et conscience de la catholicité, in Esquisse du mystère de l'èglise,* Paris: Cerf, 1953[2] .

Dulles A., 'Nature, Mission, and Structure of the Church', in M.L. Lamb—M. Levering, *Vatican II: renewal within tradition*, Oxford: Oxford University Press, 2008, pp. 25–36.

Faccani M., *Collegio e collegialità episcopali nel Sinodo 1969*, Bologna: Dehoniane, 1991.

Fenton J. C., 'Contemporary questions about membership in the true Church', in *The American Ecclesiastical Review* (1961) pp. 39–57.

Gherardini B., *La Chiesa. Mistero e servizio*, Rome: Apollinare Studi, 1994.

Hellín F. G., *Concilii Vaticani II Sinopsis. Constitutio Dogmatica De Ecclesia Lumen gentium*, Rome: LEV, 1995.

Journet C., *L'église du Verbe incarné. Essai de théologie spéculative*, Tomes I-III, Paris: Desclée de Brouwer, 1941, 1951, 1969.

Journet C., 'Le mystère de l'église selon le Concile du Vatican', in *Revue Thomiste* 65 (1965), pp. 9–14.

Journet C., *De Mystico Christi Corpore in sua ratione ad Ecclesiae membra seu de axiomate: extra Ecclesiam nulla salus*, 1961, ff. 18, in ASV, Envelope 733, Folder 45.

Kasper W., *Theology and Church*, London: SCM Press, 1989.

Komonchak J. A., 'Towards an ecclesiology of communion', in G. Alberigo (ed.), *History of Vatican II*, vol. 4, *Church as Communion. Third Period and Intersession. September 1964–September 1965*, Maryknoll / Leuven: Orbis / Peeters 2003, pp. 1–93.

Marangoni R., 'La Chiesa mistero di comunione. Il contributo di Paolo VI nell'elaborazione dell'ecclesiologia di comunione (1963–1978)', *Analecta Gregoriana* 282 (2001) Rome, PUG.

Melloni A., 'The Beginning of the Second Period: The Great Debate on the Church', in G. Alberigo (ed.), *History of Vatican II*, vol. 3, *The Formation of the Council's Identity. First Period and Intersession. October 1962—September 1963* (Maryknoll / Leuven: Orbis / Peeters, 2000) pp. 1–115;

Philips G., *L'église et son mystère*, Paris: Desclée & Cie, 1967.

Ratzinger J., 'Der Kirchenbegriff und die Frage nach der Gliedschaft in der Kirche', in Id., *Kirche-Zeichen unter den Völkern* (Gesammelte Schriften 8/1), Freiburg im B.: Herder, 2010, pp. 290–307.

Ratzinger J. (et alii), *La Chiesa del Concilio: studi e contributi*, Milan: EDIT, 1985.

Rodriguez P. (ed.), *L'ecclesiologia trent'anni dopo la 'Lumen gentium'*, Rome: Armando, 1996, pp. 42–43.

Routhier G., 'La recezione dell'ecclesiologia conciliare: problemi aperti', in Associazione Teologica Italiana, *La Chiesa e il Vaticano II. Problemi di ermeneutica e recezione conciliare*, M. Vergottini (ed.), Milan: Glossa, 2006, pp. 3–45.

Salaverri J., *De Ecclesia Christi*, Msdrid: B.A.C., 1952[2].

Semeraro M., *Mistero, comunione e missione. Manuale di ecclesiologia*, Bologna: EDB, 1996.

Tillard J. M., *Église d'Églises. L'ecclésiologie de communion*, Paris: Cerf, Paris 1987.

Tromp S., *Corpus Christi quod est Ecclesia*, 4 vols., Romæ: PUG, 1937, 1960, 1972.

Tromp S., 'De Ecclesiae membris', in *Divinitas* 6 (1962), pp. 481–492.

Walf K., 'Lacune e ambiguità nell'ecclesiologia del Vaticano I'I, in *Cristianesimo nella storia* 2/1 (1981), pp. 187–201.

Witte J. L., 'La Chiesa 'sacramentum unitatis' del cosmo e del genere umano', in *La Chiesa del Vaticano II: studi e commenti intorno alla costituzione dommatica Lumen gentium*, Florence: Vallecchi, 1967[3], pp. 491–521.

Zapelena T., *De Ecclesia Christi*, Romae, PUG 1950[5]; 1954[6].

d.3) Conciliar teaching on the Blessed Virgin Mary

AAVV., *Maria Corredentrice. Storia e teologia*, XIV vols., Frigento: Casa Mariana Editrice, 1998–2012.[1]

---

1 There is a vast post-conciliar bibliography on the mystery of Mary's co-redemption. I have drawn attention to a number of titles in the text and here limit myself to the most fundamental. For an up-dated list see: A. Villafiorita Monteleone, *Alma Redemptoris Socia. Maria e la Redenzione nella teologia*

AAVV., *Mary at Foot of the Cross*. Acts of the International Symposium on Marian Coredemption, Academy of the Immaculate, IX vols., New Bedford (MA) 2001–2010.

Apollonio A.M., 'Maria mediatrice di tutte le grazie. La natura dell'influsso della Beata Vergine Maria nell'applicazione della Redenzione', in *Immaculata Mediatrix*, 7 (2007), pp. 157–181.

Aračić D., *La dottrina mariologica negli scritti di Carlo Balić*, Rome: PAMI, 1980.

Antonelli C., *Il dibattito su Maria nel Concilio Vaticano II. Percorso redazionale sulla base di nuovi documenti di archivio*, Padua: Messaggero, 2009.

Baraúna G., 'La SS. Vergine al servizio dell'economia della salvezza', in La Chiesa del Vaticano II. *Studi e commenti intorno alla Costituzione dogmatica 'Lumen gentium'*, Florence: Vallecchi, 1967[3], pp. 1137–1155.

Besutti G., 'Note di cronaca sul Concilio Vaticano II e lo schema "De Beata Maria Virgine"', in *Marianum* 26 (1964), pp. 1–42.

Carol J., *De corredemptione Beatae Virginis Mariae*, Romae 1950.

De Aldama J. A., *De quaestione mariali in hodierna vita Ecclesiae*, Rome: PAMI, 1964.

Gherardini B., *La Corredentrice nel mistero di Cristo e della Chiesa*, Rome: Vivere in, 1998.

Goossens W., *De cooperatione immediata Matris Redemptoris ad redemptionem obiectivam, quaestionis controversae perpensatio*, Paris: Typis Desclée de Brouver, 1939.

Greco A., *'Madre dei viventi'. La cooperazione salvifica di Maria nella 'Lumen gentium': una sfida per oggi*, Lugano: Eupress FTL, 2011.

Escudero Cabello A., *La cuestión de la mediación mariana en la preparación del Vaticano II. Elementos para una evaluación de los trabajos preconciliares*, Rome: LAS, 1997.

---

contemporanea [Collana di Mariologia, 8], Lugano: Eupress FTL, 2010.

Fehlner P. D. M., 'Immaculata Mediatrix: Towards a Dogmatic Definition of the Coredemption', in *Mary Coredemptrix, Mediatrix, Advocate. Theological Foundation, II. Papal, Pneumatological, Ecumenical*, M. Miravalle (ed.), Santa Barbara 1997, pp. 259–329.

Hauke M., *Maria, 'Mittlerin aller Gnaden'. Die universale Gnadenmittlerschaft Mariens im theologischen und seelsorglichen Schaffen von Kardinal Mercier* [Mariologische Studien 17], Regensburg 2004.

Hauke M., 'Maria, "Mittlerin aller Gnaden", im Vatikanischen Geheimarchiv aus der Zeit Pius' XI.—Zwischenbericht einer Spurensicherung', in *Theologisches* 36 (2006), pp. 381–392.

Hauke M., 'Maria als mütterliche Mittlerin in Christus. Ein systematischer Durchblick', in *Sedes Sapientiae. Mariologisches Jahrbuch* 2 (2008), pp. 13–53.

Hauke M., *La mediazione materna di Maria secondo Papa Giovanni Paolo II*, in AA. VV., *Maria Corredentrice. Storia e teologia*, vol. VII, Casa Mariana Editrice, Frigento 2005, pp. 35–91.

Hauke M., 'Riscoperta: La petizione del Cardinale Mercier e dei Vescovi belgi a Papa Benedetto XV per la definizione dogmatica della Mediazione universale delle grazie da parte di Maria (1915). Introduzione teologica e testo originale francese', in *Immaculata Mediatrix* 3 (2010), pp. 305–338.

Hauke M., 'Riscoperta: la petizione del Cardinal Mercier e dei Vescovi belgi a Papa Benedetto XV per la definizione dogmatica della mediazione universale delle grazie da parte di Maria (1915)', in AAVV., *Maria Corredentrice. Storia e teologia*, vol. XIII, Frigento: Casa Mariana Editrice, 2011, pp. 183–244 (with an Italian translation of the petition).

Hauke M., 'Maria compagna del Redentore. La cooperazione di Maria alla salvezza come pista di ricerca', in *Rivista teologica di Lugano* 7 (2002), pp. 47–70.

Hauke M., 'La cooperazione attiva di Maria alla Redenzione. Prospettiva storica (patristica, medievale, moderna, contemporanea)', in Telesphore Cardinal Toppo et al. (eds.), *Maria, unica cooperatrice alla Redenzione.* Atti del Simposio sul Mistero della Corredenzione Mariana, Fatima, Portogallo, 3–7 Maggio 2005, New Bedford, MA 2005, pp. 171–219 and in *Immaculata Mediatrix* 2 (2006), pp. 157–189.

Köster H., *Die Magd des Hernn,* Limburg: Lahn, 1947.

Laurentin R., *Mary's Place in the Church* London: Compass Books, 1965.

Laurentin R., *La Vierge Marie au Concile,* Paris: P. Lethielleux, 1965.

Lennerz H., 'De redemptione et cooperatione in opere redemptionis', in *Gregorianum* 22 (1941), pp. 301–324.

Manelli S.M., 'Maria a titolo unico è corredentrice', in AAVV., *Maria Corredentrice. Storia e teologia,* vol. V, Frigento: Casa Mariana Editrice, 2002, pp. 7–31.

Perrella S.M., *I 'vota' e i 'consilia' dei vescovi italiani sulla mariologia e sulla corredenzione nella fase antipreparatoria del Concilio Vaticano II,* Rome: Marianum, 1994.

Perrella S.M., (ed.), *La Madre di Gesù nella coscienza ecclesiale contemporanea. Saggi di teologia,* Vatican City: PAMI, 2005.

Parente P., 'Il punto sulla mediazione di Maria', in *Scripta de Maria* 4 (1981), pp. 625–643.

Rahner K., 'Probleme heutiger Mariologie', in *Aus der Theologie der Zeit,* Regensburg 1948, pp. 85–113.

Roschini G.M., *La cosiddetta 'questione mariana'.* Risposta ai rilievi critici del Prof. R. Laurentin, di S.E. Mons. P. Rusch e del Prof. A. Mueller, Vicenza: Tip. S. Giuseppe, 1963.

Semmelroth O., *Urbild der Kirche. Organischer Aufban des Mariengeheimnisses,* Wurzburg: Echter, 1950.

Toniolo E.M., *La Beata Maria Vergine nel Concilio Vaticano II,* Rome: Centro di Cultura Mariana 'Madre della Chiesa', 2004.

INDEX OF NAMES